WIRE AND WALLS

RAF Prisoners of War in Itzehoe, Spangenberg and Thorn 1939-42

WIRE AND WALLS

RAF Prisoners of War in Itzehoe, Spangenberg and Thorn 1939-42

CHARLES ROLLINGS

Illustrated
with maps by Robert M Buckham

Ian Allan
PUBLISHING

Author's Note
Every effort has been made by the author and publisher to trace the
owners of copyright material.
The author bears no responsibility for any embarrassment or
inconvenience caused to individuals mentioned in this text or to their
relations or friends.

Dedication
Dedicated to all whose story this is.

First published 2003

ISBN 0 7110 2991 1

© Charles Rollings 2003

Published by Ian Allan Publishing

an imprint of Ian Allan Publishing Ltd, Hersham, Surrey KT12 4RG.
Printed by Ian Allan Printing Ltd, Hersham, Surrey KT12 4RG.

Code: 0311/A3

Contents

List of Photographs

George Booth, Larry Slattery and Laurence Edwards interviewed by German and American journalists in Wesermünde Hospital, September 1939. *(Calton Younger)*

Early RAF and *Armée de l'Air* officer POWs on their way to interrogation in Berlin, September 1939. *Left to right*: *Sous-Lieutenant* Béranger, Pilot Officer Alf Thompson, Lieutenant-Colonel Enselem and Squadron Leader Sydney Murray. *(Nora Crete)*

Murray and Thompson after their interrogation. *(Nora Crete)*

Alf Thompson, at the *Reichsrundfunk*, broadcasting the news of his capture. *(Nora Crete)*

Map of Spangenberg and Elbersdorf, 1936. *(Stadt Archiv, Spangenberg)*

The dower house at Elbersdorf prior to the outbreak of war. In September 1939 it was converted into a POW camp and designated Oflag IXA. *(Author's collection)*

Wing Commander Harry Day, shot down on Friday, 13 October 1939. *(B A James)*

The *Offiziersdurchgangslager* at Oberursel, the forerunner of *Dulag Luft*. *(Sam Flynn)*

Panoramic view of Spangenberg and Elbersdorf prior to the outbreak of war. *(L Heinlein, via Schloss Spangenberg)*

The former Spangenberg railway station, now a Kindergarten. *(Author)*

Schloss Spangenberg, Oflag IXA/H, November 1939. *(Calton Younger)*

Spangenberg castle from the north-west. *(Imperial War Museum HU20593)*

The steps from Elbersdorf leading to the castle. *(Author)*

The lower stretch of the cinder path up which POWs were marched to the castle. *(Author)*

The stone steps from the town of Spangenberg, completed in 1838. *(Author)*

The stone steps, photographed from the outer moat area. *(Author)*

The upper stretch of the cinder path. *(Author)*

The "Black Gate" leading from the outer battlements to the gatehouse. *(Author)*

The cobbled path, viewed from the gatehouse to the "Black Gate". *(Author)*

The gatehouse today. *(Author)*

The drawbridge and *Grosser Turm*, or main tower. *(Author's collection)*

The main tower and steps leading to the bottom of the moat. *(IWM HU20594)*

Prisoners relaxing in the moat. *(Author's collection)*

The courtyard and *Kommandtur* drawn by Howard Taylor for "The Quill". *(Author's collection)*

View of the courtyard and main entrance, 1940. *(Author's collection)*

The spiral staircase in the eastern tower. *(Author)*

The main Assembly Hall in the south wing in the 1930s, when the castle was a State Forestry School. During the war, newly arrived POWs were searched and given a pep-talk in the *Grosse Aula* by the Commandant. *(M Becher, via* Schloss *Spangenberg)*

The *Speisesaal*, or Dining Hall, again before the war. POWs were not allowed the luxury of glazed crockery. *(M Becher, via* Schloss *Spangenberg)*

The eastern wing and the wooden bridge leading to the gymnasium. *(IWM HU20595)*

Larry Slattery at Spangenberg after his jaw had been wired up. *(Calton Younger)*

Larry Slattery and Laurence Edwards at Spangenberg. *(Calton Younger)*

Aircrew officers photographed in the courtyard, winter 1939. *Standing left to right:* Griffiths, MacLachlan, Bewlay, Heaton-Nichols, Baughan, Thurston. *Seated left to right:* Casey, Tilsley, Murray, Day, Thompson, Edwards. *At front:* Bob Coste. *(H R Bewlay)*

Harry Bewlay *(left)* and Colin MacLachlan, 1939. *(H R Bewlay)*

Howard ("Hank") Wardle. *(Author's collection)*

Keith Milne. *(Author's collection)*

Donald S Thom. *(Author's collection)*

Squadron Leader Brian Paddon — in the cooler, as usual. *(A J Hill)*

Norman Thomas. *(Author's collection)*

Canadians at Spangenberg, 1940. *Left to right:* Aubrey Roberts, John Glover, Donald Middleton, Warren Hayward, Al Matthews, Don Thom, Robert Renison (partially hidden), George Walker, William Donaldson, Bob Coste, Alf Thompson, Hank Wardle, Keith Milne. *(Nora Crete)*

Fleet Air Arm prisoners at Dulag Luft, late 1940. *Back row, from left:* Nathaniel Hearn, Cecil Filmer, Midshipman A O Atkins, Robin Grey, Douglas Poynter. *Third row:* Guy Griffiths, Lieutenant J T Nicholson, Lieutenant W S ("Peter") Butterworth, Lieutenant J C W Illiffe, Maurice Hanrahan, Alan Cheetham, Henri Detterding, Captain R T Partridge, RM. *Second row:* Richard Thurston, Norman Quill, Lieutenant-Commander Jimmy Buckley, Lieutenant-Commander O S Stevinson, Lieutenant-Commander John Casson. *Front row:* Naval Airman A R Purchase, Naval Airman Charles Jago, Petty-Officer Alex Brims and Naval Airman H W Brown. Griffiths and Thurston had been sent from Spangenberg with "Wings" Day to form the nucleus of the British Permanent Staff at Dulag Luft. Most of the other officers would shortly be purged to Spangenberg. *(Janet Brown)*

Francis ("Errol") Flinn. *(Author's collection)*

Alex Gould in the courtyard at Spangenberg. Main gates in background. *(A H Gould)*

The purge from Stalag Luft I, Barth, arrives at Spangenberg, February 1941. In the foreground are Peter Tunstall (with Red Cross box) and Norman Forbes (directly behind him). *(Author's collection)*

Trevor Hadley and Theo Johnson, Spangenberg 1941. *(Vivien Johnson)*

Alex Gould and Peter Tunstall, Spangenberg 1941. *(A H Gould)*

Norman Forbes. *(Author's collection)*

Alf Thompson playing table-tennis at Spangenberg. *(A H Gould)*

Map showing the chain of fortresses surrounding Thorn. *(Author's collection)*

Fort XV, Thorn. *(Author's collection)*

POW accommodation at Thorn. *(Author's collection)*

Strafgefangene at Fort XV, Thorn. *From left:* Squadron Leader Murray, Rupert ("Pud") Davies and Paul Vaillant. *(A H Gould)*

Major-General Victor Fortune *(seated extreme left)*, the Senior British Officer at Fort VIII, watches the boxing match at Fort XV. *(A H Gould)*

Dan Hallifax. *(Author's collection)*

Cutaway drawing of the *Speisesaal* at Elbersdorf Lower Camp, from "The Quill". *(Author's collection)*

Wing Commander Joe Kayll, drawn by Cuthbert Orde. *(J R Kayll)*

Joe Kayll, Hornchurch Wing Leader, captured. *(J R Kayll)*

Nat Maranz. *(Author's collection)*

Officers from No82 Squadron at Spangenberg, summer 1941. *From left:* Robert Biden, Thomas Syms, Ben Newland, Ronald Ellen, Robert McKenzie, Kenneth Toft, William Keighley, Richard Wardell. *(Author's collection)*

The laundry cart in which Joe Barker and Eric Foster escaped from Spangenberg in August 1941. *(J R Kayll)*

Eric Foster and Joe Barker after recapture. *(via J R Kayll)*

Allan McSweyn. *(via J R Kayll)*

Kenneth Nichols. *(Author's collection)*

Morris Fessler. *(Author's collection)*

Flying Officer Oliver Philpot and his Beaufort crew in Dulag Luft, January 1942. *From left:* Gordon Rackow, Freddie Smith, Oliver Philpot and Roy Hester. *(Author's collection)*

Squadron Leader Thomas Calnan with his PRU Spitfire at Benson, 1941. *(Author's collection)*

Harold Bareham. *(Rosemary Bareham)*

Anthony Barber. *(The Rt. Hon. Lord Barber)*

Wing Commander R R S Tuck, air ace. *(Michael Stanford-Tuck)*

Bent props: the nose of Tuck's shot-down Spitfire. *(Michael Stanford-Tuck)*

The flak battery that shot down Tuck inspect his wrecked Spitfire. *(Michael Stanford-Tuck)*

Acting Squadron Leader Graham Campbell at Spangenberg. *(G C Campbell)*

MAPS AND LINE ILLUSTRATIONS

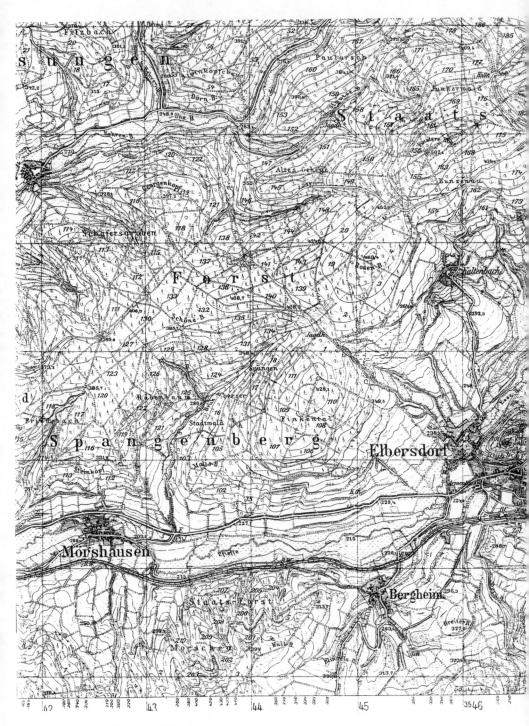

Map of Spangenberg and Elbersdorf, 1936. *(Stadt Archiv, Spangenberg)*

Preface

To begin with, the subtitle of this book is something of a misnomer, for it concerns not only Royal Air Force prisoners of war but also those of the Royal Australian Air Force, Royal Canadian Air Force, Royal New Zealand Air Force, South African Air Force, and the Royal Navy Fleet Air Arm, along with the French *Armée de l'Air* from the "Phoney War" in 1939 up until the aftermath of the invasion of the Low Countries and France in the summer of 1940.

Although the prisoner of war camps in which they were incarcerated have featured in several diaries, memoirs, biographies, histories and anthologies of escape stories published since 1945 — the relevant ones of which are listed in the Sources and Bibliography — nobody, as far as I know, has yet attempted to reconstruct a coherent history of aircrew prisoners of war in camps administered by the German Army between September 1939 and September 1942. Even in Aidan Crawley's excellent *Escape from Germany*, the official history of RAF escapes during the Second World War, the coverage of these camps is brief, and in most accounts they have appeared only as a preface to the main event, which has been the saga of Stalag Luft III and Stalag Luft VI, where the bulk of Allied aircrew prisoners were assembled under Luftwaffe authority as from 1942 and 1943 respectively.

Neither did this book start its life as the account that now appears before you. My intention, when I decided in 1989 to study seriously the subject of RAF POWs, rather than to continue passively consuming the kind of literature that I had been reading since 1970, was to write the complete history of Stalag Luft III to the exclusion of all other camps. This proved unrealistic, for two reasons. Firstly, no history of Stalag Luft III could be attempted without reference, in some detail, to the experiences the prisoners had undergone in the earlier camps, most of which had been run by the German Army. Secondly, as my appeals for information bore fruit, an abundance of material on these early camps came my way — and so fascinating was this material that it became clear to me that it would be nothing short of criminal to waste it. What finally tipped the balance was my realisation of the plain and simple fact that there was an enormous gap in the history of aircrew POWs, which would remain long after those involved had passed away — perhaps for ever — unless someone with the knowledge of and a passion for the subject did something about it.

Even then, *Wire and Walls* does not cover all the Army camps that held aircrew prisoners prior to their being gathered at Stalag Luft III. The camps described — Oflag XA, Itzehoe; Oflag IXA/H, Spangenberg, and Fort XV, Thorn (which itself was part of a larger complex of forts administered from Stalag XXA) — were only three of the many in which aircrew prisoners were held. Aircrew were also accommodated for a time in such camps as Oflag VB, Biberach; Oflag VIIC/H, Laufen; Oflag IIA, Prenzlau; Oflag XC, Lübeck; Oflag VIB, Warburg-Dössel; Stalag IIIE, Kirchhain; Stalag VIIIB, Lamsdorf; Stalag IXC, the vast POW camp at Bad Sulza from which the Army POW hospital at Obermassfeld was administered; Stalag XIIA, Limburg, and Stalag XXIB, Schubin. Most of the camps — the Stalags — were for NCOs and "other ranks". There are also many cases of aircrew officers and NCOs being held in small numbers (sometimes as low as one) for brief periods in a variety of Polish and French Army Stalags in the early summer of 1940. Holding aircrew prisoners in Army camps was a direct breach of the Geneva Convention, as was the failure, at times, to segregate officers and men. How this lamentable state of affairs came about will emerge as this narrative progresses, but the point I am trying to make here is that this history is only part of the story, and one in which many camps and all but a handful of NCOs and other ranks are conspicuously absent.

But from this complex state of affairs, a clear pattern emerges: with the exception of Stalag Luft I, where officers and NCOs shared the same camp but separate compounds, officers and men trod divergent paths on their route to Stalag Luft III. While NCOs were occasionally sent to Lamsdorf, then Barth, and then back again, officers were sent to Spangenberg, then to Thorn, then back to

Spangenberg (and finally to Warburg, which will be described in the sequel to this book, *Wire and Worse*). On one occasion a party of officers from Spangenberg was "purged" to Barth, but most were returned eight months later with a random selection of Barth "originals". On another occasion newly captured officers were sent direct to Lübeck, where they, too, were joined by another party from Barth, some of whom had initially been in Spangenberg, as well as another batch from Laufen. With the exception of three small parties of officers from the transit camp at Dulag Luft who were transferred to Spangenberg in the winter of 1941/42, all ended up, in autumn 1941, at Warburg. (As for the "Warburgers", many spent the winter of 1942/43 at Schubin, which by then had become an officers' camp, along with the bulk of those who had been at Spangenberg in 1941/42. But that is another story.) Thus a trajectory emerges: Spangenberg–Thorn–Spangenberg–Warburg. The story of these camps forms the backbone of this book and its forthcoming sequel. Future books will cover the history of the other camps, in particular Dulag Luft, Stalag Luft I and Stalag VIIIB.

Certain aspects of this narrative might need some explaining, particularly in regard to spelling the names and indicating the ranks of prisoners. The spelling of all surnames, except for those of French, Polish and Czechoslovakian prisoners, is as given in AIR 20/2336, the alphabetical list of Air Force prisoners in Germany, held at the Public Record Office. But where non-British personnel are concerned, I have tried to find the spelling preferred by themselves and their countrymen. Ranks are a thornier issue. By the time AIR 20/2336 was compiled, almost every officer captured as a Pilot Officer or a Flying Officer during the period 1939/42 had received time-promotion to Flight Lieutenant. However, to avoid confusion, I have maintained the ranks they held at the time of capture.

I have also endeavoured to describe how each of the prisoners mentioned in these pages found himself behind the wire — at least to the extent of giving his squadron number and the type of aircraft flown, and some details of the operation, especially the date. However, some shot-down stories have eluded me, and should any reader be able to throw any light on these omissions I will be grateful. However, I have deliberately omitted the capture stories of one group of prisoners who were originally in Stalag Luft I and then transferred to Spangenberg. Their accounts properly belong to the history of Stalag Luft I, and will be included in that camp history.

Some readers, particularly the ever-diminishing band of ex-POWs still living, might take issue with my rendering of some of the events of that period. However, I would point out that the keynote of this book is accuracy. I have read almost every book on the subject; interviewed and corresponded with survivors and their relatives; pored over diaries, Wartime Logs and POW letter-forms; and consulted official records in England and Germany. I have tried to cross-check every anecdote, apocryphal or otherwise, and have discarded anything that could not be verified or which seemed spurious or beyond the realms of probability.

As for service jargon and POW slang, I have kept this to the minimum required to convey the flavour of the period, and even then have limited its usage to practical and tactical situations (for example, flying on "ops", making a "brew"). Although a small percentage of the slang handed down to us may have been used widely at the time, most of it was used only occasionally, and certainly the ex-POWs who gave me the benefit of their experiences did not sprinkle their conversation or letters with such words as "goon", "Hun" and "Dienst" in the manner of postwar POW-escape books. Where I have used service and POW slang, I have followed it with an explanation in parenthesis; but only once, as I have included a Glossary to which readers may turn if their memory fails them.

Anyone who attempts a work of this nature would like to believe he is writing a "definitive" history — indeed, should set out to do so — but my aim in this book has been to lay out the material to facilitate future studies and provide a starting point for aviation, social and family historians who for either academic or personal reasons might seek information on one or a number of POWs and camps. In that respect I am more a compiler than an author, and I hope this book, the like of which nobody has yet attempted, is taken in that spirit.

At the same time, despite my best efforts, minor errors, if not major ones, are bound to creep into an ambitious project dealing with the minutiae of the day-to-day existence, over two and a half years, of more than two hundred men. Ultimately, the responsibility for any mistakes is mine. Corrections and suggestions will be gratefully received — but brickbats and lawsuits will not.

Acknowledgements

This book would not have been possible without the help, co-operation and enthusiasm of many whose story this is. They and their relatives answered detailed questions on their experiences, in both interviews and correspondence, loaned me diaries, Wartime Logs, POW letters, drawings and photographs, and egged me on when at times the mass of material confronting me made my head swim. My one regret is that during the thirteen years it has taken for the first book in this series to emerge, many of the ex-kriegies have died, and to list their names would make not only tortuous but also depressing reading. They are listed in the Sources and Bibliography, and I would like to thank them collectively for all that they have contributed.

Although to single out particular individuals is invidious, there is one I would like to mention, who does not appear in this book as he was not captured until 1943: former Flight Lieutenant R H ("Bobby") Stark from Northern Ireland, who for years gave me much encouragement and invited me to be his guest at the RAF Club whenever he flew to England on business. I would also like to thank the members of the Royal Air Force Officers' Ex-POW Association Dining Club for inviting me to their wonderful annual dinners on two occasions, and especially Captain H H Bracken, CBE, RN (Retd), who in addition to having a rich fund of anecdotes, provided me with virtually the entire proceeds of his researches in the Public Record Office on prisoner-of-war conditions in Germany and in particular on the issue of POW pay.

Thanks are also due to the Public Record Office for providing camp histories, escape reports, and the files of MI9; the Imperial War Museum, Lambeth, for allowing access to and reproduction of the photographs in its archives; the Bundesarchiv in Freiburg im Breisgau, which contains copies of almost every issue of *The Camp*; the Stadtarchiv Oberursel for allowing me access to the remains of Dulag Luft; the Stadtarchiv Spangenberg; and finally the staff at *Schloss* Spangenberg, now a plush hotel.

I would also like to extend my gratitude to Max Hastings, who permitted me to use material from his book *Bomber Command*, and to W R Chorley, whose excellent series *Royal Air Force Bomber Command Losses of the Second World War* rarely left my side during my researches.

Len Banks, an expert in Nazi German, translated German documents that were beyond my elementary German; and my wife, Isabel, checked the German throughout the manuscript. I could not have accomplished this task without them.

Glossary of Foreign Terms, Service Slang and POW Argot

AA ack-ack (qv)

AASF Advanced Air Striking Force, part of the **BEF** (qv) in France, 1939-40

Abort (Ger.) latrines

Abteilung (Ger.) section or department

Abwehr (Ger.) Military Intelligence Organisation

ack-ack AA, anti-aircraft fire (see also: **fireworks, flak, muck, stuff**)

AC1 (RAF abbr.) Aircraftman 1st Class

AC2 (RAF abbr.) Aircraftman 2nd Class

Amt (Ger.) office or service (plural, *Ämter*)

Appell (Ger.) roll-call (plural, *Appelle*)

Arbeitskarte (Ger.) worker's identity card

Armée de l'Air French Air Force

Ausweis (Ger.) card (normally an identity card)

bag (RAF slang) to seize, score or capture. One can "bag" an enemy aircraft; the Germans can "bag"
— ie, capture — one (one is thus "bagged"); one can be "in the bag" — ie, a prisoner; and one can
"bag" — ie, find or steal — something

bale out (RAF slang) to take to one's parachute

bash (service slang) feast; consume all at once

"Beehive" close formation of bombers (bees) with heavy, stepped up, fighter escort (hive)

BEF British Expeditionary Force

belly-landing (RAF slang) a landing with wheels up (see also: **wheels-up**)

black, put up a (RAF slang) boob

Blitzkrieg (Ger.) lightning war

brass-hats (Service slang) See: **top-brass**

brew (Service slang) tea; (POW slang) illicit liquor

bumf (RAF slang) paperwork; propaganda leaflets dropped from the air

bumfleteer (RAF slang) airman who drops "bumf" over enemy or enemy-occupied territory

Bürgermeister (Ger.) Mayor

'chute (colloquial) parachute

"Circus" (RAF terminology) Daylight raid by small force of bombers with heavy fighter escort, usually over German occupied-territories, with the intention of drawing up German fighters and chipping away at German air superiority

cooler (POW slang) solitary confinement cell, from the Service slang for detention cells, where hot-
heads can "cool off"

crate (RAF slang) aircraft, usually one that is obsolescent or obsolete (see also: **kite**)

duff (colloquial) incorrect, unfit, useless

duff gen (RAF slang) wrong information (see also: **gen**)

Dulag (Ger. abbr.) *Durchgangslager* — literally, "through-camp", or transit camp
Dulag Luft (Ger. abbr.) **Durchgangslager der Luftwaffe** — transit camp of the Air   Force

Ersatz (Ger.) substitute
Escadre (Fr. Air Force) Wing formation
Escadrille (Fr. Air Force) Squadron formation

Feldwebel (Ger.) Senior Sergeant
FAA (Royal Navy abbr.) Fleet Air Arm
flak (RAF slang) anti-aircraft gunfire, from the German *Flieger-(or Flugzeugs)-abwehrkanone* (air-defence cannon) (see also: **AA, ack-ack, fireworks, muck**)
Flieger (Ger.) airman
Flight (RAF terminology) one-third or one-quarter of a squadron's strength — ie, four to six aircraft — led by a Flight Commander in Fighter Command, and a Squadron Leader in Bomber Command; also slang for Flight Sergeant
footle around (RAF slang) to circle in search of a target

"Gardening" (RAF slang) mine-laying
gate, go through the (RAF slang) open the aircraft's throttle full out in order to fly at maximum speed
Geheime Staatspolizei (Ger.) *Gestapo*, Secret State Police
gen (RAF slang) information, usually genuine unless preceded by a qualification (eg. duff gen, Elsan gen, gen wallah, pukka gen)
Generalleutnant (Ger.) Lieutenant-General
George (RAF slang) automatic pilot
Geschwader (Ger.) Wing formation (Luftwaffe)
Gestapo (Ger. abr.) *Geheime Staatspolizei* (qv)
goon (Service slang) stupid person, but also any German
goonery (POW slang) squad of goons or a collective (generally unfair) act by goons
goon-skin (POW slang) fake German uniform
Grand Blessé severely wounded, sick for repatriation, etc
Groupe aérien d'observation (GAO) (Fr. Air Force) Army Co-operation Group
Groupe de bombardement (GB) (Fr. Air Force) Heavy Bomber Group
Groupe de bombardement d'assaut (GBA) (Fr. Air Force) Light Bomber Group
Groupe de chasse (GC) (Fr. Air Force) Fighter Group
Groupe de reconnaissance (GR) (Fr. Air Force) Reconnaissance Squadron
Gruppe(n) (Ger.) Group(s)

Hauptlager (Ger.) Upper Camp, also known as *Oberlager* (qv)
Hauptmann (Ger.) Captain
das Heer (Ger.) The Army
Heimatlager (Ger.) repatriation camp
Hitlerjugend (Ger.) Hitler Youth

intercom (RAF abbr.) inter-communication telephonic system of an aircraft

Jagdgeschwader (Ger.) fighter wing (Luftwaffe)
JG (Ger. abbr.) *Jagdgeschwader* (qv)

kite (RAF slang) aircraft (see also: **crate**)
Klippfisch (Ger.) frozen cod, sun-dried, issued to early POWs as part of their staple diet
Kommandantur (Ger.) administrative quarters
krank (Ger.) sick
kriegie (POW slang) prisoner-of-war, from the German *Kriegsgefangener* (qv)
kriegiedom (POW slang) prisoner-of-war life

Kriegsgefangener (Ger.) prisoner-of-war
Kriegsgefangenschaft (Ger.) prisoner-of-war life
Kriegsmarine (Ger.) Navy
Kühler German for "cooler"

Lagergeld (Ger.) camp currency
Lazarett (Ger.) hospital
Leutnant (Ger.) Second- or Sub-Lieutenant
Luftgau (Ger.) Air Defence District (plural: *Luftgaue*)
Luftwaffe (Ger.) Air Force

Machinenpistole (Ger.) machine-pistol; later known as a Tommy-gun
Mae West (official) Self-inflating life-jacket worn by aircrew, so called because it bulges in the right
    places
Met (RAF slang) Collective for Meteorological Officers
MI9 Military Intelligence 9; War Officer department set up to foster escape and evasion
MO (Service abbr.) Medical officer

Nachtjagdgeschwader (Ger.) night-fighter wing
NCO (Service abbr.) Non-commissioned officer (also: **non-com**)
"Nickel" sortie to drop propaganda leaflets over enemy territory
NJG (Ger. Abbr.) *Nachtjagdgeschwader* (qv)
non-com (Service slang) NCO (qv)

Oberkommando der Wehrmacht (Ger.) *OKH*, High Command of the Armed Force
Oberkommando des Heers (Ger.) *OKH*, High Command of the Army
Oberlager (Ger.) See: *Hauptlager*
Oberleutnant (Ger.) Full or Senior Lieutenant
Oberst (Ger.) Colonel
Oberstleutnant (Ger.) Lieutenant-Colonel
Oberzahlmeister (Ger) Senior Paymaster
OC (Service abbr.) Officer Commanding
Offizierslager (Ger.) officers' camp
Oflag (Ger. abbr.) See: *Offizierslager*
OKH (Ger. abbr.) *Oberkommando des Heers* (qv)
OKW (Ger. abbr.) *Oberkommando der Wehrmacht* (qv)
Op(s) (RAF slang) operation(s)
OR (Service abbr.) other ranks (ie, not officers or NCOs)
Ostfront (Ger.) Eastern (Russian) Front
other rank (Service jargon) rank and file below most junior NCO
OTU (RAF) Operational Training Unit

Panzer (Ger.) tank
prang (RAF) crash-land; bombing raid
pukka gen (RAF slang) absolutely trustworthy information (see: **gen**)
put up a black (See: **black, put up a**)

quick squirt (RAF slang) a rapid burst of machine-gun fire (also known as a **short burst**)

recce (abbr.) Reconnaissance
recco See: **recce**
Reich (Ger.) State
Reichsbahn (Ger.) State Railway
Reichswehr (Ger.) Defence Force
Reichssicherheitshauptamt (Ger.) *RSHA*, State Security apparatus

"Rhubarb" (RAF slang) fighter patrol, by a small number of aircraft, seeking targets of opportunity over enemy-occupied territory, usually when bad weather prohibits normal operations

Rittmeister (Ger.) Cavalry Captain

RM (Ger.) *Reichmark*, coinage

RSHA (Ger. abbr.) *Reichssicherheitshauptamt* (qv)

SBO (POW officialese) Senior British Officer

Schütze (Ger.) infantry soldier (originally, bowman or marksman)

Schutzstaffel (Ger.) *SS*, Defence Echelon

SD (Ger. abr.) *Sicherheitsdienst* (qv)

second dicky (RAF slang) Reserve Pilot on an aircraft

short burst quick squirt of gunfire

Sicherheitsdienst (Ger.) *SD*, Nazi Party Intelligence Organisation

skipper (colloquial) captain of an aircraft

SOE (abbr.) Special Operations Executive (qv)

Sonderführer (Ger.) Nominal rank, equivalent to Warrant Officer given to civilians attached to the Armed Forces for special duties

Sonderlager (Ger.) Special Camp, for hostages, persistent escapers and general nuisances

Speisefett (Ger.) literally, eating fat — sometimes real margarine, sometimes substitute, mostly lard

Special Operations Executive SOE, British clandestine organisation set up to create disruption in German-occupied territories

Speisesaal (Ger.) dining-hall

Sportplatz (Ger.) sports ground

SS (Ger. abbr.) *Schutzstaffel* (qv)

Staffel (Ger.) squad (Army), squadron (Luftwaffe)

Stalag (Ger. abbr.) See: *Stammlager*

Stammlager (Ger. Abbr.) *Mannschaftsstammlager*. Literally, team camp — a camp for NCOs and other ranks

Strafe (Ger.) punishment

strafe (RAF slang) (to) rake with gunfire

Straflager (Ger.) Punishment or Reprisal Camp

streng verboten (Ger.) strictly forbidden

top brass (Service slang) collective term for high-ranking officers, usually of Air rank (Also: **brass-hats**)

Unterlager (Ger.) Lower Camp

Unteroffizier (Ger.) Sergeant

verboten (Ger.) forbidden. See also: *streng verboten*

Vertrauensmann (Ger.) literally, "man who can be trusted" — Trusty or Man of Confidence

Wehrkreis (Ger.) (Army) Defence District

Wehrmacht (Ger.) Armed Forces

Wimpey (RAF slang) Wellington bomber — after the cartoon character J. Wellington Wimpey, partner of Popeye the Sailor

Wingco, the (RAF slang) Wing Commander (see also: **Wings**)

Wings (RAF slang) Wing Commander

WO (Service abbr.) Warrant Officer

WOp (RAF abbr.) pronounced as a word, the wireless operator of an aircraft

WOP/AG (RAF abbr.) Wireless Operator/Air Gunner

write off (RAF slang) kill, damage beyond repair

Wurst (Ger.) sausage

Zerstörer (Ger.) destroyer — ie, fighter aircraft

Zimmer (Ger.) room

Chapter One

A Fugato of Folly

London, Berlin and the Forgotten Men, 1939–42

"History," wrote Sir Cedric Gibbon, "is indeed little more than the register of the crimes, follies, and misfortunes of mankind." He might just as well have been writing about the circumstances of British and Dominion Air Force prisoners of war in the Greater Reich as about the Roman Empire, for certainly crime, folly and misfortune were their lot. Even the dogged British Prime Minister, Winston Churchill, knew how sorry their plight was. He had been a POW himself in the Boer War, and had essayed a passage in *My Early Life* much-quoted by 1939–45 prisoners, many of whom copied it into the Wartime Logs provided by the YMCA:

PRISONERS-OF-WAR! That is not the least fortunate kind of prisoner to be, but it is nevertheless a melancholy state. You are in the power of your enemy. You owe your life to his humanity, and your daily bread to his compassion. You must obey his orders, go where he tells you, stay where you are bid, await his pleasure, possess your soul in patience.

Meanwhile, the war is going on, great events are in progress, fine operations and opportunities for action and adventure are slipping away. Also the days are very long. Hours crawl by like paralytic centipedes. Nothing amuses you — reading is difficult — writing impossible. Life is one long boredom from dawn till slumber. Moreover the whole atmosphere of prison is odious — companions in this kind of misfortune quarrel about trifles, and get the least possible pleasure from each other's society.

If you have never been under restraint before, and never known what it is to be a captive, you feel a sense of constant humiliation, being confined to a narrow space fenced in by wire, watched by armed men, and webbed in by a tangle of regulations.

I certainly hated every minute of my captivity — more than I have hated any period of my whole life. Looking back on those days, I have always felt the keenest pity for prisoners and captives.

Churchill, however, did surprisingly little to help British prisoners of war, and did not even recommend the striking of a campaign medal for the strategic bombing offensive, even though for most of the Second World War it was the British and Dominion Air Forces alone who carried the offensive into Germany and the German-occupied territories, and RAF Bomber Command, with its strategic bombing campaign, which was the most aggressive arm in prosecuting the air war. Bomber Command also paid a heavy price, with 55,573 aircrew killed and 9,784 taken prisoner. Neither did Fighter Command's air supremacy come cheap. When, in November 1940, Air Marshal Sir Sholto Douglas, who had taken over from Hugh Dowding as C-in-C Fighter Command, began his policy of "leaning towards" German-occupied France, he found it was costing him more fighter pilots than his predecessor had lost during the Battle of Britain. By the time Germany surrendered, the number of British and Dominion Air Force POWs was 13,022 (4,480 officers plus 8,542 Warrant Officers and NCOs) — not counting those who had died in captivity, had been repatriated on medical grounds or had successfully escaped. They were among the finest and most highly trained material in the British Empire. It cost £10,000 to train a bomber pilot, and £15,000 for a fighter pilot — enough to send ten or fifteen men to study at Oxford or Cambridge for three years.

The earliest prisoners of the war were Regular and Short Service Commission officers, part-time Auxiliary Air Force and Volunteer Reserve officers, and senior NCOs and tradesmen other ranks. Many of the officers were ex-public schoolboys and adapted to camp life fairly quickly, being used to spending time away from home (and in any case most public schools were pretty spartan in those days). All the same, they resented the fact that their "war" had been so short and that they would never get another chance to "have a crack at Jerry". In the early days, they were the backbone of the escape committees and tunnel digging. But after two or three years, and many failed escapes, some of them became discouraged and took up other occupations — theatre, language courses, painting, music and writing. The Poles and Czechs — and the Free French to a degree — were exceptional cases. The first two were all determined to escape and get back to their own countries or England. Having had their countries raped and destroyed by the Germans, their hatred of the "Kraut" was immensely greater than that of the average Briton.

By the time Stalag Luft III, perhaps the most famous prisoner of war camp after Colditz, opened in March 1942 the Germans held almost 2,000 aircrew POWs (including British and Dominion Air Forces, Fleet Air Arm and Special Air Service). Most were already case-hardened prisoners who had at one time or another been dispersed among some of the grimmest camps in the Greater Reich. These were mainly camps for Army prisoners, several of which had originally been opened to accommodate Poles: Oflag XA, Itzehoe; Oflag IIA, Prenzlau; Oflag VB, Biberach; Oflag VIB, Warburg-Dössel; Oflag VIIC/H, Laufen; Oflag IXA/H, Spangenberg bei Kassel; Oflag XC, Lübeck; Oflag XIB, Braunschweig (Brunswick); Fort VIII, Posen; Fort XV, Thorn; Stalag IIIE, Kirchhain; Stalag VIJ, Krefeld; Stalag VIIIB, Lamsdorf; Stalag IXA, Ziegenhain; Stalag IXC, Bad Sulza; Stalag XIIA, Limburg an der Lahn, and Stalag XXIB, at Schubin in Poland.

Only two of the camps in which aircrew were accommodated had been specially built or adapted for aircrew: *Durchgangslager der Luftwaffe* (or *Dulag Luft*), at Oberursel, near Frankfurt am Main; and Stalag Luft I, at Barth-Vogelsang in Upper Pomerania. Both were run by the German Air Force, or Luftwaffe. The former was a transit camp and interrogation centre, the latter a "permanent" camp which, however, became full within less than a year, was expanded, and filled up again — with the result that, from then onwards, until Stalag Luft III opened at Sagan, aircrew prisoners were sent from Dulag Luft to Army camps. Conditions in these camps varied only from the cramped and spartan to the cramped and appalling. But aircrew were not exceptional in having to endure such privations, for the German Army treated almost all of its prisoners badly (along with its own soldiery).

This situation came about for a variety of reasons. Firstly, the German organisation for prisoners of war — under *Das Oberkommando der Wehrmacht* (*OKW*, High Command of the Armed Forces) — grew piecemeal and was chaotic. Secondly, rivalry existed between the various branches and departments of the OKW responsible for prisoners. Thirdly, Germany consistently underestimated the number of prisoners it would take as the war progressed, as a result of which its resources were constantly overstretched, with overcrowding and underfeeding as the inevitable concomitants. Fourthly — and mainly — no matter how pious the intentions of those bodies in charge of POWs, the fact remained that Germany was not only a military state but also a Nazi state. So over-arching was the ideology of Nazism that few members of the OKW, and few POW camp commandants, had the will to try to overcome the logistical problems they encountered — and many lived in constant fear of being taken before a military tribunal as "Anglophiles".

The OKW had begun formulating the policy it would take towards POWs long before the war, and evidence suggests that it intended to abide by international laws relating to POWs and to segregate them by service. Weimar Germany had been one of the first of the thirty-eight powers represented in Geneva on 27 July 1929 to sign the Prisoner of War Code and the Red Cross Convention (*see* Appendix I). These had their origins in the first, semi-official, Geneva Convention called in 1863, which was followed a year later by the first international laws of war regarding the treatment of the sick and wounded. Known collectively as the Red Cross Convention, they were ratified by forty-one states and revised in 1906. On 18 October 1907, the Red Cross Convention was extended by the Hague Convention, which for the first time in history laid down the rights and obligations of prisoners of war. But the Great War proved both Conventions inadequate and they had to be revised yet again. The 1929 Prisoner of War Code contained no less than ninety-seven specific articles.

But the provision of a Prisoner of War Code was one thing; the question of whether it would be observed and could be enforced was another. It was hardly to be supposed that Nazi Germany — a regime which had torn up the Treaty of Versailles, made a mockery of the Munich Agreement, herded thousands of Jews, Jehovah's Witnesses, communists, clerics, dissidents and intellectuals into concentration camps, and would go on to attack Poland without any declaration of war, violate the neutrality of Holland and Belgium and break the Molotov-Ribbentrop pact — would give a *Pfennig* for the Geneva Convention, particularly as it was signed by the Weimar Republic, which the Nazis did not recognise. It comes as no surprise to the historian to learn that thousands of prisoners who passed through the Greater Reich between 1939 and 1945 never even saw a copy of the POW Code; nor that, although in theory the Germans were accountable for anything that befell a prisoner once they had sent his "capture card" to the protecting power or the Red Cross, the OKW was largely indifferent to the fate of its prisoners; nor that there were no means by which to enforce the provisions of the Code.

It was possible for prisoners of war, in some camps, to appeal to German notions of fair play and thus ameliorate conditions. But the major factor in ensuring that the Germans complied with the POW Code was the fear that their own men imprisoned in Great Britain and Canada might be ill treated as a reprisal against their own unfair treatment of Allied POWs. As early as 1938 the OKW had foreseen that certain violations of international law would undoubtedly occur among all sides involved in the impending war and — on the basis of "do unto others before they do unto you" — had drawn up a tat-before-tit list of those it would violate in advance. With regard to POWs, it considered forcing them to do "war work" quite justifiable, and therefore urged that discretion be used in reproaching enemies for this practice.

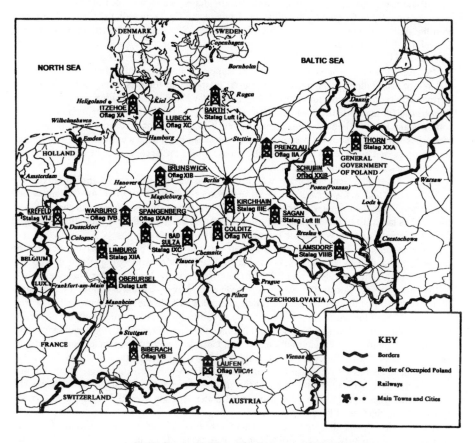

Fig 1. Camps Holding Allied Aircrew, 1939–1942

Throughout the war, POW affairs remained the responsibility of the OKW, which meant that in practice Hitler had the final say in all POW matters. His immediate subordinate in this area was General (later *Feldmarschall*) Wilhelm Keitel, Chief of the OKW and much-despised toady, who later testified at the War Crimes Trials at Nuremberg to the existence of a basic manual, *KGB-38* (Prisoner of War Directive No38), which contained all clauses in existing international agreements relative to POWs. These clauses applied equally to the Army (*das Heer*), the Navy (*die Kriegsmarine*) and the Air Force (*die Luftwaffe*). Every department down to the smallest unit had this directive and every soldier received some instruction as to its meaning and application. Furthermore, courses were instituted in Vienna to offer special training for those charged with the care of POWs. Finally, every soldier had instructions in his *Soldbuch* (pay-book) on the proper conduct towards POWs. On the other hand, German Regulation No9, Paragraph 462, advised POW camp guards that, upon seeing an escape in progress, they should shoot sooner rather than later, while Regulation No32, Paragraph 504, added that no warning shots were to be fired and that should a guard ever need to fire weapons, "they must be fired with the intent to hit".

Directly below Keitel was *General* Hermann Reinecke, who oversaw the activities of the *Allgemeines Wehrmachtsamt* (*AWA*, Armed Forces General Office), a division within the OKW generally concerned with personnel, training and equipment, which also had some influence over POWs in so far as it provided camp staff and *matériel*. Within the AWA was an office with sole responsibility over POWs, the *Abteilung Kriegsgefangenenwesen im OKW*, or the POW Office within the OKW. For most of the war the staff officer in charge of the POW Office was *Generalmajor* von Graevenitz. Prior to the expansion of Stalag Luft III in early 1943 this office was split into the *Allgemeine Abt* (General Office) and the *Organisation Abteilung* (Organisation Office). Each was divided into sections with specific duties, which were as follows:

Allgemeine Abt — Gruppe I: Discipline, punishment and legal proceedings; *Gruppe II*: Liaison with the protecting powers and Foreign Office; *Gruppe III*: German prisoners in Allied hands; *Gruppe IV*: Administration (stores, equipment, clothes and food); *Gruppe V*: Welfare and liaison with the Red Cross and YMCA; *Gruppe VI*: Return or repatriation of prisoners.

Organisation Abt — Gruppe I: Plans for new camps, changing the sites of camps and planning of large transportations of prisoners; *Gruppe II*: Responsible for personnel, eg the posting of German officers to such positions as (a) *Kommandeur des Kriegsgefangenenwesen (KGW)* in each *Wehrkreise* (defence district) or *Luftgau* (air district); (b) *Lager Kommandanten* (camp commandants) and (c) deputy camp commandants; *Gruppe III*: Camp security and investigation of escapes. Thus the first office was responsible mainly for POW affairs and contacts with foreign governments and welfare and relief organisations, while the second was in charge of camp construction, administration and personnel.

Gruppe II of the General Office was also known as the *Wehrmachtsauskunftsstelle für Kriegsverluste und Kriegsgefangene*, or Armed Forces Information Office for Casualties and Prisoners of War. At irregular intervals this body, which had originated early in the war, sent copies of its latest list of prisoners to the protecting power, the International Committee of the Red Cross in Geneva, and the War Office Information Bureau in London.

At the beginning of the war the POW system was run entirely by Army personnel, with the camps being staffed by *Wehrkreiskommandos* (military district work groups) and guarded by *Ersatzheeren* (Army reservists), and POWs of the British Army, Navy and Air Force being held in the same camps. But as the war progressed, each service assumed control of its enemy counterparts, so that the AWA found itself delegating authority to the Army, Navy and Air Force. These branches of the armed forces also had responsibility for communicating with the protecting powers — the United States of America until it joined the war in December 1941, and Switzerland thereafter — through the Foreign Office, the Red Cross and any other agencies concerned with the treatment of POWs. Representatives of the Red Cross, the protecting power and the various relief agencies had to get clearance from the OKW before visiting prison camps. Their activities were co-ordinated in the German Foreign Office by one of its under-secretaries, Baron Gustav von Steengracht, who from 1936 to 1938 had served under Joachim von Ribbentrop, then German ambassador to the United Kingdom.

Germany itself was divided into twenty-two *Wehrkreise*, or defence districts. Occupied territories were similarly divided. Prison camps were designated according to the number of the defence district in which they were located. The camps were divided mainly into three types: the *Durchgangslager* (*Dulag*, or transit camp), the *Offizierslager* (*Oflag*, for officers) and the *Stammlager* (*Stalag*, for NCOs and other ranks). Transit camps were mainly located on or near the front line. Attached to some main camps was a fourth type, the *Zweiglager*, or branch camp. This was usually designated by the letter *"Z"* following the Roman numerals. The combatant troops delivered their prisoners to *Durchgangslager*, and they in turn moved the POWs to the *Oflager, Stammlager and Zweiglager* located in Germany, Austria and Poland. Orders concerning POWs reached camp commandants through a long and tortuous route, starting with the OKW and filtering down through the *Oberkommando des Heeres* (*OKH*, Army High Command), the commander of the reserve Army, and the Army district commander before finally arriving on the commandant's desk.

Within the OKW there was, furthermore, an *Inspektor des Kriegsgefangenwesens* (Inspector of POW Affairs). Usually an Army general, he retained command of all prison camps in each district and his task was to see that OKW directives concerning prisoners were carried out. However, the function of this office changed frequently, and its power and influence rose and fell accordingly.

POW camps also fell within the orbit of the German *Abwehr* — or Intelligence and Clandestine Warfare Service of the OKW — under the command of Admiral Wilhelm Canaris. Each camp was assigned one or more *Abwehroffiziere*. They were drawn from *Abteilung III, Gruppe III-KGF. Abt III*, under *Generalmajor* von Bentivegni, was responsible for counter-sabotage, counter-espionage and security. Its work frequently overlapped with that of the Gestapo, particularly where matters of national security were concerned. As for *Gruppe III-KGF* itself, this had been set up at the beginning of the war to prevent espionage and sabotage in POW camps. The personnel from *III-KGF* attached to each camp commandant's staff were primarily interested in security, searches and escapes, but they also reported to their superiors in the *Abwehr* chain of command.

The relationship of the *SS* (*Schutzstaffel*, or Defence Echelon) and the *Gestapo* (*Geheime Staatspolizei*, or Secret State Police) with the administration of the POW camps is also worth elaborating upon, as these two organisations were mainly responsible for affairs outside, rather than inside, the camps but would increasingly involve themselves in POW affairs as the war progressed. In this sphere of operations the Gestapo worked with the *Kriminalpolizei* (Criminal Police, or *Kripo*) in an organisation called the *Reichssicherheitshauptamt* (General Security Office of the Reich, or RSHA), established, commanded and built into a ruthless terror-weapon by Hitler's favourite, Reinhard Heydrich. From its creation at the beginning of the war the RSHA was divided into seven *Ämter* (offices or services), none of which had a direct interest in the affairs of genuine prisoners of war whose governments had signed the Geneva and Hague accords. However, *Amt IV*, which was the Gestapo proper, had six *Gruppen* responsible for seeking out and repressing opponents of the Nazi regime. *Gruppe A* comprised as many as six sub-groups, charged with, among other duties, counter-sabotage and general security measures. *Gruppe C* had the powers of preventive detention, protective custody, and the compiling of dossiers and card indexes; *Gruppe E* dealt with espionage, and *Gruppe F*, the Frontier Police or *Grenzpolizei*, was responsible for issuing passports and identity cards, detecting fakes and patrolling the borders of the Greater Reich. The leader of *Amt IV* throughout the entire war was *Gruppenführer* Heinrich Müller.

Amt V was the Kripo. Led by General Arthur Nebe, it had four groups and was, strictly speaking, responsible only for the prevention and detection of civil offences. Its executive groups were: A — Criminal Police and preventive measures; B — Repressive criminal police, and crimes and misdemeanours; and C — Identification and searches. It was, however, inevitable that in the normal pursuance of its duties it would encounter, and therefore arrest, errant prisoners of war.

These two *Ämter* had their headquarters in the same building at 8 Prinz-Albrecht-Strasse in Berlin, but their respective leaders loathed each other. Indeed, it is now a matter of record that Nebe, despite a spell in one of the *Einsatzgruppen* on the Eastern front in 1942, disliked carrying out Gestapo orders concerning POWs and later became involved in the plots to kill Hitler.

The RSHA had representatives in POW camps, often holding honorary Army or Luftwaffe ranks, from as early as summer 1940, and kept duplicates of RAF prisoner of war records in its Prinz-Albrecht-Strasse HQ. Aircrew prisoners were considered important by the Reich owing to their expensive training and, therefore, their value to the Allied war effort. It followed from this that they were most likely to make escape attempts, and their records were marked with a red flag and the word *"Deutschfeindlich"* — "Enemy of Germany". In 1941 the Gestapo started to interfere systematically in POW affairs, following a meeting that July between Müller, Reinecke, General Breuer of the POW branch of the OKW, and Erwin Lahousen, a section leader from the *Abwehr*. Ostensibly, this conference was called in order to discuss measures against Russian prisoners, whose leaders had not signed the Geneva accords. However, its results, promulgated on 8 September 1941, were soon applied to other POWs:

> Insubordination, active or passive resistance, must be immediately broken by force of arms (bayonets, rifle butts, and firearms). Anyone carrying out this order without using his arms, or with insufficient energy, is liable to punishment. Prisoners who try to escape must be shot immediately, without being challenged. Warning shots are strictly forbidden... The use of weapons against prisoners of war is legal as a general rule.

In fact, this document was anticipated on 17 July 1941 by an order Müller issued to his agents in POW camps. He urged them to detect "all political, criminal or undesirable elements of whatever nature" in order to have them liquidated or subjected to "special treatment", and to seek out "all persons who could be employed in the reconstruction of the occupied territories". Any prisoners who "seemed trustworthy" should be used as spies to identify any fellow captives who needed to be suppressed.

To carry out these orders the Gestapo set up a special department, *Gruppe IVa*, under *Hauptsturmführer* Franz Koenighaus. It was hardly necessary. With agents already in all Oflags and Stalags, and Russian prisoners pouring in to them after July 1941, the RSHA already had a pretext on which to visit the camps. It was but a short walk, and a mere matter of another gate or two, for these functionaries to cross from the Russian to the British compounds.

(2)

Owing to the influence of *Feldmarschall* (later *Reichsmarschall*) Hermann Goering, Commander in Chief of the Luftwaffe, Air Force camps were a separate matter. They came under the control of the *Luftgau* (Air District) commander. Ever since Britain's declaration of war, Goering had been determined to fight according to the chivalric code of the Great War and to keep aircrew prisoners under Luftwaffe jurisdiction. In September 1939 he had told his units: "During the Great War, in which I participated as an active pilot, there reigned between the rival air forces a spirit of chivalry which lasted even after tempers got hotter... I wish and hope that the newly formed German Air Force makes this chivalry, in the fighting which is about to start, their guiding principle also." He was further motivated by a desire to ensure that Luftwaffe personnel held by the British were also well treated. During the first nine months of the war in the West, most prisoners taken by the British were from the Luftwaffe (with some from the German U-boat arm and the merchant service). Their lot in captivity would be influenced mainly by the treatment given to British and Dominion Air Force personnel in German hands. It was therefore understandable that Goering should be interested in bringing the department holding Allied aircrew under his command. Thus, Luftwaffe camps were by and large free from Army and OKW interference, a factor that would benefit aircrew POWs. The Navy was accorded the same privilege.

However, Goering was only successful in keeping the majority of aircrew prisoners under his control from March 1942 onwards (and even then the extent to which they were treated in accordance with his purported code of chivalry is open to question). For the first month of the war there was no camp in Germany for any captured British personnel, let alone aircrew. But some 700,000 Poles had been taken captive and the first RAF and FAA prisoners were held briefly in three of the Polish camps, Oflag XA, at Itzehoe; Oflag XIB, at Brunswick, and Stalag IXA at Zeigenhain. In October the Army opened Oflag IXA/H, at Spangenberg bei Kassel, for British and French officers and NCO aircrew. From December 1939 to July 1940 the only Luftwaffe camp for aircrew POWs was Dulag Luft, but this was only a transit and interrogation centre. From there prisoners were sent to Army camps. Officers went to Spangenberg (which accommodated the

RAF at various times between October 1939 and as late as January 1943) and, briefly in June and July 1940, to Stalag XIIA at Limburg an der Lahn and Oflag IIA, another Polish camp, at Prenzlau. A few officers (no more than eighteen to twenty) were also held in Stalag VIA, Hemer, and at Oflag VIIC/H, Laufen.

NCOs and "other ranks" went to Limburg; Stalag VIIIB, Lamsdorf; and Stalag XXIB, Schubin. Officers and NCOs who had been badly wounded when shot down were held at the prison hospital, Lazarett IXC, at Obermassfeld, along with the sick. (For administrative purposes, Obermassfeld hospital was attached to Stalag IXC, at Bad Sulza, near Mulhausen in Thuringia. The same camp also administered two satellite hospitals, at Meiningen and Hildburghausen; again, both were designated Lazarett IXC.)

The Army camps were considered "undesirable" by the Luftwaffe and on 5 July 1940 the first permanent aircrew camp run by the Luftwaffe was opened at Barth-Vogelsang, on the Baltic coast. As NCOs and other ranks would be in the majority, it was designated *Kriegsgefangenlager Nr.I der Luftwaffe* (or Stalag Luft I), and all subsequent aircrew camps were called Stalag Lufts even when officers were in the majority. But the Luftwaffe had underestimated the number of prisoners that would fall into its hands. By the end of 1941 Stalag Luft I held, in one compound, 128 RAF officers, about 140 officers of the Dominion Air Forces and the Royal Navy Fleet Air Arm, a sprinkling of Royal Marine, Army, Commando and Special Air Service officers, and their thirty orderlies (a mixture of Army and Air Force NCOs and ORs), and, in another compound, some 750 NCO aircrew, about six of them naval airmen. Some RAF officers were also held, by mistake, at Oflag VB, an Army camp at Biberach, and again at Oflag VIIC/H, Laufen. For a brief period, aircrew were also sent to the grim Polish forts of Posen and Thorn (Torun), administered from the nearby Stalag XXA, as a reprisal against alleged ill treatment of German prisoners in Canada.

In October 1941 Goering had ordered the construction of a new camp at Sagan, which was supposed to become a model camp where all Allied aircrew prisoners would be accommodated. In the meantime, new prisoners would be sent to Army camps: officers to Oflag IXA/H and Oflag XC (Lübeck), from both of which they would be transferred to Oflag VIB (Warburg-Dössel); and NCOs to Stalag VIIIB and Stalag IXC, and another Stalag, IIIE, at Kirchhain. Even when Stalag Luft III was opened, some officer aircrew remained at Warburg, being sent to yet another Army camp, Oflag XXIB at Schubin (formerly Stalag XXIB), in September.

Such, then, was the German state of preparedness for aircrew POWs from September 1939 up to the middle of the war. During this period, Germany breached almost every article of the Prisoner of War Code of the Geneva Convention, if not always in letter, then certainly in spirit. In some cases, newly captured prisoners were forced to march far longer distances than those stipulated, and were denied medical treatment. Under interrogation almost all were asked questions that went far beyond those required for the purposes of identification. In both transit and permanent camps many were held in substandard accommodation and denied the fresh-air exercise as laid down in Article 13; most were denied adequate food. They were collectively fined and punished for escape attempts and in some camps their food was tampered with.

(3)

While Germany had been shaping its policy towards future prisoners of war from as early as 1938, Britain did not confront the possibility that large numbers of its servicemen might end up behind barbed wire until it was forced to do so. Only after the outbreak of hostilities did the Foreign Office set up a POW Department, which would be led throughout the war by Sir Harold Satow. Not until the German offensive against the Low Countries and France was well under way in May 1940 did the War Office set up a Prisoner of War Directorate.

Initially, this tardiness was no doubt partly due to a belief that the war in the West might not develop. But for much of the war both departments, along with the Army Council, displayed a stiff-necked attitude, a distinct lack of urgency and a surfeit of confusion in dealing with prisoner of war affairs. When, in September 1939, the Foreign Office received two POW letters — one from the first squadron leader captured, the other from his observer — via Goering and his diplomatic contacts in Sweden, the civil servants complained because they had not gone through authorised Red Cross channels. Seven months later, in April 1940, the Army Council informed the

Joint War Organisation of the Red Cross and Order of St John of Jerusalem that it expected only 2,000 officers and men to be captured in the immediate future. On 15 June, when the British Expeditionary Force, driven out of Belgium and France, was evacuating through Dunkirk, the number of prisoners registered was only 1,345 — well within the Army Council's optimistic forecast. But thousands of personnel had been left behind in France, and slowly but surely the number of prisoners being registered increased. By the end of June it stood at 2,111, and by the end of July at 4,000. Even at that late stage the Army Council was unable to give the Red Cross any indication of what it thought the final figure would be. Not until November did the Council disclose the full figure of 44,000.

The Prisoner of War Directorate had representatives from all three Services and eventually spawned a number of subcommittees. They listed British POWs in enemy hands, including each man's name, rank and service number, and the designation and location of the camp in which he was held; attended to the welfare of prisoners; dealt with prisoners' pay and allowances; maintained contact with their next of kin and relatives; supplied their military clothing, which the PWD sent through the Red Cross; negotiated repatriation schemes; and regulated the voluntary organisations which helped POWs. These included the International Committee of the Red Cross (ICRC), the British Red Cross and St John War Organisation, the Young Men's Christian Association, the Relatives' Association and the International Student Body. The POW Directorate also took on responsibility for the welfare of Czechoslovakian, Polish, French, Belgian, Dutch, Norwegian and Greek POWs who had been captured while serving in His Majesty's Forces and whose governments were in exile in Britain. It also established an Imperial Prisoner of War Committee, which attended to the needs of Dominion POWs in German and Italian hands; on this sat representatives of the armed forces of Canada, Australia, New Zealand and South Africa.

Whenever it received a new list of prisoners from Germany's Armed Forces Information Office for Casualties and POWs, the Information Bureau in London notified the War Office's POW Directorate, and the POW Department of the Foreign Office, and also sent lists to the British Red Cross and St John War Organisation. The latter also established a special section called the "Wounded, Missing, and Relatives Department" to deal with the problems of missing men who could not be traced. It worked in close collaboration with the Admiralty, the War Office and the Air Ministry, each of whom sent it lists of all men missing in action. With the help of the ICRC it followed up the smallest clues in order to trace missing men.

Another means by which the POW Directorate received information about prisoners of war was by German radio. During the first year of the war, Josef Goebbels, the German propaganda minister, and his "editor and speaker" for foreign broadcasts at the *Reichsrundfunk* at Berlin-Charlottenburg, William Joyce ("Lord Haw-Haw"), had a British audience two-thirds the size of the BBC's. To keep them tuned in, Joyce regularly broadcast prisoners' names from the *Rundfunkhaus* in Masurenallee, or from satellite stations such as the *Bremensender* and *Hamburgsender*. Occasionally POWs were brought before the microphone to relate details of their capture. Lord Haw-Haw's news was passed on even when it was not heard by immediate relatives. Both the War Office and the British Red Cross Organisation treated these unofficial reports with scepticism, taking the view that they could not be checked and that, moreover, British citizens who had been informed that their husband, son or brother was a POW might be devastated when reliable details confirmed that he had in fact been killed. Such scepticism was ill founded, however, as, apart from occasionally misspelling the names of those captured, the Germans seldom communicated unreliable information on this subject except towards the end of the war when the Reich was crumbling from within as well as without. (In fact, of all the Allied nations involved in the Western theatre, it was the British who first gave up keeping accurate POW records, sometimes being three camps behind in prisoner transfers.)

In any event, the War Office forbade prisoners of all ranks from using German radio to transmit messages home under any circumstances, but a few prisoners were naturally tempted to use this means of letting their families know that they were safe. This undoubtedly owed something to the fact that very few prisoners — even the most senior officers and NCOs — were informed about Britain's POW arrangements. The same applied to their relatives. It was not until 1943 that the War Office issued *A Handbook for the Information of Relatives and Friends of Prisoners of War*, and the Government handled questions about POWs in the House of Commons only through a junior Minister. "I am astonished," says one ex-prisoner, former naval captain Hugo Bracken, "how very few questions were asked in Parliament about POWs between 1940 and 1944. I have only been able to find two in 1940, four in 1941, one in 1942 and two in 1943." Thus it was easy for both prisoners and their families back home to believe that they were being conveniently ignored.

British officialdom's attitude towards POWs is again illustrated by the reluctance with which it agreed to establish a sea route for sending them parcels of food, clothing and other essentials. On 2 September 1939 the British Red Cross Society and the Order of St John of Jerusalem had merged — as they had done in The Great War — into the Joint War Organisation, under the chairmanship of Sir Arthur Stanley, to bring relief to sick and wounded British servicemen and to ameliorate the lot of British prisoners of war. The Emergency Committee that had met to ratify this agreement had already devised the machinery to satisfy these requirements. This consisted of an Executive Committee, chaired by Lord Cromer, with Major-General Sir John Kennedy, a distinguished soldier, as vice-chairman, and fifteen departments, one of the most important of which was the Prisoners of War Department, with Lord Clarendon in charge, and Field Marshal Lord Chetwode among the distinguished members of its committee. (In June 1940 Lord Chetwode became vice-chairman of the Executive Committee. In September 1941 Lord Clarendon was succeeded by Major-General Sir Richard Howard-Vyse.)

The main task of the Prisoners of War Department was to supplement official ration scales by providing food, equipment and services that would bring the standard of prisoners' comfort up to the level the public would themselves expect. But this was by no means easy — for in effect it found itself supplying much that should have been normal issue, owing to the fact that the Germans consistently underfed their prisoners. A booklet entitled *Prisoner of War*, published by the British Red Cross in January 1942, pointed out that, in contravention of the POW Code, the food issued to prisoners sometimes fell below the standard of that issued to German garrison troops and that "if it were not supplemented from outside, British prisoners would be in a poor way". The War Office handbook went further: "...the German Government have committed serious breaches of the Convention. Of these, the most grievous is their failure to provide men with adequate food and clothing." More specifically, the Germans had estimated the cost of keeping a prisoner of war at 1.20 *Reichsmark* a day, the sterling equivalent of eleven shillings (11/-) a week. But they fed non-working prisoners — mainly officers and Senior NCOs — on one shilling and two pence a week (1/2d), that is, less than the provision for a non-working civilian. Even with Red Cross parcels, prisoners were receiving fewer than half the calories that the British and Canadian authorities were issuing to German prisoners, and were in effect being systematically starved. British other ranks engaged in heavy labour in coal mines received only slightly better rations and those working on farms were given "extras" by the farmers, who had a vested interest in ensuring they could work at their best.

Thus Red Cross food parcels became more a necessity than merely a luxury, and accordingly POWs turned to the Red Cross for their bare means of subsistence. Lord Cromer laid it down that the British Red Cross should always keep a large reserve of food parcels "in the pipe" to meet this contingency, and Mr (later Sir) Montague Eddy, in charge of transporting parcels, did his utmost to maintain the flow.

Up to the fall of the Low Countries and France, prisoners of war in Germany received Red Cross food parcels either by postal service from Britain or by road and rail from Belgium via Holland. But the 1940 campaign closed the latter route. It was not until December, by which time some members of the RAF had been prisoners for more than a year, that the British Admiralty opened a loophole in the blockade of Occupied Europe to allow ships chartered by the Red Cross to ferry vital foodstuffs, clothing and medical supplies between Lisbon and Marseilles so they could be sent on to Geneva. The first vessel, the *Julita*, sailed before Christmas 1940, and thus began a regular service controlled at all times by the Red Cross. Even then, full service was not resumed until April 1941, and the British Red Cross was subject to severe criticism by Members of Parliament, and letter-writers to *The Times*, who doubted the value and efficiency of its parcels service.

As the war progressed and the number of POWs increased, this enterprise was vastly expanded until there were ten standard types of food parcel, each containing slightly different foodstuffs but of similar calorific and nutritional value. Each contained ten shillings' worth of food, bought at cheap rates, and not subject to the usual duties and tax. The main ingredients were meat, fish, tea, cocoa, margarine (with added vitamins), pudding mixture, cheese-, egg- and milk-powders, chocolate, jam and biscuits. Cigarettes went in separate parcels.

The Red Cross also sent standard medical parcels, books, musical instruments, play-scripts, stage make-up and sports equipment, much of it supplied by the YMCA. Standard medical parcels — containing disinfectants, soap, bandages, gauze, lint, drugs and aspirins — were sent from London to Geneva every week, while the Invalids Comforts Section supplied special parcels for the sick. One was a "milk parcel" and the other an invalid parcel. A typical milk parcel contained one tin each of Benger's food, Allenbury's, Horlicks, creamed rice, lemon-curd, custard, tomatoes and arrowroot; two tins each of Nestlé's milk, Ovaltine, cheese, dried eggs and Yeatex, plus tomato sauce, barley sugar and chocolate. Hundreds of these items were packed each week into small tins. The invalid parcels contained more solid food — minced beef or sliced meat, tinned fruit, tinned salmon, meat and vegetable extracts, cod-liver oil and malt, glucose and honey. At Geneva there was usually a balance of 40,000 milk parcels and another 40,000 special food parcels. This was calculated on the assumption that five per cent of POWs at any one time would need medical attention. From Geneva they were sent to senior medical officers at prison camps and POW hospitals to use as required. In addition to these there was an occupational parcel, which contained patterns and material for making such things as slippers, waistcoats, belts, patchwork quilts, wall-pockets and tapestries.

"Utility" parcels of books could also be sent by certain specified booksellers, and cigarettes, pipes and tobacco by selected tobacconists. A prisoner's next of kin could send clothes three times a year.

Whilst utility parcels were addressed directly to individual prison camps, all other parcels had to go by what the authorities called the "Parcels Roundabout". At the beginning of the war, parcels were packed at St James's Palace, London, which sent out a mere twenty-six parcels a week. But after Dunkirk, when the number of POWs increased, the packing centre was moved to North Row, just off Park Lane, with another for next-of-kin parcels at Finsbury Circus. Many voluntary packing centres opened throughout England, the figure eventually reaching seventeen, plus another six in Scotland, including a centre for next-of-kin parcels in Glasgow. Parcels packed in Scotland were popular with prisoners because they contained oatmeal.

If a POW's wife wanted to send a next-of-kin clothing parcel it had to go first to Finsbury Circus, London, or to the packing centre in Glasgow, along with a list of contents. It was then unpacked, examined and repacked. At the Finsbury Circus centre a hundred girls — about four-fifths of them volunteers — worked at long trestle tables in a large room, and as soon as the postman delivered the parcel one of the girls unpacked it, spread its contents out on the table and examined them. First, she would check the "coupon goods". Next of kin were allowed special coupons with which to buy clothes for prisoners, and any unused coupons had to be returned when the parcel was delivered to the packing centre. However, some next of kin had been known to use the coupons for themselves. To make sure the items of clothing tallied with the number of coupons used, the girls subjected each parcel to careful scrutiny. Whenever there was a discrepancy, the parcel was delayed until it was accounted for and, if possible, rectified.

The next check was for contraband. No money, stamps, stationery or playing cards could be sent privately (playing-cards could be sent only in Red Cross games parcels). Nothing in tubes was allowed, as these could contain messages, and neither were food (except chocolate), medical comforts or cigarettes. Pictures and photographs had to go in separate letters. Dozens of parcels a week arrived at the centre containing pots of jam, homemade cakes or sweets. The girls had to take them all out and mark them "return to sender". They also had to search diligently for hidden messages — a favourite hobby with relatives, who would write endearments on thin paper and stuff them in the toes of slippers and the ends of glove-fingers. Some wives embroidered coded messages as patterns on clothes. These messages were normally innocent, but if the German censors discovered them they would naturally assume otherwise and delay issuing the parcel.

Once the girl had checked the contents, and made sure they tallied with the list inside the parcel, she had to repack them, firstly in corrugated cardboard, then in extra-strong, waterproof brown paper, which she tied up with string. (On average, the British Red Cross got through two hundred miles of string per week.) The parcel was now ready to start its journey. Until it reached Lisbon it was under the control of the General Post Office, who might receive it that same evening. However, the GPO sometimes had to hang on to it for as long as three weeks while the Ministry of War Transport awaited room on a convoy.

Vessels chartered by the ICRC sailed from Britain, the Dominions, the USA and South America to Lisbon and Genoa, where parcels from all these countries converged before being sent by sea to Marseilles and by rail to Geneva. (Experience had shown that trying to take the parcels overland through Spain was a hopeless proposition. Spain was unable to look after its own affairs, let alone help the Allies.) At Lisbon a stock of five or six weeks' food was always held over so that no ship was left idle upon its return from Marseilles. Another five million were also stockpiled at Geneva, where the Red Cross rented a huge warehouse and piled parcels from the floor to the ceiling rafters, in case of delays abroad. Later in the war a northern sea route to Gothenburg, Sweden, was established and from there stores were ferried across the Baltic to Lübeck and other ports in north Germany. From Britain there might be as many as 100,000 food parcels a week, plus five million cigarettes, as well as next-of-kin parcels. Another 100,000 food parcels a week came from Canada. Bulk food came from Argentina. Books were sent out by the British Red Cross and St John War Organisation at the rate of about a thousand a week, until by 1943 some 25,000 volumes stood on the shelves at the reserve library in Geneva.

A ship's cargo was usually made up of 75 per cent food parcels and the rest next-of-kin and other personal parcels. The latter were always given priority. When they reached Lisbon, they would go into the first available ship, and only when they were stowed away in the holds was the space left over filled with standard food parcels to add to the floating stock at Geneva. There, hundreds of people were employed on the enormous task of classifying and sorting the parcels. The food parcels were drawn from the stockpiles at a rate of one per man per week. Early in the war the parcels were addressed to individuals. But details of a new prisoner might not reach home for weeks or even months, in which case he would have to survive on the poor German diet and the charity of his fellow prisoners until his own parcels arrived. If a man moved camp he might never get the parcel meant for him. (To give the Germans credit, they set up a "lost parcels" centre at Stalag XIIA, and regularly published lists of unclaimed parcels in their POW propaganda rag, *The Camp*.) Eventually the system was changed and the parcels were sent in bulk to the camps, where they were shared out. Clothing and next-of-kin parcels were sorted out in Geneva first by country, then by camp. The ICRC then had to arrange with the German or Italian authorities for sufficient box-wagons to transport the parcels from the Swiss border to the camps.

Eventually the ICRC had eight ships in regular service. They ranged in size from the 1,000-ton *Padua* to the 5,000-ton *Malange*, which could carry 360,000 Red Cross food parcels on a single voyage. As many ships as possible were used at a time, but this was subject to the availability of crews, who had to be neutral — mainly Swedes, Portuguese and Spaniards. Each timetable and route had to be agreed between the enemy power and the detaining power, which then granted the vessel safe conduct. The Red Cross had to give the warring powers six days' notice before the ships could leave Lisbon, and make sure each ship was properly painted with large red crosses and installed with special lighting to illuminate the signs at night. Every ship's captain knew that any deviation from the agreed course could be fatal. Each ship took about a month to make the round trip from Lisbon to Marseilles and back again. Unloading at Marseilles was never easy because there was no British supervision for foreign labour. Even when the supplies were unloaded, their onward transmission could only be guaranteed after lengthy arguments between Red Cross delegates and the German authorities had secured the use of Germany's precious rolling stock. There might be anything up to five weeks' delay before the parcels moved again. The rail journey to Geneva could take as long as three weeks. A next-of-kin parcel might take as long as four or five months to make the whole journey from Finsbury Circus to its final destination.

Anything that was required urgently — such as special drugs, trusses, spectacles and false teeth — was sent by air, usually by the Invalids Comforts Section of the Red Cross Prisoners of War Department. A request would be sent from Germany by cable and the item was packed in London, if possible, on the same day. There was always a censor at the packing centre, so time was saved there straight away. Once packed, the item was immediately sent by "Clipper" to Lisbon, where it would be collected by a post office official who took it across to the office of the German airline.

The supply of artificial limbs was, however, more complex. Amputees were examined by an International Orthopaedic Commission, which had permission to investigate every single maimed British prisoner in Germany. Those who needed artificial limbs were sent to Lazarett IXC, the POW hospital at Obermassfeld.

Formerly a large agricultural school, this was a crude, ill-equipped building, which, by 1943, would house about a thousand, mainly British, Army POWs and about fifty RAF. Under the supervision of a German doctor — a jackbooted Army Colonel — and his orderlies and guards, it was run by British MOs: a former orthopaedic surgeon, Major W E Tucker; and Major W R Henderson, RAMC, a neurologist. They had a staff of about sixty officers and men of the RAMC. All had volunteered to stay behind and care for the wounded after the fall of Dunkirk. Despite the poor accommodation and inadequate equipment and medical supplies, they worked unstintingly for five years, overcoming German restrictions and carrying out major surgery on many thousands of undernourished prisoners. Dressings were sterilised daily by two orderlies from the Welsh Guards, using the boiler of a 19th-century road steam engine in an adjacent yard. Tucker, who had been an England rugby forward and a Cambridge Blue, and was well into his forties, pioneered the practice of moving muscles while still in plaster casts, and insisted that patients exercise daily. Artificial limbs were made by a team of Swiss experts in Geneva, who travelled to Obermassfeld to fit them.

Relief for POWs soon became the biggest and most expensive of the ICRC's many activities in aid of victims of war. Unfortunately, the fact that the Red Cross sent food, medical and comfort parcels did not mean they always arrived at their destination, nor that, if they did arrive, they were still intact. "The statement that parcels were released from stock at the rate of one per week," says Hugo Bracken,

gives the impression that the prisoners received parcels at that rate in the camps. That is absolute nonsense. I got part of a parcel in Dulag Luft [in August 1941] and then nothing while I was at Oflag XC, Lübeck, until I reached Oflag VIB, Warburg, at the end of October. After Stalag Luft III was evacuated at the end of January 1945 until we reached the United Kingdom in June I never saw a Red Cross parcel. In between those dates the issue of Red Cross parcels never exceeded one per room per week, or between one-eighth or one-twelfth of a parcel per man per week. I have checked this with a number of POWs, who are in general agreement with this. Had we received one parcel each per week we would all have needed a long course with Weight Watchers when we got home. Also I can recall only seeing one or two British Red Cross parcels; virtually all were either Canadian or American in Stalag Luft III.

There were from time to time rumours that the Germans had pinched some of them. These were investigated and proved to be unfounded. On the other hand, to our shame, it is a fact that Red Cross parcels were subject to a certain amount of pilfering by dockers in this country and elsewhere.

This was confirmed by the late Group Captain R B Ward, RAF, in a letter to the author in 1989. For nearly three years the officer responsible for issuing parcels in East Compound, Stalag Luft III, Ralph Ward recalled that parcels which went through Portugal were often tampered with and their contents stolen. There were also some unnecessary delays. In April 1942 there was again a serious shortage of food parcels. Packing had been cut down in Britain, and one of the ships chartered in Geneva had an accident and was out of commission for three months. The ICRC drew on its reserves in Geneva, until they, too, ran out. Eventually, normal service was resumed, and from then on POWs received Red Cross parcels at the rate recalled by Hugo Bracken. But some of the fortresses at Thorn, in which POWs were held throughout most of the war, received no parcels until 1943.

Despite these shortcomings, the activities of the ICRC, the British, American and Canadian Red Cross, and the various POW relief agencies can be looked upon as one of the great success stories of the war. The death rate among British POWs in Germany and Italy was only 5.5 per cent for the Army, 2 per cent for the Royal Navy and 1.5 per cent for the RAF — and that includes those killed trying to escape. Thus, there is hardly an ex-POW who has not at some time or another expressed undying gratitude for the help the relief agencies provided. The cost of administering such relief was also low. It cost the British Red Cross only eleven pence in the pound to collect funds, plus twopence-halfpenny in the pound for expenses in its headquarters.

Without this expenditure, the Red Cross believes, British and Dominion POWs on the continent would have died in their hundreds. However, Captain Bracken, once again, argues that

> such a catastrophe would never have been allowed to happen. Either the Germans would have been forced to increase the rations or the Allied governments would have been forced to provide the food — indeed, it can be argued that they should have done so anyway, rather than relying on private charity. In all probability there would have been reprisals against German POWs, and it should be remembered that after the German defeat in Tunisia the Allies were in an advantageous position, holding far more German prisoners than the Germans held British and Americans. It would, however, be true to say that we would have arrived back home in far worse shape than we did.

Until they received their first Red Cross parcels, prisoners taken in 1940 relied upon the charity of civilians they had encountered as they marched in POW columns through France, Belgium and Holland — and relatives and unknown benefactors on the continent — who sent personal parcels to many prisoners, who in turn shared the contents with their less fortunate fellows.

(4)

Alas, from the point of view of those who became prisoners, the same charitable outlook did not extend to most of the Whitehall departments responsible for their financial affairs. It was the job of these departments to ensure that only properly authorised expenditure was allowed and that the regulations that governed the economic blockade of Germany were enforced. But they were also responsible for ensuring that POWs continued to be paid, that their captors gave them sufficient advances on the pay accumulating back home, that the goods they bought in POW camp canteens gave value for money, that their next of kin were given a sufficient allowance throughout the war and that, finally, the detaining powers should be reimbursed after the war, while returning prisoners received the back-pay that had accumulated and were reimbursed for reasonable expenses incurred whilst in captivity. It goes without saying that it was also incumbent upon these offices to keep prisoners of war informed of their financial affairs and any other measures taken on their behalf, even if only to maintain their morale.

Pay procedure was provided for in the POW Code of the Geneva Convention and governed by private arrangements between belligerent powers. According to Article 23 of the Convention, officer prisoners should receive from the detaining power the same pay as that given to its own officers of equivalent rank who were also POWs, on condition, however, that it did not exceed that to which they were entitled from the armed forces of the country which they had served. This pay was to be granted in full, once a month if possible, and without being liable to any deductions for expenses incumbent on the detaining power, even when they were in favour of the prisoners. The Article went on to state that the rate of exchange applicable to this payment should be fixed by an agreement between the belligerents. In the absence of any such agreement, the rate adopted should be that in force at the time of the outbreak of hostilities. All payments made to prisoners had to be reimbursed at the end of hostilities by the power in which they had served. It was generally agreed that the advances in pay made by the Germans would be in the form of *Lagergeld*, or camp currency.

The conditions and pay of NCOs and other ranks were governed by Articles 30 to 34 of the Convention. Officers could not be forced to work, and neither could NCOs be forced to work outside the camps, although they could volunteer. Other ranks could be forced to work provided this did not involve direct war work — for instance, making munitions. Article 34 stipulated that prisoners should not be paid wages for work connected with the administration, management and maintenance of the camps. However, prisoners employed on other work were entitled to wages, to be fixed by agreement between the belligerents.

Article 24 of the Convention laid it down that the belligerent powers should agree to the maximum amount of ready money that POWs of various ranks should be allowed to keep in their possession. Any surplus taken from or withheld from a prisoner was to be entered into his account, the same as any deposit made by him, and was not to be converted into another currency without his consent. Pay to the credit of their accounts should be given to POWs at the end of their captivity. During their imprisonment, facilities were to be granted them for the transfer of these amounts, in whole or in part, to banks or private persons in their country of origin.

So much for the terms of the POW Code. What actually happened was markedly different. While the Germans often breached the pay provisions of the Convention, the British authorities, by and large, acted in violation of their spirit. The support of the Service Ministries for measures to mitigate the circumstances of prisoners of war was, to say the least, lukewarm. As a result of this, and Treasury-inspired opposition, the Service machinery worked very slowly and much to the disadvantage of prisoners.

In working out its pay policy, Whitehall gave consideration very early in the war to two requirements. Firstly, there was the probability that the enemy would have to be reimbursed for any issues of camp pay to officers. If deductions were not made at home from the pay of officer POWs then the money to reimburse the enemy would have to be met from the public purse. Secondly, the Government calculated all pay and allowances from the point of view of conserving as much money as possible in each prisoner's account in this country, ready for when he was repatriated. In effect, once the detaining powers had been reimbursed, the returning prisoners should receive a refund comprising camp money exchanged on arrival home, any sums credited to their accounts up to that time, and credits adjusted on the basis of any information brought back from Germany. Contributions and levies to communal funds and money spent in POW camps would not be refunded.

In anticipation, the Ministry of Defence docked a third of all officers' pay at source. In all, £1.7 million was deducted from the pay of officers in German camps throughout the war. The deductions from the pay of RAF officers and of the Dominion and Allied Air Forces serving with the RAF were held in a suspense account by the Air Ministry and eventually amounted to £646,365. However, the War Office proceeded in a dilatory manner and the steps it took to inform members of the armed forces about their financial affairs should they become prisoners were inadequate.

Hostilities commenced within hours of Britain declaring war against Germany, and a number of aircrew were taken prisoner within the next few days. Whilst sea and air warfare continued, land forces did not clash until the German invasion of Norway in April 1940. By then, more than fifty British and Dominion aircrew had been captured. The fighting in Norway went on until after the German invasion of France and the Low Countries on 10 May 1940. All Service departments had by this time realised that the so-called "Phoney War" had ended. In the event of major battles, prisoners might be taken in large numbers. Yet no agreement was reached with Germany about either the rates of pay to be issued to officers or the exchange rates to be used. Clearly, action was necessary.

Accordingly, on 16 May 1940, the War Office issued a Special Army Order, No 71/1940, which stated that from the day after capture pay would be adjusted according to the camp pay issued by the detaining power and that deductions would be made at rates notified from time to time by the Army Council. Marriage allowance would continue, but no other allowances were admissible beyond the day preceding capture. This order was followed by an Army Council Order specifying what deductions would be made from the pay of officers. The deductions announced were significantly larger than those that were subsequently agreed with the Germans, although officers' accounts were eventually adjusted and the difference refunded. It is unlikely, however, that many Army officers saw either order, as the war in the West had been going on for six days before the first was promulgated.

On 10 June 1940 Italy declared war on Britain and France. This added to the problems relating to officer POWs' pay since different deductions based on a different exchange rate would apply between those who were captured by the Germans and those captured by the Italians. Despite the greater risks of aircrew being taken prisoner, the Air Ministry issued no order until 11 July 1940. It was the only one issued by the Air Ministry throughout the entire war. AMO 463 was shorter than the Special Army Order since it dealt only with the pay of officers; otherwise it differed significantly in only one respect, in that it specified the deductions to be made: £6 a month from the pay of pilot officers and flying officers, and £8 a month from that of flight lieutenants and above. Again, these were provisional rates and were amended later on, with officers' accounts being adjusted. However, it is estimated that some 135 RAF officers were shot down and captured before this AMO was promulgated. No follow-up was ever issued giving the actual rates used, and no information was given at briefings or escape and evasion lectures prior to operations. The same applied to arrangements for the transfer home of savings — or credits — against camp pay.

Finally, the Admiralty issued Admiralty Fleet Order (AFO) 2881/40 on 1 August 1940. Again, this was shorter than the Army Order and specified the deductions to be made, which, rank for rank, were the same as those in the AMO. These, too, were subsequently amended.

Negotiations with both the Germans and the Italians started before the end of 1940. Britain and Germany reached an agreement in January 1941 that each side would provide food and accommodation for officer prisoners without charge, and on the relative ranks between the armed forces of each side. But a long wrangle ensued about exchange rates. It was difficult to apply Article 23 of the POW Code because in 1939 the Germans operated a system of multiple exchange rates which varied according to what use the foreign currency was to be put. The rate of exchange to be used was vital because it would determine the amount each side would have to reimburse the other once the war was over. Britain favoured the rate of 22 *Reichsmarks* to the pound sterling, while the Germans suggested RM10 to the pound. However, Britain was in a weak bargaining position, as the Germans by then held more than 1,500 British and Commonwealth officer prisoners while Britain held less than five hundred of theirs, and the scale of pay for German officers was lower than that for the British. Finally, in February 1941 — seventeen months after the war had started — the two sides agreed a rate of RM15. This defeated Britain's plans, which were, firstly, to secure the highest rate possible, so as to reduce the amount payable to enemy prisoners at the expense of the British taxpayer, and, secondly, to preserve the largest amount of pay due to British prisoners upon their repatriation.

British officer prisoners in Germany received news of this on 18 February 1941, when a letter reached the Army camp, Oflag IXA/H, Spangenberg, from the American Embassy. The letter, addressed to Army officers, specified that they were being paid RM15 to the pound sterling, and that deductions from their pay might be made after the war for clothes received in Red Cross parcels. However, Spangenberg was the only camp that received such information, and in any case the letter made no mention of savings. A similar announcement by the Admiralty is on record in the form of AFO 3023/41, issued on 17 July 1941. There is no evidence of an Air Ministry Order being promulgated in the RAF camp at Barth nor in Spangenberg, where the RAF were in a minority; if there was an AMO, then it was given a low priority. On 17 May 1941, these same Army prisoners, by now in Oflag VIB, Warburg, received news that all their credit and cash in hand at the end of the war would be exchanged. Again, there is no record of any such information being promulgated in the RAF camp at Barth.

As it was, the rates of pay issued each month to officer POWs in Germany, along with deductions made at home, were calculated as follows:

RN	ARMY	RAF	CAMP PAY (GERMANY)	DEDUCTIONS IN UK
Captain	Colonel	Grp Capt	RM150	£10 0s 0d
Commander	Lt-Col	Wing Cdr	RM120	£8 0s 0d
Lt Cdr	Major	Sqn Ldr	RM108	£7 4s 0d
Lieut	Captain	Flight Lt	RM96	£6 8s 0d
Sub Lieut	Lieut	Flg Officer	RM81	£5 8s 0d
A/Sub Lnt	2nd Lnt	Pilot Officer	RM72	£4 19s 0d

By 1942, a flight lieutenant in the RAF was being paid £36 5s 0d a month. After income tax and National Insurance contributions he was left with a net pay of £26 9s 0d. Even if the Germans issued the equivalent of £6 4s 0d in camp currency, it would amount to only 24 per cent of his net pay. Royal Navy lieutenants were at an even greater disadvantage. They were paid £27 4s 0d a month, and were left with £20 9s 0d after income tax and NI contributions. An RN lieutenant issued with the same amount of camp currency as a flight lieutenant would therefore have 31 per cent of his net pay deducted. An Army lieutenant, in 1942, would lose 34 per cent.

No information explaining the rates in such detail was circulated either to aircrew POW camps or at home. This was despite the formation, in late 1940, under the Prisoner of War Directorate, of the Inter-Departmental Prisoner of War Co-ordinating Committee (Finance). Chaired by the Foreign Office, it had representatives from the Treasury, all three branches of the armed forces and officials from the Dominion governments. The ICCF, as it became known, administered the pay and allowances of Allied and Dominion POWs in the European theatre, as well as those of the Allied governments in exile, and took on responsibility for financial dealings with the Germans, the Italians, the Protecting Power and the ICRC. It would recover costs at a later date, but meanwhile Dominion officers had deductions made from their pay at the same rate as British officers of equivalent rank, as did the French, Belgians, Poles and Czechs captured while serving with the British armed forces. The ICCF later became Sub-Committee B of the Imperial Prisoner of War Committee.

The failure of this committee to issue accurate and up-to-date information regarding pay and deductions was not for want of opportunity. In 1941 a pamphlet entitled "The Duties of a Prisoner of War" was distributed to the armed forces. Yet it made no mention of camp pay or credits. Aircrew also received escape and evasion briefings prior to flying on operations, and although these covered the rights and obligations of POWs, the matter of pay was again neglected.

At the end of 1941 the Air Ministry representative on Sub-Committee B voiced his concern about the paucity of information about pay so far sent to camps in Germany. He strongly urged that more information be sent. The chairman put up some resistance, but ultimately work began on a suitable document, which became known as the "Camp Leaders' Guide". Apart from information of a general nature, such as procedures for divorce and financial arrangements for prisoners' families, this guide contained, for the first time, an undertaking that the British Government would refund credits at the agreed rates of exchange after the war and pointed out that camp currency would be subject to income tax. However, administrative delays prevented it from being ready before August 1944, by which time it was too late to reach many of the camps. In lieu of this, letters were sent by each Service Ministry to the senior officers in each camp giving details of deductions in pay and credit arrangements — but not until autumn 1943, four years after the war had started. In the meantime, copies of the Geneva Convention, with its relevant clauses on pay, were seldom given to Senior British Officers in camps in Germany or even posted for prisoners to see; not that this would have helped, for the Convention did not mention deductions from pay. British POWs had no idea that the exchange rates agreed between the two sides left them much worse off than German and Italian prisoners.

It is quite clear from the foregoing that Whitehall's pay policy was poorly promulgated. However, the truth remains that even if the opposite had been the case, the policy would not have worked. For it was based on a patchy knowledge of conditions in POW camps and was therefore completely unrealistic.

In most camps, token money was usually issued monthly except during the first and last few months of war, when conditions in Germany were chaotic. Royal Navy and Royal Marine officers were paid one rank lower than the RAF by the Germans owing to a dispute about relative ranks. The pay was in the form of *"Wehrsold"*, which looked like large bus tickets and were in denominations ranging from 10 *Lagermark* to 10 *Pfennige*. The possession of genuine currency was a punishable offence, and such money was confiscated without being credited to the culprit's account. But in any case there was very little that prisoners in Germany could buy. Protecting Power and Red Cross reports of conditions in POW camps in Germany in 1941 revealed the following about camp canteens:

May	Oflag IXA/H, Spangenberg	Not bad
	Oflag IVC, Colditz	Not bad
July	Oflag IXA/H	Very badly stocked
	Stalag Luft I, Barth	Not bad
October	Oflag VIB, Warburg	No canteen
	Oflag IXA/H	Very badly stocked

To make matters worse, the Germans levied a 10 per cent tax on purchases from camp canteens, and inflation in Germany was increasing at a faster rate than in Britain, thus eroding further the value of camp money. Britain tried to get the issues halved for prisoners of both sides, but the Germans refused, as the camp canteens in Britain and Canada were well stocked and German prisoners could use their camp pay effectively. The Germans did, however, indicate that they had no objection to the British proposal being adopted unilaterally. This the British Government was unwilling to accept; it withdrew the proposal — without providing any explanation, then or since.

Even assuming that camp money was issued regularly and in full, it would have been difficult, if not impossible, for POWs to hang on to it for exchange upon repatriation. For the sad fact is that all prisoners changed camps at least once during their period of internment, while hundreds changed camps between three and nine times. Within two weeks of the letter from the American Embassy reaching Spangenberg in March 1941, for instance, the camp was cleared out and all the prisoners sent to a *Straflager* in Poland. In the year that followed, all were moved at least three times and some as many as four.

These moves frequently took place without sufficient warning or adequate transport, and often ended at squalid and disorganised camps. Prisoners on these "purges", as they were called, were lucky even to get proper rations, let alone space in which to store heaps of dirty *Lagergeld*. Escapers were even less fortunate. There was no guarantee that a man who had escaped would be returned to the same camp upon recapture, and he certainly could not expect his old pals to look after his *Lagergeld* while he spent the rest of the war in another camp. (Besides, there was a much more urgent use for *Lagergeld*, associated with the lack of toilet-paper.) Escapers also had money docked from their camp accounts as fines. On one occasion, when a tunnel was discovered at Stalag Luft I, Barth, the Germans imposed a fine of 4,500 *Reichsmark*.

Towards the end of 1941 Germany proposed that lists of credits be sent to the British authorities from the camps — but two years of negotiations were to elapse before this scheme started to operate. Even then, not all prisoners had their accounts credited, either because the Germans lost accounts when they transferred prisoners from one camp to another, or because the information from camps did not reach home, or because the authorities took no action on the information received. In the meantime, during periods in which supplies of Red Cross parcels were held up, Air Force prisoners in Stalag Luft I, existing on a meagre German diet, had perforce to spend camp pay on food that should have been issued by the enemy. They were to confront another problem later, in Stalag Luft III, when the Germans decided that administering camp pay was too much bother and the issue of *Wehrsold* to individual prisoners ceased.

The behaviour of the British Government contrasts markedly with that of other Allied administrations, who either made no deductions in pay, got the issues of camp currency reduced or undertook to refund nearly all the deductions made. Dominion officers were already better paid than those in the RAF, and neither the Australians nor the New Zealanders paid income tax while serving overseas. Nevertheless, their governments decided to adopt a more charitable stance towards the question of deductions and refunds in the light of privation, hardship and degradation that POWs suffered and in view of the very low, and at times non-existent, value of the currencies in which advances in pay were made. The British Government possessed the same knowledge, but preferred to be penny-pinching.

Thus, while British officers POWs were being underfed by their German captors and were using camp pay to supplement their paltry rations, back home the authorities who were supposed to be looking after their interests were docking one-third of their pay. After the war, the Ministry of Defence and the Treasury would go into mental contortions to wriggle out of paying them back, even going so far as to suggest that ex-POWs were already as well off, if not better off, than those who had not been captured because they had been unable to spend their pay! To add insult to the injury, they claimed that refunds to former officer POWs "would be unfair to those who continued to fight". As this book will show, the RAF continued to fight for their country even when behind barbed wire.

(5)

The Government's claim that former officer prisoners, once given refunds, would be as well off, if not better off, than "those who had continued to fight" carries with it the sneering imputation that these officers became — or at least remained — POWs by choice, and were therefore shirking their duty. In fact, they would never have been captured at all had they not been in the front line to begin with, and it is common knowledge that all officers were given to understand that the surrendering of arms did not mean they should sit out the war and await liberation by their own armed forces. It was their duty, by all possible and reasonable means, to escape. Staff officers at Bomber Command headquarters in High Wycombe, Buckinghamshire, and at the Directorate of Operations & Intelligence at the Air Ministry, spent several months preparing a memorandum to this effect, offering common-sense advice on the procedures aircrew should adopt on either baling out over, or force-landing on, enemy and neutral territory. The chief instigators seem to have been Wing Commander A J Rankin, at Intelligence, and Air Commodore N H Bottomley, Senior Air Staff Officer at High Wycombe from 1938 to the end of November 1940. Their efforts to have the memorandum ready within weeks of the outbreak of hostilities were, however, frustrated by indecisiveness and prevarication in the higher echelons of the Air Ministry, particularly, it would appear, the Deputy Chief of Air Staff.

Within the camps aircrew POWs were encouraged to escape by their senior officers. Even those who did not make escape attempts were prepared to do escape work if required and many of them bribed and demoralised guards, operated secret radios, and sent intelligence home in coded letters. In every camp in which aircrew were held, these prisoners continued to fight the war from within. Their activities were fostered in Britain by an organisation known as MI9, which, liaising with Wing Commander Rankin and Air Commodore Norman Bottomley, prepared aircrew to evade capture on being shot down and to escape from prison camps if captured.

The extent to which the War Office considered escape and evasion a duty is indicated by the fact that as early as November 1938, two staff officers in separate branches of the War Office proposed creating an organisation to train servicemen in escaping if captured and to send intelligence back from POW camps. They were Captain (later Major) A R Rawlinson and Major J C F Holland DFC. Rawlinson had been in the sub-branch of the War Office responsible in 1917/18 for interrogating ex-POWs and promoting escape and evasion. Holland would go on to create the Commandos and the Special Operations Executive (SOE). In autumn and winter 1939 the War Office and the RAF Directorate of Operations & Intelligence held consultations with Holland and escapers from the Great War to decide how help could best be given to prisoners taken in the fresh outbreak of hostilities. Their proposals were passed on to the Joint Intelligence Committee and, on 23 December 1939, MI9 was formed under Major (later Brigadier) Norman R Crockatt DSO, MC, of the Royal Scots Fusiliers, to study the problems of escape and evasion in the light of their advice. Its office was in room 424 of the Metropole Hotel in Northumberland Avenue, a couple of furlongs away from the main War Office buildings.

Initially, MI9's brief was to interrogate enemy prisoners, to organise the escape of British prisoners and debrief them, and to help maintain escape routes set up in France, Belgium and Holland by patriotic civilians. But its scope soon increased, and its objectives were later defined retrospectively as follows: (i) to supply money and radio communications to escape lines; (ii) to drop supplies; (iii) to arrange pick-ups by aircraft and naval evacuations from the coast of France; (iv) to train new agents and establish new routes; (v) to train servicemen in evasion and escaping; (vi) to provide them with escape kits; (vii) to send escape equipment to POW camps in Germany, Poland and Italy; (viii) to gather and distribute intelligence from the camps and from interrogating escapers and enemy POWs; (ix) to deny information to the enemy; and (x) to maintain POW morale. In December 1941 the side dealing with enemy prisoners became MI19, while MI9 was divided into five subsections — b for liaison with other branches of the services and interrogation of returned evaders and escapers; d for training; x for the planning and organisation of escapes; y for codes; and z for tools.

Documentary evidence shows that MI9 was highly successful in aiding evasion. But the late Airey Neave, who was the first Briton to make the home run from Colditz and who joined MI9 in May 1942, found its records difficult to interpret when he began writing the first full-length account of its exploits. They contain little of relevance to any of the prison camps in which the Royal and Dominion Air Forces were held, but it is worth going into the history of MI9 at some length in order to establish how far the War Office went to foster escape activities amongst aircrew

POWs, particularly as most of them were held in Army camps during the first half of the war.

After the Metropole suffered bomb damage in September 1940, Crockatt moved his HQ to Wilton Park, a country house on the eastern edge of Beaconsfield, in the Chilterns. Sections *b* and *d* at Beaconsfield — known as Camp 20 — collected intelligence about Allied POWs from the interrogation of escapers and other sources, and built up a system of briefing the three services on how to avoid capture. The centre of operations for escape lines in North-West Europe was Room 900 of the War Office, with MI9*b* staff at an interrogation centre in the London Transit Camp — formerly the Great Central Hotel — in Marylebone.

Room 900 also provided information for evasion briefings, sent by agents in occupied territory. This included advice on what to do when shot down, and details of German controls in frontier and coastal zones and their methods of checking passengers on trains.

Travelling MI9 lecturers started briefing operational units of the Army, Navy and Air Force at least as early as January 1940. But it was in the middle period of the war that the number of lectures reached its peak. From 1 January 1942 to 25 August 1944 — that is, from three months prior to the opening of Stalag Luft III until five months after the mass escape therefrom in March 1944 — MI9 gave 1,450 lectures to RAF personnel, 290,000 of whom attended. Many memoirs by wartime airmen, and histories of fighter and bomber operations, have included accounts of these lectures. They were often given by successful escapers from the Great War — such as Squadron Leader A J Evans MC and Flight Lieutenant H G Durnford MC — and by returned escapers and evaders from Hitler's war. However, the talks tended to concentrate on how to evade capture, rather than escape from prison camps, since in North-West Europe the main objective of MI9 was to secure the return of trained men by the Resistance.

Not only did these lectures provide information and advice which gave the men confidence in their ability to avoid arrest but they also placed great emphasis on the security of MI9's agents and helpers. Hitler and Goering knew of the existence of escape lines and appreciated the value to the Allied war effort of hundreds of airmen slipping through Axis hands. They gave orders that the lines were to be crushed. The *Feldgendarmerie* (Field Police) and Secret Field Police of the *Abwehr* repeatedly invaded the homes of helpers in the dead of night and carried them off for interrogation. In Brussels and Paris, Goering's Secret Police of the Luftwaffe collaborated with their political enemies in the Gestapo and *Sicherheitsdienst* (*SD*, or Security Service) in subjecting helpers and Allied airmen to brutality otherwise alien to the Luftwaffe. The Gestapo tortured captives by beating, ice-cold bath treatment and electric shock. Thus, MI9 warned airmen that on no account were they to put in writing the names and addresses of those who hid them. Any airman captured by the Gestapo while in the hands of escape organisations was to give only his name, rank and service number, as he was obliged to do if captured in combat.

For the same reasons, MI9 lecturers withheld concrete information regarding the locations and members of escape lines. By the end of 1942 there were four principal lines in operation, employing at the very least 12,000 helpers. The evader could only hope that once he had made contact with a patriot he would be handed on to one of these lines. The first — set up in July 1940 with the help of an MI6 agent, Donald Darling, then based in Lisbon — eventually ran from Paris, through Vichy France to Barcelona, as well as having collection points for evaders at Normandy, Rouen, the Pas de Calais, Marseilles and Toulouse; this later became known as the PAO (Pat O'Leary) Line. As many as two hundred and fifty people worked for it as couriers, forgers and clothes suppliers. Guides were recruited in Perpignan, and authorised by the Treasury to receive payment of £40 for each officer and £20 for each "other rank" they led across the Pyrenees. As frontier controls tightened, the prices increased. The cost of sheltering and feeding evaders in one year alone was at least six million French francs, all of which the Treasury credited to accounts in England. Once in Spain, successful evaders were taken by train to the consulate in Barcelona. After a brief interrogation at the British Embassy in Madrid they went by coach to Gibraltar, usually as a party of "students". There, they were interrogated by Donald Darling, who had been transferred from Lisbon in January 1942 and who arranged their passage home. The PAO Line also evacuated evaders by sea from the coast of southern France to Gibraltar. By the end of the war it would rescue more than six hundred Allied airmen and soldiers.

Even more startling successes were achieved by the Comet Line, which in 1941 had started passing soldiers and airmen through a chain of "safe houses" in Brussels and Paris and down to

San Sebastian and Bilbao. It cost 6,000 Belgian francs to pass an airman down to St Jean de Luz and 1,400 pesetas for a guide across the Pyrenees. But between July and October 1942 alone this line escorted fifty-four men to Spain. In its three years of life it would return more than eight hundred soldiers and airmen.

A third line, though less successful, was run by an MI9-trained agent, Mary Lindell, Comtesse de Milleville, who passed evaders from Paris and Bordeaux to Perpignan and across the Pyrenees. The fourth, known as "Shelburne", was established to house and feed airmen in Paris and pass them on to Brittany for naval evacuation to Dartmouth or for passage down to Spain. It would not, however, achieve its first success until January 1944. By July 1944 Shelburne would rescue three-hundred and sixty-five airmen.

MI9 provided money, radio links and trained agents for all these lines throughout the war. The officer in charge of maintaining these escape lines was Lieutenant-Colonel J M Langley MC, MBE, of the Coldstream Guards, who despite the loss of an arm at Dunkirk had escaped to England via Spain in the spring of 1941. He was based at Room 900.

There was a fifth line, however, with which MI9 had no connection: the Dutch-Paris Underground, established in 1941 by John Henry Weidner, a Seventh-Day Adventist from the Netherlands. Stretching from Holland, through Belgium and France and down to the Swiss and Spanish frontiers, Dutch-Paris would eventually employ more than three hundred helpers and save more than a thousand Jews and a hundred and twelve Allied airmen.

Running parallel to the escape and evasion briefings given by MI9d lecturers was Intelligence School 9 (IS9) at Caen Wood Towers in Highgate, North London, where Intelligence Officers of all three services were briefed on evasion and escape so they could lecture their own units. IS9 had its origins in September 1941, when the RAF started a series of Intelligence Courses at Station "Z", Harrow, which eventually became known as the "A" Courses of the RAF Intelligence School. The Air Ministry approached MI9 with a view to starting an MI9 course at the school, intended to train RAF Intelligence Officers as instructors in escape and evasion. All IOs on Operational Training Units and Operational stations would undergo the course, and at least one officer on each station would be made responsible for instructing aircrew in MI9 subjects. MI9 lecturers would continue to brief aircrew directly, and successful escapers and evaders would go on lecture tours. The first MI9 course, known as the Special Intelligence Course No1 and later called "B" Course, opened at Station "Z" on 5 January 1942 and was attended by ten Senior Intelligence Officers from No6 Group, Bomber Command. A J Evans, Senior RAF Officer attached to MI9, was appointed Chief Instructor and was responsible for drawing up the original syllabus. He was assisted by visiting lecturers from MI9 and other departments, while the administration was handled by the Intelligence School under Squadron Leader H M Parsons.

The first "B" Course covered evasion, early escape, prison camp conditions and organisation, POW security, codes, International Law, and conditions in Occupied Europe and Germany, took in a visit to MI9 Headquarters, and concluded with a short practice lecture in one of fourteen subjects by each pupil; a report was made on each pupil, assessing his suitability as a Lecturer and Instructor. It lasted five days. From then on "B" Courses ran almost continually, week by week, up to November 1944, and during this time expanded considerably in both size and scope, eventually becoming inter-service and embracing Intelligence Officers of the American Forces. Escapers and evaders detailed for lecture tours also attended. By September 1942 twenty-six of these Special Intelligence Courses had been run at Harrow.

Some aircrew fell asleep or made wisecracks during MI9 lectures — out of either cynicism or a blithe faith that they would never be shot down. There were others who, while on operations, never gave POWs a thought. But as losses — particularly on "Rhubarbs", "Circuses", "Beehives" and deep penetration raids to the Ruhr, Berlin and Nuremberg — continued to mount, so the prospect of "getting the chop" or becoming a POW preyed more heavily on the minds of aircrew. Thus, most airmen followed MI9 instructions and some took them sufficiently seriously to learn languages and study the countries over which they were due to fly on operations.

In any event, to make audiences more receptive, MI9 lecturers told true stories of the adventures of other evaders and tried to lace them with humour. (One particular anecdote, often repeated in post-war POW memoirs, concerns a shot-down airman hiding out in a nunnery. While strolling in the grounds one morning he sees an attractive back, wearing nun's habit, bending over some flowers. He makes a pass, and "the nun" turns round and says in a deep voice: "Don't be — ing silly, mate. I've been 'ere since Dunkirk!") They also briefed airmen on what to expect if their efforts to evade broke down and they were interrogated at Dulag Luft and then passed on to a permanent camp.

MI9 also asked the British Museum to comb libraries and second-hand bookshops in Bloomsbury for copies of escape classics of the Great War. In all they collected fifty — among them H G Durnford's *The Tunnellers of Holzminden*, A J Evans' *The Escaping Club*, E H Jones' *The Road to En-Dor*, Duncan Grinnell-Milne's *An Escaper's Log* and M C C Harrison and H A Cartwright's *Within Four Walls*. They had the books summarised by the sixth form of Crockatt's old school, Rugby, into guidelines for a new generation of escapers. *Within Four Walls* was published in a Penguin paperback in 1940 and issued to aircrew.

The escape kits provided by MI9 and issued before each operation also served to underline the seriousness of evasion. Crammed into flat transparent acetate boxes, they contained a variety of escape aids: silk maps, £12 in foreign currency, a small compass, a hacksaw, nourishing food for forty-eight hours (such as Horlicks malted milk tablets, boiled sweets, liver toffee, chewing gum and chocolate made with 45 per cent fat), a pint-sized water bottle, water purifying tablets (halazone), benzedrine, and such helpful items as soap, shaving tackle, a needle and thread, and a fishing line and hook. By 1942 they also contained a toothpaste tube full of concentrated milk manufactured by Nestlé. They were designed at Wilton Park under Christopher Clayton Hutton, a wayward genius who, with Charles Fraser-Smith — a civilian working ostensibly for the Ministry of Supply, but secretly under the direction of MI6 and MI9 — produced an astonishing variety of other ingenious devices. Known as "Q" gadgets, they included maps printed on rustle-free paper and hidden inside pipes, shaving brushes, hair brushes, playing cards, dominoes and chess sets; and tiny compasses hidden in tooth fillings, fountain pens, collar studs, the backs of cap badges and service buttons and, again, in pipes, shaving tackle and hair brushes. Hutton and Fraser-Smith arranged for pencils and razor blades to be magnetised, for surgical hacksaws ("Giglis") to be hidden in bootlaces and small shaving mirrors, and invented the "escape boot" — a pair of flying boots with removable leggings which could be converted into walking shoes and a waistcoat. Another one of their inventions was the escape blanket — a blanket which could be sent to a prisoner by a fictitious relative and which, when washed, revealed a pattern for a civilian suit. Their masterpiece, however, was the escape knife: as well as a strong knife-blade it had three saws, a lock breaker, a screwdriver and a small wire-cutter.

In April 1942 alone a total of 2,338 purses of foreign currency, 3,857 escape kits and 3,220 compasses were issued to RAF personnel. During the same month, 208 loaded parcels were sent to various POW camps in Germany in the guise of private parcels or gifts of some three dozen organisations invented by MI9 to sponsor their traffic — such as the Licensed Victuallers' Sports Association, the Prisoners' Leisure House Fund and the Welsh Provident Society. They contained two hundred and nine maps, ninety compasses, 5,210 *Reichsmark*, 175 *Guilder*, one dye, forty-four patterned blankets, thirty-eight hacksaws, four sets of Me110 starting instructions, two sets of Ju88 starting instructions, one set of plans for aerodromes in Holland and Belgium, and six passports. Of twenty-two RAF personnel questioned by MI9 in May 1942 after returning from Germany or German-occupied territory, ten had been briefed by MI9 and nineteen had been issued with an escape kit.

From as early as 1940 MI9y had been trying to work out a satisfactory code by which prisoners could send home information, or request escape aid, in apparently innocuous letters. Many married prisoners already had private arrangements with their wives, known as "dotty codes", since the portion of the letter in code was bracketed by a series of dots. With the help of C W R Hooker, a Foreign Office expert, the staff of MI9y, led by two of Crockatt's earliest subordinates, Major Leslie Winterbottom and A J Evans, developed a code known as "HK". The first code used by the RAF was called "Amy", which was based on a pocket English dictionary with pages measuring no more than 2 x 4 inches. By late summer 1942, Winterbottom had developed six codes, plus Hooker's; three more were in reserve by autumn. HK was a simple code, which was unusually hard to detect. The user indicated by the manner in which he wrote the date (in Roman numerals) whether the letter contained a message, showed by his opening words which part of the code he was using, and then went on to write an apparently normal, chatty letter, from which the inner meaning could be unravelled by MI9's decoders. The incoming messages, once decoded, were sent to Norman Crockatt, who then distributed them accordingly. Potential code users were chosen by MI9 from amongst the more sober and level-headed members of lecture audiences — those who would be least surprised, once in a permanent POW camp, at receiving a letter from a fictitious relation or school-chum invented by MI9y. Code users amounted to about one per cent of the Army and Navy, most fighter pilots and six per cent of other aircrew. It took less than an hour to teach them the code and instruct them on the need for maintaining strict security. The first code carrier to be shot down and made prisoner, on 20/21 July, was a flight sergeant, J N Prendergast, from No61 Squadron, Hemswell. But at the end of August 1940, when the number of British prisoners in Germany stood at about 34,000, only four aircrew officers were equipped with an MI9 code — Wing Commander H M A Day AM, RAF; Squadron Leader W H N Turner, RAF; Flying Officer J A Gillies, Auxiliary Air Force; and Lieutenant Commander J Casson, RN — although several POWs were communicating with London through coded letters by November 1940. Peculiarly, most of the RAF personnel equipped with a code by MI9 were fighter pilots, even thought they were less likely than bomber crews to get shot down over enemy or enemy-occupied territory.

However, MI9 was not without its own problems. For a long time it failed to gain the co-operation of senior officers. This owed itself in part to the distrust in which regular officers held what they chose to call "cloak and dagger" work. To them, clandestine operations seemed essentially civilian in character (hence their opposition, also, to SOE), and neither were they disposed to encourage their men to ponder on the possibilities of capture. Although they softened in their attitude after the fall of France, when many soldiers — and some aircrew — reached home through Spain, even as late as 1944 there were many whose backgrounds made them reluctant to accept the need for training in escape and evasion. The Air Ministry was especially culpable, since aircrew were much more likely than the Army or the Navy to find themselves alone and unarmed in enemy territory. For much of the war it fell to a handful of staff officers in Bomber Command and the Directorate of Operations & Intelligence to pressurise the Air Ministry into issuing instructions and escape kits to operational aircrew. Although aircrew had been receiving lectures and escape equipment since January 1940, it was not until September 1941 that the Air Ministry actually initiated evasion and escape briefings at the RAF Intelligence School, and it showed little enthusiasm for the provision of aircraft for clandestine escape operations or for the dropping of Room 900 agents, even though it succumbed to persistent pressure from SOE and other secret intelligence organisations. Military Intelligence itself considered returned POWs to be of little value to the war effort, and two years were to elapse before it would take the work of MI9 seriously. The Foreign Office suffered many attacks of "cold feet" when MI9 planned sea-borne evacuations in vessels painted in neutral colours, even though on one occasion thirty-five airmen, including the distinguished Squadron Leader Whitney Straight, were rescued in this way.

Not only were MI9's relations with other departments strained, but its own y and z sections were subject to the limitations which the global war economy imposed. POW post was slow and unreliable, and months could pass between y section asking for information and receiving a reply from a camp in Germany; seven weeks was considered fast. The alternative — for prisoners to build a radio transmitter and receiver — was accomplished in most camps, although in no case was a transmitter ever used; possession of either was, in fact, punishable by death, and MI9 gave strict instructions that prisoners should never use the transmitters except in dire emergency.

As it was, much of this activity occurred too late to be of benefit to the aircrew who became POWs in the years 1939 to 1942. Most had been shot down with no escape aids and few had heard MI9 lectures. By the end of 1941 the three services had expanded so much that visiting MI9 lecturers could not keep up. The RAF was in the worst position. With the large number of new formations, including Operational Squadrons, OTUs and Heavy Conversion Units spreading all over the country, and the demands on manpower made by the campaigns in France and Norway, the Battle of Britain and the stepping up of the Bomber Offensive, it was becoming increasingly difficult, if not impossible, for the small number of MI9 instructors to cover all these units at regular intervals. Even when instructors did visit, the prior claims of operations and flying training, leave, sickness and other causes prevented adequate attendance by aircrew. Thus in 1940 and 1941 many aircrew were operating over enemy territory with little or no knowledge of a subject which the War Office looked upon as of vital importance.

Even assuming that most had been issued with escape kits, there are several recorded instances of evaders discovering that the money was in the wrong currency or that the rubber water-bag had rotted or that the chocolate had gone sour. The escape boots were totally inadequate — they failed to keep legs warm at high altitudes and, once cut down to make shoes, proved as uncomfortable and impractical as ordinary flying boots. In the end, MI9z abandoned them.

Some of the aircrew shot down in autumn and winter 1941 were captured because the escape lines, too unwieldy for proper security to be effective, were either afraid to handle them or were infiltrated by informers and broken up. Once in POW camps, aircrew found that the lessons they had learned from reading accounts by successful escapers of the Great War were outmoded, for all *Abwehr* personnel had read the books, which had been passed on from spies in America, Cuba, Mexico and Argentina and were stocked in their escape museums. In addition, the experience that POW camp staff acquired from thwarting escapes was passed on to the *Abwehr*, who each week produced a publication called *Das Abwehrblatt* (Security News), consolidating all the information regarding escape methods employed in the past seven days and circulating it to every POW camp commandant.

Assuming the initial achievement of escaping from a POW camp in Germany, prisoners then had to avoid the inevitable manhunt (or *Fahndung*, as the Germans called it). The moment an escape was discovered (usually early in the morning), the commandant alerted the local foresters, the local railway stations, and all police stations within five kilometres (approximately three miles). They raised parties of local inhabitants on foot and bike who scanned the open country, beat forests and watched bridges, rivers and canals. The camp security officer sent off a posse of soldiers with sniffer dogs to track down the escapers within a radius of fifteen kilometres ($9\frac{1}{3}$ miles) of the camp. If, by midday, that had produced no results the dragnet would be extended to a radius of twenty-five miles. Once an identity parade, or snap *Appell* (roll-call), had ascertained exactly who was missing, the commandant phoned the area HQ of the *Kriminalpolizei*. Area HQ had duplicate records and photographs of all the POWs in the district, and could produce a profile of the escapees for publication in a *Sonderausgabe* (Special Issue) of the *Kriminalpolizeiblatt* (*Criminal Police Gazette*). Back at the camp, the *Abwehr* officers would have instituted a *Grossrazzia*, a class-one search, to discover the means of egress. It paid for the commandant and his security officers to recapture the escapees quickly and to find out their method of escape, for the *Abwehr* and OKW in Berlin would soon be on the line, asking: "How did they get out?" "When did they escape?" "What clothes are they wearing?" "Who is to blame?" "Has he been punished?" "What are you doing to stop similar escapes in the future?" And so on.

The police and the Gestapo were well aware that escapees could head in only one of four directions: north to the Baltic and across to Sweden; south to Switzerland; west to Belgium and France where they might contact an escape line, or east and south-east to Poland or Czechoslovakia, where once again they could hope to link up with Partisans. Accordingly, the railway police and the *Grenzpolizei* (Border Police) were also put on the alert. Switzerland was, however, unpopular with aircrew escapers. Once there, escapees ran the risk of either being interned for the duration of the war or of having to sneak out of the country and through France to Spain along the PAO Line, with all the attendant hazards of being captured yet again and, like their Resistance helpers, facing torture followed by death or incarceration in a concentration camp.

Of the 1939/42 crop of RAF officer POWs, only two made the home run, both from Stalag Luft I and both via Sweden. MI9's contribution to these escapes was negligible, and no aircrew officers succeeded in making it back from the Army camps, except for a small number who had been sent to "the escapers' camp" at Colditz, which was unusual in being well served by MI9. In their official history, *MI9 — Escape and Evasion, 1939–1945*, published in 1979, M R D Foot and J M Langley themselves estimate that about a third of its loaded parcels failed to reach prison camps in Germany, and that their use was difficult to evaluate. MI9 records claim that dyes, maps, money, patterned blankets and so on were continually being smuggled in to the camps. But many of Clayton Hutton's tricks for hiding escape material — such as inside gramophone records and book-bindings — were discovered early in the war, and the convertible blankets were of too good a quality to pass for civilian suits, which were often of inferior cloth. Despite all MI9 did to foster escape from prison camps, the prisoners themselves — especially those captured in the first two years of war — still had to rely mainly on bribery, theft, culling the German newspapers for information, improvised tools, papers and disguises, and the accumulation of knowledge borne of years of bitter experience in previous camps. Peculiarly, the Germans took it upon themselves to teach POWs to speak German: language lessons, by a learned professor, were featured on the back page of *The Camp*.

The escape attempts by RAF prisoners from Spangenberg and Thorn between October 1939 and April 1942 owed little to MI9. Indeed, the authors of *MI9 — Escape and Evasion* appear to have known very little at all about either camp. They inaccurately refer to Oflag IXA/H as "Haina Kloster". This is despite the fact that one of MI9's own officers, Airey Neave, had been in Oflag IXA/H between 1940 and 1941 and had filed a report on his experiences there between August 1940 and March 1941, which is included in the book's Appendices. At no time did he refer to the camp by any other name than Oflag IXA/H. Furthermore, at the end of the war MI9 de-briefed the camp's former Escape Officer, whose report, covering the period from January 1942 onwards, is on file at the PRO. Neither does he refer to the camps by any other name. It is therefore somewhat disconcerting to read an "official history" and find three entries for "Oflag IX, Spangenberg", and two entries for "Oflag IXA/H, Haina Kloster", when the authors were supposed to have been helping POWs to escape. The Spangenberg camp history is worth mentioning in another connection: only thirteen pages long, with two Appendices (one of which is missing), it makes only cursory reference to escape attempts made prior to January 1942.

According to Appendix B of this history, the following were sent to Spangenberg Lower Camp in "loaded" parcels by MI9: 33,400 Marks, 6,500 French francs, 82 special maps and plans, 119 general maps, 30 passes, seven handkerchiefs (with maps printed on them), four sets of German aircraft starting instructions, one escape photograph, three convertible blankets, one British uniform, one pair of rope-soled shoes, nine dyes, five sets of drawing materials, one magnifying glass, two sets of tracing paper, four wireless sets, one roll of insulating tape, 96 compasses, two portable cookers, seventeen files, 45 hacksaws, three keys, one sewing kit, 25 feet of rope, seven screwdrivers, two yards of wire, four pairs of wire cutters, one pair of pliers, two lock-picks, two torches (with batteries) and a theatrical make-up kit.

The Upper Camp was sent 18,110 Marks, 11,000 French francs, 20,000 Belgian francs, 1,255 guilders, ten "map" handkerchiefs, one set of aircraft starting instructions, one escape photograph, 61 special maps and plans, 109 general maps, 19 passes, five convertible blankets, eight dyes, two British uniforms, one pair of rope-soled shoes, two draughtsman's kits, three suitcases, three wireless sets, 148 compasses, two cookers, nine files, 44 hacksaws, 25 feet of rope, two yards of wire, four screwdrivers and two pairs of wire-cutters.

Almost all of this material was sent from January 1942 onwards. The RAF prisoners didn't see any of it, although the Army Escape Committee provided them with the equipment to copy maps and showed them how to make other escape paraphernalia.

The scattered references to Thorn in *MI9 — Escape and Evasion* only mention one escape by RAF officers (apart from Squadron Leader Brian Paddon's well-known home run later in the war), and even then it is a brief and inaccurate account, written for laughs in the 1970s, by an Army private doing fatigues on the airfield where the escapers were recaptured. Indeed, most of its references to escapes from POW camps are based on previously published accounts, some of them unreliable. Clearly, the history of MI9 suffers from the "bullfrog" effect.

The stark truth is that Royal and Dominion Air Force personnel captured between the outbreak of hostilities in September 1939 and the opening of Stalag Luft III in April 1942 received scant help from official sources. They had entered captivity ignorant of the existence of the POW Directorate, were begrudged their pay by the Treasury, and were poorly trained in evasion and escape by the Air Ministry and the War Office. They were the war's forgotten men.

Chapter Two
The '39 Bag

Oflag XA, Itzehoe, September–November 1939;
Offiziersdurchgangslager, Oberursel, October 1939; Oflag
IXA/H, Spangenberg, September 1939–February 1940

> *Storm on that portal,*
> *We have thee in prison!*
> *Apollo, immortal,*
> *Thou hast not arisen!*
> Rudyard Kipling, *Hymn of the Triumphant Airman*

It is 11.15am on Sunday, 3 September 1939. The place, RAF Scampton — home of No83 Squadron, part of No5 Group, Bomber Command. Aircrew from "A" Flight have just finished their morning tea, brought round by a girl from the NAAFI, and are relaxing in the Flight Commander's office, now thick with cigarette smoke. Suddenly the door opens and another officer strides in. He looks grim, and his greetings are more curt than usual. They know something is wrong. He crosses to the radio and switches it on. In silence they listen to the Prime Minister, Neville Chamberlain, as he announces the news they have been expecting ever since the Munich Crisis and his more recent demand that Germany cease all aggressive action and withdraw its troops from Poland by 11.00am: "... no such undertaking has been received and consequently this country is now at war with Germany..."

No one knows what to say. The Flight Commander, Squadron Leader A O Bridgman, draws slowly on his cigarette and blows the smoke out through his nostrils. Finally, he tells them: "Well boys, this is it. You had better all pop out and test your aeroplanes. Be back in half an hour's time. There will probably be a job for you to do."

It could be any operational RAF base, for similar scenes are being enacted on fighter, bomber and reconnaissance stations all over England and northern France. Since general mobilisation on 31 August, and the calling up of reservists on Friday, 1 September, Royal Air Force squadrons, fleet of foot and flight, have been moving from their peacetime bases to war stations throughout England, while the machines and personnel of the Advanced Air Striking Force (AASF, the expeditionary force of the RAF) have been gathering stealthily on pre-selected airfields in France. Already the AASF, comprising eight squadrons of Fairey Battles, two of Blenheims and three of Hurricanes, is dispersed to the east and north-east of Reims, along with the BEF's air component, made up of five Lysander squadrons and four squadrons each of Blenheim MkIs and Hawker Hurricanes. The atmosphere on every station is electric, each BBC news bulletin commanding instant silence and rapt attention.

For the men of Bomber Command the war begins almost immediately. Within one hour of Neville Chamberlain's announcement a Blenheim MkIV crew from No2 Group's No139 (Jamaica) Squadron, based at Wyton, is ready for its first operational sortie: a sweep across north-west Germany to search for signs of activity on airfields and harbours and for the German fleet. At 1700 hours France's ultimatum to Germany expires, by which time eighteen Handley-Page Hampdens and nine Vickers Wellingtons are preparing to seek out German warships in the North Sea. Within twelve hours, one RAF non-com and one "other rank" are in German hands — the first prisoners of the war. It is the beginning of another extension of the RAF's war: a battle in captivity that, for some, will last nearly five years. Indeed, just as the RAF's bomber offensive will be the longest campaign of the war, so its battle in captivity will last longer than that of the other two services.

But only marginally. The Royal Navy has been even quicker off the mark than the RAF. On the first day of war, the Home Fleet — with its three aircraft carriers HMS *Ark Royal*, HMS *Courageous* and HMS *Hermes* — is already north-east of the Orkneys. Having sailed to its war stations on 24 August, in anticipation of unrestricted U-boat warfare, the fleet is poised to begin hunting enemy submarines in the Western Approaches and the North-Western Approaches. Within eleven days, a Fleet Air Arm pilot and a Royal Marine from the *Ark Royal* will follow the first RAF prisoners into captivity.

In the first eight months of the war — the so-called "Sitzkrieg" — the only British and Commonwealth prisoners the Germans take are aircrew, thirty-two alone in 1939, mainly RAF but also some Fleet Air Arm. By the end of February 1940 most of them are either accommodated in, or have passed through, Oflag IXA/H at Spangenberg bei Kassel. They are, in order of capture:

Sergeant G F Booth, Aircraftman 2nd Class L J Slattery, Pilot Officer L H Edwards, Squadron Leader S S Murray, Flying Officer A B Thompson, Sergeant C A Hill, Aircraftman 1st Class S A Burry, Aircraftman 1st Class P F Pacey, Lieutenant R P Thurston, Royal Navy, Lieutenant G B K Griffiths, Royal Marines, Flying Officer R D Baughan, Pilot Officer R M Coste, Sergeant R L Galloway, Aircraftman 1st Class H Liggett, Sergeant G J Springett, Pilot Officer D G Heaton-Nichols, Flying Officer A C MacLachlan, Wing Commander H M A Day, AM, Flying Officer J Tilsley, Corporal A R Gunton, Leading Aircraftman R E Fletcher, Sergeant J W Lambert, Pilot Officer M J Casey, Sergeant A G Fripp, Aircraftman 1st Class J Nelson, Pilot Officer H R Bewlay, Sergeant S McIntyre, and Aircraftman 1st Class T P Adderley.

These men are victims of an over-optimistic view by the top brass of what aircraft and crews, at this stage of the war, are able to achieve, and the unflinching courage with which the crews themselves press home often suicidal attacks. This is no more apparent than in the raid on which Laurence Slattery and George Booth are shot down on the first raid of the war, on Monday, 4 September.

Following an early-morning reconnaissance, by a lone Blenheim, of the harbours at Wilhelmshaven and Brunsbüttel in the mouth of the Kiel Canal, twenty-nine aircraft are slated to carry out low-level attacks on German warships: fifteen of No2 Group's Blenheim MkIVs from Nos 107 and 110 Squadrons, Wattisham, and No139 Squadron, Wyton; and fourteen of No3 Group's Wellington MkIs from No9 Squadron, Honington, and No58 Squadron, Leconfield. The aircraft are inadequate for the daylight bombing task ahead of them. With a maximum speed of only 266mph fully loaded, and armed with only four Browning .303 machine-guns — two in the nose, one in the mid-upper turret, and the other firing rearward from the starboard engine nacelle — the Blenheim is easily outpaced and outgunned by the enemy's Me109, flying at 354mph and armed with four machine-guns and a 23mm cannon. The Wellington — or "Wimpey" as aircrew have dubbed it — has a maximum speed of 253mph and is armed with twin .303s in the front and rear turrets and a single .303 mounted on the beam. As the brass-hats believe in "the self-defending daylight bomber formation", they have provided no fighter escort.

Among the targets are the pocket battleships *Admiral Hipper* and *Admiral Scheer*, and the cruiser *Emden*, in the Schillig Roads; and the *Scharnhorst* and *Gneisenau* in Kiel Harbour. Take-off is between 1545 hours from Wattisham and 2219 hours from Leconfield, with the Blenheims going for Wilhelmshaven and the Wellingtons for Brunsbüttel. "Wee Georgie" Booth, a Yorkshireman, and Slattery, from Tipperary, are navigator and WOP/AG in a Blenheim from No107 Squadron, captained by Sergeant A S Prince. For them, take-off from Wattisham is at 1600 hours.

Low cloud and surface mist prevent five of the Wimpeys and the five Blenheims from No139 Squadron from finding their targets. But led by Squadron Leader Ken Doran, a gung-ho Irishman from No110 (Hyderabad) Squadron, ten Blenheims attack the *Admiral Scheer* and the *Emden* from a height of only one hundred feet. The first wave of five Blenheims — from No110 Squadron — takes the enemy by surprise. At least three bombs hit the *Admiral Scheer*, although they fail to explode and one aircraft is lost. By the time the second wave — from No107 — goes in, the flak has found its range and is coming up thick and fast. One Blenheim crashes into the *Emden*, causing damage and casualties. Three more are shot down over the target, Sergeant Prince's aircraft catching fire. Booth is leaning across his navigator's table, trying to catch a glimpse of the action, when he hears Sergeant Prince shout: "Going in!" Prince takes the Blenheim down almost to sea level, whilst Larry Slattery, strapped in to his dorsal turret, blasts away at the flak emplacements. The Blenheim finally levels out, its props skimming the waves. Booth is nervously making a weak joke about transferring to the submarine service when the aircraft hits the water at full throttle, bounces over a jetty, shoots forward and then suddenly drops nose-down in the sea. As water rushes in through the stove-in Perspex and the smashed belly, Booth is thrown forward. The engines go dead, the machine-guns stop chattering, and the disintegrating fuselage fills with sea-water; all is eerily silent except for a gentle but menacing slopping noise. Booth moves fast, throwing open the upper hatch and leaping out on to the port wing, hollering: "Princey! Princey! Get a move on!" Legs straddled across the wing to steady himself, he is about to help Prince, who is sitting still and silent in his seat, when the Blenheim, as if making a final death spasm, lurches suddenly, and tosses him into the sea. Without even pausing to think, Booth doffs his flying boots and inflates his Mae West, and is soon floating quietly on the misty sea. Although he has suffered burns and a broken ankle, and is slightly concussed, he feels no pain — just cold, wet and miserable.

Slattery is also injured when the Blenheim prangs. The impact of the aircraft against the water and the jetty throws him forward so that his face smashes into his turret-gun, fracturing his jaw in several places and almost severing his nose. He disentangles himself from his torn straps and scrambles out of the wreckage on the starboard side, unseen by Georgie Booth. As he slides in to the water, the salt stings the open wounds on his face, and he floats on the surface in agony until he hears men calling to each other — faint "Hallos" from somewhere beyond him in the surface mist. Minutes later he is being hauled into a rowing boat by German merchant sailors. Lying in the bottom, wringing out his squelching uniform, he tries to speak, but finds he can only mumble incoherently. The merchantmen transfer him to a pilot's pinnace, where crewmen hastily, and without expertise, wrap his head in bandages.

Soon afterwards Booth is scooped out of the sea by more merchantmen in another rowing boat. Wallowing in the wet bottom of the boat, he inquires after Prince and Slattery. His rescuers assure him that both men have been picked up, alive but badly hurt. They transfer him to the same pinnace in which Slattery is languishing. When he reaches the deck, Booth finds he can stand only on the toes of his left foot. Wincing, he sees through narrowed eyes another figure in RAF blue huddled in a corner of the deck. "Is that you, Princey?" he asks. Although the reply is barely audible, he recognises Slattery's Irish brogue, and is relieved that he is alive. Later, as the two men lie on bunks in one of the cabins, Slattery mutters: "I think I shall be a lot better looking when I get over this."

No hits are scored by the Wellingtons that attack Brunsbüttel. They are intercepted by German fighters, and two are lost. From the five Blenheims lost, fifteen aircrew are dead, including Sergeant Prince. But the Blenheims have achieved more than the Wimpeys against fiercer opposition. Ken Doran is awarded the Distinguished Flying Cross — the first of the war.

Larry Slattery and George Booth are sent to the *Kriegsmarine* hospital at Wesermünde. They are well treated, but find it difficult to attune their stomachs to the unpalatable food: *Volksbrot* — people's bread, black and hard — served with rice, prunes and *Wurst* (sausage) all on the same plate. Booth yearns for Yorkshire pudding, his wife Stella and their baby son, whom he left only four days ago.

(2)

Two days later, on Thursday, 7 September, Laurence Hugh Edwards arrives at Wesermünde. Edwards has the dubious triple-honour of being the first RAF officer, the first RAF pilot and the first New Zealander to fall into German hands.

A stocky, cheerful Kiwi with wavy blond hair that has earned him the nick-name "Locks", he is a former All Blacks trial and wing three-quarter. Although about to be capped for the international rugby team, he left New Zealand to take a short-service commission in the RAF. Within three days of his arrival on No206 Squadron (No16 General Reconnaissance Group, RAF Coastal Command), based at Bircham Newton in Norfolk, he flies his first reconnaissance over the North Sea.

His second and last operation is on Wednesday, 6 September, taking off early in the morning to fly his Avro Anson on a reconnaissance near the Bight of Heligoland. From a height of 300 feet he sees an aircraft in the distance. None of the crew can identify it. Eventually the observer pipes up: "It's French." Wrong. It is German — one of eight Heinkel 115 floatplanes of *1/K Ostenfliegergruppe 106*, flying from the East Frisian island of Norderney (Norder Aue) on a similar operation. Although at a top speed of 188mph the Anson is marginally slower than the floatplane, with its maximum speed of 204mph, Edwards tries to get on its tail. But it turns swiftly and is soon on top of him, emptying its 20mm cannon and machine-guns into the Anson. The turret-gunner is hit and, with his main armament unserviceable, Edwards tries to take evasive action. But for fifteen minutes the Heinkel hangs on to his tail. Then one of the Anson's wing fuel tanks explodes and the control column goes limp in his hands. With its wooden wings and its fuselage, of canvas-covered metal, now ablaze, the Anson descends in a fiery arc and hits the sea, the crew still inside. Edwards is knocked unconscious.

Some time later, when "Locks" wakes up, he finds himself floating alone on the surface in his Mae West. No Anson; no crew. How he managed to float to the surface while the rest perished he will never know. Yet there he is...half-drowned, concussed, and slightly burned, with a bullet-hole in the shoulder of his shirt and the heel of one of his shoes shot off — but otherwise in one piece.

Still Lady Luck watches over him. The pilot of the He115, flushed with victory, wants to take home proof. So he goes down, scoops Edwards out of the sea, and throws him without ceremony into the aircraft's rear compartment. Edwards is poured out on Norderney, where he receives emergency treatment for his burns at a Luftwaffe hospital. From there Edwards is sent to the mainland, where at Wesermünde naval hospital he receives further medical help. He hasn't been away from New Zealand very long and has little knowledge of the people against whom he is fighting, but, having watched the rise of Hitler, he imagines the Germans to be efficient and ruthless — and expects rough treatment. They surprise him. Local Luftwaffe aircrew drop in regularly, and after operations enter his ward and start discussions. They are, Edwards reflects, much like aircrew in the RAF — not particularly interested in the ideology of their leaders, but loyal to their country.

On the morning of Saturday, 9 September, Booth and Slattery, who occupy a separate room from Edwards, wake up to a bustle of activity. Hospital orderlies clean the ward, shave Booth and tidy Slattery's bandages. Then the burn-scarred Edwards is ushered into the room, followed by a gaggle of photographers, foreign correspondents and radio commentators carrying cumbersome microphones. They set up their equipment and begin interviewing the prisoners. The three men keep their answers non-committal, though Booth manages to insert a reference to "Yorkshire pudding". Thus, when the interview is broadcast, it is the first intimation that his squadron and his wife have that he is safe and a POW. As the interview comes to a close, an American correspondent hangs back. Leaning over Booth as if to ask another question, he whispers: "Cheer up. We'll soon be with you."

All three prisoners are getting better by the day, despite the unpalatable diet. But Slattery's nose has not been fixed back squarely, and he is taken to Bremerhaven hospital to have the nose trimmed and his jaw wired. He is fêted by the Germans, who have found out that he is something of a violinist. After his treatment they give him a violin, install him in the town barracks and make him a member of their orchestra. It is too good to be true, of course, and before long he is told that if he promises to work for the *Abwehr* (the German intelligence and counter-espionage service), he will be returned to Eire by submarine. Slattery refuses point black to co-operate, and is promptly escorted to a permanent prison camp at Spangenberg bei Kassel.

(3)

Lying in a little valley fifteen miles south of Kassel, in Hessen, is the mediæval village of Spangenberg. To the west runs the River Fulda, and the village itself sits in a triangle formed by its two tributaries, the Essebach and the Pfieffe. Running parallel to the Pfieffe are the Melsunger Strasse — the beginning of the main road to Kassel — and a *Kanonenbahn* (military railway) to Melsungen and Kassel, from which runs the main line south to Würzburg and Frankfurt. On all sides of the village are rolling, thickly wooded hills that rise about a thousand feet above the village. In many places the fields are cultivated almost to the summits, and thin grey roads meander past isolated farmhouses over ridges to the south and east, striking a happy balance between civilisation and remoteness. The village has much of historic interest to recommend it, as the houses are of attractive *Fachwerk* typical of the region: tall, of faded red — almost pink — brick, and half-timbered in black with high, sloping eaves and mellow tiled roofs. The clean, mainly cobbled streets scramble and straggle in a manner reminiscent of small towns in Ireland. The air is pungent with the smell of dung — a country smell which, though stronger than the British have been accustomed to back home, is not unpleasant. To Larry Slattery the village seems drowsy, content and very much out of touch with the war. On the northern edge of the village, perched on a conical hill of solid rock four hundred feet high, stands *Schloss* Spangenberg. From a distance, it looks every bit as romantic as the castles along the Rhine, and bears a resemblance to a print by Albrecht Dürer.

Little is known about the origins and early history of Spangenberg. To begin with, settlement was confined to the ravines and large river valleys, gradually spreading to the valley flanks and their slopes. Five shallow graves discovered near the town of Bergheim-Giflitz, to the west of Kassel, date back to the Hallstatt period, 900–50BC. The names of several mountains and rivers could also indicate a pre-Germanic settlement. Sources and discoveries for the period 50BC to the 5th Century AD are somewhat meagre. Place and river names — such as the town districts Pfieffe, Nausis and Metzebach — indicate that the Chatten, who descended from the Hessians, also settled in the area.

After the year 500, the tribal territory of the Chatten became part of France. The Frankish kings made great demands on land and property, thus diminishing the influence of tribal district leaders, and appointed foreign judiciary officers of their own choice. Little by little the rural community lost its independence. The conversion of the area to Christianity in the 8th Century resulted in the establishment of monasteries at Fulda in 744 and Hersfeld in 769; and the founding of monasteries and bishoprics, with their large manorial estates, had a profound influence on the internal organisation of the country. They provided the stimulus for settlement, which could be made possible only by the clearance of thickly wooded areas.

Spangenberg itself came into being in the first third of the 13th Century. The name "Spangenberg" might best explain the reasons leading to the construction of the castle and the establishment of the town. The word *"Spange"* generally means "clasp" or "buckle", but in middle-high German means "Wooden cross, bolt, or barrier". This meaning can be traced back to the days when the River Pfieffe and the Esse Valley linked the old army and trade routes. The castle and town performed a clasping function, protecting the river and the valley, and acting as a kind of barrier.

The old east-west long-distance trade along the Sälzer Weg — which ran west from Allendorf, over the Meissner Mountain to Lichtenau, Günsterode, Melsungen, Felsberg and Fritzlar — was parallel to the south-east axis of another route along the Lange Hessen. This ran in a north-easterly direction beginning in the Rhein-Main region further south, with a short, alternative route from Frankfurt to Butzbach, and proceeded northwards through Wetterau, Giessen, Marburg and Treysa, crossing the River Fulda at Malsfeld, south of Kassel. It split at Homburg and merged again at the foot of Spangenberg, continued in an easterly direction to Waldkappel and Reichensachsen, then reached the River Werra at Wanfried and ended at Leipzig. Further to the south-east was a third route, the Kurze Hessen, which started at Frankfurt and ran over the Alsfeld, Friedwald and Eisenach mountains to Thüringen, and there merged with the Lange Hessen. A fourth trade route, the Nürberger Strasse, ran from north to south, cutting across the other three routes west of Spangenberg and further south at Hersfeld on the River Fulda.

The routes from west to east, and south to north, could best be controlled from the steep limestone heights overlooking the Fulda. What could be more obvious than to construct a castle on those heights, under whose protection craftsmen and tradesmen could settle? The establishment of the town, which was given the same name by the lords of the castle, was also a good source of revenue through taxes and other contributions.

There is, however, a further interpretation of the name "Spangenberg". In 1755 Matthäus Merian traced the name back to the small round stones found in the Knorrenberg and the western slopes of the Teichberges (both rivers within Spangenberg), which bore a resemblance to a clasp.

Fig 2: Sketch Map of Spangenberg and Elbersdorf

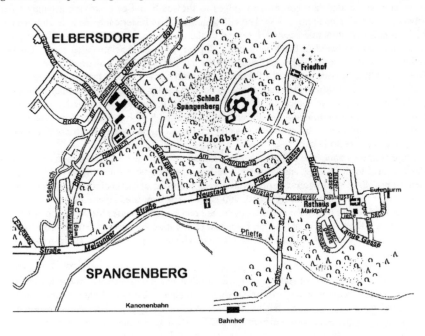

These stones derived from fossilised water lily (*encrinus lilliformis*) that once populated the bed of the limestone sea in huge quantities. Chroniclers associated these *"Spangensteinchen"* with the coat of arms. A recent etymological study on river and place names holds that Spangenberg could be derived from the word *"spayn"*, meaning "bog" or "decay" — and that such terms have been passed on to fields, woodlands, mountains, towns and villages.

In the early Middle Ages the large Imperial abbeys of Fulda and Hersfeld — on either side of the River Fulda — had become very wealthy owing to their scattered land possessions. Both abbeys attempted to gain control of the old trade routes. In order to administer their possessions they appointed special lay governors who represented the cloisters in secular dealings. The vassals to the Imperial Abbey of Fulda were the Counts of Ziegenhain-Reichenbach — who at the same time as sub-stewards safeguarded the interests of the abbey at Hersfeld. To this dynasty was bestowed the area around Morschen and Spangenberg. Sometime between 1214 and 1235 they bestowed the area on the Lords of Treffurt, who were descendants of the lower aristocracy of Thüringia. Their ancestral seat was the Normannburg, above Treffurt. As the people of Treffurt were loyal followers of the land counts of Thüringia, there were grounds for believing that they could gain a foothold on the rivers Fulda and Pfieffe and thereby protect the Lange Hessen and the connection between there and Thüringia. The Treffurts founded the domain of Spangenberg. Hermann von Treffurt, the founder of both the castle and the town, is first mentioned in a historical document as a result of establishing the Kloster Heydau in Alt Morschen on 21 January 1235 with his spouse Jutta. He names himself Hermann von Spangenberg around 1238. As Hermann *Milites de Spangenberg* — Hermann, Knight of Spangenberg — he settled a border dispute between Morschen and Wichte.

The lords of Treffurt established their castle on the summit of a 300-metre-high limestone rock, one of several mountains dominating the town. It was not as high as the surrounding mountains, but possessed the advantage of three slopes, which dropped away steeply. Their castle stood for 750 years in solitary splendour on the shelly, limestone conical peaks overlooking the confluence of the Pfieffe and Esse. The massive mountain stronghold on the *Schlossberg* stands like a sentry over the town and the landscape. It fascinates every visitor who looks back on its former historical importance.

As for the town of Spangenberg itself, this probably came into being in the middle of the 13th Century. In 1261, for the first time, a priest and a town mayor, Godefridus (Gottfried), were nominated as town officials; and in 1269 the mayor Berthold von Berterode and several knights were named as the first citizens. The conferring of the first town charter might also have occurred around the time between 1250 and 1309, when Hermann VI and squire Hermann VII confirmed and renewed the town charter, stating: "We also have possession, as our parents and predecessors."

To the west of the castle lies the small village of Elbersdorf, tucked into the foothills of the *Schlossberg* and straddling the River Essebach. The village is more or less a ribbon development, its main road, comprising Rosestrasse, Steinweg and Obersdorf Strasse, running parallel to the Essebach. Dominating the village — in a square formed by Steinweg to the north, Goldbachstrasse to the west, Blaubach to the south and Brückenstrasse to the east — is a former agricultural estate, comprising a large building that was once a country mansion, and two secondary buildings. This estate has been converted into a prisoner of war camp by the OKW.

Described by some prisoners as "a backwater", the estate, like the castle itself, is a mediæval structure — stuccoed and timber-framed with high, sloping roofs and narrow windows. The main building is a large affair shaped like a squashed "T", with a short central leg four storeys high containing a large *Speisesaal*, or dining hall, a small wing three storeys high but much longer, and a rather squat-looking wing of only two storeys. Each has, in addition, attic rooms. At the bottom of the central leg stands a long, single-storey building, overlooking the swift-flowing Essebach, which passes through the village, and providing a charming view of the period houses beyond, the cultivated and tree-fringed hills receding into the distance and, crowning them, the castle atop its conical rock. The river and the street opposite teem with life. Cackling geese make their way up-river, children paddle in the shallows, mothers push their prams to the market, and the men-folk load animal fodder into ox-drawn carts.

A few yards from the end of the smallest wing stands the third building, two floors high. (Both the smaller buildings have attic rooms.) This is the Lower Camp *Kommandantur* and guards' quarters, and will prove an effective obstacle to escape. The whole is surrounded by two parallel barbed-wire fences, nine feet apart and nine feet high, running alongside the river and down the three village streets which fringe the estate. Lamps stand on posts at intervals along the fence, and the ubiquitous wooden sentry towers overlook the compound — one from the other side of the river, and two more from the village streets. The guards within are equipped with searchlights, mounted light machine-guns and *Maschinenpistolen*.

The compound itself is only seventy-five yards square: adequate exercise space for the handful of men in the bag at this stage of the war but hardly for the two hundred or so who will fill it from 1940 onwards. Later in the war, when the Lower Camp will accommodate only a small RAF and Fleet Air Arm contingent, there will be room for prisoners to cultivate gardens and lay out a tennis court and cricket pitch. There is even a sprinkling of apple trees in which birds build their nests. Walking round the compound is far more pleasant here than it will be later on in purpose-built camps, as, apart from the river and the houses and the everyday life evolving in the streets on three sides of the compound, the prisoners can see lush green woods and a tiny chapel on a hillock along the fourth. At the corner where Goldbachstrasse crosses the main street stands a wide brick bridge over the river, partly obscured by trees, while on the northern corner of the camp is a little concrete footbridge with metal handrails leading to Brückenstrasse (Bridge Street) and the *Schlossberg* beyond.

The gabled and half-timbered buildings make the place look like a holiday camp and, indeed, before the war were used by the Hitler Youth as a *"Kraft durch Freude"* ("Strength Through Joy") hostel; Nazi slogans have been carved into the walls.

The former farming estate has been designated *Offizierslager (Oflag) IXA*, since Spangenberg is the first POW camp to be located in *Wehrkreis IX*. When the castle opens to officer prisoners in mid-September, it will be known as the *Hauptlager* or "Upper Camp", and the letter "H" appended to Oflag IXA will come to mean both camps. The Elbersdorf estate, initially intended to accommodate NCOs and "other ranks", will then be called the *Unterlager* or Lower Camp. The prisoners are guarded by *Landesschützen* (literally, land-guards, or country guards. *"Schütze"* can mean "guard" or "rifleman".)

Much to Slattery's surprise he is taken not to the castle but to the Lower Camp. At present the only British prisoners in the *Unterlager* are Sergeant Clement Hill and AC1s Sidney Burry and Peter Pacey. Members of a Whitley crew from No102 (Ceylon) Squadron based at Driffield, they have been in the bag since Saturday, 9 September. Although they are not the first prisoners of the war, Burry had been allocated POW No1, Hill No2 and Pacey No3. There will be much debate amongst NCO prisoners throughout the war as to who ought to be POW No1 — especially between Booth and Slattery, who are issued Nos 154 and 84 — and it is all the fault of "the Hun", who each time they open a new camp start numbering prisoners from No1 upwards, sometimes according to the order in which they walked through the gate, sometimes in alphabetical order of surname. "Never talk to me about German efficiency," remarked one prisoner when reflecting later on the numbering system.

The Whitley crew's pilot and "second dickey", Squadron Leader Sydney Stuart Murray and the Canadian Pilot Officer Alfred Burke Thompson, are languishing in Oflag XA, a camp for Polish prisoners of war at Itzehoe, thirty miles east of Hamburg, and ten miles north-east of the River Elbe, in Schleswig-Holstein.

Murray's is the first complete aircrew to fall into enemy hands. As a result, the two officers become the most photographed and publicised POWs in Germany. They are filmed on newsreel by American cameramen from Paramount and repeatedly photographed by German propaganda officials, while Alf Thompson also speaks on radio from the *Reichsrundfunk* in Berlin. It is because of this publicity that Thompson's father, in Penetanguishene, Ontario, discovers that he is a prisoner. The photographs and newsreels reach England, the USA and Canada. An RAF NCO from No102 Squadron watching one of the newsreels in a local cinema thinks he recognises the two officers, who have not yet been posted "Missing" by the Air Ministry. He returns to the cinema with a companion and sees the film twice more before being certain. Then he asks the manager, Mervyn Moorse, to have a shot from the film printed. Moorse sends the print to the squadron at Driffield, and the aircrew and the Station Intelligence Officer confirm that the two officer POWs are Murray and Thompson. On Saturday, 16 September — the day after the Air

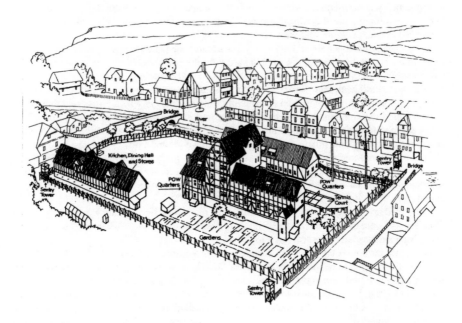

Fig 3: Oflag IXA/H, Spangenberg (Lower Camp)

Ministry posts the officers as "Missing" — the NCO sends a cable to Thompson's father saying: "Alfred Prisoner of War Germany. All well." By then, Thompson senior has already seen a picture of his son taken in Germany after his capture — for on 15 September a New York newspaper publishes a photograph, released by German censors and radioed to the USA, showing un-named British and French aircrew being escorted through Berlin. The newspaper appears in Montreal that morning and shortly afterwards an anonymous reader phones a Montreal newspaper saying that Alfred Burke Thompson is one of the men pictured. As soon as a copy of the newspaper is obtained in Penetang the picture is shown to Mr Thompson. But he does not receive a telegram from the Air Ministry confirming his son's capture until the afternoon of Monday the 18th.

The Air Ministry could have informed the prisoners' next of kin that they were safe as early as Monday, 11 September. On the morning of their capture *Generalfeldmarschall* Hermann Goering telephones Birger F Dahlerus, a Swedish businessman who acts as a diplomatic channel between him and Britain, and asks him to pass on the details. The next day, he sends his stepson, Thomas von Kantzow, to Dahlerus in Stockholm, carrying letters from Murray and Thompson, saying they are well and conveying Goering's personal assurance that they will be well treated.

Most of these events are subsequently reported in British and Canadian newspapers. But the contemporary Press either gets its facts wrong or is deliberately misinformed by the Air Ministry. Some newspapers report that Murray and Thompson have been shot down in a bombing raid on Kiel, Wilhelmshaven and Cuxhaven; others that they were on a reconnaissance flight; and still others that they are the first RAF officer prisoners of the war, a view that will persist until at least the end of the war. But the fact is that, although Murray is the first Squadron Leader, and Thompson the first Canadian, to enter captivity, the distinction of being the first RAF officer POW goes to Edwards, who is still in hospital while the two are being filmed.

Neither are they captured on a bombing mission, but instead on one of a series of leaflet raids — known as "bumf raids" — over Germany which, from 4 September to 24 December, lead to the loss of four Armstrong Whitworth Whitleys from No4 Group. Murray's, forced down over Thüringia, in the Hartz Mountains, is the first.

It is one of those ops on which everything seems to go wrong from the start. "Met" has forecast an east wind, but as the six Whitleys from No102 Squadron continue on their outward leg towards the Ruhr, it changes through 180° and strengthens. The result is that they fly much further into Germany than they intended. Alf Thompson is disgusted with the whole exercise. "We were trained to be bomber pilots," he complains. But it is on the way back that the problems really begin. As an economy measure, the Whitley's regular engines have been replaced with cheaper and less reliable types. At about 0400 hours one of them packs up. Then the other one starts to cough and drop revs, and the Whitley begins to sink. The crew are bent on staying with the aircraft, and hope that the engines will pick up. But as they near the Danish border it becomes obvious that the aircraft will not make it home. One by one they bale out. Thompson has a nasty moment when the Whitley spirals past him. He makes landfall suddenly with a thump that reverberates through his body and knocks the wind out of him.

Of the other five aircraft, only one, piloted by Flight Sergeant E L G Hall, reaches England. The other four are attacked by Belgian fighters; three — one of whose pilots, Pilot Officer T G ("Hamish") Mahaddie, will go on to become a distinguished Pathfinder — force-land in France; the fourth has to land in Belgium and its crew are interned, not being released until 16 December. (Eventually — in May 1940 — Flight Sergeant Hall and his "second dickey", Pilot Officer L Miller DFC, will enter the bag.)

Searching Germans round up Murray and his crew at dawn and lock them in cells on an aerodrome near Gotha. It is the beginning of four years and eight months of what Thompson will later describe as "an endurance contest" and "a terrible ordeal".

For the time being, RAF officers are going to war not in battle-dress but in full uniform, with starched collars, ties and shoes. Murray and Thompson are no exception. Their captors confiscate their belts, braces, ties and shoe-laces — in case, say the Germans, they try to hang themselves. For several hours they are on edge because they have heard rumours that the Germans are shooting airmen who drop propaganda leaflets.

"Wank" Murray is an RAF regular. Born in Singapore in 1901, he was in the Oxford University

Air Squadron before doing a Chinese interpreters' course, and in 1935 was appointed Assistant Air Attaché at the British Embassy in China. During the course of his appointment he also learnt French, Spanish and Italian. In October 1937, he was in one of the Embassy cars machine-gunned by Japanese airmen while carrying British residents from Nanking to Shanghai. The following August he received his promotion to Squadron Leader. To be captured as a mere "bumfleteer" is, for him, disgrace enough — but to be shot for it seems an ignoble end to a career that should really be just beginning. "Tommy" Thompson, born on 8 August 1915, descends from one of Penetanguishene's pioneering families (his father was a Member of Parliament), and after leaving school in 1933 did a stint in an insurance office in Toronto. Although his father had used his influence to secure Tommy the position, insurance was not to his liking, and he began to take flying lessons. In late 1936 he travelled to England, and in 1937 joined the RAF. He was posted to No102 Squadron on 15 November. Engaged to be married, he is only one month past his twenty-fourth birthday.

Early in the afternoon an interpreter enters and asks them if they have any last requests, because they are going on a long journey. Murray thinks this is a polite way of telling them they are about to be shot. The interpreter walks towards Thompson, holding out his tie as though to blindfold him, and Murray, his nerves taut, asks the interpreter what the devil he means. Unaware that any sinister gloss can be put on his behaviour, the German says he merely wants to know if they need anything to eat before they go by car along the *Autobahn* to Berlin. They set off at 3pm, arrive about 9.30, and spend the rest of the night in a hospital just outside the city. They are woken on Sunday at 2am and interrogated on and off for two and a half hours. No aircrew POWs at that time know anything about German interrogation procedures, so Murray and Thompson are apprehensive. But at this stage of the war German POW interrogation techniques are rudimentary, and in any case neither Murray nor Thompson has much information to spill.

Later that day they are joined by two French officers of the *Armée de l'Air*, distinctive in their full "Louise-blue" uniforms adopted in July 1934. The taller of the two is Lieutenant-Colonel Enselem, the commanding officer of *Escadre de Bombardement 31*; the other is his pilot *Sous-Lieutenant* Béranger. Enselem's wing comprised two medium bomber squadrons, *Escadrille I*, based at Connantre, and *Escadrille II*, based at Marigny-le-Grand, equipped with the Bloch MB200 and the Loire Olivier LeO451. On Saturday, 9 September, flying as second pilot, he led three Bloch 200s on a reconnaissance over the Saar. At 1445 hours they were intercepted by three Me109Ds of *I/Jagdgeschwader 152*. One Bloch was lost with its entire five-man crew, and *Oberleutnant* von Bothmer attacked Béranger's aircraft, which caught fire. Béranger stayed with the blazing aircraft, crash-landing near Saarbrücken. All of the crew survived, but *Adjudant-Chef* Charpentier, *Sergent-Senot* de la Londe and *Sergent-Chef* Audoux were wounded and taken to hospital.

The four officers are escorted to the *Reichsrundfunk*, the Ministry of Propaganda's radio broadcasting station for Europe in Masurenallee in the Charlottenburg district of Berlin, where they are given the opportunity to make a radio broadcast. Thompson alone accepts, taking the view that his family in distant Penetang are probably anxious about him. The recalcitrance of the others is, however, all for naught, as they are filmed liberally by news-hungry Paramount cameraman and snapped by newspaper photographers.

At lunchtime, Murray and Thompson are separated from the Frenchmen and taken for a mile-long walk to a wood, where they wait a while — a little mystified — until a messenger arrives and beckons them on. A little way into the wood they come to a railway siding and a string of carriages. Boarding one of the carriages, they are led out the other side and find themselves in a pleasant clearing. Under a huge, spreading tree in the middle of the clearing is a dais of trestles. There, sitting behind a large desk, is none other than the plump, bemedalled *Generalfeldmarschall* Hermann Goering, immaculately decked out in a duck-egg-blue uniform and a great cloak of soft, pale blue leather. He summons Murray to step forward and, as Murray mounts the steps, rises to his feet and waits. Murray marches up to the desk and salutes stiffly. Goering formally returns the salute, proffers his podgy hand, and motions him to sit down at a corner of the desk. Despite his antipathy towards everything German, Murray is impressed. Goering looks fit and well and seems friendly.

Although he understands a little English, Goering speaks through his interpreter and assures

Murray that he is not going to ask any questions of a military nature — Murray will not be permitted to answer them. But his first question is political, which in war is pretty much the same thing. He asks Murray what people in Britain think about the war. Murray replies that they were naturally reluctant to declare war but have faith in their Government. As the Government has decided that war is unavoidable, the people will see it through.

Goering nods, then asks Murray: "But what do *you* think?"

Murray says: "I am an RAF officer, not a politician."

Then Goering gives Murray some startling inside information. Russia, he says, is going over to the German side in two days' time and the Polish campaign will be over in a week. As history will show, he is not far wrong in both. But his next prediction is well wide of the mark. He reckons Murray and Thompson will be home by Christmas. "When Poland has been defeated," he says, "Britain will have done all she can to fulfil her pledge and there will be nothing left to fight over. Meanwhile, I intend to see that RAF prisoners are well looked after by the Luftwaffe. I know myself that men who fly are by nature the least adaptable to imprisonment. I will try to give you as many sports facilities as possible."

Goering then invites Thompson to mount the platform. He makes a weak joke about their aircraft disturbing his sleep and forcing him to take cover in a bomb shelter, but sympathises with them for having lost "the freedom of the skies". Thompson puzzles him, because Canada is not yet in the war, but he soon changes the subject to Canadian ice hockey.

After twenty-five minutes Goering ends the exchange. Before dismissing them, he asks if there is anything he can do for them at the moment. Murray tells him that his and Thompson's leather Irvine jackets were confiscated at Gotha. "Can we have them back?" Goering promises to see to it and within twenty-four hours they are handed back their jackets. They are also allowed to write letters home.

Later that day — Tuesday, 12 September — they are sent to Oflag XA. Some six hundred Polish officers and a few Polish soldiers languish in the camp, along with Enselem and Béranger, and to begin with Murray and Thompson are the only two British subjects. But on Saturday, 30 September, Laurence Edwards is removed from Wesermünde and joins them at Itzehoe.

The guards are different from those Edwards has encountered hitherto. They are older, and still remember the humiliation of the Great War and its aftermath. But in accordance with the Geneva Convention the Germans are paying the RAF prisoners the equivalent wage of a German major and lieutenant, and for a time they live fairly well. Germany is not yet short of luxuries and they have plenty of fruit and soft drinks, including "Fanta", the German answer to Coca-Cola. Each of the officers is allocated a private room, and the only thing they are really short of is recreational facilities. However, Béranger has a pack of cards, and with time heavy on their hands the five play endless rubbers of bridge.

But the wind of change comes towards the middle of October. The British Foreign Office has created a stink about the letters from Murray and Thompson that Goering passed to Dahlerus for onward transmission to London. It has requested the Swedes not to send any more POW letters as the Red Cross is the official channel. On Monday, 16 October, the two French and three RAF prisoners are packed into a lorry and after thirty-six hours on the road reach Spangenberg and Oflag IXA/H. They are sent straight to the castle, which, like the former dower house in Elbersdorf, has been converted for prisoners of war.

There are a variety of routes to the castle. From the railway station on the southern outskirts of the village you walk in a northerly direction along an almost perfectly straight road known as the Bahnhofstrasse until you reach a T-junction at Neustadt Klosterstrasse. You cross this road diagonally and then walk up Jagerstrasse, which brings you out on Neustadt Platzgasse, which runs in an arc round the western foothills of the *Schlossberg*. From then on, you need the sure-footed agility of a mountain goat, for there is no longer a proper road to the castle. You can climb up a steep flight of stone steps, built in 1838, which take you to the main-gate tower, or follow a narrow, cinder track, pretentiously called *Am Schlossberg*, which spirals the hummock and is only wide enough for a Volkswagen. In places it is so steep that, standing straight, you can almost touch the ground with an outstretched arm. It is a hill made to challenge Sisyphus. Covering the slopes of the rocky outcrop are impregnable thickets, weathered, moss-laden boulders, and forests of wind-seeded trees. At one stage the track crosses the stone steps, and it is disheartening to discover that at that point the steps have reached only the half-way mark. Some two-thirds of the way up the track you pass, to your left, the *Friedhof*, an old cemetery with a small chapel. By then you can also see the outer fortifications of the castle higher up and to your left. As the track turns sharply, almost back on itself, further up the hummock you pass the *Friedhof* again, below you and to the right. At the summit, the track levels, and you pass through an arch of the crumbling, outer-defence tower. The arch is known as the *Schwarzen Tor*, or the "Black Portal", and lacks any noticeable embellishment. Beyond it is a narrow cobbled slope that curls around the outer ramparts of a dry moat and ends at an outer gatehouse in front and to the left of a wooden bridge. The bridge straddles the moat, which, though forty feet deep and thirty feet wide, has never contained water. Its perpendicular outer walls are cut straight down into the terrain of the flattened summit, and roaming about its ferny floor are three wild boars. The only way in to the castle stronghold is by crossing the narrow drawbridge and walking under a portcullis and then through a tiny wicket gate set in a pair of massive, iron-studded doors.

It is also possible, but by no means easy, to reach the *Schloss* from Elbersdorf. Coming out of the main gate on Brückenstrasse you march up the curving hill, past the small chapel on a hillock overlooking the Lower Camp, and cross the road to mount some steps carved into the limestone rock at the foot of the mountain. Almost immediately you are enclosed by tall spindly trees and find there are two cinder paths curving up and round the *Schlossberg*, one taking a shallow route round the bottom of the mountain and another, higher track, cutting deeper into the trees and much, much steeper. Taking the higher path, you slip and trip your way up it until it joins the longer, shallower track a few yards before crossing, at right-angles, the long flight of stone steps. You then either take the steps or carry on along the path and past the cemetery.

The driver of the lorry turns in to *Am Schlossberg*, constantly revving the engine and crashing the gears as he urges it up the winding cinder track to the gatehouse. "It doesn't look very inviting," Thompson remarks. At the gatehouse they are met by the civilian castle-keeper, a tetchy civilian called Kulmer who regards all prisoners as intruders. The prisoners will come to know him as "Shagnasty".

(5)

From within, the castle is anything but picturesque: an oval structure built around a small courtyard, its walls are forbidding, appearing to sweat paranoia, its roof steep and sloping, its turrets small and round. The size and appearance of the first layout back in the 12th Century can only be guessed at. Within a circular wall that corresponds roughly to the size of the buildings that surround the courtyard in which Murray and Thompson now stand there might have been a large construction — the palace — as well as small adjacent buildings. The palace forming the main portion of the castle would have contained a central hall, living quarters, and a chapel for the family of the Lords of Treffurt-Spangenberg. This would have been made of stone, whilst the adjacent buildings would have been of timber. The western entrance was protected by a gate, but not as high as the one now squeaking closed behind the prisoners. It can be assumed that there was also a moat, but again neither as deep or wide as today's, and probably not surrounding the whole castle. Deep wells might also have been sunk by the Treffurts, but there is no definite proof.

Neither can it be said with any certainty when the original castle was built. Some historians have estimated that it took three years to build and was completed in 1238, when Treffurt named himself Hermann von Spangenberg, although the work might not necessarily have been started by Hermann himself. As the Fulda Abbey and the Counts of Ziegenhain-Reichenbach were the feudal lords, it is conceivable that they constructed the castle and conferred it upon Treffurt. However, the first references connecting Hermann von Treffurt to the political development of the area would indicate that Hermann established the castle at around the same time as the Kloister Heydau (*see below*).

In their one-hundred-year rule (1250–1350), the Treffurts provided much in the way of property that has survived the test of time, and the town expanded westwards. Unfortunately, from a monastic point of view, things were coming to a head between the families of Spangenberg and Treffurt. The representatives of both clans were leading lives of promiscuity. They became enemies, and took up arms against each other — and eventually the Treffurts became masters of

Spangenberg and the Spangenbergers became Lords of Treffurt. Both lines of descent had already offered their services in 1324 to the Hessian counts for 200 silver Marks, committing themselves and their castles and towns to providing assistance against all enemies of Hessen. The Hessian administration dominated territorial development in the last century of Spangenberg rule. Count Heinrich II, "The Iron One", used good tactics. On 6 December 1347 he concluded an agreement with the Counts of Ziegenhain in which he became a vassal of Fulda and at the same time feudal Lord of Spangenberg. On 22 May 1350, under the pressure of circumstances, Knight Hermann von Treffurt IX sold the castle, the town of Spangenberg and its associated area to Heinrich II for 8,000 silver Marks — an unprecedented sum, at that time, even for a landed prince. The amount was paid in instalments, and the Treffurts were dependent on the pledges given by the counts for the equivalent of the purchasing price. With the death of Hermann IX in Kassel, on 12 June 1376, the Treffurt dynasty died out.

However, the change in rule was not to the disadvantage of the castle or the town. On the contrary, the castle was transformed into a strong fortress and a magnificent princely residence, which maintained its importance into the 18th Century. The later Hessian counts stayed there frequently and preferred the Spangenberg residence to others on account of the thickly wooded area and its hunting prospects. For almost five hundred years the town itself remained the suburb of Hessian administrative offices and, in addition, as a favourite residence of the counts, assumed a princely status.

After the castle was taken over by the counts of Hessen (1350), some alterations were made, but to what extent is unknown. Almost certainly extensions were necessary to cope with the growing entourages of the princes who frequently resided at the castle. Because of the limitations of space imposed by the smallness of the castle a further storey was added to the southern wing.

"Otto the Bowman", the only son of Count Heinrich II, was appointed in 1340 as co-regent, but died years before his father. He resided with his wife Elizabeth of Cleve at *Schloss* Spangenberg. The marriage of Otto and Elizabeth of Cleve was childless, and Otto himself died in 1366 as a result, it is believed, of a hunting accident. The same year, his father Heinrich the Iron One appointed his nephew Hermann as successor and co-regent for his dead son Otto. (Hermann was an exceptional scholar for his times, having studied in Paris and Prague.) However, the count's grandson, Otto of Braunschweig (Brunswick), felt that the succession should have been passed on to him. It led to a military conflict, in the course of which even *Schloss* Spangenberg, the residence of the widow Elizabeth of Cleve, was to be attacked. The princess requested assistance in a letter to her husband's successor.

Count Hermann reigned for ten years, dying on 23 May 1413. He was to go down in history as "Hermann the Scholar". The reigns of Heinrich the Iron One and Hermann the Scholar were marked by constant feuds and power struggles, moral decline and a loss of prosperity. After the death of Hermann the Scholar, the business of government was passed on to his eleven-year-old son Ludwig I, the youngest of eight children. He was born in 1402 in Spangenberg castle. Next to Philipp, Ludwig was the most magnanimous of the important princes of Hessen-Kassel.

In the 15th Century a massive redevelopment was undertaken by Count Ludwig I, who particularly favoured Spangenberg, as it had been his birthplace. It was after this period that the castle received its reputation for impregnability. The old polygonal construction was surrounded by an oval-shaped outer bailey, which was reinforced with six semi-circular, roofed turrets. A new gate was added to the old approach, which with its barred frame, territorial coat of arms and three large ornamental battlements gave it an importance and dignity worthy of a princely castle. The living quarters, too, were changed in accordance with prevailing tastes. Larger windows, new doors, attractive fireplaces and stoves, as well as the painting of several rooms improved living conditions. Particularly noteworthy was the small chapel in the south wing, which was covered by a late gothic net vaulting. Also dating from the same period were several adjoining buildings to the west of the castle, such as a chancellery and a stable, with a surrounding wall and an additional gate.

The north-eastern side was most vulnerable to attack, as the slopes did not fall away so steeply. To strengthen it, a forward tower was built. Its horse-shoe shaped layout, 2.40-metre-thick walls and three firing embrasures clearly took into consideration the emergence of firearms. The rapid increase in the effectiveness of powdered weapons soon made further extensive strengthening of the fortifications necessary.

Under the aegis of Ludwig I, Spangenberg flourished. He made sound decisions for his land and people, based on clear commonsense, unprejudiced insight and energetic willpower. Known as Ludwig the Peaceful, he died under mysterious circumstances (some speculated that he might have been poisoned) on 13 January 1458 at his birthplace in *Schloss* Spangenberg. His successors — Ludwig II, Wilhelm I and his bother Wilhelm II — frequently resided at Spangenberg. After Wilhelm I abdicated in favour of his brother in 1493 he spent the remainder of his days at the residential palace until his death in 1515.

Philipp the Generous, next to Ludwig the Peaceable, was probably the most important Hessian monarch. His leading political role on the side of the evangelical princes at the time of the Reformation is undisputed in history. He is also closely associated with the history of the residential palace and the town of Spangenberg, especially on account of his bigamy with Margarethe von der Saale. Reluctantly, Martin Luther consented to the legalisation of this union. In 1540 the marriage took place in Rotenburg/Fulda "to the left side", in common parlance. Margarethe was therefore called "The Left Landgrave". In the early years of her marriage she lived in *Schloss* Spangenberg, but the Hessian nobility must have intervened, because she later moved to the patrician mansion within the town. The marriage, however, produced eight children, so that the residence became too confined, and the count transferred her to the former Boyneburgschen residence and had the manor house rebuilt.

Under Philipp and his successors, Counts Wilhelm IV (1567–92), Moritz (1592–1627) and Wilhelm V (1627–37), the fortifications were again extensively enlarged and improved, commensurate with changing tactics and firearms. A decision undoubtedly made by Count Philipp, who himself possessed considerable artillery, initiated the development of the mediæval castle into a modern fortress. Whilst most of the old castles lost their military importance on the grounds of the rapid development of weapons technology, Spangenberg was soon ranked alongside the four most powerful provincial fortresses of Kassel, Ziegenhain, Giessen and Rüsselheim.

The north-eastern side of the castle was strengthened yet again by the construction of a second fortified ring under the old forward tower. At the corner point a high battery tower with three floors was built. An earthen parapet up to ten metres thick was laid on top of the newly constructed wall leading from an outer port called the *Schwarzen Tor* up to the southern bastion. The walls of the surrounding ditches were also raised, and from them underground passageways led to the casements. The passageways merely served as a defence to the new fortifications; a supposed connection to the town has not been proved.

The battery tower was twenty-two metres in diameter, and the wall was 6.20 metres thick. Their dimensions were in keeping with those of other large fortresses, and their situation at the expected point of attack and their control and domination of the castle's approaches were similar to the developments at Marburger Castle in the years 1521–22.

The conversion work, however, appears to have been interrupted before its completion and not resumed. This suspension of work can be traced back to the compulsory measures of Karl V, namely, delivery of artillery and the dismantling of fortifications, and ended the intended conversion into a Hessian provincial fortress.

Between 1567 and 1592 Count Wilhelm IV built the castle's outer fortifications. The peaceful son of a warlike father, Wilhelm IV ("The Wise") did not continue the fortifying of the old mountain strongpoint, but transformed it into a kind of residential palace-like structure. On the north side of the courtyard, building started on a long hall, with a built-on exterior stepped tower and a brewery. The gaps between the north and south wings were closed by a four-storey annexe, which later became the *Kommandantenbau*, or the commandant's house. This was given a half-timbered façade, a steep gable of stone, and a second stepped tower with an up-to-date *Welsher Haube*, a French form of roof with curved contours.

Old and new rooms and hallways were decorated in the latest Renaissance style and embellished with figure-like representations. Although Wilhelm IV was very flexible and maintained the interior refurbishment of the castle to suit the prevailing taste, the age of frequent visits by the land counts had passed with the death of Wilhelm in 1592. During the absence of the land counts, who in the meantime had their own residences in Kassel, the castle was administered by Burgraves. According to an issue of the journal *Hessenland* for the year 1921, "Whilst in earlier times the princely Burgraves were the commanders of a fortified locality, this position was reduced, with the appearance of the foot-soldiers and the total revolution in warfare, to that of a purely administrative post."

The Burgrave's activities were many and varied, and included the diligent maintenance of the house and castle of Spangenberg. Also, as he resided there, he was to open and close the gates as and when the occasion arose, raise the drawbridge, keep all the keys safe, and oversee royal property such as bedding, household equipment, munitions, etc. In the meantime he had to carry out his own inventory, showing that all articles of property were being used fairly. In addition, he was responsible for the safekeeping of fruit, drink and provisions for the household and had to ensure that no misappropriation was taking place and that the building was maintained in good order. His supervisory powers also extended to the urban administration of the whole office of Spangenberg, and he had to attend all town and municipal court meetings together with counts and earls of high office, question people, and assist with correspondence and the payment of fines. Finally, he supervised the loans of tithes to the counts and ensured that all such matters were faithfully brought to register and settled. For this he annually received twelve *Gulden* (Florins) as Burgrave, eight *Gulden* as Treasurer, one bullock or four *Gulden*, four castrated rams, eight quarters of corn, three-quarters of a bushel of peas, two bushels of oats, two bushels of wheat, one and a half tuns of beer and, twice yearly, the usual court dress, each time four cubits of cloth and four cubits of fustian. The combined offices of Burgrave and Treasurer were therefore comparatively well paid. Subordinate to him were two gatekeepers and a scribe.

Wilhelm IV's son, Count Moritz, visited Spangenberg very rarely and ultimately converted the neighbouring former cloister, Heydau in Altmorschen, into a residential palace (1616–19). However, owing to the circumstances at the time, he was forced yet again to be involved with Spangenberg. The beginning of the Thirty Years' War (1618-48) required the fortification of the approaches to the castle and the western slopes. He constructed a list wall behind the eastern and northern ramparts of the moat, and a curtain wall protecting the western approaches. The curtain wall had a corner and a central bastion, allowing for a fully effective flanking fire. The horseshoe turret had to be partially demolished, and in its place a *Zeughaus* (arsenal) was erected for the accommodation of part of the household staff, a smith, livestock and also five metal pieces (guns). However, the course of the war interrupted the construction of the fortifications, and Moritz, as a precaution, had all the household effects sent to Kassel for safekeeping in 1625. These circumstances would explain the conspicuous lack of embellishment at the "Black Portal", which displayed neither coat of arms, nor year, nor any other décor. The construction works under Moritz were finally completed in 1635/36, and soon proved their worth. In 1623 the town had been severely pillaged, and in 1637 was reduced almost to ashes, but the fortress was one of the few in Hessen never captured during the Thirty Years' War. The fortification works were completed by Wilhelm V, and by 1631 the castle had become one of the strongest Hessian fortresses.

However, the castle's impregnable reputation was not allowed to persist. In his will, Philipp the Magnanimous had divided Hessen up amongst his four sons. Wilhelm IV received Niederhessen; Ludwig IV Oberhessen with Marburg and Giessen; Georg I the Upper Earldom of Katzenelnbogen with Darmstadt, and Philipp II the Lower Earldom of Katzenelnbogen with Reinfels. Through further increases in inherited estates Moritz of Lower Hessen had got Marburg and a part of Upper Hessen, with the proviso that the religious orders of the bequeathed lands were not to be changed. When Moritz attempted to carry through religious reforms in Lutheran Marburg, Ludwig V of Darmstadt saw a welcome opportunity to contest the line of succession in Moritz and Marburg. In 1623 the High Privy Council decided in Ludwig's favour. Moritz was to hand over the land, and was to pay back to the Darmstädter more than a million *Gulden* raised during the period from 1604 to 1623. The Emperor empowered Ludwig to safeguard his demands by pledges. This he did by taking command of a number of Hessian posts, amongst others that of Spangenberg. In October 1626 officials came from Darmstadt, and with the support of the Tillyscher Cavalry occupied the castle.

In 1627 there was a temporary settlement between Kassel and Darmstadt, but in 1643 a renewed and bloody struggle for inheritance broke out, which ended with the seizure of Marburg by Hesse and Kassel. Once more, the fury of war engulfed Spangenberg, and the town, which had numbered three hundred families, was reduced by 1644 to no more than 155 households. Although the castle was retained by its commander, Johann Stückradt, the war had left much destruction and impoverishment in its wake, and rebuilding the town took decades. Government business by the land counts was confined more and more in Kassel, to which much trade was diverted. The castle lost its military importance and by the end of the Thirty Years' War was occupied by a company of invalids.

From then on, building was confined mainly to maintenance and repairs. Although still considered a "stronghold", the castle was not really in a position to defend itself. It was converted into a prison, which required only a few alterations, above all the provision of detention cells made possible by the sub-division of available rooms. Then came the Seven Years' War (1756–63). Hessen was dragged into the conflict in the wake of other war-waging German states: Prussia against Austria, France and Russia. But only forty-three soldiers manned Spangenberg castle's company, a sure sign that its role as a fortress was considered by now to be of little importance. Indeed, its role as Hessen's strongest fortress was about to come to an inglorious end. In November 1758 the fortress was "conquered". The military historian Maximilian Freiherr von Ditfurth describes the coup:

Lieutenant-General Crillon, at the end of 1758, was ordered by the main French army encamped near Kassel to undertake with a strong corps a foraging expedition along both banks of the Fulda up to Hersfeld to collect war taxes. To safeguard these operations he deemed it necessary to take possession of the mountain fortress of Spangenberg. First of all the existing Hessian garrison there, which was considered to be much stronger than it actually was, had to be seized as quickly as possible by a cunning stratagem. For this purpose he despatched on 9 November several detachments over Mörshausen and on the heights of the Bergheim, and had them take up a position there, making themselves highly conspicuous, thus attracting the attention of the castle, and send out patrols, etc. He himself, on the other hand, would advance with other Grenadier companies out of Melsungen and conceal himself in the wooded area of Schöneberg towards Elbersdorf. As Crillon had correctly predicted, the visible detachments on the Bergheim had taken up the attention of the castle garrison to such a high degree that their vigilance to the other side had been completely neglected. And it so happened that, whilst the attention of the castle garrison was almost entirely focussed on the approaching scout patrols despatched from Bergheim, so the French detachments using various narrow passes not only passed through Elbersdorf completely undetected, but also began to ascend the north-eastern face of the castle mountain and approached the entrance situated on the south side. Captain Crillon (the son of the Commander), accompanied by two soldiers and a drummer, was to carry out a detailed reconnaissance, or at worst to demand a truce, at the castle door. When approaching the castle he became aware that the castle garrison had irresponsibly left the door open — probably in order to safeguard the withdrawal of their troops sent out on patrol — as well as the drawbridge — meaning here the external drawbridge which lay between both "Schneppern" and now exists as a solid bridge — so he considered it no longer necessary to waste time on negotiations, but with his two companions rushed on to the lowered drawbridge, cut down the sentry standing there and held the gate entrance until the arrival of the approaching Grenadiers, whereupon they forced their way into the castle. Anyhow, the castle garrison consisting of only 43 half-invalids, threw down their arms and gave themselves up. This inglorious defeat meant that the importance of Castle Spangenberg as an impregnable fortress was definitely dead.

Throughout the 19th Century little appears to have been done in the way of building other than the construction of a small guard-house in front of the drawbridge — around 1830 — along with the removal of the gateway vaulting of the "Black Portal", and the laying down, in 1838, of a long flight of stone steps leading from the southern face of the *Schlossberg* to the town. The guardhouse served many purposes in the succeeding decades, including the provision of suites for newlyweds. The castle was, however, to remain a fortress of sorts up until 1866, accommodating errant officers and political prisoners serving out their sentences. (Hitherto, confinement in a fortress had carried with it no disgrace, being referred to as *"Custodia Honesta".*) For this purpose the castle was redesigned. Anna Bölke, the daughter of the last commandant, Major Gissot, wrote:

Everything that was reminiscent of the fortified palace was swept away; the delightful balconies were torn down, as well as the terraces, the sumptuous summer-houses, arcades, and open halls. The large windows, which looked out onto the sides of the courtyard, were walled up. Without mercy the priceless frescoes of the princely halls were whitewashed. Even the magnificent stone figures and the splendid Gothic friezes were not spared. Many marvellous architectural pieces were destroyed in this manner.

The men of the watch consisted of a garrison company of long-serving NCOs and superannuated semi-invalids who, through illness or old age, were no longer fit for normal military duties but who could still be usefully employed in the provinces. The curious thing about this garrison company was that its members were not confined to their quarters, but lived with their families in and around Hessen and were free to pursue other civic duties. All the company had to provide, each day, were an NCO and two soldiers for guard duty at the castle. At about 12 noon those detailed for duty assembled in the marketplace and received their instructions from a Sergeant. Then, accompanied by two drummers playing rolls on their drums, they marched along the mountain road (*Am Schlossberg*) to the foot of the mountain and began their ascent to the castle while the drummers returned to the village.

The commandant of the castle was a staff officer. He lived with his family in the half-timbered *Kommandantenbau* in the east wing opposite the main gate to the courtyard. The guard company itself was commanded by a *Leutnant* or a *Hauptmann*. Under him were a sergeant, four other NCOs and thirty-one soldiers. Besides their guard duties they also had to escort their prisoners on daily *Spaziergang* (walks) and perform orderly duties for the commandant.

Two regular spectacles in the town were the Sunday parade at the market square and, on every fifth day, the roll-call for payment and bread. For these events the entire guard company had to present itself. Each soldier received, in addition to his pay and a loaf of bread, an extra loaf for

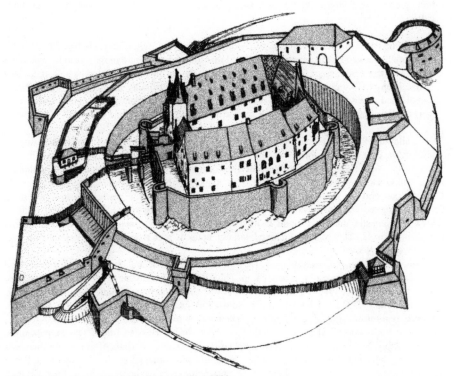

Fig 4: *Schloss* **Spangenberg from the south, c.1830**

each of his children. A much more significant event was the "Great Parade" for the sovereign's birthday, at which the commandant had to appear.

For the prisoners detained in the fortress, conditions, apart from the withdrawal of freedom, were not too bad. Adam Trabert, who with his friend and colleague Friedrich Hornfeck served a three-year sentence at the castle, kept a detailed diary so that future generations would have an insight in to everyday prison life in the castle. (Both he and Hornfeck were former journalists from Fulda and had been sentenced by the Hessian Ministry of War for advocating democratisation of the army.) The soldiers on guard duty were not allowed to converse with the prisoners during their walks, but if there were no superiors in the vicinity they would waive this rule. The guards could also be bribed to perform "small favours", and it sometimes happened that the guards almost became friends. Also, the Commandant at that time, a Major Weber, was considerate towards his prisoners. When he did his rounds of the cells he had the prison warders rattle their keys loudly to warn them of his approach. The warder then unlocked the doors, but the Major always knocked and waited outside until the prisoners invited him in. His inspection of the cells was always cursory, after which he sat down on a chair and opened conversation. The cells were sparsely furnished, but the prisoners were allowed to bring their own beds and other household effects.

But the nightly goings-on in the cells remained largely hidden from the Commandant. After the corporal in charge of the guard carried out his last inspection at 8pm, the cells became a hive of activity. Almost all of the prisoners, through one means or another, were in the possession of skeleton keys. They were therefore able to visit each other's cells and converse well into the small hours. They were also permitted to buy beer and wine, making the nights more agreeable and compensating for the boredom during the daylight hours.

Legend has it that two prisoners regained their freedom by digging the castle well, which took them seven years and was eventually 120 metres deep. However, attractive as this legend is, it is patently untrue. But an anecdote dating from 1860, which is true, concerns the day Commandant Gissot's cat fell into the well. As there existed a very real danger of the water being poisoned if the cat drowned and its corpse remained in the well, a soldier named Gerold took the risk of climbing down. In doing so, he not only saved the kitten but also the water supply. Anna Bölke recalled:

Finally, up came the barrel with the audacious diver into the light of day. He had the cat in his arms but he looked like a corpse and declared that for all the treasure in the world he would not go down there again; apart from all the horrors that the daring hero reported he also stated that it had been terribly cold down the well and that he had difficulty breathing. After the brave Gerold had received his reward he was immediately excused from guard duties, and it took several days before he recovered from the terrible anxieties that he had endured.

The vacillation of the last Hessian electoral prince, Friedrich Wilhelm I, over the Prussian dispute with Austria cost him the throne in June 1866, and Hessen-Kassel was annexed by Prussia. "Otherwise," wrote Anna Bölke, "the year 1866 swept over the old mountain castle without a trace. Up to October everything remained as it had in the old days, but on 7 October the Commandant and the garrison were sworn in, and the old princely castle had now become a Prussian fortress." In April 1867 the garrison company was dissolved. With the last military review at the castle, another chapter in its history closed. The Prussians had no use for the old mountain fortress. The rooms remained largely unused, and much-needed maintenance and repairs were neglected.

During the Franco-Prussian War of 1870/71 the deep moat and the drawbridge presented themselves as the entrance to a prison camp. The castle was ideally suited for this purpose. The walls were at least three feet thick, and the moat was sheer and flagged with stone too smooth to offer any foothold. On 22 January 1871, some 350 French POWs marched into the castle, followed by a further sixty-five in February. Their stay in the fortress, under the Prussian regime, was not to be as comfortable as it would have been during Hessian times. The French, quite understandably, gave expression to their displeasure by writing all kinds of graffiti on the walls and carving dates in the woodwork. But they were allowed home before the signing of the Peace Treaty on 6 April 1871. Three of them, however, would never see home again, as they had died during their incarceration in the *Schloss* and were buried in the old cemetery behind the village hospital.

After the departure of the French prisoners, permanent residency at the castle came to an end. The once proud fortress was now a relic of the distant past, and from the last third of the 1800s onwards its maintenance became a burden on the Prussian state, which began to dismantle parts of the castle and sell them off as scrap. Anna Bölke, paying a visit to the castle in 1896 after twenty-six years' absence, noted that even the alarm cannon, with its carriage, and the six-pounder with cleaning equipment, which had been positioned on the south-western bastion, had been sold for scrap-metal. In 1906 the Prussians put the castle up for sale. Negotiations were under way with one of the princes of Wittgenstein and a large brewery when, at the last minute, the *Hessische Heimatverein* (the Hessian Society for the Conservation of Local History and Culture), through passionate appeals to government agencies, was able to thwart the plan. Instead, the castle became an Imperial School of Forestry, thus re-establishing the old tradition of Otto the Protector and the castle's former role as a hunting lodge. As one prisoner from the Second World War, Aidan Crawley, pointed out, "With fruit trees growing along the terrace above the moat, bird-boxes in all the windows, a glorious view on all sides and excellent agricultural land at its gates, it must have been ideal."

Nevertheless, in 1906/07, sweeping changes were proposed for the castle's conversion into its new role. The preservation of the basic building structure required special consideration, which limited alterations to the exterior to a minimum, whilst for the interior many concessions were inevitable owing to the requirements of a teaching establishment. However, between them the competent government master-builder and a Spangenberg architect achieved a joint solution that bestowed on this training institution its own atmosphere and bound together generations of forestry students who regarded it as "their school".

On 20 October 1907 the first "Greencoats" moved in as boarders — fifty young forest wardens who had completed their forestry apprenticeship. After a year they sat for their first state examination. In the next thirty-two years some 1,200 young forestry students qualified at Spangenberg. The running of the classes and the boarding school was along the lines of an army cadet school, and a strict regimen prevailed from reveille to curfew. Spangenberg lived with and for the "Greencoats". In every annual intake there were students who took pleasure in brass-band music, and a school band was formed. The locals used to await with pleasure the departure of the students for the hunt or for practical instruction in the forests, accompanied by the occasional discordant note as the band played *I Shot a Stag in the Wild Forest*.

With the outbreak of the Great War the forestry school closed and the castle was converted into a military hospital. The school was re-established after the war, but was discontinued after 1921 because of a lack of free forestry vacancies. On 1 October 1926 it re-opened again, with a new class of forestry students moving into the castle. In the meantime, in 1932, the Prussian Count von Giech sold the castle to private individuals, but it remained a forestry school, and up to 1939 the number of students in each intake ranged from sixty to a hundred.

However, the further outbreak of hostilities in 1939 was the final death-knell for the school, for by October of that year the castle was already in use as a POW camp for British and French Air Force Officers. The OKW took further steps to make it impregnable. It installed searchlights to illuminate the moat at night, instituted a round-the-clock guard patrol along the parapet, and barred prisoners from the vicinity of the front gate, thus making impossible any attempt to divert the sentry's attention while an escape was in progress. The smelly boars roaming the moat were a further discouragement to escapers, as were the four machine-guns traversing the moat from four high towers, one at each corner. Nevertheless, from the point of view of would-be escapers, it still appeared to offer possibilities. Full of nooks and crannies, joints and joins, buttresses, vaults and chimneys, in which all sorts of escape paraphernalia could be hidden, the castle was a kleptomaniac's paradise. But so strong were the camp's defences that this was merely the refinement of torture.

The official history of the castle contains a brief and glowing description of its utilisation as a POW camp during the Second World War:

Soon afterwards, the French were moved out, so that only British officers remained there until

1945. The average number of officers accommodated there at any one time was about 400, with some fifty to sixty rank and file. Located at the foot of the castle mountain was the so-called *"Kreisgut"*, a former feudal possession that was used as a sub-camp. According to available official reports and evidence from the British officers themselves their treatment in every respect was correct and humane. During the war [1944] a book called *Backwater* appeared in England containing colour paintings, essays and poems by English officers in which they literally acknowledged: "We are reasonably treated." The guard lay in the hands of a local defence company, and following investigations after the war not one member of the guard company or the Commandant had any charges preferred against them. Where possible the prisoners were granted every conceivable facility and liberty. They had their own orchestra, in the castle courtyard open-air productions of Shakespearean plays were performed, and under guard they could take walks outside the camp, and were even allowed the use of a playing field and to go bathing in the stream and to have access to the cinema. In the town church they even performed concerts. Disciplinary difficulties hardly ever arose. One incident passed on by word of mouth should not be withheld: On entering the camp a prisoner was asked if he had any particular requests. His answer: "A saxophone and a beautiful woman." Understandably, one could only grant his wish for the saxophone.

(6)

Over the next few weeks Murray and Thompson were joined by seven other French officers and another six British aircrew captured during the latter half of September and the first week of October. The six British were Guy Griffiths, Richard ("Thirsty") Thurston, Reginald Douglas ("Bacchus") Baughan, Robert Maxwell ("Gonga") Coste, Derek Heaton-Nichols and Allan Colin MacLachlan.

If Laurence Edwards has the dubious honour of being the first RAF officer to fall into German hands, Guy Griffiths and Richard Thurston have the distinction of being the first prisoners from, respectively, the Royal Marines and the Royal Navy Fleet Air Arm. Skua pilots in No803 Squadron, they are captured on Thursday, 14 September. Their squadron is based on the *Ark Royal*, only completed at Birkenhead in May of 1938, and the only aircraft-carrier of modern construction in the Royal Navy. With four destroyers, it has separated from the rest of the Home Fleet, which on 6 September turned home to refuel. Since 9 September the *Ark Royal* has been cruising the Atlantic north-west of Ireland on anti-submarine patrol, for U-boats are already proving themselves a menace. Since August thirty-nine of Germany's fleet of fifty-eight submarines have been in the Atlantic, undetected by either the Navy or the RAF. On the very first day of war, in contravention of international agreements, *U-30*, commanded by *Kapitänleutnant sur Zee* Fritz-Julius Lemp wrongly identifying the passenger ship SS *Athenia* as an auxiliary cruiser, sinks the vessel. Unaware that it is a mistake, the Admiralty naturally thinks it heralds the start of unrestricted submarine warfare. To fill gaps in Coastal Command's convoy cover, aircraft-carriers are now on the lookout for enemy submarines.

The *Ark Royal* is itself attacked by another U-boat, *U-39*, on the morning of the 14th. After scoring some near misses with its torpedoes *U-39* is crippled by escorting destroyers and abandoned by its crew. Early that afternoon an SOS crackles over the *Ark Royal's* receiver: the SS *Fanad Head*, a British freighter, is under attack from a U-boat. The carrier picks up just enough to get a bearing, and estimates her position as more than a hundred miles to the west. Two destroyers swing away and race to the rescue while, from the *Ark Royal*, its flight deck heaving over a long swell, three Skua IIs, flown by the squadron's CO, Lieutenant-Commander D R F Campbell, and Thurston and Griffiths, are scrambled to attack the U-boat.

The Blackburn Skua, which came into service at the end of 1938, replaced the Hawker Nimrod as the Fleet Air Arm's main fighter. Along with the Hawker Osprey, the Fairey IIIF and the Fairey Seal, the mainstays of the Royal Naval Air Service in the 1930s, the Nimrod was a conversion from an RAF type and was not designed for naval aviation. The Skua, however, was revolutionary in 1938. Intended as a fighter/dive-bomber, it is a two-seater monoplane with a Perspex cockpit canopy, a retractable undercarriage, a variable pitch propeller, and large and powerful flaps. It is armed with four Browning machine-guns in the wings, operated by the pilot, and a Vickers, manned by the observer, in the rear cockpit. Fully loaded with one 500lb anti-submarine bomb and eight 20lb anti-personnel bombs, it has a flying duration of four and a half hours. An easy aircraft to handle, and first class as a dive-bomber, the Skua is, however, inadequate as a fighter: it is too slow; it lacks self-sealing fuel tanks; it tends to yaw in flight when fully armed and bombed-up; and the big, "conservatory"-type canopy, while affording the pilot and observer an excellent view, leaves them exposed to enemy gunfire because it is not bullet-proof and there is no armour plating behind the pilot. Even before Munich, when it was rolling off the production lines, it was obsolete by comparison with fighter aircraft of almost every other nation.

For this particular operation, the three Skuas are each loaded with one 100lb anti-submarine bomb and four 20lb anti-personnel bombs. A squadron of Swordfish torpedo-bombers is lined up to follow.

Climbing to about 3,000 feet, under a base of heavy, grey cloud, the three Skuas fly northwards independently. Half an hour later Thurston sees a thin, black shape directly ahead. He climbs quickly into the cloud to cover his approach, stays on course until he judges he is near his target, then hurtles nose-down out of the cloud. Directly below him the crippled freighter is tossing in the swell and beside it, lying at right-angles and almost touching it, is the U-boat. It is *U-30*, again, still under the command of Fritz-Julius Lemp. Too close to bomb, Thurston veers away for a few seconds, then returns and shoves his nose deeply down for the bombing dive, approaching *U-30* broadside on, so that if his 100lb bomb falls short it will not hit the *Fanad Head*. He dives as low as he dares before releasing the bomb. It falls a few feet short, its flying fragments denting the U-boat's conning-tower. Lemp begins flooding its tanks.

Hoping to drop the remaining 20lb bombs down or on the conning-tower and prevent the U-boat submerging, Thurston peels off and dives again. Time is short, as her decks are already awash. He goes in even lower this time, and when he is almost overhead he presses his button four times in quick succession, to release every bomb. Two fall on one side of the target, two on the other. As he pulls his nose up again he sees a flame shoot up in the bottom of his cockpit. A bomb splinter has pierced his unprotected petrol tank. Quicker than Thurston's brain can follow events, the flame, fed by leaking petrol, spreads and leaps up towards the controls. Strapped in his bucket seat, Thurston is unable to move his legs and agonising seconds pass as the fire burns through his thin uniform trousers. Flames surround the control column and penetrate his gloves, searing his hands and wrists. He jerks his hands on and off the stick "like a man juggling a hot potato", he recalled later. The only way out is to push the stick forward and ditch as soon as possible.

From a height of two or three hundred feet the Skua smacks into the crest of a wave. Bouncing about fifty feet into the air, it drops and hits the waves again, then ploughs to a stop, water cascading all over the cockpit. As the nose sinks, Thurston and his observer, Naval Airman McKay, unstrap themselves and flop out onto the wing. With petrol tank split and fire threatening, Thurston and McKay do not want to wait around to be fried; they tumble into the water. But McKay can barely doggy-paddle, and Thurston grabs him and pulls him out of the danger area. They have forgotten to pull the dinghy release toggle and the Skua sinks, dinghy and all, leaving them about a mile away from the *Fanad Head*, still lifting in the swell. But at least they have their Mae Wests. Thurston grabs McKay in the orthodox life-saving method and starts to swim towards the ship.

After ten minutes their progress is negligible, so Thurston releases McKay and tells him to stay afloat while he swims off alone to get help from the freighter. He struggles on for nearly an hour and is two hundred yards from the ship when the cumulative effect of shock, burns and the cold water takes over and he passes out. *U-30* captured the crew of the *Fanad Head* before Thurston's Skua arrived and a prize crew is on board. A German sailor sees his unconscious body, jumps overboard with a line, swims towards him and has him fished out of the drink. Thurston stirs later in the ship's saloon when brandy is being poured down his throat — a pleasant reawakening, all things considered. The ship's crew has by then been sent away in the boats, so Thurston gasps out to the Germans standing around him that his observer is still in the water, needing help.

Meanwhile, *U-30* has surfaced again and Griffiths, arriving a few minutes after Thurston, is making his approach. Flying low on the side of the *Fanad Head* in the lee of *U-30*, he is trying to read the name on the freighter's bow. Only when he has flown right over the freighter does he see the U-boat, its conning-tower just opening. Exhilarated, he pulls up steeply, selects his 100lb bomb, manoeuvres into position, then puts his nose down and dives. Like Thurston, he presses the button at low level. Then there is a shattering explosion and his tailplane flies off. The Skua spins violently into the sea and Griffiths passes out. When he comes to a few seconds later, floating in the foaming, white cauldron left by his sinking Skua, he feels dazed. There is no other sign of the aircraft, and again U-30 has submerged. Griffiths is not far from the freighter and he, too, is hauled on board.

Later on a great cry goes up from the anxious Germans as the U-boat once more comes to the surface. Thurston and Griffiths are hastily pushed over the side into the sea, and rough hands lug them on board U-30 and pour them into the conning-tower. The Swordfish squadron is now in earshot and the U-boat again starts diving. As the two prisoners lie half-conscious and shivering on a bunk in the U-boat's bowels, they hear explosions reverberating in the water. But the submarine survives unscathed. By the time she surfaces again there is no hope of searching for the two missing naval air observers. They are "missing, presumed drowned". For two weeks the U-boat remains on patrol before berthing at her base in Wilhelmshaven on Saturday, 28 September.

On Saturday, 14 October the two Skua pilots are sent to Oflag XIB at Brunswick— another camp, like Itzehoe, opened for Polish prisoners. Less than a week later, on Saturday, 12 October, they are escorted to Spangenberg.

(7)

As autumn fades into winter, Murray, Thompson, Griffiths and Thurston are joined by Reg Baughan and Bob Coste, whose NCOs and "other ranks", Sergeant Jock Galloway and AC1 Liggett, are inexplicably sent to Stalag IXA, a camp for Polish other ranks at nearby Ziegenhain. They are the only four survivors of a daylight sweep around Heligoland on Friday, 29 September. In response to recce sightings of German warships heading towards Wilhelmshaven, No5 Group hurriedly plans an attack on the ships — either at sea or harbour. Six Hampden MkIs from No144 Squadron, Hemswell, take off at 0640 hours led by Wing Commander J C Cunningham. They are each armed with four 500lb general purpose bombs, which have been fitted with an instantaneous fuse and must be dropped from 1,000 feet. One aircraft develops engine trouble and returns to base shortly after the take-off of six more Hampdens, led by Squadron Leader W H J Lindsay, at 0705 hours. The remaining pilots in Cunningham's formation are Flying Officers J T B Sadler, N C Beck and "Bacchus" Baughan, and Pilot Officer Coste. Jock Galloway is Sadler's navigator, and Liggett is Cunningham's WOP/AG.

Although Cunningham's formation is the first to have taken off, it arrives in the target area at about the same time as Lindsay's formation, which has taken the shorter southerly route, is turning for home. Cunningham, heading east, leads his aircraft past the south of Heligoland. Acting as lookout, he flies at 500 feet, while the other four fly 250 feet below. As they pass Heligoland, the heavy shore batteries open up. The shells fall short, but Lindsay's formation has alerted the German defences, and twenty Me109Ds from I/Zerstörergruppe 26 at Jever are preparing to attack.

The Hampdens bomb the harbour approaches singly, in line astern, and on the same heading, but with little visible success. At about 1000 hours, when they are between Heligoland and Wangerooge, flying home individually, they are jumped by what German news broadcasts will later describe as "a hornets' nest" of fighters, which attack in vics of five. Sadler's aircraft, flying at the rear of the formation, is shot down by Oberleutnant Günther Specht, who before the attack tests the Hampden's defences by coming in tight and closing up until he is tucked between its main-plane and tailplane. This puts Specht forward of the maximum arc of its rear guns and so close that other Hampden gunners cannot open up for fear of shooting Sadler down. Galloway, looking sideways and upwards, can clearly distinguish the German pilot's face. If he can reach the astrodome and open it, he might be able to shoot him down with a revolver. But even as that thought occurs to him, he sees the Me109 peel off and rejoin his formation. Suddenly Specht and four others swoop on them from the rear. Cannon-shells thrash into the sea ahead and below, and the Hampden goes into a dive, with only 200 feet of space between it and the sea. Instinctively,

Galloway lies on the floor, hoping he will be better able to withstand the crash that seems so imminent. Just then tracer streams up through the bomb bay, missing Galloway only by a few inches, and the Hampden crashes into the sea.

Galloway alone survives. He passes out from the impact of the crash, and rises to the surface through the shattered nose of the Hampden. Brought back to consciousness by the sound of German voices from a rowing boat, he is barely floating on the sea, with only a tiny pocket of air in the collar of his Mae West — which he has been unable to inflate — keeping him from going under. He again passes out, and comes to in the wheelhouse of a small patrol vessel.

The same German pilot, Specht, is probably also responsible for crippling Baughan's aircraft, which likewise hits the sea. Again, only one man, Baughan, is picked up. From Cunningham's aircraft, shot down in flames by *Unteroffizier* Pirsch, only Liggett survives. Bob Coste's Hampden, the fourth to come under attack, is hit by *Unteroffizier* Pollack. Five Me109s dive on him from 1,000 feet and open fire from a distance of about fifty yards, setting the wings and fuselage on fire and damaging the tailplane. When it hits the sea Coste is thrown clear, still sitting in his seat, with a broken right leg and deep cuts to both knees. Despite his injuries, he gathers up the bodies of his crew, but all are dead. He is six hours in the sea before being picked up.

Beck's crew, whose Hampden has been attacked by *Hauptmann* Friedrich-Karl Dickore, is killed outright. Return fire from the Hampdens hits two of the Messerschmitts, which ditch in the North Sea. The two German pilots are rescued by a German patrol boat, along with Coste, Baughan and the two NCOs. In all, eight dead bodies are retrieved from the sea, and another eight are simply "missing". The boat lands the prisoners at Wilhelmshaven, where they are taken to the naval hospital. Coste remains there for five weeks, finally arriving at Spangenberg on Saturday, 11 November.

Afterwards there is an official Air Ministry inquiry into the disaster, which reaches the not very surprising conclusion that the raid was badly planned. Of course the German fighters would have been alerted by the time the second wave arrived. Of course crews stood a good chance of being picked off if they attacked singly and in line astern. As a result, the armament of the Hampden is beefed up, and such improvements as armour-plating and self-sealing tanks are considered. But the tactical lessons are not learnt. In the months to come many other crews will attack harbours by day and in the same way, and join Baughan, Coste, Galloway and Liggett behind the wire.

Coste, a Canadian from Calgary, Alberta, was a whale of a man. He had joined the RAF long before the war. But in 1938 he put up an almighty "black". (A "black" was RAF slang for bad behaviour, also known as a "bad show" or a "shower". A typical example was being extraordinarily drunk on a Station Commander's Sunday Dress Parade, and making everyone present aware of it by whooping it up vocally, and possibly passing out in front of the troops.) The Officer i/c Postings at the Air Ministry decided to send him to an out-of-the-way spot where he wouldn't attract too much publicity if he got into any more hot water. Coste ended up as a permanent Orderly Officer at West Freugh, a bleak, isolated station a few miles east of Stranraer in Scotland. At the "Fruff" — as it was called — Coste countered the tedium of being a glorified janitor by playing poker, carousing and quaffing back an excessive amount of beer. Overflowing with bonhomie, and reeling off the latest service jokes, he was always surrounded by a crowd of admirers, fascinated by his phenomenal belly-laughs, usually at the expense of the Establishment. To the run-of-the-mill Englishman, Coste was a fearless, lovable jester — the very last man one would expect to meet at a dull, deserted, socially frost-bitten place like West Freugh.

At Spangenberg, and every subsequent prison camp, there would be many brother officers who needed his carefree laughter and envied his unquenchable spirit — and in the years ahead he would give them reason for optimism, reason to laugh...

Before long, Galloway and Liggett are joined at Ziegenhain by Sergeant Springett, captured on Saturday, 30 September. Springett, who hails from Radlett, is an observer in No150 Squadron, part of the Advanced Air Striking Force and based in France at Ecury-sur-Coole. The squadron is equipped with the Fairey Battle MkI — which crews will later dub, with typical RAF gallows humour, "the flying coffin". A single-engine, low-wing monoplane with an enclosed cockpit, it has a crew of three, carries a 1,000lb bomb-load, and has a range of 1,050 miles and a service ceiling of 23,500 feet. It has a maximum speed of 241mph — slightly lower than that of the Blenheim. Armament consists of one forward-firing .303 Browning and one Vickers Gas Operated (VGO) "K" .303 gun fired by the wireless operator/air-gunner from his position at the rear of the cockpit. Although it handles beautifully, the Battle is too slow and poorly armed to fulfil its manifold tasks as a daylight fighter, dive-bomber and reconnaissance aircraft.

At 1100 hours on the 30th, six of 150 Squadron's Battles, led by Squadron Leader W L M MacDonald, take off and head east on a photographic reconnaissance. One pilot has to turn back with engine trouble, while the rest fly on towards Saarbrücken, where they are set upon by no fewer than fifteen Me109s. MacDonald holds the formation together so all five aircraft can bring the maximum defensive armament to bear, and one Me109 catches fire and spins into a dive. But the fate of the Battles is sealed, and only one, MacDonald's, limps home — to crash and burst into flames on landing. Some crews crash-land in the Saarbrücken area and are rescued by French soldiers, but the captain of Springett's aircraft, Pilot Officer J R Saunders, and his WOP/AG, AC1 D L Thomas, are both killed, one of them during his parachute descent when the silk catches fire. They are buried in Rheinberg War Cemetery.

Another 30 September captive, this time destined for Spangenberg *Hauptlager*, is Derek Heaton-Nichols, the son of George Heaton-Nichols, the future South African High Commissioner in London. Admitted to Cranwell in 1935 as a Governor-General's cadet, he later joins No224 Squadron, No18 (GR) Group, Coastal Command, based at Leuchars and equipped with the Hudson Mk1. On a photographic reconnaissance mission over Sylt, his aircraft is shot down by gunners of *Marineflakabteilung 246*. Heaton-Nichols, wounded in the left shoulder, bales out with another member of his crew and hits the sea barely conscious. The Hudson hits the sea three hundred yards out with the rest of the crew still aboard. Despite an intensive search by the Germans only Heaton-Nichols is rescued, picked up after twenty minutes in the sea by a German fishing boat. He is then passed to the crew of a naval launch and taken ashore. Later on he learns that he was reported as "missing, believed killed" and that the Air Ministry sent a cable to his parents confirming it. His mother refuses to believe it; for once, a mother's faith is justified, as two months later the news reaches her that he is a prisoner. He is, in fact, the first South African prisoner of the war.

The next officer to enter captivity is Colin MacLachlan, a pilot in No139 Squadron, Wyton, equipped with Blenheim MkIVs. On Sunday, 1 October, on a recce of north-west Germany, his aircraft is shot down in flames over Paderborn by *Oberleutnant* Walter Adolph of *I/Jagdgeschwader 1*. He is the only survivor.

The seven French officers have similar stories to tell. They are Lieutenant-Colonel Gérardot, *Capitaine* Eveno, Lieutenants Aouach, Laemmel and Lamblin, and *Sous-Lieutenants* Lalvée and Noel. The first of these to enter captivity was Noel, the pilot of a Potez 637 in *Escadrille I* of *Escadre de Reconnaissance 33*, based at St Dizier. On Wednesday, 20 September, he was sent out on a lone reconnaissance of the Aix-la-Chapelle area and his Potez was hit by flak over Trèves. Although wounded, he nursed the blazing aircraft to the ground, where it disintegrated. His gunner, *Sergent-Chef* Leplan, was also wounded, but survived to join him in captivity. The observer, *Capitaine* Schneider, had been killed when flak struck the cockpit.

Capitaine Eveno, of *Escadrille II* of *Escadre de Reconnaissance 55*, based at Lure-Malbouhans, entered captivity on Tuesday, 26 September. He was on a recce over southern Germany when his Bloch 131 was jumped by six Me109s of *II/JG 52*. The decisive hits were scored by *Leutnant* Martin Mund. Eveno's aircraft crashed near Freiburg. His co-pilot was killed but his observer, *Adjudant-Chef* Giraud, crawled from the wreckage unscathed, and his air-gunner, Sergeant Crozon, had to be helped out of the aircraft as he was badly injured.

Lieutenant-Colonel Gérardot, commander of *Escadre de Bombardement 31*, and his pilot Paul Aouach were captured on Friday, 6 October, having set out from their base at Connantre on a lone recce over the Rhine Valley. Their Loire Olivier LeO451 developed icing problems in the carburettors, and then, at about 1350 hours, came under attack from two Me109Es from *I/JG 52*. The Messerschmitts made two passes at the bomber, *Leutnant* Hans Berthel scoring hits. The bomber was then struck by ground fire from *Flakabteilung 84*, and severely damaged. Aouach tried to nurse the aircraft to the safety of Belgium, but so badly was it crippled that it crashed two miles short of the frontier, at Euskirchen. All survived the crash, though Gérardot had broken a leg and Aouach was wounded, as were the radio operator, *Aspirant* Roy, and the gunner, Sergeant Aubert. The gunner had to have a leg amputated and died soon afterwards.

Sous-Lieutenant Lalvée, of *Groupe Aérien d'Observation 553*, was shot down five days later on Wednesday, 11 October. He took off from Sarrebourg-Buhl at 1615 hours in a Mureaux 115 to reconnoitre and photograph the Rhine bridges but was attacked by an Me109 and crashed near Lauterburg. Lalvée was wounded and his observer killed.

Lieutenant Lamblin was more fortunate: his entire crew was captured alive, although two of them were wounded. A pilot and observer in *Escadrille I* of *Escadre de Bombardement 34*, he took off in his Amiot Am143 from Abbeville on the night of 14/15 October to take part in a bombing raid. His aircraft was hit by flak and came down near Mainz. His second pilot, *Adjudant* Chable, and his radio operator, Sergeant Nomerange, were wounded, but the engineer and the gunner, *Sergent-Chef* Becqueret and *Adjudant-Chef* Bondu, crawled from the wreckage barely scratched.

Lieutenant Laemmel, an observer in *Escadrille I* of *Escadre de Bombardement 33* at St Dizier, was taking part in a large-scale reconnaissance over the Rhine on Monday, 16 October, when his Potez 637 received the undivided attention of the German flak gunners near Mainz. Yet another French recce operation ended with an aircraft in flames. The crew stayed with the aircraft, but the gunner, Sergeant Arnion, was killed, and the pilot, *Capitaine* Max Caton, fractured his skull during the crash; he lay in Darmstadt hospital for two days in a coma before dying.

One by one the officers joined the RAF in the castle, while the NCOs were taken to the Lower Camp. Also among the French NCOs were *Adjudant-Chef* Brard and *Sergent-Chef* Vergne. Brard was a Potez 637 pilot from *Escadrille I* of *Escadre de Reconnaissance 52*, based at Chaumont-Semoutiers. He was shot down on Tuesday, 26 September, while reconnoitring Konstanz (Constance). This was probably the deepest-penetration recce attempted over Germany by any French aircrew at that stage of the war. Unfortunately, on the inward leg he flew too far north and over Sigmaringen was attacked by flak and an Me109. With his crew already dead, Brard took to his parachute. Vergne was an air-gunner in a Potez 637 of *Escadrille II*, *Escadre de Reconnaissance 52*, based at Herberviller. His pilot took off on Monday, 16 October, on a photo-reconnaissance sortie over Kaiserslautern. Five Me109s homed in on the Potez and all the crew were killed in the attack, except Vergne, who had gunshot wounds in one knee. Despite the severity of his injury, he managed to escape the blazing aircraft by parachute.

(8)

As winter sets in, the number of RAF aircrew at Spangenberg and Ziegenhain swells from seventeen to nearly thirty. Of the later arrivals, seven alone were manning the short-nosed Blenheim MkIs in No.57 Squadron: Harry Day; Mike Casey, along with his navigator, Sergeant Alfie Fripp, and his WOP/AG, LAC1 James Nelson; and Harry Ryland Bewlay, with his crew, Sergeant S McIntyre and AC1 T P Adderley.

A Squadron Leader commanding an Advanced Training Squadron of Hawker Furies, Hawker Harts and twin-engined Avro Ansons at Little Rissington in early 1939, Harry Day is told that, in event of war, he will be posted to a staff job at Bomber Command. He protests and, on 1 July, is made Wing Commander and given command of No57 Squadron, a strategic reconnaissance unit stationed at Upper Heyford. At the end of September the squadron moves to Roye-Amy as part of the BEF's Air Component. In the next two months Day crams in almost a hundred hours' flying, only to be shot down on its first operation on — of all days — Friday, 13 October.

The squadron is on stand-by to provide two crews for daylight recces over the Ruhr. As the officer who commanded the squadron in the Great War, Captain (later Major) L A Pattinson MC, himself led its first action against the Germans, Day volunteers to carry out its first operation in this war. Apart from anything else, it will be good for squadron morale. But in his heart of hearts, he thinks it suicidal. The short-nosed Blenheim has a theoretical top speed of only 200mph with the nose down, and a token armament of one forward-firing Bren gun on the wing, and another in the mid-upper turret. Day considers himself doubly unfortunate. His original choice of aircraft is the one usually flown by "A" Flight's commander Sqn Ldr A H ("Judy") Garland and crewed by the latter's regular crew, Sgt Logan, observer, and LAC Sid Culver, wireless operator/gunner. For several days they fly practice flights, and an advance unit is sent to the French base at Metz to prepare for the arrival of the Blenheims on stand-by. By the time specific orders arrive, Day has decided that Logan and Culver have been on stand-by long enough and replaces them. He picks his crew from among the newcomers. His navigator, Sergeant R Hillier, is fresh from training school and his wireless operator/air gunner, LAC E G Moller, has not even completed his training.

Day is briefed to fly north to Paderborn, then west towards Dortmund, turning north-east before the Rhine complex of Bochum and Essen. After taking overlap photos of the rail traffic going along the Hanover-Hamm line into the Ruhr, he is to fly west, finally landing at either Hendon or Manston, depending on light and fuel. He takes off at 1140 hours. French "Met" has promised an overcast sky all the way. But, as often happens, the forecast is the opposite of the truth. Fifty miles inside Germany the cloud falls away to leave him looking down from a clear sky at the sun-drenched Rhineland. He is debating whether to go on or turn back when Moller warns him they are heading into a flak barrage. Day holds height and course. When Moller gives him a second warning, and Day himself sees the flak to port, he realises it is guiding fighters to his aircraft — an old trick dating from the Great War. He curses himself for a fool. As an ex-fighter pilot, he should know better. Over Birkenfeld, two Me109s — flown by *Oberfeldwebel* Ernst Vollmer and *Unteroffizier* Lütjens from *II/JG 53* — pounce on him. Attacking in line astern, from his lower port side, they pound the Blenheim with cannon-shells, hitting Moller. Day shoves the throttles through the "gate" and swings the Blenheim into a vertical turn, nose down and engines screaming. But it is useless. The self-sealing tanks are on fire and in seconds the instrument panel is masked in smoke. Day can barely see his hands, or Hillier, sitting beside him. He tells Hillier to jump. Flames are licking at him from behind, burning his face and hands. Controlling his terror, he prises open the escape hatch above him and kicks himself out. At about 1,500 feet he pulls the rip-cord, and his parachute canopy billows out above him. Debris from the Blenheim flutters past, narrowly missing him, and he finally lands in a copse outside the village of Langweiler. His navigator and air-gunner are dead, having jumped from the stricken aircraft with their parachutes already on fire. Day himself has suffered burns to his hands and face and is taken by car to the home of an Army major in Fischbach-Weierbach. The major, who is a medical officer, has Day's burns cleaned and properly dressed.

On Tuesday, 17 October Day is transferred to a local Army hospital. His escort, who arrives by chauffeur-driven staff car, is Prince Hubertus of Prussia, a not-too-distant relative of the King of England and now a Luftwaffe pilot.

Although Day is the most senior RAF officer to enter captivity, his arrival on German soil creates nothing of the sensation that surrounds the capture of Sydney Murray and Alf Thompson. In fact it is all a bit low-key. The only other patients in the hospital are German soldiers wounded in skirmishes with French troops in the Saarland back in early September. They chat amiably but are surprisingly uninquisitive. Day is given a room to himself with a sentry outside the door, which is always kept open.

That night, with nothing to do but lie on his back and stare at the ceiling, Day takes refuge in a form of self-flagellation to which every prisoner who comes after him will also resort. He blames himself for the death of his crew, and thinks about his wife, Doris. *Has she told the children I am dead? How will my mother take the news?*

As a Wing Commander, he is the equivalent of a Lieutenant-Colonel in the Army. There is every chance that a Wingco — provided he doesn't "get the chop" — will end the war with an Air rank. But now Day is in limbo: neither dead nor in the war. Confronted with a future that is uncertain and at the best bleak, he tortures himself by reliving his past and antecedents.

Born in Sarawak, Harry was educated in England and joined the Royal Marines straight from school at Haileybury. After probation he was commissioned in the Royal Marine Light Infantry. Towards the end of the Great War he was an Acting Lieutenant on HMS *Britannia*, which, on 9 November 1918, was torpedoed by an enemy submarine. Undaunted by two explosions, the ammunition going up, numerous fires, and smoke and fumes, Day went down to the wardroom to search for wounded. There he discovered the Engineer Lieutenant and a wardroom steward alive and conscious, but unable to move. Afraid he might hurt them if he moved them single-handed, he went up to the quarter deck to get help. With two stokers he returned to the wardroom, and between them they carried the wounded men up to the deck. On 7 January 1919, Day was awarded the Albert Medal, sea, 2nd Class.

His first command was as Acting Lieutenant officer-in-charge of forty Royal Marines aboard the cruiser HMS *Isis*. Afterwards he was Lieutenant of Marines on HMS *Malaya*, then commander of the Marine Detachment of HMS *Caledon*, evacuating Greek survivors of Turkish massacres at Smyrna. In 1924 he caught the flying bug and got himself seconded to the Royal Naval Air Service, then in 1929 transferred to the RAF. He went on to become one of the RAF's best aerobatic formation pilots. As a Flight Lieutenant in No23 (Fighter) Squadron, Kenley, he led the first Hendon Air Show's Synchronised Aerobatic team. By the time war broke out he had seen service in Abu Sueir, Egypt — where he was Adjutant of No4 Flying Training School — Khartoum, Aboukir, Netheravon, Rissington and Upper Heyford. In both the Marines and the RAF he was a "character", renowned not only for his professionalism, but also for his love of liquor and his gaiety in the mess. During every phase of his military career he earned a nick-name: on the *Britannia* he was called "The Boy Sprout" because he grew seven inches in two years; in the early twenties he was "Happy" Day, in the late twenties and early thirties "Pricky" Day; now, as a Wing Commander, he is "Wings", a name that will stick until his death long after his retirement — not as an Air Marshal, but as a Group Captain.

After spending forty-eight hours in the Army hospital, Day, with his head and hands still swathed in bandages, is taken by car to Oberursel. A small town of about 20,000 inhabitants near Frankfurt am Main, at the foot of the Taunus Mountains, Oberursel has an experimental agricultural school and model housing estate, which in September 1939 the Army requisitioned as a transit camp for French officer POWs. This is "Wings" Day's destination. Its official title is *Offiziersdurchgangslager*, and its commandant is an Army reservist, Major Avieni, who in peacetime was a director of a metal works at Frankfurt am Main and manager of the Obersursel model housing estate. "Wings" Day is led into a white-walled construction with high, steep roof and pale weatherboard at each end, like a Bavarian farmhouse. Tucked away in the thickly wooded hills, it has been set aside as a prison camp and surrounded by a barbed-wire fence. Twelve or fourteen small rooms, used as solitary confinement cells, lead off a central corridor, and near the entrance are a common room and a large washroom with modern conveniences. Three sentries at a time are on duty in the corridor.

Day is kept in solitary confinement at the transit camp for almost two weeks. His cell is small — about ten feet by seven — with walls of pine and a barred window. It is furnished with an iron bed, a varnished pine table, a chair and a new white-pine wardrobe. He has little room to move and, again, no way of killing time apart from recalling the past and brooding on the future. For an hour a day he is allowed to walk round the building — the only time he sees any of the other prisoners, about a dozen French Army officers captured in the Saar the previous month. Eventually Day complains to one of the German staff, a grizzled and wizen-faced civilian reservist in his early sixties called Bayer. Promising to bring him something to read, instead Bayer returns with a pencil and a wad of paper, suggesting he might wish to write home. Thus Day occupies himself writing a long letter to his wife. Bayer collects Day's jottings each evening, ostensibly to have them censored and sent home. None of it ever reaches England. It is only a means of obtaining information. But Day has merely described his cell and the scenery beyond — and, in any case, has no information to give. So for Bayer it has been a futile exercise.

On the third day Bayer tries another approach. He hands Day a form bearing the emblem of the Red Cross surrounded by the words: INTERNATIONAL RED CROSS: PRISONERS OF WAR SECTION. Headed ARRIVAL REPORT FORM and purporting, in small type, to be PRINTED IN SWITZERLAND, it is a lengthy questionnaire in duplicate, one copy of which, Bayer says, will be retained by personnel at the camp, while the other will be sent to the International Red Cross HQ in Geneva and thence to the War Office in Britain. The questions begin innocuously, asking for name, rank and service number, but then go on to ask for service trade; date and place of birth; civilian employment; religion; marital status; number of children; home address; name of next of kin; wartime salary; when, where and by whom shot down; when, where and by whom taken prisoner; Squadron number and station; Group number and station; Command; and serial number and type of aircraft. It also asks whether he is wounded, and the name, rank and number of each of his crew and whether they are wounded, killed or prisoners. Most of the information can be of no value to the Red Cross, and the Germans are in a better position than he to know when and by whom he was shot down. The form is obviously an imposture, and does not fool Day any more than Bayer's previous ploy. With a wry smile, he fills in his name, rank and number, and hands it back.

One morning at the end of October the prisoners in the farmhouse are given an hour to pack their belongings ready to move to another camp. They board a small blue Luftwaffe bus, which takes them east along the Hohemarkstrasse to Frankfurt am Main, where they turn off and drive north along the Lange Hessen to Friedberg. From there the bus trundles along the Kurze Hessen for about an hour until it reaches Grünberg, where it picks up the Lange Hessen again and passes Ziegenhain and Homberg. Further north it turns off on to a country road leading to Melsungen, then turns east along Melsunger Strasse. It is a pleasant journey, taking the prisoners through winding forest-fringed valleys and rustic *Fachwerk* towns and villages that seem untouched by Hitler or the war. After four hours' drive they see at the end of the long valley bisected by the Melsunger Strasse the classic silhouette of a German *Schloss*, perched on a conical mountain four hundred feet above two straggling villages. They have reached Spangenberg and Oflag IXA/H.

The bus does not take them directly to the castle, however, but turns left at the end of Melsunger Strasse into Schafgasse, a wide, tree-lined country road tucked into the foot of the mountain and leading to the village of Elbersdorf. Half-way along the bus stops and its cargo of prisoners is debouched on to the wet and leafy road. From here, they walk. The French — whose ranks have now swelled to twenty — carry a little light luggage and Day has none, but the walk is arduous: up the narrow, steep and muddy *Am Schlossberg*, which winds round the mountain until the panting prisoners pass through a moss-covered archway and up a cobbled slope to the gatehouse. They straggle across the wooden bridge and through the wicket gate until at last they find themselves in the cobbled courtyard. A gaggle of hungry-looking prisoners stand in the courtyard, alert eyes sweeping the column of newcomers for any sign of a familiar face. An RAF officer disengages himself from the crowd and approaches Harry Day, beaming and shaking his bandaged hand. Immediately the atmosphere of gloom is dispelled. The officer is from Day's squadron.

Michael James O'Brien Casey was captured within about three days of his former CO. Stocky, broad-faced and quick-witted, the Irish Casey was born in Allahabad, India, on 19 February 1918, the son of an inspector-general of the Indian Police. With his Imperial background he had much in common with Day, and like him was educated in England. Unlike Day, however, who could not abide any sport apart from rugby, Casey excelled in boxing and cricket as well as rugger. He was also a lot more God-fearing than Day, and paid strict attention to his religious duties. All the same, when he finished school in July 1936 he entered the RAF on a short-service commission. Casey married his girlfriend in the first week of the war but was posted to France with the rest of No57 Squadron before the month was over.

He was the second officer from the squadron to be posted "missing" — shot down on Monday, 16 October flying a route south of that which Day had followed, over Wesel-Bocholt, with the intention of carrying on northwards and going home over the North Sea. His nemesis was *Leutnant* Hans-Volkurt Rosenboom of I/JG 1, who intercepted him over Emden. An adroit and skilful pilot, Casey led Rosenboom a merry dance, diving in and out of the clouds, then going down to ground level and hugging every hill and valley, hopping over trees and hedges, scattering foliage in his wake, and skimming over rooftops. At times Casey's Blenheim was barely six feet off the ground. Finally, however, Rosenboom scored a hit, and Casey's engines packed up near Fürstenau, north-west of Osnabrück, where he pancaked into an open field. Casey, his navigator, Sergeant Alfred Fripp, and his WOP/AG, LAC James Nelson, scrambled from the wreckage just before the Blenheim burst into flames. Rosenboom circled overhead, and they gave him a hearty wave, not so much out of chivalry as of relief at coming through the ordeal unscathed.

While Casey was sent to Spangenberg, his crew joined Galloway, Liggett and Springett at Ziegenhain.

The next British arrival at Spangenberg was John Tilsley. Another No4 Group Whitley second dickey, this time from No77 Squadron, Tilsley was, like Murray and Thompson, a victim of "bumf" raids. On 15/16 October nine aircraft from No10 Squadron and four aircraft from No77 Squadron, operating from Villeneuve-les-Vertus, took off in bad weather at 1850 hours to drop leaflets over north-west Germany. The four crews of No77 Squadron, sortying over Frankfurt, ran into bad weather and flak, and Tilsley's aircraft, flown by Flying Officer R Williams, was hit. Roland Williams was killed, but the rest of the crew — Tilsley, Sergeant Lambert, Corporal Ron Gunton and LAC Fletcher — survived and went into the bag. The two NCOs were sent to Ziegenhain, and LAC Fletcher to Elbersdorf Lower Camp, but as the number of officers in the castle was swelling, two "other ranks" were transferred to the Upper Camp as orderlies. They were Larry Slattery and LAC Fletcher.

(9)

Until "Wings" Day's arrival, Murray had been Senior British Officer at Oflag IXA/H. He had decided against including German among the several languages he had learnt before the war because of his dislike of all things German, but now, of necessity, he set about rectifying that omission and would soon became fluent. His flair for languages and willingness to add German to his repertoire gained the respect of the commandant, *Oberst* von Meyer, who always treated him courteously — as would the commandants of all the camps in which he was incarcerated during the war. Now, however, Day had seniority and the lot of SBO fell to him. At forty-one, he was twice the age of all his subordinates with the exception of Murray himself. Already his brown hair, parted in the middle, was thinning, and his long face was lined and leathery. His height — a lean six feet — and a hooked nose gave him a hungry, hawk-like appearance. But his high forehead, his ready smile and his grey-green eyes, which almost always sparkled with gaiety, betrayed a youthful wildness which prison camp failed to restrain.

Day's responsibilities as SBO were hardly onerous at first. To some extent his burden in dealing with the Germans was relieved by the presence of the French, who had their own Senior Officer in Lieutenant-Colonel Enselem, and by Murray taking on the role of *Vertrauensmann* — literally, "Trusty" or "Man of Confidence" — acting as interpreter and liaison officer between the German and POW administrations. With the shooting war behind them, and no knowledge of whether the war in the West would develop or whether Hitler or the Allies would sue for peace, the aircrew at Spangenberg faced an indefinite period of confinement, and had to make the best of what cold comforts Oflag IXA/H had to offer.

In most respects, conditions are bad. The British occupy one dormitory on the ground floor. Although the windows on the outer wall allow a good view of the surrounding countryside, those on the inside give onto the tiny courtyard of sloping cobbles, on which little sun shines owing to the height of the walls. The walls of the "dorm" are whitewashed and along them are ranged single- and double-decker bunks. Destined to become standard issue throughout the Reich, they take some getting used to: for uncertain comfort, a straw-filled palliasse on wooden boards, two blankets, a straw bolster, and an envelope-type sheet of blue and white gingham. (The sheet is changed once a month, courtesy of the Reich.) Running down the middle of the dorm are two heavy, pine tables with benches either side. Here, the British have to live, eat and sleep. The French — by now there are about forty of them — inhabit a similar dormitory on the first floor. Like other rooms throughout the castle, these dorms are small and gloomy, with tiny windows, although they are at least dry in winter, which is no mean consideration when the only heat is the feeble glow given out by mediaeval carved and tiled stoves. Twice a day, at 0830 hours and 1600 hours, the prisoners parade for a roll-call (or *Appell*). Lock-up is at 2200 hours and lights-out is at midnight.

The prisoners, both British and French, spend most of the day in their respective dormitories. Exercise space in the castle is limited. The cobbled courtyard is only a hundred feet long and fifty feet wide, and one merely walks from wall to wall either in a straight line or a figure eight. The narrow battlements are about sixty paces long; there, only two or three prisoners can walk abreast.

But perhaps it is just as well, for the prison diet generates little surplus energy and is sufficient merely to keep out the cold. The Germans provide the lowest scale of rations, those for non-working civilians. Food ration cards were introduced for the German public on 28 August, covering such items as dairy products and fruit. On 25 September rationing was extended to bread

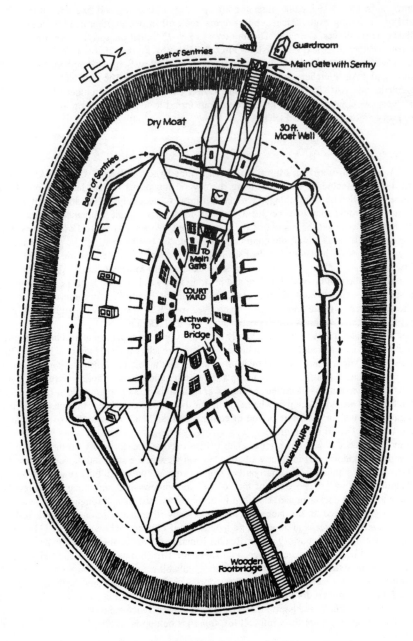

Fig 5. Bird's-Eye View of Oflag IXA/H, Spangenberg (Upper Camp)

and flour. By 1 October the weekly meat ration was down to 16 ounces. This belt-tightening by stealth within the Third Reich has a knock-on effect in the POW camps: the rations are both meagre and unpleasant. Each man receives half a loaf (ten ounces) of black *Ersatzbrot* (substitute bread) a day. Starchy, and owing much of its origin to potatoes, this bread has to last for breakfast (*Frühstück*), lunch (*Mittagessen*) and tea (*Abendessen*), when prisoners eat it with jam, honey or cheese. The honey and jam, also synthetic, are extracted from coal and sweetened with saccharine. The cheese, sticky and putrid, is made from fish residue. Bacon is also issued, but it is often raw, fatty, stringy and inedible. The only meal that whets the appetite is the midday plate of thick stew per man, cooked by the Germans with the help of eight French orderlies. Breakfast is normally served in the dining hall (*Speisesaal*) next to the kitchens, while lunch and tea are taken in the dorms. Before long, however, the British will give up eating breakfast in the dining hall, preferring instead to take their miserable fare to their room. The sight of row upon row of tables and benches, spotted with the occasional plate of thinly cut black bread and runny red jam, is too depressing. If rations are meagre, the camp canteen — if it can be called that — is pathetic. Its contents are literally brought into the castle in a suitcase by the Germans once a week, and comprise only items that enable the prisoners to maintain some semblance of decency: safety-razors and blades, toothbrushes, combs and small mirrors. These the men buy with credit allowed against camp pay, not yet issued.

Sanitary provisions are perfunctory and hardly salutary: iron wash-bowls, with running water, at the end of each dormitory; and a total of two flushing toilets. The German issue soap is guaranteed unlatherable and has a sickly smell like a cheap whore's perfume. The hand-towels — also German issue — are the size of face-flannels.

The German administrative quarters — or *Kommandantur* — occupies part of the first floor of the castle in the half-timbered and stuccoed eastern wing opposite the main gate. It is also here that the Commandant lives. A retired, white-haired cavalry colonel, von Meyer is about sixty and always sports a monocle and a sword. His adjutant is a *Hauptmann* Koch, a pompous little reservist who swathes himself in a vast, grey-green Army cloak. The Commandant rarely appears in the courtyard, and apart from the twice-daily *Appell*, contact between prisoners and the rest of the garrison is limited to occasions when rations are issued or when either side requires to complain about the behaviour of the other. The prisoners prefer it that way.

The *Lageroffizier* (camp officer) responsible for conducting *Appelle* is *Hauptmann* Gross. He is a comical figure. Tiny — under five feet tall — he can hardly stand straight because his legs are bowed from Great War service in the cavalry. His curly grey hair is flattened down with dollops of odorous brilliantine. He wears a battered peaked-cap, faded green tunic, grey riding breeches with an enormous leather seat, and cracked leather boots. Although he has risen from the ranks and is proud of his officer status, he is still a sergeant at heart, and on *Appell*, with the British assembling on one side of the courtyard, and the French on the other, he tries to make the prisoners stand as smart as a squad of his own troops. His moustache — short, pointed and waxed — twitches with dismay at their sloppy drill, and he chatters like an angry squirrel. Someone is talking, or not standing erect, is moving his head, is shuffling his feet, has not shaven, or has forgotten his cap. Consequently, Gross is the butt of many jokes by Bob Coste, whose funniest impersonation is to sit astride a make-believe horse that farts like thunder, and roll reverberating raspberries which are audible all over the castle. But for all that, the prisoners respect Gross, for he rules by the book.

"Wings" Day's meetings with the Commandant are rare, and conducted with arid formality in the presence of a *Dolmetscher* (Interpreter), *Leutnant* Helmboldt. Day complains about the lack of exercise space, mail, reading matter, and Red Cross and personal parcels. The results of these interviews are uniformly disappointing, although Red Cross parcels are supposed to be coming through from neutral Belgium and Holland. However, Day's task as SBO is helped considerably by von Meyer's giving him a copy of the Prisoner of War Convention; he also gives one to Enselem. Day soon becomes thoroughly acquainted with its Articles, and his determination to insist on the rights it grants POWs motivates him to formulate an approach to leadership at Spangenberg that he will maintain in every camp in which he is SBO. His formula is simple but effective: if he wishes the Germans to meet his demands, he and his fellow-captives should at least outwardly fulfil their own obligations. One of these is the observance of military courtesies, such as saluting German officers of equivalent or superior rank and returning their salutes. (Failure to salute Gross often carries with it the penalty of five days' solitary confinement.)

Another is discipline on *Appell*. Whereas the French have appointed a German-speaking *Vertrauensmann* to handle all routine dealings with the Germans, "Wings" takes the British roll-call himself. In a borrowed cap, he calls his little squad to rigid attention, turns sharply on his heels and faces Gross with an impressive Marine salute. Across the courtyard, the French major casually orders his men to assume a military attitude, and with minimum grace they shuffle into two wavy and barely contiguous lines. This difference in approach is the cause of several arguments between the two nationalities, with the French having the last word: "What is the good of it?" they say.

Yet another source of conflict is the food. Day wants the meat that goes into the stew to be roasted and served to the prisoners themselves, so they can cut and ration it. But the French again prevail, as their orderlies work in the kitchens and they are happy with the stew. The RAF prisoners, for their part, are constantly hungry, and as winter sets in they grow thin and peaky.

(10)

Life in the *Schloss* is brightened up in the second week of November by another familiar face from No57 Squadron, Flying Officer Harry Ryland Bewlay. Born in King's Norton, Birmingham, on 13 November 1911, Bewlay was educated at Hallfield Preparatory College, Edgbaston, and Wrekin College, Wellington. He had an uncle who was in the Coldstream Guards and who wanted young Harry to join the army as well, so after leaving Wellington he signed up with the King's Royal Rifle Corps at Whittington Barracks. But in 1936 he joined the RAF on a short-service commission, training on Tiger Moths at Perth and on Hawker Harts and Hinds at Netheravon. After training he was posted to No18 Squadron, equipped with Fairey Battles, at Upper Heyford. His unit shared the airfield with No57 Squadron, flying the short-nosed Blenheim MkI, and after a while Bewlay was transferred to that squadron, now commanded by Harry Day, whom he had known at Netheravon. Day, Bewlay and Mike Casey were an inseparable trio.

A week after Casey was shot down the squadron had moved to Rosieres-Santerre, and from there flew short-range tactical recces, mainly over the Siegfried Line. Within another week these operations had accounted for three more crews, the last of them the tall, slim Harry Bewlay himself. At midday on Tuesday, 7 November, six Blenheims, drawn equally from Nos 57 and 18 Squadrons, took off for Germany, and at about 1340 hours Bewlay was shot down over the mouth of the River Wupper by *Leutnant* Joachim Müncheberg of *III/JG 26*. Bewlay and his crew, Sergeant S McIntyre and AC1 T P Adderley, baled out, and the Blenheim crashed into the Rhine. On this occasion the Germans kept the crew together, sending McIntyre and Adderley to Spangenberg *Unterlager*.

Bewlay was a born raconteur. With a wistful expression and a pipe jammed between his teeth, he would spend hours in the Officers' Mess recalling his exploits with women. On one such occasion, Day chortled: "You bugger, Bewlay!" — and from then on young Bewlay was known as "Bugger". But, like Casey, he too married before the war, and now his wife was pregnant. Even so, in captivity, as on No57 Squadron, Bewlay endeared himself to his fellows with his habitual, brilliant smile from behind his pipe (now empty).

The Lower Camp also saw some new arrivals: apart from McIntyre and Adderley, two more French NCO aircrew turned up in November, *Adjudant* Robert and *Sergent* Barbey. *Adjudant* Robert was an air-gunner in *Escadrille II* of *Escadre de Reconnaissance 33,* based at Soissons-Saconin. His unit had taken part in a high-altitude photo-reconnaissance of Aix-le-Chapelle, Cologne, Euskirchen and the Ruhr Valley on Sunday, 5 November. Take-off was from a forward airfield at Orconte at 1430 hours, but the Luftwaffe was soon alerted and a squadron of Me109s bounced the French aircraft over Sarrebourg. In the running aerial combat that ensued, six Messerschmitts picked on Robert's Potez, flown by *Adjudant* Bernard, at about 1515 hours. Two of them attacked the Potez head-on and despite Robert scoring some hits would not be shaken off. The Potez caught fire, the pilot and observer were killed, and although badly wounded Robert was able to bale out. He never recovered from his wounds, and was to die in captivity in 23 May 1941.

The other French newcomer, *Sergent* Barbey, was a fighter pilot from *Escadrille III* of *Escadre de Chasse 2*. Five Morane 406s set out from Vitry-le-François to patrol the Wörth-Hagenau area on Wednesday, 8 November but were bounced by several Me109s north-west of their patrol line. Three enemy aircraft attacked Barbey, badly damaging his aircraft. Though wounded, he baled out. The rest of the flight returned to base and returned a report accurately describing the combat, but unusually none of the German pilots involved pressed a claim for having shot Barbey down.

During the first week in November the seven RAF aircrew at Ziegenhain saw a squad of dim-looking Jerries in civvies arrive at the gates weighed down with microphones and bulky recording equipment. The Germans were from the Ministry of Propaganda, and wanted to know if any of the prisoners would like to record messages to their families back home, which would be broadcast on the *Hamburgsender*. After allowing some of the French prisoners to speak, the compère invited the British to come to the microphone. The compère hinted that if people in England heard the broadcast, they might pass messages on to the prisoners' relatives and friends. None of the RAF prisoners had so far received any letters, personal parcels or Red Cross parcels, and this looked like a good opportunity to wake up the somnolent authorities.

Alfie Fripp, from Southampton, was first, greeting his parents in Eastbury, near Wimborne in Dorset. He was followed by Sergeant Lambert, of Brownhills, Staffordshire, who said he had been a prisoner since 9 September. He added that he was "looked after very well", sent his best wishes to his family and hoped they would enjoy Christmas as if he were with them. He also spoke on behalf of Sergeant Springett, of Radlett. Ron Gunton, from Northumberland, sent greetings to Hilda Moseley in Nottingham. James Nelson, of Belfast, also spoke. All of the prisoners asked for news from home and parcels.

A day or two later the RAF contingent were thrust unceremoniously in to the back of a lorry and moved to Spangenberg Lower Camp. They had hardly enough time to warm their bunks before another propaganda squad arrived. This time only three of the prisoners spoke: Peter Pacey, from Retford in Nottinghamshire, who said he had been a prisoner since 9 September and would like some letters; Sidney Burry, who sent greetings to his parents in Oldfield, and Clement Hill, of Saddleworth.

The recordings were spliced together and aired on Friday, 10 November. Repeated the following day, the broadcast was picked up by the Press. *The Daily Express*, which monitored broadcasts from its own radio station, reported:

> Seven British airmen, prisoners of war in Germany, broadcast short messages to their families tonight from "somewhere in central Germany."
> The German speaker who "compèred" them said at the end of the broadcast that the airmen had wanted only to tell their people that they were being treated most cordially and that they were very well.
> Added the "compère": "The German authorities asked them not to do so, to avoid comment that prisoners of war are being forced to make statements contrary to their wishes."
> The airmen said their camp was very comfortable and had such amenities as shower baths.
> Their only complaint was about the black bread, but the "compère" expressed the hope that they would soon learn to appreciate its good qualities.
> Reception was too bad to make the names of the seven prisoners, recognisable with accuracy, except in one case: Sergeant Springett, No. 561387.

An Air Ministry minute on the broadcast commented:

> This German broadcast made on Friday 10th November was repeated the next day and was therefore made on a record.
> The German announcer in introducing seven English Royal Air Force prisoners of war from a prison camp somewhere in central Germany, said that all prisoners, including about 4,000 Poles, several hundred Frenchman and a few Royal Air Force prisoners who were shot down and landed safely with their parachutes were being treated very well. The only complaint from the French was a lack of their usual wine rations and the English found it difficult to get used to black bread. The German speaker added, however, that they would no doubt soon discover its good qualities...

After the prisoners had been faded out, the German speaker mentioned that the German authorities had thought of asking the prisoners to state that they were well treated and had plenty to eat, but did not do so, and let them say what they liked, to avoid comment that prisoners were being forced to make statements contrary to their wishes.

The German announcer again stressed the wish of all the prisoners to get some letters from home.

The RAF officer writing the minute, a squadron leader in the Directorate of Operations & Intelligence, added tartly: "It will be noted that no Officer spoke." On 14 November, Wing Commander Rankin sent a memo to the SASO at Bomber Command, Air Commodore Norman Bottomley:

While it must be of tremendous relief to relatives to hear of their missing, the proper channel for this sort of thing is the International Red Cross organisation and these broadcasts are pure propaganda.

You might think it advisable to warn our personnel against this and voluntarily appearing in newsreels.

Norman Bottomley replied on the 18th: "...I agree with your last sentence – Can we not include this in our memorandum on conduct of captured personnel?"

It was, perhaps, just as well for the RAF prisoners that the Nazi Ministry of Propaganda did occasionally encourage NCOs to break the code of silence imposed on them from above. The Air Ministry seemed woefully uninformed about air force personnel imprisoned in Germany. When it compiled its first list of POWs early in 1940 it had Booth and Slattery down as "unconfirmed" and the following were not even mentioned: Edwards (the first RAF officer captured), Pacey, Baughan, Coste, Springett, Heaton-Nichols, MacLachlan, Day (the most senior RAF officer captured to date), Casey, Fripp, Nelson, Bewlay, McIntyre and Adderley.

Perhaps the most memorable occasion that winter is the Armistice Day parade on Saturday, 11 November. The day before, Enselem, who speaks no English, manages with the help of British and French officers to confide to "Wings" his intention to hold a full-dress parade. One of the French orderlies has borrowed a bugle from a German, claiming he wants to learn the instrument, while the rest have pooled their shirts, pullovers and scarves to make a *Tricolore*. At 10.55am on the day, the British and French form up into a single parade on three sides of the courtyard, under the command of Day and Enselem, the latter resplendent in dark blue tunic with the bright ribbons of the *Legion d'honneur* and the *Croix de Guerre*. The French, who have polished their shoes and dusted off their caps, right-dress into line with a military bearing which Gross is not normally accustomed to receiving from Enselem's contingent. After observing the two-minute silence, Enselem, then "Wings", address the parade. Day's speech is short and to the point. Harking back to the Great War, he points out that at the beginning of 1918 Britain thought it had lost. It might appear much the same now. But the Allies beat Germany then and would do so again. His peroration sets the tone for his future attitude towards captivity: "For us," he says, "the war is not over."

There is no evening *Appell* that day, and the Germans sedulously avoid contact with their prisoners.

(11)

Day has been at Spangenberg almost a month when *Hauptmann* Koch announces that he and the two French Colonels, Enselem and Gérardot, are to be given separate rooms as is the right of officers above the rank of captain. This is one Article of the Prisoner of War Convention that Day has no wish to observe. In the dormitory, he has the companionship of his fellow officers, some of whom are from his own squadron and several of whom were peacetime colleagues. Now he is to be robbed of the only thing that makes captivity bearable. For two or three nights he manages to avoid sleeping in his own room, remaining in the dormitory. But one evening, as lights-out approaches, someone warns him that two German NCOs are on the lookout for him. He scrambles under the bed, hoping that the Germans will not press the issue. But insist they do, and it is a disgruntled and undignified Wing Commander who hauls himself out from under the bed and lopes off between two guards.

It is the beginning, for "Wings" Day, of completely isolated leadership. But in any case the fellowship of the communal barrack would be short-lived. With a bitterly cold winter closing in, captivity is becoming increasingly irksome. Conversation turns stale, and no new prisoners arrive to provide stimulation or a vicarious glimpse of the world outside.

At this stage of the war few prisoners are thinking seriously in terms of escape. Apart from the immediate obstacle of the castle's defences, sufficient deterrence is provided by the lack of food, civilian clothing, maps and money; and winter is hardly the optimum time to be wandering aimlessly across an alien countryside. Neither is there any military purpose to be achieved. An Armistice between the warring nations is still a very real possibility, and even as late as April 1940 Hitler will still be suing for peace.

Nevertheless, the French army officers reconnoitre the castle and, more by accident than design, discover a veritable cornucopia of potential escape paraphernalia within its walls. Behind a pile of old furniture, at the end of the corridor off which their dormitory opens, they find a heavy oak door. One of them, Lieutenant Merlin, fashions a lock-pick out of a rusty iron hook he finds embedded in one of the outer walls. During a lunchtime when there is little German activity he heaves open the door. Beyond it are two more locked and shuttered rooms, the private living quarters of the Principal when the castle was an agricultural college. Merlin and his confederates conduct a search. In a sideboard are crystal bottles of schnapps, prune brandy, some bottles of wine and some biscuits. In the desks are pens, inks, documents and headed notepaper. There is even a working radio still linked to the electricity supply. Even more surprising are the contents of the wardrobe: well-worn civilian country clothing and a uniform of the German Army reserve.

Locking the doors behind them and covering their tracks, they decide to tell no one of their discovery, even keeping the secret from Enselem and Gérardot. But they are destined never to make use of their closely guarded treasure trove. Eventually they will be evacuated from the castle, which, in 1941, will become an all-RAF camp. The RAF prisoners will later rediscover the room and use the uniform for an ingenious escape attempt.

But young Bewlay wants to escape now. His wife is due to have a baby in February and he cannot bear the thought of not being there to see it. He makes his own escape reconnaissance and becomes the first prisoner of the war to start a tunnel. Undaunted by the grim prospect of chipping his way through three hundred feet of solid limestone rock, he improvises a hammer and a chisel and begins to attack the foundations of the castle.

A few days later von Meyer and Helmbolt pay a rare visit to Wing Commander Day. "Could you please tell the officer who is trying to dig a tunnel to desist," says Helmboldt. "The noise is disturbing the commandant's sleep."

(12)

During morning *Appell* at the end of the second week in December, *Hauptmann* Koch, through an interpreter, announced that six of the RAF contingent and five of the French were to pack their belongings ready for a move at 3pm to another camp. The RAF listed were Wing Commander Day, Mike Casey and "Bacchus" Baughan, along with Thurston, Griffiths and, as orderly, Casey's air-gunner, Jim Nelson. The French were the two Colonels, Enselem and Gérardot, and their pilots Béranger and Aouach, and *Sous-Lieutenant* Noel.

The British hardly needed the seven hours' notice, for their belongings consisted only of items purchased from the camp "canteen". In the time that remained, they were left to speculate upon their destination, which, once they were beyond Spangenberg in a blue Luftwaffe bus, soon become clear. They were on the way to Frankfurt am Main. Four hours later the eleven prisoners were occupying separate rooms in the same farmhouse in which Day had been held back in October.

But this time there was a difference. The Luftwaffe had taken over the camp in November, and it was now destined to become a transit camp and interrogation centre for Allied aircrew prisoners. It was now known as *Durchgangslager der Luftwaffe* (*Dulag Luft*, or Transit Camp of the Air Force). The former Spangenbergers were to form the nucleus of the British and French Permanent Staff at Dulag Luft. Their task was to acclimatise new prisoners to POW conditions before their transfer to Spangenberg.

Before the year was out two more French aircrew passed through the newly designated Dulag Luft before finally fetching up at Spangenberg. They were Lieutenant Navelet and *Adjudant* Tourel, an observer and a gunner from *Groupe I* of *Escadre de Reconnaissance 33*. Their pilot, Lieutenant Compte de Forges, set out from St Dizier on Wednesday, 20 December in his Potez 637 to photograph Saarbrücken, Kaiserslautern and Pirmasens from high altitude — pretty much the same route that "Wings" Day had taken back in October. Over Pirmasens the Potez was attacked by Me109Es of *I./JG 51*. Despite damage to his aircraft, de Forges dived down to ground level and escaped his attackers. The Potez was then hit by flak and caught fire. De Forges crashed her in the Black Forest, near the famous Landstuhl. He and his crew survived, but all were wounded. After receiving treatment at the Hohemark hospital, attached to Dulag Luft, de Forges joined the French Permanent Staff, while Navelet was transferred to *Schloss* Spangenberg and Tourel to Elbersdorf.

Mail is at last coming through, and in December the first clothing parcel from England arrives for Squadron Leader "Wank" Murray, now back to being SBO at Spangenberg. November also sees the arrival of the occasional private food parcel. Murray receives his first food parcel at 3pm and by 6pm he has polished off the lot, barring half a pound of tea and a bar of soap.

Still in Wesermünde hospital, with a ward to himself since Larry Slattery left, Georgie Booth watches the landscape beyond his wired-up window grow bleaker and then settle under a blanket of crisp-looking snow. Up to now he has been existing merely on German rations, but then personal parcels and Red Cross parcels from Belgium and Holland start coming in: the first to arrive in Germany after nearly four months of war. The Germans have to open a special store just to accommodate his parcels. He is now living well, but is lonely, and the empty days seem to merge into one another. As Christmas approaches, he recalls his home life in Yorkshire and a deep melancholy sets in.

The RAF prisoners at Spangenberg also receive their first Red Cross parcels, one each per man, but not until Christmas Eve. Their French allies receive none. Although the French in the Upper Camp are better off for food because their orderlies run the kitchen, the British cannot open their parcels without pangs of guilt, brought on by the sight of such goodies as tinned spam, margarine, powdered egg, powdered milk, condensed milk, tea, coffee, sugar, tinned fruit, tinned meat and vegetables, porridge oats, raisins and flour. Sydney Murray takes the view that the RAF contingent can hardly "bash" their parcels while their allies are eating black bread and rotten meat and potato soup, so he invites them to share Christmas dinner. He also ensures that the NCOs and other ranks in the Lower Camp have received their quota of parcels.

(13)

All is not sweetness and light in the *Unterlager*. The main problem is Corporal Ron Gunton, who is always searching for a means of escape. One night he tries to escape from the lavatory window, which faces the street. But a sentry appears at the last minute and raises the alarm. Confusion, consternation and a cacophony of shouting, screaming and hobnail-shod jackboots on metalled concrete follow. Luckily, the sentry doesn't shoot, but the game is well and truly up. The Germans soon realise that Gunton is a special case and needs to be watched; they send him from Spangenberg direct to the Napoleonic Fort VIII near Posen where they reckon a sharper eye can be kept on him. With a two-man escort he travels in a third-class railway carriage with hard wooden seats, a journey made even more uncomfortable by periodic jolting and shunting and hours spent waiting in sidings. Finally, after nearly three days of aches and pains, they arrive at Posen station.

To the usual accompaniment of shouts and yells they alight, and Gunton is marched through the streets of the beautiful Polish city, with its green trains plus their trailers clattering along the tracks in the middle of the streets, and German soldiers, airmen and Nazi Party members passing to and fro amongst the Polish civilian population, from whom Gunton receives many sympathetic looks and smiles. They pass the town cemetery and, after walking down another long straight road, eventually arrive at Gunton's new "home". It is surrounded by a high barbed-wire fence with watchtowers at each end. Gunton is led through the main gate and across a wide bridge over a dry moat, where they stand and wait in front of a huge double door. Set in the masonry above the doors is a stone tablet, which reads "G. Starmer and Co., Blackfriars, London 1884". So, his new prison is British built.

Finally the mighty doors open and Gunton finds himself in the bowels of the earth. Gunton is paraded for each guard to know and recognise, and is then led along a narrow, gloomy cobbled passage that slopes upwards slightly towards the end. When they are more than a hundred steps from daylight, they turn left, and two-dozen paces later arrive at a tunnel-shaped chamber with an arched ceiling. The place is barely illuminated by a single bulb. There is no furniture, not even bunks, tables, or benches — nothing except straw on the stone floor. Here the prisoners — mainly Polish NCOs and other ranks — sit, eat, drink, play cards, argue and sleep.

Life at Fort VIII is grim. Rations per man, per day, consist of one cup of acorn coffee for breakfast, one bowl of very thin soup at midday, and one fifth of a loaf of bread at night, with a minute portion of dripping or *ersatz* jam or one small round cheese. The "cheese" has to be experienced to be believed. The bright orange outer layer is covered with an evil smelling coat of a sticky, jelly-like substance; inside there is a white, cottage cheese-like substance. For some reason or other, it is known as "fish-cheese". It stinks, and the taste is indescribable.

Appell is thrice daily, and life in between revolves around walking along the slush-covered bed of the dry moat, washing and trying to keep clean, queuing for water and queuing for food. Before long there is an outbreak of lice — loathsome little fat grey lice. They breed anywhere it is warm and they feed on blood, even if the blood is getting thinner by the day. The best method of killing them is to strip off and run a lighted match along the seams of your uniform. Those that aren't burned are then killed by squashing them between index-finger and thumb.

Gunton's boredom is alleviated when the Germans give him a job as camp electrician, which means he can earn himself some *Lagergeld*. He is also moved to a ground-floor room overlooking the moat at the front of the fort. This room actually has a small window, albeit with two iron bars, and two prisoners can look out at once and see across the moat to the high earthen bank opposite, the trees beyond the wire and the vast Polish sky above.

It also has wooden three-tiered bunks with straw-filled palliasses, two large oblong tables and several benches. So at last he has a bed and a place to sit. To add to the luxury, dominating the room is a tall, slab-sided tiled stove, with a huge flue pipe rising from the top, turning at right-angles and leading out just above the window. Not only that, but he is very much closer to the kitchens and the toilets. Food is not plentiful and it is best to be at hand when your room number is called for soup. Equally, it is desirable to be close to the latrines, as most prisoners have some form of dysentery. The latrines consist of two narrow rooms, each with a box-like construction built along the outside wall. Round holes have been cut in this box at regular intervals. Thankfully, each hole has a hinged lid.

On New Year's Eve 1939, a cold wintry night, the lights in Fort VIII flicker and dim. It is no surprise to Gunton when, within five minutes, the German guard commander, accompanied by six guards, strides into his room and orders him to accompany them to an electrical sub-station outside the camp. At the sub-station the *Stabsfeldwebel* opens the door and indicates to Gunton that he should have a look to see if he can find the fault. Gunton doesn't want to get too deeply involved, so with a look of authority he studies the sub-station's intricate interior and announces confidently that the fault lies at the main power station. That is exactly what the *Stabsfeldwebel* wants to hear. Slapping Gunton heartily on the back, he turns to the other guards and collects his winnings from the bets he has placed about the source of the electrical fault.

Turning back to Gunton the *Stabsfeldwebel* says: "Give me your word of honour that you will not try to escape for the next twenty-four hours."

Looking at the two feet of snow in which they are standing, Gunton readily agrees. Then, indicating that he should follow, the German leads the way to where a riotous party is in progress.

Gunton sits down, and a full bottle of schnapps is pushed into his hand and several bottles of beer banged down on the table in front of him. His orders are to join the party and start drinking.

Six hours, the bottle of schnapps and a dozen bottles of beer later, the *Stabsfeldwebel* decides that it is time for Gunton to return to the Fort. A *Feldwebel* carrying a *Maschinenpistole*, another guard and Corporal Gunton begin their faltering walk back to the prisoners' quarters. The combination of the drink and the icy road surface is too much and all three collapse in a slithering, laughing heap. They pick themselves up, brush down their clothes and stagger on. The swaying men reach the camp gates, jovially shout their "goodnights" and turn to go their different ways. Gunton then realises that he has the German's sub-machine-gun slung over his shoulder. Calling him back, Gunton hands the gun back to the now red-faced *Feldwebel*. Thereafter, whenever the *Feldwebel* sees Gunton, an involuntary rosy glow spreads over his face as he recalls New Year's Eve.

When "Wings" Day and his party were moved to Oberursel in December 1939 they left the French contingent at Spangenberg without a ranking officer. But shortly after New Year 1940 the British and French were surprised to see Lieutenant-Colonel Gérardot ushered into the cobbled courtyard, protesting loudly in forceful and vivid language. Prior to being shot down, Gérardot had arranged a simple letter-code with his wife, who had contacts in the French Intelligence Service. In his food and book parcels she had hidden maps, three hundred German marks, and a compass wrapped in a rubber sheath and sealed inside a tin of condensed milk. Gérardot was preparing to escape when he blotted his copybook with the Dulag Luft commandant, Major Theo Rumpel. He had been present at a Christmas party thrown by Day and his British Permanent Staff, but had marched briskly out of the room when Rumpel had invited himself along, bringing with him two bottles of schnapps. The reason behind Gérardot's *faux pas* was understandable: before the war he had been a member of a Franco-German friendship association, but felt betrayed when he learned that one of his closest German friends was a senior officer in the Nazi Party. After that he swore never to talk to a German again. When the commandant of Oflag IXA/H informed Rumpel, via the OKW, that the camp required a Senior French Officer, Rumpel did not need to burn the midnight oil when it came to choosing between Enselem and Gérardot.

The following month news reached the commandant, von Meyer, by way of the Red Cross, that a certain Mrs Bewlay in England had recently given birth. Could her husband, who was a prisoner of war in Oflag IXA/H, please be informed? Von Meyer sent one of his flunkeys scurrying across the cobbled courtyard to the British dormitory, where the news was greeted with loud cheers and much handshaking and back-slapping. The prisoners had, of course, to wet the baby's head, and before long Bewlay & Co were chewing up rotten potatoes and spitting the resulting mess into tins, on the theory that the starch would turn to sugar and make a primitive hooch. The final "brew" was non-distillable and revolting, but prisoners would go on drinking potato-hooch for some months yet — at least until there was a regular flow of Red Cross food parcels with the right ingredients. In the meantime, von Meyer turned a blind eye to this particular (and forbidden) example of POW *"Kultur"*.

A week later George Booth was discharged from the *Kriegsmarine* hospital at Wesermünde and sent to the *Unterlager*. He was told in advance that his day of departure would be a Friday, owing to the fact that his escort, an officer and a rating from the *Kriegsmarine*, lived near the camp and had wangled some home leave for the weekend. This amused Booth, who reflected that servicemen were pretty much the same everywhere.

Booth left his ward dressed in a motley uniform comprised of Polish trousers and greatcoat, a tunic which did not match, a French forage cap and hospital issue boots. He cut a comical figure as he saluted and shook hands with the doctors and nurses who had assembled to bid him farewell and wish him luck. It was all very touching and somehow remote from the war, although his unsteady legs and walking stick were a grim reminder of the reality of the situation. He trod gingerly across the icy pavement into the passenger seat of the waiting car, German orderlies helping him in with his kit. His Red Cross parcels, accumulated since Christmas, filled the back seat. After the quiet backwater of Wesermünde hospital, he wondered what life in a proper prison camp would be like.

He needn't have given it a thought: life in the Elbersdorf camp was dull; he had gone from one backwater to another. When the NCOs and other ranks were invited by the officers to attend a church parade in the castle they accepted readily — and resolved to show "The Flag". They turned out in the best kit they could lay their hands on and with a smart step they marched up the steep hill. The German guards were unable to match their military appearance or step. As they approached the castle the prisoners at the head of the column started to sing "Colonel Bogey". *"Ruhe!"* shouted the guards, *"Ruhe!"* But when the singing stopped at the head of the column it broke out at the rear. Running frantically down the slope the guards shouted at the prisoners to be silent, only to have to run back up the slope as the singing resumed at the front. Crossing a bridge over a dry moat the contingent marched into the cobbled courtyard, halting on command with the guardsmen-like crash of their boots resounding from the high walls. "That'll show 'em," smirked Booth.

Among the officers were three RAF other ranks serving as orderlies, one of whom was Booth's old mucker Larry Slattery, who confided that one of the RAF officers intended to join the NCOs' party after the church parade and smuggle himself into the Lower Camp. The officer felt that it might be easier to escape from there than from the castle. Sure enough, as the NCOs assembled in the courtyard for their return march down the hill, young Bewlay (now known as "Pop") sneaked into their ranks. Unfortunately, the party was too small for him to escape detection, and in any case the guards knew each prisoner by sight. "Pop" was plucked from the ranks, virtuously but vainly protesting his innocence.

He would not have been out for long anyway. The weather that winter was the worst in forty-five years, with temperatures as low as -12° Celsius (10° Fahrenheit). Spangenberg castle, along with the village and the surrounding countryside, was blanketed in crisp snow and on some mornings there was 58 degrees of frost. It was time to put on every item of clothing and join the crowd huddled round the tiled stove.

Chapter Three

A Sad and Bloody Summer

Oflag IXA/H, Spangenberg, April–July 1940

Oh, to be in England
Now that April's there,
And whoever wakes in England
Sees, some morning, unaware,
That the lowest boughs and the brushwood sheaf
Round the elm-tree bole are in tiny leaf,
While the chaffinch sings on the orchard bough
In England — now!
Robert Browning, *Home-Thoughts, from Abroad*

No new prisoners arrived at Oflag IXA/H until April 1940. In the meantime the Air Ministry back home seemed to have little idea who amongst its aircrew had been captured so far and where they were being held. On 21 March the *Berliner Illustrierte Zeitung* published part of a POW group photograph that had been taken in the courtyard of the castle in December 1939. The cropped newspaper photo showed "Wings" Day, Squadron Leader Murray, "Pop" Bewlay, Heaton-Nichols, Alf Thompson, John Tilsley and Bob Coste. The caption was a gem. "Group Photo for the family Album," it began:

> Captured English officers enjoy so much freedom that — following the custom of their country — they can meticulously assemble to form this group photo.
> It will always remind them of the good and chivalrous treatment they received during their imprisonment at a Hessian castle.

A Press cutting found its way to the Air Ministry, where it was passed to the Deputy Chief of Air Staff, Air Vice-Marshal Sir Richard Peirse, who in turn passed the cutting to his aide, a Wing Commander, who on 2 April sent three copies each to Nos 2, 3, 4 and 5 Groups. "It is thought that you might be able to identify some of the Officers," he wrote to the AOCs, "and that their relatives might like to have a copy."

Then, with Hitler's invasion of Norway, the Low Countries and France, *Schloss* Spangenberg once again opened its mighty doors to officers of the RAF and Fleet Air Arm, until by mid-July the number of officer aircrew there had reached about fifty. British and French Army officers also poured in, along with more officers from the *Armée de l'Air*, bringing the strength up to two hundred.

The Air Force officers captured during the Norwegian débâcle were: Squadron Leader K C Doran DFC and Bar, from No2 Group; Flying Officers B W Hayward, T K Milne and K H P Murphy, from No4 Group; and, from No5 Group, Flying Officer M W Donaldson and Pilot Officer F D Middleton. From the Fleet Air Arm there was Lieutenant D T R Martin. Six more RAF officers from No4 Group, Squadron Leader W H N Turner DFC, and Pilot Officers J T Glover, L Miller DFC, J Plant, G E Walker and H D Wardle, had been operating over Germany, along with Pilot Officer H O Jones, from No5 Group.

The officers bagged in the campaign in the Low Countries and France were: Squadron Leader

B Paddon; Flight Lieutenants G D Clancy, J N Leyden, R I C Macpherson, G Skelton, J W Stephens and M C Wells; Flying Officers D Blew, P E Bressey, R M Burns, C A R Crews DFC, W H Edwards DFC, G E Grey-Smith, D S Hoare, A J Hudson, R H Jacoby, D F Laslett, W N Lepine, M I Murdoch, A C Peach, R E W Pumphrey, A C Roberts, M H Roth, D S Thom, N M Thomas and G O M Wright; and Pilot Officers G T Dodgshun, F Hugill, C P de Lacey Hulton-Harrop, A M Imrie, W H Lepine, E R Mullins, A W Mungovan, H M Murray, D G O'Brien, D E T Osment, I G G Potts, R J B Renison, AuxAF, H H Taylor and J Whilton. Another officer, Flight Lieutenant S G L Pepys, had been in Army Co-operation.

No fewer than ten of these new arrivals, like Coste and Thompson before them, were Canadians. Gordon Clancy hailed from Seimens in Saskatchewan. William Donaldson — known to his friends as "Weasel", because of his small stature — came from Lethbridge, Alberta; Hayward, from Dugald, Manitoba; Don Middleton, from Dauphin, Manitoba; Keith Milne, from Fort Qu'Appelle, Saskatchewan; Renison from Toronto, Ontario; Roberts, from Vernon, British Columbia; Glover, from Winnipeg; Don Thom, from Calgary, Alberta, and Howard ("Hank") Wardle, from Walkerville, Ontario. Wright was from South Africa, and the tall, lanky, wispy-haired David Osment had been born in Kingstown, on the island of St Vincent.

Some arrived from Dulag Luft in small groups — either within a week or two of being shot down, or a month or two later — but thirty arrived in one batch. Several had been badly burned or wounded and underwent treatment at the Hohemark, the hospital attached to Dulag Luft. They were not sent on to Spangenberg until the end of June or early July. The earliest 1940 arrivals, who left Dulag Luft on the morning of Thursday, 23 May and reached Spangenberg later that day, were Robert Burns, Charlie Crews, "Weasel" Donaldson, Ken Doran, Bill Edwards, George Grey-Smith, Hayward, Tony Hudson, Hulton-Harrop, Donald Middleton, Miller, Keith Milne, Ernest Mullins, Alf Mungovan, Mike Murdoch, Ken Murphy, Daniel O'Brien, Anthony Peach, Roberts, Michael Roth, Willie Turner, "Hank" Wardle and "Blackie" Wells. With them were six Frenchmen from the *Armée de l'Air*. The French were *Capitaine* Larmier; *Lieutenants* Detrie, Grandrémy and Leleu; and *Sous-Lieutenants* Besson-Guyard and Henri.

William Donaldson and Don Middleton — Hampden pilot and second dickey/navigator from No50 Squadron at Waddington — are the first RAF prisoners of the Norwegian campaign. At 0815 hours on Friday, 12 April, five Hampdens from No50 Squadron and seven from No44 Squadron, with which it shares Waddington, are sent out on a strike against the German battlecruisers *Scharnhorst* and *Gneisenau*, which are heading back to Germany with the *Admiral Hipper* after harassing the British fleet off Norway. The ships are expected to be off Kristiansand at about 1100 hours. However, bad weather — 10/10ths cloud and heavy rain — means the twelve Hampden crews have to footle around at sea level, unable to locate their targets. Suddenly, the weather, constantly fickle, clears up. Visibility is now fifty miles, and they can see enemy shipping twelve miles away in Kristiansand Bay. The formation leader, Squadron Leader J J Watts, instructs them over the R/T to carry out an attack at 9,000 feet. In sections of three, and in line astern, they drop their loads (each is armed with four 500lb semi-armour-piercing bombs). But as each section follows the other, at the same height and on the same course, the flak gunners are able to find their range and become correspondingly more accurate. A good deal of this muck comes from the *Brummer*, a gunnery training ship.

Immediately after the first section's attack, the bombers are engaged by Me109Es from the élite *II/JG 77*, flying out of Kjevik. For a full twenty-five minutes they take a terrific hammering, the fighters making beam attacks against which none of the Hampdens' guns can be brought to bear. Every bomber is either damaged or destroyed. The fourth section, in which Donaldson flies as Tail-End Charlie, gets the worst of it. All three aircraft are destroyed. Donaldson pushes his Hampden "through the gate" in an effort to catch up with the main formation, making for home and going like the clappers. But he is unable to close the gap and the Me109s set his aircraft ablaze. He manages to crash-land on a small island opposite the Norwegian fishing village of Tregve. He and Middleton survive the crash, along with Corporal A C Henry, the WOP/AG, who is badly burned.

Only six Hampdens limp back to Waddington after the raid, which, according to a subsequent inquiry, was dogged by ill-luck. The shore batteries were manned and ready for action only a few hours before the Hampdens arrived, and the crack Me109 unit that ripped them to pieces moved to Kjevik only twenty-four hours previously. But the raid has one immediate result: the equipping of Hampdens with machine-guns abeam.

The only survivors from the six Hampdens destroyed — Donaldson, Middleton and Henry — are picked up by two Norwegian fishermen who row out from the mainland. They are taken by car to the hospital at Mandal. As yet, the Germans have not reached this part of Norway, and the three are well looked after by the local inhabitants. Two days later a doctor approaches Donaldson and asks if he knows how to fly an Me109. He takes Donaldson by car to a nearby forest, where the Me109 is hidden under some cut-down branches. After a quick check, Donaldson declares the aircraft to be in flying condition. One of those which attacked the Hampdens on 12 April, it is merely out of fuel. The pilot is under arrest in the local lock-up. Together, Donaldson and the doctor — who appears to hold a military rank — scour the town for fuel and, finding only car petrol, return to the aircraft and fill her up. Donaldson rips out the seat so that he can take the survivors of his crew with him.

Eventually, Corporal Henry is squatting on the cockpit floor, Donaldson is balancing on the seat-frame and Middleton is sitting on his knees — three men in a single-seat fighter. But the "runway" is only a field a hundred yards long, and although Donaldson twice tries to take off, the aircraft will not get up sufficient horsepower on car fuel. On his third attempt he hits a tree and shears off the starboard wing.

Back they go to the hospital. Two nights later the doctor again visits Donaldson, telling him the Germans are due in town next morning. He has arranged for a guide to help him and Middleton evade capture. They dress, and are led for miles through the woods and alongside a row of summer cottages, until the guide eventually stops at one and ushers them inside. Handing them some food, he says he must leave, but promises to return later. They never see him again. Instead, they are arrested by the Germans, who have discovered Corporal Henry in hospital and warned the local people to hand over the rest of the crew — or else.

As luck would have it, their guide has been busy arranging for a boat to take them to Sweden. But the boat arrives two days late.

Howard Douglas Wardle, the next RAF officer to enter captivity, had quite another distinction: his was the last Fairey Battle to be shot down prior to the German invasion of the Low Countries. Always known as "Hank", Wardle was born at Dauphin, Manitoba, on 13 August 1915, and educated in Ontario. After working as a bookkeeper he sailed for Britain, and in March 1939 was granted a short-service commission in the RAF. In early November 1939 he joined No98 Squadron, flying Fairey Battles, and on November 27 was posted to No218, another Battle squadron in the Advanced Air Striking Force based at Auberive-sur-Suippes in France. On Saturday, 20 April he took off at 2055 hours to reconnoitre the Rhine and "Nickel" Darmstadt and Mainz. The Battle was hit by flak over Germany and the engine burst into flames. Wardle came down in near Kreilsheim, and his observer and gunner were killed. He was captured near the scene of the crash by a soldier on a bicycle.

Thomas Keith Milne and Bernard Warren Hayward had been captain and second-pilot/navigator of a No51 Squadron Whitley shot down on 23/24 April. They had taken off from Dishforth at 2210 hours on a lone bombing raid against enemy shipping in Oslofjord. But on the return flight their Whitley IV fell to deadly accurate gunfire from *Reserve Flakabteilung 603* at Aalborg. One of the crew, LAC F Hargreaves, baled out before loss of height prevented the rest escaping. Milne force-landed near Hadsund, a town on the north bank of the Mariager Fjord and some forty kilometres south-south-east of Aalborg. All the crew, which included Sergeant J B Ritchie and Corporal A W G Lyne, survived, setting fire to their aircraft before they were captured.

Kenneth Hugh Pelly Murphy — known, inevitably, as "Spud" — was shot down five nights later, during a raid by five aircraft from No102 Squadron on Fornebu airfield on 29/30 April. Taking off from Kinloss at 2000 hours and crossing the Norwegian coast, the formation came up against heavy flak. Murphy's Whitley V was hit by the gunners of *I/Flakregiment 611* and crashed at Sylling, near Drammen. One of the crew, LAC J Ellwood, was killed, but Sergeants C Warner and J F Graham, and Corporal D Magee, went into the bag with Murphy.

Kenneth Christopher Doran, an Irishman, was the last RAF prisoner that month. From No110

Squadron, he had the distinction of holding the first double DFC of the war. The gung-ho Doran earned his first Distinguished Flying Cross when on 4 December 1939 he led the first raid of the war, by Blenheims from Nos 107 and 110 squadrons, on the German fleet at Wilhelmshaven — the raid that led Larry Slattery and George Booth into captivity. Two months later, on 2 November, Doran and the officer who carried out the pre-raid reconnaissance were invested with DFCs at RAF Wyton.

The Blenheims continued with their anti-shipping sorties throughout the winter of 1939/40. These were hazardous operations, flown over the open sea in broad daylight without fighter escort and relying on tight formation for defence. On one such operation, on 10 January, Doran's formation from 110 Squadron was attacked by five Me110s. The Blenheim pilots maintained their tight formation and by co-ordinated shooting knocked one Me110 out of the sky and damaged two more. Although several Blenheims sustained damage, only one was lost. For his cool leadership, Doran was awarded a Bar to his DFC, while nine other gongs went to survivors of this action. But for Doran time was running out...

At 1630 hours on Thursday, 30 April, Doran led six Blenheim IVs from his squadron, now based at Lossiemouth, on a strike against German airfields at Stavanger/Sola. Their attack was to be followed up at intervals by sixteen Wellingtons from Nos 9, 37, 99 and 115 squadrons. As the last Wellington took off at 1815 hours, Doran's Blenheims attacked. But they did not see the results of their bombing, as four Me109Es from *II/JG 77* took off to intercept them at 1825 hours and bounced them before they could even begin their return flight. A running fight developed in which two of the Blenheims were shot down. Doran was chased by two Messerschmitts, flown by *Leutnant* Demes and *Feldwebel* Harbach, the latter making nine attacks before running out of ammunition. Demes then pitched in with his cannon and set both the Blenheim's engines on fire. It went into a steep dive from about three hundred feet and nosed into the sea, sinking straight away. Doran struggled to the surface, but his crew perished.

Flying Officer Robert Maclean Burns, flying recce Blenheims in No40 Squadron, based at Wyton, was the first RAF officer to enter captivity after the start of the Blitzkrieg on the Low Countries and France. On Friday, 10 May, No2 Group had ordered two Blenheims up at 0905 hours to observe German troop movements around Den Haag (The Hague). The reconnaissance was led by Squadron Leader Brian Paddon, who took off at 0905 hours, with Burns as his No2. By this time German airborne troops had already captured the aerodrome at Waalhaven. Paddon returned to report but Burns was shot down near The Hague and captured with his crew, Sergeant J R Brooker and Corporal G Hurford. All three were wounded.

Pilot Officer Daniel Grant O'Brien had been with No105 Squadron, flying Battles from Villeneuve-les-Vertus, and was captured later the same day. At 1530 hours two half-sections (each comprising two aircraft) had taken off to attack German columns on the Echternach-Luxembourg road. They found and attacked the target but met intense AA and small arms fire. Three of the Battles were so badly shot up that when they returned to Villeneuve they had to be written off. O'Brien was less fortunate. He and his crew — Sergeant D F Eastick and AC1 S R Wright — were wounded and taken prisoner.

Michael Heriot Roth joined the RAF in 1936 at the age of seventeen. A Fairey Battle pilot in No142 Squadron of the AASF, he has the unenviable distinction of being the only pilot from his squadron captured during the first RAF operation on the first day of the May Blitzkrieg.

Eight Battles, each carrying four 250lb bombs, take off from Berry-au-Bac at 1200 hours to attack columns of German troops advancing along the road from Luxembourg to Dippach. The enemy are expected to be some twenty miles east of Virton, flak is sure to be light, and the op should be a "piece of cake". One pilot, unable to retract his undercarriage, has to turn back, but the rest fly eastward at ceiling, wagging their wings at the tiny figures far below who wave them good luck. The weather is warm and clear, with grand visibility for twenty miles. After fifteen minutes they cross the steel cupolas of the Maginot Line into Luxembourg. They drop to two hundred feet, flying at 170mph.

When they get to Virton, from where they are supposed to fly south-east to reach the point where the Germans are rumoured to be, they are surprised to see below them, among the market booths in the cobbled square, long-barrelled guns and figures in green uniforms and grey helmets looking up at them as they munch their sandwiches.

Roth takes them to be British soldiers. But suddenly a hail of bullets strikes the belly of his Battle — sounding for all the world like the roll of a hundred kettle-drums. Stupefied, for a moment he thinks it is his air-gunner, Sergeant W F Algie, peppering away. "What the hell are you firing at, Algie?" he asks.

"It's not me, sir. They're firing at us."

"The clots! Fancy firing at their own aircraft!" Roth signals to his Number Two, Pilot Officer F S Laws, and peels off to starboard. But Laws doesn't follow. Algie sees his Battle, hit by the small arms fire, go down. It crashes. No one bales out. Three men, seventy-five years of life, gone in an instant.

From some high ground to port, machine-guns are still blasting the remaining Battles. Roth weaves between some factory chimneys and at last reaches the edge of town. He is now alone in the sky, but is out of range, and over the countryside once more. He asks Algie, and the wireless-operator, Sgt H Morris, if they are okay. "Fine, thank you, sir," they say.

"Algie, that was Virton, wasn't it?" asks Roth.

"Yes. It was Virton alright, sir."

"Good. But why would they shoot at their own aircraft? It's incredible!"

"I don't know, sir; but it was Virton alright."

As Roth flies towards the railway line, planning to follow it north, Algie reports that one of the tanks is leaking. "There's petrol all over the place back here, sir."

Roth checks the fuel gauges. The port tank is nearly empty. Must have been hit. He switches to the starboard one. It's full.

"Thanks, Algie," he says. "The other tank's okay."

He flies on, still brooding about the British soldiers firing on their own aircraft. He makes a mental note to complain to the Station Intelligence Officer when he gets back.

"Sir?"

"Yes, Algie?"

"Well, sir; it's getting pretty bad back here. Petrol's pouring in all over the place. Smells awful."

"Algie's right, sir;" — this from Morris — "it's pretty bad."

But there is nothing Roth can do. He must fly on, find a target. Can't go back with bombs still on the racks. At last — the railway line. Steep left-turn and northwards once more. Now they'll catch Jerry with his trousers down. But the crossroads east of Virton, and the fields surrounding it, are deserted; nothing but sheep, the only visible living things. What to do? He flies along roads and valleys. Apart from soldier riding west on a horse — not worth 1,000lb of bombs — there is still no sign of the enemy. Inevitably Roth, unable to match the places on the ground with those on the map, gets lost. They had better turn for home. At least his compass knows where that is.

"Any idea where we are, Algie?"

"Afraid not, sir."

"I'm lost, too. I wonder if we can find Virton again."

Then it dawns on him. The chaps firing on him at Virton were Jerries! There *is no* Allied line within twenty miles of the town, and the so-called enemy spearheads are motoring through Luxembourg unopposed. He decides to swing back and stop them the other side of Virton. As he turns west, he glimpses what looks like a procession of giraffes entering a field about a mile away and 90° to starboard. He looks again. The giraffes are guns with long barrels, pointing up like sticks, and mottle camouflage. Tractor vehicles are dragging them into the field. *No heavy flak! Some Intelligence!*

"I've found a target," he tells his crew. "An ack-ack battery for high-level stuff...We'll fix it up good and proper — and then home. At this low level they won't be able to touch us."

They snake out of the sun and over the treetops at 180mph. About two seconds to go. Then Jerry spots them. Panic on the ground. Green uniforms, waving arms, faces shouting orders, jackbooted figures scuttling like crabs among their unlimbered guns.

Bombs gone!

Instantly he banks and turns steeply to the right. *Ker-doyng!* The Battle staggers as though pounded by a giant's hammer. *We've bought it!* A well-aimed shell from a half-track among the trees. The shell explodes under Roth's feet. The instrument panel shivers to pieces. The whole world is firing at him. Glass from the gauges drops between his knees. Hot oil spurts over his face and spectacles (which he is not supposed to wear). He pulls them off and drops them in his lap; one of the lenses falls out.

They are still in a steep turn, but a level one. Roth heaves the stick to port and jams his left foot on the rudder, almost throwing the aircraft straight and level again. His uniform — from Austin Reed — is soaked in oil. *I must alter course. I must steer 270°.* The compass is still there, low down, under the frame of the instrument panel. He brings red on red and holds 270°.

Sergeant Algie again: "Smoke's pouring past us back here from the engine, sir. We're soaked in gas and oil, too, sir... D'you think we got the guns?"

"God, I hope so. Are you both okay?"

Morris: "We're okay, sir. But we're leaving a trail like a destroyer's smoke-screen."

The countryside that was so deserted only minutes ago is now swarming with soldiers, firing at them from all directions with rifles and machine-guns. Exasperated, Roth slides back the Perspex hood: "For Christ's sake stop firing at us! Can't you see we've had it?"

The oil-temperature gauge hangs limply in front of him. Its needle has gone twice round the clock — the engines will pack up any minute. Oil radiator's shot off like a clay pigeon. They're skywriting with a thick, down-slanting underline in black. *Must get down, down, before we catch fire.*

"Algie? Morris? I'm sorry — but we'll have to land. We can't possibly make it. Put your safety chains on. I'm going to land on the side of a hill just ahead."

He has already picked the spot. No choice — better to land and live than keep flying and burn. *With luck, we'll get down in one piece. Flaps down for greater breaking power — they seem to be working. Wheels down, too — their resistance will slow us up. Those idiots are still firing at us.*

"Hold tight!"

"Hope you make it okay, sir" — from Algie. *Why should they be part of this calamity?* Their presence gives Roth courage. *Throttle back, turn the ignition off to prevent fire, lower, lower, almost stalling. Nose down a trifle, gather speed, nose up...dropping, level off, down! I've judged it plumb right. Pull the stick back! Back! Hard against your stomach to stop a somersault!* Bounce, bounce, bounce, crunch! *We're down at 90mph. Terrific landing!*

With the steep gradient absorbing its momentum, the aircraft slides uphill like a glider, its undercarriage collapsing. It comes to rest with its nose and propeller (bent) tucked half-way through a hedge. Roth sits still for several seconds, listening to the hissing engine.

"You alright, sir?" asks Algie.

"Yes. Let's get out of here before the ruddy thing blows up." He yanks out the pin that holds the cockpit safety straps in place — retrieves his spectacles — pushes himself up — climbs onto the wing — waddles, parachute and all, down the camber — flops to the ground. His feet sink into grassy mud. Meanwhile, Algie and Morris are having difficulty getting out. The tail is high in the air and they have to drop to the ground from ten feet up. As they finally land beside Roth, a shot whines over the aircraft. Then another. Dashing through a gap in the hedge at the far end of the pasture are two helmeted figures swathed in camouflage capes. The three airmen stand transfixed. What else can they do?

Another shot. This is no time to fool around. Roth gives the order. "Okay, we've had it. Put your hands up." He raises one hand and with the other pulls a white handkerchief from his side-pocket. He waves it from side to side. From a distance of about thirty yards, one of the soldiers stops and beckons them out of the boggy ground. He greets them in French: "*Bonjour!*"

Good grief! Perhaps they aren't Germans after all.

"*Bonjour! Sind Sie Deutscher?*"

"*Ja! Ja! Deutsch!*"

Bugger!

The two Germans grin at each other and look very pleased. Shouting "*Komm! Schnell!*" they motion the prisoners to take off their parachute packs and hustle them out of the meadow through the gap in the hedge. One struts ahead, one behind, urging them to hurry.

"What's the bleedin' rush?" — this from Algie.

"*Los! Schnell!*"

Soon, Roth is wet through with sweat from the weight of his bullet-proof coat. He is much relieved when they stop at an *estaminet* set back on one side of the lane. One of the soldiers makes his report to a *Leutnant* — tall and young — who appears not in the least surprised. He greets the prisoners politely in heavily accented English, and after making sure they are not wounded, leads Roth inside. They stop before an *Oberst*. Middle-aged and sporting a monocle, he asks Roth a few questions and then changes the subject as he notices Roth's bullet-proof coat — specially made for pilots by the Wilkinson Sword Company — which cost him £15 from Gieves of Old Bond Street. The *Oberst* points to several places where its outer canvas is jagged with bullet-holes. "You are lucky," he says. "Remove it." Roth is glad to — it weighs 40lb.

The *Leutnant* leads him down some steps to a cellar, where Algie and Morris are washing in a basin of hot water provided by the proprietress. "You look like chimney sweeps," she says. They do, too: black oil from the aircraft engine has caked dry all over their uniforms, shirts, hands, necks, faces and hair. Several changes of water and many vigorous scrubbings later they look a bit more respectable, and the *Leutnant* takes them upstairs and locks them in a back room. The wooden window-shutters are firmly secured and the curtains are closed; the only light is from a naked bulb in the ceiling. But here is a surprise indeed! On a tapestry-covered table are three soup plates heaped high with lamb stew — a steaming concoction of thick gravy, onions, carrots, celery, huge potatoes and juicy chunks of meat — and a plate of bread-sticks, cheese and fruit. Their best meal for the next five years. They have only just settled down to eat when the door opens and the proprietress brings them three bottles of beer. Roth gives her the French francs he has left in his pocket, which she takes under protest.

Their meal is not without interruption. At intervals they have to drop their cutlery and dive under the table, as the land around the *estaminet* has become a battleground. The noise is deafening, the glass falls out of the window-frames — they hear it tinkle behind the heavy curtains — the building trembles and the soup slops over. It goes on so long the three prisoners think there may be a chance of rescue. But every few minutes the sentry outside opens the door and pops his head round to make sure they are still there. Through a chink in the wooden window-shutters they glimpse the neck of another German soldier, stationed right outside and close enough to touch. Jerry has thought of everything...

At last the sounds of battle move away. At about 3.30pm the *Leutnant* returns and orders them outside, where a tarpaulin-covered lorry awaits them. Its floor is covered with empty petrol drums and on top of them sprawl a handful of scruffy, unshaven French soldiers — prisoners — in earth-brown uniforms. They are laughing and joking amongst themselves. Obviously being captured is a great lark. But their laughter turns to inhospitable scowls when they realise they are to be joined by three more prisoners, and they make no effort to help the newcomers board. They even jeer as the British airmen try to clamber over the tailboard. Roth bends forward and makes a cradle with his hands. Like acrobats, Algie and Morris board, and pull Roth up beside them. They sit clutching the tailboard, their backs to the Frenchmen. The driver starts the engine, a pair of motorcycle escorts foot their machines behind the lorry, and the lorry lurches forward. But before it has gone ten yards, the driver has slammed on the brakes, and the prisoners are thrown forward in a heap.

The *Oberst* has decided that Roth, an officer, should ride in an open Hanomag personnel car. Roth sits in the back, with a pleasant-faced guard on his left. Both he and the driver give Roth cigarettes, and they travel like that all the way to Trier, the lorry with Algie, Morris and the French soldiers following at a distance of about a hundred yards.

As they drive westward, they pass mile upon mile of German armoured and personnel columns, nose to tail, heading towards the front. It seems to stretch right back into Germany, travelling at about 3mph — like an armoured-plated slow-worm. Once, when the Hanomag is forced off the road by a convoy of special vehicles, some youths from an engineering battalion, also waiting for the convoy to pass, engage Roth in conversation. Telling him he is lucky and patting him on the back, they assure him the war with England will be over in a month. They feel the texture of his uniform, admiring the cloth and admitting it is better than their own. They even place a machine-gun in his hands, a beautiful weapon made at Skoda — loot from the German occupation of Czechoslovakia.

When they pass through the city of Luxembourg, lined with stunned civilians watching the might of the German Army on the move, a middle-aged lady with blonde hair recognises Roth's uniform and walks alongside the Hanomag. "Oh, they caught you, you poor Englishman," she says. She runs off and returns with a bottle of water.

It is night when at last the two vehicles reach the ancient German city of Trier and halt inside the vast, empty courtyard of the castle. So high are the walls that the only light is from the stars. Roth is joined by Algie and Morris, and they wait a long time until an officer appears and takes them to their quarters for the night — a large room crowded with wooden bunks. The light bulbs have been removed, and they cannot get their bearings until Algie produces his cigarette lighter. There is no bedding. The three prisoners are cold. Roth bangs on the door. Heavy footsteps ring along the passage, a heavy key turns in the lock, the door jerks open.

"Ja?"

"Haben Sie eine Decke, bitte?"

The door is slammed and locked. But minutes later the footsteps return and a bundle of blankets is thrown into the room. Covered up, and left to themselves at last, the three prisoners sleep. It has been a long day.

The next morning, Algie and Morris are taken away — to a camp for NCOs, say the Germans. As they leave they are given a shaving brush, razors, blades and soap by a German youth who seems too young to be in the Army. Roth is given paper and envelopes and told he can write as many letters as he wishes. He writes two: one to a girlfriend, Aase, in Denmark, and another to his CO, care of the Air Ministry — and on the other sheets of paper starts a diary. For lunch he is given potato soup, bread, margarine and pork sausage. There is too much, and he leaves some of it for later. Afterwards he is moved into a room with two French Army officers. Motorcyclists. They keep going over how they were ambushed, moaning that if they had only done this, or that, they would still be free. Otherwise they are quite aloof. They seem peeved that Roth outranks them. At 4pm he is taken for a walk in a field near the castle. Afterwards he is interrogated. They seem to think there were two others in his crew, besides Algie and Morris. He wonders why.

Supper. He finishes his bread and sausage. A German officer tells him his name has been broadcast over *Bremensender* — the propaganda radio station at Bremen. News that he is safe and a prisoner will therefore have reached his family.

On Sunday, 12 May he is escorted by a guard and an interpreter to the railway station. He carries a cigar box. (It contains his jottings, his shaving kit — also a gift from the young soldier, who has relatives in Sheffield — and a picture of a blonde German film actress who resembles his Danish girlfriend. He has torn it from an old issue of the magazine *Der Adler* that he found in one of the lockers. It reminds him of happier days.) As he stands under escort on the platform civilians stare at him. Finally the train pulls in and they board — he and his escort have a third class compartment to themselves. At 8pm they arrive at Mainz. "Very steep climb up city's streets to pukka prison," he writes in his dairy:

Locked in large room with two beds on ground floor. Window barred. Barbed wire outside only a foot away — probably a civil or political prison. No evening meal. One look at the picture which reminds me of Aase, and then to sleep.

13 May. Shaken awake at 6am. Two German officers peering down at me. Why wasn't I ready to leave? Leave for where? No one had told me. Officers most impertinent. No time to wash. Outside, closed car waiting. It's chilly. I shiver. Officers wear long greatcoats. They tell me I'm going to Dulag Luft... They say that it's a special camp for pilots and has a tennis court, and that I shall be well treated.

Wonder if there'll be anyone there I know?

Two more Battle pilots captured as a result of that first day's operations are Maurice "Blackie" Wells and Aubrey Clifford Roberts. Wells is acting CO of "B" Flight, No103 Squadron, based at Béthenville. At 1345 hours four Battles take off to attack a strong German column on the main road between Echternach and Junglinster in Luxembourg. Wells leads his No2 in at low level and drops his four 250lb bombs in a stick while his gunner, LAC T H Bowen, sprays the column with machine-gun fire. The four Battles encounter a dense barrage of incendiary bullets and cannon-shells and all but one are shot down. Wells's engine is hit and catches fire, and the coolant tank bursts, covering the cockpit with smoke and steam. Wells climbs as high as he can so the crew can bale out, but is unable to order them to abandon the aircraft as the intercom has gone. He holds the Battle level at 200 feet until his legs start burning, and then the aircraft begins to lose height. At about 150 feet he jumps out. He does one swing with his parachute and makes a heavy landing not far from his burning aircraft. Wondering whether his crew have made it, he dives into a small wood but is unable to get out because it is completely surrounded by Germans, who eventually capture him. (Two years later he will meet up with his crew, Sergeant H F Bullock and LAC Bowen, at Stalag Luft III. He learns that they baled out four miles back from where the burning Battle crashed and were free for four days before the Germans caught up with them.)

At 1515 hours four Battles from Aubrey Roberts's squadron — No.150, based at Ecury-sur-Coole — are briefed to make a follow-up attack on the same German column. They take off at 1530 hours. Seeing no sign of the column, but spotting another one on the Luxembourg-Gevenmacher road, five miles west of Gevenmacher, they go in at one hundred feet with their 250lb bombs, the gunners and observers strafing the road as they fly along. All four aircraft are hit by ground fire, and Roberts's gunner, AC1 D Mayrick, is wounded. Roberts belly-lands his crippled bomber and all the crew — the observer is Sergeant E H Ward — are captured.

One of the Frenchmen, *Capitaine* Larmier, is also captured that day. While most of the French will eventually be segregated from the British and sent to their own camp, Larmier will remain with the RAF until their eventual liberation in 1945. Fair-haired, plump and in his early thirties, Larmier is an artillery observation spotter attached to *Escadrille I* of *Escadre de Reconnaissance 36*, based at Martigny-les-Gerbonvaux near the Maginot Line. On the evening of 10 May the squadron puts up a Potez 63, Type II, to observe the course of the battle over Blies. As the pilot, Lieutenant Couderq, takes the aircraft low over the battlefield, Larmier sits in the back, busily taking notes and trying to ignore the hail of fire coming up from the ground. Suddenly, the Potez shudders as flak strikes its tail assembly and renders the aileron control useless. The aircraft dives and is down to about ninety feet when Larmier heaves himself over the side. Immediately, he pulls his ripcord. Chances are the parachute will not deploy, but there is not much else Larmier can do. The canopy has just started to stream out of the pack when Larmier hits the top of a fortuitously placed haystack, bounces a little, and settles. Winded and confused, he is unsure whether he is dead or alive. Then he sits up and discovers where he is, his mind reeling at his good fortune. Looking up, he sees that the Potez, relieved of his weight, has straightened out and is pulling up over the trees and racing back towards the French lines. Then German soldiers start advancing upon him, and he has five years in which to curse his "good fortune".

The next day, Saturday 11 May, saw the capture of Cyril Paul de Lacey Hulton-Harrop and Alfred William Mungovan. Cy Hulton-Harrop had been with No17 Squadron, equipped with Hurricanes. He was involved in a combat with an Me109 of *JG51* while on an offensive patrol, and baled out when his aircraft was damaged. Alf Mungovan, a Battle pilot in No88 Squadron, based at Mourmelon-le-Grand, south-east of Reims, had been shot down on his first operation, a raid on St Vith led by the commander of "A" Flight, Flight Lieutenant John Madge. It was an experience he shared with many Battle crews.

Twice on Friday, 10 May — in the morning and the afternoon — the airfield was bombed by the Germans. They did some damage to the hangars, but the squadron's Fairey Battles, in their dispersal bays around the perimeter of the airfield, were untouched.

The following morning, Saturday 11 May, Madge was woken early and told to report to the briefing room. There he learnt he was to lead four aircraft in an attack on German troops crossing the border into Belgium. Their target was St Vith, a small town on the German/Belgian border just north of Luxembourg. Madge's crew were Sergeant E M Whittle (observer), and Corporal A C Collyer (air-gunner). Flying as his No2 was Pilot Officer B I M Skidmore. Another Pilot Officer, N C S Riddell, was to lead "B" Flight, with Alf Mungovan as his No2. Skidmore's observer was Sergeant R A P Kirby, with AC1 W L Parsons as air-gunner. Alf Mungovan's observer was Sergeant F Robson and the air-gunner was AC1 E W Maltby. The aircraft allotted Mungovan's crew for the raid was "Q", as their normal aircraft, "M", was unserviceable. Another four Battle crews were provided by No218 Squadron. None of these aircraft were destined to return.

When the crews arrived at the airfield, the aircraft engines were already being warmed up. It was a beautiful sunny morning with not a cloud in the sky. After running-up and testing the engines they trundled onto the grass airfield in formation order. Their armament was four 250lb, eleven-second delay HE bombs, one machine-gun for the gunner at the rear, one which could be fired from the bomb hatch, and one fixed gun in the starboard wing for the pilot. They took off in turn starting at 0945 hours and John Madge set course north-east for St Vith. Altitude to target was between 2,000 and 3,000 feet, and cruising speed 140mph. On approaching the target they were to descend to 250 feet and make their bombing run at that height.

Near Neufchâteau, between Vaux-sur-Sûre and Bercheux, two small towns on the Bastogne-Neufchâteau road, Madge was hit by flak and made a forced landing. None of the crew suffered any injury until then, when Madge injured his right arm (a fact not discovered until later) and Sgt Whittle, who was half-way out the bomb hatch, was thrown forward with the impact. They were captured by part of General Paul von Kleist's XII Army Group and driven to a farm on the main road to St Hubert. A large barn lay at right-angles to the road and they were taken to this by several guards. The barn was occupied by Belgian soldiers except for a space at one end where John Madge and his gunner, Corporal Collyer, flopped down on the straw.

After Madge's battle was hit, "B" Flight's leader, Pilot Officer Riddell, "indicated by hand-signal that Madge had gone down," recalls Mungovan.

...I also read into his gesture that he wanted me to move to No3 position on his left side, expecting Skidmore to fall back and join us in the No2 position. However, Skidmore continued on course for the target and made no attempt to join us. At this time I had not seen any anti-aircraft fire.

We continued to maintain altitude and the same formation until St Vith could be seen. Riddell suddenly dived very steeply and was turning to his left, apparently with the intention of attacking enemy columns, which could be seen on all roads leading from St Vith.

This left me just behind Skidmore, who began a steady descent towards a valley to the south of St Vith, which would thus place a hill between himself and the target which he could then attack from the rear. This seemed to be a reasonable plan of attack, so I followed Skidmore down and closed up on him. He looked around and saw me, and indicated that he was indeed going to approach the target from the east, keeping the hill between us and the target until the last moment. We opened our bomb-bay doors and I selected the master switch and the individual switches for the four bombs.

We turned finally around the hill and St Vith was directly in front of us. As we went over the target I was two to three seconds behind Skidmore in line astern, speed 140mph, height 250 feet. At that altitude the navigator, who also acted as bomb aimer, could not see the target in time and this function became the responsibility of the pilot. As we had no aiming gear the accepted practice was to say "Mississippi" as the target went under the nose and then move the handle across the bomb-release quadrant.

I did this and held the aircraft steady. Then the flak and machine-gun fire from the German columns opened up. It was devastating. The tracer bullets alone made it seem we were flying through a horizontal hailstorm. At that moment I felt a thud in the tail of the aircraft. Ahead was an armoured column on a road leading out of St Vith and I attacked this with the front gun. In order to bring the gun to bear it was necessary, of course, to depress the nose of the aircraft. The side of the road was lined with trees.

I eased back on the control column to go over the trees, but there was little response and the machine ploughed through the top branches, which knocked out the landing light cover in the port wing. However, we were through and I kept at treetop height. Skidmore's machine was just ahead of me and on my left and flying straight and level at about 300 feet. I saw a flash from a hill to our right and then a burst of a shell perhaps a hundred feet behind Skidmore's machine and directly in line with it and at the same height. Four more flashes followed, each shell bursting closer to Skidmore. After the sixth flash there was no sign of a hit on Skidmore's aircraft but flames began to stream back from his engine. He went into a shallow dive for about two seconds, then the nose went straight down and the aircraft exploded on impact.

After a mile or two another enemy column appeared. This time it was a horse-drawn supply column and again I attacked with the front gun. As we approached at fifty feet the soldier in charge of each cart moved to the head of the horse and stood between us and the horse, holding its harness and probably trying to calm the horse. I shall never forget those men with their backs to us, turning their heads to look up at us. What courage and discipline those soldiers displayed. Not one tried to save himself by leaving his team and jumping into the nearest ditch.

Again there was a sluggish response to the controls and the aircraft pruned a few more trees. Nevertheless, I thought we were making progress on the return flight and called over the intercom to Sgt Robson: "What is the course, Robbie?" "Bugger the course!" came the reply, "I'm firing the rear gun!"

Judging it best to leave Robson to his new-found duty I pointed the aircraft in a south-westerly direction. A second horse-drawn supply column appeared and we attacked again with front and rear guns. No results of these attacks were observed as we were over and away too quickly.

The aircraft now began to show signs of damage. I found I could not climb and the machine began to roll to the left. At first, this could be controlled by using right aileron and a touch of right rudder, but the rolls became more pronounced and more difficult to control. To counter the last roll required full right aileron with the control column back as far as I could pull it. We were then flying over gently undulating country and I thought we had a chance of making a forced landing, although there were no flat areas of ground and control was becoming impossible. "Hang on Rob," I shouted to Sgt Robson over the intercom. "I'm going to try to put her down."

My next recollection is of my head jerking backwards and forwards violently and I remember thinking quite clearly and without emotion: *This is it! I'm going to bash my brains out on the instrument panel!*

Then all was quiet and still. I opened the cockpit sliding hatch and began to climb out. We had crashed into a small pine plantation on the top of a hill. How we got to it I do not know. There was no sign of any trees ahead of us when I warned Rob to hang on.

As I stood up in the cockpit I could see flames spreading from underneath the engine through the pine-tree debris which surrounded us and which was starting to burn. This accelerated my exit, but another sharp jerk to the head reminded me to disconnect the intercom tube!

I clambered out into a sea of broken branches and tree-trunks which completely covered the wings and fuselage of the aircraft except for the pilot's cockpit and the tail plane of the Battle. I began to make my way slowly to where the rear hatch should be, but at every step I sank up to my crutch in broken pine branches without reaching the ground. I called out, and at that moment Rob appeared from behind the rudder. Apparently the fuselage had broken in half and he had crawled out through a gap in the side. "Where's Maltby?" I asked him. "He's dead," said Rob. "He was shot in the neck during the bombing run. His eyes were open and glazed."

Sgt Robson had pulled AC1 Maltby from the gunner's position and laid him on the floor of the fuselage and had then taken over the operation of the rear gun.

Again I asked Rob if he was certain Maltby was dead, and he assured me that was so. By now the front of the aircraft and surrounding timber were well alight. It was obvious there was no chance of getting through all that debris, finding the opening in the fuselage and getting to Maltby before the whole area was on fire. Robson had suffered a severe cut to his head and was bleeding. I decided the only sensible option was to get Robson and myself well clear of the immediate vicinity of the wreck.

We made our way down the hill and sat down. Rob was now beginning to ramble in his conversation. "What time is it?" "Where are we?" "How did we get here?" he asked continually. As soon as I answered his questions he would start all over again. There were two explosions from the top of the hill where the wreck was burning and ammunition was rattling away.

When Rob had recovered sufficiently we made our way to a road at the foot of the hill and began to walk. There was a properly constructed barricade of wood further along the road and as we approached I called out, but it was not manned. A house was on a slope away from the road and we made our way to it. We knocked on the door, which opened an inch or two. Rob enquired in his best French if there was any news of the Germans. "About two kilometres away," we were told. We asked if they had any transport, bicycles or whatever and the door was slammed in our faces. We pressed on, hoping to find some way to increase our progress, but there was not a soul in sight. No bicycles, cars or even horses. We passed a burnt-out Heinkel 111, and later a Fieseler Storch flew over. We hurriedly left the road and hid until it passed and then continued through the meadows. After about two hours we came to a village where a few men were gathered at the crossroads. Again we were told the Germans were about 2 kilometres away. Their attitude was surly and unfriendly and they offered no other information or assistance, nor could we see any form of transport which would help us.

As we seemed to be keeping ahead of the enemy we pushed on along a road which we hoped would take us in a south-westerly direction. An hour later we could hear the sound of transport coming from our right. We climbed to the top of a hillock and carefully edged forward until we could see the road before us. To our right a convoy of light troop transport vehicles, all fully manned, stretched to the horizon. From the column units of bicycle-equipped troops would leave at intervals apparently looking for any pockets of Belgian troops who might be lurking in the small clumps of trees with which the area abounded. Almost in front of us, slightly to our left, was a road junction. The foremost units of the column had just arrived at this point and a group of officers were talking, evidently about which road they should take as they were gesticulating and pointing in various directions. From their attitude it seemed to Robson and me that the consensus of opinion was that they should take the road to the right and not the one on the left.

Hoping to retain the advantage of being ahead of the Germans we hastened along a road at the base of our hillock which appeared to lead away from the road junction, hobbling along at our best pace, Robson with the ridiculous-looking first-aid pad which I had placed on his head-wound and tied under his chin, and me with torn trousers and cuts to my legs. The road suddenly descended between two steep banks and then turned sharply right. Our speed carried us round the corner and right into the middle of what appeared to be, at that instant, the whole of Kleist's XII Army Group! The surprise was mutual. There were no raised rifles. No shouts of *"Hände hoch!"* They just surrounded us, more curious than aggressive. I pointed to Robson's head and said he needed medical attention. He was led away and I was taken across a road junction and up a slope the other side to a shop where the local Intelligence officer had set up an office. The officer, seated at his desk, looked up at me, looked at my escort, and said in English: "I don't want to see you. I've already seen you!"

This was puzzling, but it was not for me to argue. I was taken outside again into the street, where Robson was already waiting, now with a proper dressing on his scalp. I was put into the sidecar of a motorcycle combination and Rob sat on the pillion seat behind the driver, a large man with a proportionally large pistol in his belt. We were cautioned about the consequences of trying to escape with meaningful gestures to the pistol, then off we drove...thankful to be sitting down and not walking.

After half an hour's drive they arrived at the barn where they were reunited with John Madge and his rear-gunner, Corporal Collyer, prior to the journey that was to take them to Dulag Luft. During the night they spent in the shop at Bastogne, Mungovan began to feel unwell.

At this time I must have been suffering from shock because I felt cold and was shivering although it was a fine day and we were sitting in sunshine in the garden at the back of the shop. A German officer came over and said: "Don't be afraid, you will be well treated." I was hurt by the suggestion that I was shaking from fear and replied in a surly manner that I was cold. Whereupon he told one of the guards to take a greatcoat from one of the Belgian soldiers who were also in the garden to give to me. He explained this action by saying to me: "You were captured while fighting honourably, the Belgians surrendered."

As a supplement to his account, Mungovan offers the following explanation for some of the events that mystified him at the time:

I realise I did not explain [that the reason] why the Intelligence officer who "interrogated" me after my capture...thought he had already seen me was because that morning he had seen John

Madge with whom I shared some physical similarities. This also explains why we soon met up with Madge and Collyer.

When I began writing...to you...I obtained a large-scale map of Eastern Belgium and as a result of studying the map and working out roughly the distance we must have covered on the return flight I estimate we must have come down somewhere in the vicinity of St Hubert.

When we were told by locals in Belgium the Germans were "two or three kilometres away" we assumed in our optimistic naïveté that we were ahead of the enemy, and so we tried to keep it that way. Little did we realise that the Germans were on a parallel course to ours and were, in fact, miles ahead.

Madge and Mungovan reached Dulag Luft on Thursday, 16 May. While there, Alf Mungovan, "still a bit dazed", went out on a parole walk, which included a visit to a local *Biergarten*. Mungovan was transferred to Spangenberg, but Madge stayed on at Dulag Luft and joined the British Permanent Staff.

Charles Arthur Reginald Crews and Anthony John Hudson fly two of the four No218 Squadron Battles accompanying No88 Squadron on the strafing raid on columns at St Vith, taking off from Auberive-sur-Suippes at 0930 hours. Leading his half-section at low level towards a bridge two miles to the north of St Vith, Crews takes them over the wooded area of the Ardennes, which Allied planners consider too dense for the Germans to advance through. Despite this, Crews' half-section meets German road convoys and comes under heavy fire. Almost at once, Crews sees his instrument panel, hit by machine-gun fire, shatter in front of him. But he presses on, and the Battles are peppered with gunfire of every description. Crews orders his No2 to turn for the run-in towards the bridge, but as he does so his engine is hit. Flames and glycol spew from the holes in the engine cowling, while burning petrol pours along the floor beneath his seat. Crews chokes in the smoke and heat.

Below him stretch trees in all directions — no place even to crash-land. He is well below a hundred feet so baling out seems equally impossible. But, engulfed by heat and flames, he has no choice but to jump. He shouts to his observer, Flight Sergeant T S Evans, and his gunner, Sergeant C M Jennings, to get out, while he coaxes every inch of height he can out of his crippled Battle. Holding the stick between his knees, he pulls back the cockpit canopy just as the engine starts dying. The Battle gains a little height, but is close to a stall when Crews stands up, his hands still pulling back on the control column, and bales out. Within seconds of jumping and pulling his rip-cord he is in the treetops, his face scratched by pine needles. Hanging on a tree nearby is Evans. The two stare at each other, hardly believing they have survived. Then they see Jennings — quite dead — only thirty feet away. (Although his parachute streamed, it failed to open; he was killed the instant he hit the ground.) Like Mungovan and Robson, the two survivors try to evade capture, but they, too, are picked up. Hudson, along with his observer, Sergeant N H Thompson, and his gunner, AC1 A Ellis, also goes into the bag.

The next day, Bill Edwards and George Grey-Smith are hacked out of the sky. A New Zealander, William Henry Edwards is from No107 Squadron, led by the no-nonsense Irish Wing Commander Basil Embry. Only a week has passed since the squadron, based at Wattisham, received a number of awards for distinguished service in Norway: Embry a bar to his DSO, two NCO air-gunners DFMs, and two officers, including Edwards, the DFC. Grey-Smith is on another Blenheim squadron, No139, based at Plivot as part of the AASF.

On Sunday, 12 May, Air Marshal Sir Arthur Barratt, commander of the British Air Force in France (BAFF), receives conflicting reports of what is going on in Holland and Belgium. Intelligence locally reports that the Germans are approaching the Turhout Canal in Northern Belgium, and General Alphonse Georges, French second-in-command, believes they will advance in three main thrusts: from Maastricht to Tongres and then on to Gembloux; from March to Dinant, and from Neufchâteau to Carignan. To secure the Allied thrust and disrupt at least one German line of advance, Georges gives priority to air attacks along the Maastricht-Tongres-Gembloux line. At the same time BAFF HQ receives messages from the Air Ministry in London stressing the importance of destroying the bridge across the Albert Canal, three miles south-west of Maastricht, near Vroenhaven on the Maastricht-Tongres road. The Belgians have been unable to blow up the bridge. "Ugly" Barratt has little option but to commit a force of Blenheims and Battles to knock out this and a similar bridge near Veldwezelt on the Maastricht-Hasselt road. From losses over the area during the past two days he knows it is a hotbed of flak and fighter defences, and accordingly decides that whatever squadron is assigned the task should call for volunteers.

Battles and Blenheims of Nos 103 and 139 squadrons carry out a succession of attacks on German columns at first light. Led by Wing Commander L W Dickens AFC, No139 puts up nine aircraft, taking off at 0500 hours, and No103 Squadron contributes three Battles. The Blenheims find their road targets, west of Maastricht, and Dickens signals the squadron to form into echelon and leads them in a dive-bombing approach from 6,000 feet. They are carrying a mixed bomb load of 250- and 40-pounders. Unfortunately, the Luftwaffe has also woken up early that morning, and the Blenheims are immediately attacked by Me109s and Me110s. Seven Blenheims are lost. Fifteen men are killed, four manage to rejoin their units, and two men, a WOP/AG and George Grey-Smith, are made prisoner.

Later that morning Barratt calls on No2 Group, which sends out two squadrons, Nos 107 and 15. Each puts up twelve Blenheim Mk IVs, loaded with three 250lb bombs and eighteen 40lb bombs. They are led by Embry.

It is another beautiful, clear day. Each squadron flies in two boxes of six, the crews looking out for the Hurricane escort they have been promised. All they see is a lone Hurricane, which approaches them diffidently over the Dutch coast and a few seconds later flies away. As soon as they spot the bridges they close up and approach in tight formation at 6,000 feet — a good bombing height, but it makes them perfect targets for the Germans' 88mm guns. Fifteen miles from Maastricht, No107 comes under heavy AA fire, and the nearer they get to the bridges the fiercer it becomes. Eleven Blenheims are hit on the way in, two of them dropping out. When the others in the formation release their bombs they open out to avoid the flak. Before they can close up again, they are bounced by Me109s. Bill Edwards is soon picked off, and crash-lands near Bettenhoven, about sixteen miles west-north-west of Liège. The gunner, LAC W E Palmer, has been killed. Edwards and his observer, Sergeant V G L Luter, are taken prisoner. Only then do they discover their attack was futile: the bridges have been down for at least twenty-four hours, and traffic is pouring across two pontoon bridges upstream and downstream of the main bridge.

Ernest Roy Mullins was from No110 Squadron, which shared Wattisham with Basil Embry's outfit. On Tuesday, 14 May, No110 Squadron had put up twelve Blenheim MkIVs to attack German troops at Sedan. (No107 Squadron also put up six aircraft.) Led by Squadron Leader G F Hall, No110's twelve Blenheims took off at 1330 hours and formed up over the airfield. They set course for the French coast, where they expected to rendezvous with a strong escort of both British and French fighters for the overland flight. Climbing to 6,000 feet they saw North Foreland slip away below them to starboard and nosed their way across the Channel for the continent. In a matter of minutes the low coastline of northern France came into view and they crossed north-east of Dunkirk, searching the skies for their promised fighter escort. None came, but the CO decided to press on. Their course took them over the Franco-Belgian frontier. Knowing that the Germans were by now well into the Belgian interior, they expected to meet opposition before reaching the target. They did. As they were approaching Valenciennes the sky changed to a forest of white puffs from exploding flak. In the distance other Allied aircraft were running the gauntlet — possibly their fighter escort.

They received orders to detour south and avoid the area. After fifteen minutes' flying they still hadn't shaken off the flak, and were over a wooded patch north of Mézières when another AA position opened up. Five minutes away from the target, the CO ordered the formation to break and attack in flights. The flak was getting heavy and finding the Blenheims' range and height with disconcerting accuracy. As the aircraft broke formation and fanned out, they started taking a severe beating, not only from ground fire but also from Me109s, and five Blenheims were lost. Mullins' gunner, AC2 P Aherne, was killed but he and his observer, Sergeant R Lowe, survived and were captured.

Flying Officer Michael Ian Murdoch was captured on Wednesday, 15 May. A pilot in No59

Squadron, a former Army Co-operation unit now with the Air Component and equipped with Blenheims MkIVs, Murdoch was operating from a forward base at Vitry with another Blenheim crew. Sent out on a lone recce during mid-morning, he was brought down by flak and small arms fire. He was reported in the squadron's operational records book as "missing, killed in action".

Squadron Leader William Henry Nigel Turner, a flight commander in the Whitley-equipped No51 Squadron, Dishforth (No4 Group), and his second pilot, Flying Officer Anthony Colin Peach, made an interesting pair: Turner had been born in the West Indies, on the tiny island of Dominica; Peach had travelled all the way from Hong Kong to England on the Trans-Siberian Railway to join the RAF. They had been flying together since the first Whitley operations of the war. Their last sortie together was on the night of 18/19 May, when Bomber Command put up sixty aircraft to bomb oil refineries and railway yards in Germany and enemy lines of communications in Belgium. No4 Group sent twenty-three Whitleys to attack the oil refinery at Hanover, four of them from Dishforth, which Turner led off at 2020 hours. Despite heavy flak over the target, most bombed successfully, but Turner was shot down. All the crew survived.

The remaining five French officers accompanying *Capitaine* Larmier were victims of the "Blitzkrieg" in Belgium and France, all of them flying obsolete or obsolescent aircraft, and most of these ending up in flames. Lieutenant Grandrémy, from *Escadrille I* of *Escadre de Bombardement 12*, based at Soissons-Saconin, was shot down on Saturday, 11 May. It was his first operation of the war — and his last. Twelve aircraft from *Groupement No6* were to bomb German troop concentrations between Tongres and Maastricht. Six Loire-Olivier LeO451s were drawn from *Escadrille I*, and six from *Escadrille II*, of the same bomber wing but based at Persan-Beaumont. They took off at 1600 hours and were escorted by eighteen Morane 406s from *Escadrille III* of *Escadre de Chasse 3* and *Escadrille II* of *Escadre de Chasse 6*. Over the target they met heavy flak, and LeO451 No63, flown by *Adjudant* Chamaud, was hit and crash-landed back at Soissons-Saconin, where it was written off. The captain, Lieutenant Grandrémy, and the gunner, *Sergent-Chef* Ritz, had baled out and were captured near the target area. The NCOs were held back at Dulag Luft and after various transfers were eventually sent to Stalag Luft I at Barth until being sent to an all-French NCO camp. From this period onwards, the only NCOs and other ranks sent to Spangenberg would be orderlies — mainly drawn from army *Stalags*.

Lieutenant Detrie became a *prisonnier de guerre* on Sunday, 12 May, when *Escadrille I* of *Escadre de Reconnaissance 22* put up a Potez 63.II to carry out a recce of the front lines. The pilot, *Capitaine* Lainey, took off from Metz-Frescaty, in Potez No. 444, at 1000 hours. It was attacked by several Me109s and crashed in Luxembourg. The entire crew — including Lainey, and *Adjudant* Gres, the air-gunner — were taken prisoner. Lainey was wounded and later sent to Barth.

On the same day, eleven Breguet 693s of *Escadrille I* of *Escadre Bombardment d'Assaut 54* set out from La Ferté-Gaucher at 1205 hours to attack motorised columns in the region of Tongres. They were supported by another seven Breguets from *Escadrille II*, based at Nangis. Over the target they encountered extremely dense flak; seven light bombers were lost and eleven officers and NCOs were taken prisoner. Breguet No7 crashed in flames near the target area. The pilot, *Sous-Lieutenant* Henri, survived, along with his air-gunner, *Sous-Lieutenant* Besson-Guyard. Breguet No19, flown by Lieutenant Leleu, was set alight and crashed near St Rond. Leleu and his air-gunner, Sergeant Massaux, baled out, despite the fact that the latter was wounded. Both were captured.

* * *

When these officers arrive at Spangenberg on Thursday, 23 May it is by the old blue Luftwaffe bus that took Day and his party to Dulag Luft in December 1939. It drops the new prisoners in the village and after several head-counts, a green-coated German Army NCO agrees all are present and signs the Luftwaffe's receipt. The prisoners are sorry to see the bus with their Luftwaffe guards drive away. They at least behaved like human beings. The Army guards are by contrast a miserable, mentally constipated bunch. Older men, still fighting the war of 1914–18, they are underpaid and ill fed, with no chance of promotion and only meagre pensions to look forward to; they loathe looking after young and spirited air force officers. But at least the prisoners know where they stand with them. It is less easy with the Luftwaffe. The RAF cannot help but feel that for all their apparent compassion they are only trying to curry favour, trying to use their prisoners as pawns in Goering's little game of ensuring that his "boys" in British camps are being well treated. Altogether they are like politicians throwing crumbs to get votes. Of course, the prisoners are none the less grateful for the crumbs...

As they trudge from the village to the castle road, the guards keep shouting at them to hurry. Eventually, this harassment — so uncalled for, so stupid — becomes irksome to the prisoners, who start shouting back and telling them to lay off. The commotion reaches its peak as they pass an orchard where some schoolgirls are playing "catch". A couple of the prisoners give good-natured whistles. The girls stop their game, gawk and giggle, and one waves at them. The prisoners cheer.

This fraternisation is too much for the *Feldwebel* in charge.

"Halt! Those who have insulted the citizens of the Reich will step forward immediately!"

More cheers, whistles and cat-calls.

Unsure of themselves, the guards unsling their rifles and threaten to club the nearest prisoners. As a body the prisoners yell that they will resist any violence. They are *Feldmarschall* Goering's prisoners and they guarantee that he will hear about any brutality. This gives the soldiers pause. It is a messy situation, but is unexpectedly resolved by the girls who, having gone back to their game, accidentally throw their ball amongst the column. The guards are non-plussed. So they turn on the girls in their anger, reprimanding them for being friendly with the enemy. None of the girls is any more than ten or eleven, and probably none of them knows or even cares who the strange men are. When the guards stupidly point their rifles at them, the girls freeze a second, then, squealing hysterically, dash into the depths of the orchard.

Squadron Leader Turner, the senior RAF officer, at once demands that the *Feldwebel* send a runner for a German officer, so they can report the cowardly, unmilitary-like behaviour of his guards against the innocent youth of the Reich. "We are entitled by German Army regulations to air our grievances before an officer," he insists. Turner refuses even to discuss the matter with him or his bullying squad. The *Feldwebel* is speechless. No one has ever spoken to him in such terms. He stands transfixed, legs apart, hands on hips, and froths at the mouth. At long last, unable to find the words to express his dismay, he about-faces and gives orders for the march to continue. From then on there isn't a sound, or indeed any further reference to the incident.

After forty minutes' more slogging, sweating, cursing and stumbling, they reach the top of the *Schlossberg*. It starts to drizzle. Shrouded in cloud, the castle looms bleak, gloomy — a far cry from the romantic picture they glimpsed on a faded prewar tourist poster in the village below. As their names are called, they cross the drawbridge and enter the castle through its wicket gate.

On the sloping cobbles of the courtyard a motley huddle of old prisoners are waiting to give them the once-over; with blankets draped over their heads, they look like monks. The French rush forward to embrace their countrymen, but the British take one look, recognise no friends, and disperse to their rooms at the double, anxious to get out of the rain.

Later on, while exploring the castle, Michael Roth sees the back of a huge man standing beside a window and struggling to play a scale on the saxophone. The man swings round as Roth approaches, and they immediately recognise each other; the man is Bob Coste, who Roth knows from the old days at West Freugh. Coste drops the reed from his mouth, cries "Yippee!" at the top of his voice, and rushes Roth to his room, where he makes a brew of hot chocolate.

(2)

Conditions at Spangenberg have deteriorated markedly since "Wings" Day and his party were there in autumn 1939. The 1940 crop of prisoners suffer from the same inadequate diet and cramped existence, but in addition have to contend with overcrowding. All beds in the small rooms are occupied by old prisoners, so the newcomers — "sprogs", as they are called — are shoved into one big dormitory, partially occupied by some of the French. Rows of wooden double-decker bunks are crammed into the floorspace, blocking the light from the windows. The French assume ownership of the few lockers, so the British keep their personal belongings (such as they are) either in, on or under their bunks — and hope they will not be pinched. Items thus lost are said to be "cooling off" in someone else's bunk or locker. Fortunately, acquisition by finding is not too common.

The two flushing toilets and the twenty iron washing-bowls, standing at the end of the "dorm" nearest the *Turm* (gate-tower), are inadequate for the POW complement. At a pinch, the British could get by but for the French, who add to their unpopularity by squatting on the toilet seats with their dirty boots. From birth, they have been conditioned to believe that they will catch some dreadful disease if their precious *derrières* touch the seats, and nothing can convince them otherwise. The result is that the seats are caked in mud and faeces — for which the French make no apology and which they make no effort to clean up. No habit can more effectively alienate them from the British. The *Entente Cordiale* is doomed by superstition.

The day after the arrival of the 23 May purge, a special *Appell* is held, and they line up in three rows on the cobbles of the inner courtyard ready for an address by the Commandant, von Meyer. But first, Squadron Leader Sydney Murray, who rarely smiles, gives them a "pep" talk so that the Commandant's visit will pass off without incident. He warns them to stand erect, be as smart as they can, obey all his orders at once, and not to talk or move their heads — or for that matter any part of their bodies. The prisoners are faintly amused to hear this from Murray, who wears a ragged uniform and a battered peak-cap. But he will come to impress them as a man who has accepted his lot and lives stoically in quiet desperation.

As they wait, older prisoners peer down at them from the upper windows and start barracking the Germans. Their intention is to disrupt the parade by making the sprogs cut up and the Germans mad, and then enjoy the fracas from a safe distance. Murray pleads with them: "Cut it out, now, chaps."

With his entourage of fawning subordinates, the Commandant, a seedy puppet, steps through the wicket gate and shambles across the uneven courtyard. Halting in front of the company, he returns Murray's salute, glances at the prisoners, and holds out a gloved hand to the aide beside him. The aide gives von Meyer a clipboard, without receiving so much as a sideways look or a *"Danke"*. Nattering at high speed, the Commandant reads a prepared speech from the clipboard. The prisoners don't understand a word. Speech over, the Commandant thrusts the clipboard towards his *Dolmetscher*, Helmboldt, who rephrases the whole piece of malarky in halting English.

The gist — "You are now the property of the Third and Greater German Reich. Your rights and privileges are as laid down in the Geneva Convention; they and no others will be respected." That is all. It has taken von Meyer ten minutes to say so little.

After prolonged foot-scraping, saluting and heel-clicking — rather like a ping-pong game to see who can keep the exchange going the longest — the Commandant and his aides withdraw. Relieved, the prisoners drift back to their dormitory, muttering "Senile old basket" and "What a lot of bullscheisse".

But the simple demands of the German regimen are a blessing — for they are responsibilities to be met at definite hours: first, *Appell* at 7.30am, followed by sick parade, breakfast, parcel call, gym parades, lunch; second *Appell* around 4pm, then supper; lights-out at 10pm. Six days a week *Appelle* are taken by *Hauptmann* Gross, who issues the new arrivals with captured French forage caps so that they will have no valid excuse for not saluting him whenever he appears — on parade or off. His punishment for habitual lateness on parade is compulsory bed-rest — no books or visitors allowed. He details a special guard just to see that the culprit remains there until afternoon *Appell*, when he makes a great show of asking the wretched, bored prisoner if he has had a good rest and if, in future, he will be able to parade on time. At this, the surrounding prisoners cheer and clap, and Gross returns their applause by grinning, inwardly delighted with his success as a comedian. But the prisoners respect him. He is incorruptible, and rules by the book.

All suggestions for improving their welfare have to be submitted to Gross. In turn, he passes them on to the crotchety von Meyer. A pressing problem is the paucity of toilets. Unable to make any headway with the *Oberst*, Gross advises the POWs to make representations to the Swiss Commission at Geneva. The result is a row of new toilets in another part of the castle. Gross declares on *Appell* that the old ones will be used by the French, and the new by the British. For this he receives three cheers. He beams with embarrassment.

On Sunday, 2 June, two hundred British and French Army officers, captured at Abbeville, arrive at Spangenberg Lower Camp. When Squadron Leader Murray hears that the Army contingent is without tobacco, he sends Red Cross issue cigarettes down.

(3)

In the week that follows, two more RAF officers arrive. Robert John Bristol Renison and Ian Godfrey Gwynne Potts were both Hurricane pilots. A Canadian from Toronto, Renison was in No504 Squadron, based at Martlesham Heath. He baled out of his stricken aircraft when attacked by Me109s over Mons during an offensive patrol on Saturday, 18 May. Ian Potts was from No73 Squadron, one of the first Hurricane squadrons to arrive in France. Having flown from its base in Digby, it initially operated from Le Havre-Octeville, but underwent a number of subsequent moves, until by the end of May it was stationed at Gaye. At 1915 hours on Saturday, 1 June, the squadron took off for an offensive patrol over Châlons-sur-Marne. The squadron was flying at 4,000 feet over Malmaison airfield when it came under fire from heavy and accurate flak and then from Me109s. The Messerschmitts claimed three aircraft. Of the three pilots, Potts alone survived to become a prisoner.

On Wednesday, 12 June, Michael Roth strikes it lucky. An *Unteroffizier* (sergeant) enters the courtyard and yells: "*Vier Pakete für Herrn Roth!* — Four parcels for Mr Roth!" Suddenly he is the richest man in the world. The *Unteroffizier* leads him up the spiral staircase in the eastern corner of the cobbled courtyard to a room in the *Kommandantur* where a civilian is waiting to examine the contents of the parcels. They have not been touched. The Germans at Oflag IXA/H are punctilious about opening parcels in the presence of the addressee so that no one can accuse them of filching anything.

With a sharp knife the civilian cuts through the strings: blankets, scarf and woollen gloves from the Red Cross; 10lb of food from the mother of Roth's girlfriend in Denmark; and two parcels from Selfridge's in Oxford Street, London — flannel trousers, a woollen windbreaker, a pair of brogues, shirts, socks, underwear, pyjamas, handkerchiefs, huge cakes of bath-soap, toothpaste, shaving stick, razor blades, brush, comb, scissors, two towels and four huge slabs of chocolate — sent by arrangement with his brother. The examiner lets him keep it all but, at a wink from the *Unteroffizier*, says he will not have time to use everything. He squashes his thumb against a wall-map of Paris. "*Paris ist kaputt. Frankreich ist kaputt. Bald ist England kaputt!* Two or three weeks — you go home. Then take all things with you."

"But you're wrong," counters Roth. "Germany won't win. England will win."

Laughter ringing in his ears, Roth hurries from the room.

The next day, Thursday 13 June, Squadron Leader Murray announces that he will be sending ten cigarettes per man per day down to the *Unterlager*. On the same day the German wireless interrupts its programme with a *Sondermeldung*, a special bulletin from the OKW. Paris is in German hands. Later that day the French — with the unaccountable exception of Larmier — leave the camp, bound for Oflag IIB at Arnswalde in Pomerania. The British wish them *bonne chance* and promise to meet them in Paris after the war. They feel slightly hypocritical, as inwardly they rejoice at the prospect of more elbow-room. (During the journey Lieutenant-Colonel Gérardot escapes. He reaches North Africa, where he becomes commander of the Vichy Government's air base in Tunis. Later he will be appointed Commander-in-Chief of the French Air Force.)

On Friday the 21st, Gross announces on *Appell* that France has surrendered. Much to his bewilderment, the British POWs appear indifferent, as if they have expected it all along. But when he tells them they will soon be going home, they cheer. "We know that," they tell him. "But we're waiting for England to win the war first."

The same day, the Army officers from Elbersdorf are transferred to the castle — to share the large dormitory with the RAF. With the arrival of the Army, POW organisation, hitherto loose and very much on an old pals' basis, is tightened up. Major C W Clout of the Royal West Kents becomes Senior British Officer, although he will later hand over to Captain G F W ("Tug")

Wilson, a Royal Navy officer called out of retirement to command an armed merchant cruiser that was then sunk in the North Sea. (As the war drags on, *Schloss* Spangenberg will see an apparently endless and very bewildering succession of SBOs, who at one stage seemed to change from day to day.) Squadron Leader Murray, the Senior RAF Officer, still acts as *Vertrauensmann*, and handles most of the day-to-day contact with the German staff. An entertainments committee is set up, consisting of eight Army officers, two Royal Navy and two RAF, Coste and Middleton. Arrangements are made to portion off part of the moat for exercise and to use a disused arsenal on the northern side of the moat as a gymnasium. An Escape Committee comes into being. Harry Bewlay, now known as "Pop", is appointed Escape Officer for the RAF on the basis of his experience of trying to hack his way through 300 feet of solid rock the previous December.

(4)

Before long, the prisoners are living from meal to meal. With the neutrality of Holland and Belgium violated, those countries can no longer be used as routes for Red Cross parcels, and the fall of France has disrupted lines of communication from England. No more parcels will arrive in Germany until October. In the meantime, the old prisoners eat in the dorm, drawing on their jealously hoarded stocks of delicacies from personal parcels which came in during the winter — tea, Nescafé, condensed milk, cheese, date bread and sardines — while the new prisoners eke out existing communal parcels and then rely completely on German food, based on an official German ration of a quarter of a loaf of bread per man per day. Breakfast is a perfunctory affair, but the new prisoners sit down to eat in the castle's *Speisesaal*. At intervals on the bare wooden tables are little stacks of two or three thinly cut slices of black bread, each with a glob of red *ersatz* jam, and beside each stack a blunt knife and a chinaware mug of hot *ersatz* coffee. Now the French have gone, the food is laid on by Royal Navy ratings, who work as cooks and portion out the bulk food after it comes into the castle.

For *Mittagessen* there is a bowl of watery soup per man, a boiled potato, a slice of bread, a gherkin (sometimes), salt, mustard and *ersatz* ketchup. For *Abendessen* each man receives two slices of bread, a cubic inch of *Speisefett* (literally, "eating fat" or margarine), an inch of *Wurst* (sausage) or an *ersatz* meatball, and a mug of *ersatz* coffee. (The "meatball" is as innocent of meat is the jam is of fruit — a dehydrated mixed cereal powder, moistened with water, kneaded into shape and fried.) Sometimes there is a "delicacy" called *Klippfisch* — a frozen fish dried out in the sun. Rumour has it that the fish dates from the Great War, and after twenty years of being buried under several feet of earth has been recently dug up to feed prisoners in this war. Alf Mungovan will remember it as the best German issue food in five years' captivity.

Only the smelly boars in the moat seem well fed, while the prisoners are left to daydream of foods previously taken for granted. Yet hunger has its positive side. Their taste buds become so sensitive that they can detect the flavour in a brew made from only one teaspoon of tea in two gallons of water...

Once a week the prisoners can spend their *Lagergeld* in the camp canteen, still brought to the castle in a suitcase, whose contents are now displayed in a kiosk. A list of goods for sale is pinned up on the notice boards a day in advance. Within minutes of posting, every prisoner knows the details. Apart from sauces and, very rarely, consignments of fig biscuits, the usual ration is three cigarettes and one cigar per man per week. The cigarettes are of good quality, well packed in handsomely printed boxes, and the tobacco is a mixture of Romanian and Turkish; for pipe smokers there are packets of wiry fine-cut weed that can also be rolled into cigarettes. British cigarettes were plentiful all the while there were Red Cross parcels coming in, but now the canteen stock is the only supply, and the half-starved officers are reduced to walking with their eyes lowered, searching the grounds for cigarette ends.

Regulations still in force from the Great War entitle each prisoner to one bottle of wine or two bottles of beer per week. At Spangenberg the wine is white and from the vineyards of the Rhineland. It costs three *Reichsmark* a bottle. Roth swaps his ration with one of the naval cooks for a small tin of Red Cross steak and kidney pudding. The ratings have no camp currency, but large supplies of tinned food. Roth has the currency, but no food. It is a good swap.

The hours between meals seem endless. An outside observer might easily distinguish the new prisoners from the old: the former, by their listlessness, their bad temper, their boredom, their inability to cope with the empty hours; the latter, by their clearly planned and varied activities. Bob Coste, for instance, plays a lot of poker and organises all the sport in the *Schloss* — always busy, always in a hurry, with no time to spare. The sprog prisoners sleep, walk in pairs up and down the cobbled courtyard, lie on the stones and move with the sun's rays to keep warm, and sunbathe on the outer ramparts which partially circle the steep inner walls. They play poker for *Pfennige*, listen to the German wireless music, wash clothes in *ersatz* soap powder, cut each other's hair, darn socks and share a tub of hot water in the laundry room with ten others... To young, highly trained pilots, life in the castle is like a clock without hands.

Morale amongst them is generally low. They find enforced idleness, and the realisation that they are completely at the mercy of their "hosts", extremely frustrating. The German garrison is smug, as the war is going well for the Reich, and one guard after another assures them that the war will soon be over and that they will be going home in a matter of weeks. All the same, the prisoners cull some humour out of their situation. They refer to themselves as "guests of the Reich", a phrase coined by one of the senior Army officers.

But for all that, the Germans do what they can to make life bearable, though often it comes to naught. Twice a week they let the prisoners cross the drawbridge to exercise in the small gymnasium on the far side of the moat. They also wire off a small part of the moat for a basketball court. They even try, weather permitting, laying on Sunday parole walks down the hill and across the countryside. *Hauptmann* Gross takes the walks, leading the way on an oversized horse. But Gross's Sunday strolls become strenuous route-marches, for he expects the prisoners to keep pace, march in file, and swing their arms. The prisoners, woefully underfed, cannot keep up with the horse, and Gross cannot tolerate stragglers. So eventually the *Hauptmann* goes riding by himself.

On Thursday, 20 June, there is another parade for the Commandant — a long-winded palaver, as before. He tells the POWs that the victorious German armies have found out that the French maltreated their German prisoners. There is no proof so far that Britain has done likewise, but if such evidence does come to light, then British prisoners will be subject to reprisals. He therefore strongly advises all of them to write home at once and acquaint the British Government with this knowledge, and has authorised a special issue of letter-forms for just this purpose. They take his advice, and suggest that the treatment of all German prisoners be in accordance with the Geneva Convention. But one prisoner, Potts, arouses the Germans' ire. He writes that the Erich von Stroheim type of Prussian (a reference to Jean Renoir's prewar film *La Grande Illusion* in which Erich von Stroheim plays the Prussian commandant of a Great War POW camp for French officers) is not confined to the silver screen. On reading this, the camp censors pass it to von Meyer. Back comes the *Oberst* for another parade, in which the letter is read out. Von Meyer considers the letter not only impertinent but a gross and insulting libel. Potts is given thirty days' solitary confinement on bread and water.

Potts is the first RAF officer to visit the cells. The original dungeons of the castle have been converted into a potato store, so the cells are located in the *Turm*, some of them just above the old toilets at the end of the British "dorm". The outer cells overlook the drawbridge. Furniture consists of a plank, chained to the wall, serving as a bed, and a pine table in the middle of the room. Potts is allowed no reading or writing materials and only the basic German issue rations. But the outer wall of the cell is hollow, and it is possible to drop a line through a home-made trap down to the latrines below and draw up books and extra food from confederates "in the know". The Germans never cotton on to this ruse.

Before long the number of refractory prisoners will exceed the number of cells available in The Tower, and the overspill will be sent to the cells in the *Unterlager*. They, too, will prove inadequate, and in time the backlog of prisoners awaiting sentence will swell to such an extent that months will pass before "a berth" becomes available. From the POW point of view, this is a very satisfactory state of affairs.

(5)

Despite the overcrowding, more aircrew prisoners arrived at the castle on Monday, 24 June. They were Squadron Leader Brian Paddon; Flight Lieutenants Robert Macpherson, Sam Pepys and Don

Thom; Flying Officers Don Blew, Duggie Hoare, Reg Jacoby, Des Laslett and Bob Pumphrey; and Pilot Officers Geoff Dodgshun, John Glover, Arthur Imrie, H O Jones, Len Miller DFC, David Osment, Howard Taylor and John Whilton.

Don Blew, shot down on the night of 11/12 May, was a second pilot in a Whitley V from No77 Squadron, Driffield, and the only survivor from his crew. Bomber Command had put up thirty-seven aircraft from Nos 4 and 5 Groups to bomb road and rail communications in Mönchengladbach — it was, in fact, the first raid on the town, and Don Blew's Whitley, hit near the target, was the first British bomber to crash inside Germany while carrying out an attack on a mainland target.

Arthur Macdonald Imrie entered captivity on Tuesday, 14 May. During the afternoon three wings of the AASF — a total of seventy-seven bombers — were ordered to attack enemy columns at Bouillon, Givonne and Sedan, and pontoon bridges along the upper Maas (Meuse). It was a beautiful day, with a cloudless sky and perfect visibility; too good for a daylight bombing raid. A Southern Rhodesian, Imrie was in No218 Squadron, which put up eleven Battles. To conserve manpower, only one of the aircraft carried an observer. No218 was scheduled to make the last attack, with seven of the Battles bombing and strafing the German columns, and the other four bombing the pontoon bridges. The aircraft were clearly silhouetted against the brilliant blue sky and the German gunners soon found their range. Only one aircraft was to return. Imrie's half section, led by Flying Officer D A J Foster, didn't even reach the target. They were jumped by three Me109s south-west of Sedan. Foster's aircraft was brought down in the first attack (Imrie would meet him in Dulag Luft), then Imrie himself had the undivided attention of all three Messerschmitts. His air-gunner, LAC A J Taylor, was badly wounded by the first machine-gun burst. In all, the Me109s made four attacks. Imrie was hit by splinters during the third pass and blacked out, coming round at a few hundred feet when the Me109s were making their final attack. His Battle crashed into the side of a hill, which turned out to be a hornets' nest of German soldiers. They started laying in to Imrie's stricken Battle with gunfire and rockets. Imrie stood up in his cockpit and put up his hands. The Germans helped him pull out the wounded Taylor, but he died two hours later. Imrie was then passed to the rear, reaching Dulag Luft on 22 May.

* * *

Robert Ian Cheyne Macpherson, from No53 Squadron, 2 Group, was captured on Thursday, 16 May, with his crew, Sergeant A R Morland and AC1 S Robinson. No53 squadron, formerly of No2 Group, was now part of No50 Army Co-operation Wing, sending recce-Blenheims either singly or in twos over the battlefront in broad daylight. Two Blenheims off from Poix at 0905 hours to take a "look-see" over Mézières, and Macpherson's was pounced on by Me109s.

David Ernest Thomas Osment and Howard Hamilton Taylor were captured on Sunday, 19 May. Osment was born in the West Indies and educated in England at Herne Bay, on the Kent coast. He joined the RAF on a short-service commission in 1938 and was posted to No150 Squadron, flying Fairey Battles, before the AASF moved to France. Initially the squadron was based at Ecury, near Châlons-sur-Marne, and on 30 September 1939 carried out the RAF's first whole-squadron penetration over enemy lines, led by Squadron Leader William MacDonald. The squadron was badly punished by Me109s and several aircrew badly burnt as a result of shells puncturing the 45-gallon fuel tanks in the aircraft bellies and setting them on fire. (MacDonald was awarded the DFC, and eventually became an Air Chief Marshal and a Baronet.) In the second week of May 1940 the squadron fell back to Puoan, near Troyes. On 19 May seven Battle squadrons each put up six aircraft against two German columns, which, together with mechanised infantry, were moving north towards the Neufchâtel-Montcornet road. Twenty-six Hurricanes, some from No229 Squadron, provided fighter escort. On the way in, No150 Squadron's aircraft ran into heavy AA fire from the town of Rethel. Then, when the first Battles reached the road at about 1040 hours, poor visibility made finding targets difficult. One Battle scored a direct hit but the rest bombed whatever they could find, with poor results.

Me109s, bad weather and ground fire accounted for six Battles, including Osment's. He had reached the target by flying in north-east from Troyes with Flight Lieutenant Hugo Beall in the lead. Over the target they dive-bombed whatever Beall picked out and Osment's Battle, coming under ack-ack fire, received a direct hit in the engine at 3,000 feet. Osment and his crew, Sergeant G W Clifford and AC1 W G Slade, baled out, all to be rounded up by German soldiery. Osment spent the night in a German Army barracks before starting his journey to Dulag Luft.

Howard Taylor, an Australian from Perth, was shot down on the same operation, leading three Battles of No142 Squadron, based at Berry-au-Bac, in an attack north of the Rethel-Blanzy stretch of the River Aisne. None of the three aircraft returned. Taylor was captured along with his crew, Sergeant S Lang and LAC H Long.

***

Pilot Officers John Thomas Glover and Leonard ("Dusty") Miller are from the unfortunate No102 Squadron, which has already lost "Wank" Murray, Alf Thompson and Ken Murphy to captivity. Both enter the bag on the same night, 19/20 May. Hitherto, Miller has been flying as second pilot to Flight Sergeant E L G ("Nobby") Hall, whose Hampden was the lone aircraft to make it back to England after the "bumf raid" of 8/9 September 1939 on which Murray and Thompson were captured. Since then, the squadron has lost so many crews that second pilots are being made up to captains. On 14 May Miller is told he will become a captain and that both he and Hall will be given new crews. They are given two weeks in which to train them. However, Miller never does get to be a captain of his own aircraft.

At 1300 hours on 19 May a runner rushes into Graham Hall's quarters and tells him to report to his Flight Commander. He is down for ops that night.

"With my old crew, of course," adds Hall.

"No," replies the runner. "With your new crew."

"But I haven't been given a new crew yet," Hall persists.

This is a problem, as Miller has already been put down to fly with Flight Lieutenant W G G Cogman, who has only recently returned from Belgium, where he was interned after being forced down during the 8/9 September 1939 leafleting op. Cogman is also slated for ops that night. However, some new crews have just arrived on the station from OTU, and Hall is given a new observer, Sergeant D L Dick, and Glover as a replacement second pilot. As a rear-gunner he is given AC1 A Murray, a spare gunner in the flight. The WOP/AG, LAC J McCutcheon DFM, is the only regular member of the crew. Hall is told to "get a move on" if he wants to fit in a night-flying test. The newcomers have not yet been given quarters and he has to rush about the station to find them and equip them with parachutes. Consequently, they have no time to get to know each other.

In Cogman's crew, apart from Miller, are Sergeant K V Thrift, LAC J R Nicholson and AC2 E H Bros.

Four crews are briefed to attack a synthetic oil plant at Gelsenkirchen in the Ruhr, along with aircraft from Nos 58 and 77 Squadrons. Cogman takes off from Driffield at 2010 hours, with Hall following ten minutes later. The experienced Hall reaches the target without help from his new observer, but when he makes his bombing run Sergeant Dick cannot see the refinery. Hall does another run-in, but still Dick fails to identify it. This annoys Hall, who can see the target quite plainly. Although the flak is severe he tells Glover to take over the pilot's seat and jink every ten seconds to avoid flak and searchlights, while he goes down to the bombing position and shows Dick the target. When he gets back he finds Glover is flying straight and level. The aircraft is coned and a direct hit from the flak sets one engine on fire. Hall takes over, banks the Whitley, dumps the fused bomb-load in the vicinity of the target and sets course for home. The fire dies out but, as they approach the Belgian border from Goch, it flares up again and the other engine starts giving trouble. The Whitley loses height and Hall tells the crew to bale out. All acknowledge the order, and he sees Glover and Dick go through the forward hatch. Murray, on his way out of the rear turret, accidentally pulls his rip-cord and the parachute billows out prematurely. McCutcheon goes up to the front, takes the spare 'chute and gets Murray out before jumping himself. Both land safely. After holding on for as long as possible Hall, too, bales out. Glover, the NCO and the two airmen are soon rounded up, but Hall walks west for some time before running into a patrol and being packed off by train to Dulag Luft.

Cogman is hit by flak over Holland, still on his way to the target. At about 2330 hours his Whitley crashes on a farm twelve miles outside Eindhoven. Sergeant Thrift is killed, Miller, Nicholson and Bros are captured, and Cogman evades. Eventually boarding the SS *Abukir*, he is drowned when it is sunk on 28 May.

* * *

Flying Officer Robert Edwin Welford Pumphrey had served in No607 (County of Durham) Squadron of the Auxiliary Air Force, which in November 1939 had left its base in Croydon for Merville, in France, where, flying Gloster Gladiators, it became part of the Allied Expeditionary Air Force's No60/61 Wings. In December, with Merville waterlogged, they moved to Vitry-en-Artois, where in due course they were re-equipped with Hurricanes. On Saturday, 18 May, after more than a week of intense combat in which Vitry was repeatedly attacked by enemy aircraft, the squadron was ordered to evacuate to the coast, carrying the minimum amount of kit. Burning the squadron records, the men fled in whatever vehicles were available, their progress hampered by refugees and by troops moving in the opposite direction. Eventually they had to abandon all kit except for rifles and revolvers. When the remnants of the squadron at last reached Croydon, at least ten pilots were missing, most of them believed killed. Bob Pumphrey was captured during the evacuation on Wednesday, 20 May.

Desmond Felix Laslett and Geoffrey Thomson Dodgshun had flown as pilot and second dickey on Wellington ICs with No115 Squadron, Marham. On 21/22 May, in an operation against enemy positions in the Dinant-Meuse bulge, Laslett was carrying an extra crewmember, the recently commissioned Pilot Officer Whilton, as a spare gunner. Their Wimpey was damaged by flak and Laslett force-landed near Poix-Terron. The entire crew survived to become POWs.

Humphrey Owen Jones, a second pilot in a Hampden of No144 Squadron, had a lugubrious tale to tell. Bomber Command had put up an assortment of a hundred and twenty four aircraft on 21/22 May to bomb the railway lines between Mönchengladbach and Euskirchen, which lead to the battlefront. No144 Squadron, based at Hemswell, had taken off to bomb Krefeld. Over the target, flak struck the Hampden, captained by Pilot Officer E H Coton, damaging the rudder and ailerons. Coton ordered the crew to bale out. Jones, Sergeant C J Shewry, and Corporal W G Smith duly did as they were told. (Shewry's parachute failed to deploy and he was killed in his descent.) With all but the pilot out, the aircraft righted itself and Coton coaxed her back to England. Crossing the coast of East Anglia, the Hampden was caught in the searchlights and Coton baled out, leaving the aircraft to crash in Essex. For the next five years "Humph" Jones would wonder whether baling out as ordered was the right thing to have done under the circumstances.

Flying Officer Donald Sutherland Thom, a prewar gymnast, was another one with a sorry tale to tell. A Canadian, from Calgary, Alberta, he had crossed the Pond in 1939 to join the RAF. After completing his training at No6 OTU at Sutton Bridge, he was posted to No73 Squadron, equipped with Hurricanes. However, in the first week of May Thom and three other fighter pilots were attached to No1 Squadron, based at Vassincourt. The CO, Squadron Leader P J H Halahan, was not prepared to integrate them into his team, as he reckoned there would be plenty for everybody to do if and when the Germans invaded. In any case, the officers of No1 Squadron considered themselves something of an élite outfit and Thom was definitely "not one of us". They also regarded him as "the worst navigator ever spawned". He proved them right on Saturday 25 May when the squadron was called upon to provide cover for Blenheims on a bombing operation. After escorting the Blenheims to their target, Thom flew the wrong way home. He was hit by flak at 10,000 feet and baled out of his burning Hurricane.

Brian Paddon, a wild character from Teignmouth, Devon, had taken over No40 (Blenheim) Squadron, based at Wyton, on 15 May after its CO was killed. Five days later a replacement arrived and Paddon went back to being a flight commander. He was bagged on Thursday, 6 June, when the squadron put up twelve aircraft to stem the German advance towards Bresle, near St Valéry-sur-Somme. Take-off from Wyton was at 0815 hours, and they were escorted by Hurricanes from Nos 17 and 111 Squadrons. But over the target the Blenheims encountered both flak and Me109s and, although the Hurricanes engaged the enemy fighters, five Blenheims were shot down. Paddon received the undivided attention of almost an entire Me109 squadron, who turned his aircraft into a sieve. He ordered the crew, Sergeants V C Salvage and T A Foreman, to bale out. When they had gone Paddon, too, took to his parachute. Spraining his ankle on landing, he was captured almost immediately. After being taken before a Luftwaffe Colonel who asked him his name and his squadron number, he was put in a POW column to Germany, reaching Dulag Luft on 15 June.

Paddon had already been interrogated, to no avail, at Dulag Luft, but as soon as he arrived at Spangenberg he was finger-printed and questioned again. As before, he refused to answer any questions of an operational nature. His refusal was taken for granted by his interrogators and no bullying tactics were employed.

Reginald Harold Jacoby and Samuel Guy Leslie Pepys were captured on Thursday, 23 May. A recce pilot from No53 Squadron, Pepys was a former Lieutenant in the Essex Regiment. He took off from Poix at 0430 hours to check a report that the Germans had crossed the canal running from St Omer to Aire-sur-la-Lys. His Blenheim was shot down, but his crew, Sergeant A Haygreen and AC1 H Spear, survived. Jacoby had been with No40 Squadron. Part of No2 Group at the beginning of the war, and based at Abingdon, the squadron had been sent to France on 2 September 1939 as part of No71 Wing of the AASF and operated from Béthenville until it was recalled to No2 Group in mid-May, thereafter operating from Wyton. Jacoby had seen action on the first day of the French campaign. His last sortie was against German troops at Arras, when six Blenheims, led by Paddon's successor, Wing Commander J G Llewellyn, took off from Wyton at 1010 hours and hooked up with another six Blenheims from No103 Squadron. They arrived late over the target because, before heading out to sea, they had to wait over Hawkinge for their Hurricane escort, provided by a tardy No32 Squadron. Encountering bad weather and heavy cloud over the French coast, the formation broke up, and most crews had to bomb alternative targets. Flak struck two of No40 Squadron's aircraft over Miraumont, killing the CO and his gunner, and Jacoby's two crewmen. Jacoby escaped from the pranged aircraft and went into the bag.

***

Douglas Sydney Hoare is from No74 ("Tiger") Squadron, which he joined at Hornchurch straight from Flying Training School in 1937. At 0600 hours on Friday, 24 May, 1940 Hoare takes off from the squadron's forward base at Rochford with the rest of "B" Flight to patrol the Channel off Calais. The pilots have been briefed not to cross the French coast unless chasing enemy aircraft. After about thirty minutes the Flight Commander, Flight Lieutenant W P F ("Treacle") Treacy, announces that he has spotted a Henschel Hs126 reconnaissance aircraft flying low a mile or so east of Calais. Both sections go into line astern and dive, getting to within attacking range about fifteen miles inland from the French coast. Duggie Hoare does not even get a chance to fire his guns. By the time he is in position, the Hs126 is at treetop height and on fire, having received the speedy attentions of Hoare's colleagues. A few seconds later it hits the ground and explodes.

Treacy gives the order to return to base and the Spitfires turn westwards. As they near the French coast, Hoare's engine starts boiling and streaming glycol. Checking his instruments, he sees the radiator temperature is off the clock, the oil temperature is high and the pressure low. He now has a difficult decision to make. Flying at a mere 1500 feet, he cannot be sure whether the engine will get him home, or even across the Channel. The alternative is to put her down on the AASF airfield at Calais-Marck and get a quick repair done, thus avoiding further damage to the engine. The airfield is cratered from recent bombing, so he prepares for a wheels-down landing using minimum revs and selects a line of approach that will take him between the craters. But at four hundred feet, to his astonishment, the craters vanish from sight. It is not until he actually lands that he discovers why: the grass is about three feet high and is obscuring the craters. Fortunately he is able to maintain a straight approach and come quickly to rest without falling into one of the holes. Two of his squadron's ground crew, Corporal George Higginbottom and LAC J B Cressey, having flown out in a Blenheim the day before to repair another stranded Tiger Squadron aircraft, run towards him as he climbs out of the cockpit. Hoare explains what has happened and in a matter of minutes they have removed the engine cowlings and located the trouble. Most of the glycol has leaked out through a bullet-hole in the pipe running from the header tank to the engine. In all likelihood, Hoare's section, pursuing the Hs126, crossed the enemy's line of fire. As there is no other visible damage to the engine or the airframe, Hoare calls Treacy, who is circling overhead. Treacy promises to see that spares are flown out so Higginbottom and Cressey can repair the damage.

Hoare's first instinct is to have his Spitfire towed to a hangar so that it will not present a target if the Germans bomb again. Higginbottom tells him the airfield is almost deserted; only a handful of French Air Force personnel remain in the Mess and they are having breakfast. Hoare calls in at the Mess to ask for assistance, but all he can get out of them is: *"C'est fini: la guerre est fini."* No doubt for them it is. Germans tanks are already arriving in the fields nearby. Hoare has no choice but to destroy the Spitfire and, returning to the airfield, runs towards it with Higginbottom. But enemy armour is rolling towards them from the far side of the airfield, and small arms fire is whistling through the long grass. Realising they will never reach the aircraft, the two men hit the deck, crawl off and spend the next twenty-four hours trying unsuccessfully to get away from the area. The sound of gunfire comes from all directions and Dunkirk and Calais are ablaze. Early in the evening of Saturday, 25 May, they find themselves on the beach with refugees and British Army survivors from Calais, sandwiched between tanks moving across the dunes from east and west. Hopelessly trapped, they are all rounded up. As he stands on the beach, Hoare can see Spitfires and Hurricanes patrolling above him and, just visible on the horizon, the White Cliffs of Dover. They might just as well be on the moon. Hoare will spend many months wondering if his Spitfire's Merlin engine could have got him to those cliffs after all.

(6)

The last purge of RAF officers to arrive at Spangenberg that June included Flight Lieutenants Gordon Clancy, James Leyden, George Skelton and John Stephens; Flying Officers Peter Bressey, William Lepine, Norman Thomas, George Walker and Gordon Wright; Pilot Officers Frank Hugill, Henry Murray and John Plant. They were accompanied by Lieutenant (A) D T R Martin, RN.

Henry Macale Murray had been the first of this purge to enter captivity. He had been a Fairey Battle pilot in No218 Squadron of the AASF in France and was shot down on Saturday, 11 May, during the same operation as Charlie Crews, Tony Hudson, John Madge and Alf Mungovan. Murray's observer, Sgt P Stubbs, and his gunner, LAC2 I G Adams, went with him into the bag.

Norman Maurice Thomas is shot down on the first daylight operation against the Maastricht bridges, in Belgium, on Sunday, 12 May. One other officer, Pilot Officer I A McIntosh, five NCOs and five other ranks enter captivity as a result of the raid, although Thomas will not see McIntosh again until 1943, as the latter is sent to Stalag Luft I at Barth.

Overnight, forward elements of two German panzer divisions have been pouring across the two bridges spanning the Albert Canal west of Maastricht. It looks like the main German thrust which BEF HQ has feared for eight months, and threatens the Allied position on the north-eastern front. Up to now, all RAF attacks on the two bridges, one of metal and the other of concrete, have been made at night and they have remained unscathed. Air Marshal Arthur "Ugly" Barratt reaches the conclusion that the only way to ensure the destruction of the bridges is by low-level attack in broad daylight. He gives the job to No12 Squadron, part of No76 Wing of the AASF, flying Fairey Battles from Amifontaine, near Reims. Its crews have been at Readiness since 4am. This time he takes the unprecedented step of calling for volunteers. Orders come through by telephone at 0700 hours and formal orders from AASF HQ follow at 0815 hours.

In the meantime, the crews of "The Shiny Twelfth" are called to the operations hut in the woods bordering the airfield, where the deputy CO, a grim-faced Squadron Leader B E Lowe, impresses upon them the importance of the target and calls for six crews. Fearing that few will volunteer, he phrases Barratt's orders in such a way as to leave the assembled aircrew little choice. "The raid will be carried out on a volunteer basis," he tells them. "Will anyone who doesn't wish to go please step forward?" No one moves. No one speaks. Then the hut is filled with voices, pleading to go. Lowe is about to put the names in a hat and draw a lottery, when the six crews on stand-by announce in a babble of voices: "It's our turn and we're ready to go. There's no call for volunteers." Lowe sees the force of this and they win their point. The six pilots are Norman Thomas and Pilot Officers Thomas Brereton and T D H Davy, from "A" Flight; and Flying Officer Donald Garland, Pilot Officer Ian McIntosh and Sergeant Fred Marland, from "B" Flight. Thomas is a smiling, twenty-three-year-old from Dorset who joined the RAF in 1936 and arrived in France on 2 September 1939 — one of the first RAF men to do so. His observer is Sergeant B T P Carey, and his gunner Corporal J S Campion. Davy's observer is Sergeant G D Mansell, and his gunner LAC G N Patterson, a Canadian.

The two flights are to proceed independently to the target and take a bridge each. Fighter cover has been promised by No1 (Hurricane) Squadron, based at Berry-au-Bac, which will meet them five miles south-east of Amifontaine. The attack is scheduled to begin at 0915 hours. Bomber Command aircraft will be operating against other targets in the area at about the same time, along with two Air Component squadrons.

Thomas and Garland, the two flight commanders, are left to decide tactics. Garland will be leading his formation against the metal bridge, a structure 370 feet long and thirty feet wide at Veldwezelt, on the road to Hasselt. Thomas's flight will attack the concrete bridge, a mile or so to the south at Vroenhaven, on the Maastricht-Tongres road. When Garland suggests a low-level attack as the best way to achieve surprise and avoid flak and fighters, Thomas is aghast. "It's suicide!" declares Thomas. "It hasn't had much success so far." He tells Garland that there is sufficient cloud cover in which to approach the target at high level, dive-bomb and have plenty of speed for a quick getaway. The argument becomes heated as each man fights his corner. In the end they agree to differ. Garland will go in low, and Thomas will approach at altitude.

Thomas and Davy take off first, at 0818 hours, and circle the airfield for a few minutes waiting for Brereton, Thomas's No2. Brereton has found his radio unserviceable and is transferring to another aircraft. He is held up a second time by hydraulic failure on the bomb rack and in the end is left behind.

When Thomas reaches the rendezvous there are no fighters to be seen, so he sets course for the target with neither his No2 nor his promised fighter escort. It is a bright, fresh morning with thick but broken cloud ranging across the sky at 5,000 feet. Thomas and Davy climb steadily through the cloud and level out at 7,000 feet, cruising at 160mph. Now and again, through breaks in the cloud, they get a clear view of the ground, making navigation quite straightforward; sometimes the cloud breaks up altogether to the west and they can see for miles. Thomas is aiming to cross the Meuse south of Tongres and detour twelve miles to the west of Maastricht before swinging east on the final approach. Thus they will be over friendly territory right up to the moment of attack.

Four minutes after Thomas and Davy's take-off, Garland, McIntosh and Marland follow. There is still no sign of a fighter support. In fact No1 Squadron has missed the rendezvous. Only three Hurricanes manage to locate the Battles and fly along with them; the other seven are making their way to the target with the object of drawing off any enemy fighter opposition that might appear.

Garland levels off at 2,000 feet, ready to drop down to ground level near the target. As Thomas is above cloud, and Garland below, the two Battle formations see nothing of each other.

For half an hour everything goes according to plan for the two aircraft of "B" Flight. Then, a few miles south of Tongres, flak bursts a short distance ahead of them, scattered at first, then more persistent. They have been told that the Germans are not yet across the Meuse in strength, but beneath them, fifteen miles on this — the Allied — side of the river, are German flak units. Thomas's proposed detour further west is now pointless; after a short conference with Sergeant Carey, he alters course, steering north-east direct for the target. The flak starts to thicken and he drops to cloud level at 5,000 feet, jinking to avoid enemy fighters and put the German gunners off their aim. Davy tucks in close behind him.

Suddenly, about a mile to starboard, they see a formation of Blenheims under heavy attack from flak. They are taking no evasive action, so Thomas concludes that they must be making a bombing run against German columns. As he goes below the cloud near the target the flak intensifies. Then he glimpses Maastricht dead ahead, cut in half by the winding river. All the bridges over the river are down. Picking out the Maastricht-Tongres road, he follows it with his eye from left to right until it reaches the canal and the concrete bridge he has been briefed to attack.

He turns to starboard, skirting the western edge of the town, intending to dive-bomb from the far side of the canal and make his getaway to the south-west, towards Belgium. As he is poised to dive, his gunner, Campion, alerts him to the presence of scores of enemy fighters. The three Hurricanes engage them but three more Me109s appear, starboard of the two Battles. As they close in, the flak lets up. Thomas signals to Davy to warn him about the fighters, which are coming in slightly above them and appear to be going right for him. The two gunners bring their Vickers guns to bear and wait for the 109s to come within range, while the two observers strain their necks peering into their mirror-sights without seeing a thing. Davy heads for cloud cover, with the fighters giving chase. This presents Thomas with a dilemma: to stick with Davy and offer what combined fire-power he can in defence against the Me109s, or to go ahead with the attack, hoping Davy will shake off the fighters and follow him down. Lowe's words at the briefing come back to him. He has to get that bridge — his own life, the lives of his crew, and even of Davy, are subordinate. Doggedly, he pushes the nose of the Battle forward and dives on the canal.

Focusing his eyes on the bridge, and on a building on the far side, Thomas goes into a shallow dive, then points the Battle's nose right down so that when he releases his bombs the aircraft will be almost vertical. At 4,000 feet the Battle, screaming and shuddering, gathers speed, and Carey and Campion have to struggle to hold their positions. One by one Thomas releases his four 250lb bombs — the first from 3,000 feet and the last from four hundred feet. They are fused to explode on impact, and Thomas is flying so low that he nearly blows himself up with the last explosion. Then, grunting, he heaves back on the stick to pull out of the dive.

So far the flak has remained silent. But suddenly, as he starts to climb for cloud cover, he gets the undivided attention of every flak position surrounding the bridge. The gunners are deadly accurate. Fearing the aircraft will disintegrate before he reaches cloud, he dives again and flattens out at twenty feet, hoping to make a hasty exit at low level. But the flak has followed him down and pummels the aircraft again and again.

The end comes when a shell bursts inside the starboard wing-root, splaying out all the fuel pipes leading into the fuselage. Petrol pours into the aircraft and Carey, alerting Thomas, grabs the gushing petrol pipes and tries with his gloved fingers to staunch the flow. Thomas holds the throttle wide open, and the damaged engine, still getting for the moment a sufficient feed of fuel, carries them forward at its own speed. He watches the needle flickering around 90 IAS (Indicated Air Speed). Ground batteries and a road convoy are hammering away at him, but he is too low to take evasive action. He knows how far the Germans have penetrated this side of the Meuse and sees little hope of getting clear. Then the engine dies and the aircraft sinks. Seconds later, he does a wheels-up in a field near Vroenhaven. His arrival is smooth, except that the Battle noses forward, its tail in the air. As soon as it reaches a standstill Thomas jumps from the cockpit and runs back along the wing to check on the crew. Although pretty shaken they have miraculously escaped injury. Then a hail of machine-gun fire beats against the fuselage. Yelling at Carey and Campion to stay where they are, Thomas throws himself down on the grass, looking around desperately for a ditch or some sort of cover. There is none. Even the grass is no more than two or three inches high. The hail of fire intensifies and he watches Campion standing coolly by his gun, ignoring the fire, awaiting the order to open up. A hundred and fifty yards away is the enemy convoy they saw from the air. The gunners seem not in the least bit anxious to take them alive.

Amazed at Campion's courage, Thomas realises nevertheless that their position is hopeless and that to delay surrender means certain death. As if to point the lesson, a bullet ricochets off the aircraft and strikes him a glancing blow on the face. He gets to his feet, raising his hands above his head. The firing stops and seconds later the German gunners stride across and take them prisoner.

That day, as the Germans try unsuccessfully to evacuate them east of the Meuse, the captured Thomas and his crew three times cross and recross the bridge they set out to destroy. They see craters on both sides of the bridge, one of which has reduced traffic to a single line, but the whole area is so extensively cratered they are uncertain as to whether it was they who did the damage.

The Germans show great interest in the attack, trying to establish who carried it out, but Thomas and his crew are careful to register surprise, managing to convince their captors they were on a reconnaissance flight.

The other bridge is severely damaged — by either Marland or Garland. But neither they nor their crews survive to tell the tale. Besides, it is already too late. The Germans have crossed the Meuse in strength and the temporary loss of one canal crossing and the damaging of another holds them up but little. In the event, the German attacks develop not in this sector but through the Ardennes, which the French boasted was impregnable. But whatever doubts exist at BAFF HQ about the amount of damage inflicted on the bridges, or indeed whether the raid was even worth while, there is no doubt at all about the courage of the Battle crews, seven of whom have been captured and six killed. Nearly a month later, on 11 June, Davy will be gazetted for the DFC, and his gunner, Gordon Patterson, for the DFM. Patterson will hear about his DFM in prison camp, and will be the first Canadian in the war to be thus honoured. Posthumous VCs will go to Garland and his observer, Sergeant T Gray.

***

Flight Lieutenant Skelton had been in No264 Squadron, at Martlesham Heath, since general mobilisation in September 1939. The first squadron to be equipped with the ill-fated Boulton and Paul Defiant, No264 carried out all the trials and tests, and afterwards the CO sent a damning report to the Air Ministry. Unfortunately, the Government had already placed a substantial order and the aircraft had to be used up — along with their crews. The CO was sacked and replaced by Squadron Leader Philip Hunter, who had been a Boulton and Paul test pilot.

They continued with their exercises and in December 1939 became operational, carrying out convoy patrols. In May 1940, as the Germans advanced rapidly through Holland, six Defiants from "B" Flight formed a composite squadron with six Spitfires from "A" Flight of No66 Squadron, Duxford. The Defiants were expected to defend the Spitfires from attacks from behind. On Monday, 13 May, the composite squadron took off to attack German troops moving through Breda, but got caught up with four Stukas dive-bombing the Dutch. The Spitfires and Defiants destroyed four Stukas, only to be jumped by Me109s. Five of the six Defiants were shot down. Skelton's air-gunner, Pilot Officer Hatfield, made his way back to England, but Skelton, who had badly injured an arm and a leg, was captured and spent more than a month at the Hohemark near Dulag Luft until he and other patients were purged for helping a fellow officer to escape.

Gordon Drummond Clancy, a burly Canadian from Seimens, Saskatchewan, flies his last sortie on the afternoon of Tuesday, 14 May. He, too, is a Battle pilot, from No12 Squadron. By now the Germans are across the Meuse and pouring towards Sedan, and Air Marshal Barratt agrees with the French on a combined effort to stem the advance. Each Air Force will send in two waves of bombers at two-hourly intervals, the RAF contributing more than seventy aircraft: twenty-three from No71 Wing, twenty-nine from No75 Wing, and nineteen from No76 Wing. Two-thirds will attack bridges — one south of Sedan, two at Mouzon, and one each at Douzy and Romilly — and the remainder will attack enemy columns advancing from Bouillon, through Givonne to Sedan.

No12 Squadron — still licking its wounds after the raid on the Maastricht bridges — assigns five Battles to the day's operations, and led by Clancy they start taking off at 1530 hours. They form up and fly towards the Sedan-Givonne road, where they to are attack enemy columns. When they reach the target, they see no columns and so bomb the empty road, hoping to crater it and delay the German breakthrough. Throughout the operation they meet intense AA and machine-gun fire. Then, over Pouru-St-Rémy, about eleven miles east-south-east of Sedan, they are set upon by Me109s. Four are shot down, killing five men — including Clancy's crew — and sending seven into captivity. Back at Amifontaine, the ground crews, anxiously awaiting their return so they can quickly refuel and re-arm them ready for the next operation, are sorely disappointed when only one limps back to base.

Clancy, having baled out of his damaged aircraft, gets his parachute caught up between the branches of two tall pine trees. For a day and a night he hangs forty feet above the ground, unable to reach a branch in any direction. Finally, fed up, hungry and thirsty, he takes his courage in both hands, presses his harness release, and lets himself fall. On hitting the ground he injures his spine and breaks, fractures or sprains just about every bone in his body. "If I ever get back to dear old Canada," he tells fellow POWs later, "I'll make a living selling matches in the gutter rather then leave there ever again."

It is not until much later that Clancy hears that of the seventy-one Battles operating against columns and bridges around Sedan on 14 May a total of forty failed to return.

Gordon Ormson Manly Wright is from the Blenheim-equipped No110 Squadron and is shot down on the same raid on German columns and pontoons at Sedan, on 14 May, that leads Ernest Mullins into the bag. Wright is a pilot and Sergeant J Fancy is his observer, with LAC W W Street as air-gunner. Over Mézières, where the flak opens up on them, Wright starts weaving to shake it off, and his Blenheim receives quite a buffeting before he finally gets clear. Wright decides to make the run-in to his target from the south, and tells John Fancy to keep a lookout for flak and to pick the best bridge to bomb. Once over Sedan, where thousands of refugees are streaming away to the south and east, Wright turns north, while Fancy lies down flat in the nose to get a better view of the bridges. The area seems strangely empty, with neither flak nor enemy traffic. Then Fancy tells Wright he has spotted the bridges and points out the main one. Wright banks round on a close circuit to come in on the bombing run. Just then the gunner, Bill Street, yells: "Look out to port!" and the two jump out of their skins. Wright heaves back on the stick and a flight of three Blenheims shoot past right under the nose. "A near squeak," Wright gasps as he levels out.

Fancy can still see Nos 2 and 3 aircraft flying in tight formation, so he sends a message telling them Wright is going to cross the bridge at a narrow angle at 6,000 feet and drop his bombs in a stick. As Wright turns in, Fancy's eyes are glued to the bomb-sight and he relays a few corrections as the bridge glides along the bomb-sight drift-wires towards the cross-wire, his aiming line. Then he presses the tit four times and the bombs drop out one by one. "Bombs away!" he shouts, confident of a hit. The first smacks into the water about twenty yards from the bridge; the second right alongside; the third lands directly on the bridge at about midstream; and the fourth hits the water twenty yards away on the opposite side. No2 aircraft has better luck — his first bomb scores a direct hit on the bridge and the rest overshoot only narrowly. No3 creeps progressively nearer with each bomb until his fourth lands right in the middle of the road where the bridge joins the bank. It is a highly satisfactory result, especially as all three aircraft have shared in the destruction of the bridge.

Fancy voices Wright's thanks over the R/T and hopes their efforts will cause the enemy considerable delay. He is just about to set course for home when he turns to Wright and shouts: "Look down there — Jerry troops." Glancing below, Wright sees a long line of enemy troop transports travelling south towards Sedan along a straight road running through thickly wooded country just north of the town. Immediately he goes into a strafing dive. "My kingdom for some bombs," he says wistfully. At 3,000 feet he opens up with the front guns, raking the length of the column. Then at five hundred feet he levels out and shoots his way past them as Bill Street joins in with his turret guns. Germans are diving for cover in all directions and several lorries are blazing merrily.

But their spot of ground strafing has carried them several miles from Sedan and Fancy now has to pick out new landmarks so as to set a course for home. As he is searching (it is now approaching 1530 hours) he sees gun- flashes from a clearing below; shells strike the aircraft — blowing off the nose, filling the cockpit with acrid smoke, hitting Fancy in the right leg, and tearing off his flying helmet, goggles and earphones. The next few seconds are absolute murder and time seems to stretch. Wright and Fancy are half-blind and choking, and as the Blenheim lurches and sways they are tossed about like flotsam in a gale. Wright struggles grimly to bring the aircraft back under control and Fancy gropes blindly towards him. "It's no good, chaps," shouts Wright. "I can't do a thing."

Fancy scrambles up and wrenches open the escape hatch. It clears the cockpit of smoke but they know the Blenheim is doomed. Black smoke is pouring from the engines, the wings are burning fiercely and the heat is unbearable. *If we don't get out now*, thinks Fancy, *we'll be burned alive!* But they were flying at only eight hundred feet when hit and even that was too low to bale out.

Now the ground is racing up to meet them and a crash is inevitable. Fancy grabs his mouthpiece and warns Street, in his turret, to brace himself for the crash, while Gordon Wright, unaware that the engines are useless, is the picture of torment as he fights to level out the Blenheim. Then the burning aircraft strikes the top of a tree, pivots round in the opposite direction, levels out and hits the ground with a horrible crunch, burning with a new ferocity. Mingled with the crackling flames are sounds of rending metal and snapping woodwork as she ploughs a great furrow through the earth for thirty to fifty yards. Fancy, thrown about inside the fuselage, is cut and bruised every time he makes contact with some broken part of the interior. At last the aircraft comes to rest, leaving behind a trail of wreckage, and a terrifying silence...

Then the ammunition begins to explode. In his panic to get out, Wright catches one foot behind the rudder bar. He is in agony, and as he struggles to free himself the horrible thought passes through his mind that he will be burned alive. Fancy, who feels as if every bone in his body is broken, staggers to his feet. As he scrambles through the hatch he realises that Wright isn't following him. He turns to find out what is wrong, and on seeing Wright's predicament hangs head downwards through the hatch and tries to unfasten Wright's boot-straps. After a lot of fumbling and cursing he manages to get Wright's foot out, leaving the flying boot behind. They then turn to look for Street, from whom they have heard not a sound. Fancy climbs on to the fuselage, barely aware of his own burns and injuries, and tries to kick his way through Street's hatchway. It refuses to budge. Meanwhile, Wright notices that the tail unit has broken off, carrying with it a large portion of the fuselage. It has left a gap too small for him to crawl through but big enough for Fancy. There is not a moment to lose — the fuel tanks might explode any second — and Fancy wriggles his thin body through the gap and finds Street with his feet tangled in the rudder control cables. He is more dead than alive from inhaling the fumes of the burning batteries. Coughing and spluttering, his eyes streaming, Fancy frees him and struggles towards the gap in the fuselage. Then with Wright's help he drags him feet-first through the hole.

They carry Street a good distance away from the aircraft — in the nick of time. No sooner do they lay him down than the tanks go up with a roar. Bits of wreckage fly in all directions and ignited petrol spews out and envelops the wreckage in fire. Wright and Fancy drag Street further away and wait for the fresh air to revive him. He is just coming round when they hear loud shouts nearby. Soon they are surrounded by enemy troops, poking them with automatic rifles, pointing with bayonets, and yelling: *"Hände hoch!"* The three prisoners have gone through too much of an ordeal to be intimidated by threats, but make a token effort of surrender by half-raising their hands.

The Germans lead them to a large house among some trees two hundred yards away. There they check up on their injuries. Wright has a sore ankle and burns to one side of his face. Fancy has numerous shrapnel wounds down his right leg and odd pieces of aircraft scattered about his body. His hands are badly burned and swollen to the size of footballs and most of the hair has been singed from his head. Street has miraculously escaped without injury.

Wright continually lambastes himself for getting them into this mess, and every few minutes breaks out with renewed apologies.

"Don't be a clot," says Fancy. "You're in this mess, too — and in any case all three of us are still very much alive."

Owing more to nerves than amusement, Bill Street has occasional fits of the giggles, and now the action and excitement has passed, Fancy is beginning to feel pretty sick. His leg has gone numb, and he sits down. The guards then search them and, satisfied they are unarmed, give them water. Fancy is grateful for this as he has by now developed a raging thirst. The offer of water also helps lessen the tension between captors and captives; and, although neither understands the other's language, Wright learns that they have come down near a forward wireless unit with the house as headquarters.

Before long a young officer arrives and addresses the prisoners in broken English, obviously pleased to try it out and impress the young guards.

His first words are the usual: "For you the war is over."

Then he goes on to explain that they will not be prisoners for long because in three weeks' time Germany will invade England, and three weeks after that the war will be over and they can go home. He is deadly serious. They laugh derisively, and he treats this as a form of hysteria

111

following the shock of the crash.

All the time the guards are keeping a close eye on them, but none of the prisoners is in a condition to bolt, and Fancy is content to sit leaning against the wall to rest his aching torso and leg. He and Wright have managed to hang on to their wrist-watches and, despite the buffeting they underwent in the crash, they are still going. For some reason, perhaps out of nervous reaction, the two men keep checking the time. After about an hour and a half they begin to feel hungry, but the guards provide no food. Fancy starts brooding about the bars of chocolate they have left behind in their Blenheim.

At 1730 hours a couple of lorries stop outside in a cloud of dust and the three prisoners are put aboard — Wright with two guards in one, and Fancy and Street with two guards in the other. They set off for a bumpy ride along rough country lanes, passing troops of German riflemen mounted on bicycles, and columns of motorised troops, who stare at them and yell hostile remarks at the *"Engländer"*. Village after village goes by and they are beginning to think the journey will never end when at last they pull into a farmyard, where they are directed to a large barn. Although it is still light outside, once the barn doors are closed they are in pitch darkness. Unable to see an inch in front of them, they try to find somewhere to lie down. But they find themselves treading on bodies, and hear voices complaining. The barn is full of French soldiers. Suddenly they hear voices talking in English. Street shouts: "Who the hell are you blokes?" and receives the reply: "Don't be so bloody curious. Come over here, we won't eat you!"

They pick their way through the grumbling Frenchmen and finally locate two British NCOs, Sergeants H R W Winkler and M D Smalley, pilot and observer in a Fairey Battle from No12 Squadron shot down on Monday, 13 May, attacking troops along the Sedan-Givonne road. After swapping stories all five settle down to sleep, although sleep eludes Fancy, for whom the night is one of pain, thirst and worry. That morning he received a letter from his wife announcing she was pregnant. Now he wonders how long it will be before the authorities discover he is still alive and will inform her. Later that night a fatherly Frenchman gives him some wine from his water bottle, and it helps to ease his thirst.

When dawn breaks and thin strips of daylight shine through the cracks in the barn door, the situation seems more hopeless than ever. They have passed fifteen hours in captivity and have received no food, drink, bedding or medical aid and have had no opportunity to wash.

Finally, at 0800 hours, the RAF prisoners are beckoned outside. Fancy can hardly stand up and Wright and Street have to help him into the farmyard, where they are allowed to wash at a hand-pump, drying themselves on their handkerchiefs. An ambulance is waiting in the yard to take Wright and Fancy to hospital. They scramble aboard, waving goodbye to Street, Smalley and Winkler, and after a twenty-minute ride through thick woods come to a large country house being used as a field dressing station. Their burns are treated and dressed, and two hours later they are each given a bowl of soup. It stinks like dirty socks, but hunger overcomes fastidiousness, and they wolf it down. Then their ambulance returns and they are locked in the back, the guard sitting in front with the driver. Wright keeps lashing himself for getting Fancy and Street captured. Nothing Fancy says can comfort him, and he feels even worse when he realises they are heading northwards, into Germany, and not back to the barn where Street is awaiting their return. Wright is now thinking about escape, and suggests they bust open the window and bolt for it. Fancy, knowing that in his condition he will only be a burden, tells Wright to go it alone. But no opportunity presents itself. They are travelling along narrow roads, and every few hundred yards the ambulance driver has to pull over to let troop convoys pass. The guard keeps the shutter between the driving cab and the ambulance open throughout the journey and keeps looking over his shoulder at the prisoners.

Not long after 1900 hours they pull into Neufchâteau, where the guard leads them into a schoolroom. Beds of straw have been laid on the floor round the walls, and on them slump eight other wounded prisoners, French, Dutch and Belgian. The guards, along with an NCO and an interpreter, occupy the room next door. Before long the interpreter, an elderly and benevolent gentleman, approaches the RAF prisoners and plies them with questions, none of which they answer. He stamps away and leaves them in peace.

That evening they also have their first solid food since leaving Wattisham: two rock-hard biscuits each, with a scraping of jam, washed down with a mug of revolting tea. Afterwards Fancy, who is dog-tired, sinks back on the straw and tries to get some sleep. But his wounds are still bleeding and sticking to his trouser-leg, and every time he moves during his sleep he is awakened by a sudden jolt of pain. He feels a bit better the next morning, however, although the sight of another batch of wounded prisoners — bringing the total now to twenty — and a breakfast of black bread, thinly spread with margarine and accompanied by vile tea, begins to stir feelings of resentment at Germany's treatment of its POWs. He decides to escape as soon as he is fit.

At noon they are ordered into the schoolyard, given a bowl of soup each from a field kitchen, issued with a blanket apiece, loaded into lorries, and driven to the railway station where they are transferred to cattle-trucks and locked in. Wright has to help Fancy all the time, as his hands are thickly bandaged and his right leg all but useless — it stinks so much they fear gangrene is setting in. Medical attention has become an imperative.

An hour passes before the cattle-truck is hitched up to a passenger train and starts on its way. Even then the train stops at stations for long stretches at a time to let passengers on and off. Finally, at 1800 hours, it draws into a large station. The prisoners are let out, counted and led to the end of the platform, where there is a workmen's shed behind which they are to do their business. Then more Reich rations: a thick slice of black bread, a piece of liver-sausage and a mug of *ersatz* coffee. As they are herded back into the cattle-truck, Wright complains about the lack of sanitary arrangements. One of the guards puts an old tin in one corner, and again the door is locked. The journey resumes at a crawl, and the prisoners lie silently on the straw, until at about 0800 hours the train halts at Cologne. There is a rattle of bolts, and the door slides open to reveal broad daylight and the silhouette of a young German NCO, with briefcase and revolver holster, reading from a sheet of paper. He helps Wright and Fancy out of the wagon, telling them they are going to the hospital at Frankfurt. At last! Wright supports Fancy and together they follow the German NCO down the subway and onto another platform. After another bowl of the inevitable Reich soup they embark on a Pullman train with luxuriously upholstered seats. It is their first taste of civilised comfort since leaving Wattisham. As the train winds down the beautiful Rhine Valley they are able to relax, and the German NCO, who speaks excellent English, tells them they are destined for Dulag Luft. He describes it in glowing terms, and points out places of interest along the way. It helps ease the turmoil in their exhausted minds.

At 1230 hours they pull into Koblenz, where the NCO obtains frankfurter sandwiches and coffee. Finally, at 1830 hours, they reach Frankfurt am Main, where the NCO telephones for a lorry. After a seven-mile drive they arrive at Hohemark hospital, where they are helped by Sisters into separate rooms, allowed to bathe and shave, given clean pyjamas and put between clean sheets. They are also given their first proper meal: asparagus in white sauce, fried meatballs, mashed potatoes and gravy.

Wright and Fancy spend six weeks at the Hohemark, where they meet Clancy, and will remember it as their best experience of captivity — a period in which they are well fed and receive the best of medical attention. The solitary confinement cells to which they are then sent provide a stark contrast. Each is visited by an interrogator who claims that the other has completed his Red Cross Arrival Report Form. Their reaction to this ploy is sufficiently aggressive to secure their release after only one night in the cells.

***

Flying Officer William Noel Lepine, a Hurricane pilot from No85 Squadron, based at Merville as part of the Air Component, was shot down one week later on Saturday, 18 May. Wounded when bounced by Me110s during a routine patrol, he baled out and was captured on landing.

James Napier Leyden had been a Battle pilot in No103 Squadron, based at Rheges/St Lucien Ferme. On Sunday, 26 May four Battles from his squadron, along with four from No142 and two from No150, were given the task of bombing the Château Roumont, near Ochampes aerodrome in Luxembourg, where twenty senior Luftwaffe officers were scheduled to have a meeting. They were to be escorted by Nos 1 and 73 squadrons and bomb the target at 1018 hours. Driving rain made observation difficult, but six Battles managed to find and bomb the target, one bomb bursting inside the building. All aircraft encountered light and heavy flak on the return leg. Leyden crashed near the Luxembourg town of Ucimont. His observer and gunner were killed.

An observer in the same squadron as Leyden, Frank Hugill was captured on Friday, 14 June. By this time the squadron had moved to another airfield, at Souge. Crews were briefed at dawn to attack enemy columns south of the Seine, but bad weather prevented take-off. However, by evening the weather had improved, and at 1845 hours four Battles took off. Two failed to return. Hugill and his pilot, Pilot Officer Ronald Hawkins, were captured. Hawkins, who had equipped himself with every conceivable escape aid, managed to give his captors the slip and make his way to Vichy France, then to England via Gibraltar. He was awarded the Military Cross for his escape. Eventually becoming a Squadron Leader, he commanded No3 Squadron, flying Hawker Typhoons. He was killed in action in October 1943.

George Edward Walker and John ("Pappy") Plant had been a pilot and second pilot in the same Whitley crew from No48 Squadron, No4 Group, based at Linton-on-Ouse. Along with their WOP/AGs Sergeants R R Schofield, C H Neary and H R Holmes, they are believed to be the first aircrew captured on a raid on Essen, which was to become one of the most heavily defended targets against which Bomber Command would operate. On Thursday, 20 June thirty-nine Whitleys and seventeen Hampdens had been sent out to bomb marshalling yards and industrial targets in Germany. Flak was severe. One Hampden was shot down over Hamm, and Walker's aircraft was hit over Essen, which six out of the seven Whitleys sent there had bombed. All the crew entered captivity. Both Plant and Walker were Canadians from Alberta. Walker, lean, loose-limbed, moustachioed and smooth-faced, came from Calgary, while the tall, bearded Plant looked like an Old Testament prophet — and was, in fact, a lay reader in the Episcopal Church.

Flight Lieutenant John William Stephens had fought valiantly throughout the French campaign with No107 Squadron, Wattisham, commanded first by Basil Embry and then by Squadron Leader L R Stokes. He had flown against the Maastricht bridges, motorised columns in St Omer and armoured fighting vehicles near Poix. Then, on Sunday, 23 June, the day after France surrendered, No107 Squadron attacked targets in the Ruhr and Stephens, who was aiming for Soest, was shot down. His Blenheim IV crashed in Holland and he was the only survivor.

Peter Edward Bressey was a former Imperial Airways pilot in the Reserve of Air Force Officers. He had been rounded up in May at Paris airport, trying to escape in a DC-3 along with a number of civilian pilots and cabin crews who would spend much of the war in prison camps.

***

The naval pilot, Derek Martin, had served as a Midshipman on the Skua-equipped Nos 800 and 801 Fleet Air Squadrons on the carrier HMS *Ark Royal*. On 7 May 1940, while he was on No801 Squadron, four Skuas — two from No801 and two from No803 squadron — took off from *Ark Royal* and intercepted four Heinkels from *III Gruppe*, which were bombing Ofotfjord. Between them, Martin and fellow-No801 pilot Lieutenant T E Gray shot down one of the Heinkels, peppering it with more than a hundred bullet-holes. When *Ark Royal* returned to Scapa Flow, No801 Squadron was transferred to Hatston and Martin, now commissioned, transferred to No800 Squadron, commanded by Major R T Partridge, DSO, of the Royal Marines.

On 8 June, the carrier HMS *Glorious*, en route from Bardufoss to Scapa Flow, is sighted by the *Scharnhorst* and *Gneisenau* as they are steaming to intercept Allied convoys evacuating troops from Norway. To the Germans this prize is a godsend, and they quickly seize the advantage. In a brisk engagement lasting slightly more than an hour, the *Glorious* and her twin-destroyer escort, the *Ardent* and *Acasta*, are sunk, with the loss of more than 1,500 men. Only forty-one men survive. It is a grave loss not only for the Navy but also for the RAF: the previous evening the pilots of No46 (Hurricane) Squadron, commanded by Squadron Leader K B B ("Bing") Cross, and No263 (Gladiator) Squadron, led by Squadron Leader J W ("Baldy") Donaldson, had flown their aircraft aboard the *Glorious* rather than abandon them in Norway. Cross survives, and will go on to have a distinguished career, but of the 1,207 killed or missing in *Glorious* alone, eighteen pilots are lost, along with forty-one other RAF personnel.

Even as the survivors are being plucked out of the sea, the Admiralty is bent on revenge. Admiral of the Fleet Sir Charles Forbes orders the Vice-Admiral Air, L V ("Nutty") Wells CB,

DSO, on *Ark Royal*, to send its Skuas to attack the two battle-cruisers, which are nestling in Trondheim harbour with dozens of other vessels. It comes as no surprise to Lieutenant-Commander J Casson, the CO of No803, and his opposite number in No800 Squadron, Richard Partridge, when they are summoned, separately, by "Nutty" Wells, and ordered to put on a retaliatory raid. Both point out that there are now twenty-four hours of daylight over Norway and therefore no night- or cloud-cover for the Skuas, that Trondheim lies forty-five miles up the fjord, and that the target is well protected by Me109s and Me110s based at Vaernes. Unless they have fighter cover or diversionary action of some sort the operation will fail and the losses will be unacceptable. John Casson goes further and declares that he expects losses of fifty per cent. Wells says this is "a little pessimistic". But he has planned an attack on Vaernes airfield by four Bristol Beauforts from No18 Group, while six Blenheims from the same Group will escort the Skuas to the target and back.

In the event, what happens over Trondheim exceeds even Casson's worst fears. Six Skuas from No800 Squadron and nine from No803 take off at midnight on 12/13 June. They are scheduled to attack two hours later. Both squadrons circle in formation above the *Ark Royal* until they are joined by Casson, the last to take off, and who as senior commander will be leading the operation. Swinging around on a course for the Norwegian coast and Trondheim, they climb steadily until they reach 12,000 feet. The weather is good — too good — with a completely clear sky and maximum visibility. Ideally, they should approach the target at ground level, then climb to gain height for dive-bombing. But the Skua's rate of climb with a full load is slow — making it easy meat for enemy fighters. Casson's only option is to lead them in at high altitude, hope the Beauforts will perform their diversionary task, and in the confusion slip through and lead his own attack. Both he and Partridge have ordered that should the diversionary raid not occur, and they be jumped by enemy aircraft, the formation is to scatter and each Skua crew act independently, selecting the best available target. There shall be no rendezvous point afterwards. Each crew has been given a course back to the *Ark Royal* in case it has to find its own way.

They settle down to their most economical cruising speed of 140 to 150 knots. This will only be varied later when Casson's observer/air-gunner, Lieutenant P E Fanshawe, will announce a higher or lower speed to make sure they reach their target at exactly two o'clock.

An hour or so later they fly over their first landmark, the northern end of the island of Froya. When they reach the mainland, at about 12,000 feet, Casson leads them into a shallow dive, their speed building up to about 200 knots. They are about twenty-five miles from Trondheim and scheduled to arrive in another ten minutes, but they can see no Blenheim escort and no evidence of the diversionary attack on the Messerschmitt concentrations at Vaernes. Meanwhile, the fifteen Skuas, at 9,000 feet, are building up to 240 knots, and Casson is manoeuvring them into position so they will arrive at Trondheim on time and at the pre-arranged height of about 8,000 feet. Three minutes from their target, with the town clearly visible below them, John Casson and Richard Partridge know what they have always suspected: that they will have to go it alone.

Then the German ack-ack opens up — an intense barrage from a heavy concentration of ship and shore batteries. It is the fiercest barrage the Skua crews have ever seen. Each squadron from the *Ark Royal* loses four aircraft as a result of the raid on Trondheim, and of the sixteen men who fail to return only seven survive to become prisoners: John Casson, Richard Partridge, Peter Fanshawe, Lieutenants C H Filmer and Derek Martin, Sub-Lieutenant R E Bartlett, and Filmer's Observer, Midshipman T A McKee. Martin's is the fourth Skua lost. Two Me109s, barely visible as they approach from the black mass of mountain beyond Trondheim, get in his tail and he doesn't spot them until it is too late. His observer/gunner, Leading Airman W J Tremeer, has enough time to say: "Just a minute, sir," down the Gosport tubing before the fighters are upon them. Martin turns in to one fighter, and as a result the enemy's first burst misses him. But he hasn't seen the second fighter, whose bullets thud through the back of the Skua and under the seat between his legs. It is that burst that kills Tremeer. It also shoots away all Martin's control columns and the Skua goes into dive, which he is unable to arrest. He shouts: "Jump!" several times to Tremeer, unaware that he is already dead.

Martin himself bales out and descends safely by parachute into the fjord. A German seaplane lands close by and taxies towards him. Martin is very conscious of the machine-gun in the nose of the aircraft as it approaches, and waits nervously, expecting any second to be raked with gunfire. Eventually a German airman climbs down onto the port float, calls out in clear English: "Wait a minute," and throws Martin a rope. He climbs into the aircraft, under the pilot. Two Royal Navy seamen are already aboard, one of them a survivor from the destroyer *Ardent*, sunk with the *Glorious*. Both are in a dreadful state.

Martin travels to Germany separately from the other survivors of the Trondheim raid. He is reunited with them at Dulag Luft. But Casson and Partridge are kept on as members of the British Permanent staff. The rest are sent to Stalag Luft I, with the exception of Martin, who fetches up at Spangenberg.

(7)

Wednesday, 10 July, turns out to be an eventful day. At three o'clock that morning a rumour sweeps the camp that Germans are about to invade Britain — a depressing prospect for RAF aircrew who feel helpless in their country's darkest hour. Then, on morning *Appell*, it is announced that thirty of the RAF contingent are being moved to a camp built specially for them under Goering's orders. Their names are read out. The thirty are mainly those who were shot down during May and June, with one or two victims of the Norwegian campaign. They include the three Squadron Leaders Doran, Paddon and Turner, along with Peter Bressey, Gordon Clancy, Charlie Crews, Geoff Dodgshun, Bill Edwards, Grey-Smith, Duggie Hoare, Anthony Hudson, Hulton-Harrop, Arthur Imrie, Reg Jacoby, Des Laslett, William Lepine, James Leyden, Robert Macpherson, Roy Mullins, Alf Mungovan, Ian Murdoch, Henry Murray, Daniel O'Brien, David Osment, Tony Peach, Sam Pepys, "Pappy" Plant, Ian Potts, Bob Pumphrey, Bob Renison, Aubrey Roberts, Michael Roth, John Stephens, Howard Taylor, Don Thom, Norman Thomas, George Walker, Maurice Wells and Gordon Wright. From the Navy there is Lieutenant Martin.

Later in the day, Potts is released from the cooler, and that evening, cardboard-fibre suitcases mysteriously materialise in the canteen — one to a customer — at the exorbitant price of RM21 apiece. As Roth needs two to carry the contents of his recent parcels, he buys one and gives RM21 to Gordon Wright, the South African, who does not want a suitcase and buys another for him.

The prisoners are glad to be going. Perhaps they will be better looked-after in their new camp. Before leaving they organise a rowdy sing-song, joined by some of the Army officers, who do caricature sketches.

By starlight they muster in the castle's courtyard. Naval ratings hand out travelling rations — a third of a loaf of bread and a small smoked sausage per man. Then, accompanied by a sub-machinegun escort commanded by *Hauptmann* Gross, they trudge down the hill to Spangenberg railway station, where they clamber aboard train carriages old enough to be museum exhibits. Against their apple-green paint the lustre of solid brass door-handles gleams in the lamplight. Each carriage is split into two separate compartments, each with side-door exits and a toilet. There is no corridor. The prisoners sit on hard wooden seats, eight to a compartment, covered by two guards.

The three-hundred-mile journey to the Baltic coast takes thirty-two hours, most of them spent sitting in railway sidings with the windows closed. During the night they are shunted about the marshalling yards at Halle. Someone mutters: "Hope to God none of our silly buggers get any ideas about bombing this lot. That'd be the end."

From time to time, the guards tell them about their new camp. Built on the orders of Hermann Goering, Stalag Luft I is in Pomerania. The Baltic coast climate is healthy, and there will be plenty of potatoes — Pomerania is "potato country". Best of all, there are no dormitories, only two or three prisoners to a room.

At last, at 2.30pm on Friday, 12 July, the train pulls in to Barth's small but bustling station. *"Aussteigen!"* The weary prisoners alight, and are given *ersatz* coffee by ladies of the Red Cross. After a head-count and a lot of fussing from Gross, they trudge towards their new camp.

Gross goes on leave after handing over his prisoners, and does not return to Spangenberg until the morning of Tuesday, 16 July. Left behind at the castle are the '39 bag, most of those captured in Norway, some of those captured in France, and the Frenchman, Larmier. On Saturday the 20th, they are joined by yet more Army prisoners — a Padre and nine other officers. The old lags gather

116

round to hear the latest gen from home, only to discover that the newcomers have been captives since 29 May, when Carmiers hospital was overrun by the Germans, and have been marched in a column all the way to Germany.

The Lower Camp is by then bursting at the seams, as some thirty sailors have arrived to swell the ranks. Towards the end of July the dozen RAF NCO aircrew and the newly arrived sailors are taken to the railway station and put aboard cattle-trucks, destined for the grim fortresses of Posen. The French NCOs are also purged, some going to Stalag Luft I, and some to Stalag IIA at Neu Brandenburg.

Chapter Four

Requiescat in Rumour

Oflag IXA/H, Spangenberg, July 1940–March 1941

> *Twilight and evening bell,*
> *   And after that the dark!*
> *And may there be no sadness of farewell,*
> *   When I embark;*
>
> *For tho' from out our bourne of Time and Place*
> *   The flood may bear me far,*
> *I hope to see my Pilot face to face*
> *   When I have crossed the bar.*
>
>   Alfred, Lord Tennyson, *Crossing the Bar*

Despite the existence of the all-aircrew camp at Barth, the RAF prisoners had not heard the last of Army camps. The bulk of them were still under the authority of the Army until Stalag Luft III started up in April 1942. Even in July 1940, when Stalag Luft I opened, some RAF and Fleet Air Arm officers had remained behind at Spangenberg. They included all those taken prisoner from September to November 1939: Squadron Leader "Wank" Murray; Flying Officers Colin MacLachlan and John Tilsley; Pilot Officers "Pop" Bewlay, Bob Coste, Laurence Edwards, Heaton-Nichols and Alf Thompson, and Sergeant Larry Slattery. Of the officer aircrew taken during 1940 operations over Germany and the campaigns in Norway, France and the Low Countries, the following were among those left behind at Spangenberg after the 10 July purge to Barth: Flying Officers William Donaldson, Warren Hayward, Donald Middleton and Ken Murphy; and Pilot Officers John Glover, Frank Hugill, Len Miller DFC, Keith Milne, Edward Walker, "Hank" Wardle and John Whilton.

Conditions in the *Hauptlager* at Spangenberg remained grim for some time. Red Cross parcels were being sent for only thirty officers — not the full complement of some two hundred — and the shortage of food and tobacco was making prisoners ill tempered. For lunch there was a little piece of pork, some peas, potatoes and mustard. Dinner was usually good — an *ersatz* sausage, two slices of bread and, again, peas and potatoes. Sparse though the German rations already were, they were often cut, and some mornings the prisoners had to eat breakfast without jam.

On Sunday, 14 July, Larry Slattery, on the violin, and an Army officer on the piano treated their fellow kriegies to a duet. Even the sentries on the far side of the moat craned their necks to listen, along with a German officer and his wife and daughter who had come to throw food to the wild boars. Two days later a lorry suddenly appeared under the archway laden with blankets and German and Polish tobacco and cigarettes, which were to be issued through the camp canteen at the rate of one blanket per man costing RM7, 20 *Pfennige*, and two cigars, eleven cigarettes and one-third of a packet of tobacco per man at RM1, 70 *Pfennige*. There was also a slight improvement in the evening meal: six potatoes, a piece of lettuce, blood sausage and a good butter ration.

The prisoners didn't know whether to laugh or cry about the cigarette ration. Sometimes they were issued with four German cigarettes a day, manufactured in 1924, at other times they were Polish, five a day at 10 *Pfennige*. Rumour had it that these were part of a consignment of 17,000, which the canteen could only afford to pay for by selling large quantities of beer.

By Sunday the 21st the prisoners were back on short rations for dinner. New prisoners were still not receiving mail or personal parcels and on Saturday, 3 August they asked Squadron Leader Murray if it was worth writing to the American Embassy in Berlin about the situation. He told them it would do little good. That night the canteen issued wine at RM4 a bottle, but there were few takers; it was too expensive, and in any case the prisoners had too little food in their stomachs to absorb it. The next day — a Sunday — morning *Appell* was held up because someone was missing from parade, and one of the Army officers fainted. But the meals that day were an improvement: for dinner, beans as well as potatoes and a sliver of meat; for tea, soup and hot sausage; and for supper, bread, butter, ham and condensed milk. However, during the week the bread ration was cut, and on Tuesday, 6 August, the German *Arzt* (doctor), who had arrived the previous day, said he was going to send a written complaint to Berlin. He was distressed at the condition of the prisoners, and sent one of them, George Skelton, to hospital because of the bad injury to his arm when he was shot down. He insisted that Skelton travel by aircraft and not by car, as the journey would jolt him too much. Skelton would eventually be sent from hospital to Stalag Luft I, but it would be two years before he could use his arm and in 1943 he would be repatriated.

On Saturday, 17 August, at 6pm, a lorry full of Red Cross parcels arrived and the prisoners surrounded it shouting with excitement. The parcels contained jam, condensed milk, chocolate powder, tinned plums, greengages and rusk biscuits, all from Switzerland. During the following week more parcels arrived, containing food and cigarettes (but no matches), and mail was issued.

That August, three RAF officers made the first coherent escape attempts from the *Schloss*. On the way to the gymnasium, which stood on the far side of the moat, "Hank" Wardle, one of the Canadians, climbed the high barricade and made a run for it under a hail of bullets. He was recaptured the next day when he blundered into German soldiers guarding a railway crossing. They kicked him and beat him with rifle butts, leaving him with impaired hearing and a limp. Don Middleton and Keith Milne bluffed their way through the gate by disguising themselves as civilian painters, complete with buckets of paint and a ladder, which they carried between them. Waiting until a simple-looking guard was posted, they walked past, mouthing the only German they knew, and he let them pass. Outside the castle, and half-way down the hill, they dumped the ladder and buckets, ran into the woods and doffed their disguises to reveal uniforms roughly converted into civvies. They were caught a few hours later. Their captors were particularly vengeful, not only meting out to them the same treatment as Wardle had received but also parading them through the streets to be jeered and spat at by local residents.

(2)

Stalag Luft I had been open less than two months when the Germans again started sending aircrew officers to Oflag IXA/H. The first of these purges left Dulag Luft at the end of August 1940, and included Flight Lieutenants J C Bowman and M J Fisher, RAFVR; Flying Officers R C D McKenzie, W M Nixon and P G Whitby; Pilot Officers P G Brodie, P W Cook, T F S Johnson, G Parker, J W P Perkins, R Roberts, H A T Skehill and R D Wawn; Lieutenant A Taylor, RN; Sub-Lieutenant (A) R L G Davies, RN; and Lieutenant N M Hearle, Royal Marines.

One of these officers, Robert Clifford Douglas McKenzie, had been captured during the campaign in the Low Countries and France. He had flown Blenheims in the ill-fated No82 Squadron, Watton. On Saturday, 8 June, the squadron was given the task of bombing troops, transport, tanks and houses near Horroy. The idea behind bombing the houses was to block the roads through the villages with falling masonry and rubble, thus holding up the Germans' advance. Taking off at 1022 hours, the aircraft formed up over Watton and headed for North Weald, where they linked up with Blenheims from No21 Squadron, and along with a fighter escort, set a course for France. They reached the target unmolested, but over Horroy encountered intense flak. One Blenheim from each squadron was shot down. McKenzie crashed near Eplessier, three kilometres north-west of Poix. His observer was killed but his air-gunner, Sergeant Crozier, survived.

The rest had entered captivity after the fall of France. Some had been crewed up with officers who had been sent to Barth. John Walker Philip Perkins had been "second dickey" to Pilot Officer R A G Willis, a Wellington pilot in No99 (Madras Presidency) Squadron, Newmarket (No3 Group). They were bagged on 5/6 July when Bomber Command ordered fifty-one aircraft to lay mines in Kiel Bay. One of Willis's crew was killed, but the rest, including Phil Perkins, and Sergeants K A R MacArthur and C J Scanlon, went into kriegiedom with him. Although Willis and the other survivors were sent to Barth shortly after their arrival, Perkins remained more than thirteen weeks at Dulag Luft before being purged to Spangenberg.

Lieutenant Taylor, who had recently been commissioned from the rank of Midshipman and was the spitting image of Mickey Rooney, had flown Fairey Battles in No142 Squadron, based at Eastchurch. On 22 August, the squadron, part of No1 Group, carried out two raids on E-boats in Boulogne harbour — one in the morning, and the other in the evening. These were the only No1 Group Fairey Battles operations that day. The dawn raiders encountered bad weather, and although some of them bombed they were unable to determine the results. So, that evening, Taylor, along with five other pilots, was sent out on a second raid, taking off at 1825 hours. By now the element of surprise had been lost, and the two flights met an intense flak barrage. Once again, three dropped bombs but were unable to observe the results. Taylor's Battle was hit by flak, killing his air-gunner, Sergeant L M Lowrey. But Taylor and his observer, Pilot Officer A G Middleton, survived. Like Willis, Middleton, too, was sent to Stalag Luft I. The policy of the Luftwaffe, it seemed, was to separate crews — perhaps to prevent ready-made partnerships preparing for escape attempts. George Parker was yet another Blenheim pilot, this time on No40 Squadron at Wyton. He was shot down on 14/15 August when the squadron attacked an oil refinery at Chartres. His crew evaded capture, returning to England via Spain and Gibraltar.

John Charles Bowman was an RAF regular who had served with No83 Squadron at Scampton since before the war. A cheerful, round-faced youngster, he had quite a hard luck story to spin. He had been a gunner in one of the squadron's Hampdens sent to bomb Kiel on 21 July 1940. About 5,000 feet over the harbour, the Hampden was caught by several searchlights. The pilot twisted and turned the Hampden all over the sky in an effort to clear the searchlights, eventually dropping to about five hundred feet, and still the searchlights clung like tentacles. Flak was bursting round the Hampden in venomous concentration, scoring several hits. Then the pilot's voice came loud and clear over the intercom: "Jump, Bowman! Jump for it!" By now they were dangerously low and there wasn't much time, but Bowman found he couldn't open his escape hatch. He called back over the intercom that it was jammed, but as there was no reply from the pilot he again heaved at the hatch, in a cold sweat, until suddenly it opened and he tumbled out. His parachute opened in the nick of time, but he landed heavily and broke his left leg. The Germans who found him said the Hampden had dived into the sea just seconds after he had baled out. There was no sign of the rest of the crew. During the next few weeks, while in hospital, Bowman brooded miserably on the probability that they had all bought it. Then he was sent on to Dulag Luft, and the first person he met when he came out of solitary was Pilot Officer I M ("Muckle") Muir, who had been navigator of the Hampden.

"Why, hello Tim," beamed Bowman gladly. "So you got out of the kite okay. It's good to see you. What happened to the rest?"

"Got out of the kite?" echoed Muir. "Gosh man! The skipper got the kite back under control just after you'd baled out and we all got home. I joined another crew and was shot down later. The rest are still in England."

Bowman was to reflect upon this with a gnashing of teeth for the next five years. (He was not to meet Muir again for nearly three years. Muir was sent to Barth, thence, in April 1942, to East Compound, Stalag Luft III. A year later he transferred to the new North Compound. In the meantime, Bowman had been shunted from Spangenberg to Thorn, back to Spangenberg, then to Warburg and then to Oflag XXIB at Schubin. When Schubin was cleared in April 1943 he finally reached North Compound, where Muir was already ensconced.)

Ralph Roberts, a fighter pilot, had been between postings when he was shot down during the Battle of Britain. He had been flying with No615 Squadron and was awaiting ratification of a posting to No616 Squadron. In the meantime, he was asked to fly with No64 Squadron at Kenley as it was short of pilots. On Tuesday, 13 August he claimed a Do17, but two days later, while on an offensive patrol, he got into a scrape over Calais-Marck with two Me109s at 1525 hours and was himself shot down.

Maurice John Fisher, William Maxwell Nixon, Peter George Whitby and Henry Aidan Thomas

Skehill were all shot down on the same night, 16/17 August, when Bomber Command put on a maximum effort against a wide range of targets in Holland and Germany. A hundred and fifty aircraft — an assortment of Blenheims, Hampdens, Wellingtons and Whitleys — took part, with No4 Group going for factories at Jena and Augsburg and the Bohlen power station. Seven aircraft were lost. Nixon and Whitby were pilot and second dickey in a Whitley from No10 Squadron, Leeming, nine crews from which were sent to bomb the Zeiss optical works at Jena. The other members of their crew were Sergeants H W Bradley, A W Somerville and E R Holmes. Taking off from Leeming at 2035 hours, they had the good fortune to reach Jena unmolested and encountered only light flak over the target. However, Nixon's aircraft developed engine trouble, and at 0300 hours he told his wireless-operator, Somerville, to tap out an SOS, which Leeming received. Nixon made it to the target and bombed from 5,000 feet. Somerville tapped out another message to Leeming reporting that they had bombed on target, and Nixon turned for home. However, over Holland they were hit by flak and it became clear to Nixon that the Whitley would not make it. At 0324 hours he got Somerville to send another SOS. Eventually Nixon force-landed the Whitley twenty miles from Zeugenbergen. The crew escaped without injury and were on the run for more than twenty-four hours before being picked up by the Germans, who had offered a reward over the radio for their capture.

Aidan Skehill's Hampden, from No144 Squadron, Hemswell, was shot down attacking Merseburg. Two of his crew were killed, and one survived to enter captivity with him. Maurice Fisher had been an observer in a Wellington from No149 Squadron, Mildenhall, which had bombed Koleda. The pilot, second-pilot and rear-gunner were killed, but the two WOP/AGs survived.

The night of 19/20 August saw another maximum effort when a hundred and twenty aircraft attacked targets in Belgium, France, Holland and Germany. Philip Willsteed Cook, a Battle pilot from No12 Squadron, Binbrook, was captured attacking enemy invasion barges at Boulogne. His observer and air-gunner survived. The Germans also captured another entire Whitley crew that night: Pilot Officers Peter Gascoyne ("Butch") Brodie and Theo Faire Storer Johnson, a New Zealander, and Sergeants T Entwistle, G P White and W A Kelham from No51 Squadron, Dishforth. Johnson was the least experienced member of the crew, having flown only one previous trip. Born in Wellington, NZ, on 21 May 1919, he moved to Hamilton with his parents at the age of two. After leaving school and joining the Civil Service, where he worked in the State Insurance Department, he learnt to fly near his home town. On joining the RNZAF, he trained at Wigram, and was one of thirty-six pilots who left New Zealand in March 1940 in the first RNZAF contingent bound for England. He hated flying bombers, and the thought of killing women and children gave him nightmares.

At 2010 hours on Monday, 19 August, ten Whitleys from No51 Squadron and six from No78 Squadron took off to bomb the power station at Zohornewitz. One of No51 Squadron's aircraft returned early, while the rest bombed the target. Brodie's aircraft was damaged by flak after bombing, and he ditched in the Ijsselmeer, the crew escaping unhurt. They scrambled aboard their rubber dinghy and rowed round in circles until at last they were picked up by a German patrol boat.

***

Lieutenant Nathaniel Hearle and Sub-Lieutenant Rupert ("Pud") Davies had been pilot and observer in a Swordfish from No812 Squadron, attached to RAF Coastal Command at North Coates. They had flown their last sortie together on Thursday, 22 August on a mine-laying operation off Holland. It was a stormy night, and their altimeter had been reading 200° off true. Way off course, they had run out of fuel and ditched in the North Sea. They spent fourteen hours in their rubber dinghy before being picked up by a German tanker and being landed in Holland.

"Pud" Davies was an amazing character. A portly Welshman, he had served an apprenticeship on the *Worcester* at Greenhithe, trained for the Merchant Navy, then entered the Royal Navy and finally transferred to the flying branch. He had later served on the carrier *Glorious*. John Casson, who encountered Davies while on the British Permanent Staff at Dulag Luft, takes up the story:

My first remembered meeting with "Pud" was on an evening in the autumn of 1940 soon after he had been captured. He had had the misfortune to come down in the sea off the coast of Holland while flying as an observer in a "string-bag" Swordfish that had got lost. "Pud" always called it "pilot error", but as he was the navigator there might be two opinions about his diagnosis. They floated around in a leaking rubber dinghy for nearly two days [sic] and were finally picked up by a passing German tanker when he was probably told by his captors, as we all were, "For you the war is over." And so he arrived at Dulag Luft. I remember walking into a room to meet the "new naval arrival" and saw a stalwart figure seated on a bench banging a table with enamel mugs held one in each hand. Out of his mouth came the sounds of the scream of falling bombs, the whistles of bullets and ricochets and other unidentifiable noises. This was "Pud" doing his air-raid turn. It was my first encounter with his genius for mimicry. He could imitate almost anything or anybody — and he would, too, if only you gave him the floor!

Robert David Wawn, a Hampden pilot in No50 Squadron, Lindholme, was shot down on Bomber Command's first raid on Berlin on 25/26 August. About fifty aircraft, mostly Hampdens and Wellingtons, took part, stretching the former to the limit of their fuel capacity. Thick cloud over Berlin prevented accurate bombing, most bombs falling in the country and farmlands to the south and only two falling within the city limits, destroying a wooden summer-house in the suburb of Rosenthal. On the return leg the aircraft encountered strong headwinds, which blew them off-course, and six Hampdens were lost. At 0412 hours Wawn's WOP/AG asked for a bearing. His message was heard by RAF Heston, but the Hampden ran out of fuel and Wawn force-landed at 0634 hours near Lautersheim in Germany. He and his crew escaped without injury.

(3)

It was just as well, in view of the number of aircrew arriving, that Red Cross parcels had been issued. The food, especially the condensed milk, made a great deal of difference, giving the prisoners more energy and increasing their interest in what little was going on in the castle. They read, drew, painted, and went on parole walks. Several officers in the August purge set up a gambling syndicate, betting on cards with their *Lagergeld*. Theo Johnson lost £100 at poker and was so angry with himself that he settled down to win it back and afterwards stayed clear of high stakes, although his games of bridge and chess lasted for days and weeks at a time.

But despite the parcels they were still losing weight, walking tired them out, and food was still the abiding topic of conversation. Hygiene was also a problem: their laundry was rarely taken away and a cake of soap had to last for three months. As autumn came, it brought with it a beautiful view of Spangenberg village, peeping out of the mist in the valley, and the russet leaves on the abundant trees. But it would soon bring in its train cold weather, and prisoners would need all the food they could get.

On Saturday, 8 September, the canteen issued forty cigarettes per man — French *Caporals* — which were very satisfying. But the fish-cheese for supper would have made the prisoners sick had they not been so hungry. The following day the RAF contingent had cause for jubilation: mail from home. But during the week the food situation had again deteriorated. The Red Cross supplies had been exhausted and the prisoners were reliant on meagre German rations. Having tasted the luxury of Red Cross food, they found the German issue all the less palatable. They still had plenty of cigarettes, but matches were scarce. On Sunday, 15 September they held an Arts and Crafts Exhibition, comprising models, knitting, portraits, landscapes and sketches of fruit and flowers.

The next morning the one hundred and fifty Army officers were moved to the *Unterlager* at Elbersdorf, where Army officers captured at Dunkirk had been accommodated in June 1940. Although the RAF, Fleet Air Arm and Merchant Navy contingents were remaining in the castle, all prisoners were told on morning *Appell* to hand in all canteen issue blankets and towels, even those prisoners who had bought theirs with the *Lagergeld* deducted from their service pay. Many had hidden the blankets and towels under mattresses and had to return to their rooms to get them. The weather was already bitterly cold, and the parade lasted for an hour and a half.

For the next five months the Upper Camp accommodated only RAF and Royal and Merchant Navy prisoners, including the submarine arm and the Fleet Air Arm. On Tuesday, 22 October these contingents were supplemented by yet another batch of twenty-six officers from Dulag Luft, which included: Squadron Leader A O Bridgman DFC; Acting Squadron Leader R N Wardell; Flight Lieutenants F W S Keighley, J R T Smalley DFC, and T E Syms; Acting Flight Lieutenant P F R Vaillant; Pilot Officers H R Bjelke-Peterson, RAFVR, F D Flinn, J E A Foster, RAFVR, A H Gould DFC, D K Hayes, I C Kirk, A W Matthews, B T J Newland and A J J Steel; Lieutenant-Commanders O S Stevinson and N R Quill, RN; Lieutenants (A) A O Atkins, RN, (A) M A J J Hanrahan, RN, and J C W Iliffe, RN; and Sub-Lieutenants (A) H A Cheetham, RN, (A) H Deterding, RNVR, (A) H N C Hearn, RN, and (A) D A Poynter, RN.

Albert William Matthews, who hailed from Moncton, New Brunswick, had been in No12 Squadron at Amifontaine back in May. On Friday the 10th, four crews were briefed to carry out an attack on a strong German motorised column on the Luxembourg-Junglinster road, which had already been bombed that day by Blenheims with heavy losses but no discernible results. They took off in two half-sections between 1700 and 1715 hours. One was hit before reaching the target and had to force-land at Piennes. Another dropped his bombs at low level, meeting intense ground fire, which wounded his observer. Al Matthews and his Flight Commander hedge-hopped towards the target to avoid detection by German ground observers and hostile fighters; they were fired upon by German motorcyclists — probably advanced scouting parties from the column they were seeking — but flew on unscathed. Flying down a wooded valley and hopping like sparrows over the rise at the far end, they saw a crescent-shaped wood through which ran the road from Germany to Luxembourg. Then they caught sight of the column, which had halted on the road. As they made their run-in — the Flight Commander leading — Matthews' Battle caught a packet from cannon-shells and he was knocked out by a shell fragment striking him on the forehead. Trailing white smoke, his aircraft went into a dive, bellied in, and slithered to a halt behind a belt of trees. The observer, Sergeant A A Maderson, had received a shell fragment in his elbow, smashing it, but the gunner, LAC J C Senior, was uninjured. From the wrecked aircraft Jack Senior shot up the column until he was hit by an armour-piercing bullet. The three airmen were then taken prisoner, the Germans fêting Senior as a hero.

Upon arrival at Dulag Luft, all three were admitted to Hohemark clinic. Matthews' head-wound had left him concussed. Jack Senior had a bullet-wound that required urgent attention. (He would then be sent to Stalag Luft I.) Sergeant Maderson needed treatment for his shattered elbow; he would later be transferred to the *Lazarett* attached to Stalag IXC at Bad Sulza and eventually be slated for repatriation on medical grounds.

One of the most colourful and extraordinary characters on this purge was thirty-six-year-old Pilot Officer Joseph Eric Arthur Foster, an air-gunner in the Volunteer Reserve. Born in London of a Swiss mother and a father who was one of England's top hairdressers and wig-makers, with exclusive premises in Sloane Street, Eric Foster had travelled extensively in Europe between the wars and in 1926 had actually met William Joyce, later to be known as "Lord Haw-Haw". As well as joining a glider club, he was a keen mountaineer, and in 1928, 1932 and 1933 attempted solo ascents of the 13,669-foot-high Jungfrau, despite a leg injury that would dog him for many years. After failing each time, he concentrated on his work, following his father's footsteps into the hair and beauty profession, and inventing the Trichoscope, for projecting active microscope slides during lectures, and the Trichometer, a device for measuring the tensile strength of human hair. He also had time to build his own light aircraft, which he flew at Heston. Shortly before the war he married a Danish woman, who he had met in Copenhagen, and joined the RAFVR, being commissioned Pilot Officer on 20 April 1940. He was posted to No38 Squadron, Marham, as a rear-gunner.

On 14/15 June Bomber Command put up twenty-four Wellingtons and five Hampdens against a variety of targets in Germany; Foster's pilot, Sergeant L A Morris, along with the rest of the crew, had volunteered to go on the night's raid despite the fact that they had taken part in an attack on the marshalling yards at Cologne the previous night. Morris took off in his Wellington IA at 2224 hours to bomb the Black Forest. The flight out was uneventful, but over the Schwarzwald at 12,000 feet they were boxed in by searchlights and the flak soon found its range. Two shells hit the Wimpey and set it alight. The aircraft turned and went into a shallow dive, tossing the crew about like corks in a bottle. Morris and one of the WOP/AGs, Sergeant R J Baghurst, were already dead, and Foster was wounded in the same leg that he had injured back in 1928. Sergeant J D Foulser, the remaining WOP/AG, shouted over the intercom: "The radio's gone west."

Despite the fact that the Wimpey had obviously "had it", and its dive was getting steeper, the flak kept up its barrage, and at 400 feet over Belgium one of the crew shouted: "Jump, everybody, jump! Hurry!" The remaining crew needed no further persuading. The second pilot, Sergeant W Stevens; the observer, Sergeant N Packer; and Sergeant Foulser all baled out, but Foster was sucked out by the slipstream at a dangerously low level. His parachute deployed in the nick of time. He made a heavy landing in a damp pine forest. Despite broken bones and a shrapnel wound, he burned all his papers and tried to escape from the area, crawling on all fours. By dawn, however, he was too weak to go on. He had lost a lot of blood, his head was splitting, his legs and ankles had swollen, and every movement brought pain. He slithered towards a farmhouse, weakly shouting: "Hallo," then pushed the front door open and literally fell into the hall — noticing, as he tried to call out again, a *feldgrau* uniform hanging on the wall.

There were several German soldiers in the house, and one of them asked (in German) who he was. He told them he was an English *Flieger* who had descended by parachute. *"Fallschirmjäger,"* they muttered; "Parachutist. Then where are your prisoners?" Foster then had to explain that it was he who was the prisoner, and that he was injured and wounded. He then collapsed and one of the soldiers examined his legs. They were broken. As gently as they could, three of the soldiers carried him to a bed in the front room and tried, unsuccessfully, to remove his flying boots and Sidcot flying suit. They gave him a cigarette, told him he had come down near Neufchâteau, and then turned out his pockets and examined their contents. They seemed to be regarding him as an object of curiosity, and he had continually to ask them to fetch a doctor. Finally, at 11am, the doctor arrived and had him removed to the village dressing station in Florenville, in the Ardennes Forest, where the shrapnel was removed from his knee and his wounds were cleaned and dressed. He was then put in the back seat of a car, bound for Arlon hospital, with his legs supported by a plank of wood, which rested at an angle on the front passenger seat. The ride to Arlon over the shell-cratered roads was agony. On the way they stopped and met the flak officer who had shot Foster down. He made a half-hearted attempt to question Foster, who merely gave the regulation service replies: name, rank and number.

Arlon hospital was crammed with wounded soldiers, both Axis and Allied, clothed only in white sheets. Foster was given a straw mattress and a single blanket on an open balcony. He lay there shivering for two hours, without being permitted another blanket or allowed to wash, until the doctor brought along four Luftwaffe officers who had his wounds dressed again and had him placed in another car. (In fact, a Luftwaffe general's staff car.)

The officers told him this leg of his journey would not be very long, but when they arranged him in his seat as comfortably as his condition allowed and fixed him up with cigarettes he knew he was in for a long ride. Most of the time, instead of attempting to make any real progress, they craned their heads out of the windows, looking for the rest of his crew. Eventually, after hours spent in futile detours, they arrived on the evening of Saturday, 5 June, at a village school that had been converted into a temporary hospital. They offered him some food but he was too sick to eat it; although it was a bright summer's evening he was shaking, whether from cold or shock he wasn't sure. After making a number of phone calls one of the officers bade him "Goodnight," and told him they would be flying him to Germany the next morning. However, at 10pm a nurse arrived and helped him dress, and two more Luftwaffe officers turned up to interrogate him. He was put on a stretcher and carried to an ambulance to commence the journey to Dulag Luft — 288 kilometres (179 miles) away — by road. He was covered with his torn parachute, which had been recovered by Luftwaffe personnel from a nearby airbase. Finally, at 1400 hours on Monday, 17 June, they arrived at the Hohemark clinic, where the first aircrew prisoners he saw were John Madge, who had been shot down in May on the same op as Alf Mungovan, and Flying Officer D A J Foster, shot down on 14 May. (This Foster, Donald, a Canadian and no relation to Eric, would eventually be sent to Barth.)

There were several other injured and wounded in the Hohemark at that time, some of whom would reach Spangenberg before Eric Foster and others of whom would be sent to Barth or Stalag VIIIB, Lamsdorf. They included Captain Richard Partridge; Major J B Dodge DSC, MC, of the Middlesex Regiment; Flight Lieutenants P G Leeson and George Skelton, and a sprinkling of NCOs and other ranks. Between them, they helped Eric Foster make the first coherent attempt to escape from the Hohemark, which was no mean achievement considering the condition Foster and his compatriots were in. But Foster did not get very far, twisting his damaged ankle again, and had to give himself up at 6am. As a reward for his efforts, he was sent to the solitary confinement cells but, surprisingly, was not purged for another four months. He would go on to become one of the RAF's most persistent escapers, though he received scant recognition for his efforts.

* * *

Pilot Officer Alexander Herbert Gould DFC was a New Zealander who had studied agriculture in Australia and spent a year in the infantry militia before joining the RAF on a short-service commission. Training at Netheravon, he had been one of Harry Day's pupils before seeing service at Rissington, Manston and Hemswell, where two of No5 Group's Hampden Squadrons, Nos 61 and 144, were stationed. Gould joined "B" Flight, No61 Squadron.

He was finally shot down on a "Gardening" operation on 20/21 July. This operation arose from Hitler's Reichstag speech, "My last appeal to reason", in which he offered Britain an Armistice. The speech was broadcast by the BBC on Friday, 19 July, with some humorous commentary and an outright rejection. That night Gould spoke with a priest at Lincoln Cathedral, who clearly indicated that his superiors down south had already prayed for an end to hostilities.

The following morning Gould and his crew — Pilot Officer D S Carnegie, and Sergeants J F Cowan and J N Prendergast — do a forty-minute night-flying, wireless and bomb-sight test, loaded with four 500lb and two 250lb general purpose bombs. About mid-afternoon crews are briefed to carry out an attack on shipping from 13,000 feet as a diversion for another low-level attack. However, at teatime another briefing is announced for captains only. The Group Captain, Rice, has selected fifteen crews from both squadrons to make a low-level attack on the *Tirpitz* and *Admiral Scheer* lying in harbour at Wilhelmshaven. Three aircraft from each squadron will make diversionary attacks, while three from each will attack the *Tirpitz*, and two from 61 Squadron and one from 144 Squadron will go for the *Admiral Scheer*. They should arrive at Wilhelmshaven just after midnight, approach the harbour from different directions, and drop their mines individually. Apparently, Churchill has announced to Air Vice-Marshal Arthur Harris, AOC No5 Group, that he wants this attack to be Britain's answer to Hitler. He will be refusing debate on the issue in the Commons.

The aircraft carrying out the main attack will sow Barnes Wallis's new "Special M" mines — modified sea mines with their normal detonating mechanisms replaced by fuses that will be activated by salt water after forty minutes' immersion. Each mine weighs 1500lb, with an explosive charge of 750lb of TNT. The mines must be dropped from as near to the ships as possible so that when they explode on the seabed they will cause the maximum damage to their keels, more vulnerable than their hulls because they have less armour-plating.

The briefing takes place in a state of panic. There is not enough time to change the bomb-load in Gould's aircraft, so he will take another kite, Hampden P4358, normally flown by Alex Webster. He is to approach the target from the south, passing the Jade Bucht lightship. However, photos taken that afternoon by a Spitfire PRI from the Photographic Reconnaissance Unit at Heston, and the latest Met reports, indicate a full moon, with only slight haze. Wilhelmshaven is the most strongly defended port in Germany, and in the bright moonlight and fairly clear sky the Hampdens will be sitting ducks. Gould requests permission for a westerly approach, but Rice's simple retort is: "Gould, you obey orders!"

Wallis, who is present at the briefing, is most enthusiastic about his new mines. "They must be released at 150 Indicated Air Speed and at 150 feet," he pipes up, "and at an angle of 45 degrees. Otherwise, the parachutes slowing their descent will be torn off and the mines will disintegrate on impact."

The parachutes, though, are smaller than usual. Gould queries the height, speed and angle, as normally mines are dropped from 400 to 1,000 feet at up to 200 IAS. But Wallis assures him they will work smoothly. Gould then expresses concern about the enemy's gantries and balloon-cables.

"Oh, you'll clear them," says Rice. "Hampden P4358 is equipped with cable-cutters."

It is apparent to Gould that the only simple thing about the operation is that the instructions for the fusing of the mines seem clear.

Cowan does a splendid job of navigation, taking them amidships over the German battle-cruiser *Admiral Scheer*. However, Gould's prediction that they will offer the Germans a tempting target proves correct. At midnight, as they approach the first docks, they see three destroyers anchored offshore in line abreast. The destroyers put up a terrific barrage and the Hampden is shot to hell, with both engines on fire.

When they have dropped their bombs, Cowan enquires, optimistically: "Do you want a course home?"

"I'll try to land on the beach," blurts Gould.

However, the intercom suddenly goes dead and Cowan does not hear the reply.

Despite the flames, there is still some power in the port engine and Gould manages to hold height. Passing over a stone shed, which he can see clearly through the flames, Gould pulls everything back and stalls, with nose up, on the mudflats. Cowan is thrown out and lands about ten feet away. The tide is out and he is bogged down. Gould scrambles out, forgetting to unclip his parachute harness, and tries to pull Cowan to dry sand. Until he realises his error and unbuckles his 'chute, it is a considerable struggle. When he has dragged Cowan to safety Cowan is completely covered in mud. But at least it protects him from the flames. Then they see Neil Prendergast, still in the astro-hatch, and yell at him to get out quickly. When Prendergast finally climbs down, Gould suggests he cover his hands and face with mud. Carnegie is dead. They find his body in the flightpath behind the wreckage. He looks as if he has been cut in half. He was either thrown from the aircraft as it crashed or tried to jump out beforehand, as he appears to have made an attempt to crawl towards it.

The survivors barely have time to gather their wits before a German Army officer, with two soldiers, comes squelching through the mud towards them. Indicating a small car on a track nearby, they are shouting *"Schnell! Schnell!"* They also round up the survivors from two more stricken Hampdens, Pilot Officer D H Davis, and Pilot Officer K Jones and his crew.

When Gould emerges from the cooler at Dulag Luft he hears that Churchill's official rejection of Hitler's peace offer was delivered by Lord Halifax over the BBC on Tuesday, 23 July. A day or so later Gould is marched off to see Rumpel, who tells him that Goering has telephoned and asked for prisoners' views of Hitler's Reichstag speech. Gould lies to Rumpel, claiming he has not heard it.

From then until October Alex Gould was attached to the British Permanent Staff, ostensibly as "Gardens Officer", but in reality, with his knowledge of geology, to help site a tunnel "Wings" Day was planning. He was pretty browned off when, without warning, the Jerries put his name on the list of prisoners bound for Spangenberg. Why he was suddenly purged from Dulag Luft he never did find out.

***

Four members of this purge were from Wing Commander the Earl of Bandon's No82 Squadron, Watton — recently re-formed after being almost wiped out on a daylight operation on 17 May. The first, Frederick William Spink Keighley, had been an engineer in his father's business in Darlington before joining the RAF with a short-service commission on his third application in 1936. He went on to fly the RAF's complete range of obsolete medium-bombers — the Fairey Gordon, the Vickers Wellesley, the Fairey Battle, and finally the Blenheim. But he reached No2 Group's No82 Squadron, based at Watton, on 20 June 1940 with very little experience of flying with a full bomb-load. Although Bomber Command's Operational Research Section had reported the squadron's morale astonishingly buoyant, it had in fact suffered a high death rate from flying accidents and no crew had yet lived to complete a tour of ops. Bill Keighley found that those who survived longest were those who thought least. For his part, he did not expect to last a tour.

He was in fact shot down on his ninth op, a daylight attack by four of the squadron's Blenheims on oil refineries at Hamburg on Monday, 29 July 1940. On take-off he flew through a covey of Norfolk's ubiquitous partridges, downing them all. A man who disliked killing, he felt they were in for a bad day.

The four Blenheims flew eastwards across the North Sea, then turned south on the dog-leg approach to Hamburg. The sky ahead was completely clear — not a wisp of cloud cover in sight. Only one crew risked an attack, closing in to bomb, missing the target, then narrowly escaping a pursuing gaggle of Messerschmitts. Keighley and his crew decided to divert to the secondary target, Leuwarden airfield in northern Holland. They bombed from 2,000 feet, then set course for home. After turning south-west across the coast Keighley heard the gunner, Sergeant K D MacPherson, report two Me110s closing fast. Pulling the 9lb boost lever, Keighley pushed the Blenheim through the gate towards a friendly peninsula of land. But it was soon clear to him that he would lose the race. Still minutes short of safety, Keighley felt the Blenheim shudder as the first bursts of fire began to clatter through the fuselage. As he pushed the aircraft into a steep dive for the sea, he heard an agonising cry from MacPherson: "I'm hit! I can't see!" MacPherson's turret guns hadn't fired a single shot. His intercom was dead. The German fighters came in for a second attack. They kept it up for almost five minutes, their cannon-fire ripping through the fuselage, shattering the windscreen and riddling the engine nacelles. Keighley felt splinters puncturing his leg and back.

Then suddenly they were in cloud and Keighley, oblivious of his wounds, exulted: "We've made it!" The aircraft emerged from the cloud-bank and Keighley found they were alone in a peaceful sky. For a moment he sank back, exhausted with relief. Then the propeller sheared from the port engine and spun glittering away towards the sea. The oil pressure on the starboard engine began to drop rapidly as oil poured from a fractured line. *There's no future in this*, thought Keighley, and swung back towards the German coast to crash-land. As they were losing height over the sea, he threw out his maps and the radio frequency lists. He saw the island of Texel ahead, then the mainland, and then a cornfield, in which he crash-landed. Keighley and the observer, Sergeant J W H Parsons, scrambled out, and found the gunner, MacPherson, dead in his turret. Then the Germans arrived, including a cocky young Me110 pilot who claimed he had brought them down, and took the two survivors away in an ambulance. Keighley spent six weeks in Hohemark hospital.

The other three captives from No82 Squadron were Richard Neville Wardell, Thomas Edward Syms and a South African, Ben Totham Jervois Newland. Along with the rest of the squadron they had spent two weeks practising formation flying for an operation in which would lead to No82 being wiped out for the second time in less than three months. At 0400 hours on Tuesday, 13 August, the twelve crews from "A" and "B" Flights were awoken to the cry of: "All crews to breakfast by five o'clock; briefing at five-thirty!" Assembling in Watton's former married quarters, now used as an operations briefing room, they were told by the Earl of Bandon that they were to attack Hamstede aerodrome, at Aalborg in north-east Denmark, where the Luftwaffe was building up a fleet of Ju52 transports in readiness for the impending invasion. Seventeen other No2 Group Blenheims would also be operating against aerodromes in France and Holland. Some flak and fighter opposition was expected, but the attack had to be pressed home, although the orders were to abort if cloud was less than five-tenths.

Led by Squadron Leader N C Jones, who had recently returned from India and sported a North-West Frontier "gong", "A" Flight took off from Watton; "B" Flight, led by "Rusty" Wardell, took off from the satellite aerodrome six miles away at Bodney. There was not a cloud in the sky. Forming up at 0840 hours into stacked "vics" of three, they flew out across the North Sea towards the Danish coast. As Denmark loomed ahead, one of them turned back owing to fuel shortage. The rest flew on at a steady 180mph at a height of 6,000 feet, climbing to 8,000 feet when they hit the south-east coast of Denmark. From there they intended running northwards up the coast to reach their target. Unfortunately, this approach gave the Germans ample time to scramble the Me109s of *II/JG 27*. Flying steadily northwards, the Blenheims were only twenty miles short of Aalborg when the Me109s fell on them. The fighters raked the formation continuously until, near the airfield, they broke off to allow the flak to open up.

Half the crews dumped their bombs when the Me109s made their first pass at the formation; none of the other Blenheims even reached the airfield. In the space of a few hellish minutes, all eleven were chopped down, with twenty-five men killed and thirteen on their way to captivity. The first to go down was Squadron Leader Jones, only one of whose crew, Sergeant J F H Bristow, survived. Then Sergeant Donald Blair's Blenheim, which had been in the second "vic" of "B" Flight a hundred feet lower, was hacked down. They lost an engine even before they managed to drop their bombs. Sergeant W Greenwood, the rear-gunner, got three bullets in one leg and lost consciousness; so Sergeant W G McGrath, the observer, took over his guns, though he had "little hope of hitting anything". Then the aircraft caught fire and Blair tried to ditch in the fjord. But forty feet from the ground the port fuel tank exploded and the aircraft crashed. Miraculously, all the crew came out of the wreckage alive, though Bill McGrath had broken a shoulder and was blinded in one eye. They had come down near the tiny island of Egholm. A local farmer and his son waded out and pulled them ashore.

Tom Syms was next, his observer, Sergeant K H Wright, going with him into the bag. Richard Wardell, a modest but competent officer who had seen service before the war in Egypt and Iraq, was shot up by both Me109s and flak, his aircraft being raked by cannon-fire and then damaged by a flak burst directly underneath the cockpit. The Blenheim turned turtle and disintegrated. Wardell was thrown clear, and had enough presence of mind to pull the rip-cord of his parachute. He floated down to dry land, suffering from minor burns and shock, but his observer and WOP/AG perished when the aircraft fell to pieces, as did those in Ben Newland's aircraft. The leader of the operation, Wing Commander E C de Virac Lart DSO, was killed outright with his entire crew. Only four others survived — Flight Lieutenant R A G Ellen and his observer, Sergeant V J Dance; and Sergeant J E Oates, his observer, Pilot Officer R M Biden, and his WOP/AG, Sergeant T Graham. The twenty-six-year-old Sergeant Oates broke his back when he tried to make a forced landing and the Germans fired on him again, knocking out his port and making the aircraft swing, stall and hit the ground out of control.

The Germans were not tardy in rounding up the fallen aircrew. The local *Gauleiter*, Karl Bruns, who was in charge of construction at Aalborg airfield, gathered them all in a motor-boat called the *Mira*. Within a few hours six of them — Wardell, Newland, Don Blair, Bill "Mac" McGrath, Bill Greenwood and Oates — were helped aboard an ambulance and driven to Christ's Hospital in Aalborg, where they were well treated, if underfed, and then taken by another ambulance on a six and a half hour drive to a POW hospital in Schleswig-Holstein. They were given no food during the journey, although a friendly guard allowed them two swigs each of *ersatz* coffee from his own flask.

There were thirty Polish patients at the new hospital, all of whom had been POWs for a year and most of whom were suffering from illnesses brought on by malnutrition. The NCO contingent were put in their ward, a large room with windows that stretched from floor to ceiling and furnished with about twenty two-tier metal bunks, while Wardell and Newland shared a smaller ward. At 6.30 every morning the wards were inspected by the senior *Arzt*, and the "walking wounded" had to stand to attention by their beds, while the bed patients had to lie at attention, with their arms held stiff outside the blankets. Food was a formality: one-seventh of a loaf of bread per man per day (but at this stage of their captivity white bread rather than *Volksbrot*), three evil-smelling, rotting potatoes, and a ladle of *Klippfisch* soup. During the morning of Friday, 16 August the RAF party, by now all but one of them fit to walk, were taken away by a Luftwaffe officer, an NCO and two guards, and were put aboard a lorry bound for the local railway station, where they were escorted on to a *Schnellzug* (long-distance train). The female conductor showed a great deal of interest in the young British airmen, but was warned by the Luftwaffe officer in no uncertain terms that fraternisation with the enemy was *"Streng verboten. Heil Hitler!"*

When they changed trains at Hamburg they were disappointed at the lack of bomb damage in the area of the docks. They also saw four jam-packed troop transports, and wished a flight of Blenheims would arrive and bomb the lot, even if it meant themselves getting the chop, too. As

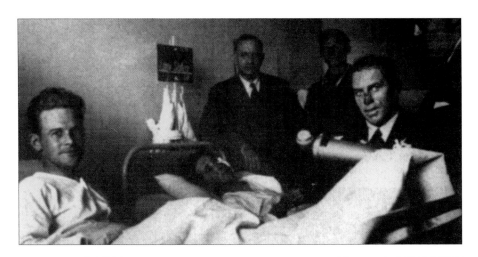

Top: George Booth, Larry Slattery and Laurence Edwards interviewed by German and American journalists in Wesermünde Hospital, September 1939. *(Calton Younger)*

Above: Early RAF and *Armée de l'Air* officer POWs on their way to interrogation in Berlin, September 1939. *Left to right: Sous-Lieutenant* Béranger, Pilot Officer Alf Thompson, Lieutenant-Colonel Enselem and Squadron Leader Sydney Murray. *(Nora Crete)*

Right:
Murray and Thompson after their interrogation. *(Nora Crete)*

Above: The dower house at Elbersdorf prior to the outbreak of war. In September 1939 it was converted into a POW camp and designated Oflag IXA. *(Author's collection)*

Below: The *Offiziersdurchgangslager* at Oberursel, the forerunner of *Dulag Luft. (Sam Flynn)*

Left: **Alf Thompson, at the** *Reichsrundfunk,* **broadcasting the news of his capture.** *(Nora Crete)*

Below: **Panoramic view of Spangenberg and Elbersdorf prior to the outbreak of war.** *(L Heinlein, via* **Schloss** *Spangenberg)*

UPPER CAMP

SPANGENBERG

LOWER CAMP

Right: **Wing Commander Harry Day, shot down on Friday, 13 October 1939.** *(B A James)*

RAILWAY STATION

Left: The former Spangenberg railway station, now a Kindergarten. *(Author)*

Below left: Schloss Spangenberg, Oflag IXA/H, November 1939. *(Calton Younger)*

Right: Spangenberg castle from the north-west. *(Imperial War Museum HU20593)*

Below: The steps from Elbersdorf leading to the castle. *(Author)*

Below right: The lower stretch of the cinder path up which POWs were marched to the castle. *(Author)*

Above left: The stone steps from the town of Spangenberg, completed in 1838. *(Author)*

Above: The stone steps, photographed from the outer moat area. *(Author)*

Left: The upper stretch of the cinder path. *(Author)*

Above right: The "Black Gate" leading from the outer battlements to the gate-house. *(Author)*

Right: The cobbled path, viewed from the gatehouse to the "Black Gate". *(Author)*

Left: The gatehouse today. *(Author)*

Below left: The draw-bridge and *Grosser Turm*, or main tower. *(Author's collection)*

Right: The main tower and steps leading to the bottom of the moat. *(IWM HU20594)*

Below: Prisoners relaxing in the moat. *(Author's collection)*

XII

Left: The courtyard and
Kommandantur drawn by Howard
Taylor for "The Quill".
(Author's collection)

Above: View of the courtyard and
main entrance, 1940.
(Author's collection)

Right: The spiral staircase in the eastern tower. *(Author)*

XIV

Above left: **The main Assembly Hall in the south wing in the 1930s, when the castle was a State Forestry School. During the war, newly arrived POWs were searched and given a pep-talk in the** *Grosse Aula* **by the Commandant.** *(M Becher, via* Schloss *Spangenberg)*

Left: **The** *Speisesaal,* **or Dining Hall, again before the war. POWs were not allowed the luxury of glazed crockery.** *(M Becher, via* Schloss *Spangenberg)*

Above: **The eastern wing and the wooden bridge leading to the gymnasium.** *(IWM HU20595)*

Left: **Larry Slattery at Spangenberg after his jaw had been wired up.** *(Calton Younger)*

Below: **Larry Slattery and Laurence Edwards at Spangenberg.** *(Calton Younger)*

Right: **Aircrew officers photographed in the courtyard, winter 1939.** *Standing left to right:* **Griffiths, MacLachlan, Bewlay, Heaton-Nichols, Baughan, Thurston.** *Seated left to right:* **Casey, Tilsley, Murray, Day, Thompson, Edwards.** *At front:* **Bob Coste.** *(H R Bewlay)*

XVII

Above: **Harry Bewlay** *(left)* **and Colin MacLachlan, 1939.** *(H R Bewlay)*

Below left: **Howard ("Hank") Wardle.** *(Author's collection)*

Below right: **Keith Milne.** *(Author's collection)*

Above left: Donald S Thom. *(Author's collection)*

Above right: Squadron Leader Brian Paddon—in the cooler, as usual. *(A J Hill)*

Below left: Norman Thomas. *(Author's collection)*

Below right: Francis ("Errol") Flinn. *(Author's collection)*

Above: Canadians at Spangenberg, 1940. *Left to right:* Aubrey Roberts, John Glover, Donald Middleton, Warren Hayward, Al Matthews, Don Thom, Robert Renison (partially hidden), George Walker, William Donaldson, Bob Coste, Alf Thompson, Hank Wardle, Keith Milne. *(Nora Crete)*

Below: Alex Gould in the courtyard at Spangenberg. Main gates in background. *(A H Gould)*

Below: Fleet Air Arm prisoners at Dulag Luft, late 1940. *Back row, from left:* Nathaniel Hearn, Cecil Filmer, Midshipman A O Atkins, Robin Grey, Douglas Poynter. *Third row:* Guy Griffiths, Lieutenant J T Nicholson, Lieutenant W S ("Peter") Butterworth, Lieutenant J C W Iliffe, Maurice Hanrahan, Alan Cheetham, Henri Detterding, Captain R T Partridge, RM. *Second row:* Richard Thurston, Norman Quill, Lieutenant-Commander Jimmy Buckley, Lieutenant-Commander O S Stevinson, Lieutenant-Commander John Casson. *Front row:* Naval Airman A R Purchase, Naval Airman Charles Jago, Petty-Officer Alex Brims and Naval Airman H W Brown. Griffiths and Thurston had been sent from Spangenberg with "Wings" Day to form the nucleus of the British Permanent Staff at Dulag Luft. Most of the other officers would shortly be purged to Spangenberg. *(Janet Brown)*

Below: The purge from Stalag Luft I, Barth, arrives at Spangenberg, February 1941. In the foreground are Peter Tunstall (with Red Cross box) and Norman Forbes (directly behind him). *(Author's collection)*

Above: **Trevor Hadley and Theo Johnson, Spangenberg 1941.** *(Vivien Johnson)*

Below left: **Alex Gould and Peter Tunstall, Spangenberg 1941.** *(A H Gould)*

Below right: **Norman Forbes.** *(Author's collection)*

Above: Alf Thompson playing table-tennis at Spangenberg. *(A H Gould)*

Below: Major-General Victor Fortune *(seated extreme left)*, the Senior British Officer at Fort VIII, watches the boxing match at Fort XV. *(A H Gould)*

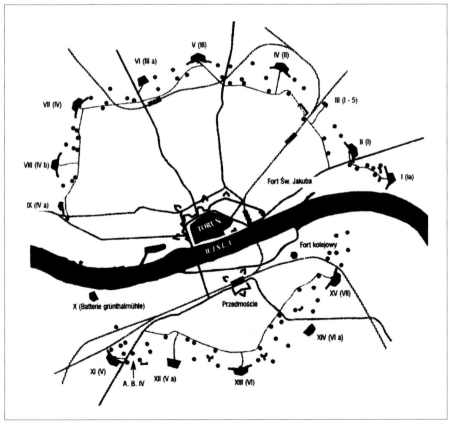

Above left: **Fort XV, Thorn.** *(Author's collection)*

Left: **Map showing the chain of fortresses surrounding Thorn.** *(Author's collection)*

Above: **POW accommodation at Thorn.** *(Author's collection)*

Below: Strafgefangene **at Fort XV, Thorn.** *From left:* **Squadron Leader Murray, Rupert ("Pud") Davies and Paul Vaillant.** *(A H Gould)*

Above: Cutaway drawing of the *Speisesaal* at Elbersdorf Lower Camp, from "The Quill". *(Author's collection)*

Below: Joe Kayll, Hornchurch Wing Leader, captured. *(J R Kayll)*

Above left: Dan Hallifax. *(Author's collection)*

Above right: Wing Commander Joe Kayll, drawn by Cuthbert Orde. *(J R Kayll)*

Below: Officers from No82 Squadron at Spangenberg, summer 1941. *From left:* Robert Biden, Thomas Syms, Ben Newland, Ronald Ellen, Robert McKenzie, Kenneth Toft, William Keighley, Richard Wardell. *(Author's collection)*

Above: **The laundry cart in which Joe Barker and Eric Foster escaped from Spangenberg in August 1941.** *(J R Kayll)*

Below left: **Nat Maranz.** *(Author's collection)*

Below right: **Eric Foster and Joe Barker after recapture.** *(via J R Kayll)*

Above left: **Allan McSweyn.** *(via J R Kayll)*

Above right: **Kenneth Nichols.** *(Author's collection)*

Below: **Flying Officer Oliver Philpot and his Beaufort crew in Dulag Luft, January 1942.** *From left:* **Gordon Rackow, Freddie Smith, Oliver Philpot and Roy Hester.** *(Author's collection)*

Above left: **Morris Fessler.** *(Author's collection)*

Above right: **Squadron Leader Thomas Calnan with his PRU Spitfire at Benson, 1941.** *(Author's collection)*

Left: Wing Commander R R S Tuck, air ace. *(Michael Stanford-Tuck)*

Above: Bent props: the nose of Tuck's shot-down Spitfire. *(Michael Stanford-Tuck)*

Below: The flak battery that shot down Tuck inspect his wrecked Spitfire. *(Michael Stanford-Tuck)*

Above left: Harold Bareham.
(Rosemary Bareham)

Above right: Anthony Barber.
(The Rt. Hon. Lord Barber)

Left: Acting Squadron Leader Graham
Campbell at Spangenberg. *(G C Campbell)*

they stood on the platform awaiting their connection, a Luftwaffe *Leutnant* approached them and boasted that he had destroyed two British aircraft, one of them a Hurricane, in the French campaign. He told them they would not be prisoners for long, as the Germans would be in London within a few days and, with the New Order established, all prisoners would be allowed home. *Poor deluded fool*, they thought. *Still, he's not a bad type, as Huns go!*

At last their train arrived, and the Luftwaffe officer turfed four German civilians out of a first-class compartment. They stood glowering in the corridor whilst the six British prisoners took their seats. Upon arrival at Frankfurt am Main, their escort saw some German infantry queuing for soup. They jumped to the head of the queue, commandeered some billy-cans and forced on their "guests" more soup than they could possibly drink. The infantrymen thought this was funny, an indication that the British had been starving for so long that their stomachs had shrunk. Patting the prisoners on the back they told them: "Cheer up, Tommy! We will soon liberate England from the grasping Jewish capitalist clique — then all will be well!"

By now Wardell and his party were tiring of Nazi propaganda, and were elated when the air-raid alarm sounded and they heard the sound of falling bombs and German ack-ack. They were shoved into a guard's van and shunted to a siding a few miles away until the raid was over. As the doors closed, they noticed that the Jerries carried on talking and guzzling their soup as though nothing was happening, and were somewhat crestfallen. Upon returning to the station four hours later they were marched on to the forecourt were a smart Mercedes-Benz saloon waited to take them on the final lap of their journey to Oberursel. An officer from Dulag Luft, who spoke English, took over, telling them that the raid had caused no bomb damage and that twenty RAF bombers had been shot down. Don Blair, pointing to a red glow in the sky about a quarter of a mile away, said: "What's that, then — someone lighting a cigarette?"

The German said: "Yes," then realised the absurdity of his position, and laughed with the prisoners. (In fact, although seven RAF bombers were lost over various targets that night, none of them was hit during the raid on Frankfurt.)

Wardell's party finally arrived at Dulag Luft at 4am. Don Blair was taken straight to the cells, and the rest to Hohemark for further treatment. Within a few weeks most of the officers and NCOs captured on the Aalborg raid were firmly ensconced in hospital at Bad Sulza, only "Rusty" Wardell, Ben Newland and Tom Syms remaining at Oberursel.

***

Acting Flight Lieutenant Paul François Reginald Vaillant was a Wellington pilot in No149 (East India) Squadron. He had been crewed up with Pilot Officer M G Butt (second pilot); Sergeant Johnny Fender (Observer); Sergeant D H G Connolly (wireless-operator); a Maori rear-gunner, Sergeant L F Mabey, RNZAF; and Sergeant R W Saywood (gunner).

On 27/28 August Bomber Command sent out a mixed force of fifty Hampdens, Wellingtons and Whitleys to bomb various targets in France, Germany and Italy. No149 Squadron's target was Kiel, where the battleships *Scharnhorst* and *Gneisenau* were harbouring. But Kiel was obscured by ten-tenths cloud, so Paul Vaillant set course for the alternative target, Wilhelmshaven. Over the Elbe they were coned by searchlights and hit in the port fuel tanks by flak. With the tanks empty, Vaillant had no option but to order the crew to abandon aircraft. They baled out safely at about 0200 hours. All were rounded up during the next few hours by searching Germans. While Vaillant remained behind at Dulag Luft for seven weeks, Maurice Butt and the rest of the crew were sent to Barth.

Ian Clark Kirk was a navigator in the Hampden-equipped No144 Squadron, based at Hemswell. The captain of his aircraft was Pilot Officer R S A Churchill, who now languished at Barth. On 2/3 September Bomber Command put up eighty-four aircraft against a variety of targets in Germany, France, Holland and Italy. No144 Squadron was to bomb Ludwigshafen. Churchill's aircraft came under attack from a night-fighter, cannon-fire ripping into the fuselage and killing the gunner and WOP/AG. The Hampden crashed between Nuth and Wijnandstrade, about nine miles north-east of Maastricht.

Anthony Orlando Bridgman (always referred to, for some obscure reason, as "Oscar") was, like Charlie Bowman, an RAF regular who had been with No83 Squadron since prewar days, commanding "A" Flight. Another No83 Squadron veteran, Guy Gibson, was to describe him in his memoirs as "quick-tempered" but a pilot who "could fly as well as any man". On 23/24 September 1940 Bomber Command pitted 129 aircraft, a mixture of Hampdens, Wellingtons and Whitleys, against eighteen separate targets in Berlin. Two nights previously, Bridgman and some of the boys had gone into Nottingham and got so drunk and belligerent that they were taken off the next night's ops. When the Hampdens took off for Berlin on the following night, Bridgman was still furious. The raid was the biggest of the war so far, but crews were dogged by cloud and flak all the way. They experienced great difficulty finding Berlin and their loop bearings were jammed continually by the enemy. Gibson later described the raid as "general chaos all round", with No83 Squadron's crews bombing at the end of their dead-reckoning position where they estimated Berlin might be. Altogether, 112 aircraft reported having bombed from heights between 4,500 and 16,000 feet, although searchlights and ground-mist made identifying targets difficult, and American journalist William L Shirer, who was in Berlin at the time, reported that few bombs actually dropped in the city itself.

However, Bomber Command's losses were small, one Wellington, one Whitley, and one Hampden — "Oscar" Bridgman's. On the return leg, crews encountered gale-strength headwinds, which took them over the most flak-infested parts of Germany. Bridgman, flying at about a thousand feet, caught a packet over Bremen that set an engine on fire. His WOP, Sergeant A G Gorwood DFM, sent a message to base saying the crew were baling out. Some time later, Gorwood tapped out another message saying Bridgman was going to try to get home. Presumably, the fire must have died down, but only temporarily, as the aircraft crashed near Bethen in Germany. Bridgman became a POW and Gorwood and the rest of the crew were killed. With the other prewar No.83 Squadron aircrew officers either dead or — like Bowman, Bridgman, Muir and Allen Mulligan — prisoners of war, Guy Gibson was now the only one left.

Harald Ridley Bjelke-Peterson, a Wellington pilot in No3 Group's No149 Squadron, was shot down when on the night of 28/29 September when bombers attacked Hanau, east-north-east of Frankfurt. All but one of his crew survived. It was a routine raid, with "B-P" taking off from Mildenhall at 2045 hours. After the navigator, Sergeant K Holden, had pin-pointed their location over the English coast, the second pilot, Sergeant W T Hallam, took over the controls. They flew through scattered low cloud, which left a layer of ice on the Wellington, but they arrived over the Dutch coast without incident and Bjelke-Peterson resumed control. Passing through several belts of flak and searchlights, he took evasive action and emerged unscathed until they reached the outskirts of Frankfurt, which were brilliantly illuminated by masses of searchlights and multi-coloured flak. As they were running up to their target, they heard several loud bangs and the port engine died. Every searchlight seemed to be shining on them and the defences were putting up a terrific barrage. It was almost impossible to control the aircraft. Whilst "B-P" tried to keep the main-plane up, Hallam held the rudder-bar with his hands, but the vibrations as the flak exploded around them made the instrument panel a blur. Then the port engine burst into flames and fumes began to envelope the cockpit. "Prepare to abandon aircraft!" yelled Harald. Then: "Jump! Jump!"

Hallam let the New Zealand front-gunner, Sergeant C McKenzie Laird, out of his turret, then opened the bottom hatch and disappeared into the maelstrom below. He was followed by Laird, then Ken Holden, then Sergeant A Botton, the W/T Operator. The rear-gunner, Sergeant Alfred B Witton, RNZAF, had considerable difficulty extricating himself from his turret, which had almost been blown off, but finally squeezed himself out, leaving only Bjelke-Peterson to jump — which he did, though nearly breaking his neck in the process.

With the exception of "Hallie" Hallam, they all made landfall safely. Hallam was killed as he left the blazing Wimpey.

Pilot Officer Donald Kenneth Hayes was the sole survivor of the only Wellington lost on 29/30 September, when No37 Squadron, Feltwell, bombed Bitterfeld. His aircraft, in which he was second pilot, was shot down near Osnabrück. Pilot Officer Arthur John Joseph Steel was one of only two survivors from another Wellington — this time from No115 Squadron, Marham — shot down during a raid on Osnabrück the following night, when Bomber Command put up 104 aircraft against a variety of targets. Steel's navigator, Sergeant R P Mogg, was sent to Stalag Luft I.

Francis Driscoll ("Errol") Flinn, a Canadian, was a Coastal Command pilot on the Beaufort-equipped No42 Squadron, based at Thorney Island. During a routine patrol on Friday, 4 October he was shot down by Me109s off the Belgian coast and ditched in the North Sea. All his crew survived. Flinn was later joined by another Coastal Command type, James Ralph Thornton Smalley, a Flight Lieutenant with a DFC who flew Spitfire PR IFs from Heston. He was shot down over Kiel on Tuesday, 8 October, and wrote an apologetic letter to his CO from Dulag Luft: "Sorry I couldn't finish the job, Sir! Don't quite know what happened — big bang and fireworks. I just managed to get out, a bit battered but safe and sound and as happy as can be expected."

* * *

Of the Fleet Air Arm contingent, Lieutenant Iliffe had been the first to enter captivity. He was an observer in No801 (Skua) Squadron, based on HMS *Furious*. On Sunday, 13 September the squadron made an attack on oil tanks at Sklaalevik, in Norway. Iliffe's pilot, Lieutenant T E Gray, crashed in his dive-bomb attack. The two officers survived, Gray being sent via Dulag Luft to Stalag XIIA at Limburg an der Lahn.

Lieutenants Hanrahan and Atkins, a pilot and an observer from No816 (Swordfish) Squadron, were also based on the carrier HMS *Furious*. The squadron was carrying out one of a series of torpedo raids on enemy shipping in Trondheimfjord on Tuesday, 22 September, when fog obscured the target. Maurice Hanrahan, his "string-bag" damaged by flak, force-landed north of the German-held Vaernes airfield. Along with the Telegraphist/Air-Gunner, Naval Airman A R Purchase, Hanrahan and Atkins had no choice but to surrender.

Also involved in the attack was No825 Squadron, led by Lieutenant-Commander Eugene Esmonde, which shared *Furious* with Nos 801 and 816. Two crews from this squadron also failed to return: Henri Deterding, his observer, nineteen-year-old Douglas Arthur Poynter, and the T/AG, Naval Airman H W Brown; and Sub-Lieutenant Hugh Hearn, his observer, Alan Cheetham, and his T/AG, Naval Airman C D Jago. No825 squadron had taken off at 0300 hours, but the weather deteriorated as they neared their target and the formation became scattered. "The CO and others returned very shortly," recalled Doug Poynter; "others ditched. We forced on." Deterding was unable to locate the target because of low cloud and flew up and down the Norwegian coast until dawn, when he headed out to sea, hoping to find the *Furious*. Hearn was also lost and heading out to sea, and the two aircraft almost flew into each other. Then together they flew back to the Norwegian coast and landed in a small field on the island of Leka, north of Namsos.

There were no Germans to be seen, so the two crews, helped by the local population, found a small fishing boat and set out for the Shetland Isles, some 500 miles away, "with enough drums of fuel to get us to the USA and back," recalled Doug Poynter. They made good progress for the first twenty-four hours, making a steady six knots, but it was difficult to steer in the rough sea, even though they took turns at the motor to conserve their strength. But at about 0800 hours on the 24th the engine packed up — salt water had entered the fuel tank. Undeterred, they tried hoisting the sail, but could make no progress against a strong south-westerly wind. For about twenty-four hours they drifted, watching the horizon for any sign of a ship. When the wind died down they managed to hoist the sail, despite the ropes being old and rotten, and headed east, back towards the coast of Norway. They reached the coast on the third night of their escapade, narrowly missing being wrecked on the jagged rocks. By now the weather had deteriorated again, with squally winds and rain. They anchored all day, waiting for the weather to clear, and after a day they set off again, hoisting the sail and paddling with lengths of driftwood. As night fell they reached an island near a lighthouse, where they decided to rest till dawn. However, a lookout on a German naval vessel had seen them, and hove to and took them on board.

The prisoners were transported to Oslo, and then to a prison in Berlin. There they remained a few days, accused of being spies, before clearing their names and being moved to Dulag Luft.

Lieutenant-Commander Stevinson was the CO of No829 (Albacore) Squadron, attached to RAF Coastal Command at St Eval. His observer was Norman Quill, with Petty Officer Alex ("Buggy") Brimms as T/AG. On Wednesday, 9 October the squadron made a night attack on seven German destroyers lying in Brest harbour, the most heavily defended port in Europe. Stevinson's Albacore was hit by light flak, but not so light that it didn't bring the aircraft down. All three aircrew were captured, with Brimms being sent to Barth.

(5)

The purge left Dulag Luft at 9.35 am on 22 October, boarding the same blue Luftwaffe bus that "Wings" Day and his French allies had travelled in the previous year and following the same route along the autobahn. Eric Foster found the journey fascinating, and for a while was able to shake off the disappointment of being recaptured after his Dulag Luft break and enjoy his surroundings. But he was looking out mainly for another chance to escape. Finally, at 1.20pm, the bus left the motorway and turned in to Melsunger Strasse. After another twenty minutes the castle of Spangenberg, perched high on its hill, hove into view, reminding Foster of Hans Christian Andersen's fairy stories. However, the twenty-six prisoners were not sent immediately to the castle, instead alighting at the Lower Camp and being marshalled into a room in the upper part of one of the buildings to be searched. The guards were rough and unpleasant. After ordering the prisoners to empty their pockets they hustled them into another room and told them to strip. Both they and their uniforms were to be de-loused. Lieutenant-Commander Stevinson protested.

"We have just come from a camp that is recognised as the best in Germany," he said. "There we bathed daily — by choice."

The *Hauptmann* in charge, Zola, was unmoved. He said they had already had Englishmen who were lousy with parasites and, therefore, all prisoners had to be de-loused.

They were issued with a towel each and after showering sat draped in blankets while they waited an hour for their clothes to be put through "the gas chamber". In the meantime, their clothes and their Red Cross boxes, containing all the worldly possessions they had accumulated at Dulag Luft, were thoroughly searched. Eric Foster lost a toasting fork, a coil of wire and some German money (*"streng verboten!"*).

After their uniforms were returned they were given a meal of meat and potato stew. It was very satisfying and they wondered if it was German issue or from the Red Cross. It seemed too good to be a German ration. They were then ordered to fall in and were marched up the long winding hill to the *Schloss*. For those officers who had been injured when shot down, the slog uphill was particularly trying. Eric Foster's foot was giving him gyp and to him the walk seemed endless. It required all the willpower he could muster to carry on, and he was relieved when Pilot Officer Arthur Steel offered to carry his load. Finally they arrived at the moat. Paul Vaillant, looking down at the three wild boars, said: "I wouldn't fancy my chances down there." At the gatehouse Kulmer, the castle keeper referred to by the prisoners as "Shagnasty", issued them with another blanket each.

They were led across the cobbled courtyard and up the winding staircase in the eastern corner to the former banqueting hall that was to be their dormitory. It was poorly lit with only four 15-watt bulbs. Because of the high altitude it was also cold, and the central heating had been turned off. When the prisoners settled down for the night in the two-tier bunks they slept in full uniform, including greatcoat and flying boots.

When Reveille came at 6am, the new prisoners were rudely awoken to repeated shouts of *"Aufstehen!"* and then, at 8.15, provided with a breakfast consisting of a slice of bread each with *Speisefett* and acorn coffee. Roll-call was now at nine o'clock, and conducted by the ubiquitous *Hauptmann* Gross. He gave his orders of the day in a full-chested bellow which left the new kriegies somewhat shaken, although in time they, like the older lags, would find him "passable enough"; he just liked to swagger on *Appell*. But on this particular day — Wednesday, 23 October — he was a man with a purpose. A sentence of ten days' solitary confinement had been passed by the Commandant on two Army officers attempting to escape from the Lower Camp. Gross then ordered Lieutenant G Wardle, a naval officer captured on 9 January 1940, to fall out. He was suspected of helping the two would-be escapers. If upon investigation the case were proven, he would join them in the *"Kühler"*.

He then ordered all the new prisoners to assemble immediately after *Appell* in the *Grosse Aula* or assembly hall. There they were allowed to sit down while camp regulations were read out in German by Gross and then in English by "Wank" Murray. The gist of Gross's boring catalogue was as follows:

"You are expected to sign parole whenever you have to cross the drawbridge. Parole ends immediately on your return. Orders have been given to the guards to fire immediately a prisoner leaves the ranks for any purpose whatsoever. In the even of prisoners trying to escape, orders are that the guards will shoot to kill."

He then gave details of some of the escape attempts that had been made — adding for good measure that all had failed ignominiously. He parroted a comment made by von Meyer: "The German guards on the Swiss frontier stand shoulder to shoulder — in fact, so close that even a tiny mouse cannot get through."

(6)

At morning *Appell* on Sunday, 27 October the naval lieutenant, Geoffrey Wardle, was again ordered to step out of the ranks. The case against him had been proved and he was sentenced to ten days' solitary confinement on German rations only. If the officers present at Gross's pep talk on the 23rd had not been convinced then of the severity of German discipline at Spangenberg, they were now. All Wardle had done was to ask an orderly to convey a message to two prisoners undergoing solitary. He was also sentenced to a further five days for being in possession of a "jemmy". On 2 December he would be sent to Colditz. Accusing prisoners of having a jemmy was the stock-in-trade of the Spangenberg security staff. They would send Padre Joseph Ellison Platt to Colditz along with Wardle for the same reason.

On Wednesday, 30 October the prisoners awoke to find the courtyard and the surrounding countryside under a thick blanket of snow. Immediately they piled into the courtyard and made snowballs.

Four days later, on Sunday, 3 November, Gross appeared on parade accompanied by another German officer. He announced that he was leaving and that the new arrival was taking over. Just as they were being dismissed a gaping hole appeared in the courtyard. A tunnel the French had started excavating back in June had subsided.

Gross's parting shot on evening *Appell* was to pronounce yet more sentences on recalcitrant prisoners. He awarded five days' solitary on German rations to two Lower Camp prisoners for "being in the possession of jemmies with a view to using them for escape" and then ordered Don Middleton and Keith Milne to fall out. "You are to be removed to another camp," he read, "because your attempt to escape proves to be a bad reflection on the discipline of this camp." He added archly: "You do not seem to like this camp. I would like you to write to me after the war telling me which was the better prison camp!"

On Monday, 4 November, Donald Middleton and Keith Milne were removed from Spangenberg, destined for Colditz; they were joined by "Hank" Wardle.

The following day was the birthday of Flying Officer Robert McKenzie, a member of the August purge. That night the men in his room threw a party and became rowdy, ending with a sing-song that included in its repertoire *"Deutschland* Unter *Alles"*. As a result, on 5 November the new *Lageroffizier* ordered prisoners to bed at 8.30pm. He also claimed that the punishment was a result of prisoners not paying enough attention to discipline and saluting. Not that going to bed early mattered: there was a fierce storm that night which played havoc with the lighting, and the lighting was not up to much anyway.

The number of Coastal Command/PRU officers in the *Schloss* had now been increased by the arrival of Squadron Leader F G L Smith DFC, Flight Lieutenant A A Rumsey, RAFO, and Pilot Officer H F Burns. Frank George Laughton Smith, formerly a Territorial Lieutenant in the 5th Battalion of the Lincolnshire Regiment, was a Beaufort pilot in "Errol" Flinn's old outfit, No42 Squadron, now based at Wick. Harry Francis Burns was his observer. On Saturday, 26 October Smith took off at 1308 hours to lead two other Beauforts in a shipping strike at Sogne Fjord. the flight was bounced by Me109s of IV/JG27, and two of the Beauforts were shot down. One crew was killed outright.   Smith, Burns and their wireless-operator survived, but the air-gunner perished.

Arnold Arthur Rumsey, of the Reserve of Air Force Operators, was another PR pilot from Heston, this time flying the Lockheed Hudson MkI. He, too, was shot down on Saturday, 26 October, while photographing invasion barge concentrations in the Scheldt Estuary. The crew baled out one by one at between 600 and 200 feet. But Pilot Officer C G Broome, the second dickey, did not survive the parachute descent. The remainder, all NCOs, went into captivity with Rumsey and were sent to Barth and Lamsdorf.

Thursday, 7 November was one of those bright winter days that hark back to summer. Despite the deep crisp snow the sky was clear blue and the sun shone brilliantly. The villages below the castle stood out in sharp relief, the rolling hills beyond looked magnificent, and even the courtyard looked less drab and uninviting than usual. Prisoners strolled along the battlements, able for a while to forget their confinement.

But the food situation was becoming grim. The kitchen orderlies posted a message on the notice board on Wednesday, 27 November announcing: "Red Cross Supplies NEARLY out!" — and that meant they were almost down to German rations only. The senior MO issued an order, backed by the SBO (at present, still Captain "Tug" Wilson, RN) that all forms of strenuous exercise should be avoided until new supplies arrived. But some personal parcels were coming in, and Eric Foster received one from a friend in Copenhagen. It contained a jumbo sausage, more than a pound of butter, jam, marmalade, sugar, biscuits, a pound of cheese and a bar of soap. He calculated that if he eked it out carefully his supply would last ten or even fifteen days. Paul Vaillant was unable to share Foster's joy: he had been waiting for a parcel from Belgium, and it was two months overdue.

The following night the lights were extinguished at 9.15 because of RAF activity overhead. Bomber Command had put up seventy-seven aircraft, including Blenheims and Hampdens, against targets as far afield as Düsseldorf and Stettin.

On Friday, 29 November letters arrived from home, some for the POWs who had reached Spangenberg in October. Several were dated as far back as mid-September.

(7)

Towards the end of 1940 the Red Cross started a scheme for POWs to be "adopted" by families in the warring countries so they could be sent money and food. One family in New Zealand, called Symonds, adopted four, one of which was Theo Johnson. He corresponded with the daughter, Vivien, and they would write to each other throughout the next four years while he was in Thorn, Warburg, Sagan and Schubin.

Christmas 1940 was one of the worst the early RAF prisoners were to endure throughout their four or more years of captivity. A heavy snow settled, and food and cigarettes were still in short supply. There was even a shortage of *ersatz* coffee and the prisoners were drinking hot water. The Upper Camp officers prepared for their "make-believe" festivities by making pudding from German bread, which they soaked in water, put through a sausage-grinder and baked. The day before Christmas Eve one of the orderlies was sentenced to solitary confinement for "purloining a tin of sausage-meat whilst on duty in the German store". The other prisoners hoped the Commandant would exercise some leniency and let him out for Christmas Day. The extent of his leniency was displayed on Christmas Eve *Appell* when the *Lageroffizier* announced: "The Commandant has seen fit to show humanity inasmuch as he has decided to allow the prisoners to have German *ersatz* coffee on Christmas Day, and again after four days." As he dismissed the parade he said to himself: "Churchill would not have done this!" Those who heard howled with laughter.

The prisoners spent most of Christmas Eve lying on their bunks, thinking of home. But that night the stillness was broken when some of the off-duty guards stealthily crept into the courtyard, their footsteps muffled by the snow, stood beneath the windows of the dormitories and sang *"Stille Nacht, Heilige Nacht"*. Even the most hardened goon-haters were moved. Afterwards the guards bade them *"Gute Nacht"*. "Goodnight," returned the prisoners. "Thank you!"

For Christmas dinner, the Army officers in the Lower Camp had a steak and kidney pudding each — saved from Red Cross parcels issued in July — and two half-bottles of Rhine wine between three. Forgetting the generosity of Sydney Murray back in June and July, they made no donation to the Air Force and Navy prisoners in the castle, most of whom had to celebrate Christmas on German issue rations. On Boxing Day, however, the gates opened and a handcart was wheeled into the courtyard, laden with Red Cross parcels — the first since the arrival of the October purge from Dulag Luft. The excitement was terrific, and cheers echoed throughout the castle. Christmas, though a little late, had been saved.

Winter dragged on, time hanging heavy like a ball and chain, and there was little excitement apart from the SBO — now Brigadier the Hon N F R Somerset of the Gloucestershire Regiment — having heated exchanges with von Meyer. One of Somerset's complaints concerned parole. The number of armed guards and dogs accompanying prisoners on parole walks was unreasonable, as was the order that the guards should "shoot to kill" any prisoner who broke ranks. The prisoner body had resolved not to give parole unless the "shoot to kill" order was revoked. Von Meyer backed down.

In February 1941 the Germans stopped the coffee issue and replaced it with leaf tea. As the weather was getting warmer they also stopped hot showers in the morning. On Tuesday the 11th they issued twenty-five parcels of cigarettes and tobacco, enough for each prisoner to have a hundred Capstan followed by either another fifty-nine Capstan or two ounces of tobacco. But there was also a rumour that *Hauptmann* Roth, the Lower Camp *Lageroffizier*, was leaving. Roth always did his utmost to lessen the privations of POW existence and the prisoners were apprehensive. However, on the 12th they discovered that he was only standing in as acting Adjutant to the Commandant for ten days to cover the Adjutant's leave. According to one of the *Unteroffiziere*, Eifert, he told his replacement, *Hauptmann* Bruntz, that the prisoners behaved tolerably well all the while they were not shouted at.

Tedium was relieved to some degree at the Upper Camp when news bulletins began to arrive via the orderlies in Elbersdorf. An influx of Army medical officers, who had remained behind in Belgium in 1940 to help the wounded, had arrived at the Lower Camp on Sunday, 2 February with a four-valve radio set. They managed to sneak it in to the compound partly because the German security personnel were more relaxed on Sundays, but also because, on seeing a gaggle of curious old-timers rubbernecking near the gate, they gesticulated towards a "medical case" one of the MOs was carrying. Captain A L Pope of the Royal Fusiliers, who had been at Spangenberg since the fall of France, instantly recognised that the "medical case" contained something of value. Fortuitously, Lance Pope spoke German, and rushed to the gate and engaged the guards in conversation, whilst three other officers grabbed the case and took it to their room. Upon opening it and discovering a radio set, the Army officers set up a syndicate to buy it for *Lagergeld* to the equivalent value of RM460. They hid it inside a medicine ball, and from then until the end of the war had a radio set which travelled with them to every prison camp. For security purposes, they nicknamed the radio "The Canary". The Lower Camp officers received the news daily, while those in the *Schloss* had to await the arrival of orderlies before they received the bulletins; but it was better than no news at all.

(9)

The "escape season", usually confined to the spring and summer months, began early in the Upper Camp. With the impending warmer weather in mind, prisoners began to think of ways to crack Spangenberg before the end of January. "Pop" Bewlay co-opted Eric Foster, a particularly keen type, on to the RAF escape committee, and between them they started brainstorming. On the face of it, breaking out of the Upper Camp was well-nigh impossible; the main gate was the most promising means of egress, but the garrison had it pretty well buttoned up by now, as a result of Milne and Middleton's bluff back in August. Short of wearing Perseus' helmet, there seemed no way through it. Such wild schemes as building a glider, catapulting men across the moat and sliding along the telephone wires on a home-made trolley were discussed and discarded. Finally — deciding that the gate it would just have to be — Phil Cook proposed to impersonate the cordially despised Kulmer and do a "walk out". He acquired a walking stick, made a shaggy moustache out of string fibres and roughly converted his uniform. Then, one morning in early

February, he approached the main gate at a slouch, looking quite convincing to the RAF prisoners who were peering furtively from the high windows. As luck would have it, however, Kulmer was in the moat just beneath the bridge, and an observant *Unteroffizier*, known by the prisoners as "Mel", was standing guard on the drawbridge. Surprised and panic-stricken at seeing double, "Mel" was speechless. While the guard was gathering his wits together, Cook considered making a dash back to his dorm, but decided to "go quietly" to prevent the Germans from meting out collective punishment.

Half-way through February the Germans announced that some land outside the camp had been set aside for prisoners to use for sports and sunbathing. This was a long-overdue right accorded them by the Geneva Convention. On Monday the 17th three of the senior Army officers from the Lower Camp were taken out to inspect it. They pronounced it too small, but decided it was better than nothing and to press for more ground later on. In the meantime, in the Upper Camp, one of the naval officers, a Sub-Lieutenant Gooch, had died of stomach cancer. Representatives of all three services from both camps were allowed to attend his funeral, which took place on the afternoon of Friday, 21 February. But no conversation was allowed between representatives from each camp. The RAF and Navy turned out in their best uniforms, and their march through the village impressed the local inhabitants. A wreath from each service was laid on Gooch's coffin. The German guard, twenty-one men commanded by *Hauptmann* Brandt, also looked smart in ceremonial dress and remained unobtrusive, attending as mourners, not as the enemy. The service was conducted by an Army Padre from the Lower Camp, Captain Norman McLean.

During the morning the prisoners in Elbersdorf had been told by *Hauptmann* Zola that the camp was soon to be completely evacuated. However, the next day another party of fifty officers arrived from Stalag Luft I and were sent to the castle.

* * *

The fifty had left Barth on Thursday, 20 February. The purge comprised two groups: most of those May and June captives who had been transferred there from Spangenberg in July; and officers who had been purged direct from Dulag Luft to Barth and whom the camp's *Abwehr* narks considered especially intransigent. In the former category were Squadron Leader Brian Paddon, who had been the SBO at Barth, Peter Bressey, Robert Burns, Charlie Crews, Geoff Dodgshun, Duggie Hoare, Tony Hudson, Hulton-Harrop, Arthur Imrie, Reg Jacoby, Des Laslett, William Lepine, James Leyden, Robert MacPherson, Derek Martin, Alf Mungovan, Henry Murray, Daniel O'Brien, Anthony Peach, Sam Pepys, Ian Potts, Aubrey Roberts, John Stephens, Howard Taylor, Don Thom, Norman Thomas, George Walker, "Blackie" Wells and Gordon Wright.

In the latter category were Flight Lieutenants F G Dutton, R H ("Pissy") Edwards, R A G ("Nellie") Ellen and R E Troward; Flying Officers P L Dakeyne, N Forbes, J C Milner, J M Taylor and P D Tunstall; Pilot Officers G M Baird, M G Butt, RAFVR, E J Clelland, R V Derbyshire, T H Hadley, J R Hoppe, RAFVR, T M Kane, P A W Thomas and K S Toft; and three naval aircrew, Lieutenant (A) R H G Grey, Sub-Lieutenant (A) R E Bartlett and Sub-Lieutenant (A) J M P Davies.

Maurice George Butt and John Ray Hoppe had intended to escape on the way to the railway station at Stralsund. However, recalls Butt, "all hopes...were dashed by the security measures employed by the guards, who were spaced out at 100m intervals, sub-machine-guns at the ready. The goons had been listening to the plans for escape, it was revealed later, when microphones were discovered under the western hut and sabotaged immediately (we learned two years later!)."

As soon as the Barth contingent arrived, Brian Paddon and John Carpenter Milner were escorted into the Lower Camp and locked in the cooler. They had escaped from Stalag Luft I by bluffing their way through the gate disguised as German workmen but had been arrested whilst walking through the streets of Barth. There was no room for them in the cooler at Stalag Luft I, so their sentence was deferred until they arrived at Spangenberg. For some reason the Germans left Milner's cell window open, so he was able to talk to passing prisoners.

The former "Spangenbergers" found there was more room in the *Schloss* than there had been in June and July 1940, as the French had been moved out and the Army officers had gone to the Lower Camp.

On Saturday, 1 March, a number of officers were summoned individually to the *Lageroffiziers'* quarters in the east wing. As each was escorted into the office he noticed that sitting at the desk before him were two SS officers and a member of the Gestapo. They invited each officer to sit down, then, playing a long shot, accused him of being the head of the Escape Committee. One such was Eric Foster, who told them he could only give two answers to any of their questions: "I don't know" and "I don't remember." They then questioned him on the whereabouts of Rupert Davies (whose presence in the camp was in fact quite conspicuous). After an hour he asked them if they were tired. They admitted they were, and asked: "Are you?"

"Yes, I am," said Foster.

"You may go," said the Gestapo official. "We understand your duty as an officer — we didn't expect any information."

It was pretty much the same scenario for each officer concerned. Evidently, the SS and Gestapo were trying to trick prisoners into giving information away as, of course, they knew absolutely nothing.

For the past two weeks all had been confusion in both the Upper and the Lower Camp. Much of the chaos in the *Unterlager* was witnessed by Paddon and Milner from their cell windows. On the morning of Gooch's funeral — Friday, 21 February — the Elbersdorf prisoners had been told by *Hauptmann* Zola that the camp would soon be completely evacuated. On Tuesday the 25th they were ordered on *Appell* to hand all clogs and German underclothes in to the quartermaster's office immediately. Suitcases were to be stacked by 9am the next day, after which the canteen would be closed. All camp money was to be handed in and credited by the afternoon. After a day of hectic preparations, the kriegies had just settled down for supper when *Unteroffizier* Eifert entered with the news that the move was off. A terrific cheer went up.

On the 27th, however, another rumour, inspired by John Milner, circulated: they were being sent to a "reprisal" camp. By 4pm the rumour was found to be true. They would have to be packed by 9am the next day. When that day arrived, Eifert appeared during breakfast to tell them to take the suitcases back to their rooms and attend an *Appell* in the *Speisesaal*. The roll-call was conducted by Bruntz, who was obviously very angry and did not understand the reason for so many orders and counter-orders. Apparently, the *Kommandantur* staff were just as confused. One of the senior Army officers demanded to know their destination, quoting the Geneva Convention. Bruntz replied that it was a silly time to bring this up, as he didn't know himself.

By Tuesday, 4 March, *Hauptmann* Roth had returned, and the rumoured evacuation took place. Carrying half a loaf of bread each, and accompanied by a platoon of guards and two dogs, the Lower Camp prisoners marched off under the steely gaze of Roth and Eifert.

The arrivals from Barth and the rest of the Upper Camp prisoners — a total of one hundred and fifty — were on the move, too. Having had so little exercise for so long they found the march down the spiralling hill and along the Bahnhofstrasse a strain. The route from the castle was lined with guards and dogs — almost at the rate of one guard per prisoner. As they passed through the archway over the cobbled road out of the castle "Errol" Flinn, who had secreted a loaf of bread under his coat, tried to make a break from the column and was seen by a guard who ran back up the road and roughly manhandled him back into the ranks.

At the station they were joined by the officers and orderlies from the Lower Camp. They became the object of curiosity by the villagers, who crowded round to gape. Ordered to form up in sixes, the prisoners then listened while a German officer read the Riot Act, to wit, if more than one man stood up at a time the guards would shoot without warning, and anyone attempting to escape would be shot without warning. Then they drew a ration of sausage and fell in again in alphabetical order. At 7pm they started boarding the train, their names being called in groups of seven already arranged by the Germans. Army officers were mixed with Navy and RAF in order to break up partnerships and thwart any escape plans. As they settled down in the third-class compartments they noticed that the windows had been secured to the lower frames with nails and barbed wire. One guard sat in each compartment with the prisoners and another guard armed with a sub-machine-gun stood in the doorway. At 9pm the train pulled out, heading east towards Poland.

Chapter Five
Strafgefangene
Fort XV, Thorn, March — June 1941

Hath fortune dealt thee ill cards? Let wisdom make thee a good gamester: in a fair gale, every fool may sail; but wise behaviour in a storm commands thewisdom of a pilot; to bear adversity with an equal mind, is both the sign and glory of a brave spirit.

Francis Quarles, *Enchiridion*, 1641

The journey east was long and tedious. The seats were hard and uncomfortable, and as only one prisoner was allowed to stand or go to the lavatory at a time, bottoms became sore and limbs stiff. No water had been supplied for either washing or drinking, and before long the prisoners were thirsty. When they pleaded for water they were promised *ersatz* coffee at Halle, but on arrival there was none forthcoming. As night approached, guards armed with rifles, some with bayonets at the ready, went up and down the train demanding the prisoners' boots and shoes. Those in Francis Flinn's compartment refused to give them up. Flinn, whose *Personalkarte I* had him marked down as *"besonders deutschfeindlich"* ("especially anti-German"), was viciously prodded with a bayonet. This argument won the day, and off came their boots. During the night two prisoners in each compartment had to sleep on the luggage racks.

Despite the security precautions, three officers escaped from the train: two former Barth kriegies, Robert Howard ("Pissy") Edwards and Ronald Alfred George ("Nellie") Ellen, and an Army officer, Lieutenant J F H Surtees of the Rifle Brigade. Edwards dived almost head-first out of the train, striking his head on the rails. He was unconscious for about an hour. When he recovered he called at a nearby house, but the residents called the police and he was arrested. Ronald Ellen had managed to retain his boots and had saved half a loaf of bread. He covered nearly two hundred kilometres and was out nearly nine days before his boots finally let him down. Not surprisingly he was in bad shape when he was recaptured.

On the morning of Wednesday the 5th the train stopped for an hour at Posen, where Nazi Party officers in brown uniforms strutted up and down the platform. The prisoners also noticed that few of the civilians were well dressed — most wore patched clothes — and that the handful of Jews they saw wore the Star of David. A number of trains were standing in the sidings, some marked *"Nur für Juden* — Only for Jews" and others *"Nur für Polen* — Only for Poles".

That evening at seven o'clock they were told by *Hauptmann* Zola that they had an hour to pack their belongings. As a result of the previous night's escape attempts, the guards went through every compartment removing the lampshades so that they had more light. By the time the train pulled into Thorn (Torun), after a fifty-two hour journey, the prisoners were hungry, thirsty, dirty and strangers to razor-blades.

The station yard was illuminated by arc lamps and the headlights of army cars. Surrounding the train was a row of guards with rifles at the ready, safety-catches off and fingers on triggers. Behind them was another group with sub-machine-guns. To the accompaniment of much shouting and bullying the prisoners were herded on to the sidings and formed up in rows of four, while guards lined up at either side with their dogs, forming a formidable corridor. An RAF officer standing next to Ernest John Clelland, another ex-Barth prisoner, remarked: "It's just like a Hollywood film." They started to laugh, whereupon a German officer drew his pistol and shouted: "It is forbidden to laugh!" Al Matthews, wearing a French general's cap and carrying a trombone, seemed oblivious to the flap, even when a corps of tanks emerged from under the trees. After their names were checked and double-checked, they were eventually marched along a muddy track, the guards with their rifles and bayonets at the charge position. Yet more guards armed with sub-machine-guns supplemented the escort; motorcycle goons, with mounted machine-guns, drove up and down the column, and cars with powerful headlights brought up the rear. As the prisoners trudged along the track, passing several forts along the way, their packs began to prove irksome. It was quite a relief when, after half a mile, they reached Fort XV, otherwise known as *"Festung* Hermann von Salza".

Thorn, which lay about a hundred miles north-west of Warsaw, was notorious for its system of five forts, built between 1857 and 1871 by Bismarck on a vast plain east of the River Vistula as a defence against Russia. The forts were numbered XIII, XIV, XV, XVI and XVII. Fort XIII was the headquarters for Stalag XXA, which was the overall POW camp designation for all the forts. Fort XIV was a hospital, and Fort XV was a punishment camp or *Straflager*. Fort XVI was the prison fort, where POWs would do "solitary". (There was another series of forts surrounding Posen, one of which, Fort VIII was a reprisal camp for NCOs and other ranks from Stalag XXIB, Schubin, and officers from Oflag VIIC/H, Laufen. Another fort, numbered XII, accommodated Poles, and a third, Fort XI, British NCOs and other ranks.) Made of stone and brick, with walls several yards thick, the forts were sunken so that the roofs were at ground level. Each fort was reputedly linked to the other by a system of tunnels. After being discarded as forts they had been used as prisons; the Germans had modernised them in the 1914-18 war, and afterwards the Poles had turned them into cadet schools and barracks. All were built along the same lines, roughly in the shape of an eagle. Surrounding each was a dry, sheer-walled moat about thirty feet wide and fifty feet deep, and an outer wall or "curtain". The only part on which the sun ever shone was a tiny square courtyard on the roof of the fort, spread with sand, used for recreation. Surrounding this courtyard was a high, turf rampart, completely hiding the outside world.

John Clelland was struck by the "terrible smell. It was coming from the rotting potatoes that would be cooked for our consumption."

The huge iron steel gates were opened and before the prisoners was an amazing scene: a forecourt about forty-five feet square, a drawbridge over the moat, and a building covered in grass and shrubbery — with the occasional tree — illuminated by searchlight beams. The upper windows of the fort were thirty feet below ground level and the lowest windows six feet from the foot of the moat. Crossing the drawbridge, the prisoners from Spangenberg were met by yet more guards armed with tommy-guns, and NCOs with Lugers and rubber truncheons. They were then herded in to a vast underground corridor, about fifteen feet wide by a hundred and fifty feet long, with an arched ceiling. Confronting them were the Commandant and his staff.

The Commandant then enumerated the reasons why they had been sent there: "Whereas the Canadians and British have seen fit to treat German prisoners of war officers at Fort Henry, Kingston, Canada, in a manner not in accordance with their dignity, and whereas protests have produced no change in these conditions, the German *Reich* is left with no alternative other than to retaliate and to treat British officers in the same way. You have been moved to this place of imprisonment by order of the German High Command." Fort XV was a "comparative camp", where British POWs would be treated the same way until conditions in Canada had improved. The camp officer, a *Hauptmann*, then read the Riot Act, which the prisoners treated with derisive remarks and a few cat-calls. Tension built up quickly and the *Hauptmann* drew his Luger from its holster. The POWs responded with a rousing cheer. "Fortunately for everyone, captives and captors alike," recalls Maurice Butt,

no shooting started, as in the confines of the long tunnel, ricocheting bullets would have killed prisoners and guards with equal impartiality.

The *Hauptmann* visibly recognised with amazement that the British prisoners before him were a most unusual lot, refusing to be cowed by threats, and changed his posture by calling on the interpreter to state the orders for the day (even though it was well into the evening).

The *Hauptmann* then shouted hysterically: "General Somerset!" The brigadier stepped forward and was escorted through a heavily barred gate and down a dark, spiral staircase to a cellar, two floors below roof level.

The rest of the prisoners were then numbered off and thrust into a corridor dripping with water.

It was at moat level and referred to by the Germans as the *"Erdgeschoss"* ("ground floor"). Reaching a series of low-vaulted subterranean rooms — which looked like short tunnels leading off the longer tunnels — the prisoners were locked in, fourteen or sixteen to a room. There were twenty-eight rooms dispersed along two floors, the ground and the basement, in which the Germans packed more than four hundred men. Each room measured about thirty feet by sixteen. Some rooms had wooden floors, some concrete. Furniture varied from room to room. In one there might be double-bunks; in another, wooden platforms, two tiers high, six feet six inches wide and running the length of the room on each side. This was the sleeping accommodation on which the prisoners lay down in rows, the space allowing eighteen inches per man. For bedclothes they were each provided with one single blanket and one half-blanket, about four feet square. Instead of the usual palliasses, they were given straw. Some rooms had two tables, measuring five feet by two feet six inches; some rooms had no other furniture at all. Each man was issued with a china bowl and spoon and a small cup. The barred windows, near the ceiling, had been boarded up, apart from fifteen square inches, even though the only view afforded was that of the surrounding moat. In the middle of each room was a stove. The stove was lit only at night, when officers were locked in their rooms from 6pm to 7.30am. This meant each man could only get on the stove for half an hour every three days. Illumination consisted of one electric light-bulb — and a dim one at that. Most of the time the prisoners were in darkness. Sanitary arrangements consisted of one small towel per man, a broom, and three buckets or jam tins — two of which were used for washing dishes and for shaving, and another for calls of nature. With anything between fourteen and eighteen, and sometimes as many as twenty-two, men using the same bucket, the results were sickening. Supper that night was two dixies of hot stew per room. After supper they were allowed a wash. The orderlies — appointed at the rate of one per room — warned the officers not to drink the water because the previous summer two hundred prisoners had died of diphtheria. One could brush one's teeth in the water provided one did not swallow any. The water had to be pumped up by hand from a well in a room next to the cesspool, with a working party at the pump all day.

Each of the two floors had a wash-house in another underground room along the corridor. Running along it was a long trough, and above this was a pipe of a radius of half an inch. Meagre droplets of water trickled from holes an eighth of an inch in diameter punched in every twenty-four inches. Only one third of the prisoners could wash at once, and the temperature of the water never varied from a degree above freezing. Three afternoons a week there were showers. The camp was divided into three Companies, each allotted one shower a week. But the showers were hotter than those at Spangenberg.

At night, when the prisoners slept, the straw was so wet they could wring the water out of it. The damp got everywhere, and within five minutes everything in the room — playing cards, notebooks, letters, tobacco, cigarettes, socks — was wet through. Ventilation was poor and the atmosphere stifling. When they were let out, during the day, they had access to two communal lavatories, one on each floor, which were primitive in the extreme. One section of the outer wall of the fort was hollow. Radiating from a central vertical pipe were wooden planks with a line of twelve holes cut through them to serve as seats. But half the holes had been securely nailed up on the ground that as the German prisoners in Canada had inadequate toilet facilities, so should the British. This communal *Abort* — which the *Strafe* kriegies called "the Cruet" — allowed no privacy at all, but Alf Mungovan recollects that it was at least "chummy": "It was not unusual to sit next to a Brigadier or other high ranking officer and talk about the war. The circumstances gave birth to many rumours which were thereafter known as 'latrinograms'." The waste from the *Abort* went into an open drain running along the middle of the moat, which stank and attracted swarms of flies. Otherwise the whole fort stank of chlorine and lime, which wafted into any room or cell when the door was left open. The senior officers, Clelland recalls, had the "privilege" of being allocated rooms next to this toilet.

Another constraint included limited access to fresh air — two one-hour breaks a day, three days a week, for exercise in the sand-covered courtyard. But, according to Alf Mungovan,

> Apart from the menacing atmosphere of the fort itself, life was not too hard except for the poor rations and few food parcels. The continual hunger led to my taking up cigarette smoking as cigarettes were plentiful, even if some of them were those dreadful Polish things, half cigarette,

half cardboard tube. The tobacco was so dry and loose the tube had to be twisted to prevent the smoker choking on a lungful of tobacco dust.

Don Blew remembers that at Thorn "we tasted the first fresh eggs for about thirteen months…the guards were as corrupt as hell, and all their gas mask haversacks were full of eggs — and no gas masks!"

Despite these occasional "luxuries", all the *Strafgefangenen* suffered from varying degrees of malnutrition, and some had been badly wounded when shot down, so most of them were constantly ill with a mild form of dysentery. Many suffered from diarrhoea, and were not even allowed out of their rooms at night to relieve themselves.

Morning Reveille was blown by a British orderly on a German cornet, echoing through the labyrinthine passages and sounding quite beautiful. After ablutions and breakfast — bread, margarine and coffee — it was time for *Appell*. On their first morning at Thorn the former prisoners from Spangenberg were herded into the courtyard to be counted and searched.

"Whenever we left a camp," recalls Maurice Butt,

it meant a search of our possessions on departure — and that didn't take too long in the early years — and another more thorough search at the new camp. There were different standards of security at the various camps. Often the searchers didn't seem to know what they were looking for. It became a game of some skill and ingenuity to get obvious items through the search. Compasses, maps, the camp radio, tools acquired from workmen or fashioned from bits and pieces found lying around, printing ink, civilian clothing — anything of use to escapers — all had to be smuggled out, and into the new camp. The drill was to be organised, the theory to wear the German searchers down and detect the easiest one to get things past. Hence the first group to be searched never had anything important to get past, and so the form of the searchers was tested.

Immediately, we found that Irvine flying jackets — the fleece-lined sheepskin leather jackets — were being confiscated. I well remember the remonstrations of one young navigator who was most reluctant to part company with his.

Realising I was next on call, I decided to test the *Abort* arrangements as a means of avoidance, and in no time was being escorted by an armed *Posten* down a long tunnel. The only hope was to leave my flying jacket in the loo. Before we reached it, the heads of two Army orderlies appeared round the door of what transpired to be the cookhouse. "Everything alright, sir?" they asked, having heard the marching feet of the goon and I approaching, priming their curiosity. "Can you hide my jacket?" I asked; and they laughed with joy at the thought of doing something against the enemy. Hence, on the way back from the loo, I outpaced the middle-aged guard, dashed into the kitchen, and flung the jacket into the helping hands of a cook-orderly. Just in time, before the alarmed guard came in, rifle at the ready, I pretended to be trying to scrounge a drink, and the guard was so relieved he didn't notice my jacket had gone — into an empty, cold oven, in fact. I collected it later, having managed to wangle a large metal file and a crossbow saw through the search.

The following day, a farm wagon appeared to collect the heap of confiscated flying jackets, tools, so-called civilian clothing and other possessions the Germans considered contraband. I was lucky to be on hand as the wagon was leaving with its load down the long sloping tunnel towards the bridge over the dry moat. A quick appraisal showed a driver with three armed guards. Just by the exit from the tunnel was a staircase either side leading into the semi-underground rooms. Without a diversion to distract the guards, I walked alongside the wagon for ten yards or so, managed to grab two jackets, and dashed down the staircase amid the roaring of enraged guards. In no time a search was mounted, but it was rather half-hearted, and so I became a baron of jackets — two flying jackets and a black horse-leather belted motoring coat confiscated from an Army type by the Germans. The latter jacket I hung on to through all subsequent searches, and eventually gave it away to the driver who took us to the airfield in Belgium on our way home four years later. The history of getting the three jackets through many searches would make a chapter of reading. The main ploy was always to study the searchers and spot the one who was either tiring of his task or rather cursory and disenchanted with his remit.

Of course, the really important things like radio, civilian clothes, maps and tools were being got through by the responsible Escape Officer of each hut or group, and this was done with much resolution by way of arranged diversions or even bribes. The most helpful asset was to apply a stance of calm and relaxation to the point of boredom. Casualness was the key to all successful escaping activities, particularly when challenged.

All the confiscated kit was taken to a store, along with bona fide clothing. After showers prisoners were allowed access to their service clothing and to take whatever they needed subject to being searched. There was no point in taking much as none of the prisoners had lockers. They took enough to last them until the next shower, and their suitcases, kitbags and Red Cross boxes were then returned to the store and put under lock and key.

At 10.30am they brewed up Red Cross tea. Another *Appell* was held at midday. On this occasion the prisoners were not numbered or inspected, so it went smoothly and quickly. Dinner was next — *Klippfisch*, potatoes, turnips and bread left over from the day before. The fish, recalls Clelland, had passed its "sell-by date" long before the war. Dinner was not accompanied by any beverage, so there was nothing to drink until at 2pm when they could draw hot water for a brew. This was a hell of a bind if the *Klippfisch* at lunch was dried and salted, as it left prisoners with a raging thirst. They had coffee at 4.40pm, and another brew (tea) at 6pm or 7pm. Between then and lock-up they made sure they visited "the Cruet" and tidied up their rooms for 8pm parade, which took place inside.

Already the prisoners had established some elementary internal organisation. Brigadier the Honourable Nigel Somerset DSO, MC, was again SBO, with "Wank" Murray as "Man of Confidence" responsible for most routine dealings with the Germans. But as at previous camps, the basic unit of POW life at Thorn was the Mess. Each room appointed a room senior. He made sure that it was kept clean and that the men in his charge were tidy. They had to wet-scrub the room twice a week, and it took hours to dry, making the atmosphere cold and damp in the meantime. When a German officer entered they were to stand to attention by their beds, while the room senior reported the room number, how many men it held, and how many were sick. If any items of clothing required mending, he made a request to the *Hauptmann* who would see that it was done. The Germans always responded well to a smart room parade, were invariably polite and asked it everything was all right. Not that they could do much had things been otherwise. Lights-out was at 9.05pm.

Polite though the officers were, the guards were not at all friendly, recalls Mungovan, "because of the reason for our incarceration and the attention the camp received from the Nazis. The camp was visited one day by a party of Brownshirt officers, who stood on the wall above us and surveyed the rabble below." At one stage the Germans also deliberately fenced off part of the tiny parade ground to make it smaller still and warned the prisoners that they would not hesitate to shoot any trespassers into the forbidden area. As well as the three roll-calls a day, prisoners had to attend an individual photograph check. Every night at sunset a small group of British orderlies would stand on the drawbridge above the moat and sing "Abide With Me". It was the only spark of hope in an otherwise dismal day. Lights-out for orderlies was not until 10.30pm, as they were not being "strafed".

Before the arrival of the *Strafgefangenen* lice had been rampant in the fort, and after less than a week more were discovered. On Sunday, 9 March, the German doctor ordered that all personnel, except naval, were to have their hair cut short and their beards removed. This would be done by two orderlies who ran a well-equipped barbers' shop. The SBO gave the order his full endorsement. They had three or four days to comply, and if they failed everyone would have their heads completely shorn. Tunics and greatcoats were also to be smartened up and boots polished for *Appelle*. This was easier said than done when clothes and boots, once removed, got wet through in five minutes. They were also to respond in kind when the *Lageroffizier* conducting the parades greeted them with *"Guten Morgen"*.

Church services, conducted by an Army Padre, were held in the chapel at 11am. The chapel was also underground, built of brick and furnished with rows of rickety wooden benches. It was cold, but the driest room in the camp. For Sunday lunch there was a good helping of stew, with tea issued by Germans from Red Cross parcels brought from Spangenberg. At three o'clock in the afternoon the prisoners were allowed out for two hours in the sandy courtyard, where the RAF played the Army at football, using coats as goalposts. Because of hunger, some fell out quite soon, while some sturdier types stayed the whole course of an hour and a half. The rest walked about feeling very cold and collecting firewood for their stoves.

That first Sunday evening "Wank" Murray visited every room with an order from the doctor that anyone who had not been inoculated against typhoid within the past twelve months must be done at once, otherwise he would be a menace to his fellow POWs.

Monday, 10 March was wet, and morning roll-call was held in the cavernous entrance hall. That afternoon all the Army orderlies left for a troops' camp, Fort XI, and the RAF orderlies for Fort VIII. The Germans doubled the coal ration and issued some Red Cross food: sausages, steak and kidney pudding, cod roe, peas and carrots.

In the meantime, the British camp staff got cracking on establishing a more elaborate POW organisation and taking measures to alleviate the generally poor conditions. They set up entertainments and PT committees, established a canteen and started an educational programme. As well as extra coal, prisoners would be allowed extra light, to write three letters and four postcards a month, and to do PT on a voluntary basis. The medical officer had recommended graded exercise courses for those up to the age of fifty. The SBO had also requested that a can of drinking water be put in each room, that showers be allowed three times rather than only once a week, that beer be issued once a week, and that a representative of the protecting power visit the fort as soon as possible. For their part, the Germans promised to try to rush through letters and parcels and to issue beer if they could get the transport.

On Thursday, 13 March, Brian Paddon received a letter from the Air Ministry informing him that after the war HM Government would refund in pounds sterling any *Lagergeld* in possession of or credited to POWs. This was welcome news to those officers who had been saving their camp currency, but not to those who used theirs for toilet purposes or had lost piles of scrip when moved from camp to camp.

The orderlies from Fort XI came back that evening because they had refused to work for officers other than their own. As it was, officers in Fort XV considered that their conduct left much to be desired, and often accused them of rudeness and indolence. In the meantime the Germans imposed further restrictions. Prisoners were forbidden to lie on their beds during the day except by the doctor's permission. Hospital patients would be discharged as soon as their temperatures were down to normal. On Friday, 14 March all soft-seated chairs which officers had bought from the Spangenberg canteen were confiscated. This was an edict from the Party, not from the German camp staff, who disliked carrying it out. Perhaps to salve their conscience, they issued some canteen produce: a small bottle of beer, six biscuits and six ginger-cakes, covered with sugar, for each man. The biscuits were about three and a quarter inches square and resembled those given to dogs. But they proved, says Maurice Butt,

a great psychological boost, an inversion to incredulity that we should have these instead of bread. The war must be ending, the last crust of bread being reserved for the VIPs of the Fatherland! Much merriment accompanied these wild speculations, until we considered what would be the next step once the biscuit supply had been exhausted. Some people actually broke teeth biting these rock-like bricks of rye. The best way of consuming them was found to be by soaking them and then boiling the mess — mixed with anything available with the mash, such as sugar or jam, though availability was the key.

Boiling up had to be [done], as all water was suspect and highly chlorinated. The MO was hot on that. To generate heat for boiling was another problem as the fuel supply was briquette coal, strictly rationed. Several methods of breaking up the dog biscuits were tried, including rolling a glass bottle to crush up the bits. This took an incredible amount of time, of which we had plenty to spare. However, on reflection, it was some days before soaking was considered a feasible proposition — which only highlights our culinary ignorance.

On *Appell* the next morning "Wank" Murray announced that the Germans had at last arranged laundry facilities. He also announced that the SBO wanted them to answer the Camp Officer's greeting with *"Guten Morgen, Herr Hauptmann"*. Roll-calls were now taking longer. For ten minutes the *Lageroffizier*, Murray and the SBO would discuss camp orders while the prisoners were being counted. Then an *Unteroffizier* would go round the rooms and the hospital counting the sick. After adding the number of prisoners at large and in the cooler, the figures would be compared.

One morning Flying Officer Peter David Tunstall (ex-Barth) entertained the prisoners in his room by starting a discussion on how people would view ex-kriegies after the war. On his aerodrome at Hemswell, news that a fellow-airman had been captured was normally greeted with the statement: "Oh well, he's alright for the rest of the war." Now he felt different. But he was willing to bet that when he got home he would be told: "You lucky devil having been a prisoner of war. You missed it all." Tunstall's room was now beginning to look like a workhouse, with laundry strung on lines above the tables and the atmosphere fuggy from damp and tobacco fumes.

On Wednesday, 19 March the prisoners were issued with next-of-kin, tobacco and clothing parcels. There was also a bulk issue from the Red Cross stores: a packet of chocolate, a tin of condensed milk, two boxes of cheese, a packet of rusk biscuits and a packet of hard biscuits per man. The hard biscuits were excellent value because they required a good deal of mastication. Less welcome was the appearance of the three escapees, Edwards, Ellen and Surtees. John Surtees, after jumping from the train to Thorn, had landed badly and cut his face. He was recaptured forty miles south of Spangenberg after three days on the run.

Next morning the Germans announced that those who had put their names down for a TAB inoculation should go for their jabs at 6pm. The following morning prisoners were warned that any letters or cards mentioning the whereabouts of the camp would be disposed of.

On Sunday, 23 March, Peter Tunstall's room had a treat for supper. One of the Army officers had collected all the spare biscuits and made two roly-poly cakes, with raisins inside and cocoa powder on top. To their jaded palates, they tasted marvellous.

"One bright morning after roll-call," says Butt,

a delegation appeared comprising a group of German officers in their best uniforms and a few civilians. In the latter group was the American Ambassador to Berlin complete with long overcoat, Homburg hat and brolly, some say with spats too, but I don't remember that. Anyway, this elegant group went round the various corners of the camp block to see the evidence with their own eyes. The main points at issue were being locked up in our rooms at night, the unnecessary obstruction to daylight — ie, the boarded-up windows — and the limitation on washing which was in part necessary as all water had to be pumped up by hand to storage tanks, a task done by orderlies (British tommies captured at Dunkirk). Lack of exercise was to be adjusted by unlimited access to the confined areas plus a promise of occasional parole walks outside the camp in order to be able to kick a football about on an open area nearby. All points were agreed in the only place where there was room to move — the area where we were counted — and the Germans were displaying a feeling of magnanimity to the point of swaggering... It was a pleasure to see.

With that, the *Strafe* started lessening. On the morning of Monday, 24 March, German workmen went round ripping off the wooden shutters over the windows. To the prisoners, soaked in rumours, this was an indication that they would soon be leaving the camp. Three days later the Germans announced a blackout at nights. When prisoners went to the washroom the next morning the blackout was still in force. Walking down the corridor was an eerie experience, with vague figures, only their naked torsos visible, feeling their way along the walls. Over the troughs they had to wash by touch. Many prisoners were missing from *Appell*, some *krank im Zimmer* (sick in their rooms) and others under room-arrest for bad behaviour on parade. The Camp Officer knew that officers pretended to be ill to get out of parading in bad weather, and promptly did a tour of the rooms, only to find several officers, supposedly ill, preparing breakfast. Those who thought they had it made on room-arrest also received a rude shock. He told them that in the German Armed Forces "room-arrest" meant the cooler. The net result was that they were all turfed out on *Appell* and that a lengthy re-count took place. One genuinely sick prisoner, however, was Peter

Tunstall, who was admitted to hospital.

On Monday, 7 April a consignment of Polish tobacco arrived at the canteen. It gave smokers the hiccups, and they found it expedient to boil the leaves and leave them to dry. The next day bookcases arrived, and kriegies now had somewhere to put their possessions. The 11th was Good Friday and it started out well, with glorious sunshine. But when the prisoners turned out on parade they discovered it was still bitterly cold. Parade was held up because one of the RAF officers was idling about and Brigadier Somerset tore a strip off him. Then Murray announced that one of the Messes had put their lights on after hours and that as a result the Germans were removing light-bulbs throughout the camp for the entire day. Some of the Army took a dim view of the RAF types. They complained that the RAF were always causing trouble, which led to reprisals for the whole camp, and that they should be put in a Company of their own. Their behaviour was considered thoroughly selfish. Another camp order was issued that night: in future all rooms were to be ready for inspection without notice and nothing was to be left lying on beds.

On the 13th, Easter Sunday, the Germans announced that officers could pin snapshots to their letters and send them home, provided no views of the fort were included. They were now officially allowed to lie on their beds between 1300 and 1500 hours. There was also an issue of two weeks' camp currency. Peter Tunstall had now been discharged from hospital but was feeling restless and depressed. He spent the day lying on his bed, staring into space or looking at snapshots of his fiancée. On the 16th a hundred letters were handed out and more parcels arrived — eight for the entire camp. The next morning, when prisoners went on parade, they saw a posse of German officers, Gestapo officials and guards enter the yard — more than a hundred of them. The guards threw a cordon round the yard and after a harangue from an *Oberleutnant*, officers were called out three at a time for a personal search in their rooms. When they reached their rooms they were confronted by ten Germans — two officers, four or five NCOs and some policemen — who spent more than half an hour making a thorough search of each man and his kit. The Germans also inspected the beds and confiscated letters, notebooks, diaries and medicaments, which they said would be returned in five days' time. Meanwhile, in the yard, other guards scoured the sandy ground. Anyone seen throwing away anything incriminating was taken before the *Oberleutnant*. The prisoners were then taken *en masse* to the top of the fort and led into another exercise yard. Surrounded by steep banks of earth and barbed-wire, and overlooked by two watchtowers equipped with light machine-guns, it afforded a good view of the moat and the countryside beyond. They stayed there until 3pm without anything to eat or drink.

The Gestapo search had caught the prisoners by surprise and resulted in quite a haul. In Paddon's room they found more pliers, files and other escape paraphernalia — more tools, in fact, than were available from the German stores. Paddon was sentenced to a term of solitary confinement in "the Bunker" for being "in possession — with intent to escape".

(2)

Via the prisoner of war newspaper, a dreadful propaganda sheet provide by the Germans called *The Camp*, the prisoners at Thorn learnt more of why they were undergoing the *strafe*.

Normally they used the newspaper for toilet purposes, but on this occasion they read the article first. It ran as follows:

According to a report received here, German officer prisoners of war were transferred in November 1940 to Fort Henry, near Kingston.

The report contains the following details:

The fort, which was built in the year 1832, is surrounded by ramparts so that it is impossible for the prisoners of war to see anything of the country beyond their camp area.

Within the area of the camp there is neither grass, bushes nor trees.

The ground is covered with fine gravel.

The prisoners of war cannot but have the intolerable feeling of being in confinement, almost really being imprisoned in a gaol.

The report expressly refers to the gaol-like character of the camp, and states it is suitable for the accommodation of criminals but not for prisoners of war, least of all for officer prisoners of war.

According to the published camp regulations the German officers in Kingston have only three times a week, for two-and-a-half hours, the opportunity to use the sports ground outside the camp.

In Fort Henry, the senior German officer has to share a casemate with three other officers.

All other casemates have to accommodate ten officers each, who are thus closely packed together in a small space.

In spite of the heating, the dampness in the walls and ceilings is still visible.

Cracks in the ceilings are only temporarily filled up, so that dust, dirt and water penetrate through them.

Each casemate has only two windows, which look onto the courtyard.

The daylight entering through them is so dim that it is impossible to read or write without artificial lighting.

During the day, only nine latrines are available for the use of the German officers.

There is no canalisation; buckets must be used with chloride of lime as disinfectant.

The latrines lie in a little shed on the courtyard, in the immediate vicinity of the dining rooms.

The report further states that all prisoners of war in Fort Henry are locked up in their casemates at eight-forty-five pm.

The doors are not opened until seven-thirty am on the following morning.

Buckets are placed in the rooms for emergency relief during the night.

All guards at Fort Henry are equipped with rubber truncheons, which do not form part of the regulation outfit of the Canadian troops but are used only for the guarding of convicts.

The *Strafgefangenen* did not give much credence to this report, nor to another rumour which reached their ears that the German prisoners had been handcuffed and chained. As for the *Strafe* itself, it was, recalls Maurice Butt, "a petty act of reprisal or revenge so dear to the typical German outlook".

In the last week of April the Germans themselves discovered that the reports concerning Fort Henry were wrong, and lifted the restrictions at Thorn without a word of explanation or apology. Several months were to pass before the kriegies learned that the German account of how POWs in Canada had been treated was the opposite of the truth. In the autumn of 1940, when the number of Luftwaffe personnel shot out of the skies and taken prisoner by the British had become a real security threat, the authorities deemed it expedient to ship them to Canada. The Canadians accommodated them in an unfenced and lightly guarded camp comprised of former private bungalows near Fort William, on Lake Superior. Just as the British would have done had the situation been reversed, the German prisoners started wandering abroad, some not to return until recaptured. Naturally, the Canadian garrison had to strengthen the defences. In turn, one group of Luftwaffe prisoners decided that the best contribution they could make to the German war effort was to burn down the camp. When the Canadian authorities issued them with canvas tents as protection against the wind and rain, the Luftwaffe prisoners were well pleased with themselves. However, they had not reckoned with the severity of the Canadian winter. Canvas did not keep out the cold, and the prisoners were reduced to begging on their knees for alternative accommodation. When the protecting power stepped in, the only accommodation available was a disused penitentiary. This the German POWs accepted in desperation, but in bad grace. A garbled report of these events had reached the OKW through the protecting power, and Hitler ordered reprisals against British POWs.

As from Friday, 25 April the garrison at Thorn allowed their prisoners up on the ramparts and earthworks from 2pm to 4pm so that they could at last see outside the camp. As winter turned to spring, the hours were extended, but they were still herded back into their rooms well before dusk. "With the new deal in operation," recalls Butt,

life was much better. What was most missing were books to read and Red Cross parcels. To feed the mind, all sorts of talks were given by different people on subjects ranging from bookkeeping, selling bananas, greyhound racing, to the tombs of Egypt. The diversity of the

Army types was most apparent, as they were older men, and consequently had so much more worldly experience...

A form of rugby was played on the parole walks, but it proved ridiculous because of lack of energy — indeed, it was extraordinary to behold a man running with a ball then suddenly stop completely for lack of stamina, the result of the steady reduction of spare fat since capture, and a starvation diet. Injuries such as simple bleeding from scratches usually became septic, and this was seen to be a hazard to avoid in order to survive. Hence rugger was out.

The level of diet was, in accordance with the Geneva Convention, to be on a scale comparable to garrison troops. In reality, the German Army could not possibly have depended on the fighting ability of their men on this diet — unless it was devised to ensure they resorted to their own initiative to supplement supplies.

The food situation was a dominant thought in most minds; hunger concentrates the mind on its own relief. The low diet was a cause for concern and, indeed, it is a well-known fact that Red Cross parcels saved the lives of many and prevented the abject misery of prolonged starvation. As with most problems, the human mind adjusted to the situation until such time as a change occurred. Initially there was an over-consciousness of hunger for which the only compensation was excessive fluid intake after everything in sight was consumed. Some individuals exercised supreme restraint and managed to save part of the bread ration (a fifth of a loaf a day) overnight for breakfast. Most didn't, and some of those who did got up in the night to finish it off in case mice intervened, or even in case there was no tomorrow.

The next phase, after any accumulated fat on the body had been consumed, was a considerable weakening in both physical and mental capacity. The warning signs were a tendency to black out when getting out of bed or standing up from a chair. These are nature's warning signs to throttle back, as it were, on excessive movement. Hence relaxed postures became a necessity, which developed into habits of resignation and in some cases despair. The real answer at that point was regular but short sessions of walking in the fresh air to maximise a "ticking over" of one's engine, and so avoid atrophy of the muscles.

...The prospect of Red Cross parcels arriving to relieve the situation was almost ruled out. What accentuated the food problem was the potatoes, which had been poorly harvested, were half rotten from frost, green from light-exposure, had come out of the winter store and were delivered in bulk into a magazine — an unventilated underground store-room. The swedes were similarly frost-bitten, and together with the potatoes stank to permeate half the rooms in the camp. This obviously caused a natural revulsion against these two vegetables, which often formed the basis of a "speciality" soup served up by the cookhouse each lunchtime...

On Thursday, 15 May the exercise period on the ramparts of the fort was extended. The Germans opened the gates from 6.30am to 8pm. But as quickly as the prisoners were granted one right, another setback occurred. The washroom trough on the ground floor became unserviceable and the two hundred officers on that floor had to share the one in the basement. It meant four hundred officers crowding around one trough — an absolute shambles. After shower days it was particularly bad, as showers used up an entire tank of water and it took all next day to fill it again — a day in which no one could wash. On the 17th, officers heard that after the war all their camp currency would be exchanged at the rate of RM15 to the pound sterling. On Sunday the 18th they awoke to a beautiful dawn. The trees seemed to have blossomed overnight, birds were singing, and they heard the first cuckoo. The ramparts were soon crowded with sunbathers.

"Then, one day," recalled Maurice Butt,

a rumour came through from the *Kommandantur* — the office which controlled the camp, with huts for interpreters etc — that Red Cross parcels were on the way. Our spirits soared. Our lethargy forgotten, there were smiling faces all round. It was indeed a breath of spring.

Rumour became reality on this score, and within two days a farm wagon loaded with parcels arrived and crossed the bridge over the empty moat, to the cheers of all on hand. We slept better that night.

The first consignment of five hundred parcels arrived on Tuesday, 20 May, and many officers came off *Appell* to find their rooms stacked with parcels, including comforts, clothing and tobacco. Rumour had it that a train-load of Red Cross parcels had arrived and that another 4,000 would be reaching the fort next day. For supper that night Peter Tunstall's Mess pooled their food and had their best meal since Christmas — curried stew, sausage, Christmas pudding and cream of rice, bread, cheese and biscuits, and chocolate, followed by a good smoke.

On Wednesday morning many officers awoke with a stomach ache. But it had been worth it. More Red Cross parcels arrived — 2,000 rather than the rumoured 4,000, but still uplifting.

(3)

Despite the privations at Thorn, more than a dozen RAF, RN and Army officers escaped between March and June. Indeed, so frequent were the escape attempts that the guards had to do extra duties. Two of the naval flyers, Alan Cheetham and John Davies, discovered an abandoned tunnel and crawled to the end, only to emerge facing the muzzle of a machine-gun. Eric Foster planned a "gate job", his intention being to hide in a cart, but had to drop this scheme because of the stringent security measures. A second attempt, which involved him changing places with an orderly working in the *Kammer* (stores), also proved abortive. On Saturday, 22 March, three of the Canadians — William Donaldson, Francis Flinn and Don Thom — exchanged identities with three members of a working party that regularly visited the fort from the main NCOs' camp, Stalag XXA, opposite the brick-built *Kommandantur* four miles away. The orderlies stood in for the escapees on parade while they were smuggled into the Stalag, from which they then escaped. Disguised as Luftwaffe ground crew, they made for Graudenz aerodrome, to the north of Thorn, and on 25 March tried to steal a Heinkel from inside one of the hangars. They actually got inside the aircraft and were still trying to start it when a harsh voice accosted them from the control tower. An enraged *Unteroffizier* mustered them to attention and started to berate them for a breach of normal take-off procedure. As their poor command of German made it impossible for them to bluff this one out, they were compelled to surrender.

While they were in the cells, the Commandant of the aerodrome telephoned Fort XV to say he had captured three RAF escapees. This was news to the Camp Officer, as all prisoners had been counted present and correct on numerous *Appelle*. At midday *Appell* the *Hauptmann* told Murray that he knew the orderlies had mingled with the officers and that they were to fall out — *"sofort!"* (immediately). One by one the three orderlies fell out...then, to the astonishment of all those present, a fourth. The Camp Officer ordered an immediate identity check, with each Company commander identifying everyone in his Company. Thus the name of a fourth escaper, Lieutenant John Hyde-Thompson (Durham Light Infantry), was revealed. The parade had taken two hours and been conducted in bitterly cold weather, but the prisoners were cheered by the audacity of the escapers. That night the Commandant passed sentence on them and the orderlies. The escapers got twenty-eight days in the cooler, with a hot meal only every three days, and the orderlies five days' solitary. On *Appell* on Thursday, 27 March, sentence was also passed on the three who had escaped from the train en route to Thorn. Three weeks later, on Monday, 14 April, Cheetham, Davies, Donaldson, Flinn and Thom were transferred to Colditz, arriving on the 16th.

On Thursday, 17 April, former Barth kriegie Norman Forbes and a Territorial Army lieutenant, Airey Neave, joined a party of officers visiting the dentist near the *Kommandantur* opposite Stalag XXA. The Germans allowed officers to visit the dentist, a captured British Army MO, every Thursday. Fortuitously, Neave was suffering from inflamed gums and had put in for dental treatment. Each time he visited the dentist he chatted to the soldiers until he found two from his own company who would be prepared to smuggle him into the Stalag and arrange for him to go out in a working party. After escaping from the working party he would make his way to Russia. He was joined by Forbes, who feigned a similar ailment, and they agreed to inform the British dentist of the impending escape, which Neave did on his next visit. An Army officer forged an *Ausweis* (identity card) for each of them, workmen's clothes were smuggled in, and they made Polish ski-caps out of Army blankets and removed the badges from two Army battledress uniforms. When they finally assembled at the main gate on the day of the escape, each was wearing thick Red Cross underwear, Army battledress, and greatcoat. In haversacks hidden under their voluminous coats they had their Polish ski-caps, a compass concealed in a matchbox, maps (including two of Graudenz aerodrome) and escape rations: tinned food — including sardines and condensed milk — and chocolate. They also had their forged passes (Neave's describing him as a carpenter from Bromberg).

The two escapers felt quietly confident as they marched through the barren Polish countryside, passing sad-eyed peasant women pushing handcarts. They reached the dentist's surgery at half past ten and sat together in the waiting room while a sentry looked impassively out of the window. After Neave had been for treatment, he returned to the waiting room, and the dentist summoned Forbes. At eleven o'clock, after waiting five minutes, Neave asked to go to the toilet. The sentry nodded, opened the wooden door, and Neave stepped into the muddy road. Two sentries lounged by the corner of the hut, their attention distracted by a British soldier trying to sell them contraband. Neave entered the lavatory, doffed his greatcoat, which he hid in a space beneath the roof, grabbed an armful of wood and waited for Forbes. He was not long in coming. Forbes performed the same ritual as Neave and, at a whistle from a tall British sergeant lurking near by, they walked one by one across to the Stalag. Passing a sentry who was chatting with a British corporal, they made straight for the warrant officers' hut.

A few hours later their absence from Fort XV was discovered, and the SS and *Feldgendarmerie* conducted a search with police dogs. Disguised as orderlies on a fatigue party, Forbes and Neave stood inside the wire and watched with fascination as the Germans flapped about near the *Kommandantur*, gesticulating and shouting furiously. The following morning the Germans mounted a hut-to-hut search. But still their quarry remained undiscovered. At 6am on Saturday, 19 April they joined a working party assembling near the main gate destined for work at a nearby farm. All morning and until late in the afternoon Forbes and Neave worked in a barn under the supervision of a British corporal, stuffing straw into palliasses. In the meantime, the corporal unravelled the wire that secured an iron bar across the doors at the back of the stable. That evening Forbes and Neave climbed up the huge haystack toward the roof-beams and burrowed their way into the straw. For several hours they lay there luxuriating while the Germans searched beneath and locked the front doors. Then, at 10pm, they doffed their uniforms and buried them in the hay. From their haversacks they drew their workmen's clothes and Polish ski-caps. Thus disguised, they left their hideout and, by match-light, went to the back door. Sliding back the iron bar, they opened the doors and stepped into the night.

Turning east, they heard a dog growling and stopped dead behind a tree in the farmyard. Fifty yards away stood a farmhouse, which was used as a German officers' Mess. After waiting a minute, they stepped cautiously across some soft turf, one behind the other, and this time the dog gave a definite bark. They crouched, shivering, by a hedge, watching as the door opened. A full minute passed before the door closed again and they heard the bolts being drawn closed. Then they were on their way again — over a wooden fence, past a thick wood on the left, and down the low, marshy hills towards an artillery training ground in the distance. They were heading towards the town of Alexandrov, on the main road from Thorn and twenty miles away. At 4.30am on Sunday, 20 April, after covering some ten miles, they rested awhile on the grass at a junction between converging forest tracks and ate some of their chocolate. A cold wind was rising and soon it brought with it a heavy rainfall. Slinging their sacks over their shoulders, which were now becoming sore, they got up and walked south-east until they reached the railway between Podgorz and Sluzewo, a few miles from Alexandrov and more than a hundred and fifty miles from Warsaw. By now dawn was breaking, wet and misty, and as they lay waiting for the coast to clear, the rain again began to fall heavily. At last they deemed it safe to cross the railway line and, scrambling down the embankment on the other side, reached the cover of dense woods. After a two-mile walk the trees gave out, and they stood at the edge of the forest in the cold grey dawn with, ahead of them and in the far distance, a road. It was the road to Alexandrov. By 8am they had reached the road. Looking at their maps, they found they had covered twenty miles in one night.

They could not use the road, as even at that time of day military vehicles and civilian cars were passing along it, all occupied by Germans or *Volksdeutsche* — Poles were not allowed motor vehicles. The two escapers left the road and ploughed through the sodden fields parallel to it, but soon reached Alexandrov. Its tiny white houses were nearly all shuttered and it was very quiet. They skirted round the town and set off towards the riverbank and a long, straight, treeless road leading to the town of Nieszawa, on the Vistula. By now they were in abject misery. The rain beat down relentlessly, soaking their thin workmen's clothes, while water dripped off their ski-caps, pulled low over their faces, and trickled down their cheeks. The skin of their thighs was sore from the motion of walking, and they hardly exchanged a word.

Later on they passed a farmhouse, and a Polish woman, leaning out of the window, invited them in and dried their clothes in front of a fire. At noon the storm passed and they carried on down the road until they were passed by an open carriage ridden by an arrogant-looking German farmer who regarded them with too much interest for comfort. They decided to leave the path and strike off across country. The going underfoot was sodden, with flooded paths and swampy ground, and the cart tracks meandered in all directions until the two escapees were hopelessly lost. Their map, which had become sodden and pulpy in the rain, was by now next to useless. Neither could they seek shelter: the countryside was barren of trees and nearly all the farms had been taken over by Germans.

At dusk they reached a farmhouse that appeared to be Polish and knocked on the door. It was occupied by an elderly Polish farmer and his two daughters, who gave Neave a pair of corduroy trousers and let them sleep in the barn.

They left at cock-crow — it was now Monday, 21 April — but as dawn broke they encountered a young man with a bicycle who asked why they were not in the Army. Forbes, who spoke a little German, told him they were trying to avoid the call-up. As he left, Forbes turned to Neave and said he was sure the man would report them. Again they decided to leave the road. Reaching some woods, they lay up beside a clear stream, bathing their feet and shaving before moving off again towards Leslau (Wloclawek). They reached the town some time after 3pm and found its buildings decked out in Nazi flags and pennants. A party of SS thugs marched through the main street, singing. It was Hitler's birthday. Poles and Germans alike raised their arms in the Nazi salute — the Poles had to — and Forbes and Neave, with weary amusement, did likewise. As they walked on they saw one of the SS beat up a frail, bent old Jew, who had failed to notice the SS and to salute. The Jew fell into the gutter and his hat spun in the wind and rolled across the road. No one dared pick it up.

Outside Leslau they tried to seek shelter at another farm, but the occupants turned out to be German and the two hurried away. Reaching the great forest stretching along the banks of the Vistula they rested there the night, huddled up together under the trees. Their sleep was disturbed by the grunting of wild boars.

On the third day of their escape — Tuesday, 22 April — they made less progress. Neave's feet were in a bad way, probably owing to the stiffness of his Army boots, and he had to rest periodically. They took advantage of these frequent rests to grab some sleep. That evening they reached Gombin. A long straggling village, it was sparsely populated and they found no shelter. They set off down the road towards Warsaw. The sun was setting and they hoped to find shelter on the way. Once they thought they had found it, when they saw what looked like a thick forest in the distance. Stumbling towards it, they discovered to their disappointment that it was one of those well-maintained fir plantations so beloved of the Germans and completely devoid of undergrowth. In the end, they had to shelter between the furrows of a ploughed field in the lee of a slight rise in the ground. But it was so cold they kept waking up. By now most of their food was gone: all they had left were sardines and condensed milk, a nauseating mixture.

At daybreak on Wednesday, 23 April they set off without breakfast, determined to reach Warsaw that night. At last they reached Itow, thirty miles from their goal, and near the frontier of the General Government of Poland. Three miles beyond Itow they came to the frontier village. Exhausted and in pain from blistered feet, they lost their sense of caution and walked straight through it until they came to the frontier post. No sentries were in sight, and they walked through that, too, and on the other side stepped off the road in the direction of a patch of forest. Then they noticed two frontier guards, twenty yards away, sitting on a grass bank with rifles beside them. Picking up their rifles, the guards walked towards the escapers, who were too tired and stupefied to run away.

The guards were amiable, and asked to see their papers. Forbes replied that they had none. Pointing to Neave, he said they were brothers who lived in Gombin and were going to visit their sick mother in Sochaczew. Unimpressed, the guards led them to the guardhouse and through a door into a back room. Another German, a hard-faced official with ruffled hair and his tunic unbuttoned at the neck, sat at the desk before them. A fourth German lay behind him on a bed. The dishevelled official ordered them to stand to attention and called them "Polish swine". When the two guards had told their story, he ordered Forbes to be taken outside while he questioned Neave, who had no choice but to confess to being an escaped POW. Forbes was then led back inside. The fourth German leapt up from the bed and together the Germans subjected Forbes to a severe cross-examination. He maintained that after escaping from the dentist's surgery at Thorn they had immediately crossed the road and hidden in the forest. He made no mention of Stalag XXA or the British soldiers who had helped them. The official told Forbes: "I do not believe you! You are lying! You are Polish spies. It is now a matter for the Gestapo!" He picked up the telephone. Another sentry appeared and escorted the escapers to the police station at Itow, and as they walked in front of him Forbes stealthily tore up his map of Graudenz aerodrome.

From Itow they were taken in the back of a lorry to Plock and handed over to the Gestapo. They were hustled into a small room, where they waited until a small civilian with blond hair and a cruel face arrived and shouted at them to turn out their pockets. He regarded their matchbox compass and broken pieces of bread and chocolate without interest, then seized upon Neave's wallet and found his map of the airfield at Graudenz. This was positive proof that they were spies! They were taken separately to an upstairs room where each was interrogated by a young SS officer. Forbes was then moved to a severe, modern prison with the forbidding title of *Strafgefängnis*, where he found Neave waiting with a civilian escort who resembled a huge gorilla. Their clothes and what remained of their belongings were taken away and replaced with rough, grey prison garments. They were then led to separate cells and ordered to remove their boots. For two days they remained at Plock, with one meal a day of bread and turnip soup and half an hour's exercise in the prison yard. They were allowed to walk side by side, separate from the other inmates, but forbidden to talk. Nevertheless, they conferred in whispers and Forbes found that he and Neave had told the same story to the SS interrogator.

When Forbes awoke from his second night's sleep he was ordered to dress. He was going back to Thorn. After bread and *ersatz* coffee for breakfast he was escorted to the prison office where he was re-united with Neave. They greeted each other with mounting excitement. Then they were taken to the prison store where they handed in the prison garb and received their escape clothes, along with their escape rations and the matchbox compass — a typical oversight by the Gestapo, who were used to dealing not with escapers but with civilians. On the train journey back to Thorn the guards were friendly and discussed the progress of the war. They were dumbfounded when Forbes and Neave insisted the Allies would win.

At last, towards evening, they reached Thorn, marching to the fort with blistered feet and hoping to return to their rooms. But it was not to be. Instead they were taken to the guardhouse and confronted by *Feldwebel* Benz, the senior German NCO whom the prisoners called "Scarface". Shouting furiously, he snatched the remains of their escape rations, flung them into a far corner and drew his revolver. At pistol-point he led them, hands raised, down to the moat, stopping and flashing his torch on two semicircular chambers in the outer wall which were used to store swedes and potatoes. Each chamber had a sheet-iron door with a circular hole on the face — the only window. Forbes was thrust into one chamber, Neave the other. Inside was the stink of rotting vegetables and, on the floor, a couple of old sacks used as bedding. Forbes passed a cold and uncomfortable night. The brick walls curved to the apex of the ceiling and only in the middle of the chamber could he, a tall man, stand upright. When he tried to sit on the pile of swedes they rolled and tumbled beneath him and he slid to the damp, earthen floor. The stink of rotting rootcrops was so overwhelming that every so often he had to cross to the hole on the door and gulp down lungfuls of air. Once, noticing a sentry passing along the edge of the moat, he shouted out in protest against the filthy conditions. The sentry pointed his rifle at the door and replied that if prisoners behaved like *Schweinehunde* they should expect to live in pigsties.

At last they were removed from the chambers and led along the moat to a keep beside the drawbridge. Inside was a room devoid of any furniture except two beds and a stove. They lay on the beds and slept the sleep of the exhausted. A few days later they were returned to their rooms in the fort.

In the meantime, Paddon and Stevinson, of the Fleet Air Arm, were caught trying to escape in a dust-cart and became involved in a violent altercation with a German NCO, who later reported that Paddon had called him a "*Schweinehund*". At 3am on Wednesday, 14 May, Paddon, Forbes, Neave and Stevinson were removed from their rooms, bound for Colditz. Paddon, shouting at the top of his voice, argued that it was contrary to the Geneva Convention to transfer prisoners without twenty-four hours' notice. His complaints had no effect on the Germans, but woke up other prisoners. While all this had been going on, Eric Foster was preparing to put his third solo escape effort from Fort XV into effect.

Foster had planned to escape from his Mess. He would lower himself from the window at night by blanket-rope, and when he was at the foot of the moat an accomplice would draw back the blankets, while a second confederate, at the lower window, would pass him a ladder, by which means he would scale the outer wall of the moat. Over a period of weeks he collected timber and manufactured the ladder, which he painted to resemble the bricks of the moat. He then made steel hooks out of hinges stolen from window-shutters and secured them to the top of the ladder. For his disguise, as a Polish workman, he acquired a naval cap, which he stripped of its insignia, and Rupert Davies gave him his tunic.

Foster was set to go on the night of 14/15 May, zero-hour being midnight when there was a guard change. He had greased all movable parts of the window with margarine, so that when he opened the window they would not squeak. Nervously, he climbed onto the sill, gently paid out the blanket rope and slid down, taking care not to thump the walls too loudly with his boots. When he reached the bottom his colleagues above hauled up the blankets, and at the same time his home-made ladder was pushed through the bars of the lower window by Captain R W Moulson of the Royal Electrical and Mechanical Engineers. Foster waited a while until all was quiet, then stealthily crossed the moat opposite a point where there was a door set into the wall. A searchlight beam flashed towards him and he threw himself to the ground until it passed by.

Gathering his wits together, he carried on, holding the ladder near to the ground, until he reached the door. Above the door, at right-angles to the wall, was a steel plate, supported by chains and forming a convenient platform. Propping his ladder against the wall, he hauled himself up to the plate, anxiously hoping that the chains would stop creaking before the approach of the sentry patrolling the ramparts above. The danger passed, and Foster pulled the ladder up to the platform and slowly climbed until he reached railings at the top of the moat. He lifted the ladder again, hooking it over the top rail. As he started the last stage of his climb, one of the chains supporting the steel platform broke and some masonry fell with a resounding clang on to the platform. The game was up: a searchlight homed in on Foster and the guard arrived, screaming at the top of his lungs. Foster was suspended in mid-air, unable to go up or down. A second guard arrived, and the two of them stood above Foster, guns at the ready, apparently debating whether or not to shoot him on the spot. A rifle was pointed directly at his head. *This*, he thought, *is the end.*

Suddenly and without warning all the searchlights, and the lights in the fort, went out. Foster could hear the guards screaming and shouting hysterically, causing themselves more confusion. He saw the erratic beam of a torch moving rapidly along the bottom of the moat, which soon resolved itself into the figure of "Scarface" Benz, waving a torch in one hand and an automatic pistol in the other. Foster dropped heavily to the ground, right at the feet of Benz, who roughly pushed him towards the guardhouse, prodding the automatic into his back. In the guardroom Benz held on tightly to Foster, pointing his gun at his chest. Benz warned Foster not to try anything while he lent his torch to a guard who was looking for candles. When by candlelight he finally recognised Foster he was momentarily taken aback. "Foster! *Mein Gott!* I nearly shot you!" But he was soon his old self again, raving at Foster for blowing the lights and wanting to know how he did it. Foster said he didn't know how it happened — it was sheer coincidence.

Benz then had him taken to "the Bunker" (see below) to undergo ten days' solitary confinement, although he was still awaiting sentence for escape activities at Spangenberg.

For those who remained at Fort XV, there was an interesting and intriguing view from the ramparts. One of the main Polish railway lines passed only two hundred yards away, and day and night long trains of vent-wagons and flat-cars rumbled along the lines towards Russia, while streams of empty trains filed back towards Germany. The nights were a bedlam of noise from Thorn railway junction. Traffic along the line became heavier and heavier until at times trains were rushing by at the rate of one every two minutes. The prisoners saw long lines of tanks, guns and lorries perched on flat-cars, and scores, then hundreds, then thousands of troops cheerfully squatting in the open doors of vent-wagons, laughing and cheering. Two roads were nearby, running up towards north-east Poland. After a while military transport began to flood along them, too — heavy lorries and guns, nose to tail, stretching as far as the eye could see and partially obscured by a heavy pall of dust. The flood increased daily and continued week after week throughout April, May and early June. Then the prisoners heard that the main roads were even more choked and that the traffic they could see on the two, lesser, visible roads was just the overflow.

At first both prisoners and guards were mystified by the convoys. The guards insisted that relations between Russia and Germany were still friendly. None of the prisoners thought for one moment that Russia would enter the war on their side. Eventually they reached the conclusion that Russia must be giving free passage to German troops through Russia and down to Iran and the Middle East. The position was then complicated further by the appearance of fighter patrols over the columns. Rumours of frontier clashes started to filter through, then more rumours of troops massing on each side of the Russo-German border. Before long the garrison at Thorn imposed a rigid black-out, preventing the prisoners from watching the troop movements. But still the prisoners could not logically consider a Russo-German conflict, especially as Germany was still supposed to be getting vast quantities of war material from Russia. They racked their brains for a solution to the puzzle, and were still figuring it out when the punishment camp was finally closed down.

*   *   *

At midday on Tuesday, 27 May Eric Foster was taken to "the Bunker" by two guards to begin a sentence for alleged escape activities at Spangenberg. He was racking up almost as much "time" as Peter Tunstall, who already held the record for the number of days spent in "solitary".

In the meantime, Maurice Butt and Flight Lieutenant Richard Eric Troward had teamed up, with the intention of escaping and making for Russia. Their attempt was co-ordinated with another scheme involving six others who were to walk out of the front gates claiming they were wanted in the *Kommandantur*. The six were John Milner, a fluent German speaker, who would act as interpreter; three other RAF types, Pilot Officer Geoff Dodgshun, "Pissy" Edwards and Peter Tunstall; and two Army officers, one of whom was Lieutenant Peter Methuen of the Queen's Royal Regiment. Butt and Dickie Troward would then become "ghosts" and disappear into the unused half of the camp. The Germans would therefore assume that they had escaped with the six. "Then after the camp was evacuated during the next week, with no guards around, we were to walk out and head east to Russia," recalls Butt. "All too simple."

For our scheme Dickie arranged maps, compass, route and clothing, and my part was to acquire sufficient rations and learn some useful Russian phrases. This latter was accomplished by the patient tutoring of an Army type whose mother had escaped from Russia after the Revolution. There were only two dozen phrases, some of which were simple words, but my tutor was appalled by my efforts at longer phrases. One of these was: "Take me to Sir Stafford Cripps, the British Ambassador, he is my uncle," which was quite untrue of course.

The night before we were to disappear I decided to visit the Senior Officers' room to top up our larder. There had been a distribution of Red Cross parcels earlier that week, the second lot to reach the camp. I was confronted by a most extraordinary situation on entering the room.

There was a Luftwaffe pilot, complete with his yellow lapel tabs, accompanied by the German Commandant in deep discussion with a roomful of senior RAF and Army officers. Germans seldom came into the camp in the evening — unless there was a crisis of some sort. I listened for fifteen minutes and decided to look elsewhere for spare rations. Later we learnt that this Luftwaffe officer was Von Werra, the one that got away from British captivity on his third attempt by jumping train on his way to a POW camp in Canada and crossing the St Lawrence River into the States. He had been sent by Goering on a tour of inspection of RAF camps and happened to visit our reprisal camp that evening whilst house-hunting in the area. He was a man of short stature but very alert and strutty, posturing and demanding full attention of everyone around. Typical extrovert fighter boy.

I went to the Padres' room as an alternative source of supplementing food. There were two in the room and they seemed to think a bible was suitable equipment to carry but I left with an extra tin of corned beef instead.

The following morning, Wednesday, 28 May, the six presented themselves at the main gate immediately after a guard change. An officer in the Royal West Kents, Captain W Earle Edwards, who shared a room with Tunstall, was detailed to engage Benz in conversation while the bluff proceeded. "Scarface" had the troublesome habit of loitering near the gate, and knew many of the officers by sight, so luring him away was imperative. Edwards chatted with "Scarface" for about fifteen minutes. The ruse worked, and the guards allowed the six impostors through. Meanwhile, Butt and Troward went into hiding. Recalls Butt:

...after watching the six leave through the front gate Dickie and I scrambled through a gap in a barred window, made by removing two one-inch diameter pre-sawn bars (the sawing having been done the previous week) stuck back into position by a glutinous mix, and these were re-stuck by our supporters after our exit.

We lay up in the doorway of a bunker into which we had a skeleton key. Unfortunately neither of us could unlock the door so we lodged in the doorway, which was about half a metre deep.

The balloon went up and we heard the pre-arranged signal that the escape had been discovered, which meant our taking maximum concealment for the inevitable search.

Despite dogs employed in checking the unused half of the camp, we survived two searches. At one stage I well remember hearing the heavy breathing of the fat *Hauptmann* standing a metre above our heads, his silhouette reflected by the sun onto the wall two metres in front of us. We had taken great care to comb and "preen" the grass and wild growth littering the approach to our hide and it had paid off.

The third search, on the second day, was a much more toothcomb affair and the *Feldwebel*, "Scarface", approached our position from in front of us and, drawing his Luger, he fired two shots to signal our discovery — or perhaps to frighten the life out of us, which it certainly did. He fired into the air above our heads but the experience was hair-raising.

We spent two days in an improvised cooler, an empty bunker on the outer side of the dry-moated area surrounding the camp. From there we watched with some satisfaction and a few cat-calls from the camp as "Scarface" went round all the barred windows opposite the central area of the camp where our colleagues were. "Scarface" was checking if any more bars had been sawn through after determining how we had exited the main camp.

(6)

Meanwhile, the other six escapers had been recaptured. None were out for long. Methuen was picked up on Thursday, 29 May. Tunstall and Milner were caught the next day. Like Donaldson, Flinn and Thom before them, they had reached Graudenz aerodrome intending to steal an aircraft. They entered the aircraft, tried to start it, and failed. While moving to another one, they were spotted, recaptured and returned to Thorn. Geoff Dodgshun, Bob Edwards and the other Army officer had walked south until dawn and then hidden in a straw barn. Setting off again at nightfall they walked until dawn the following day, but reckoned they must have been seen entering their shelter — another barn — because shortly afterwards they were arrested by the police. (They found out later that the Army officer had failed to bury his faeces — and the Germans simply followed the trail of distinctive POW excrement.)

By the end of May the *Strafgefangenen* were certain that the camp would be broken up within a week. In the meantime, because Benz, who had had to do extra duty as a result of the prisoners' repeated escape efforts, was "bloody well annoyed", roll-calls were being called at unusual hours of the day: morning *Appell* at eight o'clock instead of ten; and evening *Appell* at seven, which was normally lock-up time. The tension was eased on the last Saturday of the month when one of the army officers, Lieutenant J E Barrie-Grayson of the Royal Army Service Corps, gave an evening piano recital in one of the underground vaults, to which the RAF were invited.

On Sunday, 1 June the orderlies were divided up into three parties, destined for Spangenberg, Posen and Stalag XXA. Afterwards rumours about the impending move ran riot. That same day another two officers, Flying Officer Ken Toft and Pilot Officer Robert McKenzie, were caught trying to escape, and warned that the next prisoners who tried it would be shot. At morning *Appell* on the 2nd Squadron Leader Murray announced that all heavy luggage had to be ready at 1430 hours. Then, at 2.30, after hours of hectic packing, some Gestapo and police suddenly arrived with about thirty *Unteroffiziere* and started a search. Maurice Butt now had to turn his mind to smuggling through his three leather jackets. As it turned out, this was simply resolved

> by the Germans providing crates for our heavy items of equipment — record players, library books and personal clothing. The last of these came about because after nearly a year in prison-camp following the fall of France, the longer stay or "older" prisoners had received clothing parcels from home via the agency of the Red Cross and quite clearly could not carry all their possessions. Perhaps it was the influence of the American Ambassador's visit earlier on, but the SBO's request for the provision of packaging was granted. By luck, the three jackets were placed at the bottom of a wooden crate to be filled by another, older prisoner, and whilst we made use of the fact that the packing of the crate was not supervised, we needed another diversion to get the coats into the next camp.

Rumours of an impending move were even stronger on Tuesday the 3rd, and the destination was believed to be Spangenberg. At morning *Appell* on the 4th, notice was given that all prisoners who had not come from Spangenberg were to move out that afternoon. Finally, that evening, the Spangenberg contingent was warned to be ready to leave the next day.

On Thursday, 5 June 1941, Reveille was at 0500 hours and roll-call two hours later. Afterwards there was yet another inevitable and seemingly interminable search, this time of the person as well as of the possessions. Finally, the prisoners were moved out, marching for the last time down the narrow tunnel, but now without any screaming and shouting by the guards and no rubber truncheons. Again by contrast with their arrival back in March, the road was dusty rather than muddy. Eric Foster had never seen so much dust. At Thorn railway station a long train was waiting — about fifty wagons. The guards were much more friendly than usual, probably because they were going back to Germany, which some of them hadn't seen for years. They issued the prisoners with one Red Cross parcel each and *Hauptmann* Schmidt, the security officer from *Schloss* Spangenberg, promised a ration of water. But he still read the Riot Act with the usual "shoot to kill" warning.

The train journey was long and tiring, but considerably less arduous than the journey from Spangenberg three months previously — and this time the prisoners received a "gash" (surplus) ration of Red Cross soup. During a stop at Guesen, a minor sensation was caused by the sight of young girls in bathing suits — the first girls some POWs had seen in two years. Then the Germans issued the promised ration of drinking water — the first cold water the prisoners had had for more than three months. At 6pm the train pulled into Posen. Prisoners were not allowed out of their seats to go to the toilet, but the Germans issued plenty of drinking water and coffee, and allowed them to wash. The train left Posen at 11pm and, working up a good speed, reached Berlin by morning. For two and a half hours the train stood outside the city, while the prisoners gazed out of the wired-up windows at the well-cultivated countryside and the lilac and fir trees. The reason for the delay was that "Pop" Bewlay had dived through his carriage window. He was caught almost immediately, and the Germans spread a rumour that he had broken his neck. When the journey resumed they passed a troop train carrying a mechanised SS unit bound for the east.

On the evening of the 7th, "Wank" Murray announced that they would reach their destination between ten and eleven o'clock. Everything had to be packed by 10pm. At 11.15 they reached their previous haunt, Spangenberg castle. "As the train approached the station we could see our destination," recalls Mungovan. "A cry went up: 'Oh God! Not Spangenberg again!', which adequately expressed the feelings of all of us." Truth to tell, they had perversely enjoyed themselves at Thorn. Once the *Strafe* had been lifted, they felt, the guards had done much to make their stay pleasant, and from May onwards the weather had been good, the winter turning to summer apparently without the intervention of spring. Altogether, Thorn had been an interesting and at times exciting experience. Returning to Spangenberg was something of an anticlimax.

It was, however, to be another short stay, recalls Alf Mungovan, "with conditions much the same as before".

Chapter Six

Spangenberg — Again!

Oflag IXA/H, Spangenberg, June–October 1941

It matters not how straight the gate,
How charged with punishments the scroll;
I am the master of my fate:
I am the captain of my soul.

William Ernest Henley, *Out of the Night that Covers Me*

On arriving at Spangenberg, the Thorn old lags had been split into two parties — the Army officers going back to the *Unterlager* at Elbersdorf, and the rest to the castle or *Hauptlager*. The Elbersdorf contingent was surprised to find the compound already occupied by British Army MOs and a number of sick and wounded Army, Navy and RAF officers, who they referred to as *"Grands Blessés"*. According to Article 9 of the Geneva Convention, doctors in the armed forces were not prisoners of war but "protected personnel"; such non-combatants could be exchanged for their opposite numbers held by the enemy. Article 68 of the Geneva Convention made provision for the exchange of sick and wounded combatants. The Article stated: "Belligerents shall be required to send back to their own country, without regard to rank or numbers, after rendering them in a fit condition for transport, prisoners of war who are seriously ill or are seriously wounded." It appeared to the Thorn returnees that some form of "reconciliation", in the form of an exchange of prisoners between the British and the Germans, was about to take place to atone for the Thorn and Posen fiasco.

Preliminary negotiations for an exchange had in fact started between Whitehall and Germany's Foreign Minister, Joachim von Ribbentrop, as early as May 1940, with Geneva acting as go-between, and the *Strafe* had the curious effect of accelerated the process. In both warring nations there languished prisoners who had suffered horrible wounds when they were captured or had incurable illnesses that rendered them of no further use to the war effort. The German prisoners, numbering no more than 3,800, consisted mainly of Luftwaffe aircrew, U-boat crews, merchant seamen and paratroopers. Many of these had been shipped to Canada in the summer of 1940, along with 2,100 civilian internees. Germany, meanwhile, held tens of thousands of British and Commonwealth Army "old lags" captured during the fall of the Low Countries and France, along with captives from the campaigns in North Africa and the Mediterranean. But there were also more than a thousand from the RAF.

The War Office, however, took a bureaucratic approach to the question of repatriation — insisting, firstly, that it could not exchange an equal number of members of the armed forces, as this would imply that a bargain was being struck with the Germans and so negate the basis of the Geneva Convention; and, secondly, on the need to bring the Dominions into the discussions. However, in a memorandum to the Prisoner of War Directorate on 24 March 1941 Sir Harold Satow, head of the Foreign Office's POW Department, took the Government to task, and an exchange was at last agreed upon.

Accordingly, during the summer, a Mixed Medical Commission, made up of one German and two Swiss doctors, started visiting the camps, and more than 1,700 long-serving, sick and wounded prisoners were permitted to appear before the board. In each case the German camp doctor and the British MO presented the facts, using medical records and X-rays, and each applicant was thoroughly interviewed. Those considered by the Germans to be *Deutschfeindlich* — persistent escapers and goon-baiters — were rejected, as were those who were obviously faking and a large number of RAF, whom the OKW regarded as blacker than black.

In any event, a total of 1,153 POWs were recommended for repatriation, some of whom were from the RAF. Among the NCOs they selected were Georgie Booth, who by now had been transferred from Posen to Stalag VIIIB at Lamsdorf, and Sergeants A A Maderson, W G McGrath, J E Oates and T Paterson. From the officers at Stalag Luft I they passed Flight Lieutenant G R Guest and Pilot Officers V Kelly, I A McIntosh and W R Methven. From Stalag IXC and the accompanying *Lazarett* they selected Flight Lieutenant Skelton, Flying Officer F T Knight and Pilot Officers P J Coleson, N D Hallifax and W T Mathieson. They also hastily transferred some recent captives from Dulag Luft, including Flying Officer M M Marsh, RAFVR, and Flying Officer A K Ogilvie DFC. The RAF officers were transferred to Elbersdorf, along with some Army and Navy officers and several protected personnel.

Frederick Thomas Knight had been a Wellington pilot on No149 Squadron, Mildenhall. On the night of 21/22 April 1940 his squadron had taken part in the second of Bomber Command's night-time bombing ops against Aalborg air base. The first had been on the previous night, and the squadrons involved suffered no losses. But on this occasion, flak and night-fighters accounted for Fred Knight's aircraft. He was badly injured in the crash.

Ian Alexander McIntosh, an Australian inevitably referred to as "Digger", had been badly burned on the same raid on the Maastricht bridges as Norman Thomas on 12 May 1940. Another, much more serious, burn victim was Noel Dan Hallifax. A fighter pilot from No3 Squadron, he had been shot down on 15 May 1940. His squadron had flown from Kenley to Merville as part of No63 Wing on 9 May and on their first day of action over France engaged the enemy no fewer than three times. On Wednesday the 15th, during offensive patrols over France and the Netherlands, the squadron claimed two Do17s and one Me109, but lost three Hurricanes. Hallifax got entangled with an Me110 over Zeebrugge. His Hurricane caught fire, and so did his oxygen mask, burning off his hair and ears. His hands and face were also severely disfigured. Dan was determined to return to England as soon as possible so that plastic surgeons could get to work on him: he was worried that the longer treatment was delayed, the more difficult it would be to rebuild his hands and face.

Pilot Officer Peter John Coleson had held his commission for only four months when he was shot down on Sunday, 11 August 1940, while serving with No53 Squadron, which had been transferred to Coastal Command on 1 July. He took off from Detling at 1024 hours on a "Dundee" patrol — from Dunkirk to Dieppe — and his Blenheim was badly shot up by flak and fighters over the French coast and disintegrated. The observer, Sergeant I Inskip, was never found, but Coleson and his WOP/AG, Pilot Officer G M Bardolph, suffered grievous wounds and were taken to the German naval hospital at the Château de Dominicaines near Hardinghen. Bardolph died there on 17 August. Coleson was transferred to Bad Sulza.

William Try Mathieson was the Armaments Officer in No38 Squadron, Marham. On the night of Monday, 30 September, 1940 Bomber Command had sent 104 aircraft to various targets in Germany, and No38 Squadron was slated for the *Leunawerke,* a synthetic oil manufacturing plant in Leipzig. Mathieson, who had only recently taken up his post, felt he would be in a poor position to instruct other air-gunners on how to shoot down enemy aircraft if he had no personal experience, and asked to be included on the operation. Pilot Officer D Maclean, of Wellington "Q-Queenie", had a vacancy for a rear-gunner, and Mathieson stepped in. Although Maclean himself was fairly new, his crew were very experienced, most of them having done twenty ops.

The trip to Leipzig and back was going to be a long haul and a drain on fuel, which meant flying more or less in a straight line both ways — not much room for manoeuvre if they encountered flak or night-fighters. Ten miles from the Dutch/German border Maclean and his second pilot, Sergeant S A Williams, saw before them a curtain of searchlight beams, stretching right across their horizon. They had no option but to press on, and pray that Lady Luck would preserve them. As Q-Queenie hit the curtain of searchlights, lit up like a fly on a light-bulb, a night-fighter bounced them from the rear. Mathieson shouted a warning to Maclean, who took violent evasive action. The fighter made another pass at them. "He's coming in again!" shouted Mathieson. But it was too late. Cannon-shells ripped through the rear turret and slammed into Mathieson's legs.

"I'm hit!" he screamed. "I've been hit!" Bullets clanged along the fuselage and wings of the aircraft, and within seconds both fuel tanks were ablaze. Maclean calmly ordered: "Abandon aircraft. Abandon aircraft." Although most of the crew were able to bale out, Mathieson was too weak to move, and Maclean gamely stayed with the aircraft and attempted a forced landing. In the resulting crash he was killed. Mathieson was recovered by searching Germans and immediately taken to hospital, where he had to have a leg amputated before being transferred to the hospital at Bad Sulza for further operations and to recuperate.

Marcus Maskell Marsh, already in his fifties, slightly running to fat and with fine grey hair, had been a well-known racing horse trainer before the war. His greatest moment had been seeing one of his horses, "Windsor Lad" come in at the Derby in 1934. On the outbreak of war he joined up as air-gunner and was later posted to No214 (Federated Malay States) Squadron at Stradishall. He was crewed up with Pilot Officer I K Woodroffe. On 9 May 1941 their Wellington took off at 2226 hours to bomb Mannheim and fell victim to flak. All the crew survived and went into the bag. (Woodroffe, who was still in Dulag Luft, would turn up at Spangenberg a few weeks later)

One of the last arrivals was Flying Officer Alfred Keith ("Skeets") Ogilvie, a Canadian in the RAF who had been flying Spitfires in No.609 (West Riding of Yorkshire) Squadron, Middle Wallop, since August 1940. He had distinguished himself in the Battle of Britain by shooting down a Dornier Do17 that had bombed Buckingham Palace. He claimed another six kills, plus one shared, before getting a taste of his own medicine on "Circus No32" on Friday, 4 July 1941, when his squadron escorted Blenheims to Lille. Attacked by an Me109 of *I./JG26*, his aircraft was damaged and he was hit twice in the left arm and had his shoulder ripped open by cannon-shells. He blacked out, but came to after a while, and abandoned his Spitfire, making land-fall in a field near St Omer. Some local French people offered to help him escape, but he was weak from loss of blood and had to be handed over to the Germans for medical treatment. He was at hospital in Lille and Brussels for several weeks, while German doctors fixed him up "as good as new" before sending him to Spangenberg.

The "old lags" noticed — initially at any rate — a slightly more relaxed regimen at Spangenberg this time round. With the onset of good weather, the Germans, much to their delight, once again allowed them parole walks. Those who had them were also able to wear shorts and short-sleeved shirts. On Sunday, 13 July, there was a break in the usual POW routine: a dust storm followed by a gigantic thunderstorm the like of which none of them had ever seen, and of such severity that all roll-calls were cancelled. The next day the Germans announced that all prisoners' laundry would be done once a week by four women in the village, a policy that would later inspire a very ingenious escape by two RAF officers held in the castle. At last, at 4.45pm on Monday the 21st, a hundred and ninety-one Red Cross parcels arrived, along with cigarette and personal parcels. On the 23rd, two Army officers and three orderlies were asked by *Hauptmann* Müller, the kitchen "goon", to go to the *Kommandantur* and sort out the Red Cross, Medical Comforts and personal parcels, with the result that another consignment was immediately delivered to both the *Unterlager* and the *Schloss*.

August was an eventful month in the backwater of Elbersdorf. On Thursday the 7th there was a full meeting to discuss courses of study for next winter and the books required. But the following day, the Germans read out a new Camp Order forbidding the possession of sunglasses except those recommended by the prisoners' Medical Officer and the German camp doctor. All *verboten* sunglasses were to be handed in and a receipt given. Anyone still in possession after the 15th would be punished. The order was received with much cheering, laughter and applause.

However, it was followed the next day by the more serious threat that prisoners should give up all clothes except those which were essential and which they could carry. The atmosphere was considerably eased on Monday the 11th when a party returning from a parole walk came through the gates attended by five wild geese which waddled in a most dignified manner across the yard, cheered on by the entire camp exhorting the Mess representatives to do their stuff. They drove the geese up the *Speisesaal* steps into the kitchen. However, the joy and anticipation did not last long. Much to the disappointment of the cooks, the geese were driven out of the side door by one of the guards.

On Thursday the 14th the *Lageroffizier, Hauptmann* Roth, started a camp tidiness drive. However, as he had always done his best for the prisoners and was one of the more popular Germans, they played along. Five nights later, on 19/20 August, one of the Army officers, Lieutenant Lance Pope of the Royal Fusiliers, attempted an escape from the yard. Unfortunately, he was caught and at about 2.30am the rest of the prisoners were woken up by guards shouting and searchlights coming on in the yard. On the evening of Wednesday the 20th the Germans tightened up camp security by bringing in more coils of barbed wire to make the fences thicker and higher. It was announced on evening *Appell* that from now on walking in the yard after 9pm was prohibited, "owing to darker evenings". But the garrison was still jumpy. At 12.30am on Thursday the 28th the prisoners were again disturbed by the Germans making a thorough search of the yard, with searchlights full on.

The Lower Camp prisoners were beginning to feel acutely the privations of imprisonment. The local German girls had taken to sitting on the benches opposite, giving the prisoners come-hitherish looks and beckoning them. However, the POWs were certain they would not have to tolerate this frustration for long, as they had been told that on Tuesday, 23 August, Oflag IXA/H was to be cleared of prisoners, with the aircrew from the *Hauptlager* going to a Luftwaffe camp, the Navy to a Kriegsmarine, and the Army to their own camp. But no progress was being made about those awaiting repatriation, and they were beginning to feel uneasy.

Their suspicions were justified. The two Governments had been unable to reach agreement on the route to be taken and the means of transport. HM Government proposed that the sick and wounded be repatriated in a British hospital ship through the Channel ports. The German Government at first rejected the proposal. But on Monday, 1 September the British Government received word from the Swiss Legation that the Germans had changed their minds. Through the Swiss Government the British then confirmed the arrangement. However, the agreement covered only wounded and seriously ill prisoners — it did not include protected personnel.

In the meantime, the prisoners at Elbersdorf were bucked no end by an enormous air-raid on the night of 8/9 September. There was little flak, but flashes lit up the whole sky in the direction of Kassel.

On Tuesday, 9 September the German Government, through the American Embassy, announced that 1,153 POWs had been passed as eligible for repatriation by the Mixed Medical Commission. Negotiations still continued on the basis of an exchange of only those prisoners eligible for repatriation under Article 68, and not civilian internees and protected personnel. HM Government proposed that the exchange take place between 4 and 7 October. On Saturday, 20 September the German Government expressed the hope that it would occur as soon as possible after 1 October — adding that the exchange would also, perhaps, include sick and over-aged civilian internees. This was despite the fact that they had not previously made the repatriation of POWs conditional upon an exchange of internees. They also pointed out that they were returning nearly 1,200 British POWs, whereas Britain was returning only a hundred and fifty-odd Germans. Britain should consider its gain such as to warrant the adoption of a receptive attitude towards proposals that might follow for the exchange of civilians. Germany's attempt to wring last-minute concessions put HM Government in a difficult position. The prospect of a POW exchange after two years of war had provoked a great deal of comment in the British Press and stoked up people's expectations. If the British Government backed down it would lose face. So, for the time being, it stood firm.

Back in Elbersdorf, gloom had set in on the 20th, when *Hauptmann* Roth announced that the move scheduled for Tuesday was postponed. Relations between prisoners and captors were now very fraught. The senior British officers made it clear to *Hauptmann* Müller that if the Germans continued to treat the prisoners unfairly they could not be held responsible for their conduct. If the camp was not going to be evacuated for some days, the least the Germans could do was allow them to have their suitcases back, and some food and cigarettes. The Commandant was in Kassel — where the OKH staff responsible for the POW area, *Wehrkreis IX*, was located — trying to find out if and when the proposed move would take place. Müller promised to refer to von Meyer when he returned, but in the meantime said he had to obey the orders of the OKW. The Commandant was back before breakfast on Wednesday the 24th, but no news was given out until evening *Appell*, when prisoners learnt that the move was still on but that no date had been settled. Despite this, suitcases were not returned to the prisoners and neither did they receive any more food or cigarettes. Parole walks and visits to the *Sportplatz* were also cancelled. However, with the connivance of *Hauptmann* Roth, the prisoners were eventually allowed a consignment of Red Cross parcels.

On Friday, 26 September, HM Government received another message from Germany asking that such German civilians as women, children, and men ineligible by age for military service, be included so as to fill the space available on the hospital ships. Three days later Britain received a further message: agreement in principle for the exchange of sick and wounded combatants held in other countries, such as Eire, Uruguay and unoccupied France, was an indispensable condition to the proposed repatriation scheme. Britain agreed, adding that as a token of good faith it would include some sixty German civilians in the first batch of repatriates. Later that day the Germans at Elbersdorf announced that the *Grands Blessés* would be leaving on Sunday, 28 September for repatriation and that Army doctors should also be packed ready to leave. The prisoners gave loud and prolonged cheers and passed the day in a state of frenzy. That Sunday, the *Grands Blessés* rose at 6am, and at 9am promptly took their leave of Elbersdorf. Once they had left, surrounded by guards, the camp seemed empty, but there was a general feeling of goodwill and sympathy all round. The next day the Germans issued more Red Cross parcels.

The repatriates boarded trains for Rouen, where most of them were taken to the racecourse, which had been converted into a *Heimatlager* (Home Camp), with two Nissen-type huts surrounded by *British* barbed wire. Officers were accommodated in one, and NCOs in the other. The Germans had gathered Army and Navy "repats" from other camps throughout Germany, Poland and France at Rouen, along with RAF NCOs from Lamsdorf and Bad Sulza, but there were few German guards or security personnel in evidence. The atmosphere was quite relaxed, and the "repats" passed the time engaging in or watching sports. However, as the days passed into weeks they began to feel uneasy. Not without justification. On Thursday, 2 October, the Germans had informed Britain that its proposal of 29 September regarding prisoners in occupied territories was unsatisfactory. This made it impossible for them to adhere to the agreed date for the exchange.

Much to the astonishment of the British authorities, however, at 12.20pm on Monday, 6 October, the BBC picked up a German radio message to the British Government. "Hallo England...Hallo England...Hallo England," said the German announcer. "The German Government wish to give to the British Government important information on account of the exchange of sick and wounded prisoners of war. Please confirm on proposed wavelength of 373 metres that you are listening." Immediately the radio monitors took the message to the War Office who passed it on to its POW Directorate. It was the first of a series of exchanges over the radio that would last for six hours. Fifteen minutes later the British replied: "Hallo, Germany. Here is an important message from the British Government to the German Government. Thank you for your message, which we have heard on 514.6 metres. We are listening on 514.6 metres. We will repeat that." This was indeed a historic moment: the first time the two warring powers had spoken to each other, and discussed their plans on neutral air, since the outbreak of hostilities.

Almost half an hour passed until at one o'clock — when millions of people, unaware of what was happening in secret, were tuning in for the BBC News — Germany replied: "Hallo, England. Hospital ships having on board German prisoners of war and German civilians can leave Newhaven on Tuesday, 7 October. Please indicate correct time of departure, total number of sick and wounded prisoners, number of German Red Cross personnel, and number of German civilians — women and children — on board. The time of departure of hospital ships from Dieppe will be arranged tomorrow on this same wavelength."

Britain replied half an hour later: "Hallo, Germany. Here is an important message from the British Government to the German Government. We have received your second message and will reply in half an hour." As promised, the British were on the air again at two o'clock. "Hallo, Germany. Here is an important message from the British Government to the German Government. We have received your second message. The ships will sail tomorrow. We will give you details as soon as possible this afternoon." The message was repeated at 3pm, and was acknowledged by Germany fifteen minutes later. The British then broadcast a long statement:

Hallo, Germany. The British Government has received the German message broadcast this morning. For the sake of clarity the British Government restates the arrangements which it is going to carry into effect. The two hospital ships will sail from the anchorage off Newhaven at 15.30 hours GMT, October 7th, arriving at Dieppe at 10.30 GMT. They will carry all German sick and wounded prisoners of war due for repatriation numbering thirteen officers and forty-five other ranks, and protected personnel numbering twenty-eight officers, including one chaplain, and nineteen other ranks.

For return voyage, ships should move to anchorage off Dieppe during the night high tide. This is in order that they may sail in daylight and reach Newhaven as 12.00 GMT on October 8th. They will be loaded to full capacity with British prisoners of war and protected personnel eligible for repatriation.

The ships will sail again from Newhaven to Dieppe October 9th, carrying approximately sixty German women and children internees. The ships will return to Newhaven on October 10th loaded full to capacity with British sick and wounded prisoners of war and protected personnel. Thereafter the ships will make such further voyages as are necessary to complete the repatriation of all remaining British sick and wounded prisoners of war and protected personnel eligible for repatriation.

...The above arrangements will be put into effect provided no message to the contrary has been received by wireless from the Germans before 20.00 hours GMT today, October 6th.

The British Government reaffirms its readiness to agree to the mutual repatriation of all British and German civilian internees other than men between the ages of eighteen and sixty. The British Government will be glad to negotiate arrangements with the German Government through the intermediary of the United States Government immediately, in order that the repatriation of civilians may be carried out with the least possible delay.

The Germans replied shortly before 5pm, agreeing to the arrangements, and asking "if the hospital ships *Dinard* and *St Julien* will make the course". "Your message received," replied Britain. "Both ships *St Julien* and *Dinard* will make the course."

There the exchange of messages ended. That morning (6 October) a message from Germany had been passed to Britain through the United States Government stating that the Germans were now prepared to agree only to a "limited exchange" on the basis of one for one. The Germans were trying to welch on their agreement. The British Government cancelled the sailing of the ships, disembarked the German sick and wounded and sent them back to their respective hospitals and camps. Speaking in the House of Commons, the Secretary of State for War, Captain Margesson, accused the German Government of "a flagrant breach of faith". The Germans then opened negotiations again. But the officials at Whitehall, who did not want to be disappointed a second time, responded cautiously.

It soon became apparent to the *Grands Blessés* that repatriation had fallen through, and some of them began thinking in terms of escape. In addition to four NCOs, two of whom eventually made a home run, Dan Hallifax also took to his heels, but with his disfigured face he stood out and was soon recaptured. Afterwards the Germans warned the local civilians that anyone found harbouring escaped prisoners would be shot. At the end of November, the repatriates at Rouen *Heimatlager* (the name now had a hollow ring) were put on trains back to their respective camps and hospitals. They felt profoundly dejected and disappointed; their only consolation was that for a few weeks they had enjoyed a change of scenery.

Shortly after this débâcle, the question of an exchange was again raised by the German Government. Once more, the British procrastinated. Duncan Sandys, the Financial Secretary to the Treasury (from July 1941 to February 1943), and Churchill's son-in-law, warned in an internal memorandum on 29 January 1942: "Any suggestions of delay or indifference by Whitehall...are only too readily believed by the prisoners' relatives." But it was not until May 1943, after several successful exchanges of prisoners between Italy and Britain, that delicate negotiations, carried on in the utmost secrecy via Swiss intermediaries, resulted in Whitehall relaxing its conditions concerning numerical equality, so opening the way to successful exchanges. The first repatriates from Germany set foot on British soil on 25 October 1943. Booth was not among them, for by then his injuries had healed; but Coleson, Knight, Bill Mathieson, Skelton, Maderson, Oates and Paterson were. Dan Hallifax, who by then was imprisoned at Colditz, was not repatriated until January 1945.

The RAF and Fleet Air Arm officers in the *Schloss* had missed out on most of these events, owing to the fact that they received bulletins from "The Canary" only intermittently. A few days after his second stint at the Upper Camp, Maurice Butt was admitted to the sick bay with an inflamed leg. One evening, while *Appell* was being held in the courtyard below, Butt heard his name being called out, as he was supposed to serve his sentence in the cooler for his Thorn escape bid. "Great alarm set in when the goons couldn't find me on parade; they hastily re-checked the figures and had a careful re-count, thinking a 'cover up' job was operating for another escape. Confusion reigned for ten minutes until a goon came at the double up the spiral staircase to check my identity in the sick bay."

Now that they had proved that Fort XV was far from escape-proof, Bewlay, Foster and Co were ready to see whether the previously uncrackable Spangenberg could also be breached. In the meantime, in the first week of June, they were joined by more purges from Dulag Luft, the first of which comprised Squadron Leader D B Gericke; Flight Lieutenant L S Dunley, RNZAF; Flying Officers E F Chapman and J H Frampton; and Pilot Officers R S Ayton, DFM, R F J Featherstone, RCAF, W C Hartop, RAFVR, W Linley, D Paterson, R A R White, RNZAF, and I K Woodroffe.

These men had been made prisoners between January and May 1941. All were aircrew with the exception of Edward Chapman — known as "Tug-Boat Ted" because he commanded an Air-Sea Rescue launch. Already well into his thirties when the war started, he nevertheless volunteered and was posted to the RAF Marine Craft Section, which was equipped with high-speed launches and became the Air-Sea Rescue at the beginning of 1941. In February he was posted to Dover, where the ASR was based at the Lord Warden Hotel (then HMS *Wasp*). Dover was perilous for ASR because the Germans had sown minefields in the Channel. By the time Chapman joined, two HSLs had already been lost, and crews were warned not to exceed 20mph. Unfortunately, one day in April Chapman's HSL was going at 30mph and, inevitably, hit a mine and had to be towed into Lowestoft for repairs. After it had been rebuilt, the crew started piloting it to Dover. The Royal Navy shelled them, and eventually an MTB came up and warned that unless they diverted to Harwich to be identified they would be blown out of the water. So to Harwich they went, where they were held for ten days while awaiting confirmation of their identities.

This was enough for Chapman, who at the end of April applied for a Squadron Leader posting coming up in Gibraltar. Having been accepted for the post, he was given ten days' embarkation leave and returned to Dover on Wednesday, 7 May to collect his papers and his gear. He was due to go to Calshot HQ the next day for his final briefing. He also had to arrange modifications to his new launch, which was being fitted at the Scott Payne yard, before flying on to Gibraltar. (He was given to understand, in the strictest confidence, that he was to accompany Lord Gort.) But none of this came to pass:

After supper at the Crypt Restaurant in Dover, there were a few more drinks in the HMS *Wasp* bar and an early night, as I was to be picked up by RAF jeep at 6am. I was about to turn in when Pilot Officer H M Revill, RAFVR (HSL 143), appeared from the dock, having been skippering the duty boat that day. As I handed him a beer he collapsed in great pain and was rushed off to hospital with a suspected perforated gall bladder. Some clot told Group that I was there and I was ordered to take over HSL for twenty-four hours, pending a relief and the resumption of my journey to Calshot.

There were four high-speed launches, numbers 121, 123, 142 and 143. The last, having been the duty boat the previous day, went to the bottom of the roster and a quiet day was assumed. With the exception of the coxswain, now commissioned and whom I had met before the war, none of the crew was known to me. It was a quiet day and I was ordered back to base at 4pm and sat down to a revolting, partly warmed-up and greasy plate of mutton and sloppy vegetables. As I retchingly contemplated it, the RAF crash bell rang and I ran to the source for instructions as my crew was piped to duty by the RN bosun. The order was: 098 DGN 18 miles — or 98 degrees bearing from Dungeness lighthouse, distance 18 miles.

Arriving at Ferry Dock, where the four RAF launches and Naval MTBs were berthed, [I found that] an engineer had already started the engines…and, thinking it a false alarm, I waved back three of the crew as we shoved off. It was an uneventful trip, at first, although we saw a few Messerschmitt 109 fighters flying towards France to land. On position, just off Boulogne, I put the Perspex marker over the chart and we started a square search. As the "squares" radiated outwards, we came nearer and nearer to the shore, and figures became clearly visible as they watched our movements. A German *Seenotsdienst* (Sea Emergency Service) boat then came on the scene, their equivalent to our rescue craft, except that our launches had just had their decks painted a bright yellow with a ten-foot diameter RAF red, white and blue roundel on the foredeck for recognition from above. At the same time, the new title of the RAF Air/Sea Rescue Service had come into being. In fact, I had "starred" in a propaganda film of its innovation and was embarrassed when it was shown and was applauded at the local cinema on my recent leave.

Then the Messerschmitt 109s reappeared — seven of them — and, as we were getting dangerously close to the shore, I told the coxswain to make a bead on the Dungeness lighthouse, as both wind and tide were setting in that direction and we might pick up some debris from the aircraft we were seeking, in the light of the sun glowing upon the lighthouse. No sooner were we on that course than the fighters began to attack us. Each of them had a cannon-gun (in the propeller boss) and each of their wings carried anti-personnel, incendiary and armour-piercing weapons. Our craft had a laminated wooden hull (about an inch thick), and we were carrying some 300 gallons of high-octane fuel for our three Napier Sealion 500hp engines.

Didn't she burn!

The first attack wrecked the steering and we assumed a wide port turn to become a sitting target for the two attacks to follow. I saw an incendiary bullet penetrate the wireless operator's chest, and it came out of his back. Came the second attack and the coxswain cried out "I've been hit!" as blood streamed from his right shoulder — only a couple of inches from my left shoulder, as we stood in the wheelhouse together. "Go and lie down!" I told him, as I disregarded the useless wheel.

As he went below, I realised how helpless we were, as flames began to spread and none of the fire extinguishers worked.

The senior wireless operator was unconscious and, apart from his colleague and myself, everyone else was wounded — the three deck-hands in the legs...Then I thought of the engine-room. I rushed aft and lifted the hatch, and a blast of white-hot flames scorched off my eyelashes and moustache and singed my tunic. I immediately closed it. The engineer must have died from the first attack — but, thank God, his mate was alive, as we had left him ashore.

The whole experience was as if I were watching a film and not a participant. I could see myself, as I do now relating the story.

I flung the wooden dinghy over the side and started to abandon ship, dropping the crew into it like a cat saving her kittens. Although the dinghy was riddled with bullet-holes, I grabbed the oars to row the eighteen miles to Dover with water up to the gunwale. Then the 109s came round again and began to fire at us in the dinghy. Suddenly they sheered off and we saw that the German skipper had saved our bacon by endangering himself and his crew. In fact, he turned out to be a splendid fellow, having been an officer in our Merchant Navy prewar — in the Blue Funnel Line, I believe. As he slowly came alongside to make a lee, his craft rolled heavily and the gunwale of the dinghy was struck by his chine, throwing us all into the drink. As skipper, I did my bit from the drink end, as I was holding up the unconscious W/Op, who was gurgling blood etc all over me, while at the same time I was keeping the unwounded W/Op afloat, as he was clinging to the collar of my duffel coat because he couldn't swim.

I sent the latter up the line to give a hand on deck and then carefully placed the loop of the big-eye splice under the other W/Op and he was gently hauled aboard. Then followed the others in turn, and I was last. I didn't realise how shagged I was. The leg I had put into the splice gradually slipped out and I went down, quite blissfully, until I saw the shape of the craft way above and pulled myself together. I even threw off my tin hat. None of the "past life" nonsense happened, and I made sure that the loop was well tucked into my groin before I was eventually hauled aboard.

The German skipper handed me a bottle of brandy, and I must have glugged a good third before I began to recover. It was then that I saw my coxswain, stripped to the waist, facing aft and holding the boat's rail with his right hand. I went towards him and saw the gaping hole in his shoulder, into which the German medical orderly was inserting a probe. Suddenly, he flipped the probe and a whole cannon-shell spun out over the sea, and as it hit the water it exploded.

The remainder of the wounded had been well looked after, too. (I learned afterwards that a German nurse stayed twenty-four hours with the badly wounded W/Op until he came round.)

When we arrived in Boulogne harbour, we were met by a typical cinema Prussian with a shaven head and a monocle. This Major had had his left arm shot off below the elbow in WWI and was particularly offensive. He was soon joined by a sawn-off (five-foot nothing) Luftwaffe Major with a Van Dyke beard, the leader of the Me109s that had shot us up. He held his hand out and said: "The victor and the vanquished — you will come to our Mess to celebrate!"

"Get stuffed, you Nazi bastard! I've just learned that we were searching for one of your squadron."

The German skipper was very concerned about the entire situation, especially as we were attacked after all the publicity about Air/Sea Rescue yellow decks and special markings. This became plainer still when we arrived at the Hotel Bristol, where the *Seenotsdienst* had their HQ. There, the unwounded W/Op and I were taken to a very large room overlooking the sea from two large windows, in front of which was a partners' desk. The skipper sat one side and the Prussian on the other. All around were reporters from all the services and the Nazi papers, all very young and *Heil Hitler*-ing...

My pockets were searched and a photo of my blonde daughter was acclaimed with: "Ah! She is the true Aryan and will breed in our stud farm!"

"How about me?" I said.

"You are the squire class and will be castrated!" they responded.

The W/Op and I sat at the back of the room, each side of a small round table on which were black bread and *ersatz* coffee made from acorns. Meanwhile, we were entertained by the antics of the reporters and a very nasty argument going on between the Prussian and the skipper.

I had no knowledge of German at all then, but my wife and I had intended to take a trip up the Rhine before the war. A friend of my father — a watchmaker — had trained in Switzerland and, when he heard of our intention, had jokingly said that the only German we'd need was *"Geben Sie mir ein Doppelbett"* — give me a double bed. The row between the skipper and the Prussian had reached its pitch, and I was intrigued and gaping at them. Suddenly, the Prussian said: "You understand Cherman, no?...Vat Cherman do you know?"

"Geben Sie mir ein Doppelbett," I responded.

The Prussian glared at me, glared at the skipper, glared at the pressmen. Then he leapt to his feet, rammed on his cap and slammed out of the room.

The pressmen were hysterical, like giggling girls. They'd never seen the Major so humiliated. Then the skipper took over and ordered them out.

He then had cream cakes and real coffee brought to us, as he started to ring round his pals. Goodness knows what he said, but he always ended up slapping his thigh and saying: *"Geben Sie mir ein Doppelbett!"*

He finished our visit with an English news programme which had been preceded by Henry Hall playing "Night and Day" — the very first tune I heard after I escaped from the Russians exactly four years later, to the day!

We spent the night under guard in an old house outside the town. On the way, as we passed a filling station, a French girl gave us the V-sign. We had an uncomfortable night because the beds we slept on had springs but no mattresses. The next day I was interrogated by the Gestapo, who were confused because I was not a pilot. Later on in the day we were escorted to the railway station, bound for Frankfurt. We stopped at Lille and changed trains at Cologne. While we were awaiting our connexion the air-raid siren sounded and two women spat at us. Still, we travelled first class to Frankfurt, arriving at Dulag Luft on a beautiful, moonlit night. That was on 10 May.

I spent four or five days in solitary, and was interrogated twice. The second interrogator threatened me with a pistol. Some time later another German, impressed because I had been a district manager for Sandeman's at Buxton, arrived with two bottles of sherry. We started drinking and eventually the German flaked out under the table. I polished off the rest of the sherry. Afterwards I was bursting for a pee, and banged the door to be allowed to go to the lavatory. I got no response so threatened to pee under the door if they didn't open up. They were so exasperated that they released me into the compound.

The first person I met on entering the compound was John Casson, who had been a cadet on the *Worcester* when I was Cadet Captain. Another naval type there at the time was Peter Butterworth.

Of those 1941 kriegies at Spangenberg who were shot down as opposed to being "shot up", the first to enter the bag was John Henry Frampton, the second pilot of a Whitley MkV from No58 Squadron, Linton-on-Ouse (No4 Group). On 15/16 January Bomber Command had carried out a successful raid by ninety-six aircraft on Wilhelmshaven with the loss of only one Whitley, and decided to follow it up on 16/17 January with a further eighty-one aircraft. "Frammy" Frampton's Whitley took off at 1745 hours with Sergeant A E Barlow at the helm. The outward leg passed without incident, but as fog had closed in most crews had difficulty finding the target. It was also more heavily defended than previously, and five aircraft were lost. Barlow's crate was hit by flak from a *Marineflakabteilung*, and he struggled with the aircraft as far as Holland, where it crashed at 2115 hours at Anna Paulowna, twelve kilometres south-east of Den Helder. All the crew survived.

The next to enter *Kriegsgefangenschaft* was William Charles Hartop, a Hampden pilot in No144 Squadron, Hemswell (No5 Group). On April Fools' Day eleven of the squadron's aircraft were sent to attack Brest in broad daylight, but a decision was made to abort. Just as the formation was hitting the Brittany coast at Lannilis, on the way back, Bill Hartop's kite copped a packet from the local flak. He was the only survivor.

Pilot Officer Woodroffe, who had been Marcus Marsh's pilot on the 9/10 April op, was followed into captivity twenty-four hours later by New Zealander Stuart Dunley, a Wellington observer in No40 Squadron, Alconbury (No3 Group). On 10/11 April, eleven aircraft from No40 Squadron were briefed to bomb the airfield at Mérignac, near Bordeaux. Dunley's pilot, Flight Lieutenant F A Bowler, took off at 2040 hours. His aircraft damaged by a night-fighter and his rear-gunner killed, he was forced to ditch in the North Sea. Bowler, Dunley and the rest of the crew survived, most of them going to Stalag Luft I.

South African tough Donovan Brent Gericke was the only member of the RAF to be captured on Saturday, 12 April 1941. His squadron, No110, based at Wattisham, had been lending Coastal Command a hand by sending lone Blenheim MkIVs out on daylight anti-shipping patrols. Gericke had taken off on one such patrol at 1055 hours. Making a low-level attack on what turned out to be a flak ship, he came off the worst and had to ditch in the sea west of Westkapelle, Holland. His observer and WOP/AG were never recovered.

He was followed almost a month later by Roff Ayton, an Irishman from No97 (Straits Settlements) Squadron, Coningsby. On 10/11 May twenty-three aircraft, some of which were from No97 Squadron, set out to bomb Berlin. For Ayton and his crew — Sergeants W J Chantler, J Bryce, E W R Sykes, D H Harvey and R Anderson — this was their third operation in the Avro Manchester. As if having to fly a lousy kite was not enough, Ayton got off to a bad start when his aircraft hit an aerial mast on an English cottage just after take-off, causing a drag on the aircraft. "That started the ball rolling," he remarked later. He got the flaps up when thirty miles out at sea at a height of 100 feet, then climbed better after that and got to 14,000. The rest of the outward leg passed without incident until they got to the outskirts of Berlin. While they were looking for their target the port engine caught fire and, even though he fully feathered it, carried on burning for ten minutes. But he pressed on and bombed on one engine. Only twelve aircraft bombed targets in the city, and two Stirlings and one Manchester — Ayton's — were lost. Just as Ayton was leaving the target area the wireless set caught fire and burned out, and soon all the electrical equipment was u/s and the intercom dead. To maintain height the crew threw everything overboard except one rear gun and about 100 rounds of ammunition, but still the Manchester lost height. To cap it all, searchlights coned the aircraft over Osnabrück and Ayton had to drop 1,000 feet to get away.

Although down to 2,000 feet at the Dutch coast, he decided to make for England, with the rev counter gone on the starboard engine and the boost reading –3lbs. He flew over the sea for about seventy-five minutes. Half-way across, the starboard engine started to give trouble. By now he was flying at about fifty feet above sea level. Ayton gave the throttle full boost to try to keep height and got -½lb boost with glycol pouring out like boiling milk. He told the crew to brace themselves and, at 0342 hours, he ditched:

…a wave hit the tail and the nose went into the next one. Came to the surface shortly after, and the crew were in the dinghy. Went back for my parachute to use as a sail and, after tying it to my overalls, I jumped into the sea and swam for about 20 minutes until the crew reached me. Felt all in and had a broken ankle where my boot was yanked off on landing.

They spent three and a half days in their dinghy and were taken on board a Dutch trawler on Friday night at 2235 hours, very hungry and frost-bitten. Ayton drank three bottles of wine and slept round the clock. The rear-gunner, Sergeant R Anderson, was semi-conscious for the first two days with concussion and a twisted knee, but otherwise the crew were unharmed except for Ayton's broken ankle. They were landed in Holland and taken to Amsterdam, where they were interrogated at the Carlton Hotel, which was being used as a Luftwaffe HQ. They were questioned again at Dulag Luft, where Ayton was told that his crew held the record at that time for the number of days spent in a dinghy.

The night after Ayton ditched, the Germans bagged Johnny Featherstone, a Canadian navigator in a Hampden from No144 Squadron, which had recently lost Bill Hartop to kriegiedom. On 11/12 May eighty-one aircraft were dispatched to bomb the harbour at Bremen. On the return leg Featherstone's aircraft, flown by the Flight Commander, Squadron Leader G C Rawlins DFC, was bounced at about 0200 hours by *Oberleutnant* Helmut Woltersdorf of *II/NJG1*. Two of Rawlins' crew were killed outright and the Hampden crashed at Hoogkarspel, six kilometres west-south-west of Enkhuizen.

A lone fighter pilot amongst this crop of prisoners, New Zealander Bob White flew Hurricane IIs with No258 Squadron. On Tuesday, 21 May the squadron provided cover for a "Circus 18" operation by Blenheims over Béthune. White was shot down by an Me109.

(3)

On Monday, 23 June another batch of newcomers arrived from Dulag Luft. They were Squadron Leaders M E Redgrave and E T Smith; Flight Lieutenant J Bryks (Czech); Flying Officers T A Bax, R J E Boulding, D Bruce, AFM, and S T Sedzik (Pole); Pilot Officers A J Brewster, P S E Briggs, RAFVR, W Cebrazynski (Pole), N M Dunn, RAAF, K N Holland, K Jaklewicz (Pole), J McB Kerr, RNZAF, W A Sojka (Pole), and P P Villa; and Lieutenant E C Newborn of the South African Air Force.

Dominic Bruce, a Navigation and Bombing Leader with No9 Squadron, Honington, and Thomas Albert Bax, the unit's gunnery leader, were captured on Monday, 9 June 1941, two days after Bruce's twenty-sixth birthday. Bruce had joined the RAF in July 1935, and had originally trained as a wireless operator, then as an air-gunner. In November 1936 he joined No214 Squadron at Scampton, equipped with Virginias and Harrows. In March 1939 he re-trained as an air observer at the Bombing School, Stranraer, and in September became an instructor at OTU Harwell. He was posted to the Wellington-equipped No9 Squadron in May 1940, and in September, after twenty-five ops, became the squadron's Navigation and Bombing Leader, a staff appointment with restricted operational flying duties. Bruce was commissioned Pilot Officer in January 1941 and by June had been promoted to Flying Officer. He had in fact flown on three ops with various crews when on 9 June he was selected to fly an extra operation with the CO, Wing Commander R G C Arnold. Eighteen aircraft were down to carry out an armed reconnaissance of enemy ships off Dunkirk, The Hague and Terschelling. "This was a silly daylight raid," wrote Bruce later, "[with] no escort against shipping." The crew was formed from scratch, with Bax and the other air gunner, Sergeant R H Barratt, both being from Staff and flying "to keep in touch". All the same, Bruce merely told his wife he would be late for tea. However, the tea was ruined because the Wimpey was attacked over the Dutch coast by a gaggle of Me109s off Zeebrugge. As the crew baled out of the blazing aircraft over the North Sea, Roy Arnold stayed on board, holding it steady and ultimately giving his life for his men. Bruce was recovered with slight burns, and on reaching Dulag Luft was sent to Hohemark for treatment.

By the time he reached Spangenberg, Bruce was already in bad with the Germans, because he had become involved in an altercation with one of the guards at Dulag Luft and hit him on the head with a shelf. He was now awaiting trial.

Mark Evelyn Redgrave, a Flight Commander in No40 Squadron, which had recently lost Stuart Dunley, was bagged with his entire crew on 11/12 June, when ninety-two Wimpeys and six Short Stirlings took off at 2300 hours to raid Düsseldorf. Ground haze prevented accurate bombing, and six Wellingtons were shot down. Redgrave's aircraft didn't even reach the target. His navigator, Sergeant Cyril Rofe, had just set a new course southwards from the North Sea when at 1000 hours the machine-gun bullets from a night-fighter slammed into the Wimpey and the whole aircraft shook. It was then coned by searchlights from a marine flak unit, and all was bright lights, flashing guns and red tracer. "Where now?" Redgrave asked his navigator. Rofe pointed to a sandbank off Hellevoetsluis, Holland. "There," he said. Redgrave crash-landed on the sandbank with bombs still on board, and the aircraft started sinking. The crew scrambled out and took to their dingy. All but Redgrave and one of the WOP/AGs, Sergeant P Rockingham, were wounded. Their dingy was awash with seawater and drifting uselessly on the tide. They managed to crawl out and wade back to the sandbank, where they hollered for help. Then the tide turned, and they prayed they would get off the sandbank by daylight — otherwise they would drown. When the sun rose the water was up to their shoulders, and they kept each other afloat by forming a ring and holding hands.

At last a motor-launch arrived, and a huge Dutch sailor put out a small rowing boat and came towards them, grinning from ear to ear. As they tried to board the rowing boat the wash from the approaching launch overturned it, so the crew of the launch threw them a rope. The Dutchmen had to hand them over to the Germans, who took the stretcher cases to hospital and the walking wounded direct to Dulag Luft. Mark Redgrave and Phil Rockingham, who were not wounded, were taken to the flak post, where the Germans boasted that it was they who had shot down Redgrave's aircraft. For a quiet life, they agreed, and were pleasantly surprised when they were handed a large bowl of strawberries and cream. They then began their journey to Oberursel.

Two of the Poles, Sedzik and Sojka, were also made captive that night, flying on the same operation. They were pilot and observer in No300 (Masovian) Squadron, based at Swinderby, which had been formed in July 1940 as part of No1 Group. Like Redgrave, Sedzik was also forced to ditch, though only one of his crew, the tail-gunner, was wounded.

Pilot Officer Holland, an observer with No51 Squadron (No4 Group), was bagged on the night of 16/17 June when 105 bombers set out with HEs and incendiaries to set Cologne ablaze. No51 Squadron took off from Dishforth at 2200 hours and formed up with Nos 78 and 103 Squadrons. They caused scattered damage to the city, but on the return leg were intercepted by night-fighters from I/NJG1. Holland's Whitley, flown by Sergeant T J Baston, was attacked by *Oberfeldwebel* Reinhard Kollak, who raked it from nose to tail. The aircraft crashed at Houthalen, near Limburg, at 0226 hours. Holland was the only survivor.

Two nights later the other two Poles, Cebrazynski and Jaklewicz, were shot down during a raid by a hundred aircraft on Bremen. Cebrazynski was an observer in No300 Squadron, and Jaklewicz performed the same role on No305 (Ziemia Wielkopolska) Squadron at Syerston, also part of No1 Group and formed that August from Poles who had fought with the French Air Force. Both aircraft fell to deadly accurate fire by night-fighters. "Jacko" Jaklewicz's aircraft, piloted by Sergeant S Lewek, was attacked by *Oberleutnant* Egmont Prinz zur Lippe Weissendfeld of 4/NJG1, and with two of the air-gunners dead crashed in the Polder Het Grootslag at Hoogkarspel in northern Holland. The same unit was responsible for shooting down Cebrazynki's aircraft, flown by Sergeant W Paleniczek. The culprit was *Oberfeldwebel* Paul Gildner. They crashed into the Waddenzee at about 0300 hours, and only two of the crew came out alive.

Pilot Officer Brewster, who flew Whitleys with No51 Squadron, was brought down on 19/20 June when twenty Whitleys set out at 2303 hours to bomb Düsseldorf. Ground haze obscured the target, but not Brewster's aircraft, which was hit by flak. All the crew survived, although the tail-gunner, Sergeant Mann, was wounded. He would be repatriated in 1943.

Another victim from that night's operations was Pilot Officer Johnny Kerr, a second pilot from No99 (Madras Presidency) Squadron (No3 Group), which was now based at Waterbeach. Twenty-eight Wellingtons set out at dusk to bomb Cologne, and Kerr's aircraft, flown by Squadron Leader B J Rogers AFC, was shot down by a night-fighter. The pilot and the rear-gunner were killed.

Roger Boulding, Joseph Bryks, Norman Maxwell Dunn and Eric Smith were all fighter pilots. Max Dunn, an Australian, flew the Hurricane MkII with Rob White's old outfit, No258 Squadron. It had been using at Kenley as a forward since 14 June to provide cover for "Circus" operations. On Monday 16 June the squadron formed part of the escort for twenty-five Blenheims on "Circus 13", a coastal sweep off Holland and Germany. "The bombers were late to the rendezvous," recalled Dunn, "and then I also used up a fair bit of fuel in a fight over the target." He was then involved in a scrap with two Me109s of *JG26*:

By the time that little affair was finished, I had just enough petrol to climb up to 3,000 feet, when my engine quit and I baled out into the Channel. Picked up next morning, after seventeen hours in my dinghy, by a German MTB. Taken to Paris, then by train under guard to Dulag Luft.

Flying Officer Roger John Eric Boulding had been in No142 squadron of the AASF in France in May 1940, had afterwards requested a posting to Fighter Command, and on 22 August 1940 joined the Spitfire-equipped No74 ("Tiger") Squadron at Kirton-in-Lindsey. He scored three "kills" before being shot down on a sweep over the French coast on Tuesday, 17 June 1941.

In May the squadron had moved to Gravesend, and from there, led by "Sailor" Malan, they flew out as top-cover for twenty-three Blenheims on an early evening "Circus" (No14) to a power station near Béthune, the sort of operation that had recently brought about Bob White's undoing. Three Hurricane squadrons, Nos 56, 242 and 306, were flying as close escort. The Blenheims bombed accurately and without loss, but ten of the escorting fighters were shot down. Boulding, leading a section of four, had noticed some yellow-nosed Me109s sneaking up under the formation and warned Malan, who led the Tigers down on to them. Chasing an Me109 which was in a vertical spiral dive, Boulding couldn't line himself up for a good shot so, after a while, broke away to re-form. He followed Malan, climbing towards the sun in a weaving pattern, with what he thought was another of No74's Spits behind him. Then he heard Malan yell out to somebody to "look out behind!" He saw Malan rocking his wings, heard him shout: "Do something!" and was scanning the sky for a Spitfire in trouble when he felt a thumping behind his seat and the aileron controls went floppy. The aircraft behind had not been another Spitfire, but a Jerry. Boulding's aircraft went into a spiral dive and the only thing he could do was release the hood and bale out. That proved difficult, but as the elevator controls still worked he was able to more or less eject by pushing the stick forward. He floated down from 12,000 feet into a field occupied by an assortment of Germans who gathered round him and chorused: "For you the war is over." ("Sickening," was Boulding's pithy description, years later, of that moment.)

Two more unfortunates from that operation were Squadron Leader Eric Trenchard Smith, who had been with No242 Squadron as a supernumerary since 28 April 1941, and Pilot Officer Joe Bryks, a Czech who had joined the squadron on 14 April 1941. About fifteen miles from the target three Me109s appeared and made several passes at the close-escort Hurricanes. Unfortunately, the Spitfires providing top cover had been ordered to fly at a very high altitude and were in no position to help the escort Wing. Bryks was shot down. Then, over Béthune itself, at least fifty more Me109s joined the fray and shot down Smith.

Pilot Officers P P Villa and Paul Seth Ewart Briggs, a Volunteer Reservist, were both from No59 Squadron, no16 (GR Group), based at Detling. Despite staggering losses (36 per cent in two months alone), Coastal Command was still carrying out strikes and offensive recces, albeit with fighter escort, and on 16 June No59 Squadron contributed several Blenheim IVs to "Circus 13", the same op that had led Max Dunn into captivity. Villa took off at 1558 hours, followed a minute later by Pilot Officer D E Kennedy. The Blenheims met their escort of six fighter squadrons over Canterbury, but also met with heavy opposition across the Channel, where *JG26* pounced on them. In the ensuing combat, Villa was shot down and his crew killed. Derrick Kennedy followed him into the drink, but his observer, Peter Briggs, and his WOP/AG, Sergeant C H Edgar, survived. Air-Sea Rescue launches esorted by Nos 1 and 91 Squadrons failed to find them; they were picked up by the *Seenotsdienst* instead

The campaign in the Middle East was also bringing in its wake a large body of prisoners. Those captured by the Italians were sent to camps in Italy itself, while those who fell into the hands of the *Afrika Korps* soon found themselves on a transport plane to the Fatherland. One such was Eustace Newborn, a South African recce pilot with No24 SAAF who before the war had been an airline pilot, often flying German types. On the morning of Saturday, 14 June, Newborn was ordered to fly his Martin Maryland on a reconnaissance of Gazala South airfield, which forty-five minutes previously had been shot up by six aircraft from No73 Squadron. He was provided with an escort of five Hurricanes from No1 SAAF, led by Captain Kenneth W Driver DFC, a highly experienced South African who had been attached to No274 Squadron during its part in the Cretan campaign. When Crete fell, Driver returned to No1 SAAF Squadron. He had already shot down ten Italian aircraft over East Africa and one over the desert.

On the flight out the weather closed in and four of the fighters turned back. Despite the bad weather, Driver saw their objective but was unable to inform Newborn as they had no common radio frequency. Newborn flew on a further twenty miles until he realised something was wrong and turned back, this time spotting the airfield. Down below, the pilots of *I/JG27*, who were on Readiness, had seen the Maryland and its escort fly over the first time. The defences were now fully alerted and Newborn came under attack from 88mm guns. Then *Oberleutnant* Ludwig Franzisket scrambled into his Me109 and took off in pursuit of the escorting Hurricanes. Ken Driver made a head-on attack but his fire missed its target. His Hurricane was hit by Frantisket's return fire and the fuel tank exploded. As the two fighters approached each other, almost on collision course, the propeller of each sliced a wingtip off the other. Driver's aircraft was now ablaze and he baled out, while Franzisket, despite the damage to his wing, attacked the Martin Maryland. Only one of the crew baled out before Newborn made a forced landing, but all survived the crash.

The downed airmen were soon rounded up and taken to the *Gruppenkommandeur, Hauptmann* Springorum. He had been woken up by the flak and fighters and was very put out. In strong American English he asked the prisoners what the hell the British wanted in Africa anyway. "The same as the Germans, sir," replied Newborn, and Springorum roared with laughter. Over breakfast, Franzisket learned that Driver's wife was in Cairo. Some days later, on an operation the other side of Allied lines, he dropped her a message telling her Driver was safe and a prisoner. He would turn up at Spangenberg on the next purge from Dulag Luft.

(4)

Dulag Luft was really rushing new prisoners through now, and the next purge arrived at Spangenberg sixteen days later on Wednesday, 9 July. Under the leadership of Acting Wing Commander J R Kayll DSO, DFC, AuxAF, the party consisted of Flying Officer E T Fairbank; Pilot Officers M F Andrews, J Barker, G M Frame, RAFVR, A J C Hamilton, W H Holland, N Maranz, J D Margrie, T L W Officer, RAAF, R G Poulter and W J Sandman, RNZAF; and Captain Ken Driver DFC, of the SAAF.

Of the bomber pilots, of whom there were surprisingly few in this purge, Pilot Officer Joseph Barker had been the first to enter the bag, and in fact had been captured almost a year previously, during a raid on Bremen on 18/19 July 1940. Barker had been a Wellington second dickey to Pilot Officer W C H Hunkin on No115 Squadron, Marham (No3 Group). The rest of the crew had been sent to Barth, but Barker fell through the system, frowsting at Dulag Luft.

Edward Thomas Fairbank had flown Blenheims on No107 Squadron (No2 Group), based at Great Massingham. On Wednesday, 23 June 1941 thirty-nine Blenheims were sent out to attack Choques power station and Desvres airfield, and to carry out sweeps along the French coast. No107 Squadron, taking off at 1900 hours on "Circus 20", was heading for Desvres. Ted Fairbanks's aircraft was shot down by Me109s over Dunkirk. All his crew survived, although the

WOP/AG, Pilot Officer T Harrison, a young Londoner, had been shot through the mouth. He was taken for treatment at the hospital in St Omer.

On 27/28 June Bomber Command mounted another large-scale attack on Bremen, involving seventy-three Wellingtons and thirty-five Whitleys from Nos 10, 12, 57, 77, 102 and 142 Squadrons. On this occasion the crews encountered sever icing, storms and intense night-fighter activity. Eleven Whitleys and three Wellingtons were lost — the heaviest night loss of the war so far — and fourteen aircrew were taken prisoner, three of them officers. They included Pilot Officers James Margrie and George Murray Frame, respectively a second pilot and an observer in No10 Squadron. Their Wellington, flown by Sergeant N J Gregory, was hit by flak over Kiel and was so badly damaged that the crew had to bale out at 0300 hours, all of them ending up floating in Kiel Bay. They were rescued six hours later, by which time the tail-gunner was dead.

Pilot Officer Poulter, the other officer captive from this disastrous operation, was an observer in No102 Squadron, Topcliffe, one of the three Whitley outfits involved. His pilot, Sergeant G D Jackson, also had to ditch, and was the only member of the crew who failed to escape from the stricken aircraft.

The bulk of this purge was made up of fighter pilots — no fewer than eight. Pilot Officer Nat Maranz, an American from New York City, had joined No71 ("Eagle") Squadron at North Weald on 5 January 1941. However, he flew for only five months with No71 before being transferred to the second Eagle Squadron, No121. Then, on 9 June he was posted to RAF No1 Squadron, operating from Kenley. Twelve days later, on Saturday, 21 June, a Hurricane wing comprising Nos 1, 258 and 312 (Czech) Squadrons took off to escort six Blenheims on "Circus 16", a raid on St Omer airfield. Because of a navigation error, two Spitfire squadrons, planned to fly as top cover, failed to make the rendezvous, so the "Circus" set out twenty-four aircraft short. The formation encountered heavy flak over Boulogne, but the Blenheims were able to attack the target without interference from enemy fighters. The Me109s were waiting until the formation turned for home. Then thirty — some of them the new Me109F — swept in to attack out of the sun. A running battle continued across the Channel and Maranz was shot down, becoming one of the first "Eagle" pilots to enter captivity.

Joseph Robert Kayll, a reservist who had distinguished himself in France and the Battle of Britain, was shot down on Wednesday, 25 June — three weeks after being appointed Wing Commander Flying at Hornchurch. The Wing, equipped with Spitfires, had been flying as close escort for twelve Blenheims on "Circus 23", yet another raid on St Omer. On this occasion Kayll wasn't leading but was flying as No2, as Group Captain Harry Broadhurst, the station commander, had said he wanted to lead. It was a beautiful day, with clear visibility, and the operation went smoothly until the formation turned for home and Broadhurst decided he wanted to see a bit more action. So he turned the leading flight of four back towards France, and as they were climbing into the sun the Messerschmitts, who had had plenty of advanced warning, swooped upon them. Kayll was chased down to the ground. He thought he might be able to get out and make a run for it, but every time he tried to get the hood open he was shot at from behind. Eventually he managed to land, with the wheels up, on a stretch of land between two canals. He was trying to immobilise his Spitfire as best he could — but it was pretty difficult to destroy a very strong fighter without something like a hatchet to hand. As he was doing this, bullets started to whistle past him. *Good God*, he thought, *this is no place for me.*

He set off at a run towards the nearest farmhouse. It was a blazing hot summer's day and he was wearing heavy flying clothes. As he ran he was sweating profusely and still the gunfire continued. What he didn't know then, but learnt later, was that there had been two German soldiers standing on the far side of each canal when he had made his wheels-up landing. They could not see each other but both could see him. One had taken a shot at him, which had whistled past and nearly hit the German on the far side of the other canal. His response, thinking that it was the downed British pilot doing the shooting, was to take a shot across, which nearly hit the first German. The two Germans went on blindly shooting at each other for quite a long time. With their gunfire still resounding in the distance, Kayll reached the farmhouse and asked in schoolboy French if the owners could hide him. They said there was no chance, as the area was thick with Germans. But if he could get across the cornfield and into the woods, they would come and pick him up that night. He got into the cornfield, but the Germans were onto him in an instant, fanning out and closing in on him as though beating for pheasant. He tried to think of a way out, but he was well and truly trapped, and the Germans, along with a few of the locals, marched him off to the nearest airfield.

Usually, captured officers were invited to the Officers' Mess for a drink with the Luftwaffe pilots, but Kayll's captors told him he would not be invited as, after being shot down, he had shot at the German soldiers patrolling the canals. This surprised him, as he had been in no position to take up arms against them. (He didn't know the true story at that time.) However, they gave him food — a slice of hard, black bread. When he was given it, he thought they were trying to put one over him and said: "This must be a joke. This obviously isn't meant to be eaten." But later on he got to like German black bread.

Back home, he had been reported as "shot down in flames", which greatly upset his family. However, a week later the British captured a German Squadron Leader. During interrogation he mentioned that a British Wing Commander, shot down the previous week, had been refused access to the Mess because he had shot at German soldiers. "What day was this?" asked his interrogators. He told them, and after checking out his story they discovered that the only Wingco shot down that day was Kayll. That is how his family first heard he was still alive. Kayll himself was interrogated at Dulag Luft by *Sonderführer* Heinrich Eberhardt, a product of the Hitler Youth who knew everything about his career from reports published in the *Sunderland Echo*. "It was most disconcerting," Kayll recalled. "They knew I had performed aerobatics with No 607 Squadron at Empire Air Days and had played rugger with No603 at Edinburgh. They even knew I had recently married Annette Nisbet of Harperley Hall." Every now and then Eberhardt would cleverly slip in a question or two or proffer some information on himself. He told Kayll he had spent a year at the London School of Economics. "I've never thought much of the LSE ever since," says Kayll. (Eberhardt was, in fact, educated at the University of London.)

Two more fighter pilots, "Andy" Andrews and Bill Holland, were shot down and captured on the afternoon of Friday, 27 June, when Fighter Command put up two squadrons to cross the Channel on a fighter sweep. Pilot Officer Andrews, a Spitfire MkII pilot on No19 Squadron, was shot down in combat with an Me109. Bill Holland, flying a Spitfire MkII in No266 Squadron, entered the bag the same way. Yet another operation was mounted that evening — the third that day — when "Circus 24" was escorted to Lille by No74 Squadron. Warren Sandman, a New Zealander mounted in a Spitfire MkV, was also shot down by an Me109.

Pilot Officer Hamilton had been bagged on Friday, 6 June during the campaign in Crete. He had been in No274 Squadron, the first all-Hurricane unit in Middle East Command, based at Gerawla, Egypt. In the last week of May No274 received four new Hurricanes fitted with long-range fuel tanks, one slung under each wing. They increased the Hurricanes' range from six hundred to nine hundred miles. But they had their drawbacks. Firstly, they slowed the aircraft down and limited their manœuvrability. Secondly, the armour plating behind the seats had to be removed and the ammunition reduced to compensate for the extra fuel load. Finally, when the port tank emptied, the pilot could not guarantee that the starboard tank would take over, as the feeds were prone to air locks in the event of bad refuelling or excessive buffeting. However, on Sunday, 25 May, Hamilton and three other pilots prepared to take off from Gerawla at 0530 hours to rendezvous with two Blenheims of No54 Squadron sortying from Sidi Barrani to bomb Maleme airfield, a former RAF base on the island of Crete now in German hands. One of the Hurricanes burst its tail-wheel on take-off and aborted, while at Sidi Barrani one of the Blenheims crashed on take-off. The three other Hurricanes met up with the one remaining Blenheim, but near Crete they encountered thick cloud and became separated. Two of the fighter pilots turned for home, and Hamilton pressed on alone. His Hurricane then developed the anticipated fuel problems and he put down at RAF Heraklion. The only modern airfield on the island, Heraklion had been under siege since 20 May and was pitted with craters. As Hamilton landed he damaged his undercarriage on the cratered runway, rendering his aircraft unserviceable. Hamilton joined the airfield's ground staff and was stranded there along with them on Wednesday, 28 May when the airfield was cut off by German troops during the sea-borne evacuation of Crete. Hamilton was captured on Friday, 6 June, when more than eighty RAF aircrew, ground crew and ground staff were forced to give themselves up.

Terrence Officer, an Australian, was another captive from the campaign in North Africa to join Eustace Newborn. He was a Hurricane pilot in No274 Squadron, which had been detached to No 73 Squadron, and was shot down during the relief of Tobruk. During the afternoon No204 Group ordered up a dozen Hurricanes to carry out ground strafing along the enemy lines of communication and to attack ammunition dumps, camps and motor transport in the Sidi Omar area. Most of the aircraft, which took off at 1645 hours, were from Nos 33, 229 and 274 Squadrons, with only Terry Officer from the No73 Squadron detachment. Shortly after take-off a huge swarm of enemy aircraft appeared — Me109s escorting Stukas. A long-drawn-out dogfight ensued, in which Terry Officer was shot down and captured, along with a Frenchman from No 274 Squadron, *Sous-Lieutenant* Robert Grasset, who was sent to a POW camp in Italy.

(5)

Since their return from Thorn, the former *Strafgefangenen* had been pondering upon the troop movements they had seen in Poland. Then, one day, suddenly and without warning, they heard the unbelievable news that the Germans had invaded Russia — "to forestall the Russians", according to glib Nazi propagandists. Kriegie morale took an upward surge. Although militarily Russia was still an unknown quantity, surely this would mean the end of Germany? For a week there was little news. Then the Germans produced their first claims of a bewildering advance and astronomical Russian casualties and lists of *matériel* captured. They were so vast they staggered the imagination. But pictures in the German newspapers, showing enormous columns of dishevelled Russian prisoners, seemed to confirm them. The Russians appeared badly equipped, many without boots, and many of the wounded had lost limbs. Other photographs showed Russian weapons — most of them old and obsolete. All this rapidly forced the prisoners to conclude that Russia would go the way of Poland and the West, and that liberation would not come from that direction. Within a month of the German attack on Russia, the pendulum of optimism had swung right back until there was hardly a prisoner willing to bet that Moscow wouldn't fall within a few weeks.

Such a volatile situation produced strong reactions amongst the RAF contingent in the *Hauptlager*, who devoted a good deal of time to goon-baiting and escaping. One of their favourite tricks was to slip razor-blades into the pigswill and into the potatoes that were fed to the three wild boars inhabiting the moat. However, much to the surprise of the POWs the boars proved quite impervious to the spiked food — which, recalls Kayll, "they ate with gusto and suffered no ill-effects". From the point of view of the Air Force prisoners, this was indeed a pity, as the boars made a hell of a commotion whenever an attempt was made to use the moat as a means of escape. However, escape bids went on regardless, and nine separate attempts were made between June and September.

The first two attempts began well but ended in farce. William Lepine, who had a talent for amateur dramatics and also spoke some German, disguised himself as one of the German civilian workers who occasionally entered the castle. Accompanied by another prisoner posing as an orderly going to fetch coal, he tried to bluff the sentry on the gate to let them through. While this exchange was going on the real worker arrived outside the gate and their subterfuge was discovered. The following month Bob Coste changed identity with a British doctor who was being sent to another camp. His intention was to jump off the train on the way. The substitution worked perfectly. But Coste found no opportunity to escape during the journey and arrived safely at his destination. Once there, he discovered that the camp was seriously short of doctors and that he would have to begin medical work at once. He had no choice but to reveal himself to the Germans, and was returned to Spangenberg.

In the meantime, several officers had formed a tunnelling syndicate. Among them were Harry Bewlay (again), Peter Tunstall, John Milner, Dominic Bruce and the South African, "Useless" Eustace Newborn, who in August began to sink a shaft from a ground-floor room.

(6)

In the middle of August yet another batch of prisoners arrived from Oberursel. They were Flight Lieutenants E Hubicki (Pole), L Koslowski (Pole) and N H Svendsen DFC (Dane); and Pilot

Officers S Carter, RAFVR, W M W Fowler, W Hetherington, W F Jackman, S Z Król (Pole), W Krupowicz (Pole), A F McSweyn, RAAF, S Reeves, C I Rolfe and R A Walker.

Pilot Officers Allan McSweyn, from Rockdale, New South Wales, and Wilfred Hetherington, had been a pilot and an observer on No115 Squadron, Marham, equipped with the Wellington IC. McSweyn was shot down on his fourteenth op, a raid by a hundred and six aircraft on Bremen on 29/30 June 1941, which cost Bomber Command seven crews. No115 Squadron took off at 2300 hours and had an uneventful outward flight. But ten minutes from Bremen searchlights probed the night sky and McSweyn's Wellington was coned. He took evasive action but when the flak opened up it scored a direct hit on his starboard engine, which started to overheat. He throttled back, but did not cut the engine, instead pressing on and bombing his target from 10,000 feet before turning for home. As he did so he was again coned. But no flak followed, which could only mean one thing: enemy fighters were in the area. His fears proved correct, for suddenly one opened up from about six hundred yards and the searchlights went out. As the night-fighter closed in it gave the Wimpey another burst, smashing the wireless transmitter, putting the intercom out of action, shattering the cockpit canopy and setting on fire the already damaged starboard engine. The rear gunner, Sergeant J V Gill, returned the fire and reported an aircraft falling in flames, but from then on neither turret would operate.

Meanwhile the second pilot, Pilot Officer S W Wild, reported from his position in the astrodome that an Me110 was about to attack. It came in from below, its cannon-fire hitting Gill in the shoulder and Wild in the right hip. By this time the flames from the damaged engine had spread so far that they had set the tailplane alight. The fire was out of control and McSweyn ordered the crew to bale out, holding the aircraft steady as they jumped. As soon as they had left, he lurched towards the escape hatch, noticing on the way that there was no fabric left on the starboard wing and that the metal was melting. Then there was a terrific explosion and the whole wing came off. The Wimpey turned over on its starboard side, went straight down, and McSweyn blacked out. He came to, making a soft landing in the paddock of a farmhouse, which he later learned was near Bremervörde. Though he had miraculously escaped injury, he had lost his flying boots.

The rest of the crew had landed in wooded country some miles away. Sergeant Gill's parachute had snagged in a tree and, still dazed from his wounds and the shock of baling out, he pressed his harness release, dropped forty feet and broke his back. Wilf Hetherington and the others stayed with him until a German doctor arrived, but he died in hospital the next day. McSweyn, meanwhile, made a valiant attempt to evade capture, intending to walk towards the Dutch or Belgian borders and link up with the Resistance. He had to delay his exit from the farmyard because a German came in on a motorbike and went inside. Forty-five minutes elapsed before he came out, roared off on his motorbike and left the coast clear for McSweyn to make his getaway.

For the rest of the night he walked south, hiding up during the day and starting out again as soon as darkness fell. As he passed Bremen he saw a German night-fighter station teeming with Me110s. He decided to lie low near the airfield and examine the prospects of stealing an aircraft and flying it home. The next day, Tuesday, 1 July, he spent hiding in the wheatfield nearby and watching through the stalks as the busy German mechanics worked on the aircraft. Standing apart from the others, near the perimeter, was a lone Me110. It was only a hundred yards away from where McSweyn was crouching. A few yards behind it was a mechanics' hut, guarded by one sentry. At about six o'clock the Germans started refuelling, re-arming and preparing the Me110 for night flying. McSweyn made up his mind to fly it back to England. However, patrols were roving the perimeter, and he decided to wait until dark before making the attempt.

That night he crept cautiously from his hiding place towards the aircraft. The cockpit canopy was open. Quickly glancing around to make sure no one was watching, he climbed in, his heart pounding. The cockpit layout was completely different from that of any other machine he had flown, but he soon got the hang of the basic controls and, after a few minutes, felt sufficiently at home to reckon his chances of taking off and flying her to England in one piece as pretty good. Thinking quickly, he made a shrewd guess as to the starting procedure. Then he switched on the petrol, set the throttles, uttered a short prayer — and pressed the starter button. However, although the port engine started to tick over, he could not get it to fire, try as he might. He did not want to expend the aircraft batteries completely, so he took another thorough look around the cockpit, hoping in the meantime that no one would approach the aircraft. Suddenly, however, he was horrified to see one of the mechanics, alerted by the noise, emerge from the hut. In sheer desperation, McSweyn pressed the starter button again, hoping that he would be able to start the engine before being hauled ignominiously out of the cockpit.

To his astonishment, the mechanic walked underneath the port engine, fiddled about under the cowling, for a few seconds, then called out something. McSweyn thought the mechanic had mistaken him for the pilot and was probably helping him to start the engine. He must be shouting at the "pilot" to have another go. So once again McSweyn pressed the starter button. The propeller nearly knocked the mechanic's head off. Not in the best of moods, he climbed up to the cockpit, saw an unfamiliar, grubby face and nearly fell backwards off the wing. Yelling loudly for the sentry to come over, he pointed his rifle straight at McSweyn. A few seconds later, several guards came running to the mechanic's aid and hauled McSweyn off to the guardroom. Thus ended his attempt at evasion.

They allowed him to bath and shave, provided food and drink and gave him a very comfortable pair of boots. Afterwards, they asked him if he would like to meet the German pilots. As it was more than likely that one of them had shot down his Wimpey he was not keen, but they insisted, and so escorted him to the Officers' Mess. He found it very similar to an RAF Mess, the men the same age and all keen on flying. They believed that Germany and Britain should stop fighting each other and join forces against the Russians.

Next day he was escorted to Dulag Luft, and after spending his allotted span in the cooler met three of his crew in the compound. There were a number of stool pigeons in the camp dressed as sergeants who tended to be there one day and gone the next, so the usual form was for crew members to ignore each other so as to prevent the Germans from knowing when they were shot down. But so pleased and surprised were the three that he had survived that they shouted: "Hallo skipper, thought you had bought it," thus giving the Germans the information they required.

At Dulag Luft McSweyn learnt that Pilot Officer Wild had injured his hip on landing and was now in the hospital at Obermasfeld (he would later fetch up at Stalag Luft I), and that Sergeant J V Gill was dead.

The two Polish Flight Lieutenants, Koslowski and his observer Hubicki, were from No310 (Pomeranian) Squadron, the second Polish bomber unit formed by No1 Group, and like No300 Squadron based at Swinderby. They were shot down on the same night as Allan McSweyn and Wilf Hetherington, although their target was Bremen. All their crew survived with the exception of the WOP/AGs. Over Berlin, with their bombs still on board, they were picked up by the searchlights. Koslowski gave the order to jettison the bomb-load, for they had no hope of evading the searchlights fully laden. As Hubicki was carrying out his order a night-fighter attacked and the rear-gunner started firing. Fires broke out in the Wellington. The fuel supply was cut off, the controls had ceased to function, and the aircraft took to flying in circles with ever-increasing speed. There was nothing Koslowski could do, so he gave the order to abandon. All baled out safely, and were captured the next day.

Yet another Pole, Waclaw Krupowicz, was from No300 Squadron. A second pilot on a Wellington, he entered the bag on the night of 3/4 July when Bomber Command put up yet more aircraft against Bremen. Only Krupowicz and the observer, Sergeant M Przybylski, survived.

William Menzies Weekes Fowler was second pilot in No10 Squadron, operating Whitleys from Leeming (No4 Group). On the night of 30 June sixty-four aircraft attacked targets in the Ruhr, with No10 Squadron going for Duisburg. Fowler's pilot took off at 2347 hours; he was killed along with the observer when the aircraft was attacked over the Reichswald Forest and crashed. Two more aircrew to enter kriegiedom from that operation were Neil Hyland Svendsen and his air-gunner Stanley Carter, from No83 squadron, Scampton. Svendsen took off at 2315 hours. His Whitley was hit by flak and crashed at Düren on the east bank of the River Ruhr. His observer was killed.

Pilot Officer Walker was one of three officers from No106 Squadron, Coningsby (No5 Group), to enter captivity in 1941. His squadron took part in a raid by thirty-nine Hampdens on Duisburg on 2/3 July. Walker's aircraft was attacked by a night-fighter flown by *Leutnant* Reinhold Knacke of *II/NGJ1*. One of his WOP/AGs was killed, but the rest of the crew joined him in the bag. The observer, Pilot Officer B D Campbell, RCAF, was sent to Oflag VIIC/H at Laufen by mistake, and

Walker would meet him again when the Germans started concentrating officer POWs at Oflag VIB, Warburg-Dössel, towards the end of September 1941.

The one August captive on this batch from Oberursel was Charles Immanuel Rolfe, a Stirling pilot from No7 Squadron at Oakington (No3 Group). On the 2nd of the month fifty-three aircraft set out to bomb Berlin, Rolfe taking off at 2218 hours. The operation was not a success, with haze hampering bombing and the loss of three Wellingtons, plus Rolfe's Stirling, which was shot down by a night-fighter. The second pilot, Sergeant L R Burrows, was fatally wounded during the attack. The Stirling crashed at Werder, and only Rolfe and two of the crew, Sergeants D S Merrells and C A Tout, came out alive.

On Wednesday, 2 July, yet another pilot from No74 Squadron, Pilot Officer Stanislaw Zygmunt Król, was shot down on a fighter sweep. "Danny" Król was born on 22 March 1916, in Zagorzyce, Poland, and enlisted in the Polish Air Force on 21 September 1937. He trained at the officer cadet centre at Deblin, specialising in fighter tactics, and was commissioned on 1 September 1939. His timing was perfect, for on the next day Deblin's aircraft were bombed, and Danny and his comrades were reduced to mere spectators for the rest of the campaign. After a week, the cadets began a trek to Romania, which they reached on 17 September. The following month they reached France, where General Sikorski had re-formed the Polish Government. In February 1940, Sikorski established a Polish Air Force centre at Lyon-Bron, and most of the Poles settled in there with hopes of continuing the fight with French equipment. The Deblin cadets formed part of the Finnish Group, so named because it was destined for Finland under the terms of an agreement for assistance to that country. However, the French Government decided to keep the Finnish Group, and it remained at Lyon-Bron as part of the *Armée de l'Air*, equipped with Morane-Saulnier fighters.

The German invasion of France brought more heavy fighting for the Poles. On 10 May Lyon-Bron was bombed and, over the next month, the Deblin group moved around France to fill gaps in the defence. Eventually most of the Poles were evacuated to England and taken into the RAF for assignment to various training stations, with Danny going to No57 OTU. He was then posted to the "Tiger" Squadron at Gravesend to begin his third separate campaign of the war. He had flown on ten sweeps when he was shot down over France.

Another victim of the campaign in Crete was Stanley Reeves. He had been in No1430 Flight, detached from No112 Squadron, flying Gladiators from Heraklion. On Wednesday, 14 May about a dozen Me110s from *II/ZG 26* appeared overhead, ready to attack the airfield, and Reeves and another pilot got airborne. One of the Me110s, having attacked the airfield, then bounced Reeves. His Gladiator was badly damaged and he force-landed. He was then put in charge of the Airfield Detachment at Retimo. On Friday, 30 May the airfield was overrun by German paratroopers and some seven hundred men, including Reeves, had to surrender.

William Francis Jackman was another RAFVR officer from the Marine Craft Section to join "Tug-Boat Ted" Chapman. He had set out in his HSL on Tuesday, 1 July, to pick up a Coastal Command crew who had ditched off the Dutch coast. Told he would be given air cover, the only aerial support he got was from the Luftwaffe, who promptly shot up his launch. When the Germans picked him up, he discovered the crew he had been seeking had been rescued by the *Seenotsdienst* six hours before he had received his instructions.

(7)

Wing Commander Kayll took over as Senior RAF Officer, although Brigadier Nigel Somerset, in the Lower Camp, remained Senior British Officer. Kayll also had the ultimate say in RAF escape activities, vetting all schemes put to Harry Bewlay and his small committee. The result was an immediate, tangible improvement in conditions in the Upper Camp, along with better co-ordination in planning escapes. This owed itself partly to Kayll's seniority, experience and common sense, but also to the respect in which he was held by junior RAF officers, who were somewhat in awe of his achievements.

Joe Kayll was born in Sunderland on 12 April 1914 and educated at Stowe. He failed all his exams, so left school and at the age of sixteen started work as a mill-boy in the family business of Joseph Thompson, who owned a sawmill in Sunderland. From 1934 onwards Kayll spent weekends and holidays learning to fly on Westland Wapitis with No607 (County of Durham) Squadron. In 1939 he was called to full-time service with the squadron, which, now equipped with Gladiators, was operating from Drem in Scotland. A Luftwaffe bomber pilot shot down over the sea by one of No607's Gladiator pilots, Dudley Craig, exclaimed in fluent English: "To be shot down by a bloody barrister in a bloody biplane is more than I can bloody well bear." Luftwaffe Intelligence had led him to expect no more resistance than "a bunch of Auxiliary amateurs".

Kayll had the exceptional distinction as a fighter pilot of being awarded the DSO and DFC on the same day. In the citation for his awards, dated 31 May 1940, he was credited with the destruction of nine enemy aircraft since 10 May, when Germany launched its invasion of the Low Countries and France. This was an outstanding achievement for an Auxiliary Air Force "weekend flier" who had arrived in France in November 1939 as a flight commander. (Based at Merville, near Vitry-en-Artois, No607 was fortunate not to be seriously challenged during the Phoney War. In his sitting-duck biplane Kayll found it unnerving enough merely to fly over cemeteries from the Great War.)

In March 1940, Kayll received command of No615 (County of Surrey) Squadron, and on 2 May led it to Le Touquet to re-equip with Hurricanes. But at dawn on 10 May the airfield was attacked and four of the spanking new Hurricanes were destroyed on the ground.

Once it was back up to strength, the squadron returned to Merville. As enemy tanks, supported by Ju87s, advanced towards the English Channel, Kayll repeatedly led his gallant band of businessmen, farmers, lawyers and accountants against overwhelming fighter odds. Forced to move from airfield to inadequate airfield as Belgium and France were overrun, Kayll and his part-timers took off through curtains of falling bombs to fly six or seven combat sorties a day. On 20 May, as Belgian troops blew up an airfield prior to its abandonment, he flew to Abbeville, assembled a number of still serviceable Hurricanes and strafed enemy forces on the Arras-Douai road. Three of the aircraft were lost to ground fire.

Re-forming at Kenley with replacement pilots and Hurricanes, No615 was kept busy all that June. One day, returning from a sortie over France, Kayll found King George VI waiting to pin on both a DSO and a DFC. Shortly afterwards Kayll had another surprise when, landing back from France, he found Winston Churchill waiting to dine with the squadron and stay the night. The Prime Minister's visit provided a timely boost for No615. During the Battle of Britain it fought — with heavy losses — until the end of August, and again in October after a brief spell recuperating at Prestwick.

After the Battle of Britain, during which he notched up several further kills, Kayll was rested on Fighter Command's tactical staff until 2 June 1941, when he was given command of the celebrated Spitfire wing based at Hornchurch, Essex.

* * *

On Friday, 22 August, the walls of *Schloss* Spangenberg were breached for the first time since September 1940. With the help of two Army orderlies, John Tilsley and Harry Bewlay (again!) hid in the cart that entered the camp to collect the refuse. The orderlies covered them with rubbish, the cart proceeded through the gate and, once out of sight of the sentries, the two escapers slipped away without being seen. They were caught the following day trying to cross an *Autobahn* in daylight, unaware that the crossing of an *Autobahn* by civilians was *streng verboten*!

Three days later two more Air Force officers escaped in the laundry cart. Every Monday, a team of four orderlies wheeled the washing out of the castle in a small handcart accompanied by a guard, and took the washing to four women in the village of Spangenberg who had volunteered their services. The plan was to adapt the cart so that two officers, Eric Foster and Joe Barker, could fit inside it and make a break on the way down the hill. To remove the guard, one of the orderlies would pretend to have a weak ankle and fake an accident on the way down the hill, whereupon — they hoped — the guard and the entire party would return to the castle and abandon the cart with the two escapers inside it. The execution of the scheme was aided by an inadvertent discovery made by Foster. While in the courtyard one day he took to counting the windows and noticed that there were five windows corresponding to a passage on the first floor. Investigating the passage, he saw only four windows. Further reconnaissance revealed a room at the end of the passage. Borrowing a lock-pick from Nat Maranz, he entered the room with Joe Barker while stooges kept watch.

The room was tiny, but contained engineering drawings and more than sixty maps. One map, prepared by the Forestry Commission, gave detailed information on the area immediately surrounding the castle, even marking out every tree. Such a map would be a useful aid in a "walk-out". Foster and Barker decided to use the room as their escape workshop, and with lookouts posted, prepared for their escape every day without fear of discovery. They traced maps, forged documents and made two Hitler Youth uniforms, their proposed disguise once they were clear of the camp. Foster was to be the superior in rank, and cast his pips in metal. The moulds were made from plaster of Paris smuggled in from the sick bay, and the molten metal from a blend of foils from American tobacco and cigarette packets. Other badges, along with belt-buckles and buttons, were carved from bed boards, as were their daggers, all of which they polished to a sheen. The gold embroidered lettering on their black triangular district badges was made from pulling the cotton from yellow dusters. The armbands were made from the heavy crimson lining of a cavalry officer's coat. A linen handkerchief was cut up for the white diamond inserts and an RAF tie was used to make the Swastikas. This involved gently pulling the threads from the tie and embroidering them on to the armbands. All this was difficult enough, but finding the material for the leather belts and cross braces was an even more ticklish problem. However, with the connivance of the orderlies, Sam Brownes were donated by army officers in the Lower Camp. They also made a compass, which consisted of a darning needle suspended from a piece of thread. To magnetise the needle, they plucked the lead out of a pencil, replaced it with the darning needle, wound some flex round the pencil, and flashed each end against the contacts of an electric lamp holder. Finally, Foster had an original Hitler Youth pass, which had been stolen by Squadron Leader Bridgman. Army forgers had made copies of the pass before Bridgman handed it over to Foster.

The execution of the scheme hinged not only on manufacturing convincing uniforms for the journey beyond the walls of the castle but also on getting outside in the first place. For this, Foster and Barker had to be appointed as laundry officers, which they achieved with the connivance of the escape committee and the prisoners' administration. By now there were some two hundred officers and men in the Upper and Lower Camps, and for laundry purposes they had been divided into four groups, with each washer-woman doing laundry for fifty men. Each group of fifty men was given a colour — red, blue, green or black — and each individual was allocated a number from 1 to 200 and provided with a cardboard Red Cross box with his name and number on, along with a stripe in the appropriate group colour. In the village the orderlies delivered the soiled laundry to each of the four houses according to the coloured stripes on the boxes. Each woman was given a list itemising the contents of each box.

Foster wanted to get the guards used to the idea that he and Barker regularly accompanied the laundry party, so complained to *Gefreiter* Böttner, the camp liaison NCO, that things had gone awry with the first delivery. Böttner obtained von Meyer's permission for the two officers to accompany the next party to the village so they could interview the washer-women and explain how the system was supposed to work. On this occasion there was only one guard, which augured well for the success of the escape plan. One guard was easier to fool than two. Two more "dry runs" followed before von Meyer decided to put a stop to Foster and Barker visiting the women. He took the view that their presence was superfluous. An Army prisoner, Corporal H Barnes of the Royal Armoured Corps, agreed to take over the supervision of the orderlies and make sure they could be relied upon to co-operate in the escape. Two of the original orderlies, Corporal L M Bolitho of the Middlesex Regiment and Fusilier D Peppiatt of the Northumberland Fusiliers, were "dependable". But one had dropped out and would have to be replaced.

The two officers decided to make their break on Monday, 25 August — the anniversary of Foster's first escape attempt from Hohemark hospital, Oberursel, shortly after his capture. In the meantime, Fusilier Peppiatt feigned a weak ankle and attended the sick bay to have it bandaged — an important element in the escape plan. Another reliable orderly had also been found, Trooper W Chandler of the Royal Armoured Corps.

On the appointed day, when Corporal Barnes and his orderlies arrived in the courtyard with the handcart, Peter Tunstall emerged from the kitchens with a white-hot poker and bored air-holes into it: three in the bottom and one near each corner, about a third of the way down. Foster and Barker, who had been waiting in the shadows fully dressed in their Hitler Youth attire, climbed into the cart and lay head-to-feet, curled up like foetuses. Then came the *pièce de résistance:* Charlie Bowman slipped four nails into the air-holes that Tunstall had bored near the corners of the cart, and on them he and Tunstall mounted a wooden screen camouflaged with four Red Cross boxes. One box, which had been carefully marked, contained a packet of soap powder in which the escapers had concealed their money, maps and compass, which could be retrieved quickly and without difficulty when they made their break. The others only contained one article of soiled clothing per man, in order to lighten the weight of the screen, but it was enough to give the appearance, on cursory inspection, of a fully laden cart. However, once the lid was down the two escapers found breathing extremely difficult. Foster rapped his knuckles on the wall of the cart and complained that he and Barker were "in great distress". Charlie Bowman found the solution. He lifted the head of one of the nails and slid a match under it, providing an air-gap of about a sixteenth of an inch.

Finally, Böttner arrived, blissfully ignorant of the scheme afoot, and called to the sentry in the gatehouse on the other side of the moat to unlock the gates. The orderlies wheeled the cart over the rough cobbles of the courtyard, then across the smooth planks of the drawbridge, on the far side of which they tipped the cart into its "rest" position while the guard supplied towing ropes. The guard loaded a round in the breach of his rifle — Foster and Barker could hear it click from inside the cart, and their hearts pounded — and after ten minutes of shouting and hollering the party began its journey down the winding hill, Corporal Barnes and his orderlies behind the cart pulling on the ropes to break the speed of its descent. For Foster and Barker it was agony: not only because of the discomfort caused by the buffeting they were receiving, but also because of the serious lack of air. Finally, as they neared the foot of the *Schlossberg*, the orderlies laid on the pre-arranged "accident". Peppiatt, walking beside the cart to steady it, stuck his foot under the front wheel, which ran over his ankle. He let out a loud cry, and the cart skidded to a halt. Foster and Barker held their breath and waited to find out what the guard would do. Would he carry on to the village, or would he escort the party back to the castle, leaving the cart behind? Finally, he decided that two men should carry Peppiatt back to the castle, and he would accompany them with the other orderly, who would provide relief if one of the others tired of carrying the injured prisoner. As they abandoned the cart, one of the orderlies said: "Off we go! Back to the castle!" loud enough for the two escapers to hear.

Foster pinched Barker, slowly counted to a hundred, then gently lifted the screen, boxes and lid. They were heavier than he had expected, and he was relieved that the boxes contained only a few smalls. He peered over the edge of the cart, but could see no further than about twenty yards up the road because of a turning ahead. Nevertheless, they clambered out of the cart and ducked into the bushes, carrying the screen and the Red Cross boxes. They retrieved their escape paraphernalia from the specially marked carton without difficulty. Then, adjusting their caps, and Barker's pack and blanket roll, they emerged from the bushes and marched briskly down the road. Foster looked at his watch: it was 1.45pm.

Barely a minute passed before they came across a woman and her child. The woman raised a civilian salute and shouted: *"Heil Hitler!"* Jubilant at passing their first test, the two escapers returned her greeting with gusto.

Although the alarm was raised within fifteen minutes of their escape, and the Germans immediately set out in pursuit with sniffer dogs, Foster and Barker covered some eighty-one kilometres (fifty miles) before being recaptured. They marched through the village in a south-easterly direction, crossed the railway line and cautiously entered the *Staatsforst Spangenberg*. Rumour had it that the observation towers along the fire-breaks were manned by guards, and every time a tower loomed ahead they paused and watched to make sure the coast was clear. This slowed down their progress and, as evening wore on, torrential rain fell without them being anywhere near a suitable place to shelter. They had no choice but to march straight through the next village and hope the rain would prevent any of the villagers from venturing into the streets. As luck would have it, however, a party of women were sheltering under the veranda of a chalet.

But once again the verisimilitude of their Hitler Youth disguise was proved, and they exchanged Nazi greetings for the second time that day. All the same, the escapers felt uncomfortable and disconsolate, as the rain was pouring down in sheets. In their efforts to find a barn they had to pass through two more villages before striking out into the open country. Here they found a cowshed, but on seeing a barn further on headed for that instead. By now it had stopped raining, but it was very cold, and they urgently needed to find somewhere dry and warm, and the barn looked very substantial. Rather than break the lock on the door, however, they gained entry by climbing through a gap under the eaves. Most of the floorspace was taken up by a huge combine harvester, but a loft covered with linseed ran two-thirds of the length, and this appeared an ideal place to bed down. They used linseed to stop the gaps between the loft and the eaves and arranged several sheaves to form nests in which they could sleep. Stripping naked, they stretched out their Hitler Youth uniforms to dry and laid them out neatly near the ledge of the loft. Then they unrolled Barker's blanket and lay down to sleep. Unfortunately, sleep did not come, as the bed of linseed turned out to be very uncomfortable and in any case they were too cold. Both were shivering and Barker's teeth were chattering. They rubbed each other's back to gain some warmth and tried again to settle down. But at about 8pm they heard the voices of three people — probably the farmer and his wife and daughter — working outside the barn. The two escapers were tense with fear, but finally the talkative trio left without entering. Still the escapers could not sleep. The night was made hideous and uncanny by the hooting of owls and the scampering of rates, and seemed eternal.

When the sun came up they tried to warm their uniforms by waving them in the air. But they were still damp at 10.30 when the doors were unlocked and the farmer entered with his wife and daughter. The gimlet-eyed farmer noticed that the loft had been disturbed and climbed on to the seat of the combine harvester to peer over the ledge of the loft. Feigning sleep, they heard him say: "What goes on here?" Then his wife climbed up beside him. "Ah! *Hitler Jungen*. They are asleep. Don't wake them up, poor boys. They are tired." Down below, the girl was jumping up and down in excitement, squealing: *"Hitler Jungen! Hitler Jungen!"*

From what Foster and Barker understood of the ensuing conversation, although the farmer was convinced that they were Hitler Youths he was disturbed by their lack of respect for his personal property. As the family left the barn, Foster heard the word *"Polizei"*.

The two escapers decided to make a run for it before the police arrived, but at Barker's suggestion paused to eat some of their chocolate ration. "I don't want these bastards to have it," he added. The chocolate made them feel queasy, as their stomachs were turning over with fear. But they ate a bar each and then got dressed, not wanting to be arrested stark naked. Foster hid their German money in a glass test-tube, which he then inserted into his rectum.

The farmer had posted a yokel at the door, and he could see them through the slatted walls of the barn. He asked them what they were doing. In his best German, Foster told him: "Mind your own business, you bloody yokel, and get going!" To his surprise, the yokel departed, and as quick as they could the two escapers left the barn, using the method they had employed the night before. As they hit the ground, they saw the farmer and his wife, along with two men and another woman, in a huddle a few hundred yards away, and the yokel rapidly approaching them. The escapers headed for the woods at a fast pace and, once out of sight, cleaned their boots and daggers and finished dressing. Foster also took this opportunity to relieve himself of the discomfort of the test tube, which he put in Barker's haversack.

In the woods, they completely lost their way, and fished out their home-made compass. Finding their direction, they set off once again, leaving the forest and finding themselves in the open countryside. Once, they passed a group of French POW labourers who, much to their surprise, treated them to yet more Nazi salutations. At first, Foster was moved by this display of camaraderie between fellow prisoners, but when Barker reminded him that the French had mistaken them for Germans, Foster changed his tune and dismissed them as a bunch of bastards.

As they travelled south, again finding their direction by means of their improvised compass, they passed through some very striking scenery. As Foster commented upon each beautiful vista, Barker lapsed into ever deeper and gloomier silence. Finally, when Foster pressed him with: "Come on, Joe, you will admit it's really beautiful, won't you?" Barker replied: "No! It's German!" After that, Foster shut up.

They carried on, walking in as straight a line as possible. Often they passed groups of workers gathering in the harvest, and once they were invited to stop and have a few drinks. But worried that their accents would betray them should they engage in lengthy conversation, they politely declined, saying they were in a hurry, *"Heil Hitler!"* Most of the time they walked right through villages, this being a better alternative to thrashing through thick undergrowth or making lengthy detours through the woods. During the afternoon they found a nice spot where they could strip-wash and shave, and sat down afterwards to have their first cigarettes since their escape. They had to be careful about smoking, because their cigarettes were English and a dead give-away. The German civilian population generally had only Polish or Moravian tobacco.

Towards evening the pair passed an orchard and helped themselves to a few apples. (Scrumping from orchards, though not from private gardens, was tolerated in Germany provided it was for immediate consumption, and was known as *Mundraub* — literally "mouth theft".) Afterwards they decided to seek shelter, as they did not want to repeat the previous night's experience by waiting until the last minute and having to put up with something totally unsatisfactory or dangerous. They saw a brick building about fifteen feet square on some farmland, and waited in the woods until dusk, when they crept out of their hiding place and broke in. Unfortunately, the interior showed little promise. The building housed a tractor and the floor was of stone. But outside there were some sheaves of oats, and they carried some inside and spread them out in a far corner, using the tractor tarpaulin as a blanket. Even then, they were cold, and again their sleep was disturbed by rats. Then, suddenly, as midnight approached, they heard the wail of air-raid sirens, all within the radius of about half a mile. Removing the panel from the window they could see flak lighting up the sky over Cologne, further to the west. Whether the bombers were on their way in or on their way out they knew not. They tried to settle down again. But wearing only their underclothes, and what with rats scurrying about, they found sleep elusive. Finally, at 3am, Foster got up and dressed, spending the rest of the small hours pacing up and down the floor. Dawn brought with it thick mist, with visibility down to about ten feet, but they decided to set off nevertheless, and after a breakfast of raw cabbage they put their "bedding" back where they had found it and walked into the mist. Despite the dampness, they began to feel warm, but their shoes and socks were soon soaking wet from the morning dew. Eventually, after two hours of walking along rough roads and trudging up and down wooded hills, they came across a fire-watcher's tower that was unmanned, and they climbed into it and doffed their shoes and socks, leaving them to dry in the pale sunshine. They also tried to shave — without water — as it was essential that they kept up appearances.

At about eight o'clock a girl came into view, driving a plough being pulled by a cow — incontrovertible proof that in wartime Germany horses were in short supply. Dressed in the traditional laced bodice and coloured skirt, she sang and chirruped gaily as she ploughed the fields. Foster walked out on to the platform of the tower and showed himself off in his Hitler Youth uniform to test her reaction. She merely smiled up at him. Good. Several more farm workers passed the tower that morning, and all reacted in the same way, increasing Foster's confidence in their disguise.

By ten o'clock their shoes and socks were dry enough to wear — which didn't mean they were dry, only that they were less damp — but one of Foster's socks had developed a "potato" and needed darning. He had lost the needle and had to descend the tower to find a suitably-sized twig as a substitute. Darning the sock took the best part of an hour. At about eleven o'clock they resumed their journey, walking for the rest of the day without pausing for rest until they came across a hut where they sheltered for the night. This accommodation proved better than their previous choices, and they spent a warm and pleasant night, able at last to sleep.

At nine o'clock on the morning of Monday, 28 August they set out again, hitting a main road at midday and encountering many passers-by who neither molested nor questioned them. They even passed a number of railway officials — in Germany, state employees who were normally officious and supercilious. This did wonders for their confidence and their morale was high. Later on they heard the sound of shunting railway rolling stock and, realising they must be nearing some marshalling yards, decided to investigate. As they reached the crest of a hill they saw below them that the entire valley was one big marshalling yard. They worked out that they had reached Bebra, and in three days had walked twenty-five miles as the crow flies. After spending some time observing how the yards operated, they ventured into town. As they wandered through the streets they passed a prison for French POWs, and the sight of a guard standing outside gave Foster a shock. "Look out!" he warned Barker. "A goon!" Barker was amused. "Don't be a bloody fool," he laughed. "You're a 'goon' yourself!"

Bebra turned out to be one of those towns whose appeal quickly fades. Once you had walked around it several times you felt numb with boredom. They decided to retire back into the hills, where they discussed their plans and decided to ride the rods in order to obviate the problem of having to swim the River Fulda. In the meantime, they thought it best to stay out of the area for a while, as their continuing presence might arouse suspicion. As they walked past a cottage Barker noticed a heavily laden apple tree and was about to pick an apple from it when Foster stopped him. "Germans don't steal," explained. "At least not in public!" Barker was annoyed. "My, you are pro-German!" he said. For the second time during their escape, Barker went into a sulk, and they walked on in silence.

Later on they came to a heath that looked promising as a place to rest up. They stretched themselves out in the sunlight and Barker fell to sleep almost immediately. Foster sat gazing at the scenery, and before long saw a woman approaching with her daughter. The girl waved at him. Foster had no option but to return the wave, which only egged on the daughter to head in his direction. He woke up Barker, and told him they had better move on. They hurried off, hoping that their hasty departure would not arouse suspicion, and hid in a culvert until dusk, when they broke cover and drew water from a stream about a quarter of a mile away. Then they headed back to Bebra, scavenging some runner beans from a smallholding on the way.

By the time they reached the marshalling yard, it was pitch dark. But the yards were lit by overhead lamps, and although not brilliant they gave off enough light to be unnerving. Foster and Baker now considered their Hitler Youth imposture more a hindrance than a help. To all intents and purposes, they were now truly prisoners on the run and about to become common or garden criminals. The red and white of their Swastika armbands appeared too conspicuous, so they covered them with khaki handkerchiefs. They snaked under the barbed-wire fence and crawled on hands and knees across the railway lines, the shingles and cinders making loud crunching noises as they rolled away under their knees and boots. After crossing several lines they saw a wagon marked "Strasbourg". Looking round to make sure the coast was clear, they clambered aboard. After about half an hour the shunting staff arrived and started work, testing the door-handles of all the wagons. Foster and Barker held theirs firmly closed to create the impression it was locked. The wagons were linked up and the compressed-air pipes connected, and finally at eleven o'clock the train moved off. At last they could relax their grip on the door-handles. They also removed the handkerchiefs from their armbands.

As the train gathered speed they heard the doors being opened, and could clearly see the silhouette of a guard standing on the wooden step and holding on to the fast-moving train by the handrail. He brought up a lamp with his other hand and suddenly caught sight of Foster, lying in a far corner of the gloomy interior. "*Was machen Sie denn da?*" he asked. "What are you doing here?"

"*Ich bin ein Angehöriger der Hitlerjugendpolizei,*" replied Foster. "I am a member of the Hitler Youth police."

"*Ja, wo sind ihre Papiere,*" he pressed Foster. "Yes, but where are your papers?"

Foster dug out his genuine Hitler Youth *Ausweis* and waved it in his face. The guard appeared satisfied, and told him to produce his papers again at the next station. Hoping to get rid of him, Foster replied: "*Ja, natürlich,*" but instead of clearing off, the guard just stood stolidly looking at him. Out of the corner of his mouth Foster whispered to Barker: "Can you jump?"

"I will," said Barker — and the guard noticed him for the first time. "*Wer ist ihr Begleiter?*" he asked. "Who is that with you?" He moved his lamp towards Barker to get a better view, still hanging on to the door by his other hand.

Foster replied: "*Ich kann es Ihnen nicht sagen, es ist vertraulich.* — I cannot tell you. It is confidential." Perhaps that would satisfy him.

It didn't. "*Ist er ein Russe?*" he asked. "Is he Russian?"

"*Ja.*"

The guard finally appeared to be satisfied, but one thing was clear to Foster: they could not survive a more thorough examination at the next station. He turned to Barker, still standing behind him, and whispered: "Can you take my pack?" "Yes." "I'll kick you."

He then lunged towards the guard and pushed him off the train, pulling the door to and holding it closed with both hands. He signalled Barker with a gentle kick. They were ready to jump. But as he looked out of the window he saw the guard was still hanging on, furiously blowing his whistle. The train began to lose speed. When it dropped to twenty miles an hour Barker opened the door on the other side of the carriage and jumped, quickly followed by Foster. Both landed heavily on the sleepers of the adjacent line, and although they recovered their wind quickly they had a feeling the game was up, as they could hear men and women shouting and dogs barking further down the line. As the two fugitives scrambled across the tracks they kept tripping over signal wires, which hurt their ankles and made loud zinging noises. All the time the shouting and barking were getting nearer.

Foster had lost contact with Barker, who was well ahead and invisible in the darkness. He would now have to go it alone. He climbed over a garden fence, ran round the side of the house, crawled across a sandy road, and found himself in a potato field. He lay low in the middle of the field, waiting for the commotion to pass. Then suddenly he saw a German civilian passing close by. He flattened himself against the lumpy earth and held his breath. The civilian stopped, peered into the darkness, then moved off. Foster lay there for some time — he didn't know how long, but it seemed an age — munching on a potato that he had plucked from the earth and wiped clean on his uniform. When he felt he was safe, he stood up and walked cautiously across the field, into the wooded hills beyond. It was eerie in the forest — pitch dark, with a heavy ground mist — and impossible to tell firm ground from marshland or water. Foster was also worried about Barker, for whom he felt some responsibility. After walking for about two hours he retraced his steps and began looking for him. Although he knew it was hopeless and that he should give up, he carried on until again he could hear the trains in the Bebra marshalling yards. He stepped out of the forest on to the railway embankment, and there his search for Barker ended. He could hear voices — German voices! "*Such! Such!* — Seek! Seek!" they were shouting. Foster threw himself to the ground. Two police dogs loomed into view, stopped a few feet away from him, sniffed around a bit, then made off along the top of the embankment. Foster waited until the dogs and their handlers were about twenty yards away, then slithered down the incline.

Fortuitously, a train was passing at more or less walking pace, heading towards a steel viaduct at the bottom of the valley, and he decided to exploit the opportunity to get clear of the area. He scrambled across the numerous railway lines, and as the train was about to pass under the viaduct he tensed himself to clamber aboard. Then there was the silky sound of electricity and suddenly all the floodlights around the viaduct came on at once. He could be seen a mile away, but still he hauled himself aboard. Too late! Guards yelled out orders and yelping police dogs bounded across the railway lights. Foster felt a rush of air and teeth sinking into his arms and legs. The dogs pulled him to the ground and held him down, snarling viciously. As the posse of railway guards, police, dog-handlers and civilians approached, Foster lay still. He heard one of the police shout "*Halt! Halt!*" and immediately afterwards declared: "I surrender!"

They called off the dogs, which now stood over him, watching him intently. He tried to stand up, and they pounced on him again. The police called them off for the second time. When the posse finally reached him they handled him roughly, trying to remove his dagger. Foster explained that the dagger was a dummy, but they refused to believe him. He tried to remove his belt, but immediately felt a Luger sticking into his ribs. "*Hände hoch!*" shouted the *Polizei*.

Foster was shoved towards the signal-box, and the female operator inside snatched her handbag off the stool as if he were a thief. He told her to have no fear, as British officers did not steal. This was of course untrue — POW officers obviously stole their escape equipment, after all! — and one of the guards yelled: "*Halten Sie Ihren Mund!* — Keep your mouth shut!"

But Foster was thirsty, and asked the girl for some water. She refused. The guard nevertheless ordered her to fetch water, which she gave to Foster in a broken cup.

After about an hour a car arrived and Foster was ushered into the back, with a police guard beside him and a dog at his feet. Much to Foster's surprise the dog eventually sat up and rested its head in his lap. But if the dog was "off duty", Foster certainly was not, and knew he had to dispose of his incriminating German money and *Ausweis*. At the first opportunity, he threw them out of the window and into the night.

When they arrived at police headquarters he saw Barker standing against the wall, flanked by police officers and Army guards. His mouth was bleeding and he looked worried. Foster asked him what had happened. "You told them I was Russian…" Barker began.

The police then started to manhandle Foster, who was by now in a foul disposition. "Keep your hands off!" he shouted. "I am a British officer!"

Giving Foster a hefty shove, the policeman slapped his own chest and said: "I am an officer, too! A German officer!"

With that, he stormed off to seek out the Station Sergeant, and Foster and Barker were taken to the basement and locked in a police cell. It was tiny — no bigger than six feet by four — filthy, and alive with fleas. They spent the rest of the night *in meditatione fugae*, but could find no way out.

At daylight (it was now Tuesday, 29 August) they were escorted to the interrogation room, where they were fingerprinted, weighed and measured. All they needed now were the coffin and the undertaker, thought Barker. But this was Reich bureaucracy at work. The Station Sergeant took their details and told them he had to fill in a lengthy form, which required their fingerprints. They deliberately made his job as difficult as possible, twisting their fingers and smudging the form. He started again with a fresh form, and they did the same again. He complained to the Station Officer, saying the prisoners were *"hinderlich"* (awkward). His superior called him a *"Dummkopf"* and told him that once he had taken satisfactory prints he should transfer all the details to that form. This exchange gave the recalcitrants some satisfaction and goaded them further. Despite the advice of his superior, the Sergeant still ended up having to use five forms. Once he had completed his precious work, he ordered the prisoners back to their lice-infested, smelly cell.

Several hours passed, during which they were allowed neither food nor water. Finally they were called out of their cells again and taken before a tough-looking guard who had come from Spangenberg to take them back. "One move out of place, and I will shoot to kill," he warned.

Foster, however, was still in an obdurate mood. *"Ich habe keine Angst,"* he said. "I'm not scared."

The guard pushed him forward, sticking a Luger in his back. "Ach so! We shall see," he said.

He marched them down the street in full view of the local inhabitants, who soon formed a curious train of old men, women, children and dogs — more dogs than the two prisoners had ever seen in their lives. The guard was a particularly unpleasant type who seemed to enjoy shouting at his prisoners, and the gathering crowds acted as a further incentive to his bullying. At one stage, the guard allowed them to cross the road without him and then yelled that they were attempting to escape. They were convinced he was seeking a "legitimate" excuse to shoot them, so at the next corner Foster stopped and asked him which way he wanted them to go. "I can understand your orders in German and can hear you perfectly well if you speak normally," he added. The crowd laughed. But this had been a bad move on Foster's part, because although there were no further "misunderstandings", the guard was all the more eager to find a pretext on which to shoot them.

On the train journey, a German girl sitting opposite them — probably under the impression that they were genuine Hitler Youths in trouble for some minor infraction of the rules — made faces that indicated that they should bolt for it. But with this guard, they didn't fancy their chances.

When they reached Spangenberg, a large gang of Hitler Youths was waiting for them outside the station. On two previous occasions recaptured Spangenberg escapers had been beaten up by Hitler Youths, and Foster warned Barker that they could be in for a rough time. But to his surprise and relief, one of them approached him and joked in English: "Better luck next time, sir!"

Back in the castle they were interrogated by *Hauptmann* Schmidt — which availed the Germans of nothing — and thrown into The Tower. Foster, in one of the outer cells overlooking the drawbridge, was able to draw books and extra food up the shaft that led to the latrines, and also set about contacting Barker, who was in the next cell. He had managed to retain a penknife, which he had made into a saw by cutting into the blade at intervals with a table knife, and using this he made two traps in the wall alongside the passage and then cut through the panel of Barker's cell door to make another trap. He was thus able to visit Barker between inspections by the guard.

One Sunday evening the locks on their cell doors were picked by "Rusty" Wardell. Some of the officers were putting on a play, and Foster and Barker were "invited". However, they had to leave before the finale, as the guard on The Tower carried out his inspection earlier than usual, perhaps hoping to slope off before the appointed hour. A few nights later a guard slammed Foster's cell door too hard, and one of the traps he had made fell on the floor. There was a hell of a furore, with guards, corporals, sergeants and finally officers bellowing at each other until some semblance of sanity was restored by the decision to hold an inquiry. This, inevitably, was completely fruitless. Schmidt got not a word from Foster, Foster still had his customised penknife, and the two other traps he had cut remained undiscovered.

(8)

During the absence of Barker and Foster there had been another fatality in the Upper Camp to add to that of Sub-Lieutenant Gooch prior to the transfer to Thorn. On 29 August a second naval officer, Lieutenant Robin Grey of the Fleet Air Arm, had died of throat cancer. Grey had been shot down on 29 May 1940 and had been in three POW camps — Stalag XIIA at Limburg, Oflag IIA at Prenzlau, and Stalag Luft I at Barth — before being purged to Spangenberg and thence to Thorn. The combination of poor diet and rasping *Caporal* cigarettes had taken their toll. Grey was buried with full military honours, with senior Royal Navy and Royal Air Force officers in attendance.

On Wednesday, 3 September — nine days after the Foster and Barker effort — the RAF contingent brought off another brilliant escape attempt: the bogus "Swiss Commission", involving Dominic Bruce, John Milner, Peter Tunstall and Eustace Newborn. Bruce, Newborn and Tunstall had discovered the locked attic room that the French lieutenant, Merlin, had originally found back in 1939. The door was close to the ceiling at the top of the stone staircase. Standing on a table and chair, Tunstall broke in with a four-foot crowbar, affectionately known as "Napoleon" because it could get through anything. Brushing off the shower of plaster and wood splinters, he poked his head inside the hole and nearly fell off his chair as panic-stricken bats flapped around the attic. He had an even bigger fright when, studying the far corner, he saw a ghostly white face. Steeling himself, and firmly clutching "Napoleon", he climbed through the hole and into the attic, which was covered with dust and cobwebs. Creeping towards the white face, he was ready to commit mayhem. But the ghostly apparition turned out to be part of a bust of Franz Josef, former Emperor of Austria. Tunstall knocked the bust off its pedestal and "kicked its teeth in for frightening me".

Continuing his recce, he found the room to be a cornucopia. There were engineers' files, still wrapped in fine tissue paper, several tools, and even maps. Descending a flight of narrow, steep stairs, closely followed by Bruce and Newborn, he discovered the secret entrance to the flat that Merlin had accidentally hit upon. The flat was well furnished, and in the wardrobe the trio found a forest warden's uniform and a German officer's uniform. They also found a Luger with thirty-two rounds; a hunting rifle with, it seemed, a limitless number of rounds; and a prismatic compass. Almost on the spot a new escape plan was forming in Tunstall's mind, and he and Newborn decided to give up their places on the tunnel.

They proposed, instead, to adapt the uniforms and escape through the gate, with Bruce and Newborn disguised as Swiss representatives and Tunstall as an escort. Once clear of the camp, they would make for one of the aerodromes near Kassel, steal a German aircraft and fly home. They were hoping to find a Ju52, which Newborn had flown as a civil airline pilot. This scheme involved elaborate preparation and careful timing. They set about making Luftwaffe uniforms to wear beneath their Swiss Commission outfits, and Tunstall and Bruce decided to take the Luger with them to add a touch of authenticity. Newborn was against it. He did not feel that the usefulness of the weapon justified the risks involved. A fierce argument ensued, and Joe Kayll got to hear of it. "It is not reasonable," he told them, "for a prisoner of war to expect the protection of the Geneva Convention if he is armed." He sent a message to the SBO, Brigadier Somerset, via the Army orderlies. Somerset strictly forbade them to carry the Luger. He was less eloquent than Kayll. They would have to make a fake weapon, and like it or lump it.

Make a replica Luger they did — carving it out of wood and covering it with lead "liberated" from the roof. They polished and "blued" it until it looked near-perfect.

While the intrepid trio were in the final stages of preparing their escape, the Germans discovered the tunnel. *Hauptmann* Schmidt was beaming with triumph. He boasted on *Appell* that Spangenberg was impregnable: "It is impossible for anyone to escape by tunnel or any other way."

Schmidt was about to be proved wrong — again.

Tunstall had timed the escape to coincide with the arrival and departure, at midday, of the orderlies who carried out the pigswill. Their departure would prevent the guard from crossing the drawbridge to check at the gatehouse whether an officer and two civilians had in fact previously entered the castle.

Shortly after noon on 3 September, as the orderlies went about their usual business, Bruce, Newborn and Tunstall, none of whom could speak passable German, emerged from the castle into the courtyard attended by two British officers. One of them, John Milner, who spoke fluent German, kept up a conversation while the trio answered in monosyllables. The party dawdled a little before the gate and when it became clear that the guard was convinced by the subterfuge, Milner and the "Commission" exchanged formal farewells and approached the sentry. He opened the gate immediately and the three impostors passed through without having to exchange a word. After crossing the drawbridge they passed the guardroom, where unsuspecting, off-duty guards stood up and saluted. Tunstall, who had been carefully coached by John Milner, looked at his wrist-watch. *"Mein Gott!"* he said loudly. *"Schon viertel zwei!"* ("My God! Already a quarter past one!") Bruce replied: *"Kommen Sie, Herr Doktor! Wir müssen weiter gehen!"* ("Come, doctor, we have to get on!") He then "dropped" his *Ausweis* — actually no more than a stolen fishing permit that had been touched up and stamped with a large, official-looking seal — and made a show of picking it up. At this point, instead of turning right down the cobbled slope that led to the spiral road, they turned left and went down the stone steps until they met with one of the tracks. There, they disappeared into the woods, where they doffed their disguises and emerged a minute or two later in their home-made Luftwaffe uniforms, Tunstall as a *Felbwebel* and the other two as *Flieger*.

The trio had arranged that, should their ruse be discovered, prisoners in the castle would burn wet grass in one of the stoves, thus creating a smoke-signal from one of the chimneys. As it happened, their escape had been discovered. One of the guards had had the presence of mind to check the time the Swiss Commission had arrived. In less than a minute the ruse had been found out and every member of the garrison that could be spared had set off in pursuit. As arranged, the escapers' confederates had lit the warning fire, but as the three had been in the woods they had not seen it. However, for the time being luck was on their side. There were two tracks away from the castle and by chance they had chosen the one the garrison considered least suspect. The first intimation they had that the Germans were in hot pursuit was when they heard lorries coming up from behind, filled with armed troops. To the surprise of the escapers, the lorries thundered down the other track, giving the three Luftwaffe *Soldaten* a friendly wave from a distance.

They ate some of their escape rations and marched along Melsunger Strasse towards Kassel, spending the night in the forest, covered in bracken. Early the next morning they set off again. As they approached the city, an important military base, they passed a large number of German troops and their arms ached with having to continually return salutes. Newborn began to get fed up having to keep repeating *"Heil Hitler!"* and his companions told him in no uncertain manner that unless he displayed more allegiance to *"der Führer"* they would knock his block off. Newborn saw the humour in the situation when hordes of children ran alongside them singing the popular Luftwaffe song, *Bomben auf England.*

As planned, they sneaked into the aerodrome through a hedge, and then walked down the tarmac road as if they had every right to be there. Almost immediately they were approached by a uniformed official — some kind of airfield warden — who asked: *"Was wollen Sie?"* ("What do you want?")

Tunstall's German could not meet this kind of challenge. He altered course, waved, and said airily: *"Ich komme zurück!"* ("I'll come back!")

The official looked annoyed, but the three walked on and searched the aerodrome for a Ju52, unfortunately failing to find a suitable aircraft. They left the aerodrome and hid in the surrounding woods, where they discussed their next move. All agreed that they did not want to waste Newborn's experience on Ju52s by trying to steal a strange aircraft. Tunstall nevertheless wanted to stick around in case a Ju52 flew in. The others thought this was dangerous, and preferred to revert to

Plan B — walking to Belgium and France and contacting the Resistance. Since they had walked openly through the streets of Kassel exchanging salutes with German officers, they felt some confidence in their disguises and were sure they could brazen it out on the road in broad daylight. The majority vote won, and they decided to walk on, examining other airfields along the way.

They travelled west towards Cologne, living on apples and vegetables, and in ten days covered a distance of more than a hundred miles. They nearly came a cropper on one occasion, when, resting by a secluded stream, they dozed off. Tunstall was suddenly awoken by a young woman. Another young woman, holding a baby, was kicking Bruce and Newborn awake. Why the women had to do this the three escapers never knew; it seemed that all the young mother wanted to tell them was that her baby's father was in the Luftwaffe and had been shot down by British flak. But instead of making sympathetic noises, Tunstall grinned and said enthusiastically: *"Ja! Ja!"* The expression on her face soon told him he had given the wrong response, and the three escapers made a quick getaway.

Soon after that their luck completely deserted them. They were some seventy miles south-west of Kassel, in the village of Frankenberg, when they passed a group of soldiers speaking to a civilian. The guards saluted them, but one of them stared hard. Through ignorance of what Luftwaffe uniforms looked like, he had become suspicious of their dress. He claimed — quite wrongly, as it happened — that the caps were incorrectly made, and declared: "I think you are Englishmen!" Any attempt at argument was beyond the limited German of the three escapers. The guard unslung his rifle and instructed one of his fellows to call for the *Bürgermeister* and the *Polizei*. The Mayor arrived first, a huge man with a grey handlebar moustache, waving a Luger. He reached for Tunstall's holster. Tunstall took out his replica pistol and the Mayor snatched it out of his hand, obviously convinced it was real. The three escapers were then marched towards the town gaol, the Mayor bringing up the rear with his (real) automatic.

Back at Spangenberg, Schmidt was incensed at their audacity. How dare they escape when he had declared the camp escape-proof! And as for their Luftwaffe uniforms…! He sentenced each of them to fifty-three days' solitary, two weeks longer than the punishment permitted by the POW Code of the Geneva Convention. Bruce told him: "The Germans have no Geneva Convention — but only a German Convention." Peter Tunstall was more succinct. "Fucking Germans," he said. There were already five prisoners undergoing solitary: Joe Barker, Harry Bewlay, Bob Coste, Eric Foster and John Tilsley. The Tower did not have enough cells for the returned escapers so Foster and Barker had their sentences curtailed. Tunstall found himself in Foster's old cell, and Bruce and Newborn shared Barker's.

They took advantage of the traps Foster had made, and within hours there was once again traffic between the two cells. One night the three sat playing cards in Tunstall's cell, but became so caught up in their game that they forgot about the impending inspection by the guard. He was a pretty dim specimen. He entered the cell and counted: *"Eins, zwei, drei. Stimmt. Gute Nacht!"* ("One, two, three. Correct. Goodnight!") Then he left. The three looked at each other, without moving a muscle, waiting for the *Pfennig* to drop. Then — *"Mein Gott…!"*

Result: another ten days each in The Tower.

(9)

In the meantime, the escaping season in Spangenberg had its swansong when Allan McSweyn, Warren Sandman, Neil Svendsen, Nat Maranz and "Andy" Andrews formed another escape syndicate. After surveying the camp they decided that the drawbridge provided the only feasible means of egress. The difficulty was that after the rubbish and laundry cart escapes, and the bogus Swiss Commission, the Germans, too, knew this by now. Svendsen and Andrews came up with a scheme that at first sight looked positively brilliant. Their plan required the manufacture of a long rope and a sturdy grappling hook. One of them would toss the hook from a window, hoping it would secure itself against the side of the wooden drawbridge. They would then crawl hands and feet down the rope, ease their way onto the drawbridge and make a run for it. The plan called for a stormy night, with thunder and lightning to drown out the sounds of the escape, and driving rain to keep the sentries under shelter. In every other respect they were terrible conditions in which to flee across country.

When a suitable night finally presented itself, the escapers were ready. With utmost stealth they made their way to an unoccupied room with their camp-made rope and grappling hook. At an opportune moment, Svendsen hurled the hook out towards the drawbridge. It did not engage, so he quickly hauled it in and hurled it out again. He began to pull the rope in a second time, and the hook snagged and held. As the senior member of the group, Svendsen had elected to go across first. Andrews would follow, then McSweyn, Sandman and Maranz. Svendsen started off on his short but hazardous journey along the wet and slippery rope, hand over hand in the cold, driving rain. Then, just as he was within reach of the drawbridge, a bored guard, who had been sheltering in his sentry box, strolled out and stared idly down at the moat. To his astonishment he saw Svendsen dangling from the length of rope below him, and raised the alarm.

There was no alternative for the others but to rush back into their quarters, hide the escape gear and rations, and climb back into their bunks. Svendsen, meanwhile, was dragged off for questioning, and would later serve the mandatory ten days' solitary confinement. Soon afterwards the guards barged into the prisoners' quarters and drove the occupants out of their bunks and into the courtyard before conducting a meticulous search for any concealed escape equipment. It was cold, wet and miserable out in the courtyard, but when they were eventually ordered back into the castle it was with the comforting knowledge that the searchers had not uncovered any of the precious escape paraphernalia. (The rope and grappling hook had been hidden in the hollow central leg of a wooden table in a ground floor dormitory. It would be discovered there by another trio of prospective escapers in 1942.)

On Tuesday, 16 September the Upper Camp was evacuated. Before they left, the prisoners were lined up in the courtyard as usual and, again as usual, counted in fives and issued with a bread ration. *Hauptmann* Schmidt then screamed the warning that old lags such as Bewlay, Syd Murray, Alf Thompson and John Tilsley had already heard several times before: "You will march from the castle in formation! You will not step from the ranks! Any attempt to do so will be regarded as an attempt to escape *AND YOU WILL BE SHOT WITHOUT WARNING!* "

As Eric Foster remarked many years later, in a masterly piece of understatement: "It would be quite untrue to say that these warnings did not give rise to serious thoughts for those of us who were ever vigilant and looking for an opportunity to escape."

On the way to the rather rustic Spangenberg railway station, they were once again the objects of local curiosity, especially for the women, who had seen very few healthy young men during the past two years. However, neither side was in a position to satisfy the urges of the other, so the prisoners threw the women German bread, which was in any case too heavy for its size. The German civilian population received the same bread ration as POWs — one fifth of a loaf per day — so the women were grateful. The German officers in charge of the POWs were embarrassed and annoyed. The guards were simply jittery. As the British officers stepped out of the ranks to hand the bread over, the guards unslung their rifles and shouted: *"Zurück! Oder ich schiesse!"* ("Get back, or I shoot!") But once they realised it wasn't a trick, and that no one was trying to escape, they slung their rifles back over their shoulders and their behaviour from then on was less neurotic.

The train journey to Menne, where the prisoners were to alight for the march to Oflag VIB at Dössel, was less eventful than the previous journeys to Thorn and back. The guards were on the alert and in any case the journey lasted less than two hours, so no opportunity to escape short of the sheer bloody suicidal presented itself.

You are glad to be leaving Spangenberg — this time, hopefully, for good. You've been back and forth between one camp and another so many times, always returning, it seems, to the crumbling *Schloss*, that you're starting to feel like the man in the iterative poem:

The battle of the Nile,
I was there all the while,
I was there all the while,
At the battle of the Nile,
I was there all the while... (etc)

At last, on Friday, 10 October 1941 the Army prisoners from the Lower Camp, too, are sent by cattle-trucks to Oflag VIB. When the disappointed "repats" from Rouen return to Elbersdorf at the end of November, they find an almost empty *Unterlager*. Guest, Kelly and Methven are then returned to Barth, along with Fred Knight, and Dan Hallifax and Bill Mathieson are sent back to *Lazarett* IXC.

Chapter Seven

One of the Purge Was Missing

Oflag IXA/H, Spangenberg, November–April 1942

> *How some they have died, and some they have left me,*
> *And some are taken from me; all are departed;*
> *All, all are gone, the old familiar faces.*
>
> Charles Lamb, *The Old Familiar Faces*

Once again, Allied prisoners of war had not heard the last of Elbersdorf and Spangenberg. When these camps had been cleared in September and October 1941 a few RAF remained behind at Elbersdorf, their numbers being augmented by the return of the thwarted "repats" in November. Among those still languishing in the "Backwater" in the New Year of 1942 were John Coleson, Marcus Marsh, Keith Ogilvie and George Skelton. By mid-January the Upper Camp, too, was inhabited again, this time by some two hundred Army officers. They were nearly all of the rank of Major and above. Many of them were from the 51st Highland Division captured in the gallant rearguard action at St Valéry-sur-Somme in 1940. With their CO, Major-General Victor Fortune, they had initially been held at Stalag VIA, at Hemer bei Iserlohn, and then Oflag VIIC/H, Laufen. In March 1941 they had been sent to one of the reprisal camps at Thorn. When the *Strafe* ended, they were transferred to Spangenberg, then to Oflag VIB at Warburg-Dössel, then back to Spangenberg on 15 January 1942.

On Wednesday, 18 February, 1942 those remaining at Elbersdorf were joined by a new influx of thirty-nine prisoners from Dulag Luft. They were Wing Commanders H R Larkin (Australian) and R R S Tuck DSO, DFC and two Bars; Squadron Leaders T D Calnan, N S F Davie, AuxAF, L W V Jennens, RAFO, W Wilczewski (Pole), and V T L Wood; Acting Squadron Leader A M Crawley; Flight Lieutenants E R Abbott, H J W Bareham DFM, P J Edwards, R D Fraser, G E McGill, W H Hannigan, and W H Thallon; Flying Officers A P L Barber, G B Dawkins DFM, R J Kimbell and D Stein; Pilot Officers S B K Brackenbury, RCAF, G C Daniel, RCAF, J A R Falconer, M W Fessler (American), W D Geiger, Jnr (American), C P Hall, E R Hester, K M Jones, W D Moore, C W Murphy, RCAF, W H Nichols (American), O L S Philpot DFC, RAFVR, G M Rackow, P R Ross, RNZAF, P R M Runnacles, P S Sanders, N Smallwood, and J G Whiting, RNZAF; and Lieutenants G R Haller and B L McFarlane, SAAF.

Most had been captured during summer and autumn 1941, and winter 1941/2, and held back at Dulag Luft until 17 February, when enough officers had been assembled to warrant a purge to Spangenberg.

Abbott, Bareham, Brackenbury, Dawkins, Edwards, Fraser, Hannigan, Jennens, Kimbell, McGill, Moore, Murphy, Ross, Runnacles, Sanders, Thallon and Whiting were all bomber types.

"Abdul" Abbott, from No50 Squadron, Swinderby, had risen from the ranks, and in October 1940, while still a Sergeant Pilot, had been awarded the DFM. Now a Flight Lieutenant, he took off on 13/14 October 1941 to join thirty-eight other aircraft having yet another go at Cologne. His aircraft was hit by flak, but all the crew survived. The only other commissioned member of the crew, Pilot Officer W J Chase, was sent to Stalag Luft I. Abbott would later receive a DSO.

Pilot Officer W D Moore had been shot down on the disastrous Berlin raid of 7/8 November 1941. C-in-C Bomber Command, Sir Richard Peirse, frustrated by a long run of bad weather and poor bombing results, had decided to mount a major effort that night with Berlin as the main target. He persisted in this decision despite a late weather forecast showing that storms, thick cloud, ice and hail covered the North Sea routes by which the bombers would need to fly to Berlin and back. Air Vice-Marshal Sir John Slessor of No5 Group objected to the plan and was allowed to withdraw his part of the Berlin force and send it to Cologne instead. In all, 392 aircraft were sent out on the night's operations. This was a new record and probably represented the maximum number of serviceable aircraft and crews available at the time. For the Berlin raid, No1 Group put up twenty-two Wellingtons; No3 Group, sixty-nine Wellingtons and seventeen Stirlings; and No4 Group, forty-two Whitleys, ten Wellingtons and nine Halifaxes — a total of 169 aircraft. Meanwhile, Nos 1, 3 and 5 Groups put up 223 Hampdens, Halifaxes, Wellingtons and Whitleys to bomb Cologne, Essen, Mannheim and smaller targets, including the Channel ports, and to lay mines off Oslo.

Moore was among the eight crews detailed from No99 Squadron, flying Wellingtons from Waterbeach. None of the crews managed to identify the target because of thick cloud and severe icing, and three aircraft never made it back. Of Moore's crew, two were killed, while two others, Flight Lieutenant H H Henderson and Flying Officer H A Goodwin, were captured. They were sent to Barth.

Altogether thirty-seven aircraft were shot down that night — a 9.4 per cent loss and more than double that for previous night operations. "The Big City" alone claimed twenty-one, for no appreciable results. As for the rest, most crashed in the North Sea, suffering from icing or lack of fuel. The future of Bomber Command now hung in the balance, with Churchill himself being drawn into the debate. Three months later, Air Marshal Arthur Harris was appointed C-in-C. Significantly, Bomber Command was not to carry out another major raid on Berlin until January 1943.

Lionel William Vaughan Jennens — known to most of his fellow-POWs as "Duff Jennens", from the RAF slang "duff gen", meaning inaccurate information — had been a Flight Commander and the captain of a Stirling on No7 Squadron, Oakington (No3 Group). On Thursday, 18 December 1941, forty-seven aircraft — eighteen Halifaxes, eighteen Stirlings and eleven Manchesters — attempted a daylight bombing raid on the *Scharnhorst* and *Gneisenau* at Brest. It was the sixth raid in a month and Brest had become the most heavily defended target in German-occupied territory. Despite flak and fighters, the *Gneisenau* was hit. But aerial photography yielded disappointing results. The two battle-cruisers and their escort cruiser, the *Prinz Eugen*, were still fit to break out into open sea. Bomber Command paid the price in six aircraft, four of them Stirlings. Jennens' Stirling was bounced by three Me109s. His crew stood up to the onslaught gamely, but when the number of enemy fighters increased to five it was just too much. The "bloody old crate" — as Jennens called his Stirling, an unpopular aircraft amongst bomber types — started to fall to pieces. He lost control of the rudder. The entire crew jumped for it and all but one survived. Although not escape-minded, Jennens did not take his POW status lying down. At Dulag Luft he had emerged as a natural leader, and a constant thorn in the side of the Germans. He never lost an opportunity to remind them that their Reich was "the Third and bloody Last".

Richard ("Kim") Kimbell and C W Murphy were WOP/AGs in a No77 Squadron Whitley from Leeming. On 27/28 December 1941, Bomber Command put up 132 aircraft to attack Düsseldorf. Their aircraft, flown by Warrant Officer C H Grace, was attacked by a night-fighter killing the rear-gunner. The rest of the crew baled out, and as Kimbell floated to earth he saw the Whitley loop and fly towards him before it hit the ground.

Stuart ("Brack") Brackenbury flew Hampdens with No 408 (Goose) Squadron at Balderton (No5 Group). On 28/29 December 1941, eighty-one Hampdens bombed the chemical works at Hüls. Four aircraft were lost, Brackenbury being attacked by *Oberleutnant* Emil Woltersdorf from *III/NJG1*. His aircraft crashed in Holland. The other members of the crew were killed.

George Edwards McGill, a Canadian from Toronto, had served as an observer with No103 Squadron, which flew the most sorties and suffered the highest losses in No2 Group, Bomber Command. On 10/11 January 1942, the squadron had taken part in a raid by 124 aircraft — including Wellingtons and Hampdens — on Wilhelmshaven. It was McGill's fifth operation. The flight out passed without incident, but as the Wellington was on its bomb-run, McGill's pilot said he thought one of the bombs had hung up. So he went round for a second time, which was once too many, as flak hit the bomb-bay. The fuselage caught fire. As McGill and the two WOP/AGs fought with the blaze, a flare went off, the fuselage tunnel became a raging inferno and the three men were driven back. The skipper ordered the crew to abandon the aircraft. McGill, the WOP/AGs and the tail-gunner baled out. Then the second pilot decided to have a go with the fire extinguisher, and the pressure made the flare pop out of a hole in the fuselage skin. With his gauntleted hands, he attacked the flames and managed to put the fire out. He returned to the cockpit, and with the skipper flew the Wimpey back home. They got a DFC each. But after skulking around enemy-occupied countryside for twenty-four hours, George McGill became a prisoner.

"Sandy" Sanders, from No 40 Squadron, was up on the same night and on the same raid. He took off from Alconbury at 1645 hours, but had an engine failure and had to ditch off the Frisian Islands. Three of the crew perished, but the rest scrambled in to their dinghy. Overnight, the weather deteriorated and ice started to form a thin film on the dinghy. When they were finally picked up, Sanders' feet were frost-bitten.

Gerry Dawkins and Edwards had been in the same crew as pilot and observer in No 207 Squadron, Waddington, which had been re-formed as Bomber Command's first Manchester squadron by Wing Commander N C Hyde back in November 1940. On 14/15 January 1942, the Command put up ninety-five aircraft against shipyards and an airframe factory at Hamburg. Only forty-eight aircraft bombed, hitting Altona station and causing a dozen fires, and at least five aircraft were lost. Hit by flak, one of Gerry Dawkins' engines was put out of action, so he gave the bale out order. Of his crew, all but one of the WOP/AGs survived. Dawkins had previously served as a Sergeant Pilot on No83 Squadron, and had been awarded the DFM in March 1941.

William Herbert Thallon was a Wellington pilot with No12 Squadron. On 20/21 January twenty Wimpeys and five Hampdens set out for Emden, Bill Thallon taking off from Binbrook at 1834 hours, with Pilot P R Ross, a New Zealander, navigating. Three Wellingtons were lost. Thallon's was attacked by *Oberleutnant* Ludwig Becker of *6/NJG2*. The second-pilot and the rear-gunner were killed, but Thallon saw his co-pilot's foot move and stayed with the aircraft while the survivors baled out. Guided by the flashing light of a lighthouse, he aimed for the Dutch Frisian Islands and crash-landed on Terschelling. He then discovered that the second pilot had been dead all along; the foot movement had been caused by the vibration of the juddering aircraft.

Squadron Leader Victor Thomas Lawrence Wood, an Australian in the RAF born to be nicknamed "Woody", was bagged two nights later. He was a "B" Flight Commander in No420 (Snowy Owl) Squadron, Waddington, formed in No5 Group on 19 December 1941. Woody's claim to fame was in being the first pilot from the squadron to be shot down, on its first operation on 21/22 January 1942, one month after it was formed. That night thirty-eight aircraft went to bomb Emden, and Woody's Hampden was shot down by flak. All the crew baled out safely, and the Hampden crashed in Pietersbeirum in Holland.

***

Harold John William Bareham was a Cranwell-trained regular who had joined up in 1930, training as a navigator and then, in 1940, as a pilot. Sometimes known as "Jack", he was more often called "Bish" — short for "Bishop" — not only because he held deep religious convictions but also because once he got astride his hobby-horse he would "preach" without expecting any reply from his audience. But he was held in high regard because he was a brilliant navigator and pilot, and a genius with his hands. In a rather chequered RAF career he had served on no less than seven squadrons — bomber, fighter and Coastal Command — as well as with the Fleet Air Arm before joining No106 Squadron (Hampdens, No5 Group, Bomber Command) at Coningsby in December 1941. He had also handled ten different aircraft, ranging from training types such as the Miles Magister, Airspeed Oxford, Avro Tutor, Douglas Harvard and Prentice Proctor, through fighters such as the Mosquito, to Hampden and Manchester bombers. As passenger, wireless-operator or observer he had flown in another twelve.

Three times since the war he had flown with squadrons that had been wiped out on operations— and by good fortune had survived. Lady Luck had given him her widest smile back in 1940 when, as a Sergeant, he had been in Wing Commander the Earl of Bandon's No82

(Blenheim) Squadron at Watton, flying as observer, sometimes to Bandon and sometimes to Squadron Leader Miles V Delap. In March 1940 Delap, with "Bish" as observer, sunk a 500-ton U-boat in the Schillig Roads, one of the 250lb bombs hitting her forward of the conning-tower. It was the first U-boat sinking by an aircraft in the war. In April 1940 Bareham was selected for pilot training and on 17 May, while he was awaiting a posting to an Elementary Flying Training School, the squadron lost eleven of its Blenheims over Maastricht. The next day, when Bareham heard that the squadron might be disbanded, he marched straight to the CO's office, demanding that his posting be postponed and that he remain on what was left of the squadron as an air observer. It was this kind of pluck which prompted Group to maintain the squadron.

On the evening of 11 June, after an attack on German armour at Le Havre, Delap's Blenheim was bounced by enemy fighters. The front blister panels were blown in and all Bareham's maps and navigation tools swept away. By using the stars he navigated the aircraft back to base. Then, on 21 June, the squadron was ordered to attack an oil refinery at Bremen. After crossing the Dutch coast the formation ran into ten-tenths cloud. Yet Bareham still managed to navigate his aircraft, and the formation, to the target and reach it by the ETA. By the end of July he had flown twenty-three operations and he was awarded the DFM. The citation read: "...he is an exceptional navigator who has successfully led the formation direct to the target on every occasion. He displays great coolness and courage under fire and sets a very good example to the rest of the Squadron and inspires the formation with confidence in his navigation."

When he finally left No82 Squadron to train as a pilot, the Earl of Bandon wrote to his father, in a letter dated 30 June 1940:

> As your son has now left the Squadron I thought I would just like to let you know what wonderful work he has done. As a navigator he is quite exceptional and he has shown great courage and determination on all his flights. I hope one day I will have the pleasure of him serving under me again. We were all very sorry to lose him.

After completing his pilot training "Bish" was posted to No106 Squadron (No2 Group) at Coningsby. On 28/29 January 1942 fifty Wellingtons and twenty-nine Hampdens set out to bomb Münster. Bareham, with New Zealander J G Whiting as navigator, took off in his Hampden at 1805 hours. Visibility was poor and not one of the aircraft hit the target. Four Hampdens were lost. Bareham's aircraft was attacked by night-fighters over the Ijsselmeer. One of the gunners, Sergeant S A Dungey, was killed in the attack. The rest baled out. Sergeant E J Snelling, the other gunner, came down in the sea and was drowned. His body was found on 12 September 1942, washed up on the beach near Amrum. Pilot Officer Whiting was captured on landing. John Bareham was at liberty for forty-eight hours. He landed in the town of Nieur Loosdrecht, where a Dutch woman, Mrs Hoep, rushed out of her house, bundled his parachute up her skirt and led him indoors. She and her husband wanted to pass him on to the Underground, but a neighbour betrayed them, and two nights later the Gestapo arrived and arrested them. The Hoeps spent the rest of the war in a concentration camp, and their two blonde daughters were sent to an Aryan "race farm".

Fraser and "Hank" Hannigan had been in the same crew on No61 Squadron, North Luffenham (No5 Group), as pilot and navigator. On the night of 31 January 1942, the squadron contributed nine Manchesters to a raid by seventy-two aircraft on Brest. Three Manchesters were lost, all from No61 Squadron. Fraser's aircraft was coned by searchlights, then hit by flak and set on fire. The second pilot, Sergeant G H Marshall, was killed. The Manchester then hit a barrage-balloon cable and Fraser gave the order to bale out. Hannigan, Flight Sergeants W H Shorrock and T W Walsh, and Sergeants A W Hadley and B H Mullen, all evacuated the aircraft safely. But Sergeant S J MacLean of the RCAF was trapped in the escape hatch. Fraser tried to pull him free, but was unable to do so, and they were still in the aircraft as it hit the sea. MacLean sank with it, and his body was never recovered.

* * *

Of the Fighter Command fraternity, the first to enter captivity was Pilot Officer Kenneth Jones, of No54 Squadron, Hornchurch (No11 Group). During the afternoon of Tuesday, 22 July 1941, Group put up four squadrons on "Circus 58", which turned out to be only a fighter sweep. The Germans hadn't bothered to respond to that morning's "Circus", but this time they came up to do battle. Three Spitfire pilots were killed, one returned home wounded, and Ken Jones became a prisoner.

Gilmore Cecil Daniel, Morris ("Fess") Fessler, William Geiger and William Nichols were all Americans who had joined the first RAF Eagle Squadron, No71, formed on 19 September 1940 at Church Fenton, ten miles south of York. At first the squadron fell within the orbit of No10 Group, whose role was the air defence of the industrial Midlands, but in March 1941 it was moved into No11 Group, defending the London area. Geiger and Nichols were two of its earliest members.

Geiger had had been inducted into aviation through the Civilian Pilot Training Programme (CPTP) of the Civil Aeronautics Authority at Pasadena City College, California. The CPTP was a highly successful Federal programme offering ground training at colleges and universities, along with flight training by established civilian instructors, so as to create a reserve of college-age pilots. Both he and Nichols, a former barnstorming pilot, had joined the RAF through the Clayton Knight Committee, a recruiting organisation backed by the Royal Canadian Air Force. This had been set up in Ottawa and New York by Canada's top-scoring air ace of the Great War, Air Vice-Marshal "Billy" Bishop. He induced an American wartime flying colleague, Clayton Knight, to head the recruitment force. A wealthy Canadian, Homer Smith, was commissioned a Wing Commander in the RCAF and appointed to administer the committee. When Hitler's *Wehrmacht* invaded the Low Countries, Knight and Smith, on the basis of a manpower survey that showed that a quarter of all America's unemployed pilots lived in California, interviewed pilots in Los Angeles, San Francisco and San Diego for potential duties with the RCAF. They got into recruiting for the RAF and Ferry Command by chance. The international financier Robert Sweeny, his sons Charles and Bobby, and their uncle Colonel Charles Sweeny, had been luring pilots into the Eagle Squadron with champagne parties and showbiz publicity. Viewing this razzmatazz with some distaste, the RAF wanted the Clayton Knight Committee to screen the Sweeny organisation's recruits. Knight's committee imposed rigorous standards: to be eligible, applicants had to have at least three hundred hours' certified flying experience, a Civil Aeronautics Authority licence and the equivalent of a high-school diploma. Geiger and, several months later, Nichols met the criteria. Along with seven others, Geiger went by train to Canada, where they were sworn in as sergeant pilots by an RAF Group Captain who made them swear allegiance to His Majesty the King. Some of the recruits were unhappy about giving up their American nationality for a mere sergeant pilot's status. Two had already made up their minds to go home when the Group Captain reappeared and said he had made a mistake: they would be commissioned as pilot officers and would not have to relinquish US citizenship.

By the time the United States entered the war in December 1941 the Clayton Knight Committee had processed 50,000 applicants and approved 6,700 Americans for duty with the RCAF and RAF. About ten per cent of the RCAF enrolment at that time consisted of American volunteers, and 92 per cent of the Americans who became Eagles were products of the Clayton Knight Committee. They formed a nucleus for three squadrons, Nos 71, 121 and 133, totalling 240 US pilots, including thirty-seven who had joined the RCAF. But some of the recruits had been sold a pup, for the committee claimed they need sign up for only a year. One such was Nichols, who signed his contract in September 1940. Almost a year was to pass before he realised he had been misled.

Owing to leadership problems, No71 Eagle Squadron was not declared operational until late in January 1941 and only carried out its first operation — an uneventful patrol — on 5 February. By that time it had been moved to Kirton-in-Lindsey, near Lincoln. It had a bigger airfield and Mess than Church Fenton, and every morning RAF fighters "beat up" the station, giving it the glamour and excitement the Eagles craved.

Nichols, from Woodland, California, arrived shortly before No71 Squadron became operational and was appointed wingman for Flight Lieutenant Chesley Peterson, a flight commander who was also the American pilots' line to the British CO (Squadron Leader Stanley T Meares, a former

Battle of Britain pilot). When Nichols was shot down in September 1941 the squadron was based at North Weald and had recently converted from the Hurricane MkIIa to the Spitfire MkVb. It had become one of the best close-escort squadrons in the RAF, carrying out more ops than any of its counterparts and establishing a record in losing not one single bomber to fighter action in summer 1941. Bill Geiger alone had flown about thirty ops, most of them in close bomber escorts, and fifty or sixty convoy patrols. However, during early autumn there was a lull in the action and Nichols started fretting. He told Peterson that he wanted to go immediately on a "Rhubarb". So for the next two days Peterson and Nichols flew "Rhubarbs", initiated fighter sweeps and saw plenty of action. Then four or five days of inactivity followed. Peterson was sitting in the hot sun at North Weald reading when again Nichols came pleading for more action. "I hope I get a scramble," he said. "I have to get more fighting in this week." When Peterson asked why, Nichols explained that he had signed up for only a year and was due to return to California next week. Sceptical, Peterson went to the Air Ministry to check Nichols' records. A group captain showed him Nichols' contract, which was the same as his own, calling for service for the duration of the war and for not more than one year thereafter. He took the news to Nichols who shook his head and insisted: "I signed up for a year. I want to get fighting for the week I have left."

As it turned out, he had less than a week. On Sunday, 7 September 1941 the three squadrons of the North Weald Wing — No71 "Eagle" and two British outfits — were ordered out on a fighter sweep over France. No bombers were involved, and as the Me109s, saving themselves for attacks on bombers, rarely came up to give battle with massed fighter formations, it looked as if the operation would be no more than a practice flight. But it would be No71 Squadron's first sweep with the new Spitfires — although, owing to mechanical difficulties, only nine aircraft got off the ground.

The Spitfires were seventy-five miles inside France, near the planned turning point, when the English ground radar controller advised that he had plotted enemy bandits behind them. About a hundred Me109s, led by Adolf Galland's *JG26*, were lying in wait to trap them and overwhelm them before they turned back for the coast. The ensuing battle turned into the fiercest engagement the Eagles had yet encountered. They bore the brunt of it. Flying at 29,000 feet, they were set upon from above. Then the Messerschmitts regained altitude, re-formed and came in again. In the first pass, Peterson shot down his first enemy aircraft, but two Eagles were killed and Nichols' aircraft set on fire. He baled out and was captured on hitting French soil.

No71 Squadron's next operation took place on Wednesday, 17 September, twelve days before Bill Geiger's twenty-second birthday. It was to be his last sortie. The squadron was assigned to cover twenty-four Blenheims on "Circus 95" to Mazingarbe. Two Eagle pilots were shot down. One was killed, but Geiger survived to become a prisoner.

His Spitfire had been hit at 15,000 feet over the English Channel. The instrument panel disappeared, the gun-sight blew up in his face, the radio went dead and the cockpit stank of cordite. A little voice inside Geiger — the patter he had learned by heart during parachute drill — calmly and deliberately told him it was time to bale out. Then the voice told him: "Grab the oxygen mask and pull." (The British flying helmet was split up the back so it would fit any head-size, and you could take it off by tugging sharply on the oxygen mask). Geiger did as the little voice said, and off came the helmet. The "voice" carried on giving him the drill. Geiger tucked the helmet down beside the seat so it wouldn't wrap around his legs as he got out, pulled the little black ball overhead on the canopy, all at the voice's bidding — and nothing happened. He banged on the canopy a couple of times. It budged a little, then it stuck. He bashed it with his elbows, wrists and fists, but still nothing happened. He was now heading towards the water in a slightly inverted spin, time was running out, and the little voice within that had hitherto been so calm and helpful was curiously quiet. Geiger dropped his hands to his lap in despair and thought: *I'm going in with it.* Then he told himself: *It won't hurt.* (Thinking that brought relief and calm.) Now he was curious: what was it like to be dead? Perhaps it wouldn't be so bad after all. It was almost like embarking on a new adventure.

Suddenly he noticed that a corner of the canopy was sticking out, and felt a flicker of hope. If he stuck his elbow in the gap and pushed hard, perhaps he could bend it out further so the slipstream would grab it and pull off the canopy. In went his elbow, and off came the canopy. Now the moment of crisis was over, the voice piped up again and Geiger followed its urgings, bringing up his feet so they wouldn't get caught under the shattered instrument panel, pulling the pin in the Sutton shoulder harness, hooking his hands over the top of the windscreen, and popping smoothly out of the cockpit. Going down head first, he arched his back slightly, looking at the water below, found the rip-cord, pulled it, and threw it away. A jarring tug, then merciful silence, and he was swinging gently to and fro. He reached down and removed one flying boot, dropped it and watched it sail away below him. Taking off the second one, he held on to it until he was twenty feet above the water, so he could judge the distance at the last minute before cutting the parachute loose.

At last he hit the water, discarding the parachute and trying to figure out how to inflate the emergency dinghy in the water, for by now the voice had deserted him — he had never got as far as dinghy drill in his parachute training. The Mae Wests in those days did not come with a CO_2 bottle, and had to be blow up by lung-power. Geiger discovered that the Mae West did not keep him high enough in the water to allow him much air. It was essential he open the fighter dinghy as soon as possible. He grasped the valve on the dinghy's CO_2 bottle and twice tried to turn it, without success. In desperation he again tried to inflate the Mae West. He put the little hose in his mouth and blew, but was taking in more water than air. Frustrated, he returned to the dinghy and noticed a small pin running through the valve. He pulled out the pin, turned the valve easily, and got the dinghy inflated. At last he climbed into it and was in a position to breathe without difficulty. The dinghy did not keep him high in the water and did not keep him dry, but at least it gave him a little air.

He cast around for the paddles and — more important — the little pump that should keep the dinghy inflated. After a while he realised he had climbed into the dinghy while it was upside down. Back in the water he went, flipping over the dinghy. Climbing back in, he found all the survival gear he needed. But for several hours he progressed no more than about a hundred yards. Then he noticed a small line hanging over the stern. Retrieving it, he discovered he had left the sea anchor out. Still, at least the effort of rowing had helped keep his blood circulating.

He kept on paddling until dusk, when an E-boat turned up, plucked him out of the dinghy and took him to the French coast. He spent the night at St Omer. At four o'clock in the morning an officer and four soldiers arrived to escort him to a covered lorry full of German soldiers. Geiger had feared his escort would shoot him, and had decided to make a break for it, eyeing every alley and side-street they passed and awaiting the chance to slip away. No opportunity had presented itself, and now, as the officer ordered him to climb over the tailboard into the lorry, he was bathed in sweat, although it was a very cold morning. Then he found himself looking a German soldier right in the eye. "You are an American, aren't you?" asked the soldier, in perfect English with a slight American accent. "Yes," replied Geiger. "Don't worry," said the German. "They are going to send you to Dulag Luft. For you the war is over."

***

Gilmore Daniel, shot down a month later, was the youngest pilot ever to become an Eagle. When he enlisted at the RCAF recruiting station in December 1939 he presented a doctored birth certificate (which his father had given him) showing that he had been born on the Osage Indian Reservation in Oklahoma on 30 November 1921. Five feet eight inches tall, weighing only a hundred and forty pounds, and with a smooth, olive face, lightly freckled and framed in curly auburn hair, he looked much younger than eighteen. He was, in fact, born on 30 November 1925. Only thirteen when he graduated from Spartan Flying School, in Tulsa, he was fourteen when he joined the RCAF. Gil's parents were Osage Indians with traces of Cherokee, Choteau, French and Irish blood. His mother's grandfather was Captain Choteau, a founder of the Oklahoma Indian Territory. A cousin, Sylvester Tinker, was chief of the Osage Nation. Sylvester's brother, Clarence L Tinker, was a fighter and bomber pilot and became a Major-General commanding the 7th US Army Air Force. (He was subsequently killed at Midway, and Tinker Air Force base near Oklahoma City was named after him.)

Daniel served briefly in all three Eagle squadrons and in six other RAF squadrons, including No242 when it was commanded by the legendary Squadron Leader (later Wing Commander) "Tin Legs" Douglas Bader. After Bader was shot down and captured in August 1941, badly damaging one of his artificial legs, Daniel was among the one hundred-odd fighter pilots who escorted a flight of Blenheims over St Omer hospital to drop him a pair of replacement legs. The formation then went on to bomb Ostend.

On Monday, 13 October, Daniel himself was shot down, flying with No71 Eagle Squadron, which along with No402 (Canadian) Squadron was escorting eighteen Blenheims on "Circus 108B" to Mazingarbe. Daniel broke formation to attack three Me109s. He shot up the lead one and it exploded, knocking down the other two. Daniel was so excited he turned for home, forgetting to look out for other enemy aircraft. Flying at 28,000 feet, he was suddenly bounced by more Me109s. Within seconds Gil's cockpit was a shambles. It was a miracle he survived that first onslaught. He looked over his left shoulder and saw an Me109 off his port wing shooting at him with a 90° deflection. The enemy pilot, *Hauptmann* Philipp, got a direct hit on Daniel's starboard wing. Daniel saw a big explosion, then a gaping hole where his cannon ammunition had been. He started diving. By now smoke was pouring from two holes in the fuel tank in front of his legs. He knew it would be only a matter of seconds before fire broke out, so he jettisoned his canopy, pulled the pin out of his Sutton harness and flew out. He hit the tail, opened his parachute immediately, then saw that Me109s were still buzzing around him. They started taking pot-shots. He waved at them and they broke off. As soon as he hit the water he released his parachute. Then he felt a stabbing pain in one of his legs and realised he had been hit by shell fragments. Philipp flew off, jubilant at getting his forty-eighth victory. His first had been Flight Lieutenant D B H ("Fou") McHardy, back in October 1940. ("Fou" survived to join the British Permanent Staff at Dulag Luft, where he remained until being transferred to Stalag Luft III, Sagan, in April 1942.)

Daniel had hit the Channel about five miles off Dover. Convinced he would soon be picked up, he inflated his dinghy and clambered aboard. Then darkness descended, and he had a grandstand view of a night-bombing raid on Calais. Shortly after dawn he saw Lysanders flying overhead. He waved, but they failed to see him. This was worrying. All day he bobbed up and down in the Channel, seeing dozens of fighters and even a Walrus flying-boat. But no one spotted him. Night set in again, and again he watched a Bomber Command raid over the coast of France. The next day it started to rain. Gil found that all the while he kept his hands and face in the water, the low temperature was bearable, but once they were out, they turned frigid with cold. His legs hurt and his wounds were very sore.

On the third night he could hear the roar of the surf and picked out land. Eventually the tide carried him towards the beach. As soon as he felt some ground beneath him he starting crawling, very weakly, on all fours. It was the last thing he knew until a bright light was shined on him and he heard foreign voices. Then he blacked out again. Later in the evening he awoke in bed and saw a German sitting beside him on a chair. The German asked in English how Daniel was and whether he would like something to eat and drink. He told Daniel they had found him when they turned on the floodlights to clear the beach and fire their big guns at Dover.

Daniel had been in his dinghy for seventy-eight hours. The water had helped sterilise his wounds and kept him from freezing, but he had frost-bite and a cracked or broken leg. The Germans took him to the hospital at St Omer (the one in which Bader had been held and from which he had recently made an escape), but after two days he was removed because a typhus epidemic had broken out.

At his next hospital, in Lille, where he was to stay for a week, he was visited by a gloating *Hauptmann* Philipp. (Daniel followed Philipp's career in German newspapers all the time he was a POW. The German "ace" was killed on the Russian front three years later, by which time he had claimed 350 victories.) Daniel was then interrogated by an Intelligence officer, who wanted to know what aircraft he had been flying. "Go and ask *Hauptmann* Philipp," he replied. "He knows." The interrogator got so angry he slapped Daniel and told him he was an American mercenary and would be shot.

***

Stan Meares' wingman, the burly, laconic Morris Fessler, was captured less than two weeks later, on Monday, 27 October, during a dawn "Rhubarb" over France with Charles Wallace Tribken as his No2. Over the marshalling yards at Boulogne he attacked a large freight engine with cannons and machine-guns. But his dive was too shallow. As he pulled up to clear the target his engine misfired badly and his oil and radiator coolers packed up. Either the freight engine had blown up with him above it, or he had flown into it — he never did find out. He coaxed his Spitfire up to 2,000 feet, looked for a place to land, and set her down in a field on the outskirts of Boulogne. After setting fire to his aircraft, he set off on foot. It was 6.15am. Within fifteen minutes he was being hunted by search parties with dogs. He kept to streams, used hedgerows for cover, and played hide-and-seek with his pursuers until mid-afternoon, when they gave up. At one point he hid in a clump of bushes at a crossroads less than seventy-five feet from the search-party. But he was downwind of them and the dogs failed to pick up his scent.

For the rest of the afternoon and evening he watched a farmhouse. At about 9pm a car drove up and the occupants went into the house. Two hours later Fessler went to the back door and knocked. A woman in a long nightgown let him in, and the farmer, wearing long-johns, appeared. They invited him to sit down in the kitchen and the woman revived the dying fire and started warming some soup. Then the farmer's daughter entered, followed by two French gendarmes pulling trousers over their long-johns. One had a pistol in his belt. The police officers had been the occupants of the car and were billeted in the farmhouse. Over soup and wine, Fessler, his hosts and the policeman discussed the situation, Fessler making himself understood in schoolboy French with the aid of an English-French pocket dictionary he carried with him. One of the gendarmes told him the Germans knew he was in the area and at dawn would turn out in larger search parties. If his scent led to the farmhouse they would know the owners had helped him, even if they did not find him there. The family and the gendarmes would be arrested and killed as a warning to other French people not to help the enemy. The Germans had carried out similar reprisals before.

Fessler knew he was telling the truth. He wondered if the armed policeman would fire at him if he tried to run out of the door and into the night. At the same time, he did not want anybody to be killed on his account. He therefore accepted the inevitable, and allowed the gendarmes to hand him over to the German authorities.

* * *

Flying Officer Don Stein, of No263 Squadron, Filton (No10 Group), was another "Spangenberger" who had earned himself a singular honour: that of becoming the first commissioned officer flying a Westland Whirlwind to become a prisoner. On Thursday, 30 October 1941, because of bad weather, the only Fighter Command operation was a "Rhubarb" by two Whirlwind squadrons, Nos 137 and 263. They made an attack on Morlaix airfield and Stein was brought down by ground fire.

Polish Squadron Leader Waclaw Wilczewski, the CO of No315 Squadron, was one of two squadron commanders made prisoner on Saturday, 8 November 1941. He had originally been in No607 Squadron, which he joined on 10 October 1940 after leaving No5 OTU. On 27 November he was posted to No145 Squadron, and on 22 December to No308 Squadron. Promoted to Flight Lieutenant, he became a section leader in No316 Squadron on 24 February 1941. On 17 May he was involved in an embarrassing prang when his Hurricane had an engine failure and he tried to land in a sports field. Unfortunately, civilians gathered at the field for recreational walks thought he was about to give an aerobatic show and stood in a crowd gawping. He was unable to land and pulled the Hurricane up at the last minute, crashing into telegraph pole. The aircraft broke up, but Wilczewski escaped injury. Despite this accident, he was given command of No315 on 21 September, when the CO, Squadron Leader S Pietraszkiewicz, was shot down.

At midday on 8 November seven Spitfire squadrons escorted eleven Blenheims on "Circus 110" to Gosnay power station. The Luftwaffe put up fierce resistance, and although no Blenheims were lost, nine Spitfires were shot down, with the Kirton-in-Lindsey Wing Leader being killed, one Squadron Leader being killed, and two Squadron Leaders being captured. Wilczewski was badly wounded, and had spent much of the past month in hospital.

Pilot Officer Falconer had been on No603 Squadron, part of the Hornchurch Wing. He was shot down during the morning of Monday, 8 December 1941, when the Wing formed part of the escort for Hurri-bombers on a Fighter Ramrod to Hesdin. It was a costly exercise, with at least nine aircraft being shot down. They had just taken the Hurricanes in when they received a message from Hornchurch controller that enemy aircraft were in the vicinity. The next thing the pilots knew, the Me109s were in amongst them. Falconer's Spitfire MkVb was damaged in combat and he ended up a prisoner; all but one of the rest were killed.

***

Roland Robert Stanford Tuck had been bagged on Wednesday, 28 January 1942, less than two months after he had taken over command of the Biggin Hill Wing from "Sailor" Malan. The Wing comprised five squadrons, all flying Spitfires MkV or IX: No401 (RCAF — the "First Canadian"), and Nos 72, 91, 124 and 264 (a night-fighter squadron). By this time Tuck had been twice wounded, had four times baled out and notched up twenty-nine confirmed "kills", eight "probables" and two damaged. Once, a bullet had struck his thigh, rattling the loose change in his pocket and denting a 1921 penny-piece into the shape of a spoon-head. From then on he carried the souvenir among his coins, sometimes toying with it during conversation. His tempestuous career had earned him a DSO and three DFCs and made him a national icon. It was good copy for the Press and the stuff of which idols were made. But few were they who got to know the man behind the myth. Tuck only ever had three close friends — all of whom died in the war. One of them was Roger Bushell, whom Tuck himself had hero-worshipped on No92 Squadron back in 1940, when Bushell was his CO. Physically and temperamentally, they were poles apart. While Bushell was built for rugger, Tuck was made for athletics: only a fraction under six feet tall, as lean as a beanpole and as tough as a vine. As dark as Bushell, he was more elegant, and his gleaming, black hair, slicked back from his high, sloping forehead, lent him the appearance of a matador. His prominent cheekbones and long, thin nose added to his streamlined appearance. While Bushell could have been described as good-looking — nothing more — Tuck was handsome in an un-English and even slightly sinister way. The corners of his brown, wary eyes had an Asiatic tilt; his chin was narrow; his lips thin but strong and quick to smile, revealing perfect white teeth; his thin, black moustache was always perfectly trimmed; and down his right cheek ran a long, straight scar, white as cuttlefish, the legacy of a prewar flying accident. Altogether he looked like a villain from a Victorian melodrama. But only in the cockpit was he the cold, ruthless killer. On the ground he was restless and voluble with a great appetite for parties and a hearty laugh that was joyful to the ear. He spoke quickly — as if he were excited — in a cultivated voice with trace of neither accent nor affectation. Six years Bushell's junior, he had as colourful a vocabulary. But prison camp would effect a great change in both of them.

One of No401's pilots, Don Morrison, later admitted to being partly responsible for Tuck's capture. During the past two months the Biggin Hill Wing had seen little action and Morrison was constantly badgering Tuck to resume "Rhubarbs". On 28 January, the weather was perfect. Biggin Hill was shrouded in drizzle and mist, and leaden clouds scudded across the skies of southern England at only a few hundred feet. Tuck decided to try a few "Rhubarbs" and to lead the first one himself. He selected as his target an alcohol distillery at Hesdin, a town some twenty-one miles inland from Le Touquet familiar to early aircrew POWs who had slogged through it in May and June 1940. After lunch in the Officers' Mess, Tuck and a Canadian Pilot Officer, Al Harley, took off in their Spitfires, climbed to a hundred and fifty feet and turned east towards the coast. They flew in a neat and steady formation over Dungeness, then dived to twenty feet over the sea to avoid enemy radar. The further east they flew, the worse visibility became. The Channel was rough, a stiff wind whipping spray off the tops of the breakers. A slight misjudgement of height, and either one of them could end up in the drink. They eased a little further apart and concentrated on staying out of the water. Even when the cliffs of France appeared they hugged the wavetops until the last minute, when they pulled up sharply, grazing the brink. As they belted inland across the patchwork quilt of fields, woods, roads and villages, long lines of tracer rose lazily behind them. They had been detected by a coastal battery, and soon the whole defensive system would be alerted to their presence.

After a few miles they picked up a main railway line and followed it eastwards until Tuck, map folded on his left knee, spotted their turning-off point. A tight turn to port brought them near a second railway line with a high embankment. Beyond this lay their target. Still low, they roared towards the embankment until Tuck called to Harley to form up in line abreast and pull up sharply. As if the embankment were a slipway, the two Spitfires flew up it and shot towards cloud cover eight hundred feet above. As they levelled off, they saw the distillery grounds only a few hundred yards ahead. Suddenly 20-millimetre guns opened up on them from the rooftops and sites in the distillery grounds. But they had expected this and kept calm. "Down we go," said Tuck, without the slightest inflection in his voice. At 300mph they dived towards the four alcohol vats — poorly camouflaged affairs like small gasometers — with tracer streaming past above, below and either side of them. Each picked a vat, Harley opening fire first, Tuck holding fire until he was sure of a direct hit. Both scored, and the vats crumpled like melting candles. As they broke off, Tuck saw another building, which looked like a barracks. He raked the length of the building with machine-gun and cannon fire, and saw his shells exploding in the dark interior. Then they were up in the clouds and out of range of the flak.

Tuck set a course west, eased back the throttle to give Harley a chance to close up, and tried to pick up the main road he had intended to follow as their way out. But the weather was closing in and visibility was down to a few hundred yards. Unable to tell one arterial road from another, they picked one at random and followed it westwards. They still had plenty of ammo, so when they came upon a heavy lorry, they gave it a quick squirt and watched it roll into a ditch. Then they picked up a line of steel electricity pylons and followed it northwards, taking pot-shots at the high-tension cables. This was a favourite sport of pilots on "Rhubarbs". If they could hit the insulators, great multi-coloured flashes would light up the cables for miles. But Tuck and Harley could raise only a few sparks.

So engrossed were they in their sport that they failed to notice the line of pylons curving further and further north, taking them five or six miles off their intended course. Suddenly Tuck saw they were approaching Boulogne — notorious for its heavy flak defences. Tuck was about to make a quick 180° turn when he spotted a large, modern railway engine dead ahead of him: an irresistible target. He called Harley into line abreast and they dived on the engine together. Both scored hits, and the engine disappeared in a huge cloud of steam. As they went through the steam, Tuck lost sight of Harley, and sheered off to get out of his way. He cleared the steam at about seventy or eighty feet. Then all the flak in Boulogne seemed to open up on him. The guns were on the foothills on either side of him and were shooting almost horizontally across the valley. He was caught in the crossfire. Jerry couldn't miss. Shots smacked into the belly of his Spitfire. One shell went right up through the sump, through the cooling system, and everything stopped dead. The Spitfire started to belch black smoke and glycol. Oil covered the windscreen. Tuck slammed back the cockpit canopy and stuck his head outside to get a clear view ahead. He still had some speed — about 250mph — so he could stay aloft for about another minute. If he tried to climb and bale out they would shoot him out of the sky. His only hope was to stay close to the deck and find a space to pancake. But he couldn't find even the smallest patch of open ground. He glanced over his shoulder then and saw Harley was still following, tight on his tail. It looked as if he was going to get shot up, too. Tuck called him up on the R/T: "Get out, quick! I've had it." But when he looked again a few seconds later, Harley was still there. This time Tuck lost his cool. "Get out, you stupid twit!" he yelled. "That's a bloody order!" So startled was Harley that he yanked his stick over and was streaking out to sea before he had time to collect his shaken wits.

Meanwhile, Tuck's Spitfire was gradually losing height. At forty feet he again craned his head out of his cockpit and peered ahead for open terrain. All he saw was Jerry resolutely firing at him. At twenty feet he had a sinking feeling that this was "it". He sat back, taut and clammy, watching the tracer lurching towards him. Then he thought: *Dammit, I won't be able to see Joyce tonight!* Only seconds left now. His air-speed indicator was unwinding remorselessly towards the tiny red line at which the engine would stall and his machine would plough into the wintry French valley... Still, he had long since accustomed himself to the idea of a violent death, had given up all hope of surviving the war. *Well — here it comes, any second now...* His brain froze on these words, repeating them over and over again, like a gramophone with the needle stuck. Then, suddenly, he saw a long, narrow field ahead and to starboard. He swung the aircraft round, and it picked up height and speed. It climbed to a hundred feet and registered 140mph on the clock. Still Jerry was shooting at him, from a multiple 20mm mounted on a lorry at the end of the field, dead ahead. Tuck felt the blood rush to his temples in fury. *Surely they can see I have no engine power? Why won't they leave me alone, and give me one last chance to save my life?* As if by instinct, he shoved the stick forward, lined up his sight, checked his turn-and-bank indicator and fired his last, short burst. The gunfire stopped. Tuck was still doing 120mph but was running out of field. He took a deep breath, pushed the stick forward one last time and set her down. The first heavy impact jerked him against his safety straps. His brow struck the gun-sight and he blacked out.

When he recovered his senses, he found that his Spitfire had come to rest on a slight rise. His nose was bleeding and his right eye closing. He struggled out of his harness and clambered onto the wing. A few yards away the gun-lorry lay shattered and smoking, the mangled bodies of its crew strewn around it. His shooting — as usual — had been deadly accurate. Grey figures were running towards him from both sides of the field. *No chance of escaping them! The bastards will lynch me now*, he thought bitterly. Meanwhile, he had to destroy his aircraft cockpit and charts. Normally he carried a revolver down the leg of his right flying boot — but this time he had forgotten it. Feverishly he set to work crumpling his chart and trying to set it on fire with his cigarette lighter. But the lighter refused to work. Then he heard a bullet thud into the fuselage close to his elbow. One of the approaching Germans had seen his intention and opened up with an automatic rifle. They were closing in from all directions, yelling angrily. He saw the flash of a bayonet here and there, and looked in vain for an officer to whom he could appeal for fair treatment. Then he realised that inside his tunic pocket he still had an Iron Cross that a downed Luftwaffe pilot had given him the year before in a British hospital. It was too late to reach inside and throw it away. Slowly he raised his hands, leaning back against the fuselage and obscuring the twenty-nine swastikas stencilled below the cockpit. The lower part of his face was stiff and sticky with blood from his cracked nose, and by now he could see out of only one eye. He had to breathe through his mouth, and kept swallowing blood. His head was splitting and he wanted to vomit. But he stayed erect. Three or four Germans grabbed his arms and started to drag him towards the gun-lorry. They were shouting at him — insults, he supposed — and prodding him with rifle butts and bayonets. Some kicked him with their heavy, muddy boots. They stopped beside the wreckage of the lorry and the broken bodies of the crew. Pointing and gesticulating, and all yelling at once, they kept shoving him forward, to make sure he saw the horror he had perpetrated. *What next?* Tuck wondered. Would they beat him to death or string him up on the nearest tree? He braced himself for agony and humiliation. Then, gradually, he became aware that their attitude had changed. They had relaxed the grip on his arms and had stopped kicking and prodding him. Their yelling and screeching had changed to laughter. As if in a daze, he felt them slapping him on the back, and one was shouting in his ear over and over again: *"Goot shot, Engländer! Goot shot...!"*

Following with his good eye the direction of the pointing arms he saw that by an incredible fluke one of his shells had gone right up one of the long, slim barrels of the multiple 20mm and exploded inside, splitting it open like a half-peeled banana. Some of his captors, to get a better view of the curiously distorted barrel, were walking over the mangled remains of their friends and still roaring with laughter. Their macabre sense of humour was incomprehensible to Tuck — but he knew it had saved him from certain death. Once their mirth had subsided, they led him across some fields, giving him a cigarette on the way, until they arrived at the flak HQ. There, a middle-aged *Stabsfeldwebel* bathed his face, but was unable to staunch the flow of blood from his nose. Then, as dusk fell, they marched him about two miles to a village and handed him over to the military police, who noted his name, rank and service number and patted his uniform to make sure he was unarmed. After that, without searching his pockets, they took him across to a building resembling a village hall (the one to which Larkin and Smallwood would be taken two weeks later) and locked him in a small, dark cell on the upper floor. The cell had a small, high window with thin iron bars and was furnished with a table, a chair and a low, iron cot.

Tuck flopped onto the cot with his sodden handkerchief pressed to his nose, and suddenly began to shake violently all over. His teeth chattered, his breathing became jerky and painful, and although the cell was cold he began to sweat profusely. But before long a kindly young *Wehrmacht* doctor arrived, staunched the bleeding and gave him some pills. Afterwards a guard brought Tuck some *ersatz* coffee, and bread and cheese. A few minutes later Tuck stopped shaking and was able to eat and drink. It was only after this meagre meal and a little rest that he felt in a fit state to consider escaping. He would prise the bars loose with a chair- or table-leg, knot some blankets together and lower himself into the courtyard.

But before he could get to work on the bars he was invited to dine at St Omer Luftwaffe base by its commander, *Oberstleutnant* Adolf Galland. The German pilots greeted him so warmly that he might just as well have been back among his own pilots at Biggin Hill. Galland gave him a bottle of Scotch whisky and twenty Gold Flake — about the last of the stock the Germans had "liberated" from the BEF at Dunkirk. The meal over, Galland shook Tuck's hand and said how pleased he was that Tuck had not been wounded and that he would not have to fight again, and hoped that both would survive to meet again after the war. When he got back to his cell, Tuck was feeling sick from the injuries he had sustained when crash-landing and from the whisky, wine and greasy food he had consumed at St Omer. He spent much of the night vomiting, too weak to make his planned escape bid. The next morning he was escorted to Dulag Luft.

Tuck's loss was front-page material in British newspapers. *The Daily Express* devoted almost a whole page to an article by David Newton, "Tuck — The Man They Couldn't Keep Down". But *The Evening Standard* bungled. That same afternoon a chatty little snippet appeared in the diary columns: "ACE FIGHTS AGAIN. I hear that Wing Commander R R S Tuck, recently returned from the United States where he went to advise aircraft manufacturers on RAF requirements, is back with his squadron on an airfield near here. This is bad news for the Luftwaffe. Tuck is one of the greatest aces of this war..." Leaving aside this wholly inaccurate bit of tittle-tattle, the coverage given Tuck was exploited by the Germans, whose personnel gathered Press clippings for interrogation purposes at Dulag Luft. On Monday, 2 February, the German radio gloatingly announced that Wing Commander Tuck had been shot down and taken prisoner. News spread to Stalag Luft I. Already a legend on the home front for his many lucky escapes and the way he trotted in and out of "Buck House" as if it were the Officers' Mess, Tuck soon gained a reputation in the camps both for his dramatic entry into POW life and for his daring attempts to escape from it.

***

Roy Hester, Oliver Philpot and Gordon Rackow were Coastal Command types from the same squadron and the same aircraft. Oliver Lawrence Spurling Philpot was born in Vancouver, British Columbia, on 6 March 1913, the son of Lawrence Benjamin Philpot, a lighting engineer from London, and Catherine Barbara (*née* Spurling), from Bedford. After attending the Queen Mary School in North Vancouver, he was educated in England at Aymestrey Court, Worcester, and Radley College, Berkshire. In 1931 he went to Worcester College, Oxford (PPE Hons, MA), and underwent pilot training with the University Air Squadron. He joined Unilever as a management trainee in 1934, and in 1936 spent several months in Berlin, working with the Margarine Sales Union on a trainee exchange scheme. Later in the year Philpot was appointed Assistant Commercial Secretary of Unilever's Home Margarine Executive.

In July 1939, with the prospects of Britain taking arms against Germany increasing, the Air Ministry began calling up Reservists and Auxiliaries for full-time service. Men and units moved to "war stations" in August. Philpot, after further training, joined No42 Squadron, one of five squadrons in No16 (General Reconnaissance) Group, Coastal Command, as a Pilot Officer. From its base at Bircham Newton, No42 Squadron carried out recces in what was then the standard RAF torpedo-bomber, the Vickers Vildebeest MksIII and IV. It is now taken as almost axiomatic that at the beginning of the war Coastal Command, the "Cinderella" arm of the RAF, was ill-equipped. But the Vildebeest, a biplane with an open cockpit and a fixed undercarriage, was the most antiquated of all its aircraft. It had a radius of action of only 185 nautical miles, an endurance of only four and a quarter hours, and carried only four 250lb bombs or one eighteen-inch torpedo.

In April 1940, while based at Thorney Island, No42 Squadron became the second unit to convert to the new Bristol Beaufort MkI. However, the aircraft suffered from engine problems, and although the squadron moved to Wick, then to Leuchars, hoping to carry out operations in the North Sea, it was grounded until the Bristol Aeroplane Company could find a solution. There were two occasions when the ban on flying was lifted. On 14 June, nine aircraft attacked German shipping in Bergen as part of the RAF's effort against the German naval build-up in the Baltic. One week later, on 21 June, nine Beauforts, operating from a forward base at Sumburgh, intercepted the German battle-cruiser *Scharnhorst*. Although No42's Beauforts claimed two hits, they were in fact near misses, and four Beauforts were shot down by Me109s as they tried to escape at low level. All in all it was a frustrating period for the squadron.

From August onwards, No42 Squadron operated from Leuchars. Its role was to support Bomber Command in interdiction raids against German invasion barges and to carry out recces off Norway and "Rover" patrols in the North Sea, seeking German U-boats and targets of opportunity. However, the teething problems with the Beaufort's engines had delayed torpedo training and it was not until September that the squadron resumed operations, laying mines off Lorient on the night of the 26th and flying recces off Cherbourg, Le Havre and Dieppe. In November 1940 the squadron was transferred to No18 (GR) Group. By then it was the only fully trained stand-by torpedo strike squadron in the RAF. However, it could claim to have made only two torpedo attacks.

On 1 July 1941, by then a Flying Officer, Oliver Philpot was awarded the Distinguished Flying Cross. This was for pressing home an attack on Christiansand, Norway, even though his Beaufort was badly shot-up, and nursing the crippled aircraft back to North Coates, where he did a belly-landing. One other member of the crew survived, pulling through after some months in hospital. (After the war, Unilever presented Philpot with a specially engraved silver tray in honour of his award.) Philpot was assigned a new crew: Pilot Officer Gordon Rackow (navigator), Pilot Officer Roy Hester (wireless operator), and Sergeant Frederick Smith (turret-gunner). With three officers and only one NCO it was an unusual crew, but well knit. The four men would spend hours practising dinghy drill in the hangar in case they would have to ditch in the North Sea.

The practice paid off when, on 11 December 1941, their Beaufort, "O-Orange", was hit by a German flak ship. While on a "Rover" patrol in the North Sea, Philpot had seen a large convoy heading for Stavanger. Choosing the largest vessel, a fat freighter in the middle of the convoy, he went in low to make sure of a hit, while his turret-gunner, Smith, blazed away with his machine-guns. The return fire was intense. Flying over the deck at mast-height, Philpot dropped his load, but flak struck the Beaufort's starboard engine, which started streaming glycol. Despite a rough sea, Philpot ditched successfully. The Beaufort snapped in half behind the rear gun-turret, but all the crew escaped, spending two nights in a rubber dinghy in freezing conditions before being picked up by a German flak-ship at 9.30am on 13 December. Philpot had been wearing ordinary shoes instead of flying boots and consequently suffered numbness in both feet. Smith had injured his hand. Hester had been flying without his Irvine jacket but suffered no ill-effects. Rackow felt ruffled pride. It was bad enough being in this jam — but even worse if they had failed to hit their ship. All they had seen was a puff of smoke. The suspicion that their attack had failed made Philpot — as well as Hester and Rackow — all the more escape-minded. As it was, Philpot was anxious to return to his wife, Natalie, who was expecting twins, while Rackow, an almost stereotypical Jew, always regarded the Germans as though he were about to curse them.

Hester and Rackow were taken direct to Dulag Luft, and Philpot and Smith to the Akers Sykehus in Oslo, where they spent Christmas. After three days they went by ambulance, ship and train to Dulag Luft, spending the New Year in the cooler.

* * *

Another Coastal Command type was Squadron Leader Davie, who had been on No502 Squadron, St Eval (No16 GR Group). He had been due for leave, followed by a posting to No3 OTU as an instructor when on Wednesday, 4 February 1942 he was sent out on a daylight anti-submarine patrol over the Bay of Biscay. He was flying over the French coast at 4,000 feet when one of his Whitley's engines packed up and he had to make a forced landing in France.

Howard Rennix ("Digger") Larkin, the SBO among the February purge from Dulag Luft, was also from Coastal Command. He had not long been appointed commander of No217 Squadron (No19 General Reconnaissance Group) when he and Neville Smallwood, his leading WOP/AG, were shot down and captured on Sunday, 8 February 1942. No217, based at Thorney Island, flew Bristol Beaufort medium bombers. Their tasks included square searches, shipping strikes, mine-laying and attacks on German shipping in French ports from Brest to Bordeaux. Shortly before midnight on the 7th, three crews were put on the roster for what should have been a routine operation at 0600 hours. They were to lay mines off the German coast near Hamburg and return on a triangular course, cutting across the north bank, then the south bank, of the Thames estuary and, flying over the south-east corner of Kent, land at Thorney Island in time for breakfast. Larkin, who led the operation (his first as CO), had been lumbered with a motley crew. His Welsh navigator, Sergeant Len Evans, and Smallwood, an Englishman, had flown no more than six trips between them. However, Smallwood had topped the gunners' class on his course, and much to the annoyance of the other WOP/AG, Sergeant Frank Taylor, a Scot from Berwickshire whom he outranked, squeezed behind the two Brownings in the gun turret while Taylor sat in front of the radio. The weather was atrocious, and on the return trip Larkin lost contact with the other two Beauforts and completely missed England. Instead, at about 0900 hours — long after breakfast — Larkin was stooging along the French coast north of Dunkirk. He and Evans thought they were looking at the south bank of the Thames estuary. Suddenly Taylor rushed up from the middle of the aircraft, shouting: "Sir, sir! Get away from here! That's France!" The two gawped at him in surprise. "I *know* it's France," Taylor insisted. "I've been here before!" Then — with a fine disregard for navigational parlance — he instructed: "Turn right!"

But it was too late. They heard a loud bang and found one of their engines had been hit — probably by flak, although they never did find out. Gradually the Beaufort lost height. Taylor frantically tapped out a series of distress calls. As the Beaufort was about to hit the water he remembered to open the side escape hatch — in case it buckled on impact — took a deep breath, and braced himself. They met the Channel with a bang, and a cascade of water shot through the hatch, knocking Taylor off his feet and carrying him half-way down the aircraft. Larkin had made a good landing — tail-first on the heavy swell — and the all-metal Beaufort rose to the surface and sat there wallowing like a duck, giving the crew ample time to release the dinghy and clamber in. Sadly and silently they drifted away from their sinking aircraft. Although they had ditched close to the narrowest part of the Channel, from sea level visibility was poor and no landfall was within sight. They could easily drift out into the North Sea, or the broad Atlantic, and die of exposure or thirst before being spotted.

However, within two hours they were picked up by a French fishing boat. The captain and his crew seemed pretty jovial — smiling, shaking hands, slapping backs — so they asked him to take them to England. But he was adamant in his intention to return to France. In broken, halting schoolboy French, Larkin and his crew pleaded, cajoled, grovelled and generally debased themselves before the Frenchmen, but all their entreaties proved fruitless. In all probability the Germans would have taken reprisals against their families had the fishermen not returned, so Larkin could hardly blame them; and later on, sitting in front of the stove below deck, wrapped in blankets and sipping fiery French brandy, one or two of his crew could not help feeling a little glad that they were "out of it". Taylor was immensely relieved: WOP/AGs, most of them non-coms, had little time for "press-on types" and rated their own chances of surviving the war pretty low.

After transferring to a German patrol boat they were landed at Dunkirk and driven by lorry to St Omer, where they were taken to what in peacetime had been either a school, town hall or police station. There they were interrogated, and told by the senior officer in charge, a *Hauptmann*, that they were now officially prisoners. Tomorrow they would be sent under escort to Dulag Luft, and would be shot if they tried to escape. Looking at them quizzically, the *Hauptmann* expressed surprise that they hadn't a single decoration between them. Larkin pointed that not every airman sported the VC, DSO, DFC and DFM and that as yet no campaign medal had been struck. The *Hauptmann* appeared unconvinced. Then he revealed that the famous Battle of Britain "ace", Wing Commander Tuck, had been taken prisoner a week or so ago and that his chest had displayed a long row of medal ribbons.

***

Three of this intake were from the RAF's Photographic Reconnaissance Unit at Benson. They were Tony Barber, Tom Calnan and Chaz Hall.

Although PRU pilots might fly only four or five operational missions a week, they were getting chopped down in ever-increasing numbers. Photo-reconnaissance was a dangerous and uncomfortable business, which called for the greatest courage and endurance. The Spitfires with which PRU was equipped had no guns and no radio. This saved both weight and space and enabled each Spitfire to carry a thirty-six-inch focal length camera, mounted in the fuselage, and as much fuel, oil and oxygen as possible, increasing its duration in the air. So, while a combat Spitfire carried eighty-five gallons of fuel, the PRU Spitfire carried 220 gallons and often made flights lasting more than five hours. When fully tanked up it could fly all the way to Danzig and back and still have ten minutes for photography over the target. The lack of radio gave the aircraft another 10mph, a distinct advantage when the completely unarmed aircraft was being chased by Messerschmitts deep inside enemy territory.

But if the engine failed, for instance over the North Sea, the pilot had no means of alerting anyone or giving his position, and he knew that, even if he ditched safely, he had little or no hope of being saved by Air-Sea Rescue. The optimum height for the longer sorties was 30,000 feet, and at that height the cold was intense. Not only was there no cockpit heating, but also no pressurisation. Navigation was primitive. With no radio, no navigator, and unreliable weather forecasts, the pilot simply plotted his track and set his course, climbed to 30,000 feet, hung on to his map of Europe and prayed that when there was a break in the cloud he might recognise a landmark which would enable him to check his position. If he was over ten-tenths cloud, there was simply nothing he could do but press on and hope for the best. He could not go down below the clouds, first because fuel consumption increased as height decreased and, second, because an unarmed Spitfire stood no chance against enemy fighters attacking from above. These factors made long flights over cloud particularly hazardous. Occasionally a PRU pilot would be over cloud for the whole of the outward and return journeys. With crosswinds of up to 100mph, he seldom had much idea where he was when he finally broke through the cloud — hopefully somewhere over Britain with reasonably flat and low terrain.

Charles Piers Hall, from Buckingham, was an ex-Halton apprentice who had learned photography and photographic interpretation. He had been with No1 PRU for no more than a month when he was captured on his third operation. On Sunday, 28 December 1941 at 1010 hours he took off from Benson for a high-level photo-recce of Düsseldorf and Essen. But at about 1400 hours, over Holland, his engine cut out and his Spitfire crashed south-east of Bergen op Zoom.

The second of the Benson PRU pilots, Squadron Leader Thomas Daniel Calnan, was a career officer. Born in 1918, he had joined the RAF at seventeen as a Cranwell apprentice and in 1937 was posted to NoII (Army Co-operation) Squadron, Hawkinge, flying Hawker Hectors and receiving a Mention in Dispatches in 1940. When No1 PRU was formed he became, along with Anthony Barber, one of its earliest pilots and altogether flew thirty-seven ops. On Tuesday, 30 December 1941, he was briefed to photograph yet another daylight raid on Brest. He had, only twelve days previously, photographed the raid on which Bill Jennens had been shot down. This particular attack was to be carried out by sixteen Halifaxes from Nos 10, 35 and 76 Squadrons, loaded with armour-piercing bombs. The weather was perfect for high-altitude photography but also for the German flak: there was not a trace of cloud in the sky and visibility was excellent. Nevertheless, the attack went ahead. Calnan took off from Benson in his dark blue Spitfire MkV at exactly 1130 hours and crossed the English coast 25,000 feet above Portland Bill. At 1225 hours he was positioned a little to the north of the Rade de Brest, where he was to rendezvous with the Halifaxes. Until their arrival he flew a short patrol line on alternate easterly and westerly headings. On one side of the aircraft he had a clear view of the bombers' line of approach and, on the other, of their target. His altimeter read 31,000 feet — five hundred feet below the critical condensation level. His Spitfire was leaving no give-away con-trail, but any enemy fighter above him would leave a long con-trail behind it, visible for miles. Nothing below would have the speed to catch him. He felt safe.

The first wave of Halifaxes was due to attack at 1230 hours. He had been patrolling for nearly five minutes and still there was no sign of them. Suddenly a huge carpet of flak-bursts appeared in the air below him, not more than three miles north of Brest. Focusing his gaze on the flak, he saw a compact group of Halifaxes, surrounded by a weaving fighter escort, right in the middle of the shell-bursts. Looking over the other side of his Spitfire, he could see the gun-flashes from the anti-aircraft batteries surrounding the naval docks. The bombers moved relentlessly towards their target — so slowly it hurt him to watch. Neither weaving nor jinking, they seemed contemptuous of the black puffs around them. For half a minute he watched the bombers take their punishment.

One Halifax peeled away to starboard and went into a nearly vertical dive, trailing thick black smoke. Another two bombers, their engines on fire, dropped out of formation, but carried gamely on towards their target. By the time he turned towards the dockyard, Calnan had counted three Halifaxes which would never reach their target and another three which would never make it home. But their crews were still holding their course, determined to stay in the air long enough to reach their aiming point.

Calnan turned in towards the target exactly above the bombers, switched on his camera and reduced his speed to match theirs. He did all his photographing undisturbed. The flak was all for the bombers. When the second and third waves arrived, he repeated the process and twice more watched the flak take its toll. When the last bomb had been dropped, the Halifaxes limped home. Fourteen had dropped their bombs on target, three had been lost, and all the rest had been damaged by flak. Calnan stood off for about ten minutes, waiting for the smoke to clear, then went in to finish the film. A few minutes after 1300 hours he set course for Benson. He had completed his thirty-seventh op and was satisfied he had some good pictures.

He was not far north of Brest, steering 055°, when a burst of bright scarlet flak appeared in the sky ahead. It was nearly accurate for height, but off-beam and some three hundred yards away. Worried that it might be a directional aid to enemy fighters, he whipped into a steep turn to port, pulling all the "g" he could without stalling, and changed height and direction. Looking about him, he could see nothing but the drifting flak smoke. Not a German fighter in sight — unless one was sitting right beneath him. But at his height and speed it was unlikely that an enemy aircraft had manoeuvred itself into that position. Still taking violent evasive action, but heading home in a northerly direction, he kept his eyes on the rear-view mirror. The flak bursts were still appearing, but in diminishing intensity. Up ahead was the north coast of France.

Suddenly he heard a solitary "pop!" and saw a little hole appear in the top right-hand corner of his windscreen. His adrenalin valves opened wide and he writhed like an adder. Then he heard a dull thump under the aircraft and felt something hit him on the front of his right thigh. He was thanking the gods that the Spitfire was still flying fast and that the controls were responding normally when a searing jet of flame shot up from between his knees and played on his head and shoulders. The pain was incredible. He lost control both of the aircraft and himself. Twisting in every direction to escape the burning petrol, he tore off his oxygen mask, ripping through the straps. Eventually his survival instinct reasserted itself and his brain started to work properly. *Jump or you'll fry!* he thought, and put his right hand back into the flames and took hold of the stick. Instinctively, and without looking to either side, he righted the aircraft, forcing himself to accept the torture of burning petrol spraying into his face. As soon as the aircraft was level, he slid back the hood with his left hand, pulled the triangular harness release catch, and banged the stick forward with all his might. Immediately, he was out in space, still in a sitting position, with his legs stretched out in front of him as though on the rudder pedals.

He caught a final glimpse of his Spitfire, curling in the blue above and streaming black smoke. At last the agony was over and the fire had gone. Automatically, he felt for the rip-cord of his parachute. He jerked it, felt a violent shock, and was suddenly dangling at the end of the rigging lines some 29,000 feet over France. His next impression was of complete silence. He was alone in a desolate space where nothing whispered and nothing stirred. For almost two minutes he dangled inertly from his straps, enveloped in that intense, pervading sense of peace that comes only with relief that agony has ended. When he started to think again, he was surprised to find himself clear-headed and calm. He needed to assess his situation. Putting a hand to his face, he discovered it had swollen grotesquely. The skin, which he delicately explored with his fingertips, had the horrible texture of pork crackling. So puffed up were his eyes that he could see only through narrow slits. But he knew his eyes were undamaged because what he could see he saw perfectly. The right side of his face was covered in blood from a deep gash through the eyebrow. As he had been wearing gloves, his hands were hardly burnt at all, except where the wrists were exposed and in small patches where the gloves themselves had burned away. There was a dull pain in his right ankle and, wriggling his toes, he came to the conclusion that his flying boot was full of blood. Again probing with his fingers, he found he had a gash ten inches long on his right thigh. Flying overalls, trousers and flesh were all cleanly cut, and the wound was bleeding freely. The blood trickled down his leg and into the flying boot. He thought ruefully of all the escape and evasion lectures he had attended, of how he was landing in the midst of a friendly population, and could even speak passable French — yet was in no position to make a run for it once he landed. As he floated downwards, he tore up and threw away all his maps and personal papers.

He looked down to see where he was going to land, opening his eyelids painfully with thumb and forefinger so as to increase his field of vision. When he saw he was over the coast, suspended between land and sea, he banished all thought of escape. He would have his work cut out trying to make dry land. Although he was a strong swimmer, he doubted if he had the strength to swim the Channel, even with a Mae West, and he could hardly inflate his dinghy with his eyes closed. Then his blood ran cold — he could hear an aircraft approaching, closer, closer, so close his parachute swung violently in the slipstream. It could only be an Me109. Calnan prayed its pilot would obey the unwritten convention that you don't shoot an enemy airman dangling from a parachute. Within seconds the noise had faded into silence and his parachute was stable again. But then...yes, the Me109 was returning. Unable to see without prising open his eyes, Calnan could do nothing but cling to his webbing and watch his eyelids as he listened to the Me109 closing in... Then again the aircraft was past him and he was still alive.

Suddenly he hit solid earth and fell over. His parachute collapsed immediately. He disengaged the harness and lay there unable to see or walk; his eyelids had completely stuck together and his right ankle felt broken or fractured. He tried to smoke, but found to his immense frustration that his lips had lost any sensation of touch, and had swollen too much that he could not put a cigarette between them. He thought of the .38 he carried in a shoulder-holster under his left armpit. The ostensible reason for carrying this was so that any pilot who crash-landed in enemy territory could put a bullet in to the petrol tank and thus destroy his aircraft and the evidence it contained. The fact that a .38 bullet would have no such effect was well known to Spitfire pilots. PRU types carried the revolvers mainly for their ego, as their Spitfires were unarmed. Calnan decided he did not want to make a present to the enemy of a .38 and two packets of spare ammunition. Better to let the French find them so as to help their Resistance effort. He blindly flung the revolver and ammo as far away as he could, hoping some Frenchman would discover them. After about ten minutes he heard an indeterminate and furtive noise some feet away. Somebody was watching him: German — or French? Calnan made up his mind that only a Frenchman would need to be so furtive, so he tried to speak in French, only to find that all he could manage was a hoarse croak. Then he heard a guttural shouting and the thud of jackboots, and before long at least three Germans — one of whom, from the volume of his shouting, could only have been an NCO — arrived and helped him up. Blood poured out of his flying boot.

The Germans searched him, found nothing incriminating, and asked where he had hidden his aircraft. Calnan was too taken aback by the fact that they had left him his £50 Rolex wrist-watch to register the patent absurdity of the question, and made a noise indicating an explosion.

They took Calnan to the fighter base at Morlaix, where he was made comfortable on a couch, given first-aid and a sedative, and told he would be treated for his burns as soon as he reached the hospital. By then he was in great pain and was glad to lie still and let the sedative work. But the German fighter pilots were genuinely interested in what had happened to him and, with some embarrassment, asked him questions in halting English. One of them offered him a cigarette, and gave him a cigarette holder so he could hold it between his lips. (Calnan used it for the duration of his captivity.) Later on they brought him some peppermint tea and a boiled egg. The tea he drank through a straw so it would not burn his lips and the egg they fed him in tiny portions on the handle of a teaspoon. When an ambulance came to pick him up several hours later to take him to the naval hospital at Brest, they wished him luck and saw him off.

It was late at night when the ambulance reached the hospital, where he was immediately undressed and examined by a young German doctor who covered his face with a lint gauze from the top of his forehead to beneath his chin. The mask was covered, on the side of contact, with a thick greasy substance that stank of liver oil. Slits were cut in the mask for his mouth and nostrils but not for his eyes. This worried Calnan. He hoped he had not been written off as blind. The doctor also X-rayed his right foot. A lump of metal had lodged in the ankle. Some bones had been broken and some ligaments torn. Calnan was wheeled into the operating theatre within the hour and went out like a light when they put the needle into him. He woke up hours later with his leg in plaster.

Calnan stayed in the naval hospital at Brest for less than three weeks, and was given only the minimum care and attention. The hospital was full of German sailors, most of whom were crews of the very warships the British had been bombing almost every night, and often by day, in the naval dockyards at Brest. British airmen were so unpopular that the doctor, normally a kind and humane man, was worried about their presence and dared give them only the barest consideration. Calnan shared a ward with a nineteen-year-old RAF Sergeant Pilot, W R Joyce, a London Irishman from No234 Squadron who had been shot down flying a Spitfire MkVb escort for the big bomber raid on Brest on 18 December. A cannon-shell had burst inside the cockpit, the engine had been hit and the elevator controls rendered useless. Both of Bill Joyce's legs were peppered with shrapnel. He had already been in hospital for twelve days. During that time he had learned to speak several German phrases by talking with the two soldiers who took turns guarding them and writing down their replies phonetically.

During this time Calnan was unable to open his eyes and hardly able to move any of his facial muscles. Any movement of the jaw tended to stretch the burnt skin on his face, causing him great pain. This also made eating a problem: all he could fit between his lips was something about the size of a pip. So Joyce cut up all Calnan's food into tiny morsels and fed them to him on an egg-spoon. The food was always cold by the time it reached his mouth and he found that unless Joyce told him what it was he could not taste it. Eating took so long and was so boring that Calnan rarely ate more than a quarter of his ration.

After two or three days Calnan's face began to itch unbearably and he was warned not to scratch, as this would cause permanent scarring. He pleaded with the nurse to have the lint mask removed or replaced with a fresh one, but she insisted that the longer he kept the original one the better his face would heal. Only vanity prevented him from tearing off the mask and scratching his face. By the sixth day the irritation and his frustration had reached such a pitch that he would grip the sides of his bed, swearing and screaming. At last, after lunch on the seventh day, the doctor arrived and slowly and carefully peeled off the lint mask. When he asked Calnan to open his eyes, the eyelids would not part. The doctor told him they must be separated now, or it would mean a difficult operation later on to part them. Then he put a thumb under Calnan's left upper eyelid and a thumb on the lower and forced the eye open. It was very painful, but effective. The doctor did the same with the right eye. At first all Calnan could see was a haze of light. His eyes were full of mucus and pus. But once the nurse had bathed them, his vision returned to near-normal.

It was not until he was able to see Bill Joyce that Calnan realised just how badly injured the boy was. Joyce was thin, weak and pale, with both legs in plaster and in constant pain. He was expected to regain the partial use of one leg, but the other was so full of cannon-shell fragments that the task of removing them was beyond the hospital surgeons. He had already undergone two operations and although the bigger fragments had been removed and one leg was comparatively free of shrapnel, the other leg still held more than fifty scattered pieces of metal. Joyce would be a cripple for the rest of his life. Nevertheless, he was as determined as Calnan to escape before they were transferred to Germany, even if it meant knocking out the guard, lowering himself out of the window on knotted sheets and hobbling through the unlit streets hoping to meet up with the Resistance. Calnan was not sanguine about his own chances, let alone Joyce's, and was all for waiting until they were fitter and more mobile. Calnan went over and over the classic escape stories he had read set during the Great War, while Joyce pieced together, through conversation with the guards, a plan of the hospital.

Then one morning the doctor breezed in and told them a hospital train was leaving Brest that night. In view of the constant bombing, and the local hostility towards Allied aircrew, Calnan and Joyce would join the train for transfer to another hospital. It was with great relief that they learned that their destination was not Germany but another hospital in France some hundred kilometres to the east. This was welcome postponement of the transfer to Germany they had so much dreaded.

The new hospital was small compared to the naval hospital at Brest. It stood on the outskirts of Guingamp, a town of about 8,000 inhabitants, and was staffed entirely by Germans. The nursing sisters appeared to belong to some religious order, while the doctors and orderlies were Army personnel. Calnan and Joyce occupied a room on the fourth floor, overlooking the garden in front of the hospital. The windows were large, unbarred, and let in plenty of light. While the nursing staff looked after their British patients efficiently, they nevertheless remained distant and uncommunicative. Their doctor was a fat, cheerful Army *Leutnant*, who constantly warned them not to make any stupid attempts to escape — and made sure of it by posting a guard outside their room by day, and inside by night. He also took away their clothes. Nevertheless, the two were undeterred. Within ten days they had stolen a light metal tube — about a foot long with a rubber handle — and about forty feet of electric wire from a cupboard in the corridor near the lavatory, and had persuaded the doctor to return their uniforms. Their plan of escape was as crude as the one they had made while at Brest. It, too, was nipped in the bud by the wary German authorities. The very morning on which their uniforms had been returned they were escorted by the doctor and two guards to the railway station, where they boarded a train bound for Frankfurt am Main.

At Dulag Luft, Calnan and Joyce were separated and it was many months before they were to meet again. Joyce was sent to Stalag VIIIB, Lamsdorf, and Calnan to Spangenberg with the main party on 17 February.

The last of the Benson trio to become prisoner was Anthony Perrinot Lysberg Barber. Half-Danish on his mother's side, Tony Barber had graduated from Oriel College, Oxford, where he read Politics, Philosophy and Economics and gained an MA. At the age of eighteen he was commissioned as a Second Lieutenant in the Territorial Army. During the winter of 1939/40 he served at a small town in Northern France called Seclin — where, coincidentally, the first PRU Spitfires were based. Little did he know that in 1940, after Dunkirk, he was to be seconded to the RAF and that in due course he was to join the PRU. On one occasion, as dusk was descending and with no airfield in sight, Barber chose what seemed in the half-light to be a suitably large field only to find out the hard way, almost immediately he touched down, that it was dotted with large poles to prevent the enemy from landing. The aircraft was a write-off, but the photographs were safe.

Barber entered captivity in his unspoiled Army uniform (though not, as one memoirist later claimed, complete with Sam Browne). In January 1942, he was returning from Gibraltar, carrying some particularly sensitive photographs of ports in neutral Spain that were suspected of harbouring German submarines. At 30,000 feet he was over ten-tenths cloud. It stayed that way without a single break all over Spain and it cost him more than half his fuel. Eventually came the first welcome break in the cloud, but to his dismay there was nothing but water as far as the eye could see. He knew he must be somewhere over the Bay of Biscay, but by this time he should have been hitting the Brest peninsula. He had been flying into a strong and wholly unsuspected headwind that now made it impossible for him to reach England before his fuel ran out. But he persevered, and had reached the Channel coast by the time his fuel gauges hit zero. Because Intelligence believed (wrongly, as Barber later discovered) that the Germans did not know PRU Spitfires were unarmed, pilots had been instructed that in the event of trouble over enemy territory they should abandon their aircraft to destruction. This was doubly important in Barber's case, in view of the cargo he was carrying. The obvious answer was to bale out, which he did, watching his beautiful Spitfire spiralling to destruction while he floated down to meet the enemy waiting for him on the coast near Mont-St-Michel. Fortunately, a second set of the photographs was being sent home by more conventional means.

***

Aidan Merivale Crawley was the second of three sons — there were also two sisters — sired by the Reverend Arthur Stafford Crawley, vicar of Bishopthorpe, who was to become Canon of York and, later, of Windsor. In his youth Arthur had played cricket for Harrow and won the hundred yards and the high hurdles. He had emerged from Magdalen College, Oxford, a conservative in both religious and political matters, but sympathetic towards "gas and water" socialism. In 1915 he went to France as a chaplain in the Guards Division and in 1918 was transferred to Italy. By the time the war ended he had received two Military Crosses. In all his proclivities he followed generations of his solidly middle-class family — "a long line of well ascertained persons," Aidan later wrote, quoting E F Benson, "all of them entirely undistinguished". By tradition, the male offspring went to Harrow, excelled at games, married into the Gibbs family (as did Arthur) and entered the Church. The Gibbs family itself had come from yeoman farmer stock in Exeter and founded one of the three oldest merchant banks in England. Aidan's maternal grandfather, William Gibbs, had founded Keble College, Oxford. William's daughter Anstice — Aidan's mother — saw service in the Great War as a VAD. Three of the Gibbs family were later to earn peerages for their public service.

Until his early twenties Aidan displayed every sign that he, too, would succumb to family tradition. He fell in love with cricket from the moment he was given his first bat on his sixth birthday. In 1918 he joined his older brother Cosmo and his cousin Charles at Farnborough School, a neo-Georgian house built of stucco and grey brick during the reign of Queen Victoria, with twenty acres of playing fields that had been requisitioned by the Royal Flying Corps. He disliked the school. It was spartan and dilapidated, and seldom were the boarders allowed out through the gates. At least he enjoyed Harrow, to which he went afterwards (in 1922 there were no less than six Crawleys at the school — Aidan, Cosmo and four cousins), although he resented the time taken up by the Officers' Training Corps. His near-contemporaries at Harrow included Cecil Beaton and Terence Rattigan, who became his "fag". In the Lent term of 1926 Aidan won a History Scholarship to Trinity College, Oxford. As a reward, his history master let him take afternoons off to watch cricket at Lord's. This also had its reward. In July he made eighty-seven against Eton in one of the best innings spectators had seen in years.

That October he went up to Oxford. From Trinity he could see the dome of the Bodleian Library reading room; little did he know that in fifteen years' time he would have cause to be grateful for the Bodleian, which would send books out to prisoners of war in Germany. At Oxford he again displayed brilliance as a sportsman, playing polo, soccer, tennis and cricket. He received his cricket "blue" in 1927, was elected Secretary in 1928, hit ten sixes in a single innings in a first class match against Northamptonshire, became the first Oxford batsman to score 1,000 runs before a Varsity match, and was among twelve men picked to play for England against South Africa at Lord's. For a while he was favourite for captain of the English team. But in the midst of all this his studies lay neglected — and his scholarship had to be extended a year on condition that he played no more cricket until after the examinations. He came down in 1930 with only a Second.

His athletic prowess, charm and good looks made him a society lion-cub and it was probably the lure of society that made him rebel: no member of the Gibbs family took his fancy and he was not prepared to enter the Church. Instead, after Oxford, he went into journalism, joining *The Daily Mail* at its offices in Tudor Gate, near Blackfriars Bridge, on 5 October 1930. After a year he was appointed assistant to the Lobby correspondent in the House of Commons. For two winters he was hunting correspondent. Then he was transferred to *The Daily Dispatch*, whose editor sent him to France to write about the battlefields of the Great War. In 1932, Lord Rothermere's son, Esmond Harmsworth, sent him to work in the provinces, and during the next year he worked successively in Bristol, Swansea, Gloucester, Leicester, Derby and Manchester, mostly on evening editions and not only as a reporter but also as sub-editor, leader-writer, features editor and courts reporter, as well as trying his hand in the advertising, circulation and distribution offices. He saw more of Britain than he would had he stayed in London, and became correspondingly more aware of the growing numbers of unemployed (2,750,000 by 1932). Out with the vans, distributing newspapers to newsagents in the Welsh valleys in the early mornings, he often saw queues forming up to collect the dole. He would hand out free newspapers to them and was surprised to find them more resigned than bitter. What they hated most was being a financial burden to their fellow men. It changed his life, and he began reading Left Book Club titles: Keynes' *General Theory of Employment, Interest and Money*; Marx's *Das Kapital*; *The ABC of Communism*; G D H Cole, Harold Laski and Patrick Gordon-Walker (*An Outline of World History*).

In 1933 Crawley went to the United States to report on the New Deal and the next year was invited on a round-the-world trip by Esmond Harmsworth, who was rich, talentless and without social conscience or ambition. The association had a profound effect on the earnest, idealistic Crawley, who felt keenly the unfairness of this spoilt, languid sponger having so much wealth. It pushed him further towards socialism. The two men went to India where Harmsworth, in a moment of ennui, decided to go home. Crawley stayed, turned to acting, and visited China, Japan and New York, where for one day he shared a flat with David Niven, then about to look for work as a film extra.

On returning to London, Crawley spent two years as a sub-editor on the *Mail*. But as time went on the quality of the newspaper declined and, apart from that, he began to find himself at odds with Lord Rothermere's politics. Rothermere was becoming positively sycophantic towards Hitler and Mussolini, who his newspapers contrived to portray in a favourable light. Although Crawley did not favour military intervention in the Spanish Civil War, he had supported sanctions against Italy after its attack on Abyssinia and hoped for some resistance to Hitler's occupation of the Rhineland. But when a verbal instruction was passed round the office that nothing unfavourable to Hitler, Mussolini or the Emperor of Japan was to appear in print, Crawley knew it was time to resign. Sponsored by Cosmo Lang, the Archbishop of Canterbury, whom he had known since childhood, and financed by Lord Wakefield, the industrialist, he formed a small venture called School Films Limited and turned to producing documentary and educational films, shooting on location in the Middle East in an attempt to bring to life the Old Testament. On his return he did occasional commentating for BBC television, then in its experimental stages.

The same year — 1936 — he joined No601 Squadron of the Auxiliary Air Force, then based at Hendon. One of his contemporaries on the squadron was Roger Bushell. Although many leaders of the Labour Party were still preaching disarmament, Crawley joined the Party, and in 1938 was adopted as its Prospective Parliamentary Candidate for North Buckingham. Then came the war — and No601 Squadron, at that time equipped with the Hawker Demon, a two-seater biplane, was called up to Tangmere and the pilots sent on a conversion course to learn to fly Blenheim MkIs. Crawley came out equal top. The winter of 1939/40 they spent carrying out night-fighter patrols over the Channel, first in Blenheims, then in Hurricanes.

Bored by months of inaction, Crawley asked to be posted, and in April 1940 was seconded to the Balkan Intelligence Service, becoming an Assistant Air Attaché with the rank of Acting Squadron Leader on the staff of the Ambassador at Ankara. He spent the year in Turkey, helping to select sites for the storage of bombs the British had promised the Turks and which began to arrive in summer 1940. From time to time he carried out assignations in Bulgaria and Yugoslavia. With the fall of France the Balkans suddenly became important. It was inevitable that the Rome-Berlin Axis would occupy the Balkans, so as to ensure their supply of Romanian oil, and would probably attack Greece and even Russia. Crawley was sent to Sofia, where Cavan Elliott, another member of the Balkan Intelligence Service, was organising a resistance movement to start operating if and when the German occupation began. They also accommodated the first representatives of Special Operations Executive (SOE) and spied on Sofia airfield and the River Lom, where the Germans were rumoured to be gathering in strength. Crawley and Elliott were able to deny the rumours. Elliott's main work consisted of distributing small bombs and radios to Bulgarians who were forming resistance cells. The bombs arrived in suitcases sent by diplomatic bag and were stored in a room between his and Crawley's office in a block rented by the Embassy, and sometimes overflowed into Crawley's room. But on Saturday, 1 March 1941, Crawley heard that the Bulgarians had invited the Germany Army and Air Force into their country and that King Boris was on his way to Berlin to sign a pact with the Axis. It meant he and Elliott would have to leave Sofia. They had forty-eight hours at the outside. At eleven o'clock the next morning Crawley saw German tanks and armoured cars rolling down the main street and fanning out into the city. When he returned to the Embassy he heard from the staff that Elliott and he were to be arrested. The staff warned them not to return to their flats but to take the next train to Belgrade. They reached Belgrade without incident and within forty-eight hours were on a train to Salonika. Thirty-six hours later they arrived at Istanbul.

His career in Intelligence over, Crawley returned to flying. In June 1941 he was posted to North Africa and No73 Squadron, formed in May at Sidi Haneish, not far from the Italian-controlled border near Bardia. Given command of "A" Flight, he was told he would play an active part in leading the squadron, a position he viewed with misgivings. He had limited flying experience, had never commanded a Flight and had not yet fired a shot in anger. The squadron itself consisted of only two flights and most of its pilots were only eighteen or nineteen years old, and their flying limited to patrols over the sea. The only exceptions were Flying Officer P O V ("Ollie") Green, the leader of "B" Flight, and two Frenchmen who had fought in France in 1940.

At the end of May, No73 squadron had been given the job of protecting British barges delivering supplies to the beleaguered garrison at Tobruk, but early in July Middle East Command decided to take the offensive by putting up fighter sweeps over enemy-occupied territory. The object of these sweeps was to destroy enemy columns and aircraft on the ground. Crawley and Green were horrified. There would be no cloud cover and the Germans would see them at least twenty miles away from any ridge or escarpment they occupied. They would thus have ample warning of the approach of marauding British aircraft and make sure their forward bases were evacuated while those in the rear would be able to scramble to a convenient height from which to intercept the strike. Crawley visited the AOC, Western Desert — Air Commodore R Collishaw, a Canadian ace of the First World War — to lodge his objections and suggest alternative tactics. Collishaw was unimpressed. No73 was to lead the first sweep of eight squadrons in strafing operations against the enemy airfield at Great Gambut, about eighty miles west of the frontier. They would assemble over Sidi Haneish, the top squadron flying at twenty thousand feet and the rest in steps downwards.

At 1710 hours on Monday 7 July, six squadrons duly gathered above Sidi Haneish, where No73 Squadron joined them. The eighth squadron, which was to provide top cover, failed to show. Crawley decided to press on nevertheless. A member of his flight dropped out straight away, claiming his engine had seized up.

No73, as leading squadron, flew at a height of 8,000 feet with the others stepped up behind. They crossed the frontier south of Sollum, and as they flew across eastern Cyrenaica saw more than one airfield where Gambut was supposed to be. Oliver Green, who had been across the frontier before, broke radio silence to tell Crawley which strip was the right target. As they descended, Crawley could see that there were few aircraft on the field. But they went down to about twenty feet and swept it with gunfire. Crawley noticed that two of the "aircraft" he had hit were in fact dummies. He crossed the northern perimeter of the airfield, then heard a loud thud in front of him as a bullet struck his Hurricane. But his dials showed nothing unusual, so he turned east towards home, looking for targets along the coast road. Glancing over his shoulder he was surprised to find himself alone in the sky.

He had climbed to about a hundred feet when he saw some lorries on the road in front. He dived on them, and saw the occupants scrambling out of the back and rolling to the side of the road. One of the lorries lurched sideways. As he flew on, black puffs appeared around his aircraft. He was being fired upon by AA guns. But none of the puffs appeared within range. Away to the south he saw two columns of smoke, as if two aircraft had crashed and exploded. Then he glanced at his instrument panel and noticed that the engine temperature was off the dial. He shot up two more lorries, but by then steam was coming through his engine cowling. He could see the Mediterranean in front of him, so turned a few degrees south, hoping to cross the frontier and put the Hurricane down behind British lines. But within seconds black smoke mixed with the steam and completely obscured his forward vision. He unclipped his harness and stood up in the cockpit, looking for somewhere to land. The black puffs came closer as his speed dropped. After about half a mile he spotted what looked like a flat strip of desert, sat down in the cockpit, cut the throttle and, looking over the Hurricane's side, levelled out. The Hurricane ploughed through the desert and came to a jarring halt — an ignominious ending to a brief and ill-conceived action. (Though Crawley did not know at the time, only one of the six aircraft belonging to No73 Squadron returned to base.)

After sitting still and reflective for a few seconds, Crawley picked up his revolver and climbed out, hoping to make off into the desert. But he saw at once armed men, clad in khaki, descending upon him from all sides. The nearest was only thirty yards away. He stood and waited, feeling foolish, until a German officer came up to him waving a revolver. The German officer pointed at Crawley's revolver, which Crawley handed over, then led him away with two soldiers, armed with machine-guns, bringing up the rear. As they walked, there was a burst of machine-gun fire. One of the Germans had climbed into the cockpit of his Hurricane and pressed the firing buttons. The Hurricane was nose-down in the sand and the bullets ricocheted off the hard desert and whistled over their heads. The officer yelled at an NCO to get the man out of the aeroplane.

Crawley spent three nights in custody in North Africa before being flown in a Ju53 to Tatoi, in Greece, where he spent three days and nights in a whitewashed cell before being taken by train to Dulag 185, Salonika. There he encountered Oliver Green, who recounted the aftermath of the Great Gambut fiasco.

Green had followed Crawley down to strafe Gambut, but when he, too, saw that the aircraft on the ground were either dummies or wrecks, he turned back to the south-east with his flight to try to cross the frontier south of Sollum and reach Sidi Haneish. One of Crawley's flight joined him, but Crawley's Hurricane was nowhere to be seen. Green kept low, but his flight was bounced by an Italian squadron, which had been waiting for them further west. Three Hurricanes were shot down, then Green himself was attacked from above. His engine caught fire and, as he had just enough height to take to his parachute, he baled out. He was captured immediately, and was flown by transport aircraft direct to Salonika, where he was thrust into Dulag 185, two days before the arrival of Crawley.

Dulag 185 was a vile camp, where the Germans committed many terrible atrocities against non-British prisoners. Crawley and Green were relieved when they were summoned to the guardroom after three weeks and informed they would be leaving for Germany by train that afternoon.

Though the journey to Germany sealed their fate as prisoners it was surprisingly exciting. Soon after the train pulled out of Salonika the engine slowed to a crawl as they passed a line of railway oil tankers, derailed and lying on their sides. Altogether they passed fourteen derailed trains — mainly oil tankers — before reaching the Austrian frontier. At Belgrade their guards bought some German newspapers and magazines, which they passed to Crawley and Green once they had finished reading them. As the train wound its way through the valley of the River Sava, where the railway occasionally ran along the river bank, Green, sitting opposite Crawley, leaned forward and handed him a copy of the *Berliner Illustrierte Zeitung*, saying: "I think you might be interested in this." To Crawley's surprise the frontispiece was a picture of him, described as a great explosives expert of the former British Embassy in Sofia and a dangerous member of the British Secret Service. A long article alleged that Squadron Leader Crawley had misused diplomatic bags to import bombs, which he had distributed to the Underground before being smuggled out of Sofia. Though the article substituted him for Cavan Elliott, the real bomb-smuggler, there was some truth in the story, and Crawley supposed a member of the Embassy staff had been interrogated by the Germans and substituted him either deliberately or through ignorance. He was thankful for his dishevelled appearance — he had several days' stubble and was still wearing the dirty khaki shirt and shorts in which he had been shot down — and dropped the magazine out of the window as soon as he could.

At Dulag Luft the two lost contact. Green was transferred to the Hohemark clinic and Crawley was sent to the cells for the usual questioning. Whilst Green was subsequently purged to Oflag XC, a newly opened POW cage at Lübeck, Crawley remained at Dulag Luft until he was sent to Spangenberg in February 1942. They would be re-united in the middle of May when most RAF prisoners were collected at Stalag Luft III. From then on they would remain together until the evacuation from Sagan in January 1945

During his interrogation at Dulag Luft, mindful of the article he had read in the German newspaper accusing him of being a bomb-smuggler, he maintained his name was Stafford Crawley. (Stafford was his father's middle name.) Once in the prisoners' compound, and having established his bona fides, he reported to Lieutenant-Commander John Casson, the British camp adjutant and the officer in charge of writing coded letters to "Control" at RAF Intelligence in London. Casson wrote a coded letter informing Control that all letters and private parcels sent to Aidan Crawley were to be addressed to Flight Lieutenant Stafford Crawley. Control, in turn, notified his family, and for the rest of the war Aidan Crawley was addressed as "Stafford" in letters, on parcels and by fellow prisoners in Spangenberg, Sagan, Schubin and Tarmstedt. Throughout his years as a prisoner, Crawley would maintain a studied untidiness — just in case — and more than one ex-POW has since remarked that he was about the scruffiest officer in Stalag Luft III.

A few days after his arrival in the tiny Dulag Luft compound, Crawley was taken to Hohemark to undergo six weeks' treatment by Dr Laust, one of the five British doctors attached to the camp, for piles and numerous other ailments picked up at Salonika.

(2)

On the morning of Monday, 17 February, thirty-six officer transients at Dulag Luft were given one hour's notice of their transfer to a permanent camp. Under Luftwaffe escort, they boarded the blue Luftwaffe bus, which had pulled up outside the gates ready to take them to the railway station where they were to entrain for Spangenberg. Pilot Officer P R M Runnacles joined them at the last minute, direct from the cells. A dark, burly Argentinian, Philip ("Barney") Runnacles had left home at the outbreak of the war to join the RAF. Eventually he was posted to No10 Squadron, Leeming, as a second pilot. On 6/7 September 1941 his squadron took part in a raid on the chemical factory at Hüls along with Nos 57, 75, 77, 78 and 102 Squadrons. Barney's pilot, Flight Sergeant R M Holder, took off in his Whitley MkV at 1953 hours. Returning crews later claimed "good results", but over Holland, on the return leg, several aircraft were jumped by night-fighters who themselves were able to claim good results owing to the clear skies. Five Whitleys and two Wellingtons were shot down, with forty aircrew killed. All of Holder's crew survived, but Runnacles was handed over to the Gestapo, who sent him to a slave-labour camp. There, one of his legs, which had been smashed by a cannon-shell, became gangrenous. Fortunately, the commanding officer of the night-fighter squadron responsible for shooting him down checked with the area health officer to make sure Runnacles had been sent to Dulag Luft. The health official followed up the enquiry, personally attended to his leg at *Schloss* Mittelen, and had him transferred to Oberursel. Whilst recuperating in Hohemark clinic, Runnacles received a card from a French officer whom he had helped escape from the *Schloss*.

The first thing that Bob Tuck noticed when Runnacles boarded the bus was his luxuriant beard, which made him look like a Greek Orthodox priest. Not only were beards uncommon in the RAF but they were also illegal without the Sovereign's permission. King's Regulations and Air Council Instructions laid it down that the upper lip only may be left unshaven — as Tuck was quick to point out. Nobody believed Runnacles' excuse that he had gone a long time without shaving tackle, but he ignored their snide remarks, and, thereafter, anybody else who complained about his beard; he seldom shaved while a prisoner.

There was deep snow on the ground, and the bus had not even reached the main road, Hohemarkstrasse, before it stuck in a snowdrift. The prisoners had to get out and push, with Bill Jennens bellowing at them like a sergeant major. (Jennens would become British Adjutant at Oflag IXA/H and Stalag Luft III — hardly surprising, really, given his capacity for organising.) At the railway station the Luftwaffe relinquished control of the prisoners to the escort from Spangenberg, in whose hands they were to remain for the next three months. "I must tell you," warned the officer in charge, *Hauptmann* Roth, "that if you try to escape on this journey you will be shot. *Versteht Ihr?* — Do you understand?" The kriegies understood. They then boarded third-class carriages, with the usual hard wooden-seats and nailed-down windows. The train took twenty-four hours to reach Spangenberg, much longer than the journey by road, as it had to go via the main junction at Kassel and then crawl east along a branch line. It was hot inside the carriages, and the prisoners were hungry, uncomfortable, tired, bored and tetchy. But the scenery was beautiful — snow-covered mountains, silvery pinewoods glistening in the hard winter sun, red-roofed *Fachwerk* houses, the occasional wild animal.

At Spangenberg station they alighted not onto the platform but directly onto the railway lines between a crumbling hump-backed road bridge and the station itself. Guards with bayonets fixed to their rifles stood in line either side of the train. It was quite a reception committee for fewer than forty prisoners. Forming up, they were marched along Bahnhofstrasse in the direction of the castle. Much to their surprise, however, the escort swung to the left and took them not to the castle but to the Elbersdorf. Turning into Brückenstrasse, they were marched through the double barbed-wire gates of the Lower Camp and herded into one low-roofed room lined with two-tier bunks. The room — a *Gästezimmer* or guest-room — already accommodated seven RAF officers returned to the camp after the repatriation fiasco. In this one room more than forty officers had to eat, sleep and pass their waking hours. Eating was made easier by virtue of there being little to eat. German rations were a formality, and during their entire stay the February 1941 batch of prisoners received few Red Cross parcels. They had little in the way of personal effects, either. They passed their days playing chess with pieces cut out of paper (or horse-racing with horses cut out of paper), and staring out of the window, either at the stream below or at the villagers going about their normal activities. Occasionally they were able to purchase watery local beer with their *Wehrsold*.

Some days after their arrival the Air Force POWs were joined by a contingent of Army officers captured in Crete. They had passed through Salonika and many were suffering from dysentery.

(3)

By now there were sixty or seventy prisoners in the Lower Camp, most of them Air Force, with Brigadier R L Taverner, of the King's Shropshire Light Infantry, as the SBO, Wing Commander Larkin as senior RAF officer, Bill Jennens as Adjutant, and Barney Runnacles as official interpreter. Taverner set up an Escape Committee, with Lieutenant-Colonel W T H Peppé of the Royal Artillery in charge. The other members were Lieutenant-Colonel E K Page, also of the Royal Artillery, Major K N Wylie, Royal Engineers, and Captain J Burder, of the Royal Sussex Regiment. Brigadier Taverner lectured the RAF contingent on escape and impressed upon them the importance of being prepared — a lesson, sadly, that most of them were slow to learn. Barber, Hall and Philpot were among the exceptions. They started to harden their feet by daily walking round the yard — this only made them hungry — and traced maps onto lavatory paper. At the end of the month, however, the RAF contingent was moved uphill to join the two hundred Army officers in the castle. In the preceding search they lost several maps — although Philpot managed to save his by passing them on to another prisoner who had already been searched.

More aircrew also arrived in March: Squadron Leader R B Abraham, RAFO, and Pilot Officers R H Buchanan and E N Foinette. Ralph Bagshaw ("Honest Abe") Abraham and Eric Norman Foinette were pilot and navigator of a Wellington from No12 Squadron, Binbrook, which after service with the AASF in France had been posted to No1 Group. On 25/26 February sixty-one aircraft set out to bomb the floating dock at Kiel, and three Wellingtons were lost. Abraham took off at 2330 hours, and his Wimpey was hit by flak crossing the German coast at Sylt, some fifty kilometres off course. The radiator of the starboard engine was punctured, and the other began to ice up. They were losing height fast, so Abraham decided to make for neutral Sweden. At 0300 hours the wireless-operator, Sergeant G R Duckham, informed base of their severe engine problems and of their intended destination. However, over Denmark the engines gave up the ghost, and the crew baled out at about 1500 feet, landing safely near Odense. Foinette came down in a field. There was heavy snow and he sought shelter in some farm buildings. He encountered a friendly herdsman, who took him to his house and gave him some food. However, the Wellington had crashed in some trees at nearby Killerup, and the Danish police and the Germans were hotly pursuing the survivors. The farmer told Foinette that he would have to inform the police, and was very apologetic. Some hours later a Danish policeman, Blem Nielsen, arrived, and in turn informed the Germans of Foinette's presence. Shortly afterwards some German soldiers turned up and took him to their barracks in Odense, while the local natives were busy ransacking the crashed Wimpey.

Ralph Abraham had found a bicycle on landing and rode several kilometres before being apprehended at Rågalund Drengebjen. On the morning of Thursday, 26 February, his crew were collected together and taken to the army barracks at Odense, where they were given beds. Abraham and Foinette were put in a room together with a double bunk, and the rest of the crew, being NCOs, were held in another room. "We were given sandwiches from the shop opposite," recalls Eric Foinette, "and on pay day the German guards bought us a bottle of beer each. After a couple of days we were taken by train via Flensburg and Hamburg to Frankfurt, and then by tram to Oberursel and Dulag Luft. En route we received refreshments in the station café at Hamburg. Disappointingly, we saw very little sign of damage from our efforts anywhere." Unusually, Abraham and Foinette were not released into the transit camp, and were sent to Spangenberg straight from the cells.

Pilot Officer Buchanan was from the same squadron. His Wellington had been hit by flak over Holland when, on the night of 9/10 March, 187 aircraft set out to bomb Essen. Three of Buchanan's crew were killed. The aircraft crashed alongside a small street called Kagerweg near the town of Beverwijk, not far from Amsterdam. The survivors were interrogated at the Carlton Hotel before being set to Oberursel.

With additions and changes, the aircrew contingent in the *Hauptlager* now numbered about forty-five. The Army majority had also been augmented by the arrival of a dozen "Cretans". All were under the wise and benevolent guidance of Major-General Vic Fortune, who had a seasoned administrative staff, an Escape Committee and "The Canary". The *de facto* SBO was Lieutenant-Colonel G M Gamble of the Sherwood Foresters. He had established an Escape Committee headed by Lieutenant-Colonel H R Swinburn MC, of the Dogra Regiment. The membership including no fewer than four other Lieutenant-Colonels — Hugh L Swinburne of the Black Watch, Willie Tod of the Royal Scots Fusiliers, F B Colvin of the Dorset Regiment and W M Broomhall of the Royal Engineers — and Major Neil Rattray. General Fortune made it clear to the RAF that escape was their duty, but that all attempts had to be vetted by the committee, and that the news bulletins received over the radio should never be discussed. The RAF formed their own escape sub-committee, chaired by Wing Commander Larkin and including the more senior RAF officers among its members, which reported to the Army committee.

Conditions in the castle were an improvement on those at the Lower Camp. It had a communal kitchen run by an Army officer along with Marcus Marsh who, helped by several Army privates employed as orderlies, did their best with the meagre rations supplied by the Germans — scraps, thin soup, bread, *Sauerkraut* and, occasionally, potatoes boiled in their skins. The Germans also provided acorn coffee and mint tea and issued a litre of watery beer per man per week.

The Army old lags were kindness itself. Most of them had been in the bag since Dunkirk, and had become very organised. They received a regular flow of both Red Cross and private parcels, most from home, but some from friends they had made in the occupied countries they had marched through as POWs en route to Germany. They had real beds with pillows, blankets and sheets. Their stoves burned all day. They decorated their walls with photographs from home and even made themselves chairs out of plywood packing cases. There was also a library containing 2,000 books. But the Army prisoners did not hoard food and possessions jealously. They provided the Air Force contingent with thick woollen sweaters to help them through the hard German winter, gave them cigarettes, and invited them to dinner parties where they shared food sent from Fortnum & Mason's. From Dulag Luft the smokers amongst the RAF contingent had each brought a stock of cigarettes, delivered through Red Cross channels in sealed tins of fifty. By the time Spangenberg was cleared of officer aircrew each was down to his last twenty. Most saved their cigarette butts, so that when their stock of fresh cigarettes was exhausted they could roll themselves cigarettes from the tobacco the butts provided. A careful smoker could get twelve "second-run ciggies" from a tin of fifty. They were real "raspers", but satisfying.

Again, however, the RAF lived forty-odd men to a dormitory, just as the 1939 bag of prisoners had done; but it was now known by the Army officers as the "Arab Quarter". They slept in two-tier wooden bunks, which lined one wall. A few stools and benches and two hefty solid tables completed the furnishings. It was here that they passed most of their time, writing, reading, drawing maps, or playing cards or chess. On Sunday, 8 March, Eric Foinette wrote his first POW letter-card home to his wife in Finchley:

My residence is now a medieval castle in C[entral] Germany, as we had to bale out over Denmark. We are a mixed camp of Army & RAF officers, with high & low ranks, including one of our most famous fighter pilots. They are a grand lot & are making the best of it all. The food is quite good as we are well served by the Red Cross. If I'm away long I hope to learn a few languages, & we have a pretty good library. Don't worry about me, as I'll manage alright, though no doubt it will become irksome at times.

At nights, "Digger" Larkin, who at Dulag Luft had traded cigarettes for a guitar, kept his men amused into the small hours with an apparently endless repertoire of barrack-room ballads and bawdy songs. During the period before lights out, the "Arab Quarter" became a flourishing gambling casino. The usual games were seven- and five-card stud, Red Dog, Slippery Sam and Bridge. Soon the Army started joining in and losing their *Lagergeld* to the RAF.

"One of our number, Daniel," recalls Eric Foinette, "was a Canadian of Indian stock, who used to let out an ear-piercing wolf-cry after lights out, which scared the guards — and us!"

The RAF remained in the castle for two months. Throughout this period their morale remained high, for a number of reasons. Firstly, most were comparatively new prisoners who had either taken part in, or witnessed, the Battle of Britain, the first "Rhubarbs" and "Circuses", and the stepping-up, under Arthur Harris, of the Allied bomber offensive against Germany. Thus they had seen the threat of enemy invasion repelled and the prospect of carrying the offensive into enemy territory slowly being realised. Bomber types in particular had a terrific *esprit de corps*. Secondly, they had passed through Dulag Luft only a few months after seventeen officers, mainly those on the much-maligned British Permanent Staff led by "Wings" Day, had escaped through the first successful RAF tunnel of the war. None of the escapees reached home and the Germans purged the lot to Stalag Luft I. But Day's tunnel was still fresh in the memories of those British Permanent Staff members who had not taken part and who still remained at Oberursel. They had regaled the newcomers with colourful — and often highly embellished — accounts of the mass escape. Thirdly, most of the Army prisoners they mixed with at Spangenberg were old enough to be their fathers and took a paternal interest in the RAF contingent. Although the RAF prisoners were unruly on parade, threw snowballs at them and even made uncharitable remarks about the personal parcels they received, these old-timers taught them that in order to survive they must organise themselves, have classes and discussion groups, be tidy and have a proper routine — advice which most of the aircrew officers took to heart. The old stagers in the castle also gave them some elementary advice on escaping, encouraged them to prepare well in advance and take plenty of exercise to keep fit, and got them tracing maps, and making water-bottles, knapsacks, imitation Germans hats and even fake weapons.

A large proportion of the RAF officers were already escape-conscious, not only the senior officers like Abraham, Calnan and Vic Wood, but also several of the junior officers: Barber, Foinette, Fessler, George Haller, Hall, Philpot and Smallwood. But so far their efforts had been barren of results and the Escape Committee seemed to suffer from an infirmity of purpose. In prison in the Akers Sykehus — Oslo's main hospital — Philpot and Freddie Smith, his air-gunner, had removed three out of the four screws securing the window, only to be thwarted by the fourth, which refused to budge. Calnan's plans to escape from hospital both at Brest and Guingamp had been foiled by the alertness of the German doctors. At Dulag Luft he had pleaded with the British Permanent Staff to let him start a tunnel, but had been refused permission. The journey from Oberursel to Spangenberg had been made largely by day and the guards were alert, thus deterring would-be escapers like Barber, Calnan and Philpot from jumping off the train. When they reached the castle, overall responsibility for co-ordinating escape efforts rested with the Army types. They had more or less exhausted escape possibilities, and the German garrison was alert. For three months the Air Force contingent absorbed themselves in escape schemes, all of which it proved necessary to abort.

Oliver Philpot and Neville Smallwood hit on the notion of going through the gate disguised as Army orderlies, which were regularly replaced. The Army Escape Committee refused permission. If the Germans got wind of the scheme, the privates with whom Philpot and Smallwood swapped would get a longer spell in the cooler. Philpot then fell in with Vic Wood, the tall, dark Australian, an eccentric inventor type who was always utterly absorbed in one escape scheme or another. He would dedicate a whole day to map-making, carpentry or drawing detailed plans of the castle, and be completely oblivious to anything else going on around him. So involved did he become that he often forgot to eat. Wood conceived the idea of dangling from a trolley running along electric wires crossing the moat (a plan which had been floated and then discarded by "Pop" Bewlay's Escape Committee in 1941). But the aircrew contingent left Spangenberg before the trolley was built — much to Philpot's relief, as the path of the trolley would have led them straight into the arms of a German sentry. Apart from that, the wires would have sagged under the weight of Wood and his trolley, leaving him unable to propel himself up the incline and therefore at the mercy of gravity and the sentries' gunfire.

Tony Barber, Tom Calnan and Chaz Hall — the trio from No1 PRU, Benson — were naturally drawn towards each other and plotted to escape together. Calnan was still handicapped by the injuries he had sustained on his last operation. For three months he could walk only with the aid of two sticks, and his burnt face made him conspicuous. His eyes still filled with mucus and streamed constantly, so that he had to keep dabbing them with a handkerchief. He was determined to escape nevertheless, and with Barber and Hall he explored every idea, no matter how far-fetched. The gate had already been cracked four times: in August 1940 by the bogus painters; and in August 1941 by the rubbish-cart escape, the laundry-cart escape and the "Swiss Commission". The Germans had since strengthened the gate's defences and become doubly vigilant.

Tunnelling appeared out of the question, as they would have to start well below the moat, which would involve boring down through hundreds of yards of rock. Rumour had it that a long passage led from the bottom of the great well, through the mountain and out into the open hillside. But so far no one had yet discovered it. One tunnel, started from the gymnasium on the other side of the moat by Army officers, had nearly succeeded in 1940, and after the Air Force contingent left on 30 April 1942, a party of Army officers started a tunnel from the middle of the castle. It was discovered after almost a year's work.

That left the moat. Getting into the moat was no problem. They could do that by day during a legitimate walk along the bottom of the moat or at night by lowering themselves into it by rope. The problem was climbing up the far side, which offered no hand- or foot-hold; even then you ran the risk of falling straight into the arms of sentries patrolling the outer battlements. Finally, Calnan developed a plan based on the fact that twice a week the prisoners were taken for exercise to the gymnasium. In 1940 "Hank" Wardle had escaped by climbing the high barricades on the way to the gym, and although the alarm had been raised immediately, the idea of starting an escape outside the precincts of the castle appealed to Calnan. But to cover a respectable distance once away from the castle they needed a head start of at least twelve hours. They would have to falsify the head-count on the way out and hide up in the gym while the rest of the party rigged the count on the way back. Evening *Appell* would also have to be cooked. The three escapers could then emerge at night without arousing suspicion.

Falsifying the count proved the biggest headache. Calnan, the smallest of the trio, tried hiding under Morris Fessler's huge Polish greatcoat. It made Fessler look grotesquely fat and would certainly not pass inspection at the gate. They tried getting the Germans used to the idea of one of the prisoners carrying a sackful of gymnastic gear out of the gate, so that Calnan could eventually be smuggled out in one. But the Germans would allow no sacks through the gate. Calnan was on the verge of ditching the plan when he made a surprise discovery. Combing the "Arab Quarter" for a suitable hiding place for the saws, files, maps and odd articles of civilian clothing he had acquired, he decided to dismantle the massive circular table around which the prisoners normally sat reading, gambling and writing letters. It had a strong central leg, which might be hollow and prove a good hidey-hole. Hollow it turned out to be — but not empty. For inside was a four-pronged grappling iron, to which was attached about thirty metres of rope. This was the equipment that "Andy" Andrews, Allan McSweyn, Nat Maranz, Warren Sandman and Neil Svensden had hidden back in September after their abortive attempt on the drawbridge. The rope was rotten, but if they could replace it, the Benson trio could use it to scale the moat. An accomplice on a gymnasium party could attach the grappling iron to the top of the moat. While the attention of the sentries was diverted, he could pay the rope out to the escapers at the bottom who would climb up and hide in the gymnasium.

Calnan, under the patient tutelage of an Army Major, had by then mastered the art of picking locks, and it was this skill that led to his discovery of the replacement rope. He had spent hours taking apart mortice locks and padlocks, reassembling them and making keys to fit them. He had learned to make a master key which would open a whole series of locks of a particular type, and that 90 per cent of the locks he would encounter in Germany were of the simple mortice type which could be opened with a piece of bent wire. Armed with this knowledge, he had then made his own lock-pick. Taking a piece of stout wire some seven inches long and an eighth of an inch in diameter, he had fashioned one end into something like the handle of a sardine tin opener. The last three-quarters of an inch at the other end — the working end — he had bent at slightly less than a right-angle. He had then flattened it by hammering it between two stones, tempered it by heating it red hot then plunging it in water, and filed off the rough edges. By the time he left Spangenberg he had half a dozen lock-picks in a range of sizes. He used these to spirit himself through every door in the castle that he could work on without arousing German suspicion. Once, he found himself in a builders' store-room. It was stacked with cement, buckets and trowels, scaffolding poles, planks, barrows, spades and shovels. Calnan was convinced that he would find a serviceable length of rope in this room. He spirited himself and Charles Hall through a succession of doors and passageways, and within three minutes of entering the store had found six coils of rope, one of them about fifty metres long and very strong. It was perfect. They decided to leave it there until they needed it and, in the meantime, concentrate on planning the diversion required to cover their ascent from the moat. Oliver Philpot volunteered to head the diversion squad, and on Monday, 27 April, after discussing and rejecting several plans, Philpot, Calnan and Hall agreed that the best would be a rugby scrum against the moat wall. The Germans did not understand the game and were always fascinated by its apparent violence.

After all that, the plan had to be abandoned. Next morning the Germans took the Air Force contingent completely by surprise by mounting a search of the "Arab Quarter". Fifteen or twenty guards marched in, shouting orders, while the prisoners were still half-asleep in their bunks. The *Abwehr* officer, *Hauptmann* Schmidt, forbade them to move, get up or touch their clothes, and posted a guard next to each double-bunk to make sure his orders were adhered to. Schmidt's search party was extremely thorough — emptying mattresses of their straw fillings, dismantling the beds, carefully inspecting every piece of furniture and pulling up the floorboards. Philpot watched helplessly as a guard pulled the escape maps he had made from between the leaves of *Gone With the Wind* and removed home-made haversacks from their hiding places. Neville Smallwood saw another seize upon his collection of cloth-caps. Others confiscated tools and anything that resembled a compass. Calnan saw another searcher with a handful of original Air Ministry maps, printed on rice paper "flimsies" especially for evaders and prisoners of war. They included large-scale plans of the docks at Stettin and Danzig and the Schaffhausen re-entrant, along with smaller-scale maps of Poland, Czechoslovakia, Austria and its borders with Italy, Switzerland and Germany, central Germany, south-west Germany showing the whole Swiss border, and northern Germany including the Dutch and Danish frontiers. He was furious; no one had informed him of the existence of these maps. All but one of his lock-picks was discovered. They created a small sensation. From the remarks of Schmidt, to whom they were triumphantly presented, Calnan gathered that the German slang for lock-pick was *"Dietrich"* and that to possess one was a criminal offence. But Calnan still carried a tiny one wrapped in his handkerchief. Finally the Germans investigated the round, wooden table and started to rip off the hollow square column on which it rested. Inside the hollow leg was the grappling iron that Calnan and Co had been intending to use, much to the astonishment and annoyance of those Air Force prisoners (the majority) who had been completely unaware of its existence.

But for Calnan all was not lost. When rumours of the move to the all-Air Force camp had become insistent he had hidden most of his escape equipment by a means that the Germans had not yet discovered. Most prisoners saved the little cardboard cartons in which Red Cross provisions were packed to use as small suitcases. Calnan had acquired two of them. Their construction was simple: two outer layers of thin cardboard with, between them, a filling of stiff corrugated paper. By carefully separating the outer layer of cardboard from the corrugated filling underneath, he had cut away the filling to the exact shape of the various flat items he intended to hide: a hacksaw blade, a collection of traced maps, some notes on Junkers 87 and 88 cockpits and a small amount of German money. Once he had slotted them in, he simply glued the outer layer back into place. He had also hidden a three-cornered file in the bottom of the shaft of one of his walking sticks and sewn a 20-Mark note into the hem of his handkerchief.

Before breakfast on Thursday, 30 April, *Hauptmann* Gross strutted into the "Arab Quarter" and announced: "Today, you go. You go to your own camp." The Germans were quick to exploit their surprise. Instead of marching their baggage-laden prisoners directly to the railway station, they diverted them to a large schoolroom and proceeded to search them thoroughly. Tuck was stripped naked and made to stand publicly on a chair while the Germans examined his person and his clothes. Prisoners watched helplessly as the pile of maps and escape tools the Germans had discovered grew bigger and bigger. Between them, Marsh, Barber and Hall contrived elaborate diversions while Calnan recovered some of the maps (eleven in all). Once again, the Germans failed to discover Calnan's lock-pick, file, German money and the other booty hidden in his Red Cross boxes. Marcus Marsh also held onto about a hundred *Reichsmark*.

When the party reached the railway station their identities were thoroughly checked against their photographs and identity discs in case any had tried to change places with Army officers. The only avenue of escape now was by cutting through the floorboards of their cattle-trucks during the rail journey. When rumours about an imminent move had started circulating, Larkin had taken names from those willing to escape. From then on each pair of escapers was allocated a different fortnight; should a move occur during that fortnight, they were to escape and would be given all the help necessary. This turned out to be impracticable. When the purge finally came, none could remember whose turn it was. Besides, prisoners not on the rota took the view that if an opportunity presented itself, it could hardly be passed up simply because it was somebody else's turn. Worse than that, their latest supply of Red Cross parcels, none of which had yet been issued, was, unbeknown to most of them, locked up in a separate cattle-truck to which the prisoners had no access.

But for the Benson trio, the final blow was still to come: the Germans decided that while the bulk of the Air Force prisoners should be transported in cattle-trucks, senior, elderly, sick and wounded officers should travel in third-class carriages. There were sixteen in all, including Wing Commanders Larkin and Tuck, and Squadron Leaders Abraham, Calnan, Davie, Jennens, Wilczewski and Wood, along with Marcus Marsh, "Barney" Runnacles and "Skeets" Oglivie. Of the rest, Barber, Foinette, Hall, Hester, Philpot, Rackow and Smallwood, all bent on escape, shared the same cattle-truck.

During the rail journey from Spangenberg, several tried to escape from their cattle-trucks. Philpot and Smallwood removed the barbed wire covering the window, screened from the guard by a party of the tallest men, including Foinette, engaged in a singing concert to the accompaniment of a fiddler. Philpot was almost out of the window when he was spotted by a railway official leaning out of another window further along the train, which quickly ground to a halt. He hastily replaced the wire before a posse of guards arrived to inspect the damage. Meanwhile, Barber had been trying to saw a hole in the floor. He made little progress, and this endeavour soon fizzled out. Nevertheless, during a brief stop to stretch their legs and fetch soup at a wayside station, Barber had lost no opportunity to pull Philpot up for having made such a poor effort and to berate him for being too slow to exploit Woody's trolley scheme at Spangenberg. A heated exchange followed, in which Philpot pressed home the point that escape was one thing, suicide another.

It was then that the officers transported in the cattle-trucks heard that Calnan had escaped. This had proved a trying exercise. The second-class carriage was divided into two compartments, each the mirror-image of the other, with the windows screwed into position and one German guard armed with pistol and rifle in each compartment covering eight prisoners. Larkin — the SBO — and all his staff were in one compartment, and the rest, including Calnan and Marsh, in the other. Between the two compartments was a lavatory with a separate door leading to each compartment. On investigating the lavatory during a routine visit to answer a call of nature, Calnan found it had a sash-cord window of frosted glass locked by an arrangement outside. Heaving on the handle with all his might, he pulled the window down a fraction of an inch. He slipped a knife through the gap and entirely by feel worked out that the window was locked by two nails, one in the window frame and another, bent upwards, in the side of the carriage above, connected by a piece of strong wire. If he could rotate the bent nail 180° he could slip the wire off, pull down the window and jump out.

But it required considerable planning. To begin with, he would have to get the guard used to a constant flow of traffic between the two compartments so that his own absence while working on the nail, and after his escape, would not be noticed. Secondly, he would have to find an escape partner from amongst the other able-bodied officers in the carriage. For Calnan believed — quite rightly, as it turned out — that a successful escaper required the moral support of a staunch companion. Finally, he needed rations, especially concentrated food like chocolate, raisins and sugar. In all but the first condition he met with failure. Twice Marsh went round each compartment passing the word from one officer to another, but none offered to join him or proffered the kind of food he required. Calnan began to worry whether perhaps they were right and he was wrong. Perhaps it was suicidal for a burnt cripple to throw himself out of a speeding train at the dead of night in the middle of Germany without food, papers, civilian clothes or any idea in which direction to go. It might be even more suicidal for whoever accompanied him. But he refused to give in to defeatism. Instead, he went up to every officer in his compartment and asked directly for food. All they donated were a loaf of black bread, about a foot long and three inches square, and a one-pound tin of Lyle's golden syrup. Marcus Marsh donated fifty of his precious *Reichsmarks*. At a wayside halt for hot soup, Calnan broached the subject of food with a member of the escape committee (probably "Stafford" Crawley, whom Calnan did not seem to like). He confirmed that Red Cross parcels had been loaded on the train at Spangenberg but that the Escape Committee could not liberate any. Again, Calnan "felt the dead hand of the Escape Committee", as he put it in his memoirs, but could only shout in impotent rage. The walking stick in which his file was hidden he gave to Tony Barber for safe keeping. He suggested that Barber use the file to make another saw from a knife if the one he was using became blunt.

Back in his compartment, Calnan had satisfied himself, after three trips to the lavatory, that he could unhook the wire and have the window down in seconds. He spent the hours until dark examining the stolen maps and completing his preparations. Taking the plans of Danzig, Stettin and the Schaffhausen re-entrant, and the maps of central and south-west Germany, he gave the rest to Marsh, trusting that he would be able to get them through the search which would undoubtedly take place at the journey's end. He stowed his maps and his collar-stud compass in his pockets, along with some string, a needle and thread, one lock-pick, a penknife, the German table-knife, a Gillette razor with three new blades, a cake of soap wrapped in a small piece of towelling, a comb, a toothbrush, a spare pair of socks and half a dozen clean handkerchiefs. Apart from the maps, this was the sum total of his escape paraphernalia. Once clear of the train, he intended to remove the brass buttons from his smart officers' greatcoat, issued at Dulag Luft, and replace them with toggles whittled from wood. He had no other means of disguise, no forged papers and no cover story. The tin of syrup and the bread he slipped into the top of his tunic, so that his hands would be free.

About two hours after dark the train slowed down. Calnan waited a minute, to make sure the train was going to stop, then touched Marsh's knee and strolled nonchalantly to the lavatory. The train was now moving at a crawl, and Calnan got to work feverishly on the window, afraid that he had left it too late. Although the night was cold, he was sweating. He jerked the window down as hard as he could and got a half-inch gap through which he could work on the nail. The nail rotated easily through the first 90°, then Calnan changed position so he could work it round to the vertical. He got it down another 30° and found he could push the wire loop off the nail. The window was free.

Marsh stood behind him. They waited while the train juddered to a halt, then Calnan pulled down the window and peered out. The train had stopped at a signal way out in the country. He could see no other lights, no station and no buildings. Then he saw a man standing on the track less than ten feet away, clearly visible in the light from the firebox of the engine. The man — either the engine driver or his mate — had his back to Calnan and had seen nothing. Quickly and quietly Calnan slid the window shut, then turned and hissed his instructions to Marsh. He would wait until the train started and the man had got back on board, then get out as fast as he could. Just then the train jerked to a start. Calnan counted ten to let the man get back in his cab, then pulled down the window. By now the train was quickly gathering speed. Hurrying, Calnan leant backwards through the window, groped for a handhold above the window, and started easing out his bottom and legs. From inside the carriage Marsh was pushing and heaving. The loaf of bread jammed and Marsh took it, saying he would throw it out afterwards. Although it could have lasted only seconds, the struggle seemed to take ages to the desperate Calnan. At last his feet were out and he was dangling by his hands on the side of the train. He found a purchase for his feet and lowered his hands to the window-sill. He then found a lower platform for his feet and, with one hand free, hurled himself into the darkness with all the force of both legs and one arm. Hitting the ground with stupefying violence, he fell forward and rolled. His elbows and forearms took the brunt of the fall, but as they were well protected by his greatcoat did not get hurt. Calnan caught a last glimpse of Marsh framed in the window as the train hurtled into the night.

He lay there for a few seconds, staring at the tail-light until it had disappeared. Then he listened to the receding noise of the engine. As long as it made a regular chugging, it meant his escape had not been discovered. The noise faded into the distance. Despite all the odds against him, Calnan had made a clean getaway.

The rest were left to relish the discomfiture of the *Wehrmacht* officer who handed them over to the Luftwaffe at Sagan railway station. "These are the Royal Air Force officers from Oflag

IXA/H?" Philpot, eavesdropping from inside his cattle-truck, heard the Luftwaffe officer ask. "You have lost one, I hear." "Yes, unfortunately we have. He will be recaptured. No one can get out of Germany!" "I hope not," replied the Luftwaffe officer, tartly. The Spangenberg prisoners were cock-a-hoop at this minor victory, but it was unlikely that Calnan would remain at large for long.

(5)

Things went wrong for Calnan from the moment he found himself by the railway and alone in a night as black as pitch. First, he was overcome by depression and a complete loss of confidence in himself. This led to a feeling of lassitude, and it was some minutes before he was able to talk himself into action. Then, after searching for another ten minutes on his hands and knees, he was unable to find the loaf of bread that Marsh had thrown out after him. He was forced to go on with only the tin of golden syrup, which he would have to scoop into his mouth with a knife. Finally, when he got to his feet for the first time and looked behind him, he saw a dimly lit railway station less than a quarter of a mile down the line. This unnerved him, and although he still had no reason to suppose that his presence in the area was suspected, he ran, panicking, across the tracks, down the embankment and into the nearest woods. At last, controlling his fear, he stopped running, sat down behind a bush and lit a cigarette.

Now, thinking seriously for the first time about his escape route, he realised that he did not even know where he was. About an hour before his escape the train had passed through Erfurt. Since then he had been unable to pin-point his position. But he knew for certain that with only a tin of syrup to eat he could not hope to make the Swiss frontier on foot. Neither could he travel by train without civilian clothing or passes. His only hope was a long-shot — make for the nearest airfield, steal an aircraft and fly to Switzerland. He knew that Merseburg and Halle, on the outskirts of each of which was an airfield, lay to the north-east, possibly within three or four nights' march. Photographic reconnaissance flights had made him familiar with their layout and "Woody" Wood had marked their locations on Calnan's escape maps. Should he be able to steal food or clothes on the way, he would revise his plans and carry on north towards Stettin, where he could (in theory) board a Swedish vessel.

Using his ball of string to make a shoulder-strap and carrying his tin of syrup like a satchel, and wishing that Anthony Barber were with him, Calnan left the security of the woods and made for the nearest road, scrambling through fields, hedges and ditches before at last coming across an asphalted *Autobahn* which headed roughly north-east. This was the direction he wanted. He set out at a brisk pace and as he progressed his morale improved. Talking aloud, he recited the starting procedure for the Junkers 52, 87 and 88. Occasionally, when he felt he was far enough from human habitation, he sang in time to his marching. As long as he carried on walking, his ankle gave him no trouble. But as soon as he rested, it started to seize up. Even so, by dawn he had covered at least twenty-five miles and walked through five villages without seeing a soul. Selecting a large turnip from a pile in the corner of a ploughed field, he made for the shelter of a wood set two miles back from the road.

The wood was of conifers, disappointingly sparse and affording little cover. But on the far side was a ditch and there he hid until nightfall, eating raw turnip spread with treacle, smoking cigarettes and sleeping fitfully. With the aid of his maps he also tried to fix his position and work out how far he had to march. The road he was on should eventually lead him to Merseburg, about twenty miles from Naumburg. He had seen no signposts indicating Naumburg during the night, so must still have a considerable distance to go. But the small town of Eckartsberga, marked on the map, was nearby, and the distance from there to Merseburg was twenty-five miles as the crow flies — possibly thirty-five by road. Just for the hell of it, he measured the distances to Germany's borders. Switzerland lay 280 miles south-west, France 280 miles to the west, and Stettin 220 miles to the north. He had jumped out of the train almost slap-bang in the middle of Germany.

That afternoon he spent cutting the brass buttons off his RAF greatcoat and whittling wooden toggles to replace them. After sewing the toggles on his coat he made frogging out of Red Cross string. By then his hands were too cold to do any more sewing, and he again went over the cockpit drills for German aircraft. He slept fitfully until evening, then to kill time before dusk sewed his maps and papers into the lining of his tunic, along with two 20-Mark notes, and hid his lock-pick in the thick collar. It was nearly 7pm before it was fully dark. Leaving his hiding place, he found his ankle stiff from the previous night's march followed by resting up all day in the cold. He could walk only with a hobble. However, after limping down the road for about an hour, he felt the ankle begin to loosen up and soon he was able to walk normally.

Three hours later he walked through Eckartsberga, again without encountering a soul. He plodded on through the night, hungry, light-headed and tired after more than twenty-four hours on the run. At 3am he was approaching a much bigger town than those through which he had hitherto passed. He thought it must be Laucha, and hoped to find confirmation as he walked through. Walking quickly and quietly, hugging the houses on the south side of the road, he reached a central square, at the far corners of which were two roads, one to the left and another to the right. Flipping a mental coin, he aimed for the one on the right. At the corner of the square he saw a sign on the wall opposite indicating the road to Weissenfels. He had chosen the wrong corner, and would have to take the left-hand road to reach Merseburg. He was about to cross the road when he heard the unmistakable footfalls of two policemen approaching the square. About thirty yards to his left were the open gates of a stableyard attached to an old *Gasthaus*, or coaching inn. He slipped into the yard and hid behind one of the massive wooden gates. Watching through the gap between the gate and the gate-post, he saw the policemen round the corner into the square and pass the entrance to the inn yard. Once the sound of their footsteps on the cobbles had died away he waited another five minutes before setting out along the road to Merseburg.

Once again in open country, he was overcome by exhaustion. By now both his legs ached, his good one as much as the damaged one, and he was nearing the end of his tether. He slumped in a coppice by the roadside. But unless he ate well, he would not sleep well. The next twenty-four hours would be a nightmare and even if he carried on, flogging the last ounce of energy out of his body, he would be unable to go through the complicated process of stealing an aeroplane. His only other option was to give himself up: an ignominious end to an escape attempt that had in any case been a desperate gamble. His mind wandered to the *Gasthaus*: its kitchen would be stacked with food. He decided to go back, break in, steal some of the food, then hide up, eat and sleep. After a good night's rest on a full stomach, he would wake at dawn in a more positive frame of mind.

Painfully, he lurched to his feet and made his way back to the town. In less than ten minutes he had reached the square. Making sure it was deserted, he crossed the square, entered the inn yard, and made for what could only be the kitchen door. Opening it with his lock-pick, he went in, closed the door quietly behind him and located the pantry. A few minutes later he was back on the road to Merseburg laden with an *ersatz* leather satchel bulging with thirty potatoes baked in their jackets, about 10lb of ham, 4lb of sausages and three bottles of wine. He had left the pantry door unlocked, but had locked the kitchen door behind him, hoping the proprietor of the *Gasthaus* would think one of his guests had helped himself to a feast in the night.

After another hour's walk he hid up in a thick wood and tucked into two potatoes and several slices of ham, and polished off half a bottle of wine. Tipsy, and glowing to his fingertips, he fell into a deep sleep, using the stolen satchel as a pillow. When he awoke it was early afternoon. He had slept for nearly eight hours. He put away another enormous meal, washed down by more wine, then slept again. It was 7pm when he woke again, ready to continue his journey. Twice during the night he stopped — on one occasion to fill his water-bottle with the rest of the wine, bury the satchel and the empty wine-bottles, and eat another meal, and on the second occasion to wash and shave in a nearby stream. As he continued his journey he had to skulk by the roadside to avoid a passing car, obviously on the look-out for suspicious characters. It could only mean that the theft had been reported to the police and that his presence in the area was suspected. By now, a general warning would have gone out to all police stations. Deciding against taking to the country, as the terrain would be too difficult, he carried on down the road until he reached the river ten miles outside Merseburg. He was now so near his goal it would be foolish to risk walking through the town, which might be on the alert for him, so at last he took to the country. Crossing the fast-flowing river by means of a railway bridge, he carried on along the railway track until he spotted a well-wooded hillock in the cultivated landscape to the north. It looked as if it might offer good cover and a clear view of the countryside for miles around. As soon as he was abreast of the hill, he left the railway.

When he reached the hill, fifteen minutes later, he discovered that it completely lacked undergrowth and was very well maintained, like a park. There was no safe place to hide. But it was now too late to find an alternative. Besides, the hillock was a first-class observation post. Calnan ate some more, and fell asleep, to be woken a few hours after dawn by a violent rainstorm that soaked him to the skin.

It was now Sunday, 3 May, his third day of freedom — and his last. About four miles away was the airfield he had been seeking. It was swarming with Ju52s and at least one Fieseler Storch. That, he decided, was the aircraft for him. The Storch could be started from inside the cockpit without the presence of ground crew and was therefore the easiest aircraft to steal. When he had studied the airfield and made sure he could find his way to it blindfolded, he went to sleep. He would need all the rest he could get before approaching the airfield that night and stealing the Storch. But when he awoke a few hours later he saw a Polish slave-labourer standing less than ten feet away, looking down at him. Calnan told him he was an escaped POW and that he intended to steal an aircraft that night. The Pole promised to return at dusk to help. But he must have been seen approaching and leaving the hillock, and made to talk, because that afternoon a party of about fifteen farmers with shotguns and dogs surrounded Calnan's hiding place. His escapade was over.

They took him to the local lock-up, an evil-smelling place with a urinal where local drunks were held overnight. Undeterred, Calnan resolved to pick the lock that night and make once more for the airfield. But this plan was foiled when shortly after 7pm the local police chief turned up with four farmers — again carrying shotguns — and took him across the square to his office for finger-printing and interrogation. The police chief was anxious to get as much information as possible to impress his superiors, even to the extent of debasing himself. Calnan demanded to wash and eat before providing information and played the game for as long as possible; by the time an Army escort arrived to take him away, all he had given his interrogator were his name, rank, number, age and religion. It was still more than the Geneva Convention and RAF briefings permitted, but the police chief was so pathetic that Calnan felt he had to give him something. Besides, it hardly imperilled the British Empire. It was like giving a counterfeit coin to a blind beggar.

Calnan's escort, a *Feldwebel* and two *Soldaten*, took him to the military barracks at Weissenfels, which they reached in the small hours of Monday, 4 May. Within the barracks were the local *Militäruntersuchungsgefängnis* — Army Remand Cells. He was given a cell furnished with only a wooden double-bunk, on which lay a straw-filled palliasse. It was all he needed. Covering himself with two thin blankets, he slept almost round the clock, waking up only to eat and go to the toilet. By Wednesday, 6 May he had regained sufficient strength to take an interest in his surroundings and feel restless. He had no cigarettes and no reading matter, nobody in authority had come to see him, and he had not even been interrogated. It was as if he had been left to stew in his own juice. According to his memoirs (*Free as a Running Fox*, published in 1970), he escaped from his cell the following night, picking the lock and, from the inside, sliding back the bolts securing the door on the outside by means of a Heath-Robinson device made of bed-boards and string woven from the palliasse cover. But at the end of the corridor his way was barred by another locked door beyond which were a sentry and the guardroom. He returned to his cell, unbolting the doors of all the other cells on the way. This tale sounds rather tall, even for an audacious man like Calnan, and one wonders whether he had, after the war, seen the French film *A Man Escapes*, whose protagonist pulled a similarly ingenious stunt. Apart from anything else, Calnan's account cannot be verified, and no one he spoke to on reaching Stalag Luft III has any recollection of him mentioning it.

At any rate, on the morning of Friday, 8 May, the commandant arrived and announced that Calnan would be leaving on the 12.40 train; he would arrive at Sagan that night.

It was with immense relief that Calnan reached Sagan. Much chastened by his experiences, all he wanted was home — and home was the nearest prison camp. At Sagan he was sentenced to ten days' solitary confinement, with an hour each day for exercise in the prison yard.

(6)

It was now May 1942. The first RAF aircrew to become prisoners of war had been in the bag since

September 1939 — a total of two years and eight months. *Schloss* Spangenberg had been their "home from home in the beautiful Hessian countryside" for most of that time, and almost 250 officers, NCOs and other ranks of the Royal and Dominion Air Forces and the Fleet Air Arm had passed through the camp at one time or another. At least one fifth of these had been involved in escape activities, and at least ten per cent had made one escape attempt to escape — some as many as four. The number of individual attempts, even at a conservative estimate, exceeded thirty, several times more than the War Office listed in its official camp history and Aidan Crawley mentioned in *Escape from Germany*, the official history of RAF escapes during the war.

Still, a miss, as they say, is as good as a mile, and although ten Air Force prisoners succeeded in getting clear of the castle, several escaped in transit and ten broke out of Thorn, not one had succeeded in reaching neutral territory. Brian Paddon, who in 1941 had been transferred from Thorn to the bad boys' camp at Colditz, would return to Thorn in June 1942 to face trial for resisting a guard and from there would make a home run, ending the war as a Group Captain with a DSO. However, his story has been appropriated by the Colditz saga and in any case has been well documented.

In the meantime, two RAF officers had made the home run from Stalag Luft I at Barth. This camp had the advantage, from an escaper's point of view, of lying on the Baltic coast, whereas Spangenberg was in central Germany — not necessarily a bar to successful escape, but a formidable obstacle nevertheless, as friendly territory was much farther away. Other factors need to be taken into account, however, not least of which is that the castle itself was almost as escape-proof from within as it was impregnable from without. Aidan Crawley was not wrong when he wrote in *Escape from Germany* that it was "even better suited as a camp for prisoners of war" than the other uses to which it had previously been put. Breaking out of Spangenberg exercised one's ingenuity far more than busting the supposedly escape-proof Colditz.

Most of the prisoners there were also hampered by the fact that they were captured so early in the war. During the "Phoney War" few prisoners were escape conscious, and it was not until after the fall of France and the Low Countries in May and June 1940 that they began to consider the question of escape seriously. Even then, their methods were hardly professional, as few prisoners shot down before that period had received escape lectures, or been provided with escape kits or taught a secret letter-code. Had the War Office and the Air Ministry been less tardy, perhaps (and *only* perhaps) one or two of the "Spangenbergers" would have made it.

Even the later prisoners, however — those shot down in 1941 and early 1942 — found Spangenberg a tough nut to crack. This owed itself partly to the relatively small dimensions of the camp, which restricted escape opportunities. In addition, the guards lived on the premises in both the Upper and the Lower Camps; this, along with almost constant overcrowding, made it well nigh impossible to work on any escape project in secrecy.

Finally, the prisoners did not help themselves. Despite the pious resolutions of the numerous escape committees, there was simply not enough co-operation between committee members and the main prisoners' body. There was also some ill feeling between the Army committees and the smaller RAF committees, some of it possibly generated by the desire of a few senior Army officers to live an easy life. (One prisoner recalls being ordered not to make any escape attempts because "we are comfortable here and do not wish to lose our privileges".)

However, even in the 1941/42 period the most inured and bore-minded senior Army officers were clearly escape-conscious; the "old and bold" transferred from Warburg in January 1942 lost no time in setting up escape committees and did much to instil escape- and security-consciousness into the minds of the RAF contingent. But the RAF had their own problems. Firstly, being new prisoners, they were inexperienced in the art of escape, although some of them, such as Squadron Leader Calnan, had read the escape stories from the First World War. Secondly, they were never in any camp long enough to plan properly: they were in the Lower Camp for fewer than fourteen days, and in the Upper Camp for no more than two months. In the light of this, it is somewhat surprising that Tom Calnan felt such animosity towards the RAF Escape Committee, not only in Spangenberg but also later on in Stalag Luft III and Oflag XXIB.

As Eric Foinette pointed out in a letter to this author, Calnan had some very harsh words to say about escape committees, castigating them comprehensively in his memoirs. However, his account contains a number of factual inaccuracies, is in places self-serving, contains much that cannot be verified or which contradicts what he told his fellow-POWs at the time, and grinds a heavy political axe. Although he claimed to have started it in the 1950s and completed it in the late 1960s, much of the content was clearly a riposte to Sydney Smith's biography of "Wings" Day, published in 1968 and clearly a tribute to the work of the famous "X Organisation" which Day created in Barth and which later planned the "Great Escape". This was part of an ongoing debate between those who favoured organising escape along socialist lines (which is what "X" more or less did, "nationalising" tunnels, walk-outs and wire-jobs) and those who preferred the individualistic and gifted amateur approach. It fed into the Labour versus Conservative (collectivisation versus individual initiative) controversies of late '60s and early '70s Britain. Thus, throughout his memoirs, Calnan repeatedly lays the blame for his failed escape attempts at the feet of the Escape Committee. Aidan Crawley seems particularly to have aroused his ire, perhaps because as an Air Force Auxiliary and a socialist and a member of escape committees he stood for much that Calnan disliked.

It must be said that the RAF Escape Committee at Spangenberg in 1942 did perform poorly. In *Escape from Germany*, Crawley writes that in 1942: "the Germans were thoroughly on their guard and no attempts succeeded. The Air Force prisoners were not sorry to exchange the castle for the barbed wire encampment at Sagan where they were transferred a few months later." *Thoroughly on their guard in 1942 — but not in 1940 or 1941?* Security at Spangenberg was always tight. The problem was therefore not so much one in terms of the Germans being extra vigilant, but more one in terms of lack of organisation on the part of the RAF Escape Committee, and failure to carry out a proper escape reconnaissance. The main deterrent, however, was that there was too little time to develop plans: even assuming that one escaped from the confines of the castle, one simply would not have been able to forge adequate papers or put together a passable disguise. Hardly the fault of the Escape Committee, and certainly not the fault of Aidan Crawley! Perhaps there was some sense, after all, in waiting for a transfer to another camp.

For this, unfortunately, the Escape Committee was again ill prepared, but just how "prepared" could one have expected it to be? Wing Commander Larkin could hardly have gone up to *Hauptmann* Schmidt, the German security officer, and asked: "Excuse me, but can we have our Red Cross food parcels, please, because Squadron Leader Calnan would like to escape on the journey?" Several officers tried to escape in transit from Spangenberg to Sagan, all of them in a worse state of preparedness than Calnan. None of them succeeded, but none of them blamed Aidan Crawley or the Escape Committee, either.

Perhaps, after all, Calnan's grievance was personal. Two of his best friends, Charles Hall and Squadron Leader Ian Cross DFC, were among the fifty shot by the Gestapo as a result of the Great Escape in 1944 — an escape organised by "X". It was a tragic loss, and Calnan was not the only former prisoner to express anger at what some, with a certain amount of justification, later called "The Great Blunder". But the "X Organisation" in North Compound, Stalag Luft III, in 1943/44 was a bigger, more oligarchic and more monopolistic escape committee than the tiny affair at Spangenberg early in 1942, and planned the mass escape simply because it could. As for Aidan Crawley, he was Escape Intelligence Officer in the East Compound, from which the one hundred per cent successful "Wooden Horse" escape took place. Calnan turned down an offer to join the scheme, and the place went instead to Oliver Philpot, who made it to Sweden. So as far as getting Calnan's friends killed is concerned, and ruining Calnan's chances of getting back home, Crawley could quite honestly put his hand on his heart and say: "Look, I wasn't even there!"

Finally, even leaving aside personal rivalries and hostilities, the RAF contingent failed to pool information. The rope and grappling hook hidden by Allan McSweyn's escape team in October 1941, for instance, and discovered later by Calnan, might have proved useful to other prisoners planning an escape — such as the imperturbable Squadron Leader Vic Wood — but no one in Calnan's team saw fit to reveal its existence to anyone outside their little circle of confederates. Calnan is as much to blame as anyone else for hoarding valuable equipment and information: the unacceptable face of "individual initiative" perhaps?

Whatever the reasons might have been for the RAF failing to make a home run from Spangenberg, they must also have dogged the Army, for none of the Army escapers got through either. In the final analysis, Spangenberg did indeed prove to be an escape-proof prison camp. It was a victory for the Germans, who on this occasion showed the British "a thing or two".

Coda

O Lord God, when thou givest to Thy servants to endeavour any great matter, grant to us also to know that it is not beginning, but the continuing of the same, until it be thoroughly finished, which yieldeth the true glory; through Him that for the finishing of Thy work laid down His life, our Redeemer, Jesus Christ. Amen.

Sir Francis Drake, 1587

Despite the existence of a newly opened prison camp for aircrew, two more RAF officers were sent to Spangenberg in August 1942 to join the three-hundred-odd Army officers: Acting Squadron Leader G C Campbell DFC, and Flying Officer J Kuflik.

The Polish Jan Kuflik, whom the prisoners at Spangenberg called "John", was captured on 10/11 July 1941 when Bomber Command put on a "maximum effort" against Cologne involving 130 aircraft. The force of Hampdens and Wellingtons was given two aiming points: the city centre and the Humboldt works. Bad weather dogged the raid, preventing accurate bombing, and two Wimpeys were lost. Kuflik, then a Pilot Officer on No300 Squadron, had taken off from Swinderby at 2249 hours. It is not known how his aircraft crashed. In any event, all the crew survived, though most were badly injured. Pilot Officer J Janicki, the second pilot, was at Dulag Luft for nearly nineteen weeks before being sent to Oflag XC at Lübeck. Sergeants M Sztul, J Artymuik and A Suczynski were transferred Stalag IXC. Kuflik, after treatment at Hohemark clinic, was moved to Lazarett IXC, where he received time-promotion to Flying Officer. The observer, Pilot Officer M Kozinski, was sent to Oflag VIIC/H at Laufen.

Graham Cox Campbell had been a prisoner since 8/9 May 1942. He was born on 3 May 1914 in Nova Scotia, and when he was six his family moved to Alberta where he grew up on a wheat farm. When he graduated from the local high school in 1934 he had no funds with which to attend university so he made plans to join the RAF, which was then recruiting in Canada. To obtain enough money to pay for a private pilot's course, he worked as a farm labourer, and in August 1938 proceeded overseas and joined the RAF on a short-service commission as Acting Pilot Officer.

When he was shot down he was a Flight Commander in No420 Squadron at Waddington, which had already lost Vic Wood to kriegiedom. On the night of 8 May 1941 Bomber Command put up 193 aircraft to bomb the town of Warnemünde and the Heinkel factory at nearby Rostock. Nine aircraft were shot down, a hundred men were killed and sixteen made prisoner. Campbell's Hampden received a direct hit on the starboard wing from the local flak, causing the wing fuel tank to explode, damaging the controls and starting a fire. Campbell ordered the crew to bale out, then "controlled the aircraft in a steep dive to 3,000 feet when it broke up and I was thrown out of the a/c. Hit the ground moments after the parachute opened and broke my right ankle. Picked up some six hours later by the German Army."

Of his crew, only the lower ventral gunner, Sergeant G H Soper, RCAF, survived. The navigator, Flight Sergeant R B Peterson, RCAF, died near the aircraft, probably as a result of baling out too late. Sergeant R R Parry, the British upper gunner, "disappeared, with no early information on his fate," recalls Campbell. "Subsequent postwar information stated he was buried in Germany [in the 1939/45 War cemetery in Berlin]. Sgt Soper survived with only slight burns to his face, was subsequently commissioned and joined me in Luft III."

Graham Campbell arrived at Dulag Luft on Sunday, 10 May, and was there until Sunday, 17 May, when he was taken to the hospital at Stalag IXC. In August he and Jan Kuflik were transferred to Spangenberg and after a thorough search of their person in the Lower Camp *Kommandantur* were escorted up the hill to the *Hauptlager*. Once released into the courtyard they were interviewed by the SBO and by Lieutenant-Colonel Hugh Swinburne, the head of the Escape Committee, and then allotted their bunks in one of the large dormitories.

Prior to their arrival Lieutenant-Colonel Swinburne and a digging team had started excavating a tunnel — through practically solid rock. (The two RAF prisoners took no part in the enterprise, which was still crawling ahead when they left and was not discovered by the Germans until May 1943.) Soon afterwards two Army majors and a captain attempted to cross the moat by pushing a home-made wooden boom out of one of the windows, supported by a rope from a window further up. The spot chosen was out of sight of the two nearest guards — unless, that is, they happened to walk round the corner. Unfortunately, one of the guards did indeed start walking towards the window. He saw the boom being dismantled and raised the alarm. From then onwards that particular part of the moat was kept under stricter observation.

At the beginning of October the reason for their incarceration in Spangenberg became apparent to the two RAF officers. The Germans were instituting a *Strafe* — a familiar word to the brown jobs who had been at Thorn. This *Strafe*, however, was quite unusual. The OKW had alleged that German officer POWs had been badly treated when travelling on the SS *Pasteur*. As a reprisal, the officers at Spangenberg were ordered one morning to told to pack all their belongings and parade in the moat. As soon as they were in the moat they realised that something extraordinary was about to take place. Instead of the usual three armed sentries there were dozens of them, and mounted machine-guns controlled the drawbridge and another part of the moat.

In small groups the prisoners were taken away to a room inside the castle where their tunics and hats were removed. They were then searched and all their possessions were taken away, except for their underwear, shirts and slacks. Afterwards they were taken to the dining room and shut in. All the windows had been shut and locked and the blackout boards put up. In one corner was a metal bucket for sanitation. This room was, they presumed, supposed to represent the hold of a ship.

The last to enter the room was Major-General Fortune — hatless and in shirtsleeves, like everyone else. He read out the German order giving the reasons for their punishment, and asked them to accept this new reprisal with dignity. That evening they were allowed to leave the dining hall. General Fortune at once wrote a letter to the International Red Cross and the protecting power.

The prisoners found their tunics, greatcoats and hats in a large heap in the courtyard. All unit badges and buttons, badges of rank and medal ribbons had been cut off and taken away. From that day onwards they ceased to wear headgear.

During the day all their baggage, except blankets, had been removed from their rooms. They could no longer wash, shave, comb their hair or cut their fingernails. They had no utensils with which to eat their food. They had no other clothes to change into. They had nothing to read. This carried on for eight weeks, until on Saturday, 28 November, the *Strafe* was lifted by the OKW and the prisoners received back all their kit. By that time they had all grown fulsome beards and had shaggy heads of hair.

Campbell and Kuflik remained at Spangenberg until January 1943, when they were finally transferred to Sagan.

Appendices

KEY:

Services:

AAF	Auxiliary Air Force
FFAF	Free French Air Force
RAAF	Royal Australian Air Force
RAFO	Reserve of Air Force Officers
RAFVR	Royal Air Force Volunteer Reserve

Ranks:

Air Forces:

AC2	Aircraftman 2nd Class
AC1	Aircraftman 1st Class
LAC	Leading Aircraftman
Sgt	Sergeant
F/S	Flight Sergeant
W/O	Warrant Officer
P/O	Pilot Officer
F/O	Flying Officer
F/L	Flight Lieutenant
S/L	Squadron Leader
W/C	Wing Commander
G/C	Group Captain

Other services:

L/A	Leading Airman (RN)
Mid	Midshipman (RN)
N/A	Naval Airman (RN)
Ty S/Lt	Temporary Sub-Lieutenant (RN)
Ty Lt	Temporary Lieutenant (RN)
2/Lt	Lieutenant (SAAF)
S/Lt	Sub-Lieutenant (RN)
Sy Lt	Supply Lieutenant (RN)
Lt	Lieutenant (FFAF, RN, SAAF, Army)
Lt Cdr	Lieutenant-Commander (RN)
Cdr	Commander (RN)
Capt	(RM, RN, SAAF)

Note: The prefix "A" before a rank indicates acting rank

Decorations:

AFC	Air Force Cross
AM	Albert Medal

RCAF	Royal Canadian Air Force
RM	Royal Marines
RN	Royal Navy
RNR	Royal Navy Reserve
RNVR	Royal Navy Volunteer Reserve
RNZAF	Royal New Zealand Air Force
SAAF	South African Air Force

DFC	Distinguished Flying Cross
DFM	Distinguished Flying Medal
DSC	Distinguished Service Cross (RN)
DSO	Distinguished Service Order
MC	Military Cross
*	Bar to decoration

Prisoner of War Camps:

D185	Dulag 185, Salonika, Greece
DL	Dulag Luft, Oberursel
F8	Fort VIII, Posen
F15	Fort XV, Thorn
ODL	Offiziersdurchgangslager, Oberursel
O2A	Oflag IIA, Prenzlau
O2B	Oflag IIB, Arnswalde
O4B	Oflag IVB, Königstein
O4C	Oflag IVC, Colditz
O6B	Oflag VIB, Warburg
O9A/H	Oflag IXA/H, Spangenberg
O10A	Oflag XA, Itzehoe
O11B	Oflag XIB, Braunschweig (Brunswick)
S2A	Stalag IIA, Neu Brandenburg
S8B	Stalag VIIIB, Lamsdorf (Teschen)
S9A	Stalag IXA, Ziegenhain
S9C	Stalag IXC, Bad Sulza (Mulhausen)
S12A	Stalag XIIA, Limburg an der Lahn
SL1	Stalag Luft I, Barth
SL3	Stalag Luft III, Sagan

Appendix I

The Prisoner-of-War Code of the Geneva Convention, 1929

Weimar Germany was one of the first of the thirty-eight powers represented in Geneva on 27 July 1929 to sign the Prisoner of War Code and the Red Cross Convention. These had their origins in the first, semi-official, Geneva Convention called in 1863, which was followed a year later by the first international laws of war regarding the treatment of the sick and wounded. Known collectively as the Red Cross Convention, they were ratified by forty-one states and revised in 1906. On 18 October 1907, the Red Cross Convention was extended by the Hague Convention, which for the first time in history laid down the rights and obligations of prisoners of war. But the Great War proved both Conventions inadequate and they had to be revised yet again. The 1929 Prisoner of War Code contained no less than ninety-seven specific articles, the most pertinent of which can best be summarised as follows:

ARTICLE 2. A prisoner of war shall be under the control of the hostile power, not of the individuals or units that have captured him.

ARTICLES 2 & 3. POWs are to be protected by the detaining power from violence, insults and public curiosity, and must not be subject to reprisals for military actions. They shall be segregated according to rank—officers in one compound, NCOs and "other ranks" (ie, those below the rank of full corporal) in another.

ARTICLE 5. A POW under interrogation is obliged to give only his name, rank and service number, and must not be forced to give information on his armed forces or his country. He must not be threatened, insulted, or exposed to unpleasantness or disadvantages should he refuse to reply.

ARTICLE 6. All his personal effects are to be held initially by the detaining power and, along with identification documents, must eventually be handed back. Identity discs, badges of rank and decorations are not to be taken from him. Only arms and military equipment can be confiscated.

ARTICLE 7. Newly captured prisoners must be removed from the fighting zone as soon as possible but, "Evacuation of prisoners on foot may normally be effected only by stages of 20 kilometres (12 miles) a day, unless the necessity of reaching water and food depots requires longer stages".

ARTICLES 8 & 10. Immediately after capture or, at most, within one week of arriving at a permanent camp, a POW is entitled to write directly to his family and to POW and relief agencies, stating that he is a prisoner and indicating whether or not he has been wounded; thereafter he is entitled to send at least two letters and four cards per month. Parcels addressed to him can contain food, tobacco, clothing, medical supplies and articles of a religious, educational and recreational nature.

ARTICLE 9. Prisoners are to be given complete religious freedom, including a chaplain and provision for religious services. Captives qualified as doctors, dentists, chaplains, etc, if required to act as such, shall not then be considered prisoners of war but "protected personnel", and shall be entitled to visit prisoners working outside the camp.

ARTICLE 11. The food provided by the detaining power shall be of the same quantity and quality as that given to its own base troops (in Germany, members of the *Ersatzheer*, or Army Reserve, which guarded POWs) and means shall be provided for cooking these and any additional rations that prisoners procure. Tampering with their food as a disciplinary measure is forbidden.

ARTICLES 12-21. Prisoners are to be grouped according to nationality, language and customs, and are not to be separated, without their consent, from other prisoners from their own branch of the armed forces. POW camps must be comparable to accommodation for the detaining power's own depot troops; located in healthy areas away from the battle zone; and have sufficient running water, sanitary facilities, heating, fresh-air exercise space and bomb shelters, and a canteen stocking everyday articles such as soap, tooth-brushes, combs and hair oil at prices not above those prevailing locally. The clothing provided shall include decent underwear and footwear.

The next twenty-five articles deal with discipline and organisation. They lay it down that POWs are at all times subject to the laws of the detaining power's armed forces. Thus, all ORs are required to salute all officers of the detaining power, while officers are required to salute equals and superiors in rank. The camp commandant can put them under arrest for disobedience, disorderly behaviour or violation of camp orders. But they are only to be "reasonably restrained", and not strictly confined unless absolutely necessary. POWs are also entitled to legal counsel before signing any legal documents and to a trial for serious breaches of camp discipline. Trial is to be by military court, unless the laws of the detaining power expressly give jurisdiction to the civil authority. But no prisoner can be punished by both military and civil courts for the same act.

Prisoners are allowed to select a representative to confer with the camp commandant and his staff and to take charge of the distribution of Red Cross supplies. This individual will listen to the grievances of his men and discuss them in private with representatives of the protecting power, who are to ensure that the Geneva Convention is upheld by the detaining power. If the protecting power concludes that the grievances are legitimate, they are to be passed on to the camp commandant. Protecting power representatives, as well as representatives of the International Committee of the Red Cross and members of approved relief agencies, such as the Young Men's Christian Association, have the right to visit camps and report on their conditions.

ARTICLES 50-54 of the Code recognise the duty of a prisoner to escape, and forbid harassment or reprisals in the event of recapture, such as corporal punishment, confinement in cells not illuminated by daylight, any form of cruelty, the stripping of rank, and collective punishment for an individual act. A recaptured escapee shall be subject only to disciplinary punishment — no more than thirty days' solitary confinement. The same applies to those who have aided and abetted him, unless they have committed acts of violence or murder. (Under Article 48, however, the detaining power is permitted to create "special camps" as repositories for difficult captives.)

ARTICLE 67. Medical inspections are to be carried out once a month and prisoners given access to an infirmary on the camp site. Seriously ill POWs must be admitted to civilian or military hospitals for treatment at the expense of the detaining power.

ARTICLE 68. Inspection commissions consisting of a doctor each from the detaining power, the protecting power and the enemy power shall be permitted to examine and interview critically ill prisoners who have been put forward for repatriation or exchange. Those who pass are to be sent to a neutral port for their return home.

ARTICLE 84. A complete copy of the POW Code shall be posted "in places where it may be consulted by all prisoners" and in their native language(s).

APPENDIX II

Officers, NCOs and Other Ranks held in Itzfhoe, Spangenberg and Thorn, 1939–43

Rank and name	POW No	Date Captured	POW Camps
Officers:			
A			
F/L E R Abbott DSO DFM	1407	13/14 10 41	O9A/H SL3
S/L R B Abraham	1446	25/26 02 42	O9A/H SL3
P/O M F Andrews	1375	27 06 41	O9A/H O6B
Lt (A) A O Atkins RN	1262	22 09 40	O9A/H F15 O9A/H O6B
P/O R S Ayton DFM	1346	10/11 05 41	O9A/H O6B
B			
P/O G M Baird	61	20 10 40	SL1 O9A F15 O9A O6B
P/O A P L Barber	1411	— 01 42	O9A/H SL3
F/L H J W Bareham DFM	1412	28/29 01 42	O9A/H SL3
P/O J Barker	1370	18/19 07 40	O9A/H O6B
Sub-Lt (A) R E Bartlett RN	92	13 06 40 (31 08 40)	SL1 O9A/H F15 O9A/H O6B
F/O R D Baughan	634	29 09 39	O9A/H DL
F/O T A Bax	1352	09 06 41	O9A/H O6B
P/O H R Bewlay	—	07 11 39	O9A/H F15 O9A/H O6B
P/O H R Bjelke-Peterson	1263	28/29 09 40	O9A/H F15 O9A/H O6B
F/O D Blew	594	11 05 40	O9A/H F15 O9A/H O6B
F/O R J E Boulding	1353	17 06 41	O9A/H O6B
F/L J C Bowman	1241	21 07 40	O9A/H F15 O9A/H O6B
P/O S B K Brackenbury RCAF	1413	28/29/12 41	O9A/H SL3
F/O P E Bressey	1124	40	O9A/H SL1 O9A/H F15 O9A/H O6B
P/O A J Brewster	1354	19/20 06 41	O9A/H O6B
S/L A O Bridgman DFC	1264	23/24 09 40	O9A/H F15 O9A/H O6B
P/O P S E Briggs	1355	16 06 41	O9A/H SL3
P/O P G Brodie	1242	19/20 08 40	O9A/H F15 O9A/H O6B
F/O D Bruce	1356	09 06 41	O9A/H O6B
F/L J Bryks (Ricks) (Czech)	1363	17 06 41	O9A/H O6B
P/O R H Buchanan	1447	09/10 03 42	O9A/H SL3
P/O H F Burns	1285	26 10 41	O9A/H F15 O9A/H O6B
F/O R M Burns	595	10 05 40	O9A/H SL1 O9A/H F15 O9A/H O6B
P/O M G Butt RAFVR	241	27/28 08 40	SL1 O9A/H F15 O9A/H O6B

Rank and name	POW No	Date Captured	POW Camps
C			
S/L T D Calnan	1414	30 12 41	O9A/H SL3
A/S/L G C Campbell DFC	39635	08/09 05 42	S9C O9A/H SL3
P/O S Carter RAFVR	1386	30 06/01 07 41	O9A/H O6B SL3
F/O M J Casey	55	16 10 39	O9A/H DL
P/O W Cebrazynski (Pole)	1366	18/19 06 41	O9A/H O6B
F/O E F Chapman	1342	08 05 41	O9A/H O6B
Sub-Lt (A) H A Cheetham RN	1265	23 09 40	O9A/H F15 O4C
F/L G D Clancy	596	14 05 40	O9A/H SL1
P/O E J Clelland	358	28/29 11 40	SL1 O9A F15 O9A O6B SL3
P/O P J Coleson	—	11 08 40	S9C O9A/H S9C
P/O P W Cook	1243	19/20 08 40	O9A/H F15 O9A/H O6B
F/L R M Coste	40	29 09 39	O9A/H F15 O9A/H O6B
A/S/L A M Crawley	71	07 07 41	D185 O9A/H SL3
F/O C A R Crews DFC	328	11 05 40	O9A/H SL1 O9A/H F15 O9A/H O6B
D			
P/O G C Daniel RCAF	1415	31 10 41	O9A/H SL3
S/L N S F Davie, AuxAF	1416	04 02 42	O9A/H SL3
Sub-Lt (A) J M P Davies RN	158	30 06 40	SL1 O9A/H F15 O4C
Sub-Lt (A) R L G Davies RN	1244	22 08 40	O9A/H F15 O9A/H O6B
F/O G B Dawkins DFM	1417	14/15 01 42	O9A/H SL3
W/C H M A Day AM	37	13 10 39	ODL O9A/H DL
P/O R V Derbyshire	327	14/15 11 40	SL1 O9A/H F15 O9A/H O6B
Sub-Lt (A) H Deterding RNVR	1266	22 09 40	O9A/H F15 O9A/H O6B
P/O G T Dodgshun	508	21/22 05 40	O9A/H SLI O9A/H F15 O9A/H O6B
F/O M W Donaldson	336	12 04 40	O9A/H F15 O4C
S/L K C Doran DFC*	501	30 04 40	O9A/H SL1
Capt K W Driver DFC SAAF	1371	14 06 41	O9A/H O6B
F/L L S Dunley RNZAF	1348	10/11 04 41	O9A/H O6B
P/O N M Dunn RAAF	1357	16 06 41	O9A/H O6B
F/L F G Dutton	364	21/22 04 40	SL1 O9A/H F15 O9A/H O6B
E			
P/O L H Edwards	6	06 09 39	O9A/H F15 O9A/H O6B
F/L P J Edwards	1418	14/15 01 42	O9A/H SL3
F/L R H Edwards	—	28/29 07 40	SL1 O9A/H F15 O9A/H O6B
F/O W H Edwards DFC	326	12 05 40	O9A/H SL1 O9A/H F15 O9A/H O6B
F/L R A G Ellen	162	13 08 40	SL1 O9A/H F15 O9A/H O6B
F			
F/O E T Fairbank	1373	23 06 41	O9A/H O6B
P/O J A R Falconer	1419	08 12 41	O9A/H SL3
P/O R F J Featherstone RCAF	1345	11/12 05 41	O9A/H O6B
P/O M W Fessler(American)	1420	27 10 41	O9A/H SL3
F/L M J Fisher RAFVR	1245	16/17 08 40	O9A/H F15 O9A/H O6B
P/O F D Flinn	1267	04 10 40	O9A/H F15 O4C
P/O E N Foinette	1445	25/26 02 42	O9A/H SL3
F/O N Forbes	2257	27 05 40	S12A O2A SL1 O9A/H F15 O4C
P/O J E A Foster RAFVR	1268	14/15 06 40	O9A/H F15 O9A/H O6B
P/O W M W Fowler	1388	30 06/01 07 41	O9A/H SL3
P/O G M Frame	1380	27/28 06 41	O9A/H O6B
F/O J H Frampton	1337	16/17 01 41	O9A/H O6B
F/L R D Fraser	1421	31 01/01 02 42	O9A/H SL3
G			
P/O W D Geiger (American)	1422	17 09 41	O9A/H SL3

Rank and name	POW No	Date Captured	POW Camps
S/L D B Gericke	1341	12 04 41	O9A/H O6B
P/O J T Glover	510	19/20 05 40	O9A/H F15 O9A/H O6B
P/O A H Gould	1269	20/21 07 40	DL O9A/H F15 O9A/H O6B
Lt (A) R H G Grey RN	—	29 05 40	S12A O2A SL1 O9A/H F15 O9A/H Died 29 08 41
F/O G E Grey-Smith	—	12 05 40	O9A/H SL1
Lt G B K Griffiths RM	635	14 09 39	O11B O9A/H DL
F/L G R Guest	627	—	SL1 O9A/H SL1

H

Rank and name	POW No	Date Captured	POW Camps
P/O T H Hadley	245	10/11 09 40	SL1 O9A/H F15 O9A/H O6B
P/O C P Hall	1423	28 12 41	O9A/H SL3
Lt G R Haller SAAF	1424	—	O9A/H SL3
P/O N D Hallifax	1306	15 05 40	S9C O9A/H O6B
P/O A J C Hamilton	1376	06 06 41	O9A/H O6B
F/L W H Hannigan	1425	31 01/01 02 42	O9A/H SL3
Lt (A) M A J J Hanrahan RN	1270	22 09 40	O9A/H F15 O9A/H O6B
P/O W C Hartop RAFVR	1349	01 04 41	O9A/H O6B
P/O D K Hayes	1271	29/30 09 40	O9A/H F15 O9A/H O6B
F/O B W Hayward	204	23/24 04 40	O9A/H F15 O9A/H O6B
Lt N M Hearle RM	1246	22 08 40	O9A/H F15 O9A/H O6B
Sub-Lt (A) H N C Hearn RN	1272	23 09 40	O9A/H F15 O9A/H O6B
P/O D G Heaton-Nichols	22	30 09 39	O9A/H F15 O9A/H O6B
P/O E R Hester	1426	11 12 41	O9A/H SL3
P/O W Hetherington	1383	29/30 06 41	O9A/H O6B
F/O D S Hoare	580	25 05 40	O9A/H SL1 O9A/H F15 O9A/H O6B
P/O K N Holland	1358	16/17 06 41	O9A/H O6B
P/O W H Holland	1377	27 06 41	O9A/H O6B
P/O J R Hoppe RAFVR	371	04/05 12 40	SL1 O9A/H F15 O9A/H O6B
F/L E Hubicki (Pole)	1390	29/30 06 41	O9A/H O6B
F/O A J Hudson	329	11 05 40	O9A/H SL1
P/O F Hugill	1127	14 06 40	O9A/H F15 O9A/H O6B
P/O C P de L Hulton-Harrop	325	11 05 40	O9A/H SL1

I

Rank and name	POW No	Date Captured	POW Camps
Lt J C W Iliffe RN	1273	13 09 40	O9A/H F15 O9A/H O6B
P/O A M Imrie (S Rhodesian)	503	14 05 40	O9A/H SL1 O9A/H F15 O9A/H O6B

J

Rank and name	POW No	Date Captured	POW Camps
A/F/O W F Jackman RAFVR	1389	01 07 41	O9A/H O6B
F/O R H Jacoby	581	23 05 40	O9A/H SL1 O9A/H F15 O9A/H O6B
P/O K Jaklewicz (Pole)	1367	18/19 06 41	O9A/H O6B
S/L L W V Jennens RAFO	1427	18 12 41	O9A/H SL3
P/O T F S Johnson	1247	19/20 08 40	O9A/H F15 O9A/H O6B
P/O H O Jones	507	21/22 05 40	O9A/H SL1
P/O K M Jones RAFVR	1408	22 07 41	O9A/H SL3

K

Rank and name	POW No	Date Captured	POW Camps
P/O T M Kane	63	23 09 40	SL1 O9A/H F15 O9A/H O6B
W/C J R Kayll DSO DFC AuxAF	1374	25 06 41	O9A/H O6B
F/L F W S Keighley	1275	29 07 40	O9A/H F15 O9A/H O6B
P/O V Kelly	113	22 05 40	SL1 O9A/H SL1
P/O J McB Kerr RNZAF	1359	19/20 06 41	O9A/H O6B
F/O R J Kimbell	1428	27/28 12 41	O9A/H SL3
P/O I C Kirk	1276	02/03 09 40	O9A/H F15 O9A/H O6B
F/O F T Knight	—	21/22 04 40	SL1 S9C O9A/H SL1
F/L L Kozlowski (Pole)	1391	29/30 06 41	O9A/H O6B
P/OS Z Król (Pole)	1392	02 07 41	O9A/H O6B

Rank and name	POW No	Date Captured	POW Camps
P/O W Krupowicz (Pole)	1393	03/04 07 41	O9A/H O6B
P/O J Kuflik (Pole)	39268	10/11 07 41	S9C O9A/H SL3

L

W/C H R Larkin (Australian)	1429	08 02 42	O9A/H SL3
F/O D F Laslett	511	21/22 05 40	O9A/H SL1 O9A/H F15 O9A/H O6B
F/O W N Lepine	1129	18 05 40	O9A/H SL1 O9A/H F15 O9A/H O6B
F/L J N Leyden	1125	26 05 40	O9A/H SL1 O9A/H F15 O9A/H O6B

M

F/O A C MacLachlan	40	01 10 39	O9A/H F15 O9A/H O6B
Lt B L McFarlane SAAF	1430	—	O9A/H SL3
F/L G E McGill	1431	12 01 42	O9A/H SL3
P/O I A M McIntosh	104	12 05 40	SL1 O9A/H SL1
F/O R C D McKenzie	1248	08 06 40	O9A/H F15 O9A/H O6B
P/O A F McSweyn RAAF	—	29/30 06 41	O9A O6B
F/L R I C Macpherson	582	16 05 40	O9A/H SL1 O9A/H F15 O9A/H O6B
P/O N Maranz	1372	21 06 41	O9A/H O6B
P/O J D Margrie	1381	27/28 06 41	O9A/H O6B
F/O M M Marsh RAFVR	1344	09/10 05 41	O9A/H SL3
Lt (A) D T R Martin RN	1128	13 06 40	O9A/H SL1 O9A/H F15 O9A/H O6B
P/O E C Maskell	3738	17/18 08 41	O9A/H O6B
P/O W T Mathieson	—	30/09 01/10 40	S9C O9A/H SL1
P/O A W Matthews	1261	10 05 40	O9A/H F15 O9A/H O6B
P/O W R Methven	—	07/08 11 41	SL1 S9C O9A/H SL1
P/O F D Middleton	—	12 04 40	O9A/H O4C
P/O L Miller DFC	24	19/20 05 40	O9A/H F15 O9A/H O6B
F/O T K Milne	206	23/24 04 40	O9A/H O4C
F/O J C Milner	393/419	19 05 40	SL1 O9A/H F15 O9A/H O6B
P/O W D Moore	1432	07/08 11 41	O9A/H SL3
P/O E R Mullins	504	14 05 40	O9A/H SL1
P/O A W Mungovan	324	11 05 40	O9A/H SL1 O9A/H F15 O9A/H O6B
F/O M I Murdoch	330	15 05 40	O9A/H SL1
P/O C W Murphy RCAF	1433	27/28 12 41	O9A/H SL3
F/O K H P Murphy	207	29/30 04 40	O9A/H SL1 O9A/H F15 O9A/H O6B
P/O H M Murray	1130	11 05 40	O9A/H SL1 O9A/H F15 O9A/H O6B
S/L S S Murray	60	08/09 09 39	O10A O9A F15 O9A O6B

N

Lt E C Newborn SAAF	1360	14 06 41	O9A/H O6B
P/O B T J Newland (S Rhodesian)	1617	13 08 40	O9A/H F15 O9A/H O6B
P/O W H Nichols	1434	07 09 41	O9A/H SL3
F/O W M Nixon	1249	16/17 08 40	O9A/H F15 O9A/H O6B

O

P/O D G O'Brien	597	10 05 40	O9A/H SL1 O9A/H F15 O9A/H O6B
P/O T L W Officer RAAF	1378	17 06 41	O9A/H O6B
F/O A K Ogilvie DFC	1409	04 07 41	O9A/H SL3
P/O D E T Osment	506	19 05 40	O9A/H SL1

P

S/L B Paddon	—	06 06 40	O9A/H SL1 O9A/H F15 O4C
P/O G Parker	1250	14/15 08 40	O9A/H F15 O9A/H O6B
F/L D Paterson	1351	—	O9A O6B
F/O A C Peach	334	18/19 05 40	O9A/H SL1
F/L S G L Pepys	583	23 05 40	O9A/H SL1 O9A/H F15 O9A/H O6B
P/O J W P Perkins	1251	05/06 07 40	O9A/H F15 O9A/H O6B
P/O O L S Philpot DFC RAFVR	1435	11 12 41	O9A/H SL3

Rank and name	POW No	Date Captured	POW Camps
P/O J Plant	1126	20/21 06 40	O9A/H SL1
P/O I G G Potts	1122	01 06 40	O9A/H SL1 O9A/H F15 O9A/H O6B
P/O R G Poulter	1382	27/28 06 41	O9A/H O6B
Sub-Lt (A) D A Poynter RN	1278	22 09 40	O9A/H F15 O9A/H O6B
F/O R E W Pumphrey	598	20 05 40	O9A/H SL1

Q

Lt Cdr N R Quill RN	1279	09 10 40	O9A/H F15 O9A/H O6B

R

P/O G M Rackow	1436	11 12 41	O9A/H SL3
S/L M E Redgrave	1362	11/12 06 41	O9A/H O6B
P/O S Reeves	1405	30 05 41	O9A/H O6B
P/O R J B Renison, AuxAF	1131	18 05 40	O9A/H SL1
F/O A C Roberts	327	10 05 40	O9A/H SL1
P/O R Roberts	1252	15 08 40	O9A/H F15 O9A/H O6B
P/O C I Rolfe	1397	02/03 08 41	O9A/H SL3
P/O P R Ross RNZAF	1437	20/21 01 42	O9A/H SL3
F/O M H Roth	333	10 05 40	O9A/H SL1
F/L A A Rumsey	1286	26 10 40	O9A/H F15 O9A/H O6B
P/O P M R Runnacles	10	06/04 09 41	O9A/H SL3

S

P/O P S Sanders	1438	10/11 01 42	O9A/H SL3
P/O W J Sandman RNZAF	1379	27 06 41	O9A/H O6B
F/O S T Sedzik (Pole)	1368	11/12 06 41	O9A/H O6B
P/O H A T Skehill	1253	16/17 08 40	O9A/H F15 O9A/H O6B
F/L G Skelton	—	12/13 05 40	O9A/H S9C SL1 O9A/H SL1
F/L J R T Smalley DFC	1280	08 10 40	O9A/H F15 O9A/H O6B
P/O N Smallwood	1439	08 02 42	O9A/H SL3
S/L E T Smith	1364	17 06 41	O9A/H O6B
S/L F G L Smith DFC	1287	17 06 40	O9A/H O6B
P/O W A Sojka (Pole)	1369	11/12 06 41	O9A/H F15 O9A/HO6B
P/O A J J Steel	1281	30/09-01/10 40	O9A/H F15 O9A/H O6B
F/O D Stein	1440	30 10 41	O9A/H SL3
F/L J W Stephens	519	23 06 40	O9A/H SL1
Lt-Cdr O S Stevinson RN	1282	09 10 40	O9A/H F15 O4C
F/L N H Svendsen DFC (Dane)	1387	30 06/01 07 41	O9A/H O6B
F/L T E Syms	1288	13 08 40	O9A/H F15 O9A/H O6B

T

Lt A Taylor RN	1254	22/23 08 40	O9A/H F15 O9A/H O6B
P/O H H Taylor	584	19 05 40	O9A/H SL1 O9A/H F15 O9A/H O6B
F/O J M Taylor	256	04/05 09 40	SL1 O9A/H F15 O9A/H O6B
F/L W H Thallon	1441	20/21 01 42	O9A/H SL3
F/O D S Thom	585	25 05 40	O9A/H SL1 O9A/H F15 O4C
F/O N M Thomas	1401	12 05 40	O9A/H SL1 O9A/H F15 O9A/H O6B
P/O P A W Thomas	352	14/15 11 40	SL1 O9A/H F15 O9A/H O6B
P/O A B Thompson	59	08/09 09 39	O10A O9A/H O9A/H O6B
Lt R P Thurston RN	23	14 09 39	O11B O9A/H DL
F/O J Tilsley	38	16 10 39	O9A/H F15 O9A/H O6B
P/O K S Toft	126	17 05 40	SL1 O9A/H F15 O9A/H O6B
F/L R E Troward	340	16 11 40	SL1 O9A/H F15 O9A/H O6B
W/C R R S Tuck DSO DFC**	1442	28 01 42	O9A/H SL3

Rank and name	POW No	Date Captured	POW Camps
F/O P D Tunstall	258	26/27 08 40	SL1 O9A/H F15 O9A/H O6B
S/L W H N Turner DFC	332	18/19 05 40	O9A/H SL1

V

F/L P F R Vaillant	1283	27/28 08 40	O9A/H F15 O9A/H O6B
P/O P P Villa	1365	16 06 41	O9A/H O6B

W

F/O G E Walker	1120	20/21 06 40	O9A/H F15 O9A/H O6B
P/O R A Walker	1388	02/03 07 41	O9A/H O6B
S/L R N Wardell	1618	13 08 40	O9A/H F15 O9A/H O6B
P/O H D Wardle	—	20 04 40	O9A/H O4C
P/O R D Wawn	1255	25/26 08 40	O9A/H F15 O9A/H O6B
F/L M C Wells	331	10 05 40	O9A/H SL1 O9A/H F15 O9A/H O6B
P/O J Whilton	(?)	21/22 05 40	O9A/H F15 O9A/H O6B
F/O P G Whitby	1256	16/17 08 40	O9A/H F15 O9A/H O6B
P/O R A R White RNZAF	1350	21 05 41	O9A/H O6B
P/O J E G Whiting RNZAF	1443	28/29 01 42	O9A/H SL3
S/L W Wilczewski (Pole)	1410	08 11 41	O9A/H SL3
S/L V T L Wood (Australian)	1444	21/22 01 42	O9A/H SL3
P/O I K Woodroffe	1343	09/10 05 41	O9A/H O6B
F/L G O M Wright	599	14 05 40	O9A/H SL1 O9A/H F15 O9A/H O6B

NCOs and Other Ranks:

AC1 T P Adderley	43	07 11 39	O9A/H F8 S8B
Sgt G F Booth	154	04 09 39	O9A/H F8 S8B
AC1 S A Burry	1	08/09 09 39	O9A/H F8 S8B
LAC R E Fletcher	39	15/16 10 39	O9A/H F8 S8B
Sgt A G Fripp	5752	16 10 39	S9A O9A/H F8 S8B
Sgt R L Galloway	5760	29 09 39	S9A O9A/H F8 S8B
Cpl A R Gunton	5753	15/16 10 39	S9A O9A/H F8 S8B
Sgt C A Hill	2	08/09 09 39	O9A/H F8 S8B
Sgt J W Lambert	5751	15/16 10 39	S9A O9A/H F8 S8B
AC1 H Liggett	5759	29 09 39	S9A O9A/H F8 S8B
Sgt S McIntyre	42	07 11 39	O9A/H F8 S8B
AC1 J Nelson	5755	16 10 39	S9A O9A/H DL
AC1 P F Pacey	3	08/09 09 39	O9A/H F8 S8B
AC1 L J Slattery	84	04 09 39	09A/H F15 O9A/H O6B
Sgt G J Springett	5754	30 09 39	S9A O9A/H F8 S8B

APPENDIX III

Officer & NCO Prisoners of the *Armée de l'Air* at Spangenberg, 1939–40

Rank and name	Shot down	POW Camps
Officers:		
Lt P Aouach	06 10 39	O9A/H O2B
Sous-Lt Béranger	09 09 39	O9A/H O2B
Sous-Lt Besson-Guyard	12 05 40	O9A/H O2B
Lt Detrie	12 05 40	O9A/H O2B
Lt-Col Enselem	09 09 39	O9A/H DL
Cpte Eveno	29 09 39	O9A/H O2B
Lt-Col Gérardot	06 10 39	O9A/H DL O9A/H
Lt Grandrémy	11 05 40	O9A/H O2B
Sous-Lt Lalvée	11 10 39	O9A/H O2B
Lt Laemmel	16 10 39	O9A/H O2B
Lt Lamblin	15 10 39	O9A/H O2B
Capte Larmier	10 05 40	O9A/H F15 O9A/H O6B
Lt Leleu	12 05 40	O9A/H O2B
Lt Navalet	20 12 39	O9A/H O2B
Sous-Lt Noel	20 09 39	O9A/H DL
NCOs and Other Ranks:		
Sgt Chef Audox	09 09 39	O9A/H S2A
Sgt Barbey	08 11 39	O9A/H S2A
Adj Chef Becqueret	15 10 39	O9A/H S2A
Adj Chef Bondu	15 10 39	O9A/H S2A
Adj Chef Brard	29 09 39	O9A/H S2A
Adj Chable	15 10 39	O9A/H S2A
Adj Chef Charpentier	09 09 39	O9A/H S2A
Sgt Crozon	22 09 39	O9A/H S2A
Sgt S de la Londe	09 09 39	O9A/H S2A
Adj Chef Giraud	26 09 39	O9A/H S2A
Sgt Chef Leplan	20 09 39	O9A/H S2A
Sgt Nomerange	15 10 39	O9A/H S2A
Adj Robert	05 11 39	O9A/H S2A
Aspirant Roy	06 10 39	O9A/H S2A
Adj Tourel	20 12 39	O9A/H S2A
Sgt Chef Vergne	16 10 39	O9A/H S2A

APPENDIX IV

Officers and NCOs Involved in Escape and Cladestine Activities in Spangenberg and Thorn, 1939–1942

S/L R B Abraham	Maps O9A/H
P/O M F Andrews	Moat (abortive) O9A/H
F/L A P L Barber	Maps, moat (abortive), gate (abortive) O9A/H. Train (abortive)
P/O J Barker	Gate O9A/H
P/O H R Bewlay	Tunnels, gate, Escape Officer O9A/H. Trains
P/O S B K Brackenbury RCAF	Maps O9A/H
S/L A O Bridgman DFC	Bribery O9A/H
F/O D Bruce	Gate, tunnel (abortive) O9A/H
P/O M G Butt	Train (abortive). Gate, tunnels F15
S/L T D Calnan	Hospital window (abortive). Moat (abortive), gate (abortive) O9A/H. Train
Sub-Lt (A) H A Cheetham RN	Tunnel F15
P/O P W Cook	Gate (abortive) O9A/H
P/O R M Coste	Gate O9A/H
Sub-Lt (A) J M P Davies RN	Tunnel F15
P/O G T Dodgshun	Gate F15
F/O M W Donaldson	Gate F15
F/L R H Edwards	Gate O9A/H. Gate F15. Train
F/L R A G Ellen	Gate F15. Train
P/O M W Fessler(American)	Gate (abortive), moat (abortive), maps O9A/H
P/O F D Flinn	Gate F15. Gate (abortive) O9A/H
P/O E N Foinette	Maps O9A/H. Train (abortive)
F/O N Forbes	Gate F15
P/O J E A Foster	Moat F15. Tunnel (abortive), gate O9A/H
Cpl A R Gunton	Window, wire, gate O9A/H (Lower Camp)
P/O C P Hall	Gate (abortive), moat (abortive), maps O9A/H
Lt G R Haller SAAF	Maps O9A/H
P/O N D Hallifax	Wire (*Heimatlager*)
P/O J R Hoppe	Train (abortive).Tunnels F15
W/C J R Kayll DSO DFC	Escape Officer O9A/H
F/O W N Lepine	Gate O9A/H
P/O A F McSweyn	Moat (abortive) O9A/H
P/O N Maranz	Moat (abortive) O9A/H
P/O F D Middleton	Gate O9A/H

F/O T K Milne	Gate O9A/H
F/O J C Milner	Gate F15. Gate, tunnel (abortive) O9A/H
Lt E C Newborn SAAF	Tunnel (abortive), gate O9A/H
S/L B Paddon	Gate F15
P/O O L S Philpot DFC	Hospital window (abortive). Gate (abortive), moat (abortive) O9A/H. Train (abortive)
P/O W J Sandman RNZAF	Moat (abortive) O9A/H
P/O N Smallwood	Maps O9A/H
Lt-Cdr O S Stevinson RN	Gate F15
F/L N H Svendsen DFC (Dane)	Moat (abortive) O9A/H
F/O D S Thom	Gate F15
F/O J Tilsley	Gate O9A/H
F/L R E Troward	Train (abortive). Gate F15. Gate O9A/H
F/O P D Tunstall	Gate F15. Gate O9A/H
S/L R N Wardell	Tunnel (abortive), gate, tunnel (abortive) O9A/H
P/O H D Wardle	Gate O9A/H
S/L V T L Wood (Australian)	Moat (abortive) O9A/H

Appendix V
Chronology of Escape Attempts, 1939–42

Date and Location	Participants	Method	Result
1939			
October-December			
Oflag IXA/H Upper Camp	P/O H R Bewlay	Tunnel	Abandoned
Oflag IXA/H Lower Camp	Cpl A R Gunton	Wire/Gate/Window	Discovered
1940			
February			
Oflag IXA/H Upper Camp	P/O H R Bewlay	Gate	Discovered
August			
Oflag IXA/H Upper Camp	P/O F D Middleton	Gate	Recaptured
	F/O T K Milne		
	P/O H D Wardle	Jumped over fence on way to gym	Recaptured
1941			
February			
Oflag IXA/H Upper Camp	P/O P W Cook	Gate	Aborted
20/21 February			
In transit from Stalag Luft I	P/O M G Butt	Jumped from moving train	Aborted
to Oflag IXA/H	P/O J R Hoppe		
4 March			
Oflag IXA/H Upper Camp	P/O F D Flinn	From column leaving camp for Fort XV	Discovered
4/5 March			
In transit from Oflag IXA/H	F/L R H Edwards	Jumped from moving train	Recaptured
to Fort XV	F/L R A G Ellen		
Mid-March			
Fort XV	Sub-Lt H A Cheetham RN	Tunnel	Discovered
	Sub-Lt J M P Davies RN		
	P/O J E A Foster RAFVR	Gate	Aborted
	P/O J E A Foster RAFVR	Identity exchange with orderly	Aborted
22 March			
Fort XV	F/O M W Donaldson	Exchanged identities with working party	Recaptured
	F/O D S Thom		
	P/O F D Flinn		
17 April			
Fort XV	F/O N Forbes	From camp dentist and Stalag XXA working party	Recaptured
	(Lt A Neave, TA)		
	S/L B Paddon	Hid in dust-cart	Discovered
	Lt-Cdr O S Stevinson RN		

Date and Location	Participants	Method	Result
14/15 May Fort XV	P/O J E A Foster RAFVR	Moat	Discovered
28 May Fort XV	F/L R H Edwards F/O J C Milner F/O P D Tunstall	Bluffed their way through the gate with two gate with two Army officers	Recaptured
	P/O G T Dodgshun F/L R E Troward P/O M G Butt	Hid in camp hoping to escape later on	Discovered
June In transit from Fort XV to Oflag IXA/H	P/O H R Bewlay	Jumped from train	Recaptured
Oflag IXA/H Upper Camp	F/O W N Lepine	Gate	Aborted
July Oflag IXA/H Upper Camp	F/L R M Coste	Swapped places with army doctor being transferred	Had to reveal his true identity at POW hospital
August Oflag IXA/H Upper Camp	F/O D Bruce F/O J C Milner F/O P D Tunstall Lt E C Newborn SAAF P/O H R Bewlay	Tunnel	Abandoned
22 August Oflag IXA/H Upper Camp Recaptured	F/O J Tilsley P/O H R Bewlay	Through gate hidden in rubbish cart	
25 August Oflag IXA/H Upper camp	F/L J Barker P/O J E A Foster RAFVR	Through gate hidden in laundry cart	Recaptured
3 September Oflag IXA/H Upper Camp	F/O D Bruce F/P D Tunstall Lt E C Newborn SAAF	Through gate disguised as "Swiss Commission"	Recaptured
Mid-September Oflag IXA/H Upper Camp	P/O M F Andrews P/O A F McSweyn P/O N Maranz P/O W J Sandman RNZAF F/L N H Svendsen	Grappling hook across moat to drawbridge	Discovered
November *Heimatlager*, Rouen	P/O N D Hallifax	Wire	Recaptured

Date and Location	Participants	Method	Result
April Oflag IXA/H	S/L T D Calnan P/O C P Hall P/O A P L Barber	Intended to scale moat or escape from gymnasium	d
Oflag IXA/H	S/L V T L Wood	Across moat by trolley along telegraph wires	Aborted
30 April/1 May In transit from Oflag IXA/H to Stalag Luft III	S/L T D Calnan	Escaped from moving train	Recaptured
As above	F/L A P L Barber P/O O L S Philpot DFC P/O N Smallwood	Attempted to escape from cattle-truck	Aborted

APPENDIX VI

Selected Biographical Sketches

ABRAHAM, Ralph Bagshawe ("Honest Abe") Born Sutton Coldfield, Warwickshire, 09 02 1911. Educated at Bishop Vesey's Grammar School. Worked briefly for Wolsey Motors. Joined RAF on Permanent Commission in 1929. No504 (Bomber) Sq (Horsleys). No60 Sq, India (Wapitis), 1931–34. No7 EFTS, as Instructor, 1934–39. Promoted to F/L on 01 09 39. Then No3 Group, Bomber Command, flying Wellingtons. No12 Sq, Binbrook (Wellington IIs, No1 Group, Bomber Command), 1941–42, S/L. **Postwar:** Stayed in RAF. Transport Command; Staff College; Air Ministry appointments; Air Attaché, Lima, 1945. Changed surname to "Ward" by deed poll, 1949. Retired in 1958 as Group Captain. Lived in Devon before moving to Fairlight, near Hastings in Sussex, to farm and help run café for cliff–top walkers. Died December 1992 (married with one son and three daughters, one of whom predeceased).

BARBER, Anthony Perrinot Lysberg Born 04 07 1920. Educated at Retford Grammar School; Oriel College, Oxford (PPE, MA). Territorial Army at age 18. Seconded to RAF 1940, No1 PRU, Benson (Spitfires). In Stalag Luft III sat Law exams, 1st Class Honours. **Postwar:** Barrister, Inner Temple, 1948. Conservative MP for Doncaster, 1951–64. PPS to Under–Secretary of State for Air, 1952–55. Assistant Whip, 1955–57. PPS to the Prime Minister, Harold Macmillan, 1958–59. Economic Secretary to the Treasury, 1959–62. Financial Secretary to Treasury, 1962–63. Minister of Health (Cabinet), 1963–64. Conservative MP for Altrincham & Sale, 1965–74. Chairman, Conservative Party Organisation, 1966–70. Chancellor of the Duchy of Lancaster June–July 1970. Chancellor of the Exchequer, 1970–74. Created a Life Peer (Baron of Wentbridge) in 1974. Director, British Petroleum, 1979–88. Also Chairman of Standard Chartered Bank, and held Directorships of a number of other banks up to 1987. Took over from Lord Catto as Chairman of the RAF Benevolent Fund, May 1991.

BAREHAM, Harold John William ("Jack", "Bish") Born Norfolk 02 04 1915. Entered Cranwell College in September 1930. Trained as navigator. Postings: No29(F) Sq, North Weald, August 1933; No825 (FSR) Sq, HMS *Glorious*, April 1935; No447 Flight, HMS *Devonshire*, September 1935; No825 (FSR) Sq, HMS *Glorious*, December 1935; No233 (GR) Sq, Thornaby, January 1938; Air Observers' School, Leconfield, August 1938; Air Observation School, North Coates, November 1938; No82 (United Provinces) Sq, Cranwell (No 2 Group, Bomber Command, Blenheims), January 1939; sq on ops from Watton, September 1939. Selected for pilot training at No2 Group HQ, Huntingdon, 15 04 1940. Pilot training: No17 OTU, Upwood, July 1940; No8 FTS, Reading, January 1941; No3 SFTS, South Cerney, April 1941; No2 CFS, Cranwell, July 1941; No2 School of Air Navigation, Cranage, July 1941; No16 OTU, Upper Heyford, September 1941; No106 Squadron, Coningsby (No5 Group, Bomber Command, (Manchesters and Hampdens), December 1941. Awarded DFM with Oakleaf for King's Commendation, 1940. Mentioned in Dispatches. **Postwar:** Married 1946 (one son, two daughters). Stayed in RAF. No4 Refresher Course, Coleby Grange, June 1946; No16 OTU, Cottesmore, October 1946; No228 OCU, Leeming, July 1947. Posted: No4 Sq, BAFO, South Cerney, November 1947. As instructor: CFS, Little Rissington, September 1948; No3 FTS, Feltwell, March 1949; No1 FTS, Oakington, November 1950. Retired from RAF in 1953 as S/L. Flying Instructor BOAC (VC10s and Boeing 707s). Retired in 1979 to Norfolk. Died of a heart–attack, 15 05 1992.

BEWLAY, Harry Ryland ("Bugger"/"Pop") Born King's Norton, Birmingham, 13 11 1911. Educated at Hallfield Prep School, Edgbaston, and Wrekin College, Wellington. Joined King's Royal Rifle Corps at Whittington Barracks. Joined RAF 1936 on Short-Service Commission. Trained at Perth (Tiger Moths) and Netheravon (Hawker Hinds). Posted to No18 Sq (Fairey Battles) at Upper Heyford, then to No57 Sq, also at Upper Heyford (Blenheim Mk1s). **Postwar:** Demobbed 1945. Joined Inland Revenue in Weston–super–Mare, Somerset, then moved to Australia where 2nd child was born. Returned to UK after 18 months and worked as salesman for Orchard Tyres, retiring at age 62.

BOULDING, Roger John Eric Born 19 11 1919. Joined RAF on Short-Service Commission in June 1938. No6 E&RFTS, Sywell, Northants (Tiger Moths), 29 08 1938; No8 FTS, Montrose, November 1938; No11 FTS, Shawbury; Armament Training Camp, Penrhos, June 1939. Joined No52 Sq, Upward, July 1939, flying Fairey Battles and Avro Ansons. Commissioned P/O, 29 08 1939. No98 Sq, Hucknall, October 1939. No142 Sq, France (Battles), November 1939–May 1940. Escaped from France in an abandoned Tiger Moth, arriving at RAF Hawkinge. Volunteered for Fighter Command and posted to No74 (Tiger) Sq, Kirton–in–Lindsey (Spitfires), 22 8 1940. 1 e/a destroyed, 1 shared, 1 damaged. Promoted to F/O, 03 09 1940. Time–promotion as POW: F/L 03 09 1941 and S/L 01 07 1944. **Postwar:** Permanent Commission, 1945. Refresher training at No6 (P) AFU, 25 09 1945, and No10 OTU, Abingdon, 12 02 1945; converted to Lancasters at No1553 HCU, North Luffenham. CO, No35 Sq (Lancasters), Stradishall, 30 01 1947. HQ Bomber Command, 22 10 1948. No203 AFT, Driffield, May 1950, then two months at Central Fighter Establishment, West Raynham. CO, No249 Sq, Devesoir, Egypt (Vampires), 24 10 1950–02 05 1953. Promoted to W/C, 01 01 1954. Retired from RAF 29 11 1966. Ran hotels and restaurants with wife until retirement in 1987. Died 09 08 1993.

BUTT, Maurice Born Chislehurst, Kent, 31 08 1919. Educated at Nantwich & Acton Grammar School. Apprentice to Armstrong Whitworth Aircraft, Coventry, 1936–39, workshop and wind–tunnel. Tested Avro Manchester fuselage and wing models, autumn 1938. RAFVR, Sergeant Pilot, 1938. Flying training at Ansty. Called up for full–time service, 1939. Training at Hullavington and Ternhill, 1939/40. Assessed exceptional as pilot, February 1940. Commissioned P/O June 1940; posted to Harwell. Joined No149 (East India) Sq, Mildenhall (Wellingtons, No3 Group, Bomber Command), August 1940, as 2nd Pilot. **Postwar:** Structural engineer with steelwork contractors in Banbury and London. Senior lecturer in Structural Engineering, 1967–79. Retired to Norfolk. Has sat on Coventry Council since 1989.

CALNAN, Thomas Daniel Born 06 12 1915. Entered RAF Cranwell on Permanent Commission. P/O 19 12 1936. F/O 19 06 38. NoII (Army Co–operation) Sq. Mentioned in Dispatches. No1 PRU, Benson (Spitfires). **Postwar:** Staff College, Andover. Promoted W/C 01 01 1949. Chief Test Pilot at RAE Farnborough, 1950. Last command, Meteor night–fighter squadron. Retired from RAF as Group Captain 15 02 1959. Married with one son, born 1965. Moved with wife and son to Tuscany, farming and writing. Deceased.

CAMPBELL, Graham Cox Born 14 05 1914 in Nova Scotia and at age six moved to Alberta, growing up on a wheat farm. Matriculated from local high school 1934 and worked as farm labourer to save money for private pilot's licence so he could join RAF, then recruiting in Canada. Travelled to UK in August 1938 and joined RAF on Short-Service Commission. **Postwar:** Transferred to RCAF. Remained in the service until 1961, then worked for Canadian Government for sixteen years. Retired 1978 and lived in Ottawa.

CASEY, Michel James Born Allahabad, India, 19 02 1918. Joined RAF on Short-Service Commission.1936. Posted to No57 Sq, Upper Heyford (Blenheim Mk1). Married, 1939. Then went with No57 Sq to Amy, France, with BEF Air Component, 30 09 1939. Formed forward base at Metz, October 1939. Shot after mass escape from Stalag Luft III, 31 03 1944. Cremated at Görlitz.

CHAPMAN, Edward ("Tug–Boat Ted") Born 01 05 1906. Merchant Navy cadet, HMS *Worcester*, Greenhithe, 1921–23. Then wine trade. Married 03 03 1936, one son (Anthony, born 1945). On outbreak of war volunteered for Navy, "but Navy was full"; tried Army, but minimum length of service was seven years; then went direct to Admiralty and was accepted by Navy, also by RAF, Royal Marines and Westminster Dragoons. RAF accepted first, in February 1940, so he joined RAF Marine Craft Section (High Speed Launches). Posted to Calshott, then Grimsby, October 1940–Feb 1941; then Dover. MCS became Air–Sea Rescue Service. S/L posting, Gibraltar, March 1941, but captured before embarkation. **Postwar:** Stayed in RAF. Retired September 1966 as S/L. Supervised German market for sherry for more than twenty–five years. Pioneered plonk, 1966, creating nineteen different brands. Bought a bonded store near Sally Line at Ramsgate, working as Marketing Director. Retired in 1984 when sponsor died and his son took over. Fellow, Institute of Directors. Lived in Hove, East Sussex, until his death in late 1990s.

CLELLAND, Ernest John Born 12 12 1920, Southall. Educated at Kimbolton School. Joined RAFVR 04 07 39. Mobilised 02 09 39. **Postwar:** granted Permanent Commission. Retired in 1948 on medical grounds as S/L. From January 1957, lecturer in English Language & Literature in the interpreters' department at Louvain University, Belgium. Lives in Brussels.

CRAWLEY, Aidan Merivale ("Stafford") Born Bishopthorpe, Yorks, 10 04 1906, the son of the Canon of York (and, later, of Windsor). Educated at Harrow and Oxford. Capped for England at cricket. Journalist *Daily Mail*, 1930–36. World tour with Esmond (son of Lord) Rothermere. In India turned to acting. Joined Labour Party; Prospective Parliamentary Candidate for North Buckingham, 1938. Joined No601 (County of London) Sq, Auxiliary Air Force, 1936. Educational film producer, 1936–39. Assistant Air Attaché, Ankara, Belgrade (resident Sofia), and Balkan Intelligence Service, May 1940–Mar 1941. Escaped to Egypt, joined No73 (Hurricane) Sq. **Postwar:** Married Virginia Cowles, 1945 (killed in car accident 1983); one daughter; two sons (predeceased). Elected Labour MP for North Buckingham, 1945. Parliamentary Private Secretary to successive Secretaries of State for Colonies, 1945, and 1946–47. Appointed MBE 1946. Under-Secretary of State for Air, 1950. Defeated by 59 votes in 1951 General Election. Editor–in–Chief, Independent Television News Ltd, 1955–56. Resigned over policy dispute and turned to BBC TV, producing and photographing independent documentaries, 1956–60. Resigned from Labour Party, 1957. Re–elected to Parliament 1962 as Conservative MP for West Derbyshire. Defeated 1964 General Election. With David Frost won London Weekend TV franchise 1967, and was Chairman until 1971, President 1971–73. Wrote *Escape from Germany* (published 1956 and 1985), plus works of history and biography. Own memoirs, *Leap Before You Look*, published 1988. Lived in Farthingoe, Northants, until his death in November 1993.

DAVIS, Rupert ("Pud") Born 1916. Trained for Merchant Navy on HMS *Worcester*, Greenhithe. Transferred to RN, then FAA. Midshipman on carrier HMS *Glorious*. **Postwar:** actor in theatre, radio, film and TV. Played Georges Simenon's fictional detective, Maigret, in fifty–two episodes for BBC TV, 1960–64, and named TV actor of the year 1963. Had to struggle to shake off his Maigret image and despite a few later film appearances died of cancer, penniless, in 1976.

DAY, Harry Melville Arbuthnot ("Wings") Born Sarawak, Borneo, 03 08 1898. Educated at Haileybury, England. Joined Royal Marines 01 09 1916. Awarded Albert Medal, sea second class 09 11 1919 (gazetted 07 01 1919; upgraded to George Cross, 1971). Commissioned in RAF 16 06 1924. F/L, No23 Fighter Sq, Kenley. Leader, Hendon Air Show Synchronised Aerobatic Team, 1931. Service: Abu Suier, Egypt (Adjutant, No4 FTS); Khartoum; promoted S/L; Aboukir; Netheravon; CO, Advanced FTS, Rissington; CO, No57 Squadron, Upper Heyford, July 1939 (W/C 01 07 39). Squadron moved to Amy, France, with BEF Air Component, 30 09 1939; then forward base at Metz, October 1939. **Postwar:** DSO and OBE (Military Division), December 1945 for distinguished service as POW. Group Captain 01 10 1946. Retired from RAF 01 07 1950. Technical adviser on films *Reach for the Sky* and *The Great Escape*. Died in Blue Sisters' Hospital, Malta, 11 03 77.

DUNN, Norman Maxwell Born Sydney, Australia, 1916. Went into accountancy, then joined RAAF and was the first officer commissioned under the Empire Air Training Scheme. **Postwar:** Chairman of the Council of the Australian Telecommunications Development Association. Lives in St Ives, NSW.

FOINETTE, Eric Norman Born Stirling, Scotland, on 28 01 1915. Educated at Latymer Upper School, Hammersmith, London, 1924–33. Studied to become an actuary with an insurance company. Applied to join RAF and called up in August 1940 by Babbacombe Reception Centre for pilot training. Trained at Aberystwyth ITW and Weston–super–Mare EFTS, but failed after going solo and returned to Babbacombe in December to re–muster as an Observer. Sent to Prestwick Navigation School then to West Freugh for bombing and gunnery training on Fairey Battles. Commissioned June 1941 and sent to OTU Benson. Posted to No21 Sq, Binbrook, August 1941. **Postwar:** Civil engineer with a leading tunnel contractor for thirty–five years until retirement. Active in his squadron association and also attends annual meetings of the German Night–Fighters' Association. Lives with his wife in Ashford, Kent.

GOULD, Alexander Herbert Born New Zealand, then to USA 1918; then UK; then to Australia, 1922. Educated North and Central Queensland; New South Wales Agricultural College, Hawkesbury Agricultural School, and Sydney University. Infantry militia, 1936–37. Joined RAAF, 1937. Stations, RAF 1938–40: Netheravon, Rissington, Manston and Hemswell. Commissioned P/O 07 03 39. **Postwar:** Returned to

Australia and settled in Bundanoon, NSW, where he was active in the RAAF Ex–POW Association. Published *Tales from the Sagan Woods*, 1994.

JOHNSON, Theo Faire Storrer Born Wellington, New Zealand, 12 05 1919 then moved with family to Hamilton. Joined State Insurance Department of NZ Public Service. Joined RNZAF in 1938. Initial Training at No1 FTS Wigram. Sailed for UK, March 1940. P/O, No51 Sq, Linton–on–Ouse (Whitleys, No 4 Group, Bomber Command); flew two ops. **Postwar:** Released from RAF, 1945. Studied Town & Country Planning in UK at Manchester University, 1945–48. Married Vivien Steuart Symonds, 07 01 1947 (one son). Returned to NZ Public Service. Final post was Director of Town & Country Planning Division, Ministry of Works. Died 06 03 1972 of stomach cancer.

KAYLL, Joseph Robert Born Sunderland 1914. Educated at Aysgarth School, near Bedale, Yorkshire, and Stowe. Started work at age sixteen as mill–boy in family firm of Joseph Thompson & Co Sawmills, Sunderland. Gained "A" Licence in 1935 and joined the Auxiliary Air Force, No607 (County of Durham) Sq, Usworth. Trained on Avro 504N, Wapiti and Hawker Harts and Demons. Squadron finally equipped with Gladiator I and II. Promoted to F/L 1937. Appointed "A" Flight Commander 1939. Called to full–time service with No607 Squadron (No13 Group, Fighter Command), 24 08 1939. Moved to Merville, near Vitry–en–Artois, France, as part of Air Component, on 15 11 1939. Shared airfield with No615 Sq (also Gladiators). Appointed CO of No615 Sq (No61 Fighter Wing), March 1940. Squadron moved to Le Touquet to convert to Hurricanes, 20 50 1940; returned to Merville, 11 05 1940. Ops in Northern France from 16 05 1940. Returned to Kenley 20 05 1940. Awarded DSO and DFC on 31 05 40. Squadron "rested" at Prestwick, 31 08 1940; stationed at Northolt, 10 10 1940. Battle of Britain "ace". As fighter pilot, 12 kills, plus 1 shared and two probables. HQ Fighter Command, Bentley Priory, 30 12 1940, as S/L Tactics. Appointed W/C Flying, Hornchurch, 02 06 1941. **Postwar:** Mention in Dispatches, 28 12 45. Demobilised in 1946 as W/C. Made OBE, 26 06 46. Asked to re–form No607 Sq at RAF Ouston, Northumberland, with Spitfires. Relinquished command 1949. Returned to Thompson's Sawmills. Lived in Sunderland until his death in March 2000.

McSWEYN, Allan Frank Born Rockdale, near Sydney, in 1919. Enlisted in RAAF in September 1939 and joined No1 Course of the Empire Air Training School. Trained at Somers, Victoria, and Narromine, NSW. Shipped to Canada in 1940 to train at Uplands, Ottawa, on Yales and Harvards. December 1940 arrived in UK and sent from Uxbridge to Lossiemouth for bomber training. Posted to No115 Sq, Marham (Wellington IC). Made "home run" in 1943. After refresher course at Cranwell posted to No105 Transport OTU at Bramcote, training "operationally expired" pilots for transport and civil aviation duties. Married in Winchester on 06 03 1944. Received MC for his escape and AFC for post–escape flying work on 10 07 1945. Left RAAF as a F/L. **Postwar:** Returned to Australia. Joined Trans Australian Airlines and became their Queensland manager. After ten years with TAA he left to set up his own business, which he ran for years. After a period as general manager of an engineering business he retired to the Gold Coast.

MUNGOVAN, Alfred W ("Alf") Junior clerk, Mark Brown's Wharf near Tower Bridge, London. Joined RAF on a Short-Service Commission in October 1938. Trained at No11 FTS, Shawbury, 1939. Commissioned P/O on 03 09 39 and posted to No88 Sq. **Postwar:** Signed on for another four–year Short-Service Commission. Transferred to Administrative Branch. Served two years in India, mostly as Station Administrative Officer. Returned to UK in February 1948, then to Ballykelly, Northern Ireland. Married 1948. Transferred to HQ, No19 Group, Mount Batten, in October 1948 as Senior Personnel Staff Officer. Retired from RAF in May 1950, retaining rank of S/L. Then for seven years a sales rep for a Midlands chocolate manufacturer covering the Home Counties. Bought confectionery shop in Stanmore, 1956. Emigrated to Australia, March 1966. Settled in Modbury, South Australia, and spent six years as an arts and crafts rep. With colleague founded Premier Arts Supplies PLC, 1973, which has become the largest business of its kind in South Australia. Semi–retired since 1980, but still retained an interest in the business as a director.

OGILVIE, Alfred Keith ("Oggie"/"Skeets") Born Ottawa, 1915. Joined RAF on Short-Service Commission on 11 08 1939. Training at No1 E&RFTS, Hatfield; No9 FTS, Hullavington, 06 11 1939; and No1 Flying Practice Unit, Meir, Staffordshire, 19 05 1940. Then to CFS, Upavon, for an instructor's course, 06 06 1940, followed by posting to No7 OTU, Hawarden. Joined No609 Sq, Middle Wallop, 20 08 1940. As fighter pilot five "kills" and two "probables". Awarded the DFC on 11 07 41. **Postwar:** Transferred to RCAF, retiring on 14 09 1962. Died 1998.

OSMENT, David Ernest Thomas Born in the West Indies and educated in England at Herne Bay, Kent.

Joined RAF on Short-Service Commission in 1938. Commissioned P/O on 07 03 39. Posted to No150 Sq (Fairey Battles). **Postwar:** Permanent Commission. Retired in 1965, then spent sixteen years with a British bank.

PHILPOT, Oliver Lawrence Spurling ("Ollie") Born Vancouver, British Columbia, 06 03 1913. Educated at the Queen Mary School, North Vancouver, and in England at Aymestrey Court, Worcester; Radley College, Berkshire, and Worcester College, Oxford (PPE Hons, MA). Pilot u/t Oxford University Air Sq, RAFVR. Management trainee, Unilever, 1934; Assistant Commercial Secretary, Home Margarine Executive, 1936. Married (1st) 1938 (two daughters, one son). Called to full–time RAF service in August 1939 and trained as air–gunner. Acting P/O 15 01 1940 in No42 Sq, No16 (GR) Group, Coastal Command, Bircham Newton (Vickers Vildebeests). Squadron converted to Beauforts in June 1940, then joined No18 (GR) Group, moving to Wick, North Coates, then Leuchars. Re–trained as pilot and promoted to F/O 1941. Awarded the DFC on 01 07 1941. Time–promotion to F/L whilst POW. Home run from Stalag Luft III, 29 October 1943. Awarded MC. Lecturer with MI9. Senior Scientific Officer, Air Ministry, 1944. **Postwar:** Demobbed 1946 as F/L. Resumed business career as office manager, general manager, executive, chairman and director of various food processing and packaging companies, as well as advising and administering numerous charities. (Chairman RAF Escaping Society and its Charitable Fund, 1963–69.) Retired in 1989. POW/escape memoir, *Stolen Journey*, published 1950 by Hodder & Stoughton (15 subsequent editions, including Norwegian and Swedish translations). First marriage dissolved 1951; married (2nd) Rosl Widhalm, BA (Hons), PhD, 1954 (one son, one daughter). Died 29 04 1993.

POYNTER, Douglas Arthur Born 1921. Entered Royal Navy 1938 and trained as an Observer (Air). Served on HMS *Glorious* and HMS *Furious*. **Postwar:** MBE 19 03 46 for services as POW. From 1945 to 1955 various appointments at sea, on–shore and on courses as Lieutenant and subsequently Lieutenant–Commander. Promoted Commander, 1955, and Captain, 1962 and was Executive Officer on HMS *Terror* and Signals Officer in Far East. Deputy Director of Naval Signals, 1963. Senior Officers' War Course, 1965. Defence, Naval, Military and Air Attaché in Santiago, Lima and Quito, 1966–67. Appointed Commander of the Royal Victorian Order, 1968. Director of Naval Signals, 1969. Appointed *Aide–de–Camp* to HM the Queen, 1971. Retired from RN, 1972. Naval Regional Officer, London Area, 1972–80. Elected to Waverley Borough Council, 1983, and up to 1992 was Chairman, then Vice–Chairman, of the Finance Committee. From 1992 onwards, committee member of his local Conservative Association and Residents' Association. Lives in Farnham, Surrey.

ROBERTS, Ralph Joined No616 Sq, Auxiliary Air Force, at Doncaster in March 1939. Called to full–time service as Acting P/O on 24 08 1939 and awarded wings in September. P/O confirmed 04 09 1939. Converted to Hurricanes at Fighter Pool, St Athan. Then to Ferry Pilots Pool, Fenton. Posted to No615 Sq, Vitry (Gladiators, Hurricanes), on 01 01 1940. Squadron operated from Manston during Dunkirk evacuation and from Kenley during the Battle of Britain. Posted to No64 Sq, Kenley, in August 1940. 1 e/a destroyed. Time–promotion whilst POW: F/O 04 09 1940; F/L 04 09 1941. **Postwar:** Released from RAF on 09 03 1946 as F/L. Died 1994.

ROTH, Michael Herriott ("Maggie") Born 1919. Joined the RAF on a Short-Service Commission in 1936. Promoted to F/O 18 04 39. **Postwar:** Professional magician in Canada until retirement. Wrote a memoir of his POW experiences called "The Unhurried Years", which was accepted by an agent of William Collins & son in Canada but later turned down in favour of Eric Sydney–Smith's biography of "Wings" Day. Lived in Toronto until moving in to a retirement home in the mid–1990s.

THOMAS, Percy Ainsworth Ward Born 1913. Educated at Wellingborough. Trainee executive, London Transport. Joined RAF on Short-Service Commission and trained at Derby and Kinloss. **Postwar:** Pro–am golfer and author (as Pat Ward-Thomas): *Masters of Golf*, *The Long Green Fairway*, *World Atlas of Golf* (co–author), *Royal and Ancient*, *Shell Golfers Atlas*. Partial memoir, *Not Only Golf* (Hodder & Stoughton).

THOMPSON, Alfred Burke ("Tommy") Born Penetanguishene, Canada, 08 08 1915. Joined the RAF in 1937. **Postwar:** Osgoode Hall Law School, Toronto, 1945–48. Married Nora Jackson, 1946 (eight children, eight grandchildren). Lawyer, Penetanguishene, 1948–1967. Mayor of Penetanguishene 1957–8. Assistant Crown Attorney, Simcoe County, 1966–80. Retired in 1980. Died 09 08 1985.

TUCK, Roland Robert Stanford ("Bob") Born Catford, London, 01 07 1916. Educated at St Dunstan's Preparatory School and College, Reading. To sea as cadet with Lamport & Holt Line, 1932. Joined RAF on a Short-Service Commission, September 1935. No3 FTS Grantham, 28 09 1935. Posted to No65 Sq,

Hornchurch, 05 08 1936. Chosen to represent No65 Sq on service initiation of Spitfire, 1938. Flight Commander, No92 Sq, Croydon, 01 05 1940. CO No257 Sq, Debden, 11 08 1940. As fighter pilot, 27 confirmed "kills", 8 "probables", 6 damaged; twice wounded, twice baled out. DFC gazetted on 11 06 1940, and awarded at Hornchurch by King on 28 June. Awarded Bar to DFC on 25 10 1940, DSO on 07 01 1941, and 2nd Bar to DFC on 11 04 1941. Appointed Duxford Wing Leader, July 1941. To USA on liaison trip, October 1941, then Wing Leader, Biggin Hill. **Postwar:** RAF West Raynham, 1945. Awarded DFC (US) on 14 06 1946. Retired from RAF on 13 05 1949 as W/C. Owned mushroom farm in Sandwich, Kent. Died 05 05 1987.

WARDLE, Howard Douglas ("Hank") Born in Dauphin, Manitoba, on 13 08 1915, and educated in Ontario. After working as a book–keeper he sailed for Britain, and in March 1939 was granted a Short-Service Commission in the RAF. Early November 1939 joined No98 Sq, flying Fairey Battles, and on 27 11 39 posted to No218, another Battle squadron, in the AASF in France. Escaped from Colditz 14 10 1942 and made "home" run via Switzerland, Southern France, Spain and Gibraltar. Awarded the MC and promoted to S/L. Resumed flying as a ferry pilot to the Middle and Far East and across the Atlantic. **Postwar:** Planned to remain in the RAF but was injured in a mid–air collision, and returned to Canada. He worked for Sperry Gyroscope, retiring in the 1970s. Married and divorced three times (two sons by his first marriage). Died February 1995.

Sources and Biblography

Interviews:
H R Bewlay, H H Bracken, J Casson, E F Chapman, A M Crawley, B A James, O L S Philpot, Michael Stanford–Tuck (R R S Tuck).

Correspondence:
The Rt. Hon. Lord Barber, Mrs. Rosemary Bareham (J F W Bareham), H R Bewlay, D Blew, R J E Boulding, H H Bracken, D Bruce, Mrs M A Butler (R J E Boulding), M G Butt, G C Campbell, J Casson, E F Chapman, E J Clelland, A M Crawley, Mrs Nora Crete (A B Thompson), N M Dunn, K C Edwards, E F Foinette, P Greenhous, H Hearn, A H Gould, B A James, Mrs Vivien Johnson (T F S Johnson), J R Kayll, A W Mungovan, A K Ogilvie, D E T Osment, R Parkhouse, O L S Philpot, D Poynter, M H Roth, Michael Stanford–Tuck, R E Troward, R B Ward, Mrs P White, Calton Younger.

Unpublished manuscripts:
ROTH, M H: "The Unhurried Years"

Official Documents in the Public Record Office:
AIR 14/353: RAF Personnel taken prisoner of war: aids to escape, conduct, etc
AIR 20/2336 Alphabetical lists of RAF, RAAF, RCAF, RNZAF and SAAF POWs in Germany
MI9/S/PG(G)/805: Account of escape of S/L B Paddon
MI9/S/PG(G)/1629: Account of escape of P/O A F McSweyn, RAAF
MI9/S/PG(G)/996: Account of escape of F/L H D Wardle
WO 165/39: MI9 War Diary
WO 208/3242: Historical Record of MI9
WO 208/3293: Camp Histories: Oflag IXA/H (Upper and Lower), Spangenberg

Archives and Museums:
Bundesarchiv, Freiburg im Breisgau; Imperial War Museum, Lambeth; Fleet Air Arm Museum, Ilchester; Public Record Office, Kew; *Stadtarchiv* Oberursel; *Stadtarchiv* Spangenberg; *Stadtarchiv* Warburg.

Secondary Sources:
ADAMS, D Guy: *Backwater: Oflag IXA/H* (Frederick Muller Ltd, 1944)
ASHWORTH, Chris: *RAF Coastal Command, 1936–1969* (Patrick Stephens Ltd, 1992)
BARBER, Noel: *Prisoner of War* (Harrap & Co, 1944)
BARKER, Ralph: *Strike Hard, Strike Sure* (Chatto & Windus Ltd, 1963)
BECKWITH, E G C (Ed.): *The Mansel Diaries* (Privately Printed, 1977)
BICKERS, Richard Townshend: *The Desert Air War, 1939–45* (Leo Cooper, 1991)
BOITEN, Theo: *Blenheim Strike* (Air Research Publications, 1995)
BOITEN, Theo: *Bristol Blenheim* (The Crowood Press Ltd, 1998)
BRICKHILL, Paul: *Reach for the Sky* (William Collins & Sons, 1954)
BRICKHILL, Paul, and NORTON, Conrad: *Escape to Danger* (Faber & Faber, 1946)
CALNAN, T D: *Free as a Running Fox* (Macdonald & Co Ltd, 1970)
CHORLEY, W R: *RAF Bomber Command Losses of the Second World War:*
      Vol. 1: 1939–40 (Midland Counties Publications, 1992)
      Vol. 2: 1941 (Midland Counties Publications, 1993)
      Vol. 3: 1942 (Midland Counties Publications, 1994)
COSSEY, Bob: *Tigers: The Story of No. 74 Squadron RAF* (Arms & Armour Press, 1992)

CRAWLEY, Aidan: *Escape from Germany* (HMSO, 1985)

CRAWLEY, Aidan: *Leap Before You Look* (Collins, 1988)

CULL, Brian, and MINTERNE, Don: *Hurricanes Over Tobruk* (Grub Street, 1999)

DELARUE, Jacques: *The Gestapo: A History of Horror* (Paragon House, 1987)

DONNELLY, G L "Larry": *The Whitley Boys* (Air Research Publications, 1991)

FOOT, M R D, and LANGLEY, J M: *MI9—Escape and Evasion, 1939–1945* (The Bodley Head, 1979)

FORMAN, John: *Fighter Command War Diaries, Vol. 1: September 1939–September 1940* (Air Research Publications, 1996)

FORMAN, John: *Fighter Command War Diaries, Vol. 2: September 1940 to December 1941* (Air Research Publications, 1998)

FORRESTER, Larry: *Fly For Your Life* (Frederick Muller Ltd, 1973)

FOSTER, Eric: *Life Hangs by a Silken Thread* (Astia Publishing, 1992)

FRANKS, Norman: *Valiant Wings* (William Kimber, 1988)

GIBSON, Guy: *Enemy Coast Ahead* (Michael Joseph Ltd, 1946)

GRETZYNGIER, *Robert: Poles in the Defence of Britain* (Grub Street, 2001)

HAMMERTON, Sir John (Ed.): *ABC of the RAF* (The Amalgamated Press Ltd, 1941)

HASTINGS, Max: *Bomber Command* (Michael Joseph Ltd, 1979)

JACKSON, Robert: *Before the Storm: The Story of Bomber Command 1939–42* (Arthur Barker, 1972)

MIDDLEBROOK, Martin, and EVERITT, Chris: *The Bomber Command War Diaries* (Midland Publishing Ltd, 1996)

MOORE, Bob, and FEDOROWICH, Kent (Eds.): *Prisoners of War and Their Captors in World War II* (Oxford: Berg, 1996)

MOYLE, Harry: *The Hampden File* (Air Britain, 1989)

NEAVE, Airey: *Saturday at MI9* (Hodder & Stoughton Ltd, 1969)

NEAVE, Airey: *They Have Their Exits* (Hodder & Stoughton, 1953)

PAINE, Lauran: *German Military Intelligence in World War II: The Abwehr* (Military Heritage Press, 1984)

PFEIFFER, Ludwig: *Die Geschichte des Schlosses Spangenberg* (Horst Schreckhase, Spangenberg, 1987)

PRITTIE, T C F and EDWARDS, W Earle: *South to Freedom* (Hutchinson & Co, 1946)

REID, Major P R, MBE MC: *Colditz: The Full Story* (Macmillan, 1984)

SAUNDERS, Hilary St George: *The Red Cross and The White* (Hollis & Carter, 1949)

SHAW, Michael: *No.1 Squadron* (Ian Allan Ltd, 1971)

SHORES, Christopher: *Dust Clouds in the Middle East* (Grub Street, 1996)

SHORES, Christopher, et al: *Fledgling Eagles* (Grub Street, 1991)

SHORES, Christopher, et al: *Air War For Yugoslavia, Greece and Crete, 1940–41* (Grub Street, 1987)

SLIZEWSKI, Grzegorz: *The Lost Hopes* (Kozsalin, 2000)

SMITH, Sydney: *"Wings" Day* (William Collins & Sons, 1968)

WRAGG, David: *The Fleet Air Arm Handbook* (Sutton Publishing, 2001)

WYNN, Kenneth G: *Men of the Battle of Britain* (CCB Associates, 1999)

Newspapers and Periodicals: *The Camp, The Kriegie, The Times, The Daily Telegraph, The Daily Mail.*

Index

253

259

mentioned: 12, 13, 20, 23-4
Offiziersdurchgangslager, Oberursel,
　69-70
Oflag IIA, Prenzlau, 12, 20, 25, 185
Oflag IIB, Arnswalde, 99
Oflag IVC, Colditz, 20, 34, 36, 41,
　133, 148, 152, 162, 225, 249
Oflag VB, Biberach, 12, 20, 25
Oflag VIB, Warburg-Dössel, 12-13,
　20, 25, 30, 33, 34, 134, 175,
　188-90, 225
Oflag VIIC/H, Laufen, 12, 20, 25,
　139, 175, 190, 227
Oflag IXA/H, Spangenberg and
　Elbersdorf, 12-13, 20, 24-25, 33-
　35, 43, 49-50, 53, 61-2, 64-7, 70-
　1, 75-8, 80-2, 94, 96-101, 105-6,
　116-120, 122-23, 125-26, 132-41,
　143, 152-53, 155-61, 163, 166-68,
　170, 173, 176-79, 184-190, 209,
　213-20, 222, 225-28
Oflag XA, Itzehoe, 12, 20, 24, 43, 50,
　53, 64
Oflag XC, Lübeck, 12-13, 20, 25, 30,
　213, 227
Oflag XIB, Braunschweig
　(Brunswick), 20, 24, 64
Oflag XXIB, Schubin, 120, 134, 213,
　225 (*See also*: Stalag XXIB)
Stalag IIA, Neu Brandenburg, 117
Stalag IIIE, Kirchhain, 12, 20, 25
Stalag VIA, Hemer bei Iserlohn, 25,
　190
Stalag VIJ, Krefeld, 20
Stalag VIIIB, Lamsdorf, 12-13, 20,
　25, 125, 134, 158, 161, 209
Stalag IXA, Ziegenhain, 20, 24, 64-5,
　67, 70-1, 75-77
Stalag IXC, Bad Sulza, 12, 20, 25,
　123, 129, 158-59, 161, 227
Stalag XIIA, Limburg an der Lahn,
　12, 20, 25, 29, 131, 185
Stalag XXA, Thorn (Torun), 12, 25,
　139, 148, 151, 155
Stalag XXIB (later Oflag XXIB),
　Schubin, 12-13, 20, 25, 139
Stalag Luft I, Barth-Vogelsang, 12-13,
　20, 25, 33-35, 41, 96, 106, 116-20
　(*passim*), 123, 125, 129, 131, 134,
　136-38 (*passim*), 144, 148, 158,
　166, 170, 175, 185, 189-91 (*pas-
　sim*), 217, 225
Stalag Luft III, Sagan 12, 20, 22, 25,
　30, 35, 37, 42, 90, 120, 134, 197,
　202, 213-14, 222, 224-28 (*pas-
　sim*), 244-45, 248
Stalag Luft VI, Heydekrug, 12
Stalags, 12, 20, 23, 24, 96
Straflager, see: Fort XV
Transit camps: 69, 78 (*See also*:
　Dulag Luft; Dulags)
Prisoner of War Code, *see*: Geneva
Convention
Prisoner of War Directorate, *see*: Prisoner
of War Organisation, British
Prisoner of War Organisation, British, 25-
34, 42, 157, 161
Prisoner of War Organisation, German,
22-25, 160
Prisoners of War, *passim*
　American, 31, 171, 190, 194-97
　Argentinian, 214

Army (British), 25, 30, 33, 42, 82, 96,
　99-100, 116-17, 122, 134, 137,
　138-39, 142-45, 147-48, 154-55,
　157, 159-61, 177-78, 185, 188-90,
　215-18, 226-28
Army Commandos, 25
　Australian, 12, 26, 103, 158, 167,
　169-70, 171, 173-75, 190, 192
Auxiliary Air Force, 19, 170, 226
Belgian, 26, 34, 112
Canadian, 12, 26, 51, 65, 83, 99, 104,
　107, 109, 114, 125, 131, 148, 159,
　163, 167, 190-91, 217, 227
Czechoslovakian, 13, 20, 26, 34, 167
Danish, 173
Dominion Air Forces, 19, 20, 24, 25,
　32, 42, 225
Dutch, 26, 112
Fleet Air Arm, 12, 20, 24, 25, 43, 49,
　62, 82, 118, 122-23, 131-32, 152,
　163, 185, 225
French, 12, 13, 20, 24, 26, 34, 51-2,
　61, 66-9, 71, 73-8, 80, 82-3, 88,
　90, 96-9, 112, 117, 132-33, 214
German, 21, 24, 25, 31, 33, 34, 35,
　101, 139-40, 145-46, 154,
　157,161-62, 228
Greek, 26
Italian, 34
Maori, 129
Merchant Navy, 100, 117, 122-23
New Zealand, 12, 26, 45, 94, 121,
　125, 163, 166-67, 170, 172, 190,
　192-93
Norwegian, 26
Polish, 12, 13, 20, 24, 26, 34, 50, 53,
　64, 75, 79, 128, 139, 167-68, 173,
　175-76, 190, 198, 224, 227
RAF, *passim; mentioned*: 23-5, 26-7,
　30, 32-3, 40-3, 49, 77-8, 82, 90,
　96-100, 116, 118, 122-23, 134,
　136-37, 143, 145, 148, 155, 157-
　58, 160, 163, 171-73, 176, 185,
　215-17, 219-20, 225-27
RAF NCOs and other ranks, 12, 19-
　20, 24, 25, 26, 43, 75, 80, 117,
　128, 133, 143, 158, 161-62, 225
RAF officers, 24-25, 32, 43, 45, 61,
　68, 74-5, 80, 118-19, 128, 190,
　225
RAF Volunteer Reserve (RAFVR),
　19, 136, 158, 163, 167, 169-70,
　173, 190
Reserve of Air Force Officers
　(RAFO), 114, 134, 190
Royal Marines, 25, 43, 62
Royal Navy, 30, 33, 100, 117, 123,
　136-37, 148, 160-61, 185
Russian, 24
South African, 26, 66, 83, 116,
　166-67, 173, 190
Southern Rhodesian, 102
Special Air Service, 20, 25
Propaganda, 26, 50, 75-6, 82, 89, 129,
　145 (*See also: Camp, The*)
Protected Personnel, 158, 161-62
Protecting Power, 34, 157, 160
Przybylski, Sgt M, 175
Pumphrey, F/O R E W, 83, 102, 104, 116,
　236
Purchase, N/A A R, RN, 131
Pyrenees, 37-38

Q
Queen Mary School, Vancouver, 248
Queen's Royal Regiment, 153
Queensland, Australia, 246-47
Quill, Lt Cr N R, RN, 123, 132, 236
Quito, Ecuador, 248

R
Rackow, P/O G M, 190, 202-03, 220,
　236, 236
Radio, 26, 52, 75-6, 89, 126, 135, 161
　(*See also*: BBC; "Canary, The";
　Propaganda)
Radlett, 65, 75
Radley College, Berks, 202
Rågalund Drengebjen, Denmark, 215
Ramsgate, Kent, 245
Ramrod operations, 198-99
Rankin, Wing Commander A J, 36, 76
Rattigan, Terence, 210
Rattray, Major N
Rawlins, S/L G C, DFC, 167
Rawlinson, Captain A R, 36
Reading, Berkshire, 248
Red Cross, 21, 25-31 (*passim*), 34, 69-70,
　76, 80, 98-9, 116, 132, 134, 142, 155,
　161, 216, 222, 228
Reach for the Sky (film), 246
Red Cross Convention, *see*: Geneva
　Convention
Redgrave, S/L M E, 167-68, 236
Reeves, P/O S, 173, 176, 236
Reichssicherheitshauptampt, see: RSHA
Reichsrundfunk, 26, 52
Reichswald Forest, 175
Reims, 90, 106
Reinecke, General Hermann, 22, 23
Relatives' Association, 26
Renison, P/O R J B, AuxAF, 83, 99, 116,
　236
Repatriation, 157-62, 189-90, 214
Reprisals, 101,132-33, 139, 146, 187,
　190, 228 (*See also*: Fort XV)
Resistance, The, 37, 174
Retford, Notts, 75, 244
Rethel, France, 102-3
Revill, P/O H M, RAFVR, 163
Rheinberg War Cemetery, 66
Rhine, River, 74
Rhine Valley, 66-8, 84, 113
Rhineland, 211
"Rhubarbs", 38, 195, 197, 199-200, 217
Rice, G/C, 125-26
Riddell, P/O N C S, 90-1
Rifle Brigade, 138
Ritchie, Sgt J B, 84
Ritz, *Sergent-Chef*, 96
Road to En-Dor, The (E H Jones), 39
Robert, *Adjudant*, 74, 238
Roberts, F/O A C, 83, 89-90, 116, 136,
　236, 236
Roberts, P/O R, 119-20, 236, 236, 248
Robinson, AC1 S, 102
Robson, Sgt F, 90-4
Rockdale, NSW, 173, 247
Rockingham, Sgt P, 168
Rofe, Sgt Cyril, 168
Rogers, S/L B J, AFC, 169
Rolfe, P/O C I, 173, 175-76, 236
Romania, 176
Romilly-sur-Seine, France, 109
Room 900, 37 (*See also*: MI9)